Real World Photoshop 5

Real World Photoshop 5

Industrial Strength Production Techniques

David Blatner
Bruce Fraser

Peachpit Press

David

For Fay, Harry, Ann, Abe, Katie, and Rita,
who laid the foundation in my family.

Bruce
For Pamela.

Real World Photoshop 5

David Blatner and Bruce Fraser

Copyright ©1999 by David Blatner and Bruce Fraser

Peachpit Press
1249 Eighth Street
Berkeley, CA 94710
510/524-2178
Fax: 510/524-2221

Find us on the World Wide Web at: http://www.peachpit.com
Peachpit Press is a division of Addison Wesley Longman

Interior design by Stephen F. Roth/Open House
Cover Design: Lynn Brofsky Design
Illustration Production: Jeff McCord
Image credits and permissions, page 681

ISBN 0-201-35375-X

9 8 7 6 5 4 3 2 1

Printed and bound in the United States of America

Overview

The Big Picture

Contents

What's Inside

Author! Author!

Where to Reach Us

David Blatner is a Seattle-based graphic-arts consultant specializing in electronic publishing. He has authored or coauthored several books, including the award-winning bestseller *The QuarkXPress Book, Real World Scanning and Halftones, Real World QuarkImmedia,* and *The Joy of Pi.* David presents at conferences around North America and Japan, including MacWorld, Seybold Seminars, and The Photoshop Conference. His email address is david@moo.com.

Bruce Fraser spent 25 years in Edinburgh, Scotland before moving to the equally gray fog belt of San Francisco, which may explain his fascination with color. Bruce is currently a contributing editor for *eMediaweekly* and *MacWorld,* and has authored several books on desktop publishing, in addition to a groundbreaking industry study on color management systems. He also lectures on color reproduction topics. Bruce has been a Photoshop user since the program made its first appearance as BarneyScan XP, and is also an avid amateur photographer. You can reach him via email at bruce@pixelboyz.com.

We'd love to hear from you. You can contact us by mail c/o Moo.com, 1619 Eighth Ave. N., Seattle, WA 98109. Or fax: 206/285-0308.

Foreword

Photoshop Conquers the World

"How hard can it be to change the color of a pixel?"

That question was originally asked as a taunt at the Photoshop engineering team by another product group within Adobe, but it is actually a rather interesting question.

It is, of course, relatively easy to change the color of a single pixel. But how do you know which color to change it to? What do you do when the color you want cannot be expressed in the medium where that pixel will be reproduced? And what do you do when you want to change not one but a million or several million pixels?

Photoshop provides a large collection of tools for changing the color of pixels, and it attempts to embody a certain amount of intelligence about those pixels and their colors. But when it comes right down to it, as far as Photoshop is concerned, those pixels are just a bunch of numbers: it has no notion of what they represent. Ergo, while Photoshop will do the grunt work of making the changes, it has to rely on your judgment about what changes to make.

This book will help you develop that judgment.

It's a book about production issues. In general, it addresses the question "How do I make my images look best when reproduced?" and, specifically, it addresses questions involving color correction, color conversion, color reproduction, image retouching, and efficient use of the computer, the printer, and most importantly your time.

David and Bruce take pride in the fact that this book does not discuss Photoshop special effects such as creating chrome or using the pinch filter. Not to denigrate those capabilities of Photoshop or the books that cover them, but you won't miss the coverage. The absence of those topics makes room for *Real World Photoshop* to take Photoshop's core functions apart, look at how they work, and show you how to use them to get the day-to-day production tasks done.

Photoshop gives you the power to change the color of pixels to your heart's content. *Real World Photoshop* strives to give you the insights about what changes to make.

Mark Hamburg
Principal Scientist and Architect for Adobe Photoshop
Adobe Systems Incorporated

Preface

Photoshop in the Real World

If you're reading this book because you want to produce embossed type, fractalized tree branches, or spherized images in Photoshop, you're in the wrong place. If you're after tips and tricks on how to get the coolest special effects in your images, look elsewhere. There are (at least) half a dozen good books on those subjects.

But if you're looking to move images through Photoshop—getting good scans in, working your will on them, and putting out world-class, camera-ready film—this is the book for you. Its *raison d'être* is to answer the questions that people in production environments ask every single day (and not without some frustration).

▶ What settings should I use in the CMYK Setup dialog box?

▶ How do I bring out shadow details in my images without blowing away the highlights?

▶ What methods are available to neutralize color casts?

▶ How do I calibrate my monitor? (And should I?)

▶ What problems will I run into with the Dust and Scratches filter? Are there better alternatives?

▶ What screen angles should I use for duotones?

▶ How do I put a drop shadow on top of a process-color tint in Quark-XPress or PageMaker?

▶ What's the best way to silhouette an image for catalog work?

These questions, and dozens of others, face Photoshop users all the time. And unfortunately, the books we've seen on Photoshop—much less Photoshop's own manuals—simply don't address these crucial, run-of-the-mill, day-in-and-day-out production issues.

This book does.

Ask Your Printer

We wrote this book for a lot of reasons, but the biggest one was probably our frustration with the knee-jerk advice we kept hearing about desktop prepress: "Ask your printer."

Go ahead. Ask your printer what values you should enter in the RGB Setup, CMYK Setup, and Profile Setup dialog boxes. In our experience, with nine out of ten printers you'll be lucky if you get anything better than wild guesses. You can just forget about black generation curves or anything similarly esoteric.

In this new age of desktop prepress, there's simply no one you can ask (whether you're a designer, a prepress shop . . . or a printer). *You're* in the pilot's seat, with your hand on the stick (and the trigger). Where do you turn when the bogies are incoming?

We're hoping that you'll turn to this book.

Developing Your "Spidey Sense"

Flipping through several hundred pages isn't exactly practical, though, when you've got a missile on your tail. So we try to do more with this book than tell you which key to press, or what value to enter where. We're trying to help you develop what our friend and colleague Greg Vander Houwen calls your "spidey sense" (those who didn't grow up on Spiderman comics may not relate completely, but you get the idea).

When you're in the crunch, you've gotta have an intuitive, almost instinctive feel for what's going on in Photoshop, so you can finesse it to your needs. Canned techniques just don't cut it. So you'll find a fair amount of conceptual discussion here, describing how Photoshop "thinks" about images, and suggesting how you might think about them as well.

The Step-by-Step Stuff

Along with those concepts, we've included just about every step-by-step production technique we know of. From scanning to silhouettes and drop shadows, to tonal correction, sharpening, and color separation, we've tried to explain how to get images into Photoshop—and back out again—with the least pain and the best quality.

And yes, in the course of explaining those techniques, we *will* tell you which key to press, and what values to enter in what dialog boxes.

History is Important

We hear some of you mumbling under your breath, "We've been doing prepress for thirty years, and we don't need to learn a new way of doing it." We don't want to be too confrontational, but we can only reply, "Okay, put down this book, ignore the new tools and techniques, and go out of business like almost every other typesetter and color house that hasn't yet entered the '90s."

The key to succeeding in today's prepress market is understanding both the digital and the traditional realms. Our goal in this book is to help you with both. If you're new to prepress, we try to give you the background you need. If you're an old pro, we try to provide an entry into the heart of digital imaging—the world of zeros and ones.

Our goal is not to detract from the way you've been doing things. It's to show you how those approaches can be incorporated with the new tools, improved, and pushed to new limits.

Whither Photography?

This book isn't just about prepress. It's also about photography and about images. We believe that photographers understand tone and color as well as any other skilled group of professionals, and one of our aims has been to help photographers translate their own understanding of images into Photoshop's digital world.

Digital imaging will undoubtedly change the practice of photography, but images still come from an intentional act on the part of the image maker, and that isn't going to change—no matter whether the photons are captured by goo smeared on celluloid or by photoelectric sensors. We believe that digital imaging offers the photographer as many opportunities as it creates pitfalls. To all the photographers out there who are nervous about the digital revolution, we say, "Come on in, the water's fine." And more to the point, we can't *do* this stuff without you.

The Depth of Understanding

We were crazy to take on this book. If we weren't, we wouldn't have tried to unravel such an insanely complex subject. Writing this book has been a humbling experience—we thought we knew how Photoshop worked when we started, but as the book grew, we realized how much we still had (and have) to learn. The process of acquiring knowledge is largely a matter of remapping the boundaries of our ignorance.

We don't claim to have the ultimate answers, but the answers we do have are tried, tested, and effective. The methods we discuss in this book may not be the only way to get good results from Photoshop, but they're the product of many long days and nights of research and testing, of badgering anyone we thought might have an answer with endless questions, and of even more long nights of experiments, more testing, and trying to present these insights in some coherent form. (Bruce vaguely remembers wondering, while making coffee at 4 AM, why one of his kitchen faucets was labeled "cyan" . . . .)

While our grasp on reality may have occasionally been tenuous during the production of this book, the techniques we present are firmly grounded in the real world—hence the title.

How the Book is Organized

The biggest problem we've faced in writing about Photoshop is not just that it's the "deepest" program we've ever used, but that almost every technique and feature relies on every other technique and feature. In that way, Photoshop is impossible to talk about without circular reasoning. Nevertheless, we've tried to impose some order by breaking our topics down into five general sections.

The world of Photoshop. In the first five chapters, we attempt to lay the groundwork for the rest of the book. We put all this information first because it's patently impossible to be effective in Photoshop without it.

▶ Building a Photoshop System

▶ Essential Photoshop Tips and Tricks

▶ Image Essentials

▶ Color Essentials

▶ Color Settings

Image corrections. Now that we've laid the groundwork, we jump into really working with images. In these chapters, we explore techniques you'll want to employ with almost every image you work with in Photoshop.

▶ Tonal Correction

▶ Color Correction

▶ The Digital Darkroom

▶ Sharpening

Images. The origin and type of the images you work with determine what you can or need to do with them.

▶ Spot Colors and Duotones

▶ Line Art

▶ Scanners

▶ Capturing Images

Fine tuning. In the next two chapters, we really get down to the nitty-gritty of manipulating images—selecting pixels, pushing them into place, and being really efficient with the sort of editing that we all have to do every day.

▶ Selections

▶ Essential Image Techniques

After Photoshop. Sometimes it's hard to remember that there is life outside of Photoshop. In the last three chapters of the book, we show how to get those images out of Photoshop into the real world.

▶ Storing Images

▶ Output Methods

▶ Multimedia and the Web

A Word to Windows Users

This book covers tips and techniques for both the Macintosh and Windows versions of Photoshop. However, we have chosen to illustrate dialog boxes, menus, and palettes using screen shots from the Macintosh version. Similarly, when discussing the many keyboard shortcuts in the program, we include the Macintosh versions. We apologize to all you Windows users, but because the interface between the two programs is so transparent we picked one platform and ran with it.

As for keystrokes, in almost every case the Command key translates to the Control key and the Option key translates to the Alt key. In the few cases where this is not true, we have included both the Macintosh and the Windows versions.

Thank You!

We'd like to give special thanks to a few of the many people who helped evolve a shadow of an idea into what you hold in your hands. Our first vote of thanks goes to the editor of the first edition, Steve Roth, who continually challenged us to make the book better and clearer, and forced us to learn things we only thought we knew. Nancy Davis, our editor of this third edition, was very helpful and patient. Jeff Carlson of Never Enough Coffee Creations handled the gargantuan task of bringing all the elements together in time to meet our deadlines. Carl Juarez built and rebuilt huge numbers of pages, and Angela Reitz caught an embarrassingly large number of typos and inconsistencies at the 11th hour.

Cindy Bell of Design Language, Agen Schmitz, and Debbie Carlson made sure we didn't sound like complete fools, and Robb Kerr of Digital Iguana provided invaluable advice on Windows arcana.

We particularly appreciate Mark Hamburg, Photoshop's chief architect, for writing the Foreword to this edition, for providing patient and clear answers to a constant string of arcane e-mail questions, and for Photoshop 4 and 5. Thanks also go to Chris Cox, Bryan Lamkin, John Leddy, Sean Parent, John Cornicello, and Andrei Herasimchuk at Adobe, who all helped and inspired us in their diverse ways.

Other vendors were generous in providing equipment, support and encouragement. Special thanks go to Karl Lang of Radius, Marla Robinson and David Eigelhart of Intergraph, Joe Runde, Cliff Wilson, Hapet Berberian, Mike Shea, and Jay Kelbley at Kodak, Luc Colle and Wendy Bosley at Barco, Jan deClippeleer and John Phillips at Agfa, Ed Grainger and Fred Bunting at Light Source, Andy Chang at Imacon, Eckhard Huebner at Heidelberg CPS, Michael Stokes at Hewlett-Packard, and Barry Weiss at Minolta.

Many third-party software vendors provided invaluable help too, including Herb Paynter at ImageXPress, Dr. Stefan Brues at Logo Software, Eric Walowit and Mark Geeves at Color Savvy, John Grimaldi at Candela, Bill Hilliard at Sonnetech, and Stephen Herron at Isis Imaging.

We owe Sam Merrell, Steve Pollock, Andrew Rodney, and Scott Sandeman-Allen a great vote of thanks for their ongoing support. Thanks also go to Stephen Johnson for his generosity of spirit, his constant encouragement, and for the many hours he spent with us in deep discussions that ranged from the technical to the philosophical.

If we see further than others, it's because we stand on the shoulders of true Photoshop giants, including Greg Vander Houwen, Katrin Eismann, Jeff Schewe, Lynda Weinmann, Doug Peltonen, Bob Schaffel, Glenn Mitsui, Chuck Weger, Eric Reinfeld, David Biedny, Deke McClelland, and Bill Niffenegger, pixelmeisters all.

And thank you to the regulars on CompuServe's DTP Forum, Adobe Forum, and Photo Forum, for questions as well as answers.

We also want to thank all our friends at Peachpit Press—Nancy, Keasley, Cary, Amy, Paula, Hannah, Jim, and at least a dozen others. And, finally, thanks to the folks at Thunder Lizard Productions, Glenn Fleishman, and Olav Martin Kvern.

convinced that price and performance are at parity on the two platforms: The Mac has somewhat richer third-party support in terms of plug-ins and color measurement equipment. The PC has a much greater range of general business software.

The major difference we see between Macs and PCs for Photoshop use is that, if you want to build a system that lets you work visually rather than by the numbers, it's still easier to do so on the Mac, largely because of the very different ways the two platforms handle the monitor. We should add that building a Mac system that lets you work visually isn't a trivial undertaking either, but it's doable. Windows 98 has much more robust color management than Windows 95, but that's not in and of itself a reason to upgrade. Bruce has been quite successful in implementing a visually-based Photoshop system on Windows NT 4, which has no color management features whatever. The key ingredient is an accurate ICC monitor profile, and while there are many more tools for creating monitor profiles on the Mac than on any flavor of Windows, it's possible to do so on any of the platforms Photoshop supports.

The bottom line: if you're happy with your current platform, there's probably no reason to switch.

Macintosh. Many Photoshop operations involve really large quantities of number crunching, so the speed of your Mac's processor makes a big difference. Photoshop 5 is the first version that requires a Power Mac—it won't run at all on 680x0-based systems—and the new G3-based systems are much faster than their predecessors.

Fast multiprocessor Power Macs like the Daystar Genesis MP machines can still hold their own against the G3—a few operations may even be faster—but if you're still running a single-processor 604 (or even worse, a 601), you may want to investigate one of the third-party G3 accelerators, or consider buying a new machine entirely.

The Pentium II. Pentium II-based machines are handy Photoshop workhorses, particularly those in the 300–400MHz range. Today's Pentium IIs are all MMX-enabled, which accelerates some time-consuming Photoshop tasks such as Unsharp Masking and RGB-to-CMYK conversion by 300 to 500 percent. If you're running an older, non-MMX Pentium or Pentium Pro, you may want to consider a processor upgrade.

The Pentium Pro. Pentium Pros are significantly faster than a same-clock-speed Pentium II, so they're optimal for Photoshop in a Windows environment, and the current generation are all MMX-enabled, though the early ones were not. However, to really achieve the full benefit of a Pentium Pro you probably want to run Windows NT 4, which is a completely 32-bit operating system. If you want to use a multiprocessor Pentium Pro system you must run Windows NT—Windows 95 and Windows 98 don't support multiprocessing.

RAM

You can never be too thin, too rich, or have too much RAM. Just how much RAM you need depends on your file size—remember that additional layers and channels increase the size of the file—but we don't recommend even trying to run Photoshop on a system with less than 32MB of RAM. It's doable—barely—but you have to kill all your INITs or TSRs and other RAM-gobblers, and it generally becomes an exercise in frustration.

For optimum performance on the Mac, you should allocate to Photoshop an amount of RAM equal to at least three times the size of your file, plus about five megabytes for the program itself (see Figure 1-1). Note that a 5 MB file becomes a 10 MB file as soon as you add a layer, so the file size can add up quickly, particularly if you use a lot of layers or channels. Nonetheless, the biggest single factor affecting Photoshop performance is the availability of enough RAM. Copying pixels takes RAM; taking a snapshot takes RAM; History states take RAM; in fact, doing anything takes RAM because Photoshop always saves a version of your image in a memory buffer so that you can quickly undo. The new History feature takes up gobs of RAM—if you want a supercharged History palette, you may want 20–50 times the file size in RAM for optimal performance. See "Tip: Turning Off History" in Chapter 2, *Essential Photoshop Tips and Tricks.*

Under Windows, memory allocation is dynamic, so you can't allocate a specific amount of RAM to Photoshop. A safe recommendation seems to be to allocate Photoshop 75% of the remaining memory—if you give it much more than that, Windows may become unhappy.

If you're working with 2 MB images, you should have at least 11 or 12 MB allocated to Photoshop. If you're working with 18 MB Photo CD images, you better have at least 64 MB in your machine. For larger images you need even more.

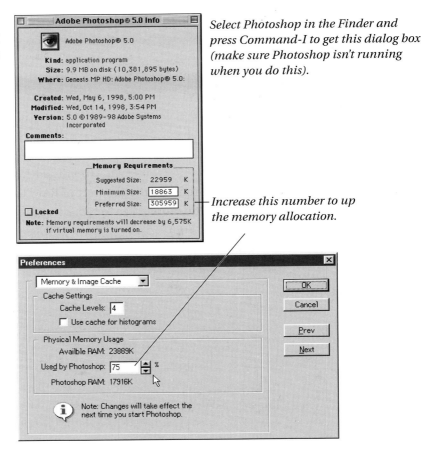

Figure 1-1
**Allocating RAM
to Photoshop**

Select Photoshop in the Finder and press Command-I to get this dialog box (make sure Photoshop isn't running when you do this).

Increase this number to up the memory allocation.

Note that a few Photoshop filters (Lens Flare, for instance) require that you have enough physical RAM to load the entire image into memory. Even though Photoshop has a virtual-memory scheme (see below), if you don't have the RAM, these effects just won't work.

Virtual memory. Since Apple instituted a virtual-memory scheme in System 7, there's been an ongoing debate over whether or not to use it while running Photoshop. Virtual memory lets you run more applications at one time because it sets aside hard disk space as "temporary RAM." (On Power Macs, virtual memory has the side effect of reducing the amount of memory that you need to allocate to programs.) But hard disks are nowhere near as fast as RAM, so you get a significant slowdown.

Photoshop has its own virtual-memory scheme that comes into play anytime it needs more RAM than you have allocated to it (see "Scratch Disk Space," later in this chapter).

Nonetheless, you can use virtual memory (either the Mac's—invoked through the Memory control panel—or Connectix's RAM Doubler) in conjunction with Photoshop, but only in a limited, specific way. Do not use virtual memory in order to allocate more RAM to Photoshop than you physically have. Your performance will suffer horribly, because Apple's (or RAM Doubler's) virtual memory will work at cross-purposes with Photoshop's own very efficient virtual-memory scheme.

Ultimately, the only time we turn on virtual memory is when we are working on a Power Mac with too little RAM (like 32 MB). In this case, turning it on reduces the amount of RAM the actual program takes up, so there's a little more room for your images, and you can run additional programs. One other drawback to Apple's virtual memory is that the system "freezes" temporarily whenever it's reading from the disk; if you're painting at that moment, your work might be interrupted.

Tip: Disk Cache Settings. Photoshop 5 ignores the Macintosh's disk cache, which you set in the Memory control panel. The only impact it has is that memory allocated to the disk cache isn't available to Photoshop. If you have enough RAM, and you find that the disk cache helps other programs significantly (which it does with disk-intensive applications like page layout), then by all means devote a couple megabytes to it. If you need to give Photoshop every ounce of available RAM, set it to the lowest possible setting instead.

Windows Swapfile

Windows always uses the startup drive for its swap file unless you have told it otherwise. You can change the swap file setting by bringing up Properties for "My Computer," selecting the "Performance" tab, pressing the "Virtual Memory" button and selecting the "Let me specify my own virtual memory settings" (Win95/98) or "Change" (Windows NT) option. This lets you specify maximum and minimum sizes for the swap file as well as which drive gets used.

Our Windows guru, Robb Kerr, adds the following advice: "Do not disable Windows' virtual memory scheme or crank its size way down like you do on the Mac. Very bad things happen. System lock-ups, inability to reboot, required reloading of Win95, etc."

Things go much faster if you put the swap file on a different drive from

Photoshop's scratch file. Since Photoshop also defaults to using the startup drive for its scratch file, you'll always want to change the configuration of either the Windows swapfile or the Photoshop scratch disk. (See "Contiguous Scratch Disk Space," below.)

Scratch Disk Space

Photoshop requires scratch disk space equal to the amount of RAM you've allocated to Photoshop. That means if you've given Photoshop 120 MB of RAM, you must have 120 MB of free disk space. If you have less, Photoshop will only use an amount of RAM equivalent to the free space on the scratch disk.

Photoshop constantly optimizes the scratch space. Those of you who learned in the stone age to regard disk access as a warning signal that things are about to get very slow should learn to accept this behavior as a necessary and normal part of Photoshop's functioning. People are often especially concerned when they see disk access immediately after opening a file. This, too, is normal: Photoshop is simply setting itself up to be more efficient down the line.

Tip: Contiguous Scratch Disk Space. Photoshop runs faster and more smoothly when the scratch disk space is contiguous and unfragmented. If you can, dedicate an entire hard disk to Photoshop's scratch space. If you have a partitioned hard drive, you can set one partition to be the scratch disk. However, *don't* use one partition for the scratch disk and the other partition for the system, the program, or the image. If you do, the hard drive head has to move all over the hard drive between reading the image and writing the scratch space, which can really slow you down.

On Windows systems, you'll get much better performance if your Windows swapfile is pointed to a different drive than Photoshop's scratch disk, for the same reason. We recommend letting Windows manage its own swap file and allocating a second disk for Photoshop's scratch disk.

Tip: Use the Efficiency Indicator. Unless you've got way too much RAM, or you work on files that are mighty small, there's a good chance that Photoshop is going to start using its built-in virtual memory technique. That means that Photoshop is going to be reading and writing to your scratch disk (whatever hard drive you've specified in the Scratch Disk preferences under the File menu). Here's a way you can check to see if

Photoshop is writing to your scratch disk.

In the lower-left corner of the document window, there's a popup menu that shows document size, scratch size, or "efficiency" (see Figure 1-2). If you set this to Scratch Sizes, the first number shows the amount of RAM being used by all open documents, and the second number shows the amount of RAM that's allocated to Photoshop. If the first number is bigger than the second, Photoshop is using your hard drive as virtual memory. When the indicator is set to Efficiency, a reading of less than 100 percent indicates that virtual memory is coming into play.

Figure 1-2
Scratch size

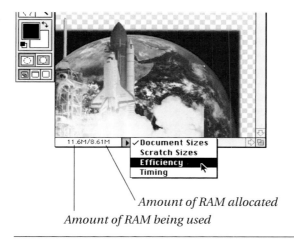

11.6M/8.61M

✓ Document Sizes
　Scratch Sizes
　Efficiency
　Timing

Amount of RAM allocated

Amount of RAM being used

Tip: Watching Your Windows Scratch Disk. Norton Utilities for Windows contains a mini-app called Norton System Doctor. You can leave the dialog for this app open all the time: it gives you dynamic updates on available disk space for all your attached drives, system resource usage, and CPU usage. It's very useful in diagnosing a slow machine, and for watching Photoshop's usage of the swap disk.

Tip: Use the Purge Commands. You know that Photoshop gets sluggish when you run out of RAM. And you know that whenever you take a new snapshot, or copy a large chunk of your document to the clipboard, Photoshop guzzles down two or three times your document size in RAM. If you don't have two to three times the document size of RAM in your machine, life slows down significantly. You can clear up the amount of RAM that Photoshop is using by "emptying" the Histories, Clipboard, Pattern, and Undo buffers. In old versions of Photoshop we resorted to all sorts of clever tricks to do this. Nowadays, we simply select Clipboard,

Histories, Pattern, Undo, or All from the Purge submenu (at the bottom of the Edit menu). If a Purge command is dimmed, it means the buffer is already empty, so there's nothing there to purge.

You can always check to see if the Purge is working by looking at the Scratch Sizes (see "Tip: Use the Efficiency Indicator," earlier in this chapter).

RAID arrays. A striped RAID hard disk array can be a very worthwhile investment, particularly if you're dealing with images too large for your available RAM on a regular basis. It won't give you the performance you'd get from having enough RAM, but it's cheaper per megabyte than buying more RAM, and because Photoshop can write to a RAID disk much faster than to a single fixed disk, your performance is going to improve.

Opening and saving large files will also be faster with a RAID hard disk array. However, given sufficient RAM, relatively few Photoshop tasks are dependent on disk speed, so if you have a choice between buying RAM and buying a fast hard drive, you should invest in RAM first (unless opening and saving large files already constitutes a significant bottleneck in your workflow). Windows NT has built-in RAID software, but a hardware RAID array is faster.

Video Acceleration

There's a widespread belief that accelerated video boards speed up Photoshop. Unfortunately, it's ill-informed. The bottleneck in redrawing Photoshop images on the screen is almost never in the video system—it's in getting the image data out of RAM (or even worse, from disk) to the video system. A super-fast video card may make your system feel faster and more responsive, but if you take the time to analyze what's going on, you'll typically find that the difference is a screen redraw of two-tenths of a second rather than five-tenths of a second. (Of course, those tenths of a second can add up—in a month you may even save enough time to grab a cup of coffee.)

On the other hand, many Windows systems, especially those "special-of-the-week" machines people are so fond of buying at office supply stores, often have less-than-optimal video boards. We generally advise people to get a Matrox video board; if you've got something else, it might be okay, or it might be slowing you down considerably.

The only other reason to add a third-party video board is to obtain higher resolutions than the built-in video offers. You really need to be able to run at your desired resolution in 24-bit (millions) color—16-bit color is fine for viewing images, but not for editing them.

A fairly widespread misconception is that a video board with a lot of VRAM will be somehow faster than one with less. Not so. More VRAM simply translates into more pixels on the screen—as long as your monitor can display them (see Table 1-1). Some Windows video cards will, given sufficient VRAM, buffer the image behind dialog boxes. This speeds up performance because when you dismiss the dialog box, the screen doesn't have to redraw—the underlying image is already there.

Table 1-1
Monitor resolutions and VRAM

VRAM	Monitor resolution	Bit Depth
2 Mb	832-by-624	24-bit
	1280-by-1024	16-bit
4 Mb	1360-by-1024	24-bit
	1600-by-1200	16-bit
8 Mb	1600-by-1200	24-bit

Video LUT Animation. A video lookup table (Video LUT) can help a video card "drive" the monitor by offering a quick method for converting a digital signal into an analog one. One great feature about Video LUT is that it can offer software control; that is, by changing the Video LUT settings, a computer program (like Photoshop) can actually control what you see on the screen. This is called Video LUT Animation.

However, while some cards (notably those on Macintoshes) use Video LUT, many others (notably many of those in the Windows environment) do not. Instead, they use fixed digital-to-analog converters (DACs), which makes Video LUT Animation impossible—there's no lookup table to animate. Other cards may use a Video LUT, but they supply no means of addressing it, so again, Video LUT Animation is impossible. We also know of some cases where the video card supplies Video LUT Animation, but only when the screen is set to 256 colors (which is less than optimal when working in Photoshop, of course).

We'll look at how Photoshop uses Video LUT Animation in Chapter 6, *Tonal Correction*. You may find you just don't need it. However, if you do want it and your video card won't support it, we can only suggest that you ask the vendor why it doesn't. If it's simply a driver problem it can be fixed in software. If the card has fixed DACs, though, you're out of luck.

The Power of Photoshop

Photoshop is not a island, complete unto itself. Rather, it's surrounded by hardware and software that supports or hinders it. If you focus on any piece of the whole and ignore the rest, you'll undoubtedly run into trouble (or at the very least, you'll be less efficient than you might have been).

We're going to focus on Photoshop for the rest of the book, but while you read, keep in mind these other factors: memory considerations, hardware, and third-party software. That way, you'll really be prepared to harness the power of Photoshop.

2

Essential Photoshop Tips and Tricks

Making Photoshop Fly

Photoshop is deep. Really deep. It's like those National Geographic movies that talk about the world below the surface of the ocean: on the surface it's smooth and straightforward, but down below you'll find things that'll knock your socks off.

In this chapter, we dive down deep and map out some of the canyons along the sea bed. You can dog-paddle around Photoshop without these tips, but you'll never really swim with the sharks until you've explored these territories.

Don't forget your flippers!

Upgrading to a New Version

There are few things as inevitable as death, taxes, and upgrading your software. Some people upgrade as soon as the box hits the proverbial shelf; others take years, buying a new version only after their service bureau or printer refuses to take their old files anymore. Sooner or later, though, you'll be faced with new features, new challenges, and a new bottle of aspirin.

We have found that there are many people who, afraid of being left behind by the march of time, are only now quickly upgrading from

Photoshop 3 to version 5. Others have already taken the intermediate step to version 4. If you're in this latter group, you can just skim over this next section and start reading at "What's New in Version 5."

No matter what version you're upgrading from, we urge you to be cautious when using Photoshop 5, as there are some significant changes that can bite you hard where you expect it least (primarily in how Photoshop handles color).

Upgrading from Version 3

Those accustomed to Photoshop 3 will be jolted by several improvements that were first found in Photoshop 4, including new keyboard shortcuts and methods for navigating through the document. Here are a few things to think about when working with the new version. (These certainly aren't the majority of the new features that appeared in Photoshop 4, but they're the ones most likely to stick in your craw.)

Selections. Draw out a selection, then click in the center of the selection and move it. In version 3, this moved the pixels within the selection. Now it moves the selection itself and leaves the pixels alone. If you want to move the pixels, you need the Move tool, which you can get from the Tool palette or—even better—by holding down the Command key. This takes some getting used to, even though it's much more logical.

Pasting. Every time you paste something into a document, Photoshop places it on a new layer (and deselects it). For some reason, this makes version 3 users insane. You must keep two things in mind. First, the Command key temporarily gives you the Move tool, with which you can move the new layer wherever you want it. Second, you can always press Command-E to merge the new layer with the layer beneath it. This merges *only* these two layers; the other layers remain separate.

Type tool. The Type tool has the same result as pasting pixels: you automatically get a new layer. This, too, is really a godsend, because you almost always want type on a separate layer (just in case the copy editors change their minds about how something should read). Photoshop 5 now puts text on a special kind of layer (which we'll discuss in the next section).

Keystrokes. Adobe changed many familiar keystrokes in version 4, and it's worth learning them to get the most out of the program. One of the best ways to learn these keystrokes is to turn on the Tool Tips option in General Preferences (press Command-K). When Tool Tips is on and your cursor lingers over one of the tools for more than two or three seconds, a small label appears displaying that tool's name and keystroke.

Some changes to keystrokes are significant. For example, Command-zero used to display your image's color composite; now, it zooms to Fit in Window. To get the color composite, you must press Command-~ (tilde), which used to switch to the layer mask (if there was one). Now, to switch to the layer mask you must press Command-\ (backslash).

Cropping tool. It's a little thing, but it makes people angry that Adobe changed the way the Cropping tool works. In Photoshop 3, clicking inside the cropping rectangle told Photoshop to go ahead and perform the crop. Now, you have to press Enter or Return, or double-click inside the rectangle in order to crop. Adobe had to change this because now, single-clicking in the rectangle lets you move the cropping rectangle, and clicking outside the rectangle lets you rotate it. Also, to cancel the Cropping tool, you have to press Command-period (on the Macintosh) or press Escape (if you're using Windows).

Commands palette. The Commands palette no longer exists, replaced by a much more powerful set of tools in the Actions palette. We discuss actions and what you can do with them in Chapter 15, *Essential Image Techniques*.

Big data. Remember how in Photoshop 3, you always had to be careful of moving something outside the edges of the image, because if you painted or ran a filter or something, the pixels hanging off the side would be clipped off? Well, no longer! Now, Photoshop always remembers image data off the sides of an image (as long as you save the image in Photoshop format; formats like TIFF and EPS can't handle this).

What's New in Version 5

Those of you familiar with Photoshop 4 will be pleased with most of the interface changes in version 5, though some might throw you off a little at first. The most drastic change in version 5 is Photoshop's internal color management, which is so important that we've devoted a whole chapter to it (see Chapter 5, *Color Settings*). We don't want to scare you, but without a thorough understanding of the Color Settings dialog boxes, you'll be lost in this new version (and you may not even know how lost you are).

Here are a few other important changes in version 5 (again, we're not listing every new feature in Photoshop 5 here; just the ones you'd better know about before jumping into the rest of the book).

Type layers. When you use the Type tool, Photoshop 5 places your text on a new kind of layer, called a *type layer*. The primary benefit to a type layer is that you can edit the text on it later by double-clicking on the layer's tile in the Layers palette. There are two other important changes to the Type tool. First, you can now format type (set its font, size, kerning, and so on) character by character. Second, if you want your text to sit vertically rather than horizontally, you have to use the Vertical Text tool instead (found on the Text tool's popout menu on the Tool palette).

History palette. One of the most incredible features of Photoshop 5 is the History palette, which not only provides multiple Undos, but also a method of selectively undoing portions of your image. The cost to use the History palette is high, however: you need lots (lots!) of free RAM. (See "When Things Go Worng," later in this chapter, for more on this feature.)

Layer Effects. By now you probably know that we're not into special effects; rather our focus is how to get the job done fast and well. However, there are some effects that real-world people do every day—drop shadows, for instance. Photoshop 5 lets you apply several special effects (including drop shadows) to your layers. As far as we're concerned, there's hardly any reason to build drop shadows using the old methods anymore; just use Layer Effects. (See Chapter 15, *Essential Image Techniques*, for more on Layer Effects.) Note that Photoshop 5 also lets you align and distribute layers from the Layers menu.

Spot color. For years we were reduced to saying, "Sorry, Photoshop doesn't do spot color except for duotones." Fortunately, that's all changed now. Spot colors are still somewhat nonintuitive, but we explain it all for you in Chapter 10, *Spot Colors and Duotones*.

Transforms. The Free Transform feature, now found under the Edit menu (or press Command-T), lets you rotate, skew, scale, and move a selection all in one fell swoop (see Figure 2-1). That's not new, but this is: Command-Shift-T, which used to display the Numeric Transform dialog box, now applies the last-used transform settings on whatever you have selected. If you add the Option key to either of these keystrokes, Photoshop copies the pixels before transforming them, so you don't end up with a "hole" in your image. By the way, version 5's Transform feature also lets you specify the center point of the transformation (so you can rotate a selection from the lower-left corner, for example).

As with the Cropping tool, you can press Command-period (Mac) or Escape (Windows) to cancel anything you've done. Unlike the Cropping tool, you can press Command-Z at any time to undo the last modification you made. Note that even when you're in "transform mode," you can still use the various other transformation tools on the Transform submenu (under the Layer menu). For instance, you can rotate and skew a layer with Free Transform, and then select Flip Horizontal from the Transform submenu.

If you think in numbers rather than visually, you might prefer selecting Numeric Transform from the Transform submenu (under the Edit menu). Here, you can enter values for scale, rotation, skew, and so on, very precisely.

Figure 2-1
Free Transform

Drag any handle to scale

Command-drag to distort

Drag outside of the selection to rotate

Command-drag a side handle to skew

Command-Option-drag to distort opposite handles in opposite directions

Command-Option-Shift-drag a corner handle to give perspective

Selections and paths. Photoshop 5 offers several enhancements to the already powerful group of selection tools. The Magnetic Lasso, the Magnetic Pen, and the Freehand Pen tools, for instance, are very cool for making certain kinds of selections quickly. Even better, in our book, is the ability to perform transformations (scaling, rotation, skewing, and so on) to both selections and paths (choose Transform Selection from the Select menu, or Transform Path from the Edit menu; see Chapter 14, *Selections*, for more on these features).

Keyboard shortcuts. We get the sense that Adobe would feel like they hadn't really done their job if they didn't change at least a few keyboard shortcuts between versions. Fortunately, the changes aren't as dramatic between versions 4 and 5 than they were between 3 and 4. While you could switch between similar tools by repeatedly pressing their shortcut key (such as pressing M once for the rectangular Marquee tool, and M again for the oval Marquee tool), now you must hold down the Shift key to change from one tool to the next (in this case, Shift-M switches to the oval Marquee tool).

If you use the Airbrush tool, note that its shortcut is now the letter J, because the direct-select Path tool has changed to A (for "arrow"). You can also change blend modes (Normal, Screen, Multiply, and so on), by pressing Shift-hyphen and Shift-plus, or by holding down Shift and Option and pressing the first letter of the mode (such as Shift-Option-S for Screen). If you have a painting tool selected (like the Brush tool), this changes the mode of that tool; otherwise, it changes the mode of the layer itself.

You've always been able to press Option-Delete to fill a selection or layer with the foreground color. In version 4, Photoshop added the ability to automatically preserve transparency on the layer when you add the Shift key (slightly faster than having to turn on the Preserve Transparency checkbox in the Layers palette). Similarly, you can fill with the background color by pressing Command-Delete (add the Shift key to preserve transparency).

What's more, in Photoshop 5, Command-Option-Delete fills your selection with the current source state on the History palette; and, of course, you can add the Shift key to this to fill with Preserve Transparency turned on.

Windows

Screen space is at almost as great a premium as memory these days—every little bit helps. We like to work in full-screen mode with Photoshop (see Figure 2-2) instead of wasting space on title bars, scroll bars, and the like. You can switch to either of two full-screen modes in the Tool palette, or by pressing F. The first time you press F (or when you click on the middle icon on the palette), the image window takes over the screen (up to the menu bar) and the background becomes 50-percent gray. The second time, the menu bar disappears, too, and the background becomes

Figure 2-2

Full-screen mode

Click here or press F. . .

. . . to switch to full-screen mode.

black. (See "Make the Palettes Go Away," later in this chapter, for an important related tip.)

Tip: Show the Menu Bar. When you're in either of the full-screen modes, you can hide or show the menu bar by pressing Shift-F.

Tip: Rotating Through Your Windows. We often find ourselves in Photoshop with five or more windows open at a time—a frustrating situation when we need to move through them all quickly. In Photoshop for Windows, you can use the Control-Tab and Control-Shift-Tab keystrokes to switch among open documents. There's no such keystroke on the Macintosh, however. CE Software's QuicKeys to the rescue! We rely on the Select Rear Window shortcut (under QuicKeys's Specials submenu; see Figure 2-3). When you press the appropriate keystroke (David has it set to Command-Shift-Tab), the back window pops to the front. This way,

Figure 2-3

Defining a QuicKey shortcut to toggle through windows

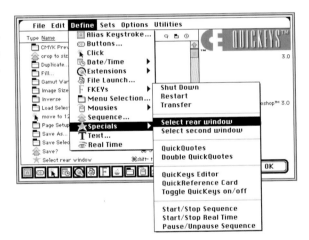

you can rotate through the windows without taking your hands off the keyboard, even if you're in full-screen mode with no menus.

Tip: Use New Window. You often want to see your image at Actual Pixels view (where screen pixels equal image pixels), but work at some other magnification. Instead of jumping back and forth between magnification views, try opening a second window by selecting New Window from the View menu. You can leave one window set to one hundered percent, and change the other window to whatever view you want to work at. Whenever you change something in one window, Photoshop updates the other window almost immediately. You can also use this technique to display an image in RGB and CMYK Preview modes simultaneously.

Navigation

In this section, we first explore some of the fastest ways to move around your image, including zooming in and out. Then we move on to moving pixels around within your document, and from one document to another. If you've just upgraded from version 3, note that the zooming behavior and many of the shortcuts changed substantially in Photoshop 4, so we urge you to read this section even if you think you already know all there is to know about navigating in Photoshop.

Magnification

Images got pixels. Computer screens got pixels. But how does one type of pixel relate to the other type of pixel? When you display an image on your screen, Photoshop has to match image pixels to screen pixels (see Figure 2-4). The percentage in the title bar of the document window tells you how Photoshop is matching those pixels up.

The key to understanding this percentage stuff is to remember two things. First, at 100-percent view (otherwise known as Actual Pixels), each image pixel is represented by a single screen pixel. This view is not necessarily how big the image will be in print or on a computer screen (if it's destined for the Web). Second, at any percentage other than 100, you're probably not seeing a fully accurate view of your image.

At 400 percent, the image is magnified four times. At 50 percent, it's reduced by half, so you're only seeing half the pixels in the image because you're zoomed farther out and Photoshop has to downsample the picture on the fly. When you're viewing at an integral multiple of 100 (meaning 25, 50, 200, 400 percent, and so on), Photoshop displays image pixels evenly. At 200 percent, two screen pixels equal one image pixel; at 50 percent, two image pixels equal one screen pixel, and so on.

However, when you're at any "odd" percentage, the program has to jimmy the display in order to make things work. Photoshop can't cut a screen pixel or an image pixel in half, so instead it fakes the effect using anti-aliasing. The moral of the story is always return to Actual Size (100

Figure 2-4
Matching pixels

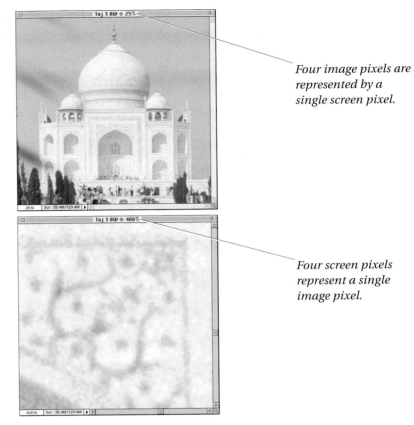

Four image pixels are represented by a single screen pixel.

Four screen pixels represent a single image pixel.

percent) view to peruse your image, particularly if you're trying to evaluate the effects of Unsharp Masking.

Tip: Don't Use Image Cache for Histograms. When the Use Image Cache for Histograms option is turned on in the Preferences dialog box (Command-K), as it is by default, the histogram you see is a histogram of what you see on screen, *not* the histogram of your data. The anti-aliasing you get at any view other than 100 percent can produce a very smooth histogram when in fact your data is already severely posterized. We can't really envisage a situation where you need to see a histogram of the screen display instead of a histogram of your data, so turn this option off.

Tip: Don't Select the Zoom Tool. We never select the Zoom tool from the Tool palette. You can always get the Zoom tool temporarily by holding down Command-spacebar (to zoom in) or Command-Option-spacebar (to zoom out). Each click magnifies from actual size to two-thirds

(66.7 percent), to one-half (50 percent), to one-third (33.3 percent), and so on when zooming out, and in one-hundred-percent increments when zooming in. (Actually, it jumps from 800 to 1,200 percent, and from 1,200 to 1,600 percent, which is the maximum magnification available.)

You can also drag around an area with the Zoom tool. The pixels within the marquee are magnified to whatever arbitrary percentage best fills the screen.

Tip: Zoom with Keystrokes. If you just want to change the overall magnification of an image, press Command-plus (+) or Command-minus (-) to zoom in or out. We find this especially handy because it resizes the window at the same time if necessary (but if any palettes are open, this keystroke won't increase the document window beyond the edges of the palettes). Note that adding the Option key to this mix tells Photoshop to zoom in or out without changing the size of the window.

Tip: Get to 100-Percent View Quickly. You can jump to 100-percent view quickly by double-clicking on the Zoom tool in the Tool palette. This is just the same as clicking the Actual Pixels button in the Zoom Tool or Hand Tool Options palette or choosing Actual Pixels from the View menu. Even faster, press Command-Option-0 (zero).

Tip: Fit Window in Screen. Double-clicking on the Hand tool, on the other hand (no pun left unturned), is the same as pressing Fit on Screen in the Zoom Tool or Hand Tool Options palette, or pressing Command-0 (zero)—it makes the image and the document window as large as it can, without going out of the screen's boundaries.

Tip: Zoom Factor. At the bottom-left corner of the window, Photoshop displays the current magnification percentage. This isn't only a display: you can change it to whatever percentage you'd like (double-click to select the whole field). Type the zoom percentage you want, then press Return or Enter when you're done. If you're not sure exactly what percentage you want, note that you can press Shift-Return instead of Return and the field remains selected after Photoshop zooms in or out, letting you enter a different value (See Figure 2-5).

Figure 2-5
Zoom factor

Moving

If you're like most Photoshop users, you find yourself moving around the image a lot. Do a little here . . . do a little there . . . and so on. But when you're doing this kind of navigation, you should rarely use the scroll bars. There are much better ways.

Tip: Use the Grabber Hand. The best way to make a small move around your image is with the Grabber Hand. Don't choose it from the Tool palette. Instead, hold down the spacebar to get the Grabber Hand. Then just click and drag to where you want to go.

Tip: End Up Down Home. We like the extended keyboard—the kind with function keys and the built-in keypad. Most people ignore the very helpful Page Up, Page Down, Home, and End keys in Photoshop, but we find them invaluable for perusing an image for dust or scratches.

When you press Page Up or Page Down, Photoshop scrolls the image by almost an entire page's worth of pixels up or down. It leaves a small band of overlap, just in case. While there's no Page Left or Page Right button, you can jump a screen to the left or right by pressing Command-Page Up or Command-Page Down. You can also scroll in 10-pixel increments by pressing Shift-Page Up and Shift-Page Down (or, again, add the Command key to go left or right).

Also note that pressing the Home button jumps you to the upper-left corner, and the End button jumps you to the lower-right corner of the document. David often uses this technique when using the Cropping tool. He lazily sets the cropping rectangle approximately where he wants it, then zooms in to the upper-left corner to precisely adjust that corner point. Then, with one hit of the End key, he's transported to the lower-right, where he can adjust that corner.

Tip: Use the Control Key on the Mac Standard Keyboard. If you have a Macintosh Standard Keyboard, you don't have the Page Up, Page Down,

Home, and End keys, but you can use Control-key equivalents. Press Control-K (*not* Command-K) instead of Page Up, Control-L for Page Down, Control-A for Home, and Control-D for End. (Add the Command key to Control-K and Control-L to move left and right, and the Shift key to move the display in 10-pixel increments.)

Tip: Moving Among the Layers. The Grabber Hand and scroll bars only let you move around your image on a two-dimensional plane. What about moving into the third dimension—the layer dimension?

You can move among layers (without ever touching the Layers palette) by using keystrokes: Option-[or Option-] (the square brackets) move to the previous or next visible layer. If you add the Shift key to that, Photoshop jumps to the bottom or top layer (very helpful if you've got a mess o' layers).

One cool feature here is that if only one layer is visible when you press these keystrokes, Photoshop hides that layer and shows the next layer. This is great for cycling through a number of layers.

In Photoshop 3, Command-[and Command-] switched from one layer to the next. However, now these keystrokes move the targeted layer backward and forward. Command-Shift-[and Command-Shift-] move the layer to the bottom and top of the layers stack, respectively.

Tip: Context-Sensitive Menus. When you Control-click (Macintosh) or click with the right mouse button (Windows), Photoshop displays a context-sensitive menu that changes depending on what tool you have selected in the Tool palette. We find the menu for the various painting tools pretty useless (though if you had to do a lot of painting, it might be helpful). But the menus you get when you Control-click (or right-mouse-button click) with the Move tool and the selection tools are great.

The context-sensitive menu for the Move tool lets you choose a layer to work on. If you have four layers in an image, and three of them overlap in one particular area, you can Control-click (or right-mouse-button click) on that area and Photoshop asks you which of the three layers you want to jump to. (Note that you can always get the Move tool's context-sensitive menu by Command-Control-clicking or—on Windows—clicking the right mouse button when the Control key is held down.)

The context-sensitive menu for the Marquee tool contains a mish-mosh of features, including Delete Layer, Duplicate Layer, Load

Selection, Reselect, and Color Range (we have no idea why they picked these and left other features out). Many of these features don't have keyboard shortcuts, so this menu is the fastest way to perform them.

Tip: Click on Your Layer. Here's another way to select a different layer without clicking on it in the Layers palette: Command-Option-Control-click (with any tool; in Windows, you Control-Alt-click with the right mouse button). If you click on pixels that "belong" to a different layer than the one you're on, Photoshop jumps to that layer. For instance, if you've got a picture of your mom on Layer 3, and you're currently on the background layer, you can Command-Option-Control-click (or Control-Alt-right-mouse-button click) on your mom with the Move tool to jump to Layer 3.

This typically only works when you click on a pixel that has an opacity greater than 50 percent. (We say "typically" because it sometimes *does* work if the total visible opacity is less than 50 percent—see "Info Palette," later in this chapter.) If your mom has a feathered halo around her, you may not be able to get this to work if you click on the feathered part.

Navigator Palette

The Navigator palette acts as command central for all scrolling and zooming (see Figure 2-6). We rarely use this palette because we find that it's usually either too precise or not precise enough, and it takes too much mousing around. Of course, this is largely a personal bias on our part; if you find it useful, more power to you.

Figure 2-6
Navigator palette

Most of the palette is occupied by a thumbnail of the image, with a red frame indicating the contents of the active window (if your image has a lot of red in it, you might want to change the frame color by choosing Palette Options from the palette's popout menu). Dragging the outline pans the contents of the active window. Command-dragging lets you define a new outline, thereby changing the zoom percentage.

The percentage field at the lower left of the palette functions identically to the one at the lower left of the image window. Clicking the zoom-in and zoom-out buttons has the same effect as pressing Command-plus and Command-minus. David's favorite feature in this palette is the magnification slider, which lets him change the zoom level dynamically. It's not a particularly useful feature, but it's mighty fun.

Moving Pixels

If you simply make a selection, then drag it with one of the selection tools, you move the selection boundary but not its contents. If you want the pixels to move as well, you have to use the Move tool. Fortunately, no matter what tool is selected, you can always temporarily get the Move tool simply by holding down the Command key. Note that you can hold down the Option key while you drag to copy the pixels as you move them (moving a duplicate of the pixels).

When you move or copy selected pixels with the Move tool, you get a floating selection (sort of like a temporary layer that disappears when you deselect). While the selection is still floating, you can use the Fade command (in the Filter menu) to change its opacity or blend mode.

With the Move tool, you can move an entire layer around without selecting anything. When you do have something selected, you don't have to worry about positioning the cursor before you click and drag. This is a great speedup, especially when working with heavily feathered selections.

Tip: Arrow Keys Move, Too. When moving pixels around, don't forget the arrow keys. With the Move tool selected, each press of the key moves the contents of your selection by one pixel. If you add the Shift key, the selection moves 10 pixels. Modifier keys work, too: hold down the Option key when you first press an arrow key, and the selection is duplicated, floated, and moved one pixel (don't keep holding down the Option key after that, unless you want a *lot* of duplicates).

Remember that you can always get the Move tool temporarily by adding the Command key to any of the above shortcuts. Pressing the arrow keys with any tool other than the Move tool moves the selection without moving the pixels it contains. This is an essential technique for precision placement of a selection.

If you've got the Move tool selected (press V), and nothing is selected when you press the arrow keys, the entire layer moves by one pixel. Add the Shift key to move 10 pixels instead.

Tip: Moving Multiple Layers. One of the problems with layers is that you often can't do the same thing to more than one layer at a time. But remember: there are always workarounds!

If you want to move more than one layer at a time with the Move tool, you can link the layers by clicking in the second column of the Layers palette (see Figure 2-7). Whichever layer tile you click on (other than the one that's already active) is linked with the current layer. Now when you use the Move tool (with no selections), both layers move.

Tip: Duplicating Layers. Duplicating a layer is a part of our everyday workflow, so it's odd that until recently it's been kind of a pain to do. There are various ways to duplicate a layer in Photoshop 5.

► You can drag the layer's tile on top of the new layer icon in the Layers palette.

► You can press Command-A (to select everything on the current layer), and then Command-J.

► You can select Duplicate Layer from the Layer menu.

► You can select Duplicate Layer from the context-sensitive menu you get when Control-clicking (Macintosh) or right-mouse-button-clicking (Windows) with the Marquee, Lasso, or Cropping tools.

The method you use at any given time should be determined by where your hands are. (Keyboard? Mouse? Coffee mug?)

Tip: Duplicating and Merging Layers. You can merge a copy of all the currently visible layers in a document with the currently selected layer by holding down the Option key when selecting Merge Visible from the Layer menu (or, better yet, just press Command-Shift-Option-E).

Figure 2-7

Linking layers
for moving

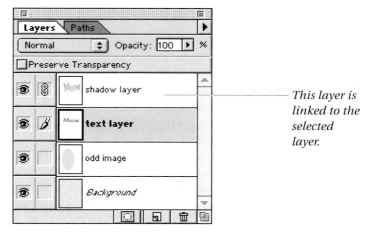

This layer is linked to the selected layer.

Tip: Move Tool Options. The Options palette for the Move tool contains two mysterious-sounding checkboxes, labeled Pixel Doubling and Auto Select Layer. When Pixel Doubling is turned on, Photoshop gives you a lower-resolution preview when you move a layer. Lower resolution typically means you get a more snappy redraw, which is great when working on larger files. We turn it on and leave it on. Note that Pixel Doubling only works when the Image Cache preference is set higher than 1 (see "Preferences," later in this chapter).

When the Auto Select Layer option is turned on, Photoshop looks to see what pixel you're clicking on before moving. If you click on a pixel that belongs to a layer other than the one currently selected, Photoshop switches to the layer that contains that pixel. This is a great feature, but one that can get you into hot water if you're not careful where you click. We typically turn this on only occasionally (when we've got a lot of layers that we need to move around quickly).

Tip: Copying Pixels. Layers are a fact of life, and with Photoshop it's not uncommon to find yourself with more layers than you know what to do with. If you make a selection and select Copy, you only get the pixels on the currently active layer (the one selected on the Layers palette). If you want to copy all the visible layers, select Copy Merged instead (or press Command-Shift-C).

However, we find some people using this technique in order to make a merged copy of the entire image (not just a selection). Sure, you can do it, but it's faster and less memory-intensive to use the Duplicate feature (under the Image menu) and turn on the Merged Layers Only checkbox. (This label makes no sense to us; it really should be called "Merge Visible Layers in Duplicate.")

Tip: Pasting Pixels. Pasting pixels into a document automatically creates a new layer. So what about the Paste Into (Command-Shift-V) and Paste Behind (Command-Shift-Option-V) features (which are available when you've made a selection)? When invoked, each of these also adds a new layer, but they also add a layer mask to that layer in the form of the selection. This is one of the fastest ways to build a layer and a layer mask in one step: draw a selection the shape of the layer mask you want, then perform a Paste Into or a Paste Behind (depending on the effect you're trying to achieve).

Tip: Drag-and-Drop Selections and Layers. Those of us who were properly indoctrinated on the Macintosh can't envision a world without Cut and Paste. However, there are times to use the clipboard and times not to. In Photoshop, you often want to avoid the clipboard because you're dealing with large amounts of data. Every time you move something to or from the clipboard, you eat up more RAM, or hard drive space, which can slow you down.

If you want to move a selection of pixels (or a layer) from one document to another, you can do so by dragging it from one window into the other (if you've got a selection, remember to use the Move tool, or else you'll just move the selection boundary itself). Photoshop moves the pixels "behind the scenes," so as to avoid unneeded memory requirements. If you're trying to copy an entire layer, you can also just click on its tile in the Layers palette and drag it over the other document's window.

Tip: Placing Your Drag-and-Drop Selection. In the last tip we talked about how you can drag and drop a selection or layer from one image into another. When you let go of the mouse button, the selection is placed into the image right where you dropped it. However, if you hold down the Shift key, Photoshop centers the layer or selection in the new image. If the two images have the same pixel dimensions, the Shift key "pin-registers" it—the layer or selection falls in exactly the same place as it was in the original document.

Guides, Grids, and Alignment

Moving pixels is all very well and good, but where are you going to move them to? If you need to place pixels with precision, you should use the ruler, guides, grids, and the alignment features. The ruler is the simplest: you can hide or show it by pressing Command-R. Wherever you move your cursor, faint tick marks appear in the rulers, showing you exactly where you are (you can also follow the coordinates on the Info palette).

Guides. You can add a guide to a page by dragging it out from either the horizontal or vertical ruler. Unfortunately, there is no way to specify a specific placement for a guide (like "put a guide at two inches over"), but if you care about specific placement, make sure you watch the measurements on the Info palette carefully. (If you don't think in inches, you can change the default measurement system; see "Tip: Switch Units," later in this chapter.)

You can always move a guide with the Move tool (don't forget you can always get the Move tool temporarily by holding down the Command key). Table 2-1 lists a number of grids and guides keystrokes that can help you use these features effortlessly.

Table 2-1	To do this ...	Press this ...
Grids and guides keystrokes	Hide/Show Guides	Command-; (semicolon)
	Snap To Guides	Command-Shift-;
	Lock/Unlock Guides	Command-Option-;
	Show/Hide Grid	Command-' (quote)
	Snap To Grid	Command-Shift-'

Tip: Snap to Ruler Marks. We almost always hold down the Shift key when dragging guides out from a ruler; that way, the guide automatically snaps to the ruler tick marks. If you find that your guides are slightly sticky as you drag them out without the Shift key held down, check to see what layer you're on. When Snap To Guides is turned on, objects snap to the guides *and* guides snap to the edges and centers of objects on layers.

Tip: Switching Guide Direction. Dragged out a horizontal guide when you meant to get a vertical one? No problem: just Option-click on the guide to switch its orientation (or hold down the Option key while dragging out the guide).

Tip: Mirroring Guides. If you rotate your image by 90 degrees, or flip it horizontally or vertically, your guides will rotate or flip with it. You can stop this errant behavior by locking the guides down first (press Command-Option-semicolon).

Tip: Guides on the Pasteboard. Just because your pixels stop at the edge of the image doesn't mean your guides have to. You can place guides out on the gray area outside the image canvas and they're still functional. This is just the ticket if you've got a photo that you need to place so that it bleeds off the edge of your image by .25 inch.

Tip: Changing Guides and Grids. Guides are, by default, blue. Grid lines are, by default, set one inch apart. If you don't like these settings, change them in the Guides and Grid Preferences dialog box (you can select this from the Preferences submenu), or just double-click on any guide with the Move tool (or Command-double-click with any other tool).

Alignment and distribution. Page-layout programs have had alignment features for years, but this capability is new in Photoshop 5, and it's a godsend for anyone who really cares about precision in their images (we find it particularly useful when building images for the Web). Here's how you can align objects on two layers.

1. Choose which layer you want "locked"—that is, which one stays put while the other layer moves—by selecting it in the Layers palette.

2. Click in the second column of the Layers palette next to the layer you want to move (a link icon should appear next to it). If you want to align more than two layers, link all of them.

3. Make sure you have no selections by pressing Command-D (or choosing Deselect from the Select menu), and then choose among the options on the Align Linked submenu (under the Layer menu; see Figure 2-8).

Figure 2-8

Aligning layers

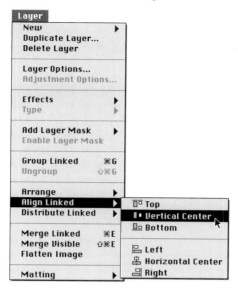

4. When you're done aligning objects, don't forget to turn off the link icon in the Layers palette (unless you want these layers to be linked so that they move in tandem from now on).

If you select three or more layers (or, to be more precise, select one layer in the Layers palette, and then link two or more other layers to it), you can also distribute the layers instead of aligning them. For example, if you have five small pictures that you want evenly spread across your Photoshop image, you could put each one on a separate layer, link them all together, and choose Horizontal Center from the Distribute Linked submenu (under the Layer menu; see Figure 2-9).

Note that Distribute Linked doesn't care which layers are selected and which are linked. When distributing layers vertically, Photoshop "locks" the layers that are closest to the top and the bottom of the image canvas; when distributing horizontally, it locks the left-most and right-most layers. All the layers in between get moved. For example, if you choose Vertical Center from the Distribute Linked submenu, Photoshop moves the layers so that there is an equal amount of space from the vertical center point of one layer to the next.

While we think this interface is pretty clunky (after all, when you link layers together, they aren't supposed to move independently of each other), once you align or distribute layers once or twice, you'll find that it's not that bad.

Figure 2-9 Distributing layers

Align Linked: Top,
Distribute Linked: Horizontal Center

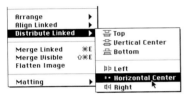

Tip: Aligning to the Canvas. Aligning two layers together is all well and good, but we often find we want to align something to the image canvas itself. For instance, you might want to center some text horizontally in the picture. If the background layer is a "real" background layer (that is, it's labeled "Background" on the Layers palette), you can just select the layer you want to move, link the background layer to it, and align horizontally. Make sure you don't select the background layer and link the type layer to it; in this case, the background itself will move!

If you don't have a real background layer, you can still align to the image's canvas.

1. Press Command-A to select the whole image.

2. Select the layer you want to move.

3. If you want to align more than one layer, link those layers to the selected layer.

4. Choose from the Align to Selection submenu (under the Layer menu). If you choose Horizontal Center from this submenu, then Photoshop centers your layer to the selection (which, in this case, is the size of the canvas).

Note that when you have a selection, the Align Linked submenu changes to the Align to Selection submenu (that's why you have to deselect your selections before aligning two or more layers).

Dialog Boxes

Dialog boxes seem like simple things, but since you probably spend a good chunk of your time in Photoshop looking at them, wouldn't it be great to be more efficient while you're there? Here are a bunch of tips that will let you fly through those pesky beasts.

Tip: Scroll 'n' Zoom. The most important lesson to learn about dialog boxes in Photoshop is that just because one is open doesn't mean that you can't do anything else. For instance, in many dialog boxes—such as the Levels and Curves dialog boxes—you can still scroll around any open documents (not just the active one) by holding down the spacebar and dragging. You can even zoom in and out of the active window using the Command-spacebar and Command-Option-spacebar techniques.

Note that some dialog boxes, most notoriously the Distort filters, don't let you scroll or zoom at all. Pity.

Tip: Turning On Checkboxes. You don't have to painstakingly aim your cursor at the middle of a checkbox to turn it on or off. Instead, just click anywhere on the box, or even on the word(s) to the right of it. This is true in almost all Macintosh and Windows applications.

Tip: Save Your Settings. Many dialog boxes in Photoshop have Save and Load buttons that let you save to disk all the settings that you've made in a dialog box. They're particularly useful when you're going through the iterative process of editing an image.

For instance, let's say you're adjusting the tone of an image with Curves. You increase this and decrease that, and add some points here and there . . . . Finally, when you're finished, you press OK and find—much to your dismay—that you need to make one additional change. If you jump right back into Curves, you degrade your image a second time—not good (see Chapter 6, *Tonal Correction*). If you undo first, you lose the changes you made the first time.

But if you've saved the curve to disk before leaving the dialog box, you can undo, go back to the dialog box, and load in the settings you had saved. Then you can add that one last move to the curve, without introducing a second round of image-degrading corrections.

Just for reference, here's a list of the dialog boxes in Photoshop that have Load and Save buttons.

▶ Levels

▶ Curves

▶ Hue/Saturation

▶ Replace Color

▶ Selective Color

▶ Variations

▶ Halftone Screen

▶ Screen (in Page Setup)

▶ Transfer Function (in Page Setup)

▶ RGB Setup

▶ CMYK Setup—Built-In Model

▶ CMYK Setup—Tables

▶ Color Range

Tip: Instant Replay. There's one other way to undo and still save any tonal-adjustment settings you've made. If you hold down the Option key while selecting *any* feature from the Adjust submenu (under the Image menu), Photoshop opens the dialog box with the last-used settings. Similarly, you can hold down the Option key when pressing the adjustment's keyboard shortcut. For instance, Command-Option-L opens the Levels dialog box with the same settings you last used. This is a great way to specify the same Levels or Curves (or Hue/Saturation, or any other adjustment) to several different images. Unfortunately, as soon as you quit Photoshop, it loses its memory.

Tip: Opening Palettes from Dialog Boxes. We almost always work with the Info palette open. However, every now and again it gets closed or covered up with some other palette. Unfortunately, while you're in a dialog box (like the Curves or Levels dialog boxes), you cannot click on any palette without leaving by pressing OK or Cancel. Fortunately for efficiency, you *can* select a palette from the Windows menu. To display the Info palette, select Show Info from this menu.

Keystrokes

We love keystrokes. They make everything go much faster, or at least they make it *feel* like we're working faster. Here are a few keystrokes that we use all the time while in dialog boxes.

Option. Holding down the Option key while in a dialog box almost always changes the Cancel button into a Reset button, letting you reset the dialog box to its original state (the way it was when you first opened it). If you want to go keystrokes the whole way, type Command-Option-period to do the same thing.

Command-Z. You already know Command-Z (what Seattle's Mac user group calls "Just Undo It"), because it's gotten you out of more jams than you care to think about. Well, Command-Z performs an undo within dialog boxes, too. It undoes the last change you made. We use this all the time when we mistype.

Arrow keys. Many dialog boxes in Photoshop have text fields where you enter or change numbers (see Figure 2-10). You can change those numbers using the Up and Down arrow keys. Press once, and the number increases or decreases by one. If you hold down the Shift key while pressing the arrow key, it changes by 10. (Note that some dialog boxes change by a tenth or even a hundredth; when you hold down Shift, they change by 10 times as much.)

A few dialog boxes use the arrow keys in a different way, or don't use them at all. In the Lens Flare filter, for instance, the arrow keys move the position of the effect, and arrow keys just don't do anything in most of the Distort filters.

Figure 2-10
Numerical fields
in dialog boxes

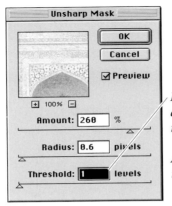

Pressing the Up or Down arrow key changes this number.

Add Shift to change in increments of 10.

Tab key. As in most Macintosh and Windows applications, the Tab key selects the next text field in dialog boxes with multiple text fields. You can use this in conjunction with the previous tip in dialog boxes such as the Unsharp Mask filter, or you can simply tab to the next field and type in a number if you already know the value you want.

Previewing

Most of Photoshop's tonal- and color-correction features and many of its filters offer a Preview checkbox in their dialog boxes. Plus, all the filters that have a dialog box have a proxy window that shows the effect applied to a small section of the image (some dialog boxes have both). It often takes Photoshop a significant amount of time to actually apply an effect to the whole image, particularly if it's a large, high-resolution one, so using the previewing features efficiently can save you lots of time.

Preview checkbox. When you turn on the Preview checkbox, the effect is applied to the current selection, or if nothing is selected, to the entire image. If you leave the Preview option unchecked, nothing happens to the image as you move the sliders or type in new values (see Figure 2-11).

The Preview options in several of the Image Adjust commands—including Levels, Curves, Hue/Saturation, and Color Balance—behave a little differently. When Preview is turned on, the preview works exactly the same as it does anywhere else. But when it's turned off, Video LUT Animation kicks in (if it's turned on and if your video card can handle it—see Figure 2-12 and the description of Video LUT Animation, below).

Figure 2-11
Preview

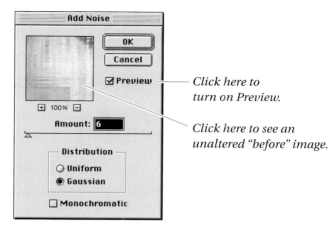

*Click here to
turn on Preview.*

*Click here to see an
unaltered "before" image.*

If Video LUT Animation is turned off, the previews in the four Image Adjust commands behave exactly the same as all other previews—they apply the effect to the image when they're turned on, and they do nothing when they're turned off.

Video LUT Animation. Video LUT stands for "video lookup table." The circuitry that drives your monitor, whether it's an add-on card or built-in video, uses a lookup table to convert digital RGB values to the analog voltages that actually drive your monitor. Most monitor calibrators work by manipulating the values in this table to produce the requested gamma and white point. But Adobe Photoshop also uses it to perform another nifty trick.

Figure 2-12
Turning on
Video LUT Animation

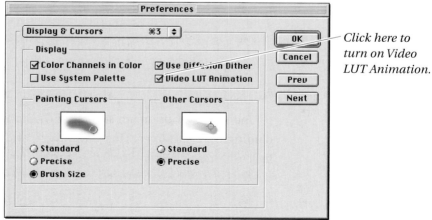

*Click here to
turn on Video
LUT Animation.*

When you change an image using one of the Image Adjust features with Preview turned on, Photoshop has to recalculate every pixel being displayed to show you a preview (see Figure 2-13). This can take some time, particularly with a large screen on a slower computer.

When you use the Video LUT Animation feature instead, Photoshop simply changes the lookup table. It can do this in real time (or, as we used to say when we were lads, "instantly") so you always get constant feedback as you move the controls. The catch is that the *entire screen* changes, not just the image.

When you have Video LUT Animation turned on, the Preview checkbox acts as a manual override: when you check Preview, you get the real, honest-to-goodness calculated pixels, and when you turn it off, you get the simulation created by manipulating the lookup table.

There are three major benefits to turning on Video LUT Animation.

▶ You can see tonal adjustments as you make them in Levels, Curves, Hue/Saturation, and so on.

▶ Video LUT Animation is much faster than the preview you get while the Preview checkbox is turned on.

▶ It allows you to use the indispensable black-point and white-point clipping display in Levels (see Figure 6-17 on page 222).

We turn Video LUT Animation on and leave it on. However, there are three good reasons *not* to use it, so we often turn on the Preview option to override it.

▶ First, although it's faster than the real preview, it's less accurate. Sometimes, particularly in Duotone or CMYK modes, it can be *very* inaccurate indeed—the results vary with different video cards—but even in RGB or grayscale, you'll see subtle differences between the Video LUT Animation preview and the real thing.

▶ Second, it applies the effect to the entire screen, not just to the selection or the image. As a result, you lose the context in which you view the image. If you're trying to set a neutral balance and your neutral desktop turns green or blue or magenta, it plays havoc with your color perception.

Figure 2-13
Preview and
Video LUT
Animation

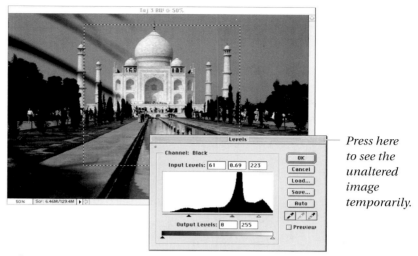

*Press here
to see the
unaltered
image
temporarily.*

When Preview is turned off, the entire screen appears to change.

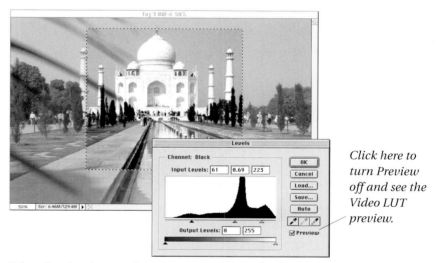

*Click here to
turn Preview
off and see the
Video LUT
preview.*

When Preview is turned on, the screen reflects the final image.

▶ Finally, it simply doesn't work on most Windows computers (because
most video cards for the PC can't deal with it). If you find it not working on your Windows machine, you might as well just turn it off.

On the other hand, when we're working on a selection or when we're
working in CMYK, we turn the Preview checkbox on. We *always* check the
real preview before we press OK to apply the changes to the file.

Tip: Seeing Before-and-Afters. You can always toggle between a preview of the effect and the unaltered image, but the method for doing so is different with Video LUT Animation on and with it off.

With Preview turned off, you can toggle between the corrected and uncorrected versions of the image by clicking on the dialog box's title bar. This temporarily turns off Video LUT Animation.

With Video LUT Animation off in General Preferences, when you turn off the Preview checkbox you see the unaltered image ("before"). Turn Preview on again to see the effect of the changes ("after").

Proxies. The proxy in dialog boxes shows only a small part of the image, but it updates almost instantly. Previewing time-consuming filters such as Unsharp Mask or Motion Blur on a large file can take a long time, and some very time-consuming filters such as the Distort filters don't offer a preview at all, so we rely on the proxy a lot.

Tip: Before and After in Proxies. You can always see a before-and-after comparison by clicking in the proxy. As long as you hold down the mouse button, you can see the unaltered version.

Tip: Changing the Proxy View. To see a different part of the image, click and drag in the proxy (no modifier keys are necessary). Alternatively, you can click in the document itself. The cursor changes to a small rectangle—wherever you click shows up in the Preview window.

Similarly, you can zoom the proxy in and out. The *slow* way is to click on the little (+) and (-) buttons. Much faster is to click the proxy with either the Command or Option keys held down—the former zooms in, the latter zooms out.

Note that proxies only show the layer you're working on at any one time. This makes sense, really; only that layer is going to be affected.

New Dialog Box

Before we move on to essential tips about tools, we need to take a quick look at the New dialog box, which has a few very helpful hidden features.

Tip: Clairvoyant Image Size. The New dialog box tries to read your mind. If you have something copied to the Clipboard when you create a new document, Photoshop plugs the pixel dimensions, resolution, and color model of that copied piece into the proper places of the dialog box for you.

If you'd rather use the values from the last new image you created, hold down the Option key while selecting New from the File menu (or press Command-Option-N).

Tip: Copying Sizes from Other Documents. Russell Brown, that king of Photoshop tips and tricks, reminded us to keep our eyes open. Why, for instance, is the Window menu not grayed out when you have the New dialog box open? Because you can select items from it!

If you want your new document to have the same pixel dimensions, resolution, and color mode as a document you already have open, you can select that document from the bottom of the Window menu. Voilà! The statistics are copied.

This trick also works in the Image Size and Canvas size dialog boxes.

Tools

After you're finished moving around in your image, zooming in and out, and moving pixels hither and yon, it's time to get down to work with Photoshop's tools. Photoshop's tools have all sorts of hidden properties that can make life easier and—more important—more efficient. Let's look at a number of tips and techniques for getting the most out of these instruments of creation.

Tip: Tool Keystrokes. The most important productivity tip we've found in Photoshop to date has been the ability to select each and every tool with a keystroke. Unlike most programs, the keystrokes for Photoshop's tools do not use any modifier keys. You press the key without Command, Option, or Shift. Figure 2-14 shows the keystroke for each tool.

Some tools in the Tool palette have multiple modes. For instance, the Dodge tool also "contains" the Burn and the Sponge tools. The slow way to access the different modes is to press the tool icon to bring up the

Figure 2-14
Keystrokes
for tools

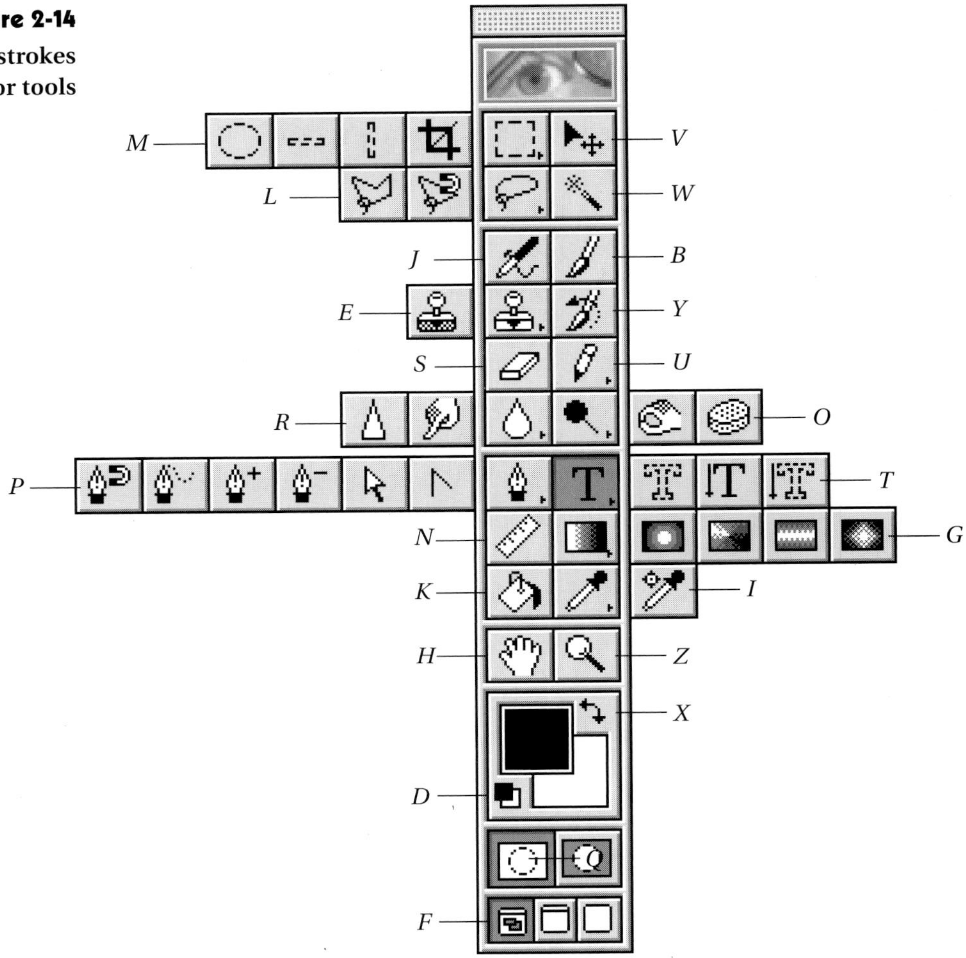

popout palette containing the different modes. A faster method is to press the tool's keystroke once to select it, and then hold down the Shift key while pressing it again to toggle among the choices. Press M once, and you jump to the Marquee tool; then press Shift-M, and it switches to the elliptical Marquee tool; press Shift-M once more, and it switches back to the rectangular Marquee tool. Note that the keystroke doesn't cycle through the single-row marquee, the single-column marquee, or the Cropping tool (you can get the Cropping tool by pressing C).

Note too that there are speedy routes to the Options and Brushes palettes. We'll cover those in "Palettes," later in this chapter.

Tip: Swap Tool Effect. While we rarely use the Blur, Sharpen, Dodge, or Burn tools (the first two are kind of clunky and we prefer to use adjustment layers rather than the last two), it is kind of fun to know that if you hold down the Option key, the Blur tool switches to the Sharpen tool (or vice versa), and the Dodge tool switches to the Burn tool (and vice versa).

Eyedropper

Matching colors by eye can be difficult. Instead, use the tool designed for the job: the Eyedropper.

Tip: Eyedropper Keystroke. You can always grab the Eyedropper from the Tool palette (or press I), but if you already have a painting tool selected, it's faster just to use the Option key to toggle between the Eyedropper tool and the painting tool.

Tip: How Many Pixels Are You Looking At? Almost every image has noise in it—pixels that are just plain wrong. If you're clicking around with the Eyedropper tool, there's a reasonable chance that you'll click right on one of those noise pixels, resulting in a color you don't expect (or want). The key is to change what the Eyedropper is looking at.

David usually changes the Sample Size popup menu in the Eyedropper Options palette to 3 by 3 Average. This way, the Eyedropper looks at nine pixels (the pixel you click on, plus the eight surrounding it) and averages them. If he's working on a very high-resolution image, however, he switches to 5 by 5 Average. Bruce, on the other hand, lives on the edge: he always leaves the Eyedropper set to Point Sample. If he thinks there's a danger of picking up a noise pixel, he just zooms in far enough to see exactly which pixel he's sampling.

Tip: Don't Limit Your Eyedropping. Don't forget that when you're working with the Eyedropper tool, you can click on *any* open document, or even the Picker, Swatches, or Scratch palettes. This usually even works when a dialog box is open.

Tip: Lock Your Sample Points. Photoshop 5 includes a new tool in your arsenal: the Color Sampler (which is hidden as an alternate to the Eyedropper tool). When you click on your image with the Color Sampler,

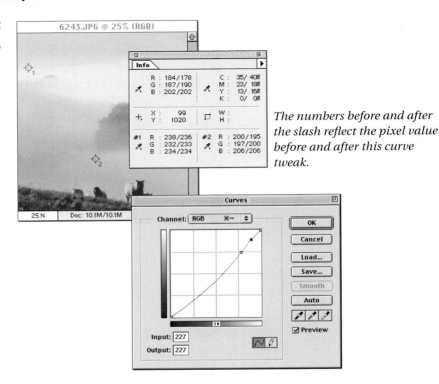

The numbers before and after the slash reflect the pixel value before and after this curve tweak.

Photoshop places a sample point at that location and expands the Info palette to show the readings at this coordinate (see Figure 2-15). This is most helpful when performing color or tonal adjustments because you can quickly see how your tweaks are affecting various areas of your image while you're making changes. (See Chapter 6, *Tonal Corrections,* for more on this technique.)

We almost never choose the actual Color Sampler tool from the toolbox. Instead, we just Shift-click with the normal Eyedropper tool, which does the same thing. If you want to move a sample point someplace else, you can just click and drag it with the Color Sampler tool (or Shift-drag with the Eyedropper tool). To delete a sample point, just Option-click with the Color Sampler tool (or Option-Shift-click on it with the Eyedropper tool).

Type Tool

Photoshop is not renowned for its typographic prowess. In fact, it's often downright painful to get good-looking type out of it. However, as we said earlier, Photoshop 5 offers a number of improvements in the type department—namely the ability to edit text after placing it, and to format it character by character. In earlier versions, David got into the habit of just clicking with the Type tool, typing the text, and then quickly setting the font, size, and so on. Photoshop 5 trips him up because he must add one more step to the process: select the text he wants to format.

Here are a couple of tips that may help in the process of making type. (Note that there are also some Type tool tips in Chapter 15, *Essential Image Techniques*.)

Tip: WYSIWYG Text Editing. Years behind the curve, Photoshop still doesn't let you edit text directly on your image—you must use that big ugly dialog box. The folks at Adobe did offer one concession, however: the Preview checkbox. As long as this option is on, you can see how text will appear in the image proper while you create, format, or edit it in the dialog box. We turn this on, leave it on, and move the dialog box out of the way. (This, of course, usually requires something bigger than a 15-inch screen.)

Tip: Editing Type Layers. There are several ways to edit text on a type layer.

▶ You can double-click on the type layer's tile in the Layers palette. (If you double-click on the thumbnail instead of the tile, you open the Layer Options dialog box instead, which lets you rename the layer, among other things.)

▶ You can click on top of the text with the Type tool. You know your cursor is in the right place when the Type tool's cursor changes to a regular "I-beam."

▶ Best yet, when you have both the Type tool selected in the Tool palette and the type layer selected in the Layers palette, you can select Edit Type from the context-sensitive menu: Control-click on the Macintosh, or right-mouse-button click in Windows anywhere on the layer.

Tip: Rendering Type Layers. Type layers are special; you can't paint on them or run filters on them or anything else that relies on pixel-editing.

If you need to perform anything like that, you have to render them (turn them into proper bitmaps) by selecting Render Type from the Type submenu (under the Layers menu) or from the context-sensitive menu you get with the Type tool (see the previous tip).

However, note that in general, it's best to do all the transformations (rotating, scaling, positioning, skewing, and so on) and layer effects (drop shadows, and so on) you need before rendering the type layer. That way, you can be assured of the highest quality type.

Tip: Making Text Masks. While Photoshop 5 offers four different tools for type (two type tools that create type layers, and two that create selections in the shape of type), we only use one: the regular horizontal Type tool. If we want to get a selection in the shape of type, we create a type layer with this tool and then Command-click on it in the Layers palette. By actually making a type layer, we can preview it in the image before clicking OK, we can edit it later, or use the type someplace else (even in another image). If we had just used the Type Selection tool, we'd have nothing but an ephemeral group of marching ants.

By the way, if you already have a selection made, don't forget that you can add to that selection by Command-Shift-clicking on the type layer in the Layers palette. Conversely, you can remove from the selection by Command-Option-clicking.

Note that we don't use the vertical type tools either, because we can always Control-click (Mac) or right-button-click (Windows) on the type layer, and select Vertical or Horizontal from the Type tool's context-sensitive menu.

Tip: Rebuilding the Font List. Previous versions of Photoshop were a bit dull when it came to your adding or removing fonts while the program was running. There were various silly ways of forcing Photoshop to update its internal font list (the fonts you see in the Edit Type dialog box), but it always felt kind of kludgy. Fortunately, Photoshop 5 is more on the ball; you can now add fonts while the program is running and they'll show up on the Font menu without extra help. We've noticed some strangeness when disabling fonts (they sometimes still appear on the font list, but are not useable), but we're not complaining.

Tip: Keyboard Type Shortcuts. There are a number of keyboard shortcuts that can help you speed up your text formatting (see Table 2-2). Remember that the extra time you take to learn these now will come back as time saved later.

Gradient Tool

One of the complaints Adobe heard most in times gone by was that blends in Photoshop resulted in banding. The answer they always gave was to "add noise" to the blend. It's true; noise reduces banding significantly. And fortunately, when Photoshop 3 came out, the program started adding the noise for us. You can stop it by turning off the Dither checkbox in the Gradient Options palette, but there's almost no reason to do so. You *may* want to turn dithering off if you're going to a continuous-tone device that can actually reproduce the gradient without banding.

Tip: Adding More Noise. If you're still getting banding even with Dither turned on, you may want to add even more noise to a blend. However, note that you don't always need to apply the Add Noise filter to the entire gradient; use the filter selectively.

Instead, you might find it better to add noise to only one or two channels. View each channel separately (see Chapter 14, *Selections*) to see

Table 2-2 Keyboard shortcuts in the Type dialog box

To do this . . .	Press this . . .
Select All	Command-A
Select one word to left/right	Command-Shift-Left Arrow/Right Arrow
Increase size by two pixels or points	Command-Shift-> or < (period or comma)
Increase/Decrease size by 10 pixels or points	Command-Shift-Alt-> or <
Kern by 20/1,000 em	Option-Left Arrow/Right Arrow
Kern by 1/10 em	Command-Option-Left Arrow/Right Arrow
Increase/Decrease leading by two points	Option-Down Arrow/Up Arrow
Increase/Decrease leading by 10 points	Command-Option-Down Arrow/Up Arrow
Increase/Decrease Baseline Shift by two points	Shift-Alt-Up Arrow/Down Arrow
Increase/Decrease Baseline Shift by 10 points	Command-Shift-Alt-Up Arrow/Down Arrow
Exit Type Tool dialog box	Enter (on keypad) or Command-Enter
Left, Right, Center alignment	Command-Shift-L, R, or C

where the banding is more prevalent. Then add some noise just to the blend area in that channel.

Tip: Blends in CMYK. Eric Reinfeld pounded it into our heads one day: if you're going to make blends in Photoshop images that will end up in CMYK mode, create them in CMYK mode. Sometimes changing modes from RGB to CMYK can give you significant color shifts in blends.

Tip: Gradients on Layers. Some people make hard work of creating a blend that fades away into transparency. They go through endless convolutions of Layer Masks and Channel Options, or they spend hours building Custom Gradients, and so on. They're making it difficult for themselves by not opening their eyes. On the Gradient Options palette, there is a Style popup menu that gives you the options of blending from Foreground to Transparent, or from Transparent to Foreground. Seek and ye shall find . . . .

Paint Brushes

We can't tell you how to make great art using Photoshop's painting tools, but we can give you some hints about how to use them more efficiently. One of the key speedups in painting is to alternate brush sizes with keystrokes (we talk about that in "Palettes," later in this chapter). Here are some other quickie tips that might help, too.

Tip: Touching Up Line Art. We talk about scanning and converting to line art in Chapter 11, *Line Art*, but since we're on the topic of tools, we should discuss the Pencil tool for just a moment. One of the best techniques for retouching line-art (black-and-white) images is the Auto Erase feature on the Pencil Options palette.

When Auto Erase is turned on, the Pencil tool works like this: if you click on any color other than the foreground color, that pixel—along with all others you touch before lifting the mouse button—is changed to the foreground color (this is the way it works, even with Auto Erase turned off). If you click on the foreground color, however, that pixel—along with all others you encounter—is changed to the background color.

This effectively means you don't have to keep switching the foreground and background colors while you work.

Tip: Sample Merged. If you're working on a multilayer image, you may find yourself frustrated with the Smudge, Blur, Sharpen, Magic Wand, or Rubber Stamp tools. That's because sometimes you want these tools to "see" the layers below the one you're working on, and sometimes you do not. Fortunately, Photoshop gives you a choice for each of these tools with the Sample Merged checkbox on the Options palette.

When Sample Merged is turned off, each tool acts as though the other layers weren't even there. But if you turn it on, look out! Photoshop sees the other layers (both above and below it) and acts as though they were merged together (see Figure 2-16).

Figure 2-16

Sample Merged

Using the Rubber Stamp to copy from here . . .

. . . to here

Sample Merged turned on: the clouds in the layer below get picked up with the rubber stamp.

Sample Merged turned off: the clouds don't get picked up.

The benefit of this is great, but people often don't see the downfall. Let's say your background contains a blue box, and Layer 1 has an overlapping yellow box. When you paint or smudge or blur or whatever with Sample Merged turned on, Photoshop "sucks up" the blue and paints it into Layer 1. If you think about it, that's what it should and has to do. But it can really throw you for a loop if you're not prepared.

Cropping Tool

We almost always scan a little bigger than we need, just in case. So we end up using the Cropping tool a lot. The nice thing about the Cropping tool (as opposed to the Crop feature on the Image menu) is that you can make fine adjustments before agreeing to go through with the paring. Just drag one of the corner handles. Here are a couple more ways you can fine-tune the crop.

Tip: Rotating While Cropping. If cropping an image down is the most common postscan step, what is the second most common? Rotating, of course. You can crop and rotate at the same time with the Cropping tool: after dragging out the cropping rectangle with the Cropping tool, just place the cursor outside the cropping rectangle and drag. The rectangle rotates. When you press Return or Enter, Photoshop crops and rotates the image to straighten the rectangle. It can be tricky to get exactly the right angle by eye—keep an eye on the Info palette.

Tip: Resampling While Cropping. The Options palette for the Cropping tool lets you specify output size and resolution. If you set the Height and Width, the aspect ratio of the crop is constrained. If you set Resolution, when you press Return or Enter to perform the crop, Photoshop also resamples the image to that resolution. This is handy when you want to resample down, but be careful that you don't ask for more resolution than you really have; resampling up is best avoided. You don't have to specify three values. If you leave Height or Width blank, the aspect ratio isn't constrained. If you leave Resolution blank, no resampling occurs.

Tip: Moving the Cropping Rectangle. If the cropping rectangle isn't in the right place, you can always move it—just place the cursor inside the cropping rectangle and drag.

Tip: Expand the Canvas by Cropping. Once you create a cropping rectangle with the Cropping tool, you can actually expand the cropping rectangle past the boundaries of the image. Then, after you press Enter, the canvas size actually expands to the edge of the cropping rectangle. This is new in version 5 and is our favorite new way to enlarge the canvas.

Tip: Cropping Near the Border. If you're trying to shave just a sliver of pixels off one side of an image, you'll find it incredibly annoying that Photoshop 5 snaps the cropping rectangle to the edge of the image whenever you drag close to it. There's no menu item to turn this off. Fortunately, you can hold down the Control key to temporarily disable the snapping behavior.

Tip: Watch Out for Your Fonts. As we go to press, there appears to be a bug in Photoshop 5 that can cause fonts on type layers to change when you use the cropping tool. Let's say you have text on a type layer in a particular font, and then you disable that font or move the image to another machine that doesn't have that font. Photoshop is smart enough to remember what the fonts looked like . . . until you use the Cropping tool. At this point, your fonts revert to some other font (usually Helvetica). Ugly! We hope that Adobe will fix this problem by the time you read this, but be warned.

Eraser Tool

The Eraser tool has gotten a bad rap. "Never use it," people say. But that's just holdover resentment for the pathetic pre-3.0 Eraser. The primary advancement in the Eraser is that you can erase using any brush—soft or hard. Plus, you can make the Eraser tool work like the Airbrush, Pencil, Brush, or Block (the original, MacPaint-like eraser). And what's more, you can control the opacity of the Eraser. This makes the eraser fully useable, in our opinion.

Tip: Switching Eraser Mode. You know that you can press E to get the Eraser tool. But wouldn't it be great if there were a keystroke to jump to a different *type* of eraser? Fortunately, there is. Press Shift-E, and you move through the list of eraser types: Airbrush, Paintbrush, Pencil, and Block. Then if you want to change opacity, you can press a number key from 1 to 0 (1 is ten percent, 2 is twenty percent, and so on). To vary the opacity in finer increments, press two number keys in rapid succession—for example, pressing the 3 key twice will get you 33-percent opacity.

Tip: Erase to History. Earlier versions of Photoshop included a feature called Erase to Saved, which let you use the Eraser tool to replace pixels

automatically subtracts it from 90 degrees, assuming that you want to rotate it counterclockwise to align with the vertical axis instead of the horizontal axis.

Palettes

Bruce has a second monitor set up on his computer just so he can open all of Photoshop's palettes on it and free up his primary monitor's precious space. There's little doubt that palettes are both incredibly important and yet incredibly annoying at times. Fortunately, Photoshop has some built-in but hidden features that make working with palettes a much happier experience. For instance, palettes are "sticky"—if you move them near the side of the monitor or near another palette, they'll "snap-to" align to that side or palette. (Even better, you can hold down the Shift key while you drag a palette, to force it to the side of the screen.) This (if nothing else) helps you keep a neat and tidy screen on which to work.

Tip: Make the Palettes Go Away. If you only have one monitor on which to store both your image and Photoshop's plethora of palettes, you should remember two keyboard shortcuts. First, pressing Tab makes the palettes disappear (or reappear, if they're already hidden). We find this absolutely invaluable, and use it daily.

Second, pressing Shift-Tab makes all palettes except the Tool palette disappear (or reappear). We find this only slightly better than completely useless; we would prefer that the keystroke hid all the palettes except the Info palette.

Tip: Making Palettes Smaller. Another way to maximize your screen real estate is by collapsing one or more of your open palettes. If you double-click on the palette's name tab, the palette collapses to just the title bar and name (see Figure 2-18). Or if you click in the zoom box of a palette (the checkbox in the upper-right corner of the palette), the palette reduces in size to only a few key elements. For instance, if you click in the zoom box of the Layers palette, you can still use the Opacity sliders and Mode popup menu (but the Layer tiles and icons get hidden).

Figure 2-18

Collapsing palettes

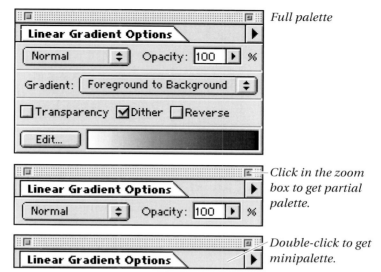

Full palette

Click in the zoom box to get partial palette.

Double-click to get minipalette.

Tip: Mix and Match Palettes. There's one more way to save space on your computer screen: mix and match your palettes. Palettes in Photoshop have a curious attribute: you can drag one on top of another and they become one (see Figure 2-19). Then if you want, you can drag them apart again by clicking and dragging the palette's tab heading.

For instance, David always keeps his Layers, Channels, and Paths palettes together on one palette. When he wants to work with one of these, he can click on that palette's tab heading. Or better yet, he uses a keystroke to bring it forward (see Table 2-3; see "Actions" in Chapter 15, *Essential Image Techniques,* for more on how to define your own keyboard shortcuts).

While you could, in theory, put all the palettes into one, he finds it much more useful to have several palette bunches: Layers/Channels/Paths, Colors/Color Picker/Scratch Pad, and Brushes/Options.

Table 2-3

Default keyboard shortcuts

To do this ...	Press this ...
Show/Hide Brushes palette	F5
Show/Hide Colors palette	F6
Show/Hide Layers palette	F7
Show/Hide Info palette	F8
Show/Hide Actions palette	F9

Figure 2-19

Mixing and
matching palettes

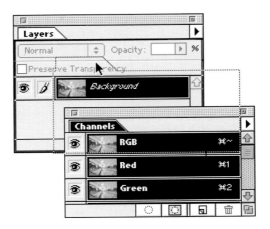

Bruce, on the other hand, always keeps the Layers and Channels palettes and the Brushes and Options palettes separate, even when he's
working on a single-monitor system. Neither of us ever mixes the Info
palette with another palette, because we want it open all the time.

Options Palette

The tools on the Tool palette only go so far. You often need to modify their
default settings in the Options palette. Try this: select the tool, then press
Return. The Options palette, even if hidden, appears at this command.
Plus, if there is a number-input field on the palette, Photoshop selects it
for you. For instance, when you press Return with the Lasso or Marquee
tools selected, the Lasso Options or Marquee Options palette appears
and the Feather field is highlighted on the palette.

If there is more than one number-input field on the palette, you can
press Tab to jump from one to the next. Finally, when you're finished with
your changes, press Return again to exit from the palette and resume
work.

Tip: Resetting the Tools. Photoshop power users are forever changing
the settings for palettes, especially the Tool Options palette. But every
now and again, it's nice to level the playing field. In this case, you can
reset the tool options for either a single tool or for all the tools on the
Options palette's popout menu (see Figure 2-20).

Figure 2-20
Tool Options palette

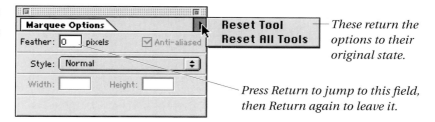

These return the
options to their
original state.

Press Return to jump to this field,
then Return again to leave it.

Brushes Palette

If there's one thing that makes us crazy in Photoshop, it's forever moving the cursor around the screen to change options, to change tools, or (especially) to change brush sizes. We can't tell you how happy we were to discover this next little technique.

Tip: Brush Keystrokes. Did you know that the [and] keys (the square brackets) move left and right through the Brushes palette? We now keep one hand on the keyboard and one on our mouse (or tablet pen); when we want to change tools, we press the key for that tool. When we want to change brush size, we cycle through the brushes with the [and] keys until we find the size we like.

If you want to go for extremes, you can also type Shift-[and Shift-]. These jump to the first and last brushes on the palette.

Tip: Opacity by the Numbers. In between changing brush sizes, we're forever changing brush opacity while painting or retouching. If you're still moving the sliders around on the Brush Options palette (or the Options palette for any other painting/editing tool), don't; instead, just type a number from 0 to 9. Zero gives you 100-percent opacity, 1 gives you 10 percent, 2 gives you 20 percent, and so on. For finer control, press two number keys in quick succession—for example, pressing 45 gets you 45-percent opacity.

Layers Palette

In every version since 3.0 (the first time that the layers feature was introduced), the Layers palette has become increasingly important to how people use Photoshop. With such a crucial palette, there have to be at least a few good tips around here. No?

Tip: Displaying Multiple Layers. Every click takes another moment or two, and many people click in the display column of the Layers palette (the one with the little eyeballs in it) once for each layer they want to see. Cut out the clicker-chatter, and just click and drag through the column for all the layers you want to see.

Tip: Click to Turn Off Layers. Another way to make multiple layers appear or disappear is by Option-clicking in the display column of the Layers palette. When you Option-click on an eyeball, Photoshop hides all the layers except the one you clicked on. Then, if you Option-click again, it redisplays them all again. Even though this trick doesn't save you a lot of time, it sure feels like it does (which is often just as cool).

Info Palette

In a battle of the palettes, we don't know which Photoshop palette would win the "most important" prize, but we do know which would win in the "most telling" category: the Info palette. We never close this palette. It just provides us with too much critical information.

At its most basic task, as a densitometer, it tells us the gray values and RGB or CMYK values in our image. But there's much more. When you're working in RGB, the Info palette shows you how pixels will translate into CMYK or Grayscale. When working in Levels or Curves, it displays before-and-after values (see Chapter 6, *Tonal Correction*).

But wait, there's more! When you rotate a selection, the Info palette displays what angle you're at. And when you scale, it shows percentages. If you've selected a color that is out of the CMYK gamut (depending on your setup; see Chapter 5, *Color Settings*), a gamut alarm appears on the Info palette.

Tip: Finding Opacity. When you have transparency showing (*e.g.*, on layers that have transparency when no background is showing), the Info palette can give you an opacity ("Op") reading. However, while Photoshop would display this automatically in earlier versions, now you have to do a little extra work: you must click on one of the little black eyedroppers in the Info palette and select Opacity (see Figure 2-21).

Figure 2-21

The Info palette

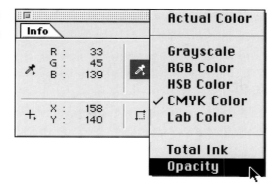

Tip: Switch Units. While we typically work in pixel measurements, we do on occasion need to see "real world" physical measurements such as inches or centimeters. Instead of traversing the menus to open the Units dialog box (on the Preferences submenu under the File menu), we find it's usually faster to select from the Info palette's popout menus. Just click on the XY cursor icon (see Figure 2-22). Another option: double-clicking in one of the rulers opens the Units Preferences dialog box.

Figure 2-22

Changing units

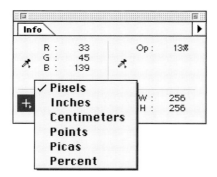

Color Palettes

The Scratch Pad, the Color Picker, and the Color palette all fit into one category, so we almost always group them together into one palette on our screen and switch between them as necessary.

Most novice Photoshop users select a foreground or background color by clicking once on the icons in the Tool palette and choosing from the Color dialog box. Many pros, however, have abandoned this technique, and focus instead on these color palettes. Here are a few tips to make this technique more . . . ah . . . palettable.

Tip: Switching Color Bars. Instead of clicking on the foreground color swatch in the Tool palette, you might consider typing values into the Color palette. Are the fields labeled "RGB" when you want to type in "CMYK" or something else? Just choose a different mode from the popout menu on the palette. If you like choosing colors visually rather than numerically, you can use the color bar at the bottom of the palette (no, the Color Bar is not just another place to meet people). While the spectrum of colors that appear here usually covers the RGB gamut, you can switch to a different spectrum by Shift-clicking on the area. Click once, and you switch to CMYK; again, and you get a gradient in grayscale; a third time, and you see a gradient from your foreground color to your background color. Shift-clicking again takes you back to RGB.

Tip: Editing the Color Swatches. You've probably ignored all those swatches on the Swatches palette because they never seem to include colors that have anything to do with your images. Don't ignore . . . explore! You can add, delete, and edit those little color swatches on the Swatches palette. Table 2-4 shows you how.

You can't actually edit a color that's already there. Instead, you can click on the swatch (to make it the current foreground color), edit the foreground color, then Shift-click back on the swatch (which replaces it with the current foreground color).

Preferences

There's a scene in Monty Python's *Life of Brian* where Brian is trying to persuade his followers to think for themselves. He shouts, "Every one of you is different! You're all individuals!" One person raises his hand and replies, "I'm not."

This is the situation we often find with Photoshop users. Even though each person uses the program differently, they think they need to use it just like everyone else. Not true. You can customize Photoshop in a number of ways through its Preferences submenu (under the File menu). We're not going to discuss every preference. Instead, we'll take a look at some of the key items we think you should be aware of on the Preferences submenu. First we'll cover the General Preferences dialog box (press

Table 2-4

Editing the Swatches palette

To do this . . .	Do this . . .
Add foreground color	Click any empty swatch
Delete a color	Command-click
Replace a color with foreground color	Shift-click
Insert foreground color between two others	Shift-Option-click

Command-K); then we'll look at some other preferences. (We explore Photoshop's color preferences more in Chapter 5, *Color Settings*.)

Tip: Return of Preferences. If you make a change in one of the many Preferences dialog boxes and then—after pressing OK—you decide to change to some other preference, you can return to the same dialog box by pressing Command-Option-K.

Tip: Propagating Your Preferences. Any time you make a change to one of the Preferences dialog boxes, Photoshop remembers your alteration, and when you quit, saves it in the "Adobe Photoshop 5 Prefs.psp" file in the Adobe Photoshop Settings folder, inside your application folder. If anything happens to that file, all your changes are gone. Because of this, we recommend keeping a backup of that file someplace (people often back up their images without realizing they should back up this sort of data file, too).

Certain kinds of crashes (mostly caused by software other than Photoshop) can corrupt Photoshop's Preferences file. If Photoshop starts acting strange on us, our first step is always to replace the Preferences file with a clean copy (if no copy of the Preferences file is available, then Photoshop will build a new one for you).

Note that if you administer a number of different computers that are running Photoshop, you may want to standardize the same preferences on all machines. The answer: copy the Photoshop Prefs file to each computer. Finally, note that Photoshop doesn't save changes to the preferences until you Quit. If Photoshop crashes, the changes don't get saved.

Export Clipboard. When the Export Clipboard checkbox is on, Photoshop converts whatever is on the clipboard into a PICT or WMF format when you leave Photoshop. This is helpful—indeed, necessary—if you want to paste a selection into some other program. But if you've got a megabyte or two or 10 megabytes on the clipboard, that conversion is going to take some time. In situations when you're running low on RAM, it can even crash your machine, though this is rarer than it used to be.

We recommend leaving Export Clipboard off until you really need it.

Dynamic Sliders in Picker. This one is very subtle. When Dynamic Sliders in the Picker is turned on, the bars for the sliders on the Picker palette change color as you drag. The target color changes as you drag, whether it's turned on or not—it just affects the sliders themselves. On a slower machine you may want to turn it off, as it can exact a slight performance penalty, but we've never noticed it.

Save Palette Locations. This does what it says—it remembers which palettes were open, which were closed, and where they were located on the screen the last time you quit. However, if you change your monitor resolution, the palettes return to their default locations. We leave this turned on.

By the way, there's a button at the bottom of the Preferences dialog box labeled Reset Palette Locations to Default. Every now and again, your palettes might get really messed up—placed partly or entirely off your screen, and so on. Don't panic; that's what this button is for. Just click once, then click OK, and you'll be back in business.

Image Previews. When you save a document in Photoshop, the program can save little thumbnails of your image as file icons. These thumbnails can be helpful, or they can simply be a drag to your productivity. We always set Image Previews to Ask When Saving, so we get a choice for each file (see "Preview Options" in Chapter 16, *Storing Images*).

Include Composited Image with Layered Files. We used to think that the Include Composited Image with Layered Files feature (previously known as 2.5 Format Compatibility) was completely brain-dead. Photoshop files that have no layers in them can be opened in older versions with no trouble even with this turned off. If you do have layers, you have to turn this on in order for Photoshop 2.5 people to open the file; however, if they do anything to the file and resave it, all your layers are deleted. Not very helpful.

What's worse, this feature (which is on by default) makes your image sizes larger on disk (sometimes several times larger) than they would otherwise be, because the program saves the information in the layers, and then it saves a duplicate flattened version of the image, too.

We've always said: turn this off and leave it off. However, now there are several programs that claim to open native Photoshop files, layers and all. The trick is that very few of them can actually read the layers themselves; rather, they depend on the duplicate version of the image. This includes Macromedia FreeHand and Adobe Illustrator. If you turn off this preference, these programs won't be able to import the image. So now we say: turn it off most of the time, but if you really need to open layered Photoshop files in some other program (instead of saving them as flattened TIFFs or EPSes or whatever), then turn it on.

Save Metric Color Tags. The Save Metric Color Tags option is only useful if you're using PostScript color management to convert your colors while printing from Photoshop to a PostScript Level 2 or PostScript 3 device. We've yet to see this work in the real world, perhaps because so few vendors bother to create good CRDs (Color Rendering Dictionaries) for their printers. However, if you've gone to the bother of building a CRD, you'll be glad to know that Save Metric Color Tags embeds a CSA (Color Space Array) in the image, which PostScript can then use as the "source profile" for an in-RIP color transform to the color space defined by the CRD.

Diffusion Dither. If, for some bizarre reason, you work in 8-bit color (we hardly ever work with Photoshop in less than "Thousands" of colors), Photoshop has to do even more work at displaying its plethora of colors on your screen. This is usually done with dithering of some sort. You can choose the method: when Use Diffusion Dither is turned on in the Display & Cursors Preferences dialog box, Photoshop generates colors using a "random" pixel placement. Otherwise, it uses a standard pattern. Neither of these methods is particularly attractive, though Diffusion Dither often produces a nicer look when zoomed in closer than 1:1.

Video LUT Animation. We talked about Video LUT Animation back in the Previewing section of "Dialog Boxes," earlier in this chapter. Quick recap: turn it on and leave it on, unless you primarily work with images in CMYK mode.

Brush Size. When you painted or edited pixels in pre-3.0 versions of Photoshop, the program would display the cursor only as a Brush icon (or Rubber Stamp icon, or whatever you were using). Because it was sometimes difficult to tell which pixel the tool would affect, Photoshop implemented the crosshairs feature—when Caps Lock is down, the cursor switches to a crosshair icon displaying precisely which pixel Photoshop is "looking at."

But most brushes affect more than one pixel at a time, so now when you set Painting Cursors to Brush Size (in the Display & Cursors Preferences dialog box), Photoshop shows you exactly how large the brush is while you're painting or editing (see Figure 2-23). After working with this for awhile, you'll wonder how you could ever go back.

You can still get the crosshairs with the Caps Lock key. Note that Photoshop can't show Brush Size cursors for brushes over 300 pixels in diameter.

Gamut Warning. Bruce thinks the Gamut Warning is basically useless—he'd rather just see what's happening to the out-of-gamut colors when they're converted—but for the record, when you turn on Gamut Warning from the View menu (or press Command-Shift-Y), it displays all the out-of-gamut pixels in the color you choose here (for more on Photoshop's out-of-gamut display features, see "Gamut Alarm" in Chapter 7, *Color Correction*).

If you do want to use this feature (David likes it), we recommend you choose a really ugly color (in the Transparency & Gamut Preferences dialog box) that doesn't appear anywhere in your image, such as a bright

Figure 2-23
Brush Size

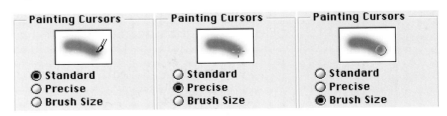

Figure 2-24

Transparency
preferences

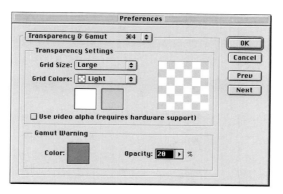

lime green. This way, when you switch on Gamut Warning, the out-of-gamut areas are quite obvious.

Transparency. Transparency is not a color, it's a state of mind. Therefore, when you see it on a layer, what should it look like? Typically, Photoshop displays transparency as a grid of white and gray boxes in a checkerboard pattern. The Preferences dialog box lets you change the colors of the checkerboard and set the size of the squares, though we've never found a reason to do so (see Figure 2-24).

Image Cache. Adobe has been getting yelled at for years about their handling of large images. Finally, in version 4, Photoshop introduced a nominal concession toward large-image handling with the Image Cache feature. It wasn't a great step forward, but it was a step nonetheless (Photoshop 5 didn't progress any farther down the road). When Image Cache is on (it is by default), Photoshop saves several downsampled, low-resolution versions of your image. That way, if you work on your image at 50-, 33- or 25-percent view (the particular views depend on the number of downsampled images cached), Photoshop is able to update your screen preview more quickly.

If you're low on RAM, you should probably turn off image caching (set the number of caches to 1 in the Image Cache Preferences dialog box; see Figure 2-25), because these downsampled versions of your image take up extra RAM (or space on your scratch disk, if you don't have enough RAM available). If you've got plenty of RAM and you spend a lot of time working at zoom percentages less than 100 percent, an Image Cache setting of 4 or higher could help speed you up. Each cache level caches one

Figure 2-25

Image Cache

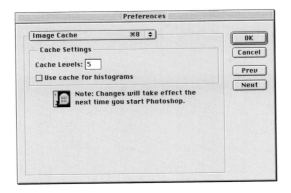

increment of zoom, so a setting of 4 caches the 66.7-, 50-, 33.3- and 25-percent views, while a setting of 6 adds the 16.7-percent and 12.5-percent views. The highest setting, 8 levels, caches all the views down to 6.25 percent. This is really only useful on very large images, but the incremental difference in RAM footprint between 6 levels and 8 levels is so small that even if you'd benefit from a setting of 8 only occasionally, you'd probably be best off just setting the Image Cache to 8 and leaving it there.

Note that we strongly urge you to turn off the Use cache for histograms checkbox in this Preferences dialog box. While turning it on will speed up your histograms at views other than 100 percent, it renders these histograms useless (see "Turn Off Use Image Cache For Histograms" in Chapter 6, *Tonal Correction*).

When Things Go Worng

It's 11 PM on the night before your big presentation. You've been working on this image for thirteen hours, and you're beginning to experience "pixel vision." After making a selection, you run a filter, look carefully, and decide that you don't like the effect. But before you can reach Undo, you accidentally click on the document window, deselecting the area.

That's not so bad, is it? Not until you realize that undoing will only undo the deselection, not the filter . . . and that you haven't saved for half an hour. The mistake remains, and there's no way to get rid of it without losing the last 30 minutes of brain-draining work. Or is there? In this section of the chapter, we take a look at the various ways you can save yourself when something goes terribly wrong.

The first two techniques are pretty obvious. However, the third technique, the History palette, is a major new feature in Photoshop 5, and some of you will find it's worth every penny of the upgrade cost.

Undo. The first defense against any offensive mistake is, of course, Undo. You can find this on the Edit menu, but we suggest keeping one hand conveniently on the Command and Z keys, ready and waiting for the blunder that is sure to come sooner or later. Note that Photoshop is smart enough not to count some things as "undoable." Taking a snapshot, for instance, doesn't count; so you can take a snapshot and then undo whatever you did just before the snapshot. Similarly, you can open the Histogram, hide edges, change foreground or background colors, zoom, scroll, or even duplicate the file, and Photoshop still lets you go back and undo the previous action.

Revert to Saved. This command is pretty easy to interpret. If you've really messed up something in your image, often the best option is simply to revert the entire file to the last saved version by selecting Revert to Saved from the File menu. It's the same as closing the file without saving changes, then reopening it. Any changes you've made since then are lost, however, so proceed with caution.

The History Palette

There is a school of thought that dictates, "Don't give people what they want, give them what they need." The Photoshop engineering team appears to be an advocate of this—they spend a lot of time listening to and thinking about what people ask for, but then they often come back with a feature that goes far beyond what anyone had even thought to request. For example, people have been asking for multiple Undos (the ability to sequentially undo steps that you've taken while editing a Photoshop image). The result is the History palette, which goes far beyond a simple Undo mechanism into a whole new paradigm of working in Photoshop.

The History palette, at its most basic, remembers what you've done to your file and lets you either retrace your steps or revert back to any earlier version of the image. Every time you do something to your image—paint a brush stroke, run a filter, make a selection, and so on—Photoshop saves this change as a *state* in the History palette (see Figure 2-26). At any time, you can revert the entire image to any previous state, or—using the

Figure 2-26

The History palette

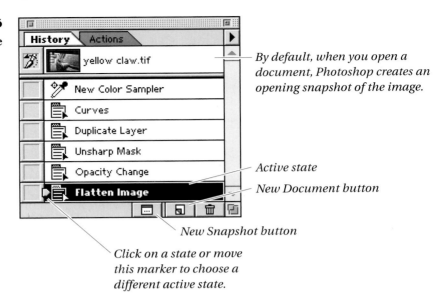

By default, when you open a document, Photoshop creates an opening snapshot of the image.

Active state

New Document button

New Snapshot button

Click on a state or move this marker to choose a different active state.

History Brush tool or the Fill command, which we'll discuss in a moment—selectively paint back in time.

There is, however, an itty-bitty problem with the History palette: it can take up a lot of RAM. Sorry, did we say "a lot"? We meant "vast, awe-inspiring, mind-boggling quantities" of memory. As we pointed out in Chapter 1, *Building a Photoshop System*, Photoshop can require as much as 10 to 20 times your file size in RAM—or more—to perform efficiently (that's 200 to 400 MB of RAM for a 20 MB image). Performing simple tasks such as opening, rotating, sharpening, and saving may take significantly longer when the History feature is turned on (which it is by default in Photoshop 5).

Tip: Turning Off History. If you're doing straight-laced production work all day (the kind of work for which a single Undo is perfectly adequate), you may want to avoid the History feature's RAM overhead by changing the Maximum Remembered States value to 1 and turning off the Automatically Create First Snapshot option in the History Options dialog box (which you can find on the History palette's popout menu). You might also want to turn off these functions if you're going to batch-process a number of images using actions or the Automate "wizards."

The History palette has two sections: snapshots and states. Let's take a look at each of these and how you can use them.

Snapshots. Earlier versions of Photoshop let you save a single snapshot of your document, representing a moment in time for your image. The History palette lets you save any number of snapshots so that at any time you can return to a specific state. There are two primary differences between snapshots and states.

▶ Photoshop records everything you do to an image as a state. Snapshots are only recorded when you first open an image and when you click the New Snapshot button in the History palette.

▶ When the number of states on the History palette exceeds the Maximum Remembered States value (in the History Options dialog box), the oldest states start dropping off the list. Snapshots don't disappear until you close the document.

Tip: What's in the Snapshot. When you click the New Snapshot button on the History palette (or select New Snapshot from the palette's popout menu), Photoshop saves the whole document (individual layers and all). Depending on how many layers you have and how large your document is, this might require a lot of RAM. If you Option-click the button, Photoshop offers two other less-memory-intensive snapshot choices: a version of the image with merged layers, or just of the currently selected layer.

Stepping through states. As we mentioned above, Photoshop saves every brush stroke, every selection, every *anything* you do to your image as a state on the History palette (though the state only remains on the palette until you reach the maximum number of states or you close the document). There are several ways to move among states of your image.

▶ To revert your image back to a state, you can click on any state's tile in the History palette.

▶ You can also move the active state marker to a state on the History palette.

▶ You can press Command-Z to step back to the last state (just like you've always been able to do). However, you can also press Command-Option-Z to move backward one state at a time, and Command-Shift-Z to move forward one state at a time.

In general, when you move to an earlier state, Photoshop grays out every subsequent state on the History palette, indicating that if you do anything now these grayed-out states will be erased. This is like going back to a fork in the road and choosing the opposite path from what you took before. Photoshop offers another option: if you turn on the Allow Non-Linear History checkbox in the History Options dialog box, Photoshop doesn't gray out or remove subsequent states when you move back in time (though it still deletes old states after you reach the maximum number of states limit).

Non-Linear History is like returning to the fork in the road, taking the opposite path, but then having the option to return to any state from the first path. For example, you could run a Gaussian Blur on your image using three different amounts—returning the image to the pre-blurred state in the History palette each time—and then switch among these three states to decide which one you wanted to use.

The primary problem with Non-Linear History is that it may confuse you more than help you, especially when you're dealing with a number of different "forks on the road."

The History Brush. Returning to a previous state returns the entire image to that state. But Photoshop's History feature lets you selectively return portions of your image to a previous state, too, with the History Brush and the Fill command. Before painting with the History Brush, first select the source state in the History palette (click in the column to the left of the state from which you want to paint). For instance, let's say you sharpen a picture of a face with Unsharp Masking (see Chapter 9, *Sharpening*) and find that the lips have become oversharp. You can select the History Brush, set the source state to the presharpened state, and then brush around the lips (though you'd probably want to reduce the opacity of the History Brush to 20 or 30 percent by pressing 2 or 3 first).

The History Brush tool (press Y) is very similar to the Eraser tool when the Erase to History checkbox is turned on in the Options palette, but the

History Brush offers two additional features over the "magic erase" tool. First, you can paint with modes, such as Multiply and Screen. Second, you can turn on the Impressionist checkbox in the Options palette, which lets you paint and blur and smudge all at the same time. (As much as we like the works of the great Impressionists, we simply don't ever use this feature.)

Tip: Snap Before Action. If you run an action in the Actions palette that has more steps than your Maximum Remembered States preference, you won't be able to "undo" the action. That's why before running the action you should either save a snapshot of your full document or set the source state for the History Brush to the current state. The latter works because Photoshop never "rolls off" the source state in the History palette, so you don't have to worry about its getting deleted after reaching the maxiumum number of states.

Fill with History. The last technique that can help in case of a catastrophic "oops" is the Fill command on the Edit menu (or press Shift-Delete). This lets you fill any selection (or the entire image, if nothing is selected) with the pixels from the current source state on the History palette. We usually use this in preference to the History Brush or Magic Eraser tools when the area to be reverted is easily selectable. Sometimes when we paint with those tools, we overlook some pixels (it's hard to use a brush to paint *every* pixel in an area at 100 percent). This is never a problem when you use the Fill command. (Even faster than opening the Fill dialog box is to press Command-Option-Backspace, which always fills from the source state.)

Tip: Persistent States. Remember that both snapshots and states are cleared out when you close a document. If you want to save a particular state or snapshot, drag its tile over the Create New Document button on the History palette. Now that state is its own document that you can save to disk. If you want to copy pixels from that document into another image, simply use the Rubber Stamp tool (you can set the source point to one document and then paint with it in the other file).

Tip: Revert when Revert Doesn't Work. Deke McClelland taught us a trick at a recent Photoshop conference that has already saved David's buttocks several times. Because David has a tendency to type fast and loose, he'll often press Command-S (Save) when he meant to press Command-A (Select All) or Command-D (Deselect). Of course, this saves over his file on disk, often ruining his original scan. The History palette to the rescue! Remember that the default preference for the History palette is to create a snapshot of the image when you first open it. If you save over your original image, you can drag the snapshot's tile over the Create New Document button in the History palette to recreate the original data in its own file.

Tip: Copying States. Although Photoshop lets you copy states from one document to another simply by dragging them from the History palette onto the other document's window, we can't think of many good reasons to do this. The copied state completely replaces the image that you've dragged it over.

Tip: When History Stops Working. Note that you cannot use the History Brush or the Fill from History feature when your image's pixel dimensions or color mode has changed. Pixel dimensions usually change when you rotate the whole image, use the Cropping tool, or use the Image Size or Canvas Size dialog boxes.

Tip: Purging States. As we said earlier, the History palette takes up a lot of memory. If you find yourself in need of some RAM, you might try clearing out the History states by either selecting Clear History from the popout menu on the History palette or choosing History from the Purge submenu (under the Edit menu). The former can be undone in a pinch; the latter cannot. Curiously, neither of these removes your snapshots, so you have to delete those manually if you want to save even more RAM. Remember that closing your document and reopening it will also remove all snapshots and history states.

Easter Eggs

It's a tradition in Macintosh software to include Easter Eggs—those wacky little undocumented, nonutilitarian features that serve only to amuse the programmer and (they hope) the user. Note that if your friends think you have no sense of humor, you might want to skip this section; it might just annoy you.

There are (at least) three Easter Eggs in Photoshop: two hidden screens and one quote list.

Strange Cargo. A tradition even older than Easter Eggs is code names. Almost all software has a code name that the developers use before the product is christened with a real shipping name. Photoshop 4 was code-named Big Electric Cat (it's an Adrian Belew reference, if you care). Photoshop 5 was code-named Strange Cargo. To see the original Strange Cargo splash screen, hold down the Command key while selecting About Photoshop from the Apple menu (or press Control-Alt and select About Photoshop from the Help menu in Photoshop for Windows). The name of the cat is Udo; type his name. Now tell him to burp. Gotta love it. (Note that if you make a typo, the trick may not work until next time you open the dialog box or start Photoshop.)

Quotes. If you watch either the standard About Photoshop screen or the Strange Cargo splash screen, you'll notice that the credits at the bottom of the screen start to scroll by, thanking everyone and their dog for participating in the development process. Don't get impatient—the last person on the list is someone special. (Actually, if you *are* the impatient type, try holding down the Option key once the credits start rolling; that speeds them up.)

At any time before or during the rolling credits, try clicking once between the big word "Adobe" and the picture. If the screen disappears, you've clicked in the wrong place. If nothing happens, you've done it right. Now just wait until the scrolling credits are finished, and you'll be treated to some very funny quotations. (Again, this seems to be a Mac-only thing.)

Merlin lives! Finally (at least, this is the last one we know about), there's a little hidden dialog box nestled away. When you hold down the Option key while selecting Palette Options from the popout menus in either the Paths, Layers, or Channels palette, Merlin happily jumps out. If you're on a Mac, don't forget to try clicking on Merlin for that extra kick.

The World of Photoshop

If our publisher weren't screaming bloody murder to get this book to the printer, we'd still be writing tips. But instead of waiting until the next edition of the book, try finding them for yourself. The more you *play* with Photoshop, the more you'll be rewarded with treasures from the deep.

3 Image Essentials

It's All Zeros and Ones

Let's get one thing perfectly clear: this book is not about pictures or work flow or even computers. This book is about zeros and ones. As Laurie Anderson so plainly pointed out, no one wants to be a zero and everyone (at least in America) wants to be "number one." The digital age is built entirely on the interplay between the two.

To be sure, the digital world (in which zeros and ones, offs and ons, and whites and blacks frolic together in cooperation, not competition) is not as confusing as some people make it out to be. And, as it turns out, you can't really be efficient with digital imaging without knowing a little bit about that dark underworld. In this chapter we're going to break it all down for you. To some of you, most of this chapter is going to sound pretty basic, but we urge you to peruse it anyhow. You might be surprised at how many "power users" find themselves stumped by something as small as a misunderstanding of how—and why—bitmapped images work.

Bitmapped versus Object-Oriented Graphics

In all the grand canon of computer imaging, there are really only two kinds of graphics: bitmapped and object-oriented.

Bitmapped images. Bitmapped images are simply collections of dots (we call them *pixels* or *sample points*) laid out in a big grid. The pixels can be different colors, and the number of dots can vary. No matter what the picture is—whether it's a modernist painting of a giraffe or a photograph of your mother—it's always described using lots of dots. This is the only way to represent the fine detail and subtle gradations of photorealistic images.

Just about every bitmapped image comes from one of three sources: capture devices (such as scanners, video cameras, or digital cameras), painting and image-editing programs (such as Photoshop), and screen-capture programs (like Exposure Pro, the System, and a host of others). If you create a graphic with any of these tools, it's a bitmapped image.

Object-oriented graphics. Object-oriented graphics are both more complex and simpler than bitmapped images. On the one hand, instead of describing a rectangle with thousands (or millions) of dots, object-oriented graphics just say, "Draw a rectangle this big and put it here." Clearly, this is a much more efficient and space-saving method for describing some images. However, object-oriented graphics can include many different types of objects—lines, boxes, circles, curves, polygons, and text blocks, and all those items can have a variety of attributes—line weight, type formatting, fill color, graduated fills, and so on.

To use an analogy, object-oriented graphics are like directions saying, "Go three blocks down the street, turn left at the 7-11, and go another five blocks," while bitmapped images are more like saying, "Take a step. Now take another step. And another . . . ." When you work in Photoshop, you're working with bitmapped images (though you can import some object-oriented graphics, converting them to bitmaps, and you can use object-oriented techniques to create selections and masks).

Most object-oriented graphics come from two primary sources: drawing programs (FreeHand, Canvas, Illustrator, and so on), and computer-aided design (CAD) programs. You might also get object-oriented graphics from other programs, such as a program that makes graphs.

Bitmaps as objects. It turns out that the distinction between bitmapped and object-oriented graphics is slightly fuzzy, because object-oriented graphics can include bitmaps as objects in their own right. For instance, you can put a scanned image into an Adobe Illustrator illustration. The scan actually acts like an object on the page, much like a rectangle or

Words, Words, Words

While terminology might not keep you up at night, we in the writin' business have to worry about such things. In fact, one of our first controversies in writing this book concerned the term *bitmap*.

Bruce maintains that, strictly speaking, bitmaps are only black-and-white images. This is how Photoshop uses the term. He prefers to describe images made up of colored dots as *raster* images (the word "raster" refers to a group of lines—in this case, lines of pixels—that collectively make up an image). David thinks that only people who wear pocket protectors (some of his best friends do) would use the word "raster." With the first controversy comes the first compromise: we'll call these creatures we're working with in Photoshop "bitmapped images"—whether

they're black and white, gray-scale, or color.

Another problem we've encountered is what to call all those little dots in a bitmapped image. As we mentioned earlier, when we talk about points in a bitmapped image, we like to call them *pixels, samples,* or *sample points*.

The phrase "sample points" comes from what a scanner does: it samples an image—checking what color or gray value it finds—every 300th of an inch, every 100th of an inch, or whatever. However, not all bitmapped images are scanned. "Pixel" is a more generic term because it specifies the smallest "picture element" in an image. Occasionally, you'll run into someone who refers to pixels as "pels." They may not wear pocket protectors, but they've almost certainly had an unnaturally close relationship with an

IBM mainframe computer somewhere in their past.

When we talk about scanning an image in, or printing an image out, we talk about samples or pixels per inch (Bruce prefers the latter, or *ppi;* David likes the former, or *spi*); and when we talk about the resolution of a bitmapped image saved on disk, we just talk about the total number of pixels. Note that many people use "dots per inch" (*dpi*) for any and all kinds of resolution. We prefer to reserve the term "dots per inch" (dpi) for use when speaking of printers and image-setters, which actually create dots on paper or film.

We use the term "pixels" for one other thing: screen resolution. However, to be clear, we always try to specify "screen pixels" versus "image pixels."

oval. If you include a bitmap as an object in an illustration, you can rotate it and scale it, but you can't go into the image and change the pixels.

Note that an object-oriented graphic file might include a bitmap as its *only* object. In this situation, the file is a bitmapped image that you can open for editing in a painting or image-processing application. Photoshop's EPS (Encapsulated PostScript) files are good examples of this. While EPS is typically an object-oriented file format, you can create a bitmap-only EPS in Photoshop.

Objects in bitmapped graphics. Just to round out the confusion, we should mention that Photoshop lets you include an object called a *clipping path* in bitmapped images. A clipping path in an image is invisible; it simply acts as a cookie cutter, allowing you to produce irregularly shaped images such as the silhouetted product shots you often see in ads (see "Clipping Paths" in Chapter 16, *Storing Images*).

Bitmapped Images

Photoshop lets you open, create, edit, and save bitmapped images. Bitmapped images are its *sine qua non*, its *raison d'être*, its "precious bodily fluid." So to get the most out of Photoshop, you've got to understand bitmapped images inside and out.

Every bitmapped graphic has three basic characteristics: dimension, bit depth, and color model (which Photoshop refers to as *image mode*).

Dimension

Bitmapped images are always big rectangular grids. Like checkerboards or chessboards or parquet floors in your kitchen, these big grids are made of little squares (see Figure 3-1). The *dimensions* of the bitmap grid refer to the number of pixels wide and tall it is. A chessboard is always eight squares by eight squares. The grid of pixels that makes up your computer screen might be 640 by 480.

Figure 3-1

Bitmaps as grids of squares

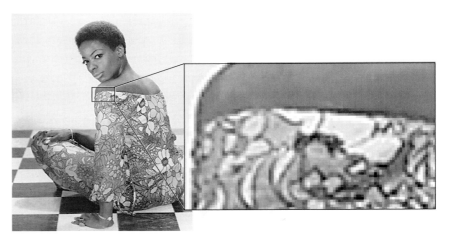

A bitmapped image can be any dimension you like, limited only by the capabilities of your capture device, the amount of storage space you have available, and your patience—the more pixels in the image, the more space it takes up, and the longer it takes to do anything with it.

Note that *dimension has nothing to do with physical size* in inches or picas. Bitmapped images in their pure digital state have no physical size; they're just data. They exist as Platonic ideals, waiting to be realized by reproduction in some physical form. No matter how you stretch or shrink a bitmapped image, it still contains the same number of pixels.

When you print a bitmapped image, you print it at a specific size, and the relationship between that size and the number of pixels the image contains is called the *resolution* of the image. But it's very important to understand that resolution isn't innate to the digital image; it's a rubber measurement that changes depending on the physical size at which you reproduce the image. We'll discuss resolution and why it's important in more detail later in this chapter.

Bit Depth

Each pixel in a bitmapped image is represented by a particular number of zeros and ones, otherwise known as *bit depth* (one bit can be either a zero or a one). That number dictates the range of possible values for each pixel, and hence the total number of colors (or shades of gray) that the image can contain.

A 1-bit image (one in which each pixel is represented by one bit) can only contain blacks and whites. If you have two bits of information describing a pixel, there are four possible combinations (00, 01, 10, and 11), hence four possible values, and four possible colors or gray levels (see Figure 3-2). Eight bits of information give you 256 possible values; 24 bits of information result in over 16 million possible colors. (With 24-bit RGB images, each sample actually has three 8-bit values—one each for red, green, and blue; see Color Plate 1 on page 677.)

Figure 3-2
Bit depth

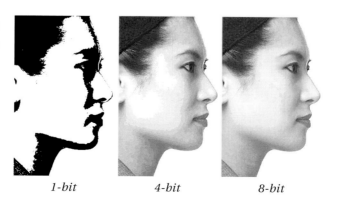

1-bit   *4-bit*   *8-bit*

Figure 3-3

A "deep" bitmap

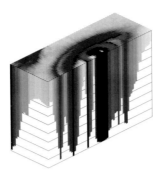

We call 1-bit images *flat* or *bilevel* bitmaps. A *deep* bitmap is any image that has more than one bit describing each pixel (see Figure 3-3).

Bit depth has an important relationship to the quality of an image, which we'll cover more fully later in this chapter.

Image Mode

The problem with bit depth is that it doesn't really tell us (or Photoshop) what each color (numerical value) means. A 1-bit image is easy: each pixel can only be on or off. It doesn't have to be black or white, though; if you were twisted enough, you could make this orange or blue.

But as we've seen, each pixel in an 8-bit image can be described using one of 256 values. Are those 256 levels of gray? Or 256 colors? Or something else? We'll let you in on a sad, sordid little secret here. Everyone who works with color on computers discovers it eventually anyway: computers don't understand color at all—they just understand numbers: zeros and ones.

The color model—otherwise known as image mode—is the missing piece of the puzzle, the magic decoder ring that tells how to translate each pixel's numerical value into a color or a shade of gray. Actually, image mode and color model aren't exactly the same thing, but they're so closely related that it makes sense to discuss them as aspects of the same thing.

If the image mode is set to Grayscale under the Mode menu, the value of each pixel is a grayscale value: 0 is black, 255 is white. If image mode is Indexed, then each value is tagged to a specific, arbitrarily chosen color. (An indexed color image can only have 256 different colors in it; see "Indexed Color," later in this chapter.)

However, if the image mode is set to RGB, Lab, or CMYK, then the color of the pixel is actually made up of multiple 8-bit values. For instance, in an RGB image, each pixel is described using three 8-bit values, each of which specifies a level of brightness for the red, green, and blue channels (see Color Plate 1 on page 677). In a CMYK image, Photoshop looks at and composites four 8-bit images.

You can look at the individual channels and view each one as a grayscale image. The color image is made by colorizing each channel with the appropriate color and stacking them one atop the other.

Note that unless you're working with esoteric scientific or medical imaging equipment, you won't have to tell Photoshop which image mode to use: virtually every file format that Photoshop recognizes has the secret decoder ring built in. But you need to understand image modes and their related color models if you want to do much useful work with Photoshop. (For a fuller discussion of color models, see Chapter 4, *Color Essentials.*)

We'll look at each mode that Photoshop uses, and why you'd want to use one or another, later in this chapter.

Resolution

Resolution is one of the most overused and under-understood words in desktop publishing. People use it when talking about scanners and printers, images and screens, halftones, and just about anything else they can get their hands on. Then they wonder why they're confused. Don't worry; resolution is easy.

As we noted earlier, a bitmapped image in its pure digital state has no physical size—it's just a bunch of pixels. But you can't see a pure digital image unless you can decipher zeros and ones in your head. So whenever you give an image tangible expression, whether it's as an ephemeral representation on the screen or as a permanent printed form, you confer upon it the property of physical size. And with size comes resolution.

The resolution of a bitmapped image is the number of pixels in each unit of measurement. If we're talking in inches, then we talk about the number of pixels per inch (ppi), which is what most people mean when they say "dots per inch" (dpi).

If your bitmapped image has 72 pixels per inch, and it's 72 pixels long on each side, then it's an inch long on each side. If you print it at half the size, you'll still have the same number of pixels, but they'll be crammed

Figure 3-4

Scaling and
resolution

25 percent
(288 ppi)

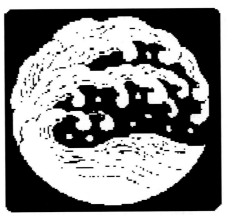

50 percent
(144 ppi)

100 percent (72 ppi)

50 percent
(144 ppi)

100 percent (72 ppi)

300 percent (24 ppi)

into half the space, so each inch will contain 144 of them. If we take the same bitmapped image and change it to 36 pixels per inch (changing its resolution), suddenly the image is two inches on each side (same number of pixels, but each one is twice as big as the original; see Figure 3-4).

You can also look at bitmap resolution in another way: if you know the size of an image and its resolution, you can figure out its dimensions. When you scan a picture that is three inches on each side at 100 pixels per inch, you know that the bitmapped image has 300 pixels on each side (100 per inch). If you scan it at 300 pixels per inch, the dimensions shoot up to 900 pixels on each side.

The key to making resolution work for you (rather than against you) is in knowing how many pixels you need for the intended purpose to which you'll put the image. We discuss how much data you need for different purposes later in this chapter.

How Much Is Enough?

If bigger were better, we'd be out of business (you'd be hard pressed to call us statuesque). And when it comes to resolution of bitmapped images, bigger is not only worse, but costly, too. The higher the resolution of an image, the longer it takes to open, edit, save, or print. Plus, while the cost of hard drives has come down in recent years, you're still paying between 50 cents and a dollar per megabyte of storage. That means you'll save $100 just by reducing ten 8-by-10-inch images from 300 ppi to 225 ppi (see "Bitmaps and File Size," later in this chapter).

Figure 3-5

Pixelation in too-low-resolution images

100 percent
200 ppi

300 percent
66 ppi

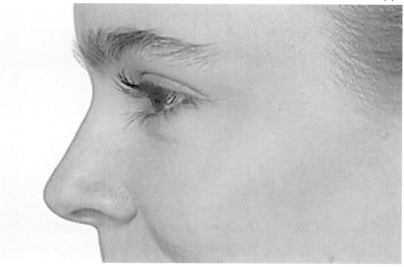

Of course, smaller isn't necessarily better, either. If your image resolution is too low, your image will look pixelated (see Figure 3-5); you'll start to see the pixels themselves, or adverse effects due to excessively large pixels. Loss of detail and mottling are the two worst offenders in this category.

Terms of Resolution

Not everyone talks about resolution in terms of ppi. Depending on the circumstance, your personality, and the time of day, you might discuss a file's resolution in a number of ways, but they're all different ways of talking about the same essential concept: *how much information* the file contains. Here's a quick rundown of your options.

Image size. The first way to discuss resolution is the way we've done it up until now (and the way we do it in most places in this book): spec both the physical size and number of pixels per inch. For example, you might say a file is 4 by 5 inches at 225 ppi. This makes the most sense to someone doing page layout, because they're typically concerned with how the image is going to look on the printed page. Note, however, that you have to specify both the size and the

resolution; otherwise you're only telling half the story.

Dimensions. You can sidestep the question of resolution by simply specifying the dimensions of the bitmapped image; that is, the number of pixels on each side of the bitmap grid. This doesn't tell you what physical size it is, but if you understand how much resolution you need for different output methods, it's useful shorthand for expressing how big the image *could be*, depending on what you wanted to do with it. It tells you how much information there is in the file. Hard-core Photoshop users like to talk in dimensions because they don't necessarily know (or care) how large the final output will be.

For instance, you could say a scan from a 35 mm original is a 2,048-by-3,076 image. What does that tell you? With experience,

you'd know that your file size is 18 MB, and at 225 ppi you could print a full-bleed letter-sized page. Later on we'll discuss how you can figure all this out for yourself.

File size. The third way to discuss resolution is by the file's size on disk. You can quickly get a sense of the difference in information content of two files when we tell you that the first is 900 K and the second is 12 MB. In fact, a lot of digital imaging gurus *only* think in file size. If you ask them, "What's the resolution of that file?" they look at you like you're an idiot.

Once you become accustomed to working with a number of different sizes, you'll recognize that the 900 K RGB file is about the size of a 640-by-480 RGB image. At 72 ppi (screen resolution) that's pretty big, but at 300 ppi (typical

Maybe you thought you could save even more money by reducing those eight-by-tens down to 150 ppi. However, when the client rejects the job because the image is too pixelated, that savings will be more than wiped out when you have to redo the job. So if bigger isn't better, and too small is even worse, then how much is enough? How much image data do you need? The first consideration is image mode: the requirements are very different for line art than they are for grayscale and color.

Line art

For bilevel (black-and-white, 1-bit) images, the resolution never needs to be higher than that of the printer you're using. If you're printing to a resolution for a high-quality print job), the image is only about two inches wide.

The resolution of Photo CD images is often specced by file size. The highest-resolution Photo CD image is 18 MB; the highest resolution of Pro Photo CD is 64 MB.

Single-side dimension. People who work with continuous-tone film recorders, such as the Solitaire or the FIRE1000, frequently talk about a file's resolution in terms of the dimension of one side—typically the width—of the image. For instance, they might ask for "a 4 K file." That means the image should be exactly 4,096 pixels across.

"K" usually means file size (kilobytes). However, in this case it's 1,024 pixels (see Table 3-1).

The height of the image is relatively unimportant in this case, though if you're imaging to film, it's usually assumed that you know the other dimension of the image because it's dictated by the

Table 3-1 Resolution in K

K	Number of pixels across
1	1,024
2	2,048
3	3,072*
4	4,096
5	5,120*
6	6,144*
7	7,168*
8	8,192

* rarely used

aspect ratio of the film you're using. High-quality film recorders usually write out to 4-by-5-inch chromes (positive transparencies), so if you want to fill the image area, it's usually assumed that the short side of your 8 K image will contain somewhere around 6,550 pixels.

Res. One other method of discussing resolution uses the term *res*. "Res" is simply the number of pixels per millimeter, and if we had anything to say about the matter, it'd be stricken from common us-

Table 3-2 Resolution in res

Res	Pixels per inch
1	25.4
2	50.8
3	76.2
4	101.6
5	127
6	152.4
7	177.8
8	203.2
9	228.6
10	254
11	279.4
12	304.8
20	508
40	1,016
60	1,524
80	2,032

age. People usually talk about res when they're discussing scanning resolution. For example, a file scanned at res 12 is scanned at 12 sample points (pixels) per millimeter—which is 120 sample points per centimeter, or—in common usage—304.8 sample points per inch (see Table 3-2).

300-dpi desktop laser printer, there's no reason to have more than 300 pixels per inch in your image (the printer can only image 300 dots per inch, so any extras just get thrown away). However, when you print to a 1,200-dpi imagesetter, that 300-ppi image appears jaggy.

If you're printing to an imagesetter, you should plan on using an image resolution of *at least* 800 ppi—preferably 1,000 ppi or more (see Figure 3-6). Line art with an image resolution of less than 800 shows jaggies and broken lines. Of course, if you're then going to print that artwork onto newsprint or porous paper, you can often get away with a lower resolution such as 400 or 600 ppi, because the jaggies will disappear with the spreading ink.

Figure 3-6
Resolution of
line art

144 ppi

300 ppi

800 ppi

1,200 ppi

See Chapter 11, *Line Art*, for techniques to increase the resolution and appearance of line art images at lower resolutions.

Grayscale and Color Halftones

There's a relatively simple formula for figuring out the proper resolution for printing grayscale and color ("deep") bitmapped images to halftoning devices like laser printers and imagesetters: image resolution should be two times the screen frequency *at most*. For instance, if you're printing a halftone image at 133 lpi, the image resolution should be no larger than 266 ppi (see Figure 3-7, and Color Plate 2 on page 678). Any higher resolution is almost certainly wasted information.

We've heard from people who claim to see a difference between 2 times the screen frequency and 2.5 times the screen frequency, but no one has ever shown us a print sample that supported this contention. It's absolutely certain that anything higher than 2.5 times the screen frequency is wasted if you're printing to a PostScript output device.

Figure 3-7 Resolution of grayscale images

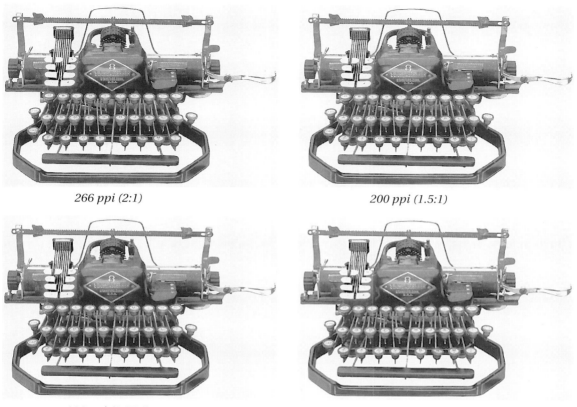

266 ppi (2:1)   *200 ppi (1.5:1)*

166 ppi (1.25:1)   *133 ppi (1:1)*

If you go to print an image whose resolution exceeds that multiplier, Photoshop warns you, and PostScript just discards the extra information when it gets to the printer. You can print the image, but it takes longer to print, and you don't get any better results than you would with a lower-resolution version.

In fact, we rarely use even twice the line screen. With a good 80 percent of images, you can use 1.5 times the screen frequency, and you can often get away with less, sometimes even as low as 1.2 times the screen frequency. That means the resolution of the image that you're printing at 133 lpi *could* be as low as 160 ppi (but if you want to play it safe, you might use 200 ppi).

So which multiplier should you use? It depends on your quality requirements, the quality of your reproduction method, the kind of images you're reproducing, and your system. If you're working with a less-powerful computer, less RAM, or a smaller hard drive, think lower resolution.

Quality requirements. The only reliable way we've found to answer the question of what's "good enough" is whether the person paying for the job smiles when they sign the check. There's no absolute index of quality, and clients have widely differing expectations. The best course of action is to prepare Match Prints or other high-quality laminated film proofs of a few different images, using different multipliers to see where the trade-off works for you.

Reproduction method. Images destined for uncoated stock and newsprint can generally withstand a lower multiplier than those printed on coated stock at a high screen frequency, because the more porous stock causes greater dot gain: the halftone dots grow larger because the ink bleeds into the paper. If you're producing a rag or a newspaper and you're still using the two-times-frequency rule, you're wasting someone's time and money—we hope it's not yours.

Image detail. The need for higher resolution also depends on the content of the image itself. Reducing the multiplier reduces the clarity of small details, so higher resolution is most important with images that have small (and important) details.

Most pictures of people work fine at 1.25 times the screen frequency, but trees with fine branches and leaves might do best with 1.5 times screen frequency. And if the image has a lot of fine diagonal or curved lines (such as rigging on a sailboat, or small text), you may want to use a resolution of 2 times the frequency, particularly if you're paying through the teeth for a 200-lpi print job on high-quality coated stock. Of course, in those cases it's probably worth spending a little extra on Match Prints or other high-quality laminated proofs to test some of the more difficult images at different resolutions.

Many Photoshop neophytes assume that if they have a 300-ppi scanner, they should scan at 300 ppi even if the image is going to be reproduced at actual size with a 133-lpi screen. If you use a 2x multiplier or 266 ppi instead, that's a savings of one megabyte for a little 4-by-5-inch image. A 1.5x multiplier saves you almost three megabytes, and 1.25x brings your original 5 MB image down to only 1.58 MB. That could mean quite a large difference in printing time or costs. (See Chapter 13, *Capturing Images,* for more information on scanning resolution, and Chapter 17, *Output Methods,* for a fuller discussion of halftone output issues.)

If a lot of this halftone talk is going over your head, we recommend a book that David coauthored with Steve Roth and Glenn Fleishman called *Real World Scanning and Halftones.*

Grayscale and Color Continuous-Tone Output

If you're printing to a continuous-tone output device such as a dye-sublimation printer or a film recorder, you can forget all that fancy math. In an ideal world, you simply want the resolution of your file to match the resolution of the output device. If you're printing to a 300-dpi dye-sublimation printer, you want 300-ppi resolution—about 18 MB for a letter-sized page. If you're printing to an 8 K film recorder, you really do want 8,096 pixels on the short side of the image. That's a lot of data: about 240 MB for a 4-by-5-inch piece of film!

Sometimes, though, this simply isn't practical; you may not be able to make a scan that large. More important, the original may not contain enough useful information in the first place. It's possible to scan a 35 mm slide to a 75 MB file, but you'll see a lot of film grain, and the scan may not contain any more *useful* information than one that's half that size.

Some high-end continuous-tone output devices such as the FIRE1000 film recorder and the Iris ink-jet printer have extremely sophisticated resampling algorithms, much better than anything Photoshop provides. You may be able to produce a very acceptable 4-by-5 digital chrome (positive transparency) or a 16-by-20 Iris print from a 75 MB file, even though its resolution is only about half that of the output device. Again, it's worth making some tests using different resolutions.

On-screen Output (Multimedia and the Web)

Multimedia is another form of continuous-tone output, but where you often need very high resolution for film recorders, on-screen multimedia projects require very little. It's generally misleading to think in terms of resolution when you prepare images for use on screen. All that really matters is the pixel dimensions.

When people talk about monitor resolution, they almost invariably specify the number of pixels on the screen—640 by 480, 800 by 600, 1024 by 768, and so on. The polite fiction that screen resolution is 72 ppi is no more than that. You can run a 21-inch monitor at 640 by 480 (great for games) or a 17-inch monitor at 1,600 by 1,200 (great for images, bad for reading small type). These extreme cases produce actual resolutions much lower and higher than 72 ppi. You can't control the actual size at which your images will appear on other people's monitors. All you can do is suggest the ideal number of pixels on the screen for viewing your project.

We almost never scan an image at screen resolution, however. We like to scan at a higher resolution so that we can crop and resize the image to get it just right; then we downsample it (see the next section).

Resampling

One of the most important issues in working with bitmapped images—and, unfortunately, one which few people seem to understand—is how the resolution can change relative to (or independently of) the size of your image.

There are two ways that you can change resolution: scaling and resampling. You can scale or resample an image or part of an image in several ways, but you get the most control through the Image Size dialog box (see "Tip: Faster File Figuring," later in this chapter).

In Photoshop, you can scale an image without altering its resolution. Or you can change the resolution of a bitmapped image without changing its size. These processes are called *resampling*, because you're changing the number of pixels in the image. You're adding or removing pixels.

If you take a 2-by-2-inch, 100-ppi image and change the size to 1 inch square without changing the resolution, Photoshop has to throw away a bunch of pixels; that's called *downsampling*. If you double the size by *upsampling*, it has to add more pixels by *interpolating* between other pixels in the image (see Figure 3-8).

Upsampling versus Downsampling

The rule to remember with upsampling is, "Just don't do it if you can avoid it; and if you *can't* avoid it, use bicubic interpolation." Adding pixels to a file can reduce aliasing (a.k.a. the jaggies) and mottling in some situations (and exaggerate them in others), but it can't add details that weren't there in the first place: you don't get something for nothing, and

Figure 3-8
Resampling

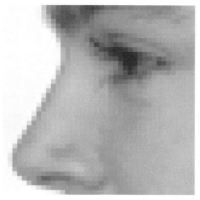

Original image

Downsampled

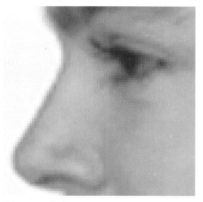

While downsampling is a normal and necessary procedure, there's almost never any reason to upsample. It simply adds data, not information, so your image is blurry instead of pixelated.

Upsampled

there's no such thing as a free lunch. (The one place that upsampling is really useful is in creating line art; see Chapter 11, *Line Art*.)

Downsampling is much less problematic, because it's simply throwing away data in a more or less intelligent manner. In fact, it's a common and necessary practice: we often scan at a higher resolution than is strictly necessary, to allow for cropping and for unanticipated changes in output size or method. We downsample to the required resolution before printing to save time and storage space.

Resampling methods. Photoshop can downsample and interpolate using three methods: Nearest Neighbor, Bilinear, and Bicubic. You choose which you want in the General Preferences dialog box or in the Image Size dialog box (see Figure 3-11 on page 94).

Image Size Dialog Box

The folks at Adobe revised the Image Size dialog box in version 4, and we thought it was about time (see Figure 3-9). For those of us who have to teach Photoshop as well as use it, Image Size was one of the biggest sources of frustration because of its confusing labels and odd workings. The current arrangement is a great step forward, but it takes some getting used to if you're coming from Photoshop 3.

The Image Size dialog box is split into the two most important ways of describing an image's resolution: its pixel dimensions and its print size.

▶ **Pixel Dimensions.** The best way to specify an image's size is by its pixel dimensions—these tell you exactly how much data you have to work with. The Pixel Dimensions section shows you both the dimensions and the file's size, in megabytes (or K, if it's under 1 MB).

▶ **Print Size.** A bitmapped image has no inherent size—it's just pixels on a grid. The Print Size section lets you tag the image with a size and resolution, so that when you import the file into some other program, it knows the image size.

Resample Image. The most important feature in the Image Size dialog box is the Resample Image

Figure 3-9 Image Size dialog box

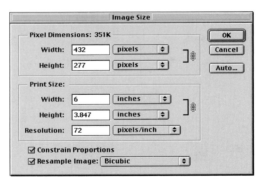

In Photoshop 3, the Image Size dialog box was split into two areas showing the current size and the new size. You could only change values in the new size area.

In Photoshop 4 and 5, the Image Size dialog box is split into two editable areas: pixel dimensions and print size.

checkbox. When this is turned on, Photoshop lets you change the image's pixel dimensions; when off, the dimensions are locked. In other words, unless you turn this checkbox on, you cannot add pixels to or remove pixels from the image (upsample or downsample).

In older versions of Photoshop, the Resample Image checkbox was labelled Constrain File Size

and it worked just the opposite (when it was *off*, you could resample the image). The reason the current dialog box is better is that it's always immediately apparent if or when you're going to resample the image (possibly causing damage to the image). You also have the ability to choose what kind of resampling method Photoshop should use (see Upsampling versus Down-

Figure 3-10 Image Size dialog box, continued

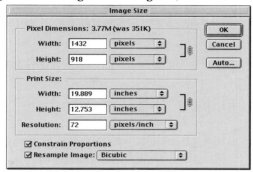

With Resample Image turned on, when you change the Pixel Dimensions, the Print Size changes, but the Resolution is locked.

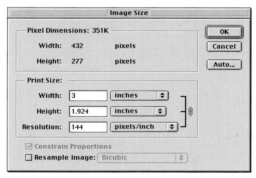

With Resample Image turned off, the Pixel Dimensions never change. Changing Print Size affects Resolution and vice versa.

sampling, earlier in this chapter).

Note that when the pixel dimensions change, so does the size of the file. Photoshop displays both the old and new size in the Pixel Dimensions section of the dialog box.

Changing Sizes. Like we said, the Image Size dialog box takes some getting used to. One element which is confusing is that whenever you make a change to one field, some other fields change and others don't. Here's a quick summary of what to watch for.

When Resample Image is turned on and you change the Pixel Dimensions, the Print Size changes, but the Resolution is locked. If you change the Print Size, the Pixel Dimensions change, too, and the Resolution remains locked. If you change the Resolution, the Pixel Dimensions change, and the Print Size stays the same.

When Resample Image is turned off, the Pixel Dimensions never change, and changing either Print Size or Resolution always affects the other one (see Figure 3-10).

If the previous two paragraphs didn't make any sense, don't bother trying to memorize them; just go and play with the Image Size dialog box until you see what's going on.

Tip: Adjusting by Percent. The word "Percent" appears in both the Pixel Dimensions and the Print Size popup menus. Percent isn't a size; it's based on the current size of the image you're working on. For example, if you have a 2-by-2-inch image and you type in 200 percent for Print Size Width and Height, the result would be a 4-by-4-inch image. The number of pixels in the image would depend on whether you had Resample Image turned on or off.

We find this especially helpful when we have to recreate an image that was stretched or resized "for position only" in a program such as QuarkXPress. First we write down the scaling values from XPress on a piece of paper, then we open the image in Photoshop and type the percentages into Photoshop's Image Size dialog box.

Figure 3-11

Photoshop's resampling (interpolation) methods

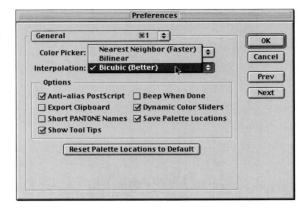

▶ **Nearest Neighbor** is the most basic, and it's very fast: to create a new pixel, Photoshop simply looks at the pixel next to it and copies its value. Unfortunately, the results are usually lousy unless the image is made of colored lines or shapes (like an image from Illustrator or FreeHand).

▶ **Bilinear** is slightly more complex, and produces somewhat better quality: the program sets the color or gray value of each pixel according to the pixels surrounding it. The effect is similar to averaging the neighboring pixels, but Photoshop is actually using a more sophisticated algorithm. The result is that some pictures can be upsampled pretty well with bilinear interpolation. However, we really have never found a good reason to use it; instead, we use bicubic.

▶ **Bicubic** interpolation creates the best effects, but takes the longest. Like bilinear, it looks at surrounding pixels, but the equation it uses is much more complex and calculation intensive (see Figure 3-12), producing smoother tonal gradations.

Image Mode

As we said earlier, pixel depth can tell you that pixel number 45 has a value of 165, but that doesn't mean anything until you know what image mode the bitmapped image is saved in. That 45 could represent a level of gray, or a particular color, or that might only be one value in a set of three or four other 8-bit values. Fortunately, Photoshop makes it easy to see

Figure 3-12 Results of different interpolation methods

Original   *Nearest Neighbor*   *Bicubic*

what image mode a bitmapped image is in, as well as to convert it to a different mode, if you want.

Ultimately, an image mode is simply a method of organizing the bits to describe a color. In a perfect world, you could say to a printer, "I'd like this box to be navy blue," and they'd know exactly what you were talking about. However, even Bruce and David can't agree on what "navy blue" looks like, much less you and your printer. So color scientists created a whole mess of ways for us to describe colors with some precision—to each other and to a computer.

Photoshop only reads and writes a handful of the many different modes they came up with. Fortunately, they're the most important of the bunch, at least for those in the world of graphic arts. Each of the following image modes appears on Photoshop's Mode menu. Note that what mode your image is in determines the file formats you can save in. For instance, you cannot save as PICT if the file is in CMYK mode. We'll talk more about this in Chapter 16, *Storing Images*.

Bitmap

David really wishes that Adobe had picked a different word for this image mode. All images in Photoshop are *bitmapped*, but only "flat" black-

and-white images, in which each pixel is defined using one bit of data (a zero or a one), are *bitmaps*. Perhaps "B&W" would have been more user-friendly to those of us who think that "rasters" have something to do with reggae.

One-bit pictures have a particular difference when it comes to PostScript printing: the white areas throughout the image can appear transparent, showing through to whatever the image is printing over. Ordinarily, images are opaque, except for the occasional white silhouetted background made with clipping paths (see "Silhouettes" in Chapter 15, *Essential Image Techniques*).

There's one other major difference between the other image modes and Bitmap mode: you're much more limited in the sorts of image editing you can do. For instance, you can't use any filters, and because there's no such thing as anti-aliasing in 1-bit images, you just cannot use tools that require this, such as the Smudge tool, the Blur tool, or the Dodge/Burn tool.

Bilevel bitmaps are the most generic of images, so you can save them in almost any file format (though there are some quirks that can cause transparency weirdnesses; see "Drop Shadows" in Chapter 15, *Essential Image Techniques*).

Grayscale

Although you can spec grayscale images with various numbers of bits per pixel in other programs, grayscale files in Photoshop are always either 8- or 16-bit images: anything less than 8-bit gets converted to 8-bit, anything more than 8-bit gets converted to 16-bit. Eight-bit is by far the more common, although an increasing number of scanners allow you to bring more than eight bits into Photoshop.

With 8-bit grayscale, each pixel has a value from 0 (black) to 255 (white), so there are a maximum of 256 levels of gray possible. With 16-bit grayscale, each pixel has a value from 0 (black) to 65,535 (white), for a theoretical maximum of 65,536 possible gray shades.

However, in practice, few scanners can actually deliver all those gray shades, so 16-bit files usually have rather a lot of redundancy. Photoshop's support for them is still fairly limited, but much more comprehensive than in previous versions. With scanners that capture 12 or more bits per pixel, it's well worthwhile bringing the high-bit data into Photoshop.

Eight-bit grayscale images are also pretty generic, so you can save them in almost any format this side of MacPaint. But if you want to save 16-bit grayscale images, your choices are limited to Photoshop format and TIFF.

Duotone

When you print a grayscale image on a printing press, those 256 levels of gray often get reduced to 100 or so because of the limitations of the printing press. You can counter this flattening effect considerably—increasing the tonal range of the printed image—by printing the image with more than one color of ink. This is called printing a *duotone* (for two inks), a *tritone* (for three inks), or a *quadtone* (for four).

The key is that the extra colors aren't typically used to simulate colors in the image; rather, they're used to enhance the underlying grayscale image. Those expensive Ansel Adams books on your coffee table were very likely printed using three or four (or even five or six) *different* black and gray inks.

Duotones also allow you to exploit the presence of a spot color in a two-color job. However, you have to take some care in matching the spot color to the subject in a duotone: duotones of people generally look ghastly if the second color is a green shade.

Photoshop has a special image mode for duotones, tritones, and quadtones, and even though the file may appear to be in color, each pixel is still saved using only eight bits of information. The trick is that Photoshop saves the 8-bit grayscale image along with a set of contrast curves for each ink.

Creating a good duotone is an art as much as a science. We'll discuss it in some detail in Chapter 10, *Spot Colors and Duotones*. Note that if you want to place resampling duotone images in a page-layout application for spot-color separation, you have to save the file in EPS format, the only non-native format that Photoshop supports for duotone-mode images.

Indexed Color

As we said, each pixel in a grayscale image is defined with eight bits of information, so the file can contain up to 256 different pixel values. But each of those values, from 1 to 256, doesn't have to be a level of gray. The Indexed Color image mode is a method for producing 8-bit, 256-color files. Indexed-color bitmaps use a table of 256 colors, chosen from the full 24-bit palette. A given pixel's color is defined by reference to the table: "This pixel is color number 123, this pixel is color number 81," and so on.

While indexed color can save disk space (it only requires eight bits per sample point, rather than the full 24 in RGB—see below), it only gives you 256 different colors. That's not a lot of colors, when you compare it to the 16.7 million different colors you can get in RGB mode. However, because many computer screens only display in 8-bit mode, indexed-color images are perfect for multimedia or screen presentation applications.

There are also a few (severe) limitations with Indexed Color mode. First, you can't use any filters or tools that require anti-aliasing (such as the Smudge tool or the Dodge/Burn tool) because Photoshop can't anti-alias in this mode. Therefore, you should always do your image editing in RGB mode and then convert to Indexed Color mode as a last step.

Another problem with indexed color stems from a problem with the color lookup tables. If the table changes when you move the picture from one program to another, so do all the colors in the image (see Color Plate 3 on page 679). Pixel number 123 might still have a value of 81, but "color number 81" may have changed from red to blue in the process.

Lastly, note that you can't separate indexed-color images into CMYK values using a program such as QuarkXPress or Adobe PageMaker. If you're printing these images to paper, you might consider converting them to RGB or CMYK while still in Photoshop. However, you won't improve the image any in the process—you're still only getting 256 colors.

Note that indexed-color images can be used with some success for spot color work.

You can save indexed-color images in Photoshop, CompuServe GIF, PNG, PICT, Amiga IFF, or BMP formats (see "Reasonable Niche File Formats" in Chapter 16, *Storing Images*).

RGB

Every color computer monitor and television in the world displays color using the RGB image mode, in which every color is produced with varying amounts of red, green, and blue light. (These colors are called *additive primaries* because the more red, green, or blue light you add, the closer to white you get.) In Photoshop, files saved in the RGB mode typically use a set of three 8-bit grayscale files, so we say that RGB files are "24-bit" files.

These files can include up to approximately 16 million colors—more than enough to qualify as photographic quality. This is the mode in which we prefer to work when editing color images. Also, most scanners save images in RGB format. The exception is high-end drum scanners; these usually include "color computers" that automatically convert files to CMYK mode (see below) as they're scanned.

If you're producing images for multimedia, or you're outputting files to a film recorder—to 35 mm or 4-by-5 film, for instance—you should always save your files in RGB mode (see Chapter 17, *Output Methods*).

Tip: To RGB or to CMYK. A great philosophical debate rages on whether it's better to work in RGB or in CMYK for prepress work. As with most burning philosophical questions, there's no easy answer to this one, but that doesn't deter us from supplying one anyway. If you get CMYK scans from a drum scanner, work in CMYK. In all other cases, we recommend staying in RGB for as long as possible. We discuss this question in much more detail in Chapter 7, *Color Correction*.

You can save 24-bit RGB files in Photoshop, EPS, TIFF, PICT, Amiga IFF, BMP, JPEG, PCX, Pixar, Raw, Scitex CT, or Targa formats, but unless you have compelling reasons to do otherwise, we suggest you stick with Photoshop, TIFF, or EPS.

Photoshop also lets you work with 48-bit RGB files, which contain three 16-bit channels instead of three 8-bit ones. Despite the limited tools available for 48-bit images, we're bringing more and more 48-bit files into Photoshop for the great editing flexibility they offer (see "Working with a High-Bit Scan" in Chapter 7, *Color Correction*).

Of course, if you're building images for multimedia or the Web, you want to stick with RGB and avoid ever switching to CMYK.

CMYK

Traditional full-color printing presses can only print four colors in a run: cyan, magenta, yellow, and black. Every other color in the spectrum is simulated using various combinations of those colors. When you open a file saved in the CMYK mode, Photoshop has to convert the CMYK values to RGB values on the fly, in order to display it on your computer screen. It's important to remember that when you look at the screen, you're looking at an RGB version of the data.

If you buy high-end drum scans, they'll almost certainly be CMYK files. Otherwise, to print your images on press or on many desktop color printers, you'll have to convert your RGB images to CMYK. We discuss Photoshop's tools for doing so in Chapter 5, *Color Settings*.

You can save CMYK files in Photoshop, TIFF, EPS, JPEG, Scitex CT, and Raw formats, but the first three are by far the most common.

Lab

The problem with RGB and CMYK modes is that a given RGB or CMYK specification doesn't really describe a *color*. Rather, it's a set of instructions that a specific output device uses to produce a color. The problem is that different devices produce different colors from the same RGB or CMYK specifications. If you've ever seen a wall full of television screens at a department store, you know what we're talking about: the same image—with the same RGB values—looks different on each screen.

And if you've ever sat through a printing press run, you'll know that the 50th impression probably isn't exactly the same color as the 5,000th or the 50,000th. So, while a pixel in a scanned image may have a particular RGB or CMYK value, you can't tell what that color really *looks like*. RGB and CMYK are both *device-specific* color modes.

However, a class of *device-independent* or *perceptually-based* modes has been developed over the years. All of them are based, more or less, on a color space defined by the Commission Internationale de l'Éclairage (CIE) in 1931. The Lab mode in Photoshop is one such derivative.

Lab doesn't describe a color by the components that make it up (RGB or CMYK, for instance). Instead, it describes *what a color looks like*. Device-independent color spaces are at the heart of the various color management systems now available that improve color correspondence between your screen, color printouts, and final printed output.

A file saved in the Lab mode describes what a color looks like under rigidly specified conditions; it's up to you (or Photoshop, or your color management software) to decide what RGB or CMYK values are needed to create that color on your chosen output device.

Photoshop uses the Lab mode as a reference when switching between CMYK and RGB modes, taking the values in your RGB Setup and CMYK Setup dialog boxes into account (see Chapter 5, *Color Settings*, for more information on this conversion). You can save Lab images in Photoshop, EPS, TIFF, or Raw formats.

It's a good thing that there's seldom reason to work in Lab mode, because it's almost impossible to wrap your head around this model. While RGB or CMYK can actually make some sense, Lab is almost entirely undecipherable (worry for your sanity if this mode starts to makes sense to you). Nonetheless, every now and again Lab mode is essential for some techniques (like cleaning up images from digital cameras or doing subtle brightness tweaks).

Tip: L Is for Luminosity. One useful property of the Lab mode is that it stores the luminance information (the "L" channel) separately from the color information (the "A" and "B" channels). This can be handy if you want to adjust the tonal values in the image without affecting the hues. It's also useful for some sharpening tricks.

Multichannel

The last image mode that Photoshop offers is the Multichannel mode. This mode is the generic mode: like RGB or CMYK, multichannel mode has more than one 8-bit channel; however, you can set the color and name of each channel to anything you like.

This flexibility can be a blessing or a curse. Back in the days when color scanners cost a fortune, we used to scan in color on grayscale scanners by scanning the image three times through red, green, and blue acetate, combining the three images into a single multichannel document that we then turned into RGB. Fortunately we don't have to do that anymore.

These days, many scientific and astronomical images are made in "false color"—the channels may be a combination of radar, infrared, and ultraviolet, in addition to various colors of visible light. Some of our gonzo digital photographer friends are using Multichannel mode to combine infrared and visible-spectrum photographs into composite images of surreal beauty.

However, we mostly use Multichannel mode as an intermediary step. For instance, you can use it to store extra channels for transparency masks or selections in other images. Your only options for saving multichannel images are the Photoshop and Raw formats.

Bitmaps and File Size

As we said at the beginning of this chapter, bitmapped images are rectangles with hundreds, or thousands, or hundreds of thousands of pixels. Each of those pixels has to be saved on disk. If each pixel is defined using eight bits of color information, then the file is eight times bigger than a flat bitmap. Similarly, a 24-bit file is a full three times bigger than that, and a 48-bit file is twice the size of a 24-bit one.

Big files take a long time to open, edit, print, or save. Many people who complain about how slow editing is in Photoshop are simply working with files much bigger than they need. Instead, you can save yourself the complaining and reduce your file size when you can. Here's a quick rundown of how each attribute of a bitmapped image affects file size.

Dimensions and resolution. When you increase the number of pixels in a bitmap, you increase the file's size by the square of the value. That means if you double the resolution, you quadruple the file size (2×2); triple the resolution, and your file is nine times as large (3×3). There can easily be a multimegabyte difference between a 300-ppi and a 225-ppi image.

Bit depth. Increasing bit depth increases file size by a simple multiplier. Therefore, a 24-bit image is three times as large as an 8-bit image, and 24 times as large as a 1-bit image.

Image mode. Image mode doesn't necessarily increase file size, but going from RGB (24-bit) to CMYK (32-bit) mode does because it alters bit depth.

Figuring File Size

Now that you know the factors that affect the size of bitmaps, it's a simple matter to calculate file size using the following formula.

$$\text{Resolution}^2 \times \text{Width} \times \text{Height} \times \text{Bits per sample} \div 8,192$$

For example, if you have a 4-by-5-inch, 1-bit image at 300 ppi, you know that the file size is 220 K—$300^2 \times 4 \times 5 \times 1 \div 8192$. A 24-bit image of the same size would be 5,273 K (just about five megabytes). In case you were wondering, this formula works because 8,192 is the number of bits in a kilobyte.

Figure 3-13

The Image Size
dialog box

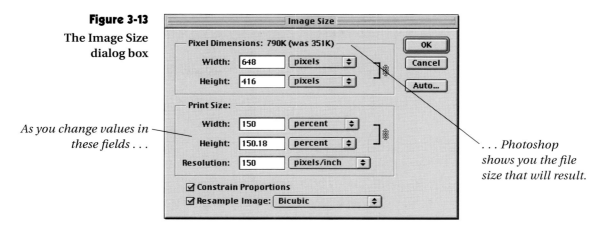

*As you change values in
these fields . . .*

*. . . Photoshop
shows you the file
size that will result.*

Tip: Faster File Figuring. There's an even easier way to calculate file sizes than doing the math yourself—let the computer do it for you. Photoshop's New Document and Image Size dialog boxes are very handy calculators for figuring dimensions, resolution, and file size. Simply type in the values you want, and Photoshop shows you how big the file would be (see Figure 3-13).

Billions and Billions of Bits

Would you hire a carpenter who didn't know anything about wood? Bitmapped graphics are the wood of Photoshop; they're the material you use to construct your images. Without a firm understanding of the strengths as well as the weaknesses of your material, you won't get very far with this power tool of a program.

In the next chapter, we move away from the wood, and start looking at the hammer-and-nails aspects of Photoshop: the essential tools you need to get your work done efficiently.

4 Color Essentials

What Makes a Color

You may have been taught back in kindergarten that the primary colors are red, yellow, and blue, and that all other colors can be made from them. Bruce still vividly recalls the day when his first-grade teacher, Mrs. Anderson, told him that he could make gray by using equal amounts of red, yellow, and blue. After looking at the lurid, weird, multicolored mess that was supposed to be a gray cat, he quite sensibly started over using a 2B pencil, and concluded that Mrs. Anderson was either color-blind or clueless. He traces his sometimes-inconvenient tendency to question authority to that day.

The details of Mrs. Anderson's lesson were certainly fallacious, but they contained an important kernel of truth—the notion that we can create all colors by combining three primary constituents. People have many different ways of thinking about, talking about, and working with color, but the notion of three ingredients that make up a color occurs again and again. Art directors may feel comfortable specifying color changes with the terms *hue*, *lightness*, and *saturation*. Those who came to color through the computer may be more at home with levels of RGB. Scientists think about color in all sorts of strange ways, including CIE Lab, HSB, or LCH. And dyed-in-the-wool prepress folks think in CMYK dot percentages.

Although Photoshop tries to accommodate all these ways of thinking about color—and it does a pretty good job—many Photoshop users find themselves locked into seeing color in only one way. This is natural and understandable—we all have one way of thinking about color that seems to make more sense than the others—but it can make life with Photoshop more difficult than it needs to be. If you understand that all the different ways of looking at color are based on the same notion—combining three ingredients—you can learn to translate among the ways Photoshop lets you work with them, and choose the right one for the task at hand.

"Wait a minute," you say. "CMYK has four constituents, not three!" You question authority too, when that authority doesn't make sense. Well, in our role as temporary authority figures, we'll do what authority figures often do when asked hard questions: we ask you to trust us. Set this issue aside for the moment. We promise we'll deal with it later.

In this chapter, we take a hard look at some fundamental color relationships and how Photoshop presents them. This stuff might seem a little theoretical at times, but we urge you to slog through it; it's essential for our later discussions about tonal and color correction.

Primary Colors

The concept of *primary* colors is at the heart of much of the color work we do on computers. When we work with primary colors, we're talking about three colors that we can combine to make all the other colors. We can define colors by specifying varying proportions of primary colors, and we can color-correct images by adjusting the relationship of the primary colors. Ignoring for the moment which specific colors constitute the primaries, there are two fundamental principles of primary colors.

▶   They are the irreducible components of color.

▶   The primary colors, combined in varying proportions, can produce an entire spectrum of color.

The *secondary* colors, by the way, are produced by combining two primary colors and excluding the third. But we don't much care about that.

Additive and Subtractive Color

Before becoming preoccupied with the behavior of spherical objects like apples, billiard balls, and planets, Sir Isaac Newton performed some experiments with light and prisms. He found that he could break white light down into red, green, and blue components, a fairly trivial phenomenon that had been known for centuries. His breakthrough was the discovery that he could *reconstitute* white light by recombining those red, green, and blue components. Red, green, and blue—the primary colors of light—are known as the *additive primary* colors because as you add color, the result becomes more white (the absence of colored light is black; see Figure 4-1). This is how computer monitors and televisions produce color.

Figure 4-1
Additive and subtractive primaries

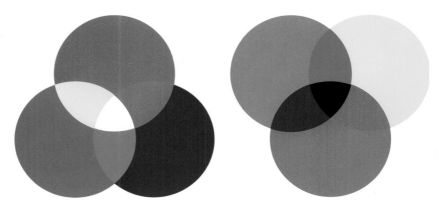

But color on the printed page works differently. Unlike a television, the page doesn't emit light; it just reflects whatever light hits it. To produce color images in print, we don't work with the light directly. Instead, we use pigments (like ink, dye, toner, or wax) that *absorb* some colors of light and reflect others.

The primary colors of pigments are cyan, yellow, and magenta. We call these the *subtractive primary* colors because as you add pigments to a white page, they subtract (absorb) more light, and the reflected color becomes darker. (We sometimes find it easier to remember: you *add* additive colors to get white, and you *subtract* subtractive colors to get white.) Cyan absorbs all the red light, magenta absorbs all the green light, and yellow absorbs all the blue light. If we add the maximum intensities of cyan, magenta, and yellow, we get black—in theory (see Figure 4-1).

Mrs. Anderson had the right idea about primary colors; she just picked the wrong ones. No matter how hard you try, you'll never be able to create cyan using red, yellow, and blue crayons.

An Imperfect World

A little while ago, we asked you to trust us on the subject of CMYK. Well, we just told you that combining cyan, magenta, and yellow would, *in theory,* produce black. In practice, however, it produces a muddy brown mess. Why? In the words of our friend and colleague Bob Schaffel, "God made RGB . . . man made CMYK." To that we add: "Who do you trust more?"

Imperfect pigments. If we had perfect CMY pigments, we wouldn't have to add black (K) as a fourth color. But despite our best efforts, our cyan pigments always contain a little red, our magentas always contain a little green, and our yellows always contain a trace of blue. So when we print in color, we add black to help with the reproduction of dark colors. Plus, by adding black, we can reduce the total amount of ink needed to create dark areas, which not only saves money but solves some . . . uh . . . *sticky* printing problems. See Chapter 5, *Color Settings,* for more on this.

Imperfect conversions. If we only had to deal with CMY, life would be a lot simpler. However, a large part of the problem of reproducing color images in print is that scanners—since they deal with light—see color in RGB, and we have to translate those values into CMYK to print them. Unfortunately, this conversion is a thorny one (see "How the Color Preferences Interact" in Chapter 5, *Color Settings,* for more on this subject).

The Color Wheel

Before moving on to weightier matters such as gravity, calculus, and his impending thirtieth birthday, Sir Isaac Newton provided the world of color with one more key concept: if we take the colors of the spectrum and arrange them around the circumference of a wheel, the relationships among primaries become much clearer (see Figure 4-2).

The important thing to notice about this color wheel is that the additive and subtractive primary colors are opposite each other, equidistant around the wheel. These relationships are key to understanding how color works. For instance, cyan sits opposite to red on the color wheel because it is, in fact, the opposite of red: cyan pigments appear cyan because they absorb red light and reflect blue and green. Cyan is, in short, the absence of red.

Figure 4-2
The color wheel

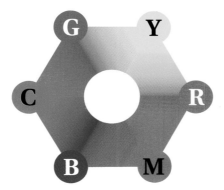

Emitted and reflected (additive and subtractive) colors are complementary to one another. Red is complementary to cyan, green to magenta, and blue to yellow.

Colors that lie directly opposite each other on the wheel are known as *complementary* colors.

Figuring Saturation and Brightness

So far, we've talked about color in terms of three primary colors. But there are other ways of specifying color in terms of three ingredients. The most familiar one describes color in terms of hue (the property we refer to when we talk about "red" or "orange"), saturation (the "purity" of the color), and brightness.

Newton's basic two-dimensional color wheel lets us see the relationships between different hues, but to describe colors more fully, we need a more complex, three-dimensional model. We can find one of these in the Apple Color Picker (see Figure 4-3).

In the Apple Color Picker, we can see the hues are arranged around the edge of the wheel, and colors become progressively more "pastel" as we move into the center—the farther in you go, the less saturated or "pure" the color is. Beside the wheel, we have a slider that makes the color lighter or darker. The Color Picker is a graphical representation of the HSB (hue, saturation, and brightness) color model.

Tristimulus Models and Color Spaces

Ignoring the inconvenience of CMYK, all the ways we've talked about of specifying and thinking about color involve three primary ingredients. Color scientists call these *tristimulus* models. (A *color* model is simply a way of thinking about color and representing it numerically: a tristimulus model represents colors by using three numbers.) If you go deep into

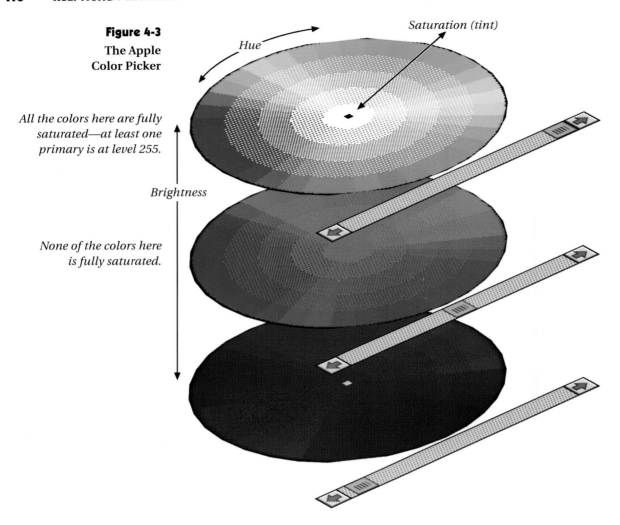

Figure 4-3
The Apple
Color Picker

Hue

Saturation (tint)

*All the colors here are fully
saturated—at least one
primary is at level 255.*

Brightness

*None of the colors here
is fully saturated.*

the physiology of color, you'll find that our perceptual systems are actually wired in terms of three different responses to light that go together to produce the sensation of color. So the tristimulus approach is more than just a mathematical convenience—it has a solid basis in the way our nervous systems work.

But tristimulus models have another useful property. Because they specify everything in terms of three ingredients, we can (with very little effort) view them as three-dimensional objects with X, Y, and Z axes. Each color has a location in this three-dimensional object, specified by the three values. These three-dimensional models are called *color spaces*, a term that gets thrown around a great deal in the world of color.

We like to think of the HSB color space as a giant cylinder; the brightness slider in the Apple Color Picker determines which "slice" of the cylinder we're looking at. But, like any metaphor, there's a good side and a bad side to looking at color this way.

▶ **The good side.** The Apple Color Picker is a great way to start learning about color, and how changing a single primary changes your colors.

▶ **The bad side.** The simple HSB model can't really describe how we *see* colors. For instance, we know that cyan appears much lighter than blue; but in our HSB cylinder, they both have the same brightness and saturation values.

Therefore, while the color picker is a step in the right direction, we have to go further to understand how to work with color.

How Colors Affect Each Other

There are a lot of times in Photoshop when we find ourselves working with one color space, but thinking about the changes in terms of another. As you'll see in Chapter 7, *Color Correction*, for instance, we often recommend that you use curves to adjust RGB values, but base your changes on the resulting CMYK percentages as displayed in the Info palette. So it can speed up your work a lot to take some time and figure out how color spaces interact—what happens in one space when you work in another.

Here are some ways to think about RGB, CMY, and HSB colors, and how they relate to each other.

Tone. One of the least understood—yet most important—effects of adding colors together is that adding or removing primaries not only affects hue and saturation; it also affects tone. When you increase any RGB component to change the hue—adding light—the color gets lighter. The reverse is true with CMY because you're adding ink, and hence making the color darker.

Hue. Every color, except for the primaries, contains opposing primary colors. In RGB mode, red is "pure," but orange contains red alongside a good dose of green (and possibly some blue, too). In CMYK, magenta is pure, and red is not—it contains some amount of yellow in addition to magenta. So to change a color's hue, you add or subtract primary colors.

In the process, you will probably affect the color's tone—adding or removing light (or ink) so the color gets lighter or darker.

Saturation. A saturated RGB color is made up of only one or two primaries; the third primary is always zero. When you add a trace of the third color—in order to change the hue slightly, for instance—you desaturate the color.

Likewise, if you increase the saturation of a color using the Hue/Saturation dialog box (or any other), you're removing one of the primaries. If you get out to the edge, where one of the primaries is maxed out and the other two are still changing, you're going to change the hue and the tone.

There's another important consideration pertaining to saturated colors. When you saturate a color in an RGB image, you wind up with detail in only one of the three channels. One of the others is always solid white, and the other is always solid black. It's this—not just the difficulty of reproducing them—that makes saturated colors in images difficult to handle, because all the detail is being carried by only one channel.

Neutrals. A color made up of equal values of red, green, and blue is always a neutral gray (though we may have to do quite a bit of work to make it come out that way on screen or—once we've converted it to CMYK—on press). The "darkness" of the gray depends on how much red, green, and blue there is—more light makes for a lighter gray. This is important for a number of reasons, including monitor adjustments and correcting color casts.

For a quick summary of relationships among the color spaces, see the sidebar "Color Relationships at a Glance," later in the chapter.

Device-Independent Color

Basically, the problem with HSB, RGB, and CMY (and even CMYK) is that they don't describe how a color looks; they only describe the color's ingredients. If you've ever walked into a television store, you know what we're talking about. There are about a hundred televisions on the wall, each of them showing the same image (they're receiving the same color

Color Relationships at a Glance

It's worth spending however long it takes to understand the color relationships we're discussing in this chapter. We all have a favorite color space, but if you can learn to view color in more than one way—understanding how to achieve the same results by manipulating CMY, RGB, and HSB—you'll find the world of color correction much less alien, and you'll be much more able to select the right tool for the job.

We suggest memorizing these fundamentals.

► 100% cyan = 0 red

► 100% magenta = 0 green

► 100% yellow = 0 blue

► Increasing RGB values corresponds exactly to reducing CMY values, and vice versa.

► Reducing saturation (making something more "gray") means introducing the complementary color; to desaturate red, for example, we add cyan.

► The complement of a primary color is produced by combining equal amounts of the other two primary colors.

► Lightening or darkening a saturated color desaturates that color.

► Changing the hue of a color often changes lightness as well.

► Saturation changes can cause hue changes.

Saturated Primaries—CMY versus RGB

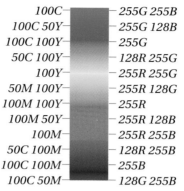

100C	255G 255B
100C 50Y	255G 128B
100C 100Y	255G
50C 100Y	128R 255G
100Y	255R 255G
50M 100Y	255R 128G
100M 100Y	255R
100M 50Y	255R 128B
100M	255R 255B
50C 100M	128R 255B
100C 100M	255B
100C 50M	128G 255B

The colors at left are fully saturated—each contains 100 percent of one or two primaries. The additive and subtractive primaries have an inverse relationship.

Desaturating Saturated Colors

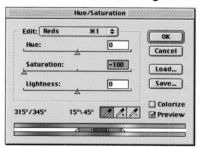

255R 255G
64R 128G 192B
128R 128G 128B
64R 192G 128B
255R 255B

Desaturating the reds removes red and adds other primaries to the red areas. Adding a third primary "pollutes" the saturated color, causing it to go gray. It may or may not affect lightness.

Lightness and Saturation

Lightening or darkening a saturated color (here, +50 and -50) desaturates it; either it pulls the primaries back from 100 percent, or it pollutes them with a third primary, or both. Also note the hue shift in the darkened version.

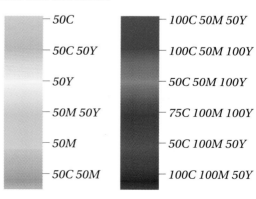

50C	100C 50M 50Y
50C 50Y	100C 50M 100Y
50Y	50C 50M 100Y
50M 50Y	75C 100M 100Y
50M	50C 100M 50Y
50C 50M	100C 100M 50Y

information), but *none* of them displays the colors in the same way.

In fact, if we send the same RGB values to ten different monitors, or the same CMYK values to ten different presses, we'll end up with ten different colors (see Figure 4-4). We call RGB and CMYK *device dependent*, because the color we get varies from device to device.

So, Photoshop has a problem in trying to display colors properly on your monitor: it doesn't know what the colors should *look like* to you. It doesn't know what those RGB or CMYK values really mean.

Plus, the program has to take all the little quirks of human vision into account. For instance, our eyes are more sensitive to some colors and brightness levels than to others, and we're more sensitive to small changes in bright colors than we are to small changes in dark ones (if you've had trouble teasing all the subtle shadow details out of your scanned images, this is one reason why). RGB and CMYK don't give Photoshop the information it needs to know what color is actually being described.

Figure 4-4 Device-dependent color and color gamuts

Since this figure is printed with process inks on paper, it can only simulate the results of sending the same RGB or CMYK values to various devices. It depicts relative appearances, not actual results. Likewise, the color wheel just represents the gamuts of different devices, rather than actually showing those gamuts. See also Figure 7-5 on page 269.

Screen display

Dye-sublimation printer

Process inks, coated stock

Process inks, newsprint

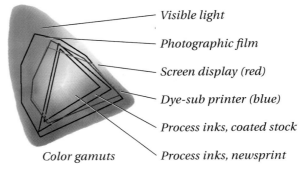
Color gamuts

— Visible light
— Photographic film
— Screen display (red)
— Dye-sub printer (blue)
— Process inks, coated stock
— Process inks, newsprint

Lab Color

Fortunately, there's CIE Lab, which appears on the Mode menu simply as Lab. Lab is designed to describe what colors *look like*, regardless of the device they're displayed on, so we call it *device independent.*

Whereas in HSB the hues are represented as lying around a wheel, Lab color uses a more accurate but significantly less intuitive arrangement. In Lab, the third axis (which lies perpendicular to the page and is roughly equivalent to brightness in HSB) is the luminance axis—it represents how bright the color appears to the human eye. But unlike brightness in HSB, it takes into account the fact that we see green as brighter than blue.

Whole books have been written on Lab color (we've even read some of them), and while they may be of interest to color scientists, they're unlikely to help you get great-looking images on a deadline. For now, there are really only three things you need to know about Lab color.

▶ While HSB, HSL, and LCH are based on the way we think about color, and RGB and CMYK are based on the ways devices such as monitors and printers produce color, Lab is based on the way humans actually *see* color. A Lab specification actually describes the color that most people will see when they look at an object under specified lighting conditions.

▶ Photoshop thinks in Lab when it does mode changes. For instance, when you switch from RGB mode to CMYK mode, Photoshop uses Lab to decide what *color* is being specified by each device-dependent RGB value, then comes up with the right device-dependent CMYK equivalent. We'll see why this is so important in the next chapter, *Color Settings.*

▶ Finally, you shouldn't feel dumb if you find it hard to get your head around Lab color. It *is* difficult to visualize, because it's an abstract mathematical construct—it isn't based on amounts of things we can understand readily, like RGB or HSB. It uses amounts of three primaries to specify colors, but those primaries don't correspond to anything we can actually experience.

Working with Colors

When you work with Photoshop, it lets you view and adjust your colors in all sorts of different ways. It's difficult to adjust saturation in an image, for example, by manipulating RGB or CMYK values directly, so Photoshop provides tools that let you apply changes in hue, saturation, and brightness to the underlying RGB or CMYK data. Likewise, if you have an RGB image but you plan to print it in CMYK, you can use Photoshop's Info palette to keep track of what's happening to the CMYK values you'll eventually get when you do the mode change from RGB to CMYK.

We do face two fairly large problems, however. The first is that every time we do a mode change, we lose some image information, because our images only have 256 shades of each color, and as we convert from one color space to another, some of these get lost due to rounding errors. Photoshop lets us work around this by providing information about what we'll get after we've done the color-space conversion, without our actually having to do so until we've perfected our images. We discuss this in much more detail in Chapter 7, *Color Correction.*

The second problem is that the color spaces in which most of our images are stored, RGB and CMYK, are device dependent—the color we'll get varies depending on the device we send it to. Worse, each device has a range of colors it can reproduce—called the *color gamut*—and some devices have a much wider gamut than others (see Figure 4-4 on page 114). For example, color film can record a wider range of colors than a color monitor can display, and the monitor displays a wider range of colors than we can reproduce with ink on paper; so no matter what we do, some of the colors captured on film simply can't be reproduced in print.

Fortunately, Photoshop has tools that let us remove some (if not all) of the variability from our RGB and CMYK color definitions, and it lets us specify the gamut of our monitor and our CMYK output devices. The next chapter, *Color Settings*, is devoted to explaining what those tools are, how they work, and how to use them.

5 Color Settings

Configuring Photoshop's Color Engine

Warning: Photoshop has drastically changed the way it handles color. So much so that many people have already needlessly ruined their images based on their own ignorance and Photoshop's strange default settings, threatened to sue Adobe, and ended up getting angry at everyone but themselves. It doesn't have to be that way. If you're familiar with earlier versions, be prepared to re-learn a lot. Whether you're a Photoshop newbie or an old pro, be prepared to spend some time in this chapter, 'cause we're going spelunking deep into Photoshop's dark color caverns; without this information, you're gonna be one lost puppy.

In the last chapter, we broke the sad news that RGB and CMYK are very ambiguous ways of specifying color, since the actual color you get will vary from device to device. In this chapter, we'll look at the tools Photoshop gives you to try to keep your color consistent from original image to your screen to your color proofer to the final printed output. Photoshop 5 not only offers these tools, but demands that you use them correctly in order to get quality output.

While at first glance it seems like the folks at Adobe just rearranged some dialog boxes between versions 4 and 5, in fact the two versions have drastically different methods of dealing with color. If you open the same image side by side in Photoshop 4 and Photoshop 5, it's almost certain that they'll display and print differently.

Stop the clock! There are those who believe that Adobe was wrong to change the way it handles color because it forces people to change their workflow. We strongly disagree—we think that the initial inconveniences you may encounter are simply the price of getting things right this time around. However, if you've been avoiding the topic of color management—calibrating your monitor, and all that—you're going to be in for a rude awakening. For instance, there are folks (we're sure you're not one of them) whose idea of color calibration is to print something, then screw up their monitor to match that print. This is a kludge akin to using a kitchen knife as a screwdriver, and it's pretty much impossible to replicate in Photoshop 5. It's an approach we've always discouraged, even if it has been a depressingly widespread practice.

If you're in this situation, you have essentially two choices:

▶ Stay with Photoshop 4 (which we don't recommend as a long-term solution, especially now that you've bought this book).

▶ Bite the bullet, adopt Photoshop 5's new workflow, and get ready for the 21st century.

We'll do our best to make the process painless—we'll even hold your hand through the process of dealing with your old legacy files—and we hope you'll quickly come to realize the many benefits the new color architecture can offer.

Color Settings

It seems a little odd to devote an entire chapter to four dialog boxes, but the preferences settings that deal with color—RGB Setup, CMYK Setup, Grayscale Setup, and Profile Setup (all found on the Color Settings submenu, under the File menu; see Figure 5-1)—are so important that it's essential to spend the time learning what they do and how they do it. These settings affect almost everything you do with tone and color in Photoshop, sometimes in ways that are less than obvious.

In some respects, these dialog boxes do something very simple: they let you tell Photoshop what red, green, blue, cyan, yellow, magenta, and black look like. (If you've just started reading at this chapter, and you don't know that these color names don't actually mean anything, we sug-

Figure 5-1
Color Settings

gest you stop and read the previous chapter immediately.) More precisely, they let you configure Photoshop to work with either its own internal color management system or with a third-party color management system such as Apple's ColorSync or Kodak's KICC.

Previous versions of Photoshop used a proprietary and fairly limited color management system (in fact, it was so closed and limited that most people didn't even recognize it as such). Color management in Photoshop 5 is much more powerful and much more open. Unfortunately, it's also much more confusing, particularly if you're new to the concepts behind color management. So before we look in detail at the Photoshop 5 color management features, let's step back a little and look at just what color management is, and how it's supposed to work.

Color Management Systems Explained

A color management system (CMS) is a set of software tools that attempts to maintain the appearance of colors on different devices (monitors, printers, and so on). We stress the word "appearance" because it's impossible to reproduce many of the colors found in color film in print, or even on a color monitor. However, it is possible to simulate the appearance, which is usually good enough.

There are a number of CMSes available besides the one built into Photoshop, and while they differ in the details, they all do the same thing, in more or less the same way. Best of all, Photoshop 5 provides a consistent interface for interacting with the different CMSes it supports, so let's concentrate on the similarities rather than the differences.

CMS Components

All CMSes employ three basic components.

▶ *Device profiles* describe the color behavior of scanners, monitors, and printers. Basically, they tell the color management system what a color on this particular device looks like. Remember, fully saturated red on one monitor is different than fully saturated red on another monitor, so the device profile says, "This is what red looks like." Good profiles are the key to making a CMS work. Unfortunately, most of the problems with color management systems lie in creating, using, and editing profiles.

▶ The *color matching engine* (sometimes known as the *color matching method*, or *CMM*) is the software that actually converts one device-specific color into another device-specific color space, based on the profiles of the two devices. Photoshop 5 supports several different color matching engines—including a new Adobe-branded one that we expect to see in other future Adobe products—and this multiplicity of CMMs may lead to some confusion. In general, though, the differences between the various CMMs are slight.

▶ The *reference color space* is the device-independent, perceptually based color space that the CMM uses as an intermediary between the two device-specific color spaces (see "Conveying Color Meaning," below). Most current CMSes use either a CIE-defined color space such as CIE Lab, or a proprietary derivative of a CIE color space such as Kodak's RCS. You never have to worry about the reference color space; it's the theory behind how the software works.

Earlier versions of Photoshop included a really basic color management system: Monitor Setup and Printing Inks Setup were like profiles (they let you specify what the RGB and CMYK colorants looked like) and Photoshop used Lab color as a reference when it converted color between device-specific color spaces. The major difference is that the device profiles used in version 5 typically provide a much more detailed description of the device's color space than Photoshop's old Color Settings did.

Conveying Color Meaning

The key concept in using a CMS is conveying color meaning—making those ambiguous RGB and CMYK values unambiguous. If the system is going to keep the color consistent among different devices, it needs to know how each device in the process sees, displays, or prints colors. If a CMS knows enough about a particular scanner, it can *interpret* the incoming color information to find out what the colors in the original really look like. Then, if it knows how colors appear on your screen, it can adjust the image's colors to make the image on your screen match the original. Finally, if it knows about a printer, the CMS can adjust the colors to make them look right on that printer.

Source and target profiles. In short, the CMS needs to know where the device-specific color values came from, and where you want to send them. Whenever you open or create an image, you have to give the CMS this information by specifying a *source profile* and a *target profile*.

The source profile says, "This RGB data is from such-and-such a scanner," or "This RGB data was last edited on such-and-such a monitor." This tells the CMS what the colors really look like. The target profile tells the CMS where the image is going, so that the engine can maintain the color in the image.

For example, imagine that color management systems work with words rather than colors. The purpose of the word-CMS is to translate words from one language to another. If you just feed it a bunch of words, it can't do anything. But if you give it the words and tell it that they were written by a French person (the source), it all of a sudden can understand what the words are saying. If you then tell it that you speak German (the target), it can translate the meaning faithfully for you.

The process. Back to pictures: when you scan some artwork, you end up with a lot of RGB data. But for Photoshop to know what specific colors those RGB values are meant to represent, you have to tell it that the RGB data came from a specific scanner. When you choose your scanner's device profile as the source profile, you're telling Photoshop that this isn't just any old RGB data; it's the RGB data carefully defined by the scanner's device profile.

To make the image on the monitor match the original, you choose your monitor profile as the target profile. The CMS uses the scanner profile as the secret decoder ring to convert the RGB colors in the scanned image into the reference color space (that is, it figures out what the colors really look like to humans). Then it calculates new RGB values based on the monitor profile, to produce the same colors when they're displayed on your monitor. (Actually, note that we're still talking somewhat conceptually; the reality is that Photoshop 5 introduces a new wrinkle into this workflow, but we'll get to that a little later.)

If you just want to print the image, and you don't care what it looks like on the monitor, you could choose a profile for a CMYK output process as the target instead. The CMS would produce a CMYK file targeted for that output process. In theory, the printed output matches the original.

This is really the only thing CMSes do. They convert color data from one device's color space (one "language") to another. Pretty much everything you do with a CMS involves asking it to make the colors match between a source and a target profile, and this same two-step is integral to the way Photoshop 5 handles color. But before we look at Photoshop 5's Color Settings in detail, a cautionary note is in order.

Tip: Space Conversions and Data Loss. Bear in mind that even the best CMS degrades your image slightly when you convert it from one color space to another (any color-space conversion involves some loss, due to rounding and quantization errors). Even though the conversions may be very accurate, you still want to limit their number. Converting once or twice probably isn't going to harm your image; but avoid using the CMM to convert your image five or 10 or 20 times from one color space into another.

Color Management in Photoshop

Ordinarily, if you wanted an image to appear the same on five different monitors, the CMM would have to convert the image data five different times, degrading the image quality. Clearly, there's got to be a better way; and indeed there is. Adobe introduced the somewhat unusual (but very practical) concept of a device-independent RGB working space.

How previous versions managed color. In earlier versions of Photoshop, the program looked to your Monitor Setup dialog box to figure out what RGB colors looked like. But the real problem was that Photoshop simply sent your image's RGB values straight to the screen, assuming that your Monitor Setup settings accurately described both your screen and the RGB colors in the image. The result: the same image could look very different when you moved it from one monitor to another.

How Photoshop manages color now. Now, in Photoshop 5, your image's RGB is uncoupled from the monitor (and from any other physical device, for that matter). If there's a profile attached to your RGB image, then Photoshop knows what the colors in your image really look like. If you have a profile for your RGB monitor, then Photoshop knows what particular colors on your monitor look like. With this information, Photoshop can use its CMM to convert on the fly from the image's RGB space to your monitor's RGB space. The result: your image looks the same, no matter what monitor you display it on (even cross-platform). Even better, Photoshop only converts the data to display it; behind the scenes, your image data doesn't change, so you don't suffer from repeated color-space conversions.

While the benefits of this approach are clear, there are several less-obvious problems. First, you have to choose an RGB editing space that you're going to use for all your images. Second, you have to convert each image from whatever RGB space you used in previous versions to this new editing space. Finally, you have to spend some real time making sure your profiles are accurate. Once again, we believe that these problems are more than outweighed by the advantages that you gain by buying into the idea of an RGB editing space. Of course, old habits die hard, and there's certainly a learning curve to this new method.

For the rest of this chapter, we're going to discuss each of the tools Photoshop offers for managing this workflow, including converting your RGB images into CMYK and working with grayscale images (yes, that's right: grayscale images can be affected by the color settings, too).

Color Settings Overview

Remember that Photoshop relies heavily on *you* telling *it* what red, green, blue, cyan, yellow, magenta, and black look like on your screen, from your scanner, on your printing press, and so on. Of course, there are a bunch of default settings built into Photoshop. But just as you wouldn't drive a new car without adjusting the mirrors and the position of the seat, it's not safe to drive Photoshop without configuring it to you, your images, and the way that you work.

Color Settings at a Glance

RGB Setup lets you specify which RGB color space you're editing in (this is the RGB editing space that will be attached to your images). CMYK Setup lets you tell Photoshop what your particular inks look like, how you want to use those inks to reproduce your RGB colors, and which separation engine you want to use to convert images from one color space to another. Here's how the preferences affect different kinds of images.

▶ When you open a grayscale file, Photoshop always uses RGB Setup to convert it to RGB for display (remember that monitors are RGB). If "Display Using Monitor Compensation" is turned off in RGB Setup, Photoshop just throws this RGB data on the screen. If it's turned on (which it usually is), Photoshop does an on-the-fly conversion from the RGB working space to your monitor's RGB. If

Grayscale Setup is set to Black Ink, Photoshop *also* takes into account the Black dot-gain setting in CMYK Setup when it displays the image.

▶ When you display an RGB file, Photoshop interprets the image's RGB values according to the settings in RGB Setup. If "Display Using Monitor Compensation" is turned on in RGB Setup, Photoshop does an on-the-fly conversion from the RGB working space to your monitor's RGB.

▶ When you display a CMYK file, Photoshop converts the CMYK colors to RGB (for the screen), using the CMYK Setup settings to interpret the colors (the source profile, as it were) and RGB Setup settings (the target profile). If "Display Using Monitor Compensation" is turned on in RGB Setup, Photoshop does an on-the-fly

conversion from the RGB working space to your monitor's RGB. (If it's turned off, then the plain ol' RGB colors are sent directly to the screen, which isn't very helpful.)

▶ When you display a Lab file, it uses RGB Setup to convert the colors to RGB for display. If "Display Using Monitor Compensation" is turned on in RGB Setup, Photoshop does an on-the-fly conversion from the RGB working space to your monitor's RGB.

▶ When you convert an RGB file to Lab, Photoshop uses RGB Setup to interpret the RGB colors.

▶ When you convert an RGB file to CMYK, Photoshop uses RGB Setup to interpret the RGB colors, and CMYK Setup to arrive at the CMYK equivalents.

The primary method for telling Photoshop 5 what the colors on your monitor look like is the ColorSync System Profile (on the Macintosh) or the Adobe Gamma Preferences (in Windows). We'll cover setting these up in "RGB Setup and the Monitor," later in this chapter. The primary method for telling Photoshop just about everything else is the Color Settings dialog boxes, found under the File menu. That's what we're going to explore now.

The four Color Settings dialog boxes contain all the controls you use to configure Photoshop's color management system. Mastering them is key to producing reliable, consistent color from Photoshop, but the way they interact can be confusing; so before we consider the Color Settings individually, let's take in a 30,000-foot overview of how they work.

You can think of the settings in RGB Setup, CMYK Setup, and Grayscale Setup as behaving like device profiles. Whenever you convert your image between RGB, CMYK, and grayscale, Photoshop transforms the image's colors into Lab, then from Lab into the destination space. The Color Settings dialog boxes define the image and destination spaces.

The fourth color setting, Profile Setup, lets you control whether or not Photoshop embeds profiles in images, and also lets you instruct Photoshop on how to handle images that either lack profiles, or are in a different RGB, CMYK, or grayscale space from the ones you've set in Color Settings.

Together, these four settings provide all the global color controls for Photoshop 5. Let's look at how they affect each other.

RGB Setup. The settings in RGB Setup define Photoshop's RGB color space, also called "the RGB editing space" because all your edits to RGB data are performed in this space (see Figure 5-2). Photoshop only allows you to use a single RGB color space at a time, and it applies to all RGB images you have open. Later, we'll look at the various options in this dialog box, and explain why you want to convert all your files to a single editing space.

Photoshop uses the settings in RGB Setup to attach a specific color meaning to your RGB data. It uses that information in the following situations.

▶ Translating RGB data to your monitor's color space (for display only).

▶ Translating RGB data to CMYK, Lab, or Grayscale.

Figure 5-2
RGB Setup

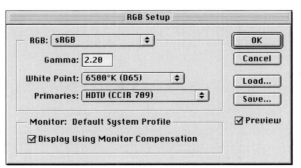

The RGB Setup dialog box lets you specify which actual colors your RGB values represent.

► Translating CMYK, Lab, or grayscale data to RGB. Of course, when you open a CMYK, Lab, or grayscale image, Photoshop has to display an RGB representation of the data (there's no such thing as a CMYK monitor). So these files always get converted for display only. If the "Display Using Monitor Compensation" option is turned off, Photoshop just throws these RGB values at the screen. However, if you turn this option on (which we heartily recommend you do), then Photoshop takes the conversion one step further with an on-the-fly RGB-to-RGB transformation from the RGB space defined in RGB Setup to the RGB space defined by your monitor profile. This is the only way that the CMYK, Lab, or grayscale image can be displayed correctly on your monitor.

► Embedding profiles in RGB images. The only profile Photoshop ever embeds in an RGB image is the one defined by the settings in RGB Setup.

CMYK Setup. The CMYK Setup dialog box lets you define the actual color of your process-color inks, the behavior of those inks on paper (dot gain), and how colors should be converted into (and out of) CMYK (see Figure 5-3). It also lets you choose which CMM you want Photoshop to use, so you may have to visit this dialog box, even if you never touch CMYK images.

Photoshop only allows you to use a single CMYK color space at a time, and it applies to all CMYK images you have open. Note that the CMYK Setup dialog box replaces both the Printing Inks Setup and Separation Setup dialog boxes from previous versions of Photoshop. Because Photoshop 5 offers so many more options for converting to CMYK than its predecessors did, it's become something of a monster, but it essentially does the same things as those old features.

Photoshop uses the CMYK Setup settings in the following situations.

► Translating RGB, grayscale, or Lab images to CMYK.

► Translating CMYK files to RGB, Lab, or Grayscale.

► Translating CMYK data to the RGB working space, in order to display it on screen. Then, if "Display Using Monitor Compensation" is turned on in RGB Setup, Photoshop transforms the data to your

Figure 5-3
CMYK Setup

*The CMYK Setup
dialog box lets you tell
Photoshop what color
your CMYK inks are,
and how you want
Photoshop to use them.*

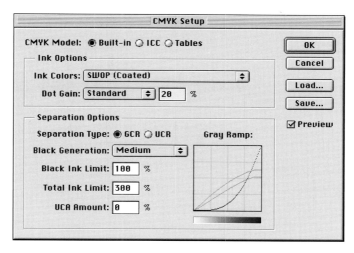

monitor's color space so that the CMYK image is then displayed correctly on your monitor.

▶ Translating grayscale images to the RGB working space in order to display it on the screen, if you set Grayscale Setup to Black Ink (see "Grayscale Setup," below).

▶ Embedding profiles in CMYK images. The only profile Photoshop ever embeds in a CMYK image is the one defined by the settings in CMYK Setup.

Grayscale Setup. The Grayscale Setup dialog box offers a single choice: should your grayscale images be considered RGB or as Black Ink (see Figure 5-4). As RGB, grayscale images take on the gamma of the RGB working space (this would be most appropriate for images destined to be viewed on screen). As Black Ink, grayscale images use the dot gain specified in CMYK Setup (this is best for images destined for print). Photoshop uses the Grayscale Setup information in the following situations.

▶ Translating RGB, CMYK, or Lab images to Grayscale.

▶ Translating grayscale images to RGB, Lab, or CMYK.

▶ Translating grayscale data to the RGB working space in order to display the image on screen. Note that when you elect to treat grayscale images as RGB, the grayscale data is simply converted on the fly to the

Figure 5-4
Grayscale Setup

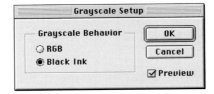

The Grayscale Setup dialog box lets you tell Photoshop whether to make grayscale images use the gamma of your RGB Setup space or the dot gain settings for Black Ink in CMYK Setup.

RGB space defined by RGB Setup. If you choose Black Ink instead, Photoshop first applies the Black dot-gain curve in the CMYK Setup dialog box, and then converts the image to the RGB space defined by RGB Setup. Either way, as we said earlier, it's then converted to your monitor's RGB space (based on the monitor's profile) or not, depending on the "Display Using Monitor Compensation" option, so that the grayscale image is displayed correctly on your monitor.

▶ Embedding profiles in grayscale images. Photoshop can embed a miniprofile in your grayscale image (it's really just embedding a tone curve). When Grayscale Setup is set to RGB, the program embeds the gamma of the RGB working space; when it's set to Black Ink, it uses the Black dot-gain curve, or the black generation specified in the ICC profile or Separation Table selected in the CMYK Setup dialog box.

Profile Setup. The Profile Setup dialog box differs from the other three Color Settings in that it doesn't define a color space. Instead, it lets you control how Photoshop handles profiles when saving and opening images (see Figure 5-5). For instance, what should Photoshop do when opening a legacy image (a file from a previous version of the application) which has no embedded profile? Should Photoshop embed profiles in images when saving them to disk? What about images whose profiles don't match the settings in RGB Setup or CMYK Setup?

▶ It lets you choose whether or not to embed profiles in RGB, CMYK, grayscale, and Lab images. The profiles that get embedded are always those defined by the current Color Settings.

▶ It lets you designate "assumed profiles" for RGB, CMYK, and grayscale that Photoshop will use when it encounters an image with no profile embedded.

▶ It lets you instruct Photoshop how to handle images whose profiles do not match the current RGB, CMYK, or grayscale settings.

Figure 5-5
Profile Setup

Figure 5-5
Profile Setup

*The Profile Setup
dialog box lets you
control profile
embedding and profile
mismatch handling.*

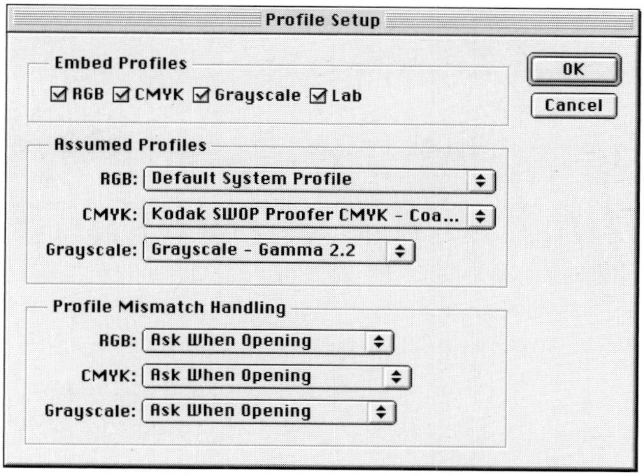

The RGB Editing Space

The biggest challenge facing you in Photoshop 5 is understanding the new RGB behavior. It affects everything you do with RGB files, and also affects the display of CMYK, grayscale, and Lab images. In other words, just about anything you do in this program is affected by the decisions you make in RGB Setup, so it's important to choose an RGB editing space that will work for your needs.

What is this strange thing called "the RGB editing space"? The RGB editing space contains all the possible colors you can use in your image. Like any color space, it defines the boundaries of color: how red is red, what color is fully saturated green, and so on. When you edit an RGB image, you're actually editing in this color space, so you're not bound to the limits of your own monitor. Ultimately, it's an arbitrary, device-independent RGB space.

(Some folks quibble with the application of the term "device-independent" to an RGB space, preferring to reserve the term for purely synthetic, perceptually based color spaces like CIE Lab. However, while a useful distinction can be made between perceptually based spaces and RGB spaces, that distinction does not revolve around device independence. Ultimately, Photoshop's RGB editing space doesn't depend on the vagaries of any given piece of hardware, so it's device-independent.)

Why is device-independent RGB better than Monitor RGB? In previous versions of Photoshop, your image's RGB was always defined as your

CIE xyY and Colorants

Whenever Photoshop asks you to enter custom colorant values (white points for working space or display, custom RGB primaries, or custom ink colors), it demands values in the CIE xyY color space. In theory, you can convert values from any CIE color space to any other CIE color space, but be warned that the accuracy of those conversions varies from application to application.

Photoshop now lets you enter CIE Lab values for custom ink colors: the more observant among you will notice that the Ink Colors dialog box is the only place in Photoshop 5 that allows you to enter Lab values that have a figure after the decimal point. The significance of this is that it's OK to measure custom ink colors using Lab values. However, for monitor chromaticities, white points, or RGB primaries, you really need to use xy values. Most of the current crop of low-end measuring instruments and virtually all mid-range and high-end tools can make xyY measurements directly, including hand-held devices like the X-Rite DTP 22, X-Rite DTP 92, and the Light Source Colortron II. You need ColorShop version 2.5 or higher, so if you're still using an older version of ColorShop with your Colortron, xyY support is a good reason to upgrade.

monitor's RGB, however you had set that up in the Monitor Setup dialog box. This approach had the benefit of simplicity: if your Monitor Setup settings were correct, Photoshop knew what colors you were seeing on the monitor. But it also had some profound disadvantages.

▶ While the gamut of most monitors is larger than that of most CMYK print processes (the *gamut* is the range of colors a device can produce or the range of colors within a color space), it's still much smaller than that of film or of high-end digital cameras. Photoshop 4 limited your image's RGB to the gamut of the monitor, so the original image's gamut was compressed into this smaller space. That's undesirable if you plan to output on an RGB film recorder, or on any other device with a wider gamut than the monitor.

▶ Most people don't realize that most monitors simply cannot display a considerable part of the gamut of CMYK output, particularly in the pure cyans, and in those greens and blues adjacent to them. Limiting your image's RGB to the gamut of the monitor means that you cannot produce all the colors that the CMYK output process offers.

▶ Monitor color spaces are not generally perceptually uniform. When you edit your image in a monitor space, the same editing increment in Levels (or Curves, or Hue/Saturation), may have a much larger effect on some parts of the tonal range and color gamut than on others.

will almost inevitably result. It also does a rather poor job of reproducing blue, which goes black very quickly.

CIE RGB may be of interest to users with wide-gamut capture devices such as scanning digital camera backs that can provide 16-bit files, particularly if they are also going to high-chroma output devices. For 8-bit channels, though, it's simply too large a gamut.

ColorMatch RGB. Based on the Radius Pressview monitor space, Color-Match RGB could fairly be called the conservative choice for print work. It has a reasonably large gamut, though it still clips some of the cyans. If you've been using a calibrated Pressview monitor, you can use ColorMatch RGB as an editing space, and simply open your legacy files with no conversion at all. If you've been using a high-quality monitor calibrated to D50, with a gamma of 1.8, ColorMatch RGB is the closest space to your old Photoshop RGB that Photoshop 5 offers.

The only real strikes against it are that it uses a gamma of 1.8, which gives fewer bits in the shadows, and that its gamut is still on the small side.

NTSC (1953). For many years, NTSC (1953) was the standard for broadcast video in North America, and is still in use in some systems. It has a wide gamut and a very yellow white point. The gamut isn't too large for 8-bit work, but when the white point mismatch is taken into account, posterization becomes a real issue. If you're working on images for broadcast video, NTSC is a rational choice. For other applications, avoid it.

PAL/SECAM. You may be aware that the standard color space for broadcast video in Europe and much of Asia is PAL/SECAM. Its gamut is similar to that of AppleRGB, and is on the small side for print work. Use it if you're doing video for PAL/SECAM systems; otherwise, ignore it.

Adobe RGB (1998). Early adopters of Photoshop 5 may also know this space as SMPTE-240M (Adobe changed the name of this space in their first maintenance upgrade). The *real* SMPTE-240M is a proposed standard for HDTV that's very little different from sRGB. Adobe RGB (1998) is, we believe, much more useful. In fact, if ColorMatch RGB is the conservative choice for print work, Adobe RGB (1998) is the radical option. Its gamut comes extremely close to encompassing the entire CMYK gamut —cyan maxes out at around 98-percent cyan, 2-percent magenta, and 2-percent yellow—and the gamma of 2.2 is perceptually uniform.

The downside of Adobe RGB (1998) is that it has a huge excursion into the greens, and hence wastes some bits on colors that you're unlikely to be able to capture, let alone display or reproduce. Nevertheless, it's eminently worth considering, and if you use a 16-bit workflow rather than an 8-bit one, posterization is unlikely to be a problem with Adobe RGB (1998). (We discuss high-bit workflows in Chapter 7, *Color Correction* and Chapter 13, *Capturing Images.*)

SMPTE-C. The current U.S. broadcast video–production standard, SMPTE-C has the worst gamut of all the spaces being offered, and there's probably no reason to use it unless you're generating images for U.S. video broadcast. (What does this tell us about what Americans are watching on television?)

(For those who care, SMPTE stands for the Society of Motion Picture and Television Engineers, the body that developed this and other SMPTE standards.)

Wide Gamut RGB. The Wide Gamut RGB color space is aptly named— the primaries are the pure wavelengths of red, green, and blue light. This space has a huge gamut, and will cause 24-bit files to fall apart at the slightest tweak of a curve, particularly in the light greens. For the adventurous soul who uses a wide-gamut 48-bit capture device, it may be a useful tool, but it's totally unsafe for 24-bit work.

Simplified Monitor RGB. Simplified Monitor RGB is basically your monitor ICC profile with any kinks ironed out. You can think of it as the "work like Photoshop 4" option. Unlike all the other spaces offered, this one isn't device-independent, because it's tied directly to your specific monitor—it will be different on someone else's machine. It has all the disadvantages of the old color architecture, and none of the benefits of the new one. It may be useful as a source profile for converting legacy images into the RGB working space, or as a transition space as you're trying to get familiar with the new color architecture. But in the long run it's not the best choice—you're much better off letting the "Display Using

Monitor Compensation" feature handle the translation to your specific monitor, and using one of the larger and more uniform RGB spaces for editing.

Custom RGB Spaces

There's nothing special about any of the above color spaces, other than in each case, a group of people have gotten together to decide that it's good for some particular use. If none of Photoshop 5's preset RGB working spaces meets your needs, you can define your own RGB working space. This is easier than it sounds, because an RGB working space is defined by just three xy values (for red, green, and blue), plus xy values for the white point and a single gamma value.

For instance, since none of the RGB spaces that Photoshop 5 offers is ideal for 24-bit RGB images destined for print—ColorMatch RGB is a tad too small, and Adobe RGB (1998) is a tad too big—Bruce has developed a compromise we call BruceRGB, which is defined as follows:

▶ White point = 6500K

▶ Gamma = 2.2

▶ Red xy = 0.6400 0.3300

▶ Green xy = 0.2800 0.6500

▶ Blue xy = 0.1500 0.0600

In the next section, we'll discuss exactly where you can type these values. For now, though, here's why we like it: The red and blue primaries are the same as Adobe RGB (1998), but the green is a bit more conservative. The gamma 2.2 is perceptually uniform, and the 6500K white point is, we feel, a better reflection of the real world than the 5000K (D50) standard. When it comes to finishing your image for output, you can still aim toward D50, but D65 is almost certainly closer to the native white point of most images.

If you want to hammer the political analogy to death (where ColorMatch RGB and Adobe RGB [1998] are the two ends of the spectrum), you can think of BruceRGB as the social-democratic alternative for print work. Many professionals (including us) have been using this space since early beta versions of Photoshop 5 with good results, and we're confident that it's a safe choice for working with 24-bit images that

Figure 5-7

xy chromaticities

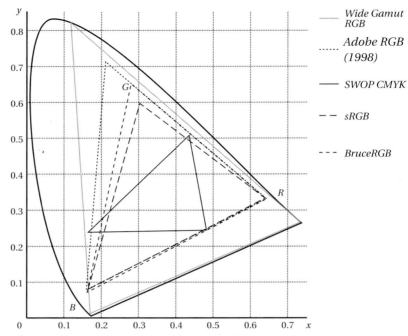

This figure shows the gamuts of several of Photoshop's working RGB spaces, and the gamut of SWOP CMYK, plotted in CIE xyY space. It illustrates the trade-off inherent in choosing an RGB space between clipping the gamut of CMYK and wasting bits on unprintable colors.

will eventually end up in print, whether from a $500 ink-jet printer or from a printing press.

There are other reasons to build a custom RGB editing space. You may, for example, want to define a working space whose primaries are the same as those of your scanner or digital camera, thereby ensuring that your working space matches your input device. Or if the bulk of your work is destined for an RGB output device, you may want to define an RGB space that matches the gamut and gamma of that output device. Generally, we don't advise you to adopt a device color space as your working RGB space, even though it may be possible.

Figure 5-7 shows a chromaticity plot of BruceRGB and some of the built-in spaces in Photoshop 5, compared with the chromaticities of SWOP inks. A word of caution: color gamuts are complex three-dimensional objects, and a chromaticity plot is very much an abstraction. We include this figure primarily as a visualization tool to help you get your head around the implications of different RGB primaries, not as the final word on the comparison of the color gamuts they offer.

Tip: If You Just Want to Go by the Numbers . . . It's quite possible to do good work with Photoshop using an uncalibrated, uncharacterized monitor—you just can't trust what you see on the screen. If you want to simply go by the numbers—reading the RGB levels and the CMYK dot percentages—you can use the Info palette to check your color, and simply ignore what you see on the monitor. Even with a calibrated monitor, you should *always* check those numbers anyway.

If you aren't concerned with the monitor's appearance, simply uncheck "Display Using Monitor Compensation" in RGB Setup. We don't advocate this—we much prefer being able to work visually—but it *is* possible, particularly if you're working in a closed-loop environment where you always go to the same output conditions.

Bruce has five very different monitors in his office (his old house had to be retrofitted to handle the electrical load): a Barco calibrated to D65 with a gamma of 2.2, a Radius Pressview 17SR calibrated to ColorMatch RGB (which has a D50 white point and a gamma of 1.8), a Mitsubishi SpectraView calibrated to D65 with a gamma of 2.2, and two monitors— an older Hitachi EBU and a Matsushita 21-inch hooked to an NT box— that aren't calibrated at all, but were simply measured in their native state as they came out of the box. Within the limits of their varying color gamuts and dynamic ranges, all five monitors display images identically in Photoshop 5, because Photoshop corrects the data that gets sent to the display on each machine. If you've ever tried to calibrate two monitors from different vendors so that they show the same result, you'll realise right away that this is a big deal!

Again, to make this magic happen, you need an accurate monitor profile, and you need to let Photoshop know which profile it should use for the monitor. Creating a profile is basically the same on all platforms, though each has its peculiarities. The mechanisms for getting Photoshop to use that profile, however, differ depending on which platform you're using.

First let's look at the profile-creation part of the exercise. There are three basic scenarios: using a measuring instrument with a smart monitor, using a measuring instrument with a dumb monitor, and measuring by eyeball using Adobe Gamma.

Creating a Consistent Environment

Getting an accurate profile that describes the behavior of your monitor is only part of the story: the environment in which you view the monitor is also extremely important, and is often overlooked. So before you start trying to characterize and calibrate your monitor, you need to optimize your viewing conditions.

Three factors combine to produce the sensation we describe as color: the object, the light source that illuminates the object, and the observer. You are the observer, and your color vision is subject to subtle changes brought on by things as disparate as age, diet, mood, and how much sleep you've had. There isn't a lot you can do about those, and their effects are relatively minor, but it's good to bear them in mind because they remind us that the phenomenon of color is very subjective. The other factors that affect your color vision are, fortunately, easier to control.

Lighting. Consistent lighting is vital to creating a calibrated system. In the United States, color transparencies and print proofs are almost always evaluated using light with a controlled color temperature of 5000 Kelvins (K). In Europe and Asia, 6500 K is the standard—it's a little more blue. (Strictly speaking, the relevant standards—D50 and D65—are daylight curves that aren't absolutely identical to the black-body radiation described by the Kelvin scale, but for all practical purposes they're interchangeable.)

You need to provide a consistent lighting environment for viewing your printed output, otherwise the thing you're trying to match—the original image or the final output—will be constantly changing. You can go whole hog and install D50 lighting everywhere, bricking up any offending windows in the process, but for most of us that's impractical. You can, however, situate your monitor so that it's shielded from direct window light, turn off room lights for color-critical evaluations, and put a D50 bulb in a 10-dollar desk lamp for evaluating photographs and printed material. (Be careful, though—some D50 lamps require a special fixture to avoid overheating, because the unwanted wavelengths are reflected through the back of the lamp into the fixture.)

Theoretically, the ideal working situation is a low ambient

Using Measuring Hardware with a Smart Monitor

The best-case scenario is to create a profile using a third-party hardware measuring unit on a smart monitor. A *smart* monitor has a serial connection to the host computer, which lets the calibrator set the screen's white point by adjusting the gains on the voltage amplifiers that drive the electron guns. For instance, the Barco Reference Display Calibrator (and its less-expensive sibling, the PCD 321), the Radius Pressview 21SR and 17SR, and the Mitsubishi SpectraView are all smart monitors. Smart monitors are much more common for the Macintosh than for Windows, but we expect that to change over the next year or two.

Hardware measuring units are also called "suckers" because they use suction cups to clamp a spectrophotometer onto the monitor while the calibration/characterization process takes place. This device can "see" light (almost dark) environment. This maximizes the apparent dynamic range of the monitor, and ensures that no stray light is distorting your color perception. However, some shops that have tried this have noted a significant drop in the productivity of the employees forced to work in dark windowless rooms, so go as far toward approaching that ideal as you feel is reasonable.

Consistency is much more important than the absolute color temperature of the light source—the variations we've measured of the color temperature of viewing booths at various commercial printers is strong evidence of that. If you work in a studio with a skylight and floor-to-ceiling windows, the color of the light will change over the course of the day, and hence so will your perception of color. In a situation like that, you really need to create an area where you can view prints and transparencies under a light source that's shielded from the ambient light.

A hood to shield the monitor from stray reflections is also very worthwhile—a cardboard box spray-painted matte black may not be elegant, but it's every bit as effective as more expensive solutions, and doesn't distort the color the way most antiglare shields do.

Context. Your color perception is dramatically affected by surrounding colors. Again, you can go to extremes and paint all your walls neutral gray. (Bruce wound up doing this because his office was painted pale pink when he first moved in, and he found that it was introducing a color cast into almost everything—including his dreams.)

It's easier and more important, however, to make your desktop pattern neutral. Pink-marble, green-plaid, or family-snapshot desktop patterns may seem fun and harmless, but they'll seriously interfere with your color judgment. We also recommend not wearing Hawaiian shirts when you're making critical color judgments. Designer black, you'll be happy to know, is just great.

Tip: Neutral-Gray Desktops.
Pattern number 24 in Macintosh System 8 or later's Desktop Pictures control panel is a solid 50-percent gray, and provides a nondistracting background. On Windows, you can change the background color on the Appearance tab of the Display control panel.

what color is displayed on the screen and then feed that information to the calibration software, which can then tweak the monitor. With smart monitors, the easiest approach is to use the hardware device (and its accompanying software) to calibrate the screen to a known standard, and then generate a profile that describes this standard. The question is then: To what standard should you calibrate?

While we've long advocated that people involved with prepress calibrate their monitors to D50 white with a gamma of 1.8, several factors have brought us to temper that recommendation. It still holds good if you're on a Macintosh, if you're happy with the brightness of the monitor at D50 (that is, if it looks white, not dingy yellow), and if you have to deal with applications that don't support ICC-based color management. On the other hand, if you're a Windows user, have a darker-than-

Evaluating Your Monitor

Monitors lose brightness over time, and eventually they simply wear out. Long before the menu bar is burned into the screen, the monitor has lost so much of its brightness range that it probably can't be accurately calibrated to ideal settings.

Calibration utilities work by selectively *reducing* the brightness of the red, green, and blue channels (making them dimmer). So

when you calibrate your monitor, the first thing you'll notice is that it isn't as bright as it was in its uncalibrated state. If the monitor's not very bright to begin with, it's a problem.

Here's our simple rule of thumb. Turn the brightness and contrast controls all the way up. If the monitor is brighter at those settings than you like, it's a worthwhile candidate for hard-

ware calibration. If it isn't as bright as you'd like, it's a candidate for replacement—it's only going to get dimmer over time, and you'll find it very difficult to bring it to a specific white point. You can still get some life out of the monitor by running it in its raw state and simply profiling that state, but it won't last forever.

preferred monitor, or use your machine for just about anything other than Photoshop, we offer the following suggestions.

▶ Calibrate to a white point of D65 rather than D50. Monitors find it much easier to achieve satisfactory brightness levels at D65 than at D50. If you're a believer in D50 simply because much of the graphic arts industry worldwide uses D50 as the proofing illuminant, check out our thoughts on the subject in the sidebar "How White are Your Whites?"

▶ If you're running a PC whose video card doesn't allow the calibrator to adjust the gamma (which includes almost any video card running under Windows NT), simply use the sucker device to measure the native gamma of the monitor, and use it.

▶ If you're running Windows, and your video card does allow your calibrator to adjust the gamma, you're probably better off shooting for a target gamma of 2.2 than one of 1.8. PC-based systems generally aim for a gamma of 2.2, and the closer to the native monitor gamma you aim, the fewer levels in the video card's lookup table you lose. Mac users should continue to aim for gamma 1.8 for the same reason—the native gamma of most Mac display systems is close to 1.8.

Using Measuring Hardware with a Dumb Monitor

We don't mean anything pejorative by the term "dumb monitor"—just that it doesn't talk to the host computer. Most monitors are dumb standalone devices. You can use a hardware measuring device to either calibrate a dumb monitor to a specific standard or simply leave the monitor in its native state and let the sucker device build a profile that describes it. Monitor measuring devices include spectrophotometers such as the Light Source Colortron and the Gretag Spectrolino, and colorimeters such as the X-Rite DTP92 Monitor Optimizer. In addition, many monitor-profiling software packages, such as The Color Partnership's OptiCal and ViewOpen from Heidelberg CPS (formerly LinoColor), include a measuring device.

Calibration. In the calibrate-to-a-standard scenario, all the calibration is done by the calibration software (the stuff that came with the measurement device) forcing a change in the video card's lookup table. This almost invariably means that the monitor ends up displaying fewer than 256 levels per color. How many fewer levels depends on how far you're trying to take the monitor from its native state—the farther you go, the more levels you lose.

If you're running Windows NT, or Windows 95 or 98 with a video card that doesn't allow software to change the video lookup table, you can't do this, so characterizing your monitor—building a custom profile that simply describes your monitor's current state—is really your only alternative—see "Characterizing," below.

However, if your platform actually allows you to calibrate the monitor, we suggest calibrating it to something close to its native white point and gamma, to minimize losses in the video lookup table. A good place to start would be D65 gamma 1.8 on the Macintosh, and D65 gamma 2.2 on Windows systems.

Characterizing. You can also simply measure the monitor, and create a profile from the measurements. That way, you'll get your monitor to perform optimally, delivering the full range of brightness and color of which it's capable. The downside to this approach is that monitors drift—some drift a lot more than others—so you need to check the measurements and update the profile on a regular basis.

In the past, this would have led to a nasty situation where you had multiple profiles for the same device applied to different images. But if you follow our recommendation to use a standard RGB editing space in conjunction with the "Display Using Monitor Compensation" feature, you don't need to keep your old monitor profiles—you only need a profile that describes what your monitor is doing now, since your RGB images are no longer in monitor RGB.

Visual Calibration using Adobe Gamma

There's no doubt that a hardware device can measure your monitor better than your own two eyes can. Nonetheless, if you don't have a sucker-cup instrument, you can still do a reasonably good characterization using the Adobe Gamma utility, which you can find in the Calibration Folder inside the Goodies folder inside the Adobe Photoshop 5.0 folder. Remember that getting accurate color on screen with Photoshop 5 depends heavily on having an accurate monitor profile; so even if you don't have a hardware calibrator, you should definitely go through the simple steps to create a profile with Adobe Gamma.

Note that eyeball-based calibration is extremely dependent on the ambient viewing conditions. A stable viewing environment is vital for this process to work. See the sidebar "Creating a Consistent Environment," earlier in this chapter.

Tip: Watch Your Gamma Versions. Adobe Gamma has changed radically with version 5. If you're using Photoshop 5 for the Mac, do not use the Gamma control panel device that shipped with earlier versions of Photoshop. In fact, make sure that these are all deleted from your hard drive (and restart your computer) before you try to characterize your monitor with the new version.

While the new Adobe Gamma is much improved, we do have some observations that supplement the on-screen instructions. Our suggestions are based on the order of the process that Adobe Gamma steps you through. (If you're on a Macintosh, you have the choice of using the Control Panel mode instead; either method offers the same controls, but we prefer the step-by-step, at least for the first couple of times you perform this task. See Figure 5-9.)

Figure 5-9
Adobe Gamma

Adobe Gamma allows you to choose the Step-by-Step wizard or the Adobe Gamma control panel.

Pick a Profile. In the first step of the process, Adobe Gamma tells you which profile it will base the calibration on, and offers you the opportunity to load a different one (see Figure 5-10). On the Mac it picks up the ColorSync System Profile, on Windows 95/98 it picks up the default ICM profile, and on Windows NT it starts out with a generic display profile installed by Photoshop. Unless you've previously set up a system profile, its choice will almost certainly be incorrect, no matter what platform you're on.

Figure 5-10
Picking a profile

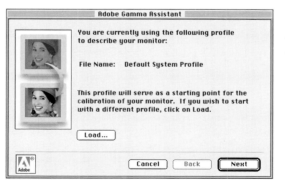

You start by choosing an existing profile as a starting point.

The results you get from the calibration will vary, depending how far away this profile is from your monitor's real behavior. If you don't have any profiles that are even slightly appropriate for your monitor, you'll have some opportunities to address this later in the calibration process, but if you do have a profile that describes at least your model of monitor, choose it now. (You can sometimes get generic monitor profiles from the manufacturer's Web site.)

Setting Brightness and Contrast. The next screen deals with setting brightness and contrast (see Figure 5-11). Note that Adobe Gamma actually expects you to be in a low ambient-light setting; if you're working in bright surroundings, some of the recommendations given by the software may be problematic.

Figure 5-11

Setting brightness and contrast

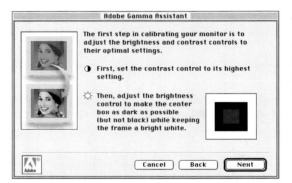

Adjust the brightness and contrast until the center square is very slightly lighter then the black surround while keeping the white frame white.

Adobe Gamma suggests that you set your monitor's contrast control to its maximum. For many users this will work well, particularly if the monitor is more than a year or two old. However, if you're running Windows NT4, which doesn't allow system-wide monitor calibration, you may find that your monitor is uncomfortably bright when you exit Photoshop. In this case, simply set the contrast (which is really the monitor's overall gain control) to the brightest level at which it's comfortable, or perhaps just a hair brighter.

Next, you're instructed to set the brightness control (which is really the black level) so that the center box is as dark as possible while maintaining a bright white in the surrounding frame. Note that there are three concentric boxes. The center box should end up being a dark gray, the outer box should be white, and the one in between should be a true black (or as close to a true black as your monitor can display).

Overriding a starting profile. The next screen lets you choose a phosphor set, in case you want to override those indicated by the starting profile (see Figure 5-12). If you know that your starting profile was incorrect, this is your chance to fix it. If you know that your monitor uses one of the phosphor sets listed on the menu, you can choose it, although if the monitor is more than a few months old, the phosphors will likely have changed. Similarly, you might be able to obtain the phosphor chromaticities from your monitor's documentation or from the vendor. If you can beg, borrow, or steal a measuring instrument that provides xyY values, measure the *current* state of the red, green, and blue primaries, choose Custom from the Phosphors popup menu, then type in the measurements (see Figure 5-12).

Figure 5-12

Overriding the phosphor settings

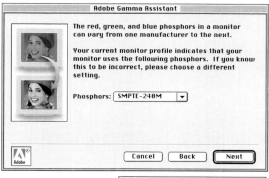

If you know that your starting profile has incorrect primary values, you can choose the correct ones from the pop-up menu, or choose custom to enter custom values.

If you know know the xy chromaticities for your monitor's phosphors, you can enter them here.

Setting the Gamma. The next screen lets you set the monitor gamma (see Figure 5-13). Unless you have compelling reasons to do otherwise,

Figure 5-13

Gamma

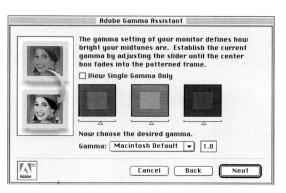

Adobe Gamma lets you pick a target gamma, then adjust the monitor to that target gamma.

we suggest that Macintosh users pick a gamma of 1.8, and Windows users choose a gamma of 2.2—that way, you'll lose the fewest possible number of levels in the video card.

We strongly recommend turning off the View Single Gamma Only checkbox so you can adjust the red, green, and blue gamma settings independently. When you're adjusting the sliders, it helps to move as far back from the monitor as you can and unfocus your eyes so that the red, green, and blue squares become slightly blurry. This makes it much easier to find the sweet spot where the solid center boxes merge with the striped backgrounds.

You'll probably find that it's much harder to make the green square merge into the background than the red or blue squares. If you use a neutral gray desktop pattern, you can watch the color balance change as you manipulate the green slider: when the desktop looks neutral, you've probably come as close as you possibly can to making the central green square match its background.

Setting the white point. The last setting lets you choose a white point (see Figure 5-14). If your monitor has hardware that lets you manually change its white-point setting, we suggest you choose D65—the D50 setting will probably look dim and yellow, while settings higher than D65 will likely be very blue. On most of the monitors we've measured, the hardware white points are strictly a ballpark estimate, so go ahead and use the Measure button to let Adobe Gamma help you figure out what your monitor's white point really is. (Again, if you have access to a measuring instrument, you can measure the monitor white, choose Custom from the popup menu, and type in the xy values.)

Figure 5-14
Setting the white point

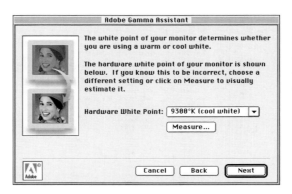

You can choose a different white point from the one in the profile, or use the Measure feature to estimate it visually.

On the next screen, Adobe Gamma lets you change the white point that you've just measured. For instance, if the measured white point was 7900K, you could adjust this to D65. (This screen—see Figure 5-15—only appears on systems that allow software to adjust the video lookup table; if you're running Windows NT, you won't see it.) We suggest choosing Same as Hardware, which will minimize any losses in the video lookup table, unless you need to work with a specified white point to deal with non-ICC applications—in which case you can choose it from the popup menu.

Figure 5-15
Adjusting the white point

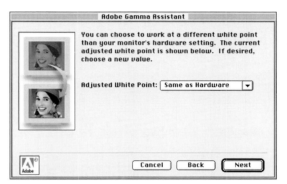

Once you've established your monitor's native white point, you can tell Adobe Gamma to set it to a different white point or leave it unadjusted.

Saving the profile. On the next screen, you can compare the before-and-after results of the calibration (see Figure 5-16). If your phosphors are correct, and you use the Same as Hardware setting for white point, probably the only difference you'll see is a slight midtone shift from the gamma correction. If at this stage you find that the After setting makes the monitor too dim, your best bet is to go back to the beginning and turn up your monitor's contrast setting. If the contrast was already set at its

Figure 5-16
Saving your profile

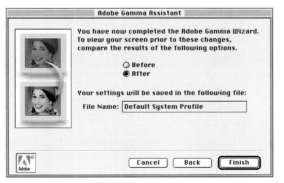

You can compare the unadjusted and adjusted behavior of your monitor, and save a profile.

maximum, you're probably as close as you can get, but it may be time to think about replacing the monitor.

When you're satisfied with the calibration, type in an appropriate file name, and click Finish. You'll be prompted to save the profile, which you should do in the appropriate location for your platform.

▶ On the Macintosh, save it in the ColorSync Profiles folder. (In ColorSync 2.5, this folder lives at the root level of the System Folder; in earlier versions, it lives in the Preferences folder inside the System Folder.)

▶ In Windows 95/98, save the profile in the Windows/System/Color directory.

▶ On Windows NT systems, save the profile in the WinNT/System32/ Color directory.

Loading the Monitor Profile

If you used Adobe Gamma to create the monitor profile, you needn't do anything else—Photoshop is smart enough to automatically load the correct monitor profile. On the other hand, if you used a third-party package to create the profile, you probably have to load it manually.

▶ **Macintosh.** To load a third-party profile on the Macintosh, open the ColorSync control panel (ColorSync 2.5; see Figure 5-17), or the ColorSync System Profile control panel (earlier versions of Color-Sync). Here you can choose your custom profile.

Figure 5-17
Specifying the
System Profile

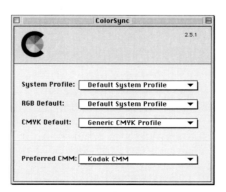

To make Photoshop use a third-party monitor profile on the Macintosh, load it as the System Profile in the ColorSync control panel.

cyan would appear as PMS 286 on screen. In Chapter 10, *Spot Colors and Duotones*, we discuss some of the pros and cons of this technique. The problem is that it's difficult to know what color you'll get when spot colors overlap. Fortunately, another new feature in the Ink Colors dialog box is the Estimate Overprints option. When this is on, Photoshop simulates the colors for cyan+magenta, cyan+yellow, and so on. Be aware that this is a highly experimental procedure, and the strongest possible closed-track, professional-driver, don't-try-this-at-home caveats apply. But if you're in a situation where you're forced to do a job using spot inks instead of process, loading the spot inks into Custom Ink Colors and using Estimate Overprint will give you at least some idea of what can be done with those inks.

Dot Gain

When ink hits paper, it smooshes some, bleeds some, and generally "heavies up on press." That means that your 50-percent cyan halftone spot won't look like 50 percent when it comes off a printing press. It's your responsibility to take this *dot gain* into account when building images. Your primary tool for doing this is the Dot Gain field in the CMYK Setup dialog box (see Figure 5-24).

While the changes to the Custom Ink Colors feature in Photoshop 5 are relatively minor, the changes to the Dot Gain feature are major, to the point where various industry pundits have had loud hissy-fits on the subject. It seems that Adobe received a significant number of complaints about SWOP separations printing too dark in earlier versions. We believe that much of this was due to user error: most Photoshop users simply never took the time to do what you're doing now—learning how this stuff really works. Nonetheless, it's also true that the old method of calculating the dot-gain compensation had built-in numerical errors that minimized dot gain around 30 percent and became increasingly severe the farther from that value you went.

The result: Adobe's engineers completely revamped the way dot gain was calculated internally. While some people find that their images are now more accurate, others are finding that their images now print way too light.

To make matters worse, the changes are largely undocumented (one possibly apocryphal story tells of a member of the documentation team who decided that the change didn't make any sense, and simply cut it from the manual). Or to be more precise, they've been undocumented until now.

There are now two options for dot gain: Standard and Curves. We're going to take a look at each of these in a moment.

By the way, if you just want to make the dot gain behave like it did in previous versions, you can skip ahead to "Tip: Make Dot Gain Behave the Old Way," later in this chapter. But you should be aware that the old way wasn't necessarily the best way.

In fact, the old way had some real problems, particularly when used with custom inks—the often-baffling Gray Balance feature in the old Photoshop Printing Inks Setup was basically a kludge necessitated by some fundamental problems in dot-gain modeling. In version 5, these problems have now been fixed, and the Gray Balance feature has gone away, being replaced by the much more accurate and understandable Dot Gain Curves feature, which we believe offers the best method of compensating for dot gain, though it does require careful measurement.

Tip: Where to Adjust Dot Gain. Photoshop automatically compensates for dot gain when it converts images to CMYK for printing. It's much less work to build the dot-gain compensation into the separation process than to try to compensate for it manually on an image-by-image basis. In a pinch, you can make slight compensations for dot gain in an already separated CMYK file using Curves, but you'll generally get better results going back to the original RGB image, adjusting the dot-gain value in CMYK Setup, and generating a new CMYK file using the new settings.

Standard. The default Dot Gain setting, Standard, lets you specify a single dot-gain value. This one value has an enormous effect on the contrast and brightness of the printed image, so the number you enter here is critical.

You'll hear all sorts of numbers bandied about with reference to dot gain, so it's important to understand that Photoshop and your service providers often differ on what they're talking about when they use the term "dot gain" (see the sidebar "Dot Gain: Coping with Midtone Spread," later in this chapter). To make matters even more complicated, the way

Figure 5-24

Dot Gain

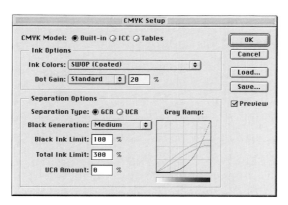

Enter a single value for Dot Gain, or choose Curves to specify a dot gain curve for each ink.

the standard dot-gain compensation is calculated in Photoshop 5 has changed significantly.

Unfortunately, when you select one of the SWOP ink sets, the default dot-gain values are the same as in previous Photoshop versions. The results, however, are different—the separations will print lighter than before. Curiously, Adobe did change the default dot-gain values for the other built-in ink sets so that the new values will produce results similar to the old defaults in the previous versions.

In any case, the default dot-gain values in the built-in ink sets shouldn't be considered as much more than a starting point. Table 5-1 shows some rough-and-ready numbers for typical dot gain, but they're guidelines, not rules. If you come up with values vastly different from these, double-check your calculations, reread the sidebar "Dot Gain: Coping with Midtone Spread" (later in this chapter), and talk to your service providers to make sure that there isn't some misunderstanding. Bear in mind that higher halftone screen frequencies have more dot gain than low ones. The values in the table are based on 133- to 150-line screens with the exception of newsprint, which is based on an 85-line screen.

Curves. Many people don't realize that different-colored inks have different dot gains; yellow, for instance, often gains more than magenta. The standard, single-value dot gains work reasonably well if you're using one of the built-in ink sets, because the differential gain for each ink has already been factored in. But if you're using a custom ink set (or even if you just want to better your results from the built-in ink sets), Photoshop 5 offers a new, easy, unambiguous way to define the anticipated dot gain in the form of the Dot Gain Curves feature.

Table 5-1	Press and stock	Typical dot gain
Dot gain settings	Web press, coated stock	17–22%
	Sheetfed press, coated stock	12–15%
	Sheetfed press, uncoated stock	18–22%
	Newsprint	30–40%
	Positive plates	10–12%

The only disadvantage to using Dot Gain Curves is that you need to use a densitometer (or a colorimeter or spectrophotometer that can read dot area) to read printed swatches. (You can almost always piggyback the swatches onto another job by printing them in the trim area, and if you don't have one of these devices, your printer or service bureau probably does.)

Choosing Curves from the Dot Gain popup menu opens the Dot Gain Curves dialog box (see Figure 5-25). Here, you can enter the actual dot values measured from 2-, 4-, 6-, 8-, 10-, 20-, 30-, 40-, 50-, 60-, 70-, 80-, and 90-percent patches for each ink. Measuring all the patches is probably overkill. At a pinch, you can simply measure the 50-percent dot, and type in the measured value, but we recommend taking measurements of at least the 4-, 6-, 8-, 10-, 40-, 50-, and 80-percent swatches for each ink. Don't be tempted by the All Same checkbox—it's very unusual to find exactly the same dot gains on all four inks.

It's worth noting that the combination of Custom Ink Colors and Dot Gain Curves provides a very effective means of profiling a press or other halftone output device. While most profiling tools require hundreds or even thousands of measurements, Photoshop gets by with a relatively small number of measurements. You can even create an ICC profile from this setup (see "Saving ICC Profiles" in the Tables section, later in this chapter).

Tip: Make Dot Gain Behave the Old Way. There are various formulae floating around for converting old Photoshop dot-gain values to Photoshop 5 dot-gain values, but none of them work for all dot-gain percentages, so we suggest you ignore them. Instead, if you had found an effective dot-gain value in Photoshop 4, here's how you can replicate that behavior in Photoshop 5.

Figure 5-25
Dot Gain Curves
dialog box

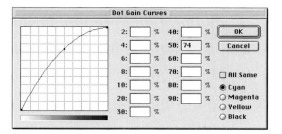

Enter the measured dot area for a swatch to build a custom dot gain curve. You can enter a single value for the 50-percent dot, or take more measurements to increase accuracy.

1. In Photoshop 4, open the Printing Inks Setup dialog box and click the Save button to save this setup to disk.

2. Quit Photoshop 4, launch Photoshop 5, and open the CMYK Setup dialog box.

3. Click the Load button and select the file you just saved. The dot-gain number will be different in Photoshop 5, but the results will be effectively identical. You *may* see a one-percent difference in some colors: this is no big deal. In fact, if you can find a service bureau that guarantees precision of 1 percent on their film, we'd like to hear about it.

If you want to include your old Separation Setup info as well as the Printing Inks Setup settings, you can save Printing Inks Setup and Separation Setup together out of Photoshop 4 as a Separation Table, then load them into CMYK Setup in Photoshop 5 by switching the CMYK Model to Tables, and then clicking Load.

Tip: Use Transfer Functions for Finer Control over Dot Gain. The dot-gain mechanism in CMYK Setup works well, as long as the imagesetter you're using has been properly calibrated and linearized. (In fact, this book and Photoshop both assume that you or your service bureau have linearized the imagesetter.) But if you need to compensate for an unlinearized imagesetter, or if you're printing to a nonlinear device such as a color laser printer, you may get better results using a transfer function instead (see "Page Setup" in Chapter 17, *Output Methods*).

Similarly, if you need to correct the dot-gain compensation in an existing CMYK file, the dot-gain field in CMYK Setup won't help you: it only operates when you convert an image from some other color space to CMYK. To correct dot gain in an existing separation, you can either change the image data itself using the Curves command, or you can use a transfer function.

Some caveats apply to using transfer functions. You're limited to the EPS file format, and it isn't readily obvious to anyone who tries to work on the file that it has a transfer function embedded, so there's considerable potential for confusion. But sometimes it's the only way to get things to work (see "Controlling Dot Gain with Transfer Functions" in Chapter 6, *Tonal Correction*).

Separation Options

The Separation Options part of the CMYK Setup dialog box replaces Photoshop's old Separation Setup feature (see Figure 5-26). It lets you control the total amount of ink you'll put on the paper, and also controls the black generation—the relationship between black and the other colors. Note that this section has no effect on the display of CMYK images.

Figure 5-26
Separation Options

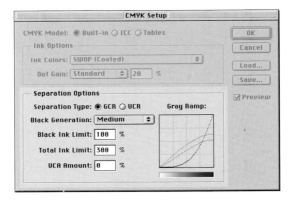

Separation Options lets you specify a total ink limit, a black ink limit, and a black generation method.

The decisions you make in Separation Options can make or break a print job, and there's no single correct answer, no hard-and-fast rules—every combination of press, ink, and paper has its own optimum settings. When it comes to determining what these are, there's no substitute for experience. But understanding the way the separation options work is key to making sense of your own experience, and even if there are no rules, there are at least some valuable guidelines.

Rules, guidelines, and caveats. It's important to remember that these guidelines are useful starting points, nothing more. You'll hear all sorts of recommendations from experts; most are valid, but it's unlikely that

Dot Gain: Coping with Midtone Spread

Dot gain is the name given to the tendency for halftone dots to increase in size from film to press. The biggest cause is the ink spreading as it hits the paper—the more absorbent the paper, the greater the dot gain—but some dot gain occurs when the ink is transferred from the ink roller to the blanket roller on press, and some may even creep in when the film is made into plates. Because dot gain makes your images print darker than anticipated, compensating for it is essential.

Photoshop's dot gain is always measured at the 50-percent value, because that's where its effect is greatest. The larger the circumference of the halftone dot, the more it's subject to dot gain, but above 50 percent the dots start to run together, so they don't gain as much. For the same reason, high screen frequencies are more prone to dot gain than low screen frequencies, because there's more circumference to the dots.

The subject of dot gain attracts more than its fair share of confusion because people measure different things with the term "dot gain." Then, to make matters worse, they have different ways of expressing that measurement.

Photoshop's Dot Gain. The Photoshop manual states that Photoshop's dot-gain measurement is the dot gain from film to press. However, since Photoshop also assumes that it's printing to a linearized imagesetter—one that will produce a 50-percent dot when asked for one—we think it's less confusing to say that Photoshop's dot gain is really talking about the difference between the digital data and the final printed piece.

Photoshop's reckoning of dot gain is the absolute additive amount by which a 50-percent dot increases. So if a 50-percent dot prints as 72 percent, Photoshop would call this a 22-percent dot gain.

When you ask your printer about the dot gain anticipated for your job, they may give you the gain from color proof to final print. There's a simple way to remove this ambiguity. Ask your printer, "What will happen to the 50-percent dot on my film when it hits the press?" If the response is that it will print as a 78-percent dot, that's 28-percent dot gain as far as Photoshop is concerned, and that's the number you should use for your dot-gain setting in the CMYK Setup dialog box.

Now Photoshop 5 offers an even simpler way to remove the ambiguity: just use a densitometer to measure the dot area of the 50-percent dot, then simply plug that value into the 50 percent field in Dot Gain Curves—that way, no guesswork or arithmetic is involved.

Who makes the proof? Many service bureaus will make a laminated proof such as a MatchPrint when they run your film, but it's unlikely that their proofing system is set up to match the press and paper stock on which your job will run. If you give this proof to your printer, they may tell you they can match it, but they're guessing. If the printer makes the proof, there's no guesswork involved, and responsibility is clear.

any of them will apply perfectly to your particular situation. Just how far it's worth going to optimize your color seps for a specific press depends in part on the economics of the situation, and in part on the degree of process control used by the commercial printer. It's the exception rather than the rule for every impression in a print run to be identical, but the amount of variation within a press run varies widely from shop to shop—typically, the less variation, the higher the prices.

Creating *ideal* separations for a given press is an iterative process—you have to run press proofs and measure them, then go back to original RGB files, reseparate them, and repeat the whole process until you arrive at the optimum conditions. This is both time-consuming and expensive, and for most jobs the economics simply don't justify it.

If you're aiming for "pleasing" color from an inexpensive, one-time, midrange job, you just want to aim somewhere in the middle of the range the press can deliver, make a film-based proof such as a MatchPrint or Fuji ColorArt, and ask the press operator to match the proof as closely as possible. But if you're publishing a magazine or newspaper and are constantly working with the same press, it's worth doing much more work to fingerprint the press—each job you do can serve as a proof for the next job. Likewise, if you're working on a premium job, it makes sense to pull press proofs, measure them, and reseparate the images if necessary, or if press proofs are prohibitively expensive, consider doing more than one round of conventional proofing. Most high-end color houses end up scanning and proofing each image two or three times before they get ideal separations. You have to determine reasonable expectations for each job, and decide how far you want to go.

Tip: Don't Bother Converting to CMYK. When you're evaluating the effect of different Separation Setups, you don't actually have to convert images to CMYK. Instead, open an RGB image, and use the Info palette to display the CMYK values you'll get. If you use the new Photoshop 5 lockable color samplers, you can see the effect that changes in Separation Setup have on the CMYK values generated for key areas in the image. Similarly, you could change to CMYK Preview mode (Command-Y). In fact, we'll sometimes open a duplicate window (select New Window from the View menu) and turn on CMYK Preview mode for this second view of the image. This way we can quickly compare the two versions.

Tip: Testing on a Budget. Remember that a printer can sometimes piggyback a test onto someone else's print job, particularly if you show that you can offer them a significant amount of business. Preparing several different versions of an image (and a few color bars, too) and ganging them on a page can tell you a lot when they're printed.

UCR vs. GCR. The Photoshop Classic separation engine offers two different methods of black generation, UCR (Undercolor Removal) and GCR (Gray Component Replacement). Both reduce the total amount of ink used to compensate for ink-trapping problems that appear when too much ink is applied to the page. (In this context, trapping is the ability of one ink to adhere to another ink—it has nothing to do with building chokes and spreads to compensate for misregistration on press.)

▶ UCR separations replace cyan, magenta, and yellow ink with black *only* in the neutral areas. This uses much less ink in the shadows.

▶ GCR extends into color areas of the image as well—it replaces the proportions of cyan, magenta, and yellow that produce neutral gray with a corresponding percentage of black ink.

GCR separations are generally considered easier to control on press than are UCR separations, at least by the theoreticians. The downside of GCR is that it can make the shadow areas look flat and unsaturated since they're being printed only with black ink, so many commercial printers distrust GCR separations. UCA (Undercolor Addition) allows you to compensate for flat shadows by adding some CMY back into the neutral shadow areas (see "Undercolor Addition (UCA)," later in this chapter).

Even though some experts contend that UCR separations are better for sheetfed presses and that GCR is better for web presses, we just don't buy it. We almost always use GCR separations with some UCA. On the other hand, we've found that UCR sometimes works better than GCR when printing to newsprint with a low total ink limit—say, 220 to 240 percent—but your mileage may vary. Ask your printer, but test whenever possible. We suspect that many printers who profess to hate GCR seps often run them unknowingly, usually with good results, as long as the black generation amount isn't too extreme.

Black Generation. The Black Generation popup menu is only available when Separation Type is set to GCR. This feature lets you control the areas of the tonal range that Photoshop replaces with black (see Color Plate 5 on page 680). For the vast majority of situations we prefer a Light black setting, in which Photoshop only begins to add black after the 40-percent mark. Often, however, a Medium black (where black begins to replace colors after only 20 percent) may work better for newsprint. We almost never use the Heavy or Maximum black settings, with one exception: a Maximum black setting can do wonders when printing images that were captured from your screen (like the screen shots in this book).

Custom black generation. The Custom option allows you to create your own black generation curve. This isn't something you should undertake lightly—the black plate has an enormous influence on the tonal reproduction of the image. However, if you want to make slight modifications to one of the built-in black generation curves, you can—choose the curve you want to view, then choose Custom. The Black Generation dialog box appears with the last selected curve loaded (see Figure 5-27).

Figure 5-27
Custom black generation

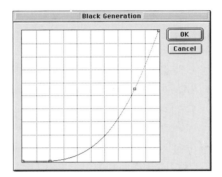

Choose Custom to create a custom black generation curve.

If your printer asks for a skeleton black, you can use the Custom option to create a skeleton black curve, a very light black setting that still extends high up into the tonal range, typically to 25 or 30 percent. You should only attempt to do this if the printer demands it, and even then only if you have considerable experience in evaluating images by looking at the individual color plates—the values on the black plate are critical, and you'll almost certainly need to run press proofs to get it right.

Black Ink Limit. Black Ink Limit does just what it says—it limits the amount of black ink used in the deepest shadows. In general, we recommend leaving this set at 100 percent, because it seems to produce the best overall balance between the black and the CMY inks. This doesn't mean that you'll actually wind up laying down 100-percent black ink. You can (and in many cases should) reduce the black shadow dot for individual images by changing the target black color of the black eyedropper in Levels or Curves (see "Reducing the Black with the Eyedropper" in

Chapter 7, *Color Correction*). But if you're working with newsprint or another process that requires low total ink densities—280 percent or less—you may want to try setting the Black Ink Limit between 70 and 80 percent, particularly if you're using UCR rather than GCR. Your printer is the best source of advice on the maximum black the press can handle.

Total Ink Limit. Total Ink Limit also does what it says—it limits the total amount of ink used in the deepest shadows. Photoshop's separation engine seems to provide the best balance between the colored inks and black when the Total Ink Limit is set somewhere between 300 and 320 percent.

The ideal value depends on the combination of press, ink, and paper, but bear in mind that it isn't necessarily desirable to use the maximum amount of ink that the printing process can handle. It's generally true that more ink will yield a better image (within the limits of the press), but it also creates more problems with ink trapping and drying, show-through, and offsetting, and (for printers) it costs more because you're using more ink. Your printer will know, better than anyone else, the trade-offs involved.

For high-quality sheetfed presses with coated stock, a total ink limit of 320 to 340 percent is a good starting point—you may be able to go even higher with some paper stocks. For newsprint, values can range from 220 to 280 percent (see "Typical Photoshop Classic Setups," below).

Undercolor Addition (UCA). UCA (Undercolor Addition) is used with GCR to compensate for loss of ink density in the neutral shadow areas. Using UCA lets you bring back richness to the shadows, yet still retain the benefits of easier color-ink balancing on the press that GCR offers.

The need for UCA is image-dependent. If your shadows look flat, the image can probably benefit from modest amounts of UCA. We rarely use more than 10 percent, and typically use less.

Typical Photoshop Classic Setups

Table 5-2 gives some general guidelines for different types of print jobs. The dot-gain values are based on 133- to 150-line screens, except for newsprint, which assumes an 85-line screen. If you use these values, you should get acceptable separations, but every combination of press, ink, and paper has its own quirks, and your printer should know them better than anyone else. View these values as useful starting points, and get as much advice from your printer as you can.

Table 5-2 Suggested separation settings

Sheetfed Press

Coated	Uncoated	
Ink colors: SWOP (Coated)	Ink colors: SWOP (Uncoated)	
Dot Gain: 12–15%	Dot Gain: 17–22%	
GCR, Light Black Generation	GCR, Light Black Generation	
Black Limit: 100%	Black Limit: 100%	
Total Ink Limit: 320–340%	Total Ink Limit: 270–300%	
UCA: 0–10%	UCA: 0–10%	

Web Press

Coated	Uncoated	Newsprint
Ink colors: SWOP (Coated)	Ink colors: SWOP (Uncoated)	Ink Colors: SWOP (Newsprint)
Dot Gain: 17–22%	Dot Gain: 22–30%	Dot Gain: 30–40%
GCR, Light Black Generation	GCR, Light Black Generation	GCR, Medium Black Generation
Black Limit: 100%	Black Limit: 100%	Black Limit: 95–100%
Total Ink Limit: 300–320%	Total Ink Limit: 280–300%	Total Ink Limit: 260–280%
UCA: 0–10%	UCA: 0–10%	UCA: 0–10%
		Or:
		Ink Colors: SWOP (Newsprint)
		Dot Gain: 30–40%
		UCR, Black Limit: 70–80%
		Total Ink Limit: 220–240%

ICC

The second method of dealing with CMYK colors, the ICC model, lets you bring Photoshop into the brave new world of ICC-based color management. ICC stands for International Color Consortium, an industry group of color-management and operating-system vendors. The group's main achievement so far has been to agree on a standard format for device profiles—the files that tell a color management system how a device behaves.

ICC-based color management has been canonized by some pundits and demonized by others. We feel that it's simply another tool, one that doesn't differ fundamentally from the old Photoshop way of doing things—it's just another way to convert image data from the color space of one device to the color space of another.

Gamut clipping versus compression. The main difference between color separations created using ICC profiles and those using the Photoshop Classic separation engine is in how it handles RGB or Lab colors that it can't reproduce in CMYK (because the gamut of CMYK is a different size than RGB or Lab). The Photoshop Classic separation engine simply converts these colors to the nearest printable equivalent. In other words, it clips them (this is also called *colorimetric* rendering). This can create problems where detail is carried by differences between out-of-gamut colors, particularly in strong reds, which Photoshop has an unfortunate tendency to turn into oversaturated, brightly colored blobs.

On the other hand, a well-made ICC profile can compress a large gamut (like that of many RGB images) into a smaller gamut (like CMYK; see Figure 5-28). Scaling the entire gamut of the source to fit inside the gamut of the target device changes almost every color in the image, but the overall relationship among colors is maintained. Our eyes are much better at seeing relationships between colors than they are at picking absolute colors, so in general, as long as the color relationship is

Figure 5-28

Out-of-gamut
color mapping

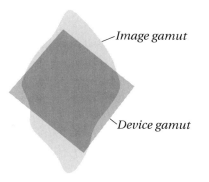

Image gamut

Device gamut

One of the big jobs of a color management system is mapping out-of-gamut colors to colors that the target device can reproduce. Gamut clipping distorts the relationships between colors. Gamut compression retains those relationships, preserving the differences between colors, which is what you want for reproduction of natural images.

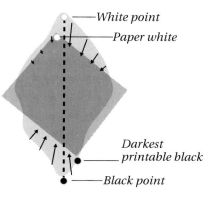

White point

Paper white

Darkest
printable black

Black point

Gamut clipping

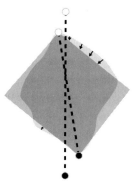

Gamut compression

maintained, the image appears the same, even if it's being reproduced using a far smaller gamut than in the original.

We stress the phrase "well-made ICC profile" because in current implementations of ICC-based color management, all the intelligence is built into the profile. Remember that the whole idea of a profile is to describe your particular device or process; the canned profiles that come with Photoshop or that are available commercially almost certainly do not (see the sidebars "Canned versus Custom Profiles" and "Creating ICC Profiles," below).

As it turns out, making a good custom profile is very difficult and the results are not always worth the trouble. If your images are often heavily saturated, or if you have an uncommon printing process, building a custom profile and using the ICC mode might be worthwhile. However, we have come to believe that taking 61 measurements (to create a high-quality custom-ink setup plus dot-gain curves) is often a more reasonable solution than using expensive equipment to sample the hundreds or thousands of colors you need to build a reasonable ICC profile.

Who Does the Conversion?

There's one more wrinkle in all of this. When you change color spaces by doing a Mode change (choosing Mode from the Image menu), Photoshop always uses the Photoshop Classic engine to do the actual conversion, even if you have chosen ICC in the CMYK Setup dialog box. The key is that when you choose ICC rather than Built-in as the CMYK model, the selected ICC engine is used to build the color lookup tables used by the Photoshop Classic engine. Therefore, the difference is generally so subtle that you wouldn't even notice it.

Nonetheless, if you really want the ICC-compatible CMM to do the conversion, you have to use the Profile-to-Profile command. Again, there are very few reasons when it's important to know this. In fact, we only bring up the subject for two reasons. First, every now and again you may run into a bug in one of the CMMs (or even in Photoshop itself, though we haven't found any yet). Second, if you're as geeky about color as we are, you may notice a tiny difference depending on whether you convert an image using the Mode menu or Profile-to-Profile. Usually, the differences boil down to a difference of one level in one channel on colors that are extremely out of gamut, and the only way you can detect them is by

Canned versus Custom Profiles

Canned profiles—profiles supplied by a third party that are based on something other than measurements of your specific device—have earned a bad reputation, often deservedly so. But under the right circumstances, generic ICC profiles can be very useful. It's definitely true that generic monitor profiles are worse than useless, because when you factor in the viewing environment and the user's preferences on contrast and brightness settings, everyone's monitor is basically unique. It's also somewhat true that each combination of printing press, ink, and paper is unique. However, virtually every press operator can match a contract proof such as a Matchprint, AgfaProof or Fuji ColorArt—if they couldn't, color printing would be basically impossible.

Proofer profiles. Proofing systems are generally very consistent from shop to shop. This makes them good candidates for canned profiles—stable, repeatable, consistent output processes like contract proofers simply don't need custom profiles. You need to make sure that the profile you choose has the correct ink limits, black generation, and substrate for your job, but as long as you pay attention to these variables, you can produce excellent results using generic proofer profiles.

Sheetfed press. While sheetfed presses vary a little more than do proofing systems, we've seen excellent results from generic sheetfed press profiles too, providing the paper stock isn't too weird. Bear in mind that the press operator has a great deal of control over the final result: a profile only has to be a reasonable match to the press.

Composite color printers. You *may* be able to get good results from a canned profile for a composite color printer. The critical variables tend to be the consistency of the inks, dyes, or toner from lot to lot, and the choice of substrate. We've had success with generic profiles for Kodak and NewGen dye-sublimation printers—the dyes tend to be consistent from lot to lot, and there's only one substrate to worry about. Inkjet and color laser printers are a much more uncertain proposition, but even then we hear the occasional success story.

The bottom line in all this is that it's often worthwhile to start out with a canned profile if you're printing to a reasonably stable and consistent process, but keep in mind that a profile is usually built with a particular ink set and substrate in mind. If these aren't documented, you're flying blind. Apple Computer's ColorSync Web page (www.colorsync.com) offers a decent collection of generic profiles for a variety of output conditions. To use them on Windows systems all you need to do is to add an .icm extension to the file name—the profile format is cross-platform.

comparing the images on a pixel-by-pixel basis using the Apply Image command set to Subtract.

Differences this small aren't visible to the naked eye, either on screen or in print. Precious few devices can even reproduce a difference this small with any reliability. So, in case you are of a bent to spend hours trying to chase down tiny discrepancies between different separation methods, this is where the differences stem from.

Installing ICC Profiles

Before you can use an ICC profile, you have to put it in the appropriate folder on your system.

▶ Under Windows 95 and Windows 98, you should put your profiles in the Windows/System/Color directory.

▶ Under Windows NT, put them in the WinNT/System32/Color directory.

▶ To use ICC profiles on the Macintosh, all you need to do is place them in the ColorSync Profiles folder. For ColorSync versions prior to 2.5, the ColorSync Profiles folder is in the Preferences folder (in the System Folder). For ColorSync 2.5 and later, the ColorSync Profiles folder is at the root level of the System Folder.

Note that once you install a new profile, you probably have to quit and relaunch Photoshop in order for the program to recognize it.

Tip: Cross-Platform Profiles. One of our favorite characteristics of ICC profiles is that they are completely cross-platform. To use ColorSync profiles on Windows systems, you only need to add an .icm extension and install them in the appropriate folder.

Tip: Remove Unused Profiles. We've heard many complaints, particularly from Windows users, about the length of time Photoshop 5 takes to launch. A good deal of this time is spent cataloguing the ICC profiles installed in the system. We strongly recommend that you keep only the profiles you're likely to use in the profiles folder (the Color directory in Windows, or ColorSync Profiles on the Mac). Loading times will be significantly reduced, particularly on Windows systems. ColorSync on the Mac caches profiles, so on the Mac it's less of a critical issue, but we still advise keeping your ColorSync Profiles folder lean and mean, if only to cut down on the number of profiles on the various menus.

ICC Options

If you've decided to go for the gusto and try to use ICC profiles with a color matching engine, then select ICC in the CMYK Setup dialog box

Creating ICC Profiles

Building ICC profiles for output devices is not a task for the faint of heart. In fact, Bruce often questions whether it's something any normal person would ever want to do. In addition to a substantial investment in measuring hardware and profiling software, it requires patience (particularly if you're using a handheld measuring instrument), skill, a good deal of knowledge about the behavior of the process you're profiling, and approximately equal parts of art and rocket science.

A comprehensive discussion of profiling is well outside the scope of this book; however, we'd like to make it clear that building an output profile is not simply a matter of taking some measurements, plugging them into a profiling tool, and spitting out a profile, no matter what the profiling-software vendors would have you believe. So here are a few pointers to issues that are often overlooked.

Process Control. Without strong process control, building a profile is like measuring a moving target with a rubber ruler. The first step in building an output profile should always be to gauge the variability of the process you're profiling, and to eliminate as much of that variability as is humanly possible. If you're profiling a composite color printer, there may be little that you can do to eliminate variation from one lot of consumables to another, and if you're dealing with an old printing press you're likely at the mercy of the press operators. When you're dealing with an inherently variable process, you need to take pains to make sure that the data you're collecting is actually a good representation of the process.

Data Averaging. The only reliable way to profile a variable process is to collect data that accurately represents the range in which the device or process operates. Some processes exhibit variation from one impression to the next. In these cases, the best approach is to pick several targets that fairly represent the working range, measure them, and average the results. An autofeeding instrument like the X-Rite DTP-41 is invaluable for this task.

Other processes, such as newsprint, or ink-jet on rag paper, may be noisy—that is, they display variation within the color patches on the target. For noisy processes, the best remedy is to make multiple measurements within each patch, and average the results. The Gretag Spectro-Lino/SpectroScan combination is probably the ideal instrument for this purpose—you can program it to take readings at locations specified to one-tenth of a millimeter.

Ink Limits and Black Generation. Most profiling packages have default settings for total ink and for black generation. It's unlikely that these are good settings for the process you're profiling. Many profiling tools make the naive assumption that processes like CMYK dye-sub and color laser can handle 400-percent coverage. They can, but typically you achieve maximum density long before that point. In the case of dye-subs, density can actually decrease as you increase coverage beyond a critical point. It's usually a good idea to find out, by making measurements, what combination of inks gives you the maximum density, then use that as your maximum coverage. You also need an awareness of what kind of black generation works for your process. For example, color laser printers usually benefit from a heavy black generation, while CMYK dye-sub usually needs a very light black.

(see Figure 5-29). The ICC options part of the CMYK Setup dialog box lets you designate a profile to represent your CMYK output conditions, choose an engine (or CMM) to perform the conversions, select a *rendering intent*, which controls how the source gamut is mapped into the target gamut, and optionally turn on black-point compensation. Let's look at each of these options in turn.

Figure 5-29

ICC options

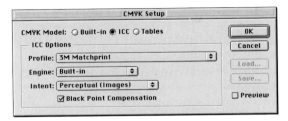

In ICC Options, you can choose a profile, a color management engine and a rendering intent, and you can enable or disable black point compensation.

Profile. The Profile popup menu lists the ICC profiles for CMYK devices that are installed on your system. Choose the profile you want to use from this list. Remember, this profile both describes how CMYK colors look (in order for Photoshop to display them properly on screen) and also how to convert images into a CMYK space (GCR, black generation amount, ink limits, and so on).

Engine. The Engine popup menu lists the ICC-compatible CMMs that are installed on your system. If you do a standard installation of Photoshop 5.0, you should see both the Built-in Adobe CMM (this is different from the Built-in CMYK model that we refer to as "the Photoshop Classic separation engine") and the Kodak CMM available, no matter what platform you're running on. (By the way, in Windows, the Kodak CMM is called "Kodak Digital Science ICC CMS"; on the Macintosh it simply appears as "Kodak CMM.")

Other CMMs may also be available. For instance, on the Mac, your choices will likely include LinoColor CMM and Apple ColorSync. The difference between these two is that choosing LinoColor CMM always invokes the LinoColor engine (which is the default CMM under Color-Sync), while choosing Apple ColorSync will invoke whatever CMM you have chosen in the ColorSync 2.5 control panel. (By the way, don't select Automatic in the ColorSync control panel; if you do, each profile calls its "preferred CMM," which pretty much ensures that you'll never know which CMM is doing what to whom.)

Which engine should you choose? Generally speaking, all the CMMs we've tried (which we believe means all the CMMs currently available) produce very similar results from the same pair of profiles. The results are generally visually identical, with the differences only being apparent when you do a pixel-by-pixel comparison of the images. In a very few cases, we've seen one CMM or another fail with a specific pair of profiles—"fail" in this context means that the result was obviously unacceptable to the naked eye. In short, if a CMM fails, it will be immediately obvious that it has done so, and you can undo your conversion and try a different engine.

We've yet to experience any problems with the Adobe (Built-in) CMM, and we tend to believe that it's the best of the bunch, with the Kodak CMM a close second. However, we've also been producing great results for several years using the LinoColor CMM built into ColorSync—the differences are generally very subtle. Unless you have a compelling reason to use one of the other CMMs—you may, for example, want to use the same CMM in several different applications—we recommend using the Adobe CMM because we've found it to be bullet-proof.

Intent. The Intent popup menu lets you choose one of the four standard *rendering intents* specified in the ICC profile format. In this dialog box, you should almost always choose Perceptual (Images) as your rendering intent. (We might use one of the colorimetric intents when using images that were created synthetically, like in Illustrator or FreeHand.)

▶ *Perceptual rendering* attempts to map the gamut of the source device into that of the target device. In the process, all the colors in the image may change, but their relationships (and hence the overall appearance of the image) remain largely unchanged. When mapping a larger gamut to a smaller one, this is called "gamut compression."

▶ *Relative Colorimetric rendering* scales the white point of the source to the white point of the target, then it reproduces in-gamut colors exactly, and clips out-of-gamut colors to the nearest printable equivalent (gamut clipping). It generally gives very similar results to the Photoshop Classic separation engine, but since the Photoshop Classic engine lets you control the separation options easily, we recommend using it rather than ICC when you want this kind of behavior.

▶ *Absolute Colorimetric* performs similarly to Relative Colorimetric, only without white-point scaling. It can be useful in proofing transforms when you want to simulate, say, the color of newsprint on a dye-sublimation or ink-jet printer using the Profile-to-Profile command, but it's rarely if ever a good choice for RGB-to-CMYK conversions. (See "Profile-to-Profile," later in this chapter.)

▶ *Saturation (Graphics) rendering* maps fully saturated colors in the source gamut to fully saturated colors in the target gamut. It's really only useful for business graphics like pie charts, and we suspect that the only reason it's been included here is to comply with the ICC specifications.

Black Point Compensation. Black Point Compensation maps the black of the source to the black of the target, ensuring that the entire dynamic range of the output device is used. For RGB-to-CMYK conversions you always want this option turned on, though in many cases you'll find little if any perceptible difference whether it's turned on or off.

However, viewing CMYK files is another story. If your print process can produce a blacker black than your monitor (a sheetfed press on good coated stock probably can), it makes little difference whether Black Point Compensation is on or off, but if you're printing to newsprint, to an ink-jet on rag paper, or to some other process that produces a black lighter than your monitor's black, you need to turn Black Point Compensation off to make the printed black display accurately on your screen.

What about CMYK Preview? As it turns out, Black Point Compensation has no effect on the CMYK numbers shown by the Info palette when you're working on an RGB image; it just affects the screen display. Our recommendation, therefore, is to leave Black Point Compensation turned off *except* when you're actually doing an RGB-to-CMYK mode change. Even then, it's possible you may encounter a situation where you want Black Point Compensation off when doing a mode change with specific profiles; we haven't encountered any CMYK profiles like this, but they may exist. See the sidebar "Black Is Black (or Is It?)," below, for a detailed look at the Black Point Compensation feature. Note also that a different set of rules apply when using Black Point Compensation in the Profile-to-Profile command. See "Profile-to-Profile," later in this chapter.

Tip: Use Actions to Turn Black Point Compensation On and Off. Bruce quickly tired of going into CMYK setup to reset the Black Point Compensation setting, so he created a pair of actions, one to turn it on, the other to turn it off—it would be nice if Actions allowed you to create one action that simply toggled the setting, but unfortunately it doesn't. So Bruce did the next best thing, using an function key shortcut to turn it on, and a Shift-plus-function key shortcut to turn it off.

Tables

The third and final CMYK mode is Tables (see Figure 5-30). The Tables feature has changed somewhat from previous versions: the old Tables mechanism just let you save a Printing Inks Setup and a Separation Setup together in a single file. This is no longer necessary, as Photoshop 5 has combined these in a single dialog box. (When you save a file from the CMYK Setup dialog box's Classic settings, you get an .API file which contains both the ink and setup information.) On the other hand, the new Tables feature lets you do three useful things.

Figure 5-30
Tables in CMYK Setup

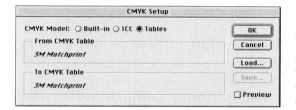

Tables lets you load Separation Tables from previous versions of Photoshop, and save Built-in settings as ICC profiles.

▶ Load CMYK tables from previous versions of Photoshop (legacy tables) and from third-party applications that can write separation tables.

▶ Save Photoshop Classic setups (including those that you've loaded from older versions) to disk as ICC profiles. (Note that there is no way to save an old-style separation table, or .AST file, from the Tables dialog box; see "Custom Separation Tables," later in this section.)

▶ Fool Photoshop into displaying a (more or less) accurate soft proof of an RGB device (or devices that act like they're RGB, such as inexpensive ink-jets).

Black Is Black (or Is It?)

We usually think of black as being "just black," but of course black on different devices appears differently, and now Photoshop's Black Point Compensation forces us to think about this fact. The information here is fairly complex, but the basic principle is quite simple. When you transform from one color space to another, there are two ways of transforming the black point, absolute and relative. Transformations involve mapping the source gamut to the reference color space, also known as the Profile Connection Space (PCS) which in most cases is Lab, then mapping the Lab values to the destination space. In a relative black-point transformation, the source black is mapped to a L* value of 0 in the PCS, but in an absolute black-point transformation, it's mapped to the actual L* value that the device can produce, which is usually substantially greater than zero. (A zero L* value represents the total absence of any reflected light, which is blacker than any real device can ever reproduce.) ICC profiles define the transform between device space and the PCS, and some profiles are built with relative black transforms while others are built with absolute ones.

This can lead to undesirable results. For example, Radius ColorMatch RGB profiles map RGB 0,0,0 to L*a*b* 3,0,0 in the PCS. A CMYK profile that uses absolute black encoding may map to a black value in the PCS of L*a*b* 7,0,0. If you convert an RGB image to CMYK using this pair of profiles, your shadow detail will get clobbered because the first few levels in the RGB document will convert to L* values in the PCS between 3 and 7. Since these are all darker than the output device can produce, they'll be clipped to black, and your shadow detail goes bye-bye.

If the same RGB profile is used with a CMYK profile that maps device black to L*a*b* 2,0,0, you'll get very different, equally undesirable results. The RGB black will convert to L*a*b* 3,0,0, which is lighter than the black the output device can produce.

Most Photoshop users will have no need to use the Tables feature. Nonetheless, it is a very powerful little tool in your arsenal, and one that you should know about (we'll explore how to do each of these in a moment). There are two simple rules to remember when using Tables.

▶ You can open old-style separation tables (.AST) and some (but by no means all) CMYK ICC profiles in the Tables dialog box. (The profiles have to be really basic; most ICC profiles contain too much information for Photoshop to grok; besides, it's probably better to just load profiles in the ICC section of the dialog box.)

▶ Anything saved from the Tables dialog box becomes an ICC profile.

Loading Tables

There are two ways to load settings into the Tables section of the CMYK Setup dialog box. The obvious way is to click the Load button. This is

The resulting image will appear washed out because it contains no true blacks.

If you want a transform that uses the entire dynamic range of the output device, you need a relative black transform both from source to PCS and from PCS to output. Photoshop's Black Point Compensation provides such a transform between profiles using absolute black encoding, or between one that uses absolute black encoding and another that uses relative black encoding. It works by estimating the black point for the source and the target. If they're the same, as they would be if both profiles use relative black encoding, the feature does nothing. But if the black levels are different, it adds an extra processing step: after the source color is converted into the PCS, Black Point Compensation adjusts the PCS to map the source profile's black to the destination profile's black via a straightforward linear transformation of the L* values in the PCS. This ensures that the entire dynamic range of the source is mapped into the entire dynamic range of the target, without shadow clipping or washed-out blacks.

To accomplish this, Photoshop needs to know the black levels of both the source and the target profiles: this isn't a standard part of the ICC profile, so Photoshop has to make some educated guesses. Sometimes its estimate of one or both profiles' black levels is inaccurate, and black-point compensation makes the results look worse—either washed-out blacks or clipped shadows. This is quite rare—we've only seen it with a few profiles for RGB output devices such as film recorders or photo printers—but if you see shadow clipping or washed-out blacks when Black Point Compensation is turned on, try turning it off to see if matters improve.

The other occasion when you'd want to turn Black Point Compensation off is when you're doing a proofing transform from a narrow–dynamic-range process like newsprint to a wide–dynamic-range process like a monitor or a dye-sub printer, and you want to see the washed-out blacks on the proof as they'll appear on newsprint.

useful for loading separation tables (.AST) files created by previous versions of Photoshop. (It also lets you load some ICC profiles, but as we noted earlier, this is a pointless exercise.) The less-obvious technique is to create your settings in CMYK Setup using the Photoshop Classic (Built-in) model, then click the Tables button to switch to Tables.

Saving ICC Profiles

Photoshop 5 has a nifty method for converting CMYK Setups (either Classic or imported tables) to ICC profiles. The primary reason you'd want to do this is to use the same settings in other ICC-savvy applications—such as QuarkXPress 4, PageMaker 6.5, or FreeHand 8.0—to provide accurate display of placed CMYK images.

Some of you are thinking, "Why not just build an ICC profile and then use it in both Photoshop and the other program?" The answer is that most profiling tools demand that you take somewhere between 500 and 6,000 or so measurements, while a custom ink setup in Photoshop can be made with as few as 12 measurements (though you can take 60 or so samples to get an even better profile).

The conversion is a simple three-step process.

1. Open CMYK Setup, choose the Built-in model (what we call "Classic"), and dial in (or load) the settings you want to turn into an ICC profile.

2. Switch the model to Tables. Notice that the From CMYK Table is named to reflect the ink-set and dot-gain settings you made in the Built-in model, while the To CMYK Table is named to also reflect the black generation settings you chose. That's because "From CMYK" means "when converting *from CMYK* to another space" (like when displaying CMYK images on screen). Conversely, "To CMYK" means "when converting another color space *to CMYK*" (in which case, you need the black generation settings).

3. Click the Save button to save the file to disk as an ICC profile into the directory where you keep your profiles (see "Installing ICC Profiles," earlier in this chapter). Don't forget to name the profile appropriately.

You can now use your profile in any application that understands ICC profiles.

By the way, there's one other use for these profiles. We also use them to temporarily convert our CMYK images so that we can print inexpensive "preproofs" on desktop color printers—the desktop printer's profile becomes the target profile, and the profile created by Photoshop becomes the source. When we're done printing, we just revert the file to its pre-transformed space.

Longing for the Old Days

As we noted previously, the dot-gain compensation in Photoshop 5 is considerably improved from previous versions. However, if you have a Printing Inks Setup and a Separation Setup from an older version of Photoshop that you want to preserve, Tables offers a simple way to bring that setup into Photoshop 5. Here's how.

1. In the older version of Photoshop (any version prior to 5), set up the Printing Inks Setup and Separation Setup dialog boxes, then choose Separation Tables from the Color Settings submenu (under the File menu).

2. Make sure that the To CMYK table is set to Use Separation Setup and that the From CMYK table is set to Use Printing Inks Setup, then save this table to disk (click Save).

3. Quit the old version of Photoshop and launch Photoshop 5. Choose CMYK Setup from the Color Settings submenu, and click Tables.

4. Click Load, then load the table you just saved from the older version of Photoshop.

Using this table, you'll be able to produce separations that are virtually identical to those produced by the previous version—we say "virtually" because you may see on a few colors a one-percent difference in a single channel between the Photoshop 5 separations and the earlier ones. In real-world production terms, this is a meaninglessly small difference.

Of course, if you want, you can now click Save to save the old table as an ICC profile.

Custom Separation Tables

As we said earlier, the Tables section of the CMYK Setup dialog box only saves ICC profiles, not old-style separation tables (.AST files). Nonetheless, there are some tricky and tweaky methods that involve using the mysterious Calibration Sources files (the Photoshop files inside the Calibration folder, within the Photoshop application folder). While we're finding fewer and fewer reasons to bother with these techniques, they're still worth considering.

Custom RGB-to-RGB tables. One situation where we've found custom tables useful is for soft-proofing RGB output devices, whether they're real RGB devices (such as the Fuji Pictrography, the Durst Lambda, the Cymbolics LightJet, or a film recorder) or simply ones that pretend so assiduously to be RGB devices that you have to treat them as such (most inexpensive color ink-jet printers fall into this category, since their drivers convert everything to RGB before processing the image).

In this case, the tables let you use CMYK Preview to soft-proof the RGB output. We don't recommend actually using these tables to transform your files before printing them (that's better done by Profile-to-Profile), but the soft-proofing is reasonably accurate, and certainly better than having to print a proof, then tweak it, then print again and tweak, and so on.

The trick is to fool Photoshop into thinking that an RGB device is actually a CMY device. The downside is that you lose CMYK as a real space while you have the table for the printer loaded. Note that to make this work, you need a reasonably good ICC profile for the printer. (We're grateful to Mark Hamburg, Photoshop's Chief Architect, for figuring this one out.)

1. Open the Calibration Sources files named Lab Colors and CMYK Colors (located in the Calibration folder, inside the Goodies folder) without color conversion.

2. Add an alpha channel filled with white to the Lab Colors file.

3. Using Profile-to-Profile (we talk about this feature later in this chapter), convert the Lab Colors file from Lab to the profile for the RGB device you are interested in proofing. Use the intent that you would use for doing mode conversions—almost always Perceptual—and turn *off* Black Point Compensation.

4. Save this file, calling it something like "<Profile Name> to CMYK" in the Raw file format. In the Save as Raw dialog box, use these settings: Type = 8BST, Creator = 8BIM, Header = 0, Interleaved Order.

5. Close the file.

6. Convert the CMYK Colors file to Multichannel mode, and then convert it to RGB mode (thereby relabeling the channels).

7. Discard the fourth (black) channel in the Channels palette.

8. Use Profile-to-Profile to convert from the profile for the RGB device to Lab. In this case, you should probably use the Relative Colorimetric intent, with Black Point Compensation turned *on*, to match Photoshop's standard proofing behavior.

9. Save the result, calling it "<Profile Name> from CMYK" as Raw format. In the Save as Raw dialog box, use these settings: Type = 8BST, Creator = 8BIM, Header = 0, Interleaved Order.

10. Close the file.

11. Choose CMYK Setup and go to the Tables section.

12. Load the files saved in steps 4 and 9 (one at a time, of course). They should end up in the appropriate portions of the dialog box.

13. (Optional) Click Save to create an ICC profile representing the result of combining these two tables.

The CMY portion of CMYK now works just like the RGB for the target device. The K portion has no effect. You can now use CMYK Preview to proof the appearance of the file on the RGB device. Just don't try printing using CMYK.

Custom RGB-to-CMYK tables. Here's how to create a custom RGB-to-CMYK table using a third-party separation package (though most people will never need or want to do this). Note that you must find a way to make Photoshop's RGB Setup definition match the definition of RGB in the separation program.

1. In Photoshop, open the file named Lab Colors (located in the Calibration folder, inside the Goodies folder), convert it to RGB, and save it to disk with another name, *e.g.,* "Photoshop RGB."

2. In the color-separation application, open this RGB file, convert it to CMYK, and save it with another name, *e.g.,* "Scitex CMYK."

3. In Photoshop, open this CMYK file *without conversion* (see "Profile Setup" for more on when Photoshop does or does not convert images upon opening) and save it as Raw. In the Save as Raw dialog box, use these settings: Type = 8BST, Creator = 8BIM, Header = 0, Interleaved Order (see Figure 5-31).

That's it. Believe it or not, this graphic file is the complete custom table. You can load it by choosing Tables in the CMYK Setup dialog box, clicking the Load button, and opening the Raw file you just saved.

We've never had much success creating tables going in the other direction, from CMYK to RGB. To control the display of CMYK images created by your custom table, you're almost certainly better off simply tweaking the Ink Colors and Dot Gain settings in the Built-in model.

Figure 5-31
Saving in the
Raw file format

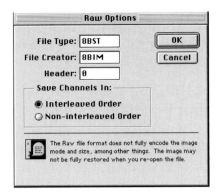

*Save your custom Separation
Table in the Raw format, using
the settings shown at left.*

Grayscale Setup

After slogging through the monster CMYK Setup dialog box for so long,
it's a pleasure to switch to Grayscale Setup, which is really very simple
(see Figure 5-32). Essentially, this one dialog box replaces the "Use dot
gain for grayscale images" checkbox that sat in the old Printing Inks
Setup dialog box.

Grayscale Setup contains only two options, RGB and Black Ink. If you
choose RGB, grayscale images use the gamma setting in RGB Setup. If
you choose Black Ink, grayscale images use the Dot Gain Setting for Black
Ink in CMYK Setup. Choose RGB if your grayscale images are destined for
the screen (multimedia, World Wide Web), and choose Black Ink if they're
destined for print. We told you this one was simple!

Figure 5-32
Grayscale Setup

*Grayscale Setup lets you target
grayscale images for the monitor,
or for print.*

Profile Setup

At the beginning of this chapter, we indicated that Photoshop 5 shipped
with some less-than-optimal settings which could have the effect of ruining your images without your even knowing about it. The Profile Setup
dialog box is the central headquarters for determining how (or whether)
Photoshop acts on images when you open them (see Figure 5-33). If you set

Figure 5-33
Profile Setup

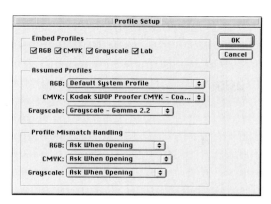

Profile Setup lets you control profile embedding, and lets you configure the "cop at the door" to handle missing and mismatched profiles.

the Profile Setup settings correctly, you can do marvelous things with Photoshop, but if you set it up incorrectly, Photoshop can easily destroy your images without even notifying you that it's doing so. Unfortunately, the default setting in Photoshop 5.0 did the latter (though by the time you read this, a maintenance release will almost certainly have changed that behavior).

Profile Setup performs two distinct functions. First, it acts as "the cop at the door," offering you a method of ensuring that images get translated correctly into the working space. Second, it lets you embed ICC profiles in images so that Photoshop and other ICC-savvy applications can interpret them correctly. In concept, it's quite simple. The devil, as always, is in the details.

The Profile Setup dialog box is divided into three sections: Embed Profiles, Assumed Profiles, and Profile Mismatch Handling. Let's look at these options in detail.

Embed Profiles

The Embed Profiles section is about as straightforward as they come. By default, the checkbox is turned on for all color spaces, meaning that Photoshop automatically embeds a profile in every image that you save. If it's an RGB image, Photoshop embeds the profile for whatever space you've set in RGB Setup; if it's a CMYK image, Photoshop embeds the profile for whatever space you've set in CMYK Setup, and so on.

Note that Photoshop will also embed a profile for Lab images. Why would you need a profile for a Lab image? Well, in previous versions of Photoshop, Lab was always just Lab, because the white-point scaling algorithm it used (the von Kries white-point transform, for all you hardcore color geeks) would always produce the same Lab values from a given set of RGB values, no matter which white point the Lab space had. In Photoshop 5, however, the more visually accurate Bradford white-point transform is used, and the net result is that the white point of Lab *does* matter. In Photoshop 5, Lab is always D50, 2-degree observer Lab, which exactly matches the ICC profile interchange space. Some other applications, particularly those of European origin, use D65 2-degree observer Lab. By embedding the profile, Photoshop makes clear exactly which flavor of Lab the image uses.

To embed, or not to embed. In the vast majority of situations, we recommend that you embed profiles. When you embed a profile, you're telling all ICC-savvy applications that the values in the file aren't just any old random RGB or CMYK values, but that instead, they're colorimetrically defined, calibrated RGB or CMYK values. In most cases, the worst that can happen is that the profile will be ignored by applications that don't understand it.

There is, however, always the possibility of stupid human intervention . . . . Some people have all sorts of strange ideas about color management, and some shops are definitely ICC-phobic. They'll probably have conniption fits if they accidentally discover that your CMYK images contain profiles. Eventually, they'll probably realize that profiles are their friends (if they don't go out of business first), but if you're dealing with an ICC-phobic service bureau, prepress house or printer, it's probably best to deliver final CMYK with no embedded profile, along with very clear instructions that the CMYK values in the file are the ones you want printed.

Similarly, if you open and save a calibration target file, you also generally don't want to embed a profile in it. You always want those to keep the same RGB or CMYK values, irrespective of the device you're sending them to. When you save a file without an embedded profile, Photoshop actually places a tag in the file that indicates it was deliberately saved that way.

If you're saving JPEG files for the Web, and you are really obsessive about file size, you can probably shave about 500 bytes (that's one-half K) off your images by telling Photoshop not to embed an RGB profile. However, as there's a possibility that Web browsers may someday be able to read this profile and display the image appropriately, we leave it in.

In almost every other situation we can envision, you want to embed profiles in your images.

Tip: Grayscale Profiles and PageMaker. Adobe PageMaker doesn't apply color management to grayscale files (it handles color files fine). It does, however, read the profiles that may be in a grayscale image, and it tends to get very confused. If you're preparing grayscale TIFFs for import into PageMaker, turn off profile embedding for Grayscale in the Profile Setup dialog box—your life will be a lot easier.

Assumed Profiles

The Assumed Profiles section lets you specify a profile for Photoshop to use when it encounters an image that doesn't contain an embedded profile. However, Photoshop doesn't actually do anything with this information unless you tell it to in the Profile Mismatch Handling section (see below). In short, it's a convenience and automation feature.

For example, if you know that all the old, legacy Photoshop 4 RGB images you're going to be opening today came from such-and-such a calibrated monitor (for which you just happen to have a profile), you could set the Assumed Profile popup menu to that monitor profile. Then you can set up your Profile Mismatch Handling so that it converts the files automatically to your new RGB editing space. When you're done opening and saving these images from Photoshop 5, you could reset the Assumed Profiles setting to a safer setting: Ask When Opening.

You almost always want to convert legacy RGB images into your chosen working space, but unless you're deliberately repurposing a CMYK image, you usually just want to open it with no conversion—you just want to see how it will print. Therefore, the safest course, and the default settings we suggest, are to set Assumed Profiles for RGB and Grayscale to Ask When Opening, and to choose None for the CMYK setting. That way, when you open RGB or grayscale images that don't contain profiles, Photoshop will ask you which profile you want to use as the source, providing you also follow our recommendations in Profile Mismatch Handling.

Profile Mismatch Handling

Profile Mismatch Handling is possibly the most dangerous setting in the Profile Setup dialog box, particularly if you don't understand what it's doing. Unfortunately, Photoshop 5.0 shipped with default settings that we think are very dangerous indeed, although they may be changed in a maintenance release by the time you read this.

When you open an image that either has no embedded profile or a profile that doesn't match your color settings (in RGB Setup, CMYK Setup, and Grayscale Setup), Photoshop consults the Profile Mismatch Handling popup menus to decide what to do. The default behavior is to convert any RGB image, based on either the assumed profile or whatever profile is embedded. It transforms the image, of course, to the settings in your RGB Setup dialog box. If you don't change anything about Photoshop's color settings, the program automatically converts legacy RGB images to sRGB, which can effectively kill your data.

If your legacy images were created on a system where you never calibrated the monitor, and you left the Monitor Setup settings at their defaults, this may not be a total disaster; but unless all your images are headed for the World Wide Web, converting them to sRGB is probably the last thing you'd want to do, since the sRGB gamut is so limited.

Let's look at the options for Profile Mismatch Handling in detail, explaining exactly what each one does.

Ignore. This option simply opens the image into the current color settings space (defined in RGB Setup, CMYK Setup, or Grayscale setup), without converting the image data at all. With most RGB images, this is not what you want because you're redefining the values in the file to be those of the current RGB Setup space. The numbers in the file don't change, but the colorimetric meaning of those numbers becomes whatever the RGB Setup dialog box says they are. The color will look different, and print differently.

With CMYK images, though, preserving the values in the file probably *is* what you want—you usually just want to know how this data will print on the CMYK process for which Photoshop is configured. When you open a CMYK file with no conversion, what you see on the screen is a soft proof of the file as it will print to your current CMYK Setup.

With grayscale images, it really depends on what you want to do with them. If you have Grayscale Setup set to Black Ink and you just want to look at how the images will print, setting the popup menu to Ignore might be just the ticket. If, on the other hand, you want to preserve the character of the image as it appeared on the system on which it was

Figure 6-1

Adjusting gamma

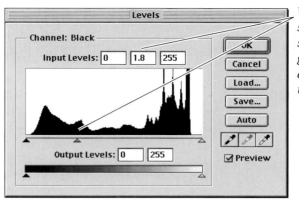

While it's not labeled as such, the middle Input slider controls the gamma setting, which adjusts the midtone values in an image.

4. Choose Levels again, and change the gamma to 0.45. The midtones are back almost to where you started, but you should be able to see that, instead of a smooth gradation, you have some distinct bands in the image (see Figure 6-2 on page 208).

What happened here? With the first gamma adjustment, you lightened the midtones—stretching the shadows and compressing the highlights. With the second gamma adjustment, you darkened the midtones—stretching the highlights and compressing the shadows.

But with all that stretching and squeezing, you lost some of the levels. Instead of a smooth blend, with pixels occupying every value from 0 to 255, some of those levels became unpopulated—in fact, if we're counting right, some 76 levels are no longer being used.

Call up the Levels dialog box again, and you'll see that the histogram is comb-like—there are missing areas, with no pixels. You've thrown away somewhere between a quarter and a third of the tonal information, and in the process you've introduced our arch-enemy: posterization.

If you repeat the pair of gamma adjustments, you'll see that each time you make an adjustment, the banding becomes more obvious as you lose more and more tonal information. Repeating the gamma adjustments half a dozen times will give you a file that contains only 55 gray levels instead of 256. And once you've lost that information, there's no way to bring it back.

Difference Is Detail: Tonal-Correction Issues

What do we mean when we talk about image information? Very simply, adjacent pixels with different values constitute image detail. If the difference is very slight, you won't be able to see it (especially in shadows); but it's there, waiting to be exploited. You can accentuate those differences—making those adjacent pixels *more* different—to bring out the detail.

The color of noise. Difference isn't always detail, though. Most scanners—particularly low-cost desktop flatbeds—introduce spurious differences between pixels (see Figure 6-3). Those differences aren't detail, they're just noise (like static on the radio that drowns out the weather report), and they're one of our least favorite things. Photoshop can't tell the difference between genuine image information and device-induced noise. You need to decide what is desirable detail and what's noise, accentuating the detail while minimizing the noise.

Posterization. Noise isn't the only problem to deal with when you're doing tonal correction, however. There's also *posterization*—stair-stepping of gray levels in distinct, visible jumps, as opposed to smooth gradations (see Figure 6-4).

Photoshop only gives you 256 possible values for a gray pixel (unless you're working with a high-bit image; see "The High-Bit Advantage" in Chapter 13, *Capturing Images*). When you start making dark pixels more

Figure 6-3 What noise looks like

A dirty scan. This type of noise poses problems during tonal correction.

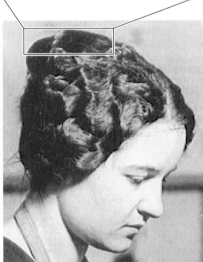

A cleaner scan makes it much easier to adjust tone.

Data Loss in Perspective

This loss of image information may seem scarier than it really is. In most cases, the corrections you make to images are much less drastic than in the example above. Moreover, while there's considerable debate over exactly how many shades of gray can be successfully represented in print,

Figure 6-4 The effects of posterization

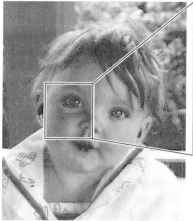
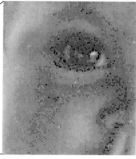

not detail. And the posterization is accentuated by sharpening.

Lost highlight detail. When you accentuate detail in one part of the tonal range, making slightly different pixels more different (*expanding* the range), you lose detail in other areas, making slightly different pixels more similar (*compressing* the range).

For instance, if you stretch the

different, you eventually make them *so* different that the image looks splotchy—covered with patches of distinctly different pixels, rather than smooth transitions. This is a problem especially with noisy images, because those distinct patches may be noise,

shadow values apart to bring out shadow detail, you inevitably squeeze the highlight values together (see Figure 6-5). If you make two different pixels the same, that detail is gone forever. That's what we mean in real-world terms when we say that information is "lost."

Photoshop's tonal controls let you improve your images immeasurably, but they'll also let you wreck an image irreparably. Various clichés come to mind—you can't make a silk purse out of a sow's ear, there's no such thing as a free lunch, and so on—but however you slice it, *any* tonal manipulation you do in Photoshop throws away some image information. The trick is to make the image look better than it did before, even though it contains less information.

Figure 6-5 Loss of highlight detail

Bringing out shadow detail with tonal correction inevitably loses some highlight detail.

Before tonal correction   *After tonal correction*

our experience leads us to believe that it's significantly less than 256. Nonetheless, this simple demonstration should serve to hammer home the following lessons, and the ensuing pieces of advice.

▶ All tonal manipulations incur some data loss.

Figure 6-2

Data loss due to
tonal correction

*While the effect of
successive tonal-
correction moves on
images may be subtle, the
effect on the data within
the image—as expressed
in the histogram—
is profound.*

*Histogram for the
gray wedge at the
right side of the image*

Before tonal correction   *After three gamma moves*

▶ Once the data is gone, you can't bring it back.

▶ Successive tonal manipulations lose data at an increasing rate.

Get good data to begin with. As we emphasize in Chapter 13, *Capturing Images,* if you've got a high-bit scanner, it's better to get the image as close to "right" as you possibly can as you scan it. The whole point of a high-bit scanner is to let you manipulate the high-bit data during the scan, so that you get the *right* 8-bit data out of the scanner.

Use Adjustment Layers. You can avoid the penalties incurred by successive corrections and cover yourself by using an Adjustment Layer instead of applying the changes directly to the image. However, there are trade-offs involved—you need more RAM, and some features aren't available when you use Adjustment Layers. In any case, because the various tools offered in Adjustment Layers operate identically to the way they work on flat files, we're going to discuss how the features (Curves, Levels, Hue/ Saturation, and so on) work on flat files first. For a detailed discussion of Adjustment Layers, see Chapter 8, *The Digital Darkroom.*

Use high-bit data. If your scanner allows it, you can bring the 10-, 12-, 14-, or 16-bit-per-channel data directly into Photoshop—you're effectively telling your scanner "just grab all the data you can capture"— and then edit it in Photoshop. In the 16-bit-per-channel space, you have much more editing headroom before you run into posterization. You won't have access to all Photoshop's tools in 16-bit-per-channel mode, but you'll probably have more tools than your scanner control software offers.

Minimize tonal correction. Small tonal moves are much less destructive than big ones. The more you want to change an image, the more compromises you'll have to make to avoid obvious posterization, artifacts due to noise, and loss of highlight and shadow detail.

Avoid successive corrections. Since multiple manipulations lose more data than a single change does, it's worth putting in a little extra work to create one tonal adjustment that does everything you want. This is almost always an iterative process (that means trial and error), but we'll show you how to refine your tonal adjustments while you experiment, without degrading the image.

Cover yourself. Since the data you lose is irretrievable, you should try to leave yourself a way out by working on a copy of the file, or by saving your tonal adjustments in progress separately, without applying them to the image (or both).

Data loss can be good. Sometimes you want to throw away information. For example, none of these restrictions applies when you're working on masks or alpha channels—in fact, you usually *want* to throw away data on those, since you're often trying to exaggerate a feature or isolate it from its background. (See "Step-by-Step Silhouettes" in Chapter 14, *Selections.*)

With these caveats in mind, let's look at Photoshop's tonal-manipulation tools.

Tonal-Correction Tools

Almost everything you need to do to tone and color your images can be accomplished using only four of Photoshop's tools.

▶ Histogram

▶ Info palette

▶ Levels dialog box

▶ Curves dialog box

The Histogram and Info palette let you analyze the image and the effect of your tonal manipulations. Levels and Curves are the tools you use to actually make the adjustments (if you're still using Brightness/Contrast, check out the sidebar "The Nonlinear Advantage," later in this chapter). These four tools simply offer different ways of viewing and changing the same data.

The Histogram

The Histogram is a simple bar chart that plots the levels from 0 to 255 along the horizontal axis, and the number of pixels at each level along the vertical axis (see Figure 6-6). If there are lots of pixels in shadow areas, the bars are concentrated on the left; the reverse is true with "high-key" images, where most of the information is in the highlights.

Some of the information offered by the histogram may not seem

Figure 6-6

Histogram dialog box

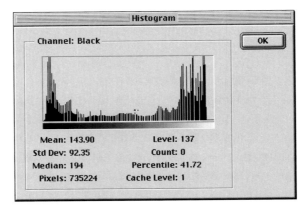

particularly useful—for normal image reproduction tasks you really don't need to know the median pixel value, or how many pixels in the image are at level 33. But histograms do show some very useful information at a glance.

Highlight and Shadow Clipping

With a quick look at the histogram, you can immediately see whether or not your scanner has clipped the highlights or shadows (see Figure 6-7). If there's a spike at either end of the histogram, the highlight or shadow values are almost certainly clipped—we say "almost" because there are some images that really do have a very large number of pure white or solid black areas. But they're pretty rare.

Figure 6-7

Highlight and shadow clipping

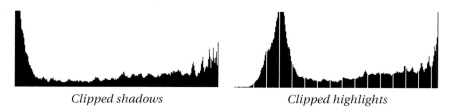

Clipped shadows   *Clipped highlights*

How Much Information Is Present

The overall appearance of the histogram also gives you a quick, rough-and-ready picture of the integrity of your image data (see Figure 6-8). A good scan uses the entire tonal range, and has a histogram with smooth contours. The actual location of the peaks and valleys depends entirely on the image content, but if the histogram shows obvious spikes, you're probably dealing with a noisy scanner. If it shows a comb-like appearance, it's likely that the image has already been manipulated—perhaps by your scanning software.

Figure 6-8

Comb-like histogram suggesting a noisy (or previously manipulated) image

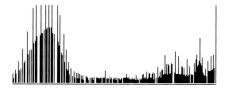

The histogram also shows you where to examine the image for signs that you've gone too far in your tonal manipulations. If you look at the histograms produced by the earlier experiment in applying gamma adjustments to a gradient, you can see at a glance exactly what each successive adjustment did to the image—spikes and gaps start to appear in the histogram.

Note that a gap of only one level is almost certainly unnoticeable in the image—especially if it's in the shadows or midtones—but once you start to see gaps of three or more levels, you may start to see visible posterization in the image. The location of the gap gives you a good idea of where in the tonal range the posterization is happening.

Histograms Are Generalizations

Once you've edited an image, the histogram may look pretty ugly. This is normal; in fact, it's almost inevitable. The histogram is only a guide, not a rule. Histograms are most useful for evaluating raw scans. A histogram will show clipped endpoints and missing levels, but a good-looking histogram isn't necessarily the sign of a good raw image. And an image with a bad histogram can still look good.

Fixing the histogram doesn't mean you've fixed the image. We have plenty of tricks that will make the histogram look better: smoothing out the peaks and filling in the gaps (resampling the image), or rotating the image clockwise, then counterclockwise by the same amount will do it, for example. But none of those tricks brings back image detail that was lost through overly aggressive tone manipulation. They just interpolate pixels in the missing levels, based on the data that's left. You can use these tricks to salvage a posterized image when there's really no other alternative, but it's better to avoid the posterization in the first place. Extract what useful information you can from the histogram, but don't let yourself be ruled by it.

Our next tool, however, is very specific. It tells you exactly what's happening to a specific pixel or group of pixels in the image.

Tip: Turn Off Use Image Cache For Histograms. In the Image Cache Preferences dialog box (press Command-K, then Command-8) Photoshop offers you an option labelled "Use Image Cache for Histograms." When this is on (it is by default) Photoshop displays histograms much faster; unfortunately, the histograms it gives you are of the antialiased screen display of your image. That means if you're working at a zoom level other than 100 percent, the histogram you see may be quite different from the histogram of your actual data. In particular, these histograms hide posterization, giving you an unrealistically rosy picture of your data. We recommend turning the option off, permanently.

The Info Palette

Like the Histogram, the Info palette is purely an informational display. It doesn't let you do anything to the image besides analyze its contents. But where the Histogram shows a general picture of the entire image, the Info palette lets you analyze *specific* points in the image.

When you move the cursor across the image, the Info palette displays the pixel value under the cursor, and its location in the image. More important, when you have one of the tonal- or color-correction dialog boxes (such as Levels or Curves) open, the Info palette displays the values for the pixel before and after the transformation (see Figure 6-9).

Figure 6-9
Info palette

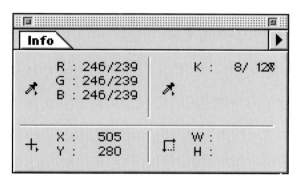

When you're working in one of the Image:Adjust dialog boxes, such as Levels or Curves, the Info palette shows the pixel value before and after the correction.

Tip: Look for Differences. The Info palette lets you sample the actual values of different pixels, but it also lets you hunt down hidden detail, particularly in deep shadows and bright highlights where it can be hard to see on the monitor. Move the cursor over a deep shadow, and watch the Info palette. If the numbers *change* as you move the cursor, there's difference lurking in there—it may be detail waiting to be exploited or it may be noise that you'll need to suppress, but *something* is hiding in there.

Palette Options

You can control what sorts of information the Info palette displays in one of two ways. First, you can select Palette Options from the Info palette's popout menu (see Figure 6-10). The second method is to use the Info palette's hidden popup menus (see Figure 6-11). We have several different palette setups that we use for different kinds of work, and we dearly wish

Figure 6-10

The Info palette's Info Options dialog box

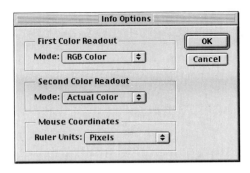

Figure 6-11

The Info palette's popup menus

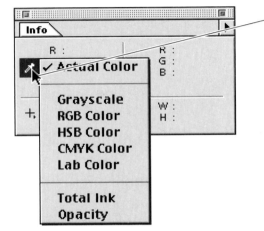

Click on the little arrow to bring up the Options menu.

we could save and load them. Alas, we still can't—maybe we'll be able to do so in Photoshop 6?

For grayscale, duotone, or multichannel images, we generally set the First Color Readout to RGB, and the Second Color Readout to Actual Color (Actual Color causes the readout method to change, depending on what type of image you're viewing). We almost always display the mouse coordinates as pixels, because it makes it easier for us to return consistently to the same spot in the image.

Why display RGB values for a grayscale image? Because it's the only way to display the values as levels from 0 to 255, the most precise display possible. The other options show percentages instead, on a scale of 100 instead of 255. The numbers for R, G, and B are always the same in a grayscale image, so the level just displays three times. Setting the second readout to Actual Color lets us read the dot percentage, so we can display levels

The Nonlinear Advantage

Linear transformations (such as those applied by Brightness and Contrast) throw away image information, and they do so in a pretty dumb way. They're called "linear transformations" because they do exactly the same thing to each pixel in the image. If you're trying to modify the brightness or contrast of an image, Brightness/Contrast is a bad approach, because you lose detail at one or both ends of the tonal range, and probably do severe violence to the image in the process.

For example, the Brightness control simply shifts all the pixel values up or down the tonal range. Let's say you increase Brightness by 10. Photoshop adds 10 to every pixel's value, so value 0 becomes 10, 190 becomes 200, and every pixel with a value of 245 or above becomes 255 (you can't go above 255). This is called "clipping the highlights" (they're all the same value, so there's no highlight detail). Plus, your shadows go flat because you lose all your true blacks.

The Contrast control stretches the tonal range when you increase the contrast, throwing away information in both highlights and shadows (and potentially posterizing the tones in between); and it compresses the tonal range when you reduce the contrast, so either way, you lose gray levels.

Don't use the Brightness and Contrast controls on images! You can use them to good effect with channels and masks, but that's another story; see Chapter 14, *Selections.*

The nonlinear transformations applied by Levels and Curves throw away some image information too (losing some highlight detail, in most cases), but they don't throw away nearly as much, and they do it in a much more intelligent way. They let you adjust the values in the middle of the tonal range without losing the information at the ends, so you can improve your images dramatically and still preserve important highlight and shadow detail.

Figure 6-12 Linear versus nonlinear correction

| Uncorrected | Brightened | Increased contrast | Corrected with Levels |

and percentages at the same time. We use different setups for working in color, which we'll cover in Chapter 7, *Color Correction.*

Now let's look at the tools we use to actually change the image.

Levels and Curves

Levels and Curves are the two Photoshop features that we use the most for global tonal and color correction. The Levels command is the easier of the two for beginning Photoshop users, and (in some situations) for experienced ones too. The Curves command is a little more difficult to master, but it's a lot more powerful once you've done so.

We liken Levels to an automatic transmission and Curves to a stick shift. Levels is quick and easy. Curves lets you do all the same things (and more) that you can do with Levels but it demands a bit more skill, coordination, and experience.

Levels and Curves both do the same thing—they let you apply transformations to the image that change existing (input) pixel values to new (output) pixel values—but they offer different ways of controlling the relationship between input and output.

They also share an important property that differentiates them from the Brightness and Contrast controls: they allow you to apply *nonlinear transformations*, as distinct from the linear transformations applied by the Brightness and Contrast controls (see sidebar, "The Nonlinear Advantage," earlier in this chapter).

Levels

Photoshop's Levels command opens a tonal-manipulation powerhouse. For grayscale images, it's often the only tonal-manipulation feature we use. This deceptively simple little dialog box lets us identify the shadow and highlight points in the image, limit the highlight and shadow dot percentages, and make dramatic changes to the midtones, while providing real-time feedback via the on-screen image and the Info palette. For color work, or for very detailed tonal corrections on grayscale images, we use the Curves command instead; but there are a couple of things that we can only do in Levels, and for a considerable amount of grayscale work, it's all we need (see Figure 6-13).

The Levels dialog box not only displays a histogram of the image, it lets you work with it in very useful ways. If you understand what the histogram shows, the workings of the Levels controls suddenly become a lot less mysterious.

Figure 6-13
How Levels works

This tonal range is being expanded...

This tonal range is being compressed...

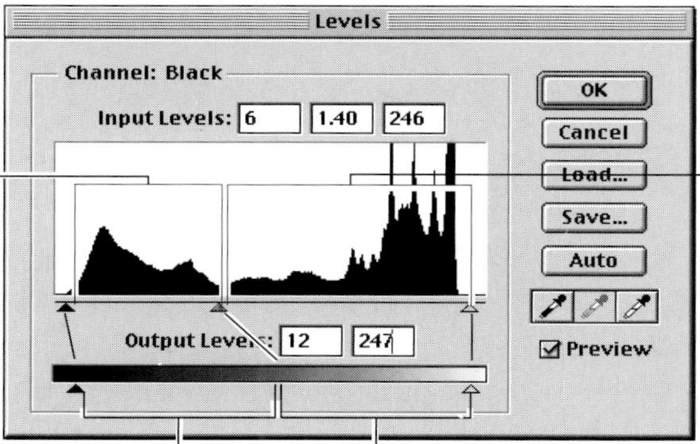

...to this range, spreading the pixels out and making them more different, so detail is more apparent.

...to this range, making the pixels more similar (and in some cases, identical), so detail is less visible or completely lost.

Input Levels

The three Input Levels sliders let you change the black point, the white point, and gamma in the image. As you move the sliders, the numbers in the corresponding Input Levels fields change, so if you know what you're doing, you can type in the numbers directly. But we still use the sliders most of the time, because they provide real-time feedback—by changing the image on screen—as we drag them. Here's what they actually do.

Black- and white-point sliders. Moving these sliders in toward the center has the effect of increasing the overall contrast of the image. When you move the black-point slider away from its default position at zero to a higher level, you're telling Photoshop to turn all the pixels at that level and lower (those to the left) to level 0 (black), and stretch all the levels to the right of the slider to fill the entire tonal range from 0 to 255.

A look at the histogram in Figure 6-14 shows that the tweak clips some extreme shadow details, but increases contrast and detail in the remaining shadows (as a result, a few gaps appear in the histogram).

Moving the white-point slider does the same thing to the other end of the tonal range. As you move it away from its default position at level 255 (white) to a lower level, you're telling Photoshop to turn all the pixels at that level and higher (those to the right of the slider) to level 255 (white), and stretch all the levels to the left of the slider to fill the entire tonal range from 0 to 255.

Figure 6-14 Black- and white-point tweaks

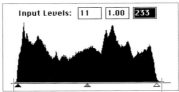

Input Levels: 11 1.00 233

*These pixels
go black . . .*   *. . . and these
                         go white.*

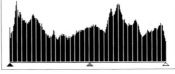

*Postcorrection histogram,
displaying some black- and
white-point clipping*

Gamma slider. The gamma slider lets you alter the midtones without changing the highlight and shadow points. When you move the gamma slider, you're telling Photoshop where you want the midtone gray value (50-percent gray, or level 128) to be. If you move it to the left, the image gets lighter, because you're choosing a value that's darker than 128, and making it 128. As you do so, the shadows get stretched to fill up that part of the tonal range, and the highlights get squeezed together (see Figure 6-15).

Conversely, if you move the slider to the right, the image gets darker because you're choosing a lighter value and telling Photoshop to change

Figure 6-15
Gamma tweak

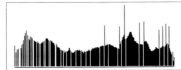

*Adding a gamma adjustment of 1.2 to
the image in the previous figure brings
out some shadow detail, though
highlight detail is lost, and the
histogram displays some
additional combing.*

it to level 128. The highlights get stretched, and the shadow values get squeezed together. (David likes to think of this as grabbing a rubber band on both ends and in the middle, and pulling the middle part to the left or right; one side gets stretched out, and the other side gets bunched up.)

The ultimate effect of changing gamma is to lighten or darken the midtones without affecting the extreme highlight and shadow points. If you make too large a gamma correction, you end up with obvious posterization where levels get stretched too far apart; but smaller moves (less than 1.4) are very effective. However, you're often forced to make larger corrections, especially with images from low-cost desktop scanners. That's just one of the many trade-offs you have to work with in digital imaging.

Output Levels

The Output Levels controls let you compress the tonal range of the image into fewer than the entire 256 possible gray levels. Mostly, they're useful for targeting—setting the maximum shadow and minimum highlight dot on grayscale images that don't contain any *specular highlights* (the small, very bright reflections you get from glass or highly polished metal). If you know that the press for which the image is destined can't hold a dot smaller than five percent, for example, you can compress the tonal range so that the brightest pixels have a value of level 242, which corresponds to a five-percent dot on the press.

When we have a color or grayscale image where we want small specular highlights to blow out to white paper, we use the black and white eyedroppers instead, and we use them later in the image-editing process (after sharpening). But even then, if we're dealing with a low-quality reproduction medium like newsprint—where the minimum highlight dot is more like 10 percent—we use the Output Levels sliders to do some preliminary tonal compression, then use the eyedroppers for fine tuning.

Black Output Levels. When this slider is at its default setting of 0, pixels in the image at level 0 will remain at level 0. As you increase the value of the slider, it limits the darkest pixels in the image to the level at which it's set.

This is different from the behavior of the black *Input* Levels control, which actually clips the data: if you set the black Input Levels slider to 5, then all pixels at levels 0 through 5 turn to level 0. If you set the black *Output* Levels slider to 5, on the other hand, the distinction between the levels is maintained; but the pixels that were at level 0 go to level 5, those at level 1 go to level 6 (or thereabouts), and so on. You lose contrast and

Figure 6-18

Curves dialog

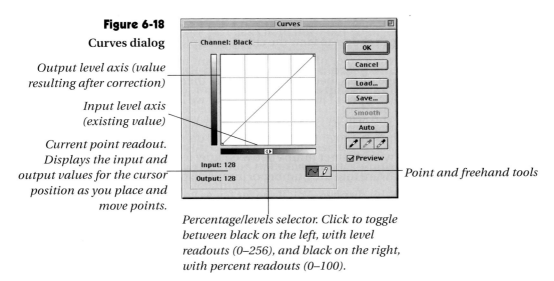

Output level axis (value resulting after correction)

Input level axis (existing value)

Current point readout. Displays the input and output values for the cursor position as you place and move points.

Point and freehand tools

Percentage/levels selector. Click to toggle between black on the left, with level readouts (0–256), and black on the right, with percent readouts (0–100).

Curves versus Levels. Anything you can do in the Levels dialog box, you can also do with Curves (see Figure 6-19). When you move the middle Input slider in Levels to adjust gamma, for instance, it's almost the same as moving the midpoint of the curve right or left. Setting the other four sliders is equivalent to setting the endpoints of the curve.

Figure 6-19

Levels and Curves

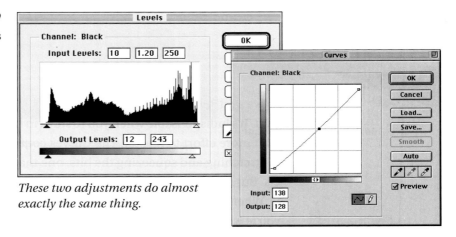

These two adjustments do almost exactly the same thing.

Tone curves are probably the most useful global image-manipulation tool ever invented—they're indispensable for color correction, but they're also very useful for fine control over grayscale work. Gamma corrections like the one in Levels let you change the broad distribution of midtones, but they only let you create very basic curves ("move the 50-percent point to here") with two endpoints and a single midpoint. The Curves command lets you make very precise adjustments to specific parts of the tonal range.

You change the relationship between input level and output level by changing the shape of the curve, either by placing points or by drawing a curve freehand (with the pencil tool). We vastly prefer placing points on the curve to drawing freehand, because it's much easier to be precise that way. All the settings you can make with Levels—white point, black point, midtones, maximum shadow, and minimum highlight—you can make with Curves too, but the way you go about it is slightly different.

Before we get into adjusting curves, though, there are a couple of ways to customize the Curves dialog box to your preferred way of working.

Tip: Customizing the Curves Dialog Box. Some people are happy thinking of tone in terms of levels from 0 to 255. Others want to work with dot percentages. The Curves dialog allows you to switch from one to the other by clicking the arrowheads in the middle of the gray ramp.

When you display levels, the 0,0 shadow point is at the lower left, and the 255,255 highlight point is at the upper right. When you display using percentages, the 0,0 highlight point is at the lower left and the 100,100 shadow point is at the upper right. You can switch freely between the two modes at any time.

Tip: Change the Grid. You can also change the gridlines of the Curves dialog box. The default displays gridlines in 25-percent increments, but if you Option-click anywhere in the graph area, the gridlines display in 10-percent increments instead (see Figure 6-20). We like the 10-percent increments because they give us a good idea of the percentages, even when we're displaying levels instead. But it doesn't really change the functionality of the controls.

Figure 6-20

Changing the grid in Curves

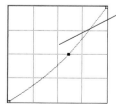

Option-click anywhere in the grid area to toggle between 25-percent and 10-percent gridlines.

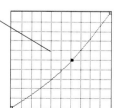

The curve. The great power of the Curves command comes from the fact that you aren't limited to placing just one point on the curve. You can actually place up to fourteen curve points, though we rarely need that many. This lets you change the shape of the curve as well as its steepness (remember, steepness is contrast; the steeper an area of the curve, the more definition you're pulling out between pixel values).

For example, an S-shaped curve increases contrast in the midtones, without blowing out the highlights or plugging up the shadows (see Figure 6-21). On the other hand, it sacrifices highlight and shadow detail by compressing those regions. We often use a small bump on the highlight end of the curve to stretch the highlights, or on the shadow end of the curve to open up the extreme shadows.

Figure 6-21

S-curves

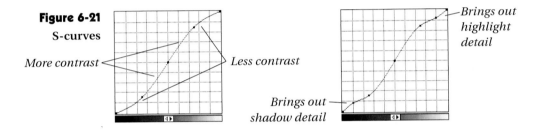

More contrast

Less contrast

Brings out highlight detail

Brings out shadow detail

The info readout. Whenever you move the cursor into the graph area, the Input and Output levels display at the bottom of the dialog box changes to reflect the cursor's x,y coordinates on the graph. For example, if you place the cursor at Input 128, Output 102 and click, the curve changes its shape to pass through that point, and the readouts become editable fields. All the pixels that were at level 128 change to level 102, and the rest of the midtones are darkened correspondingly (see Figure 6-22).

Figure 6-22

The numeric entry fields

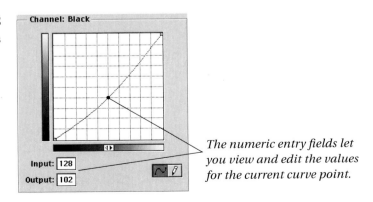

The numeric entry fields let you view and edit the values for the current curve point.

Taking the midpoint of the curve and moving it left or right is analogous to moving the gamma slider in Levels. You can follow the shape of the curve with the cursor, and watch the info readout to determine exactly what's happening to each level.

Handling black and white points. You can clip the black or white points by moving the endpoints of the curve horizontally toward the center of the graph (just like moving the Input sliders in Levels; see Figure 6-23). For instance, if you move the black end of the curve directly to the right so that the info readout reads Input 12, Output 0, you've clipped all the pixels at level 12 or below and made them all level 0. This is exactly the same as moving the black Input slider in Levels from 0 to 12.

Figure 6-23

Clipping and compressing in Curves

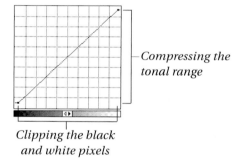

Compressing the tonal range

Clipping the black and white pixels

You can also limit the highlight and shadow dots by moving the endpoints of the curve vertically toward the center of the graph (like moving the Output sliders in the Levels dialog box). For example, to limit the highlight dot to 5 percent, move the highlight end of the curve until the Output Level displays as 243—or (if you're displaying percentages) 5 percent.

The eyedropper. While the Curves dialog box lacks the black and white clipping displays of Levels, it has an extra cool feature that shows you at a glance where any point in the image lies on the tonal curve. When the Curves dialog box is open, the cursor automatically switches to the eyedropper when you move it over the image. If you hold down the mouse button, the info display in the Curves dialog shows the Input and Output levels of the pixel(s) under the eyedropper, and a hollow white circle shows the location of that point on the curve (see Figure 6-24). This makes it very easy to identify the levels in the regions you want to change, and to see just how much you're changing them.

Figure 6-24

Curves dialog with eyedropper

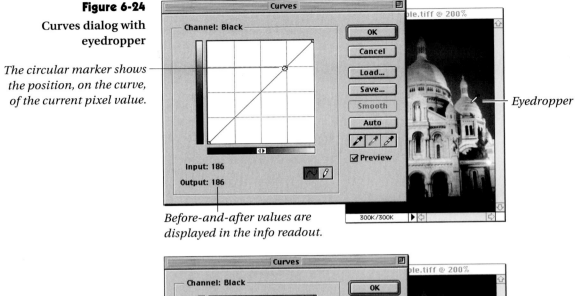

The circular marker shows the position, on the curve, of the current pixel value.

Eyedropper

Before-and-after values are displayed in the info readout.

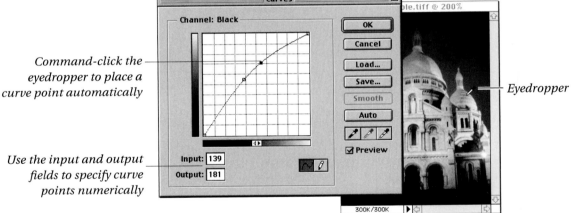

Command-click the eyedropper to place a curve point automatically

Eyedropper

Use the input and output fields to specify curve points numerically

For some reason the eyedropper feature doesn't work when you're adjusting the composite (CMYK) channel in a CMYK image, though it does when you adjust individual channels.

Automatic Curve Point Placement. One of the niftier new features in Photoshop 5 is automatic curve point placement. When you Command-click in the image, Photoshop automatically places a point on the curve for the input value of the pixel on which you clicked. Once the point is placed you can adjust it by dragging, or by using the following tip.

Tip: Numeric Curve Entry. Another nifty new feature in Curves is that you can specify curve points numerically. We use this in two ways:

▶ When we know the input and output values we want, we place a curve point by clicking anywhere on the curve, type in the input value, press Tab to move to the output field, and type in the output value.

▶ When we want to set a specific point in the image to a specific output value, we Command-click on the image to place the curve point, then we press Tab and type in the output value.

Other Curves command goodies. Like Levels, Curves has some hidden goodies. The Preview feature and the instant before-and-after work exactly the same as in Levels, with the same constraints, and the Option key provides the same auto-reset feature—Option-click Cancel to reset the curve.

We'll take you through the process of using Curves to correct an image a little later in this chapter, but first let's look at those oft-misunderstood little critters, the black and white eyedropper tools.

White Points and Black Points and Grays, Oh My!

Correcting images is only half the battle. You also have to target them—you have to compensate for the shortcomings of the output process the images are aimed at. If you're going to an output process other than halftone printing, targeting grayscale images is simply a matter of matching the contrast of your image to the contrast behavior of the output device. But when the image is destined for print, you have to do two things.

▶ Set the endpoints of the tonal range so that your highlights don't blow out and your shadows don't plug up.

▶ Adjust your midtones to compensate for dot gain on press.

You can build in these adjustments while you correct flaws in the image, or you can perform them as a separate step, after you've fixed all the other problems in the image.

Endpoints and limits. Some people use the terms "white point" and "minimum highlight," or "black point" and "maximum shadow" interchangeably. But an important distinction can be drawn between the two.

▶ White point and black point are defined by the image itself. They're simply the lightest and darkest pixels in the image, normally (but not always) levels 255 and 0, respectively.

▶ The minimum highlight and maximum shadow values, on the other hand, are dictated by the limitations of your output process. Each combination of printing press, ink, and paper has limits for both the smallest and largest dots it can print. Dots that are too small don't print (you get white paper instead), because the ink doesn't adhere to the plate. Dots that are too large simply plug up, and print as solid ink coverage. In either case, the detail in those areas is lost, because the differences between adjacent pixels are gone—they're all black or white.

Setting Endpoints with Levels

In many cases, we can simply set our white point to the value that we know will produce the minimum highlight dot, and our black point to the maximum shadow dot. With many images, however, the white and black points need to lie inside or outside of the printable range.

True blacks and whites. If the image has detail all the way up to the level-255 highlight and all the way down to the level-0 shadow, we can simply set these values to our minimum highlight and maximum shadow dots. To do so, we use the Output Levels sliders in Levels (see Figure 6-25).

For example, if we know that a particular press can handle a minimum highlight dot of five percent and a maximum shadow dot of 95 percent, we set the white Output slider to 243 and the black Output slider to 13.

Figure 6-25

Setting endpoints with Levels

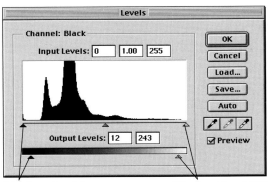

Pixels at level 0 change to level 13 (a 95-percent dot).

Pixels at level 255 change to level 243 (a 5-percent dot).

This ensures that all our gray values fall into the range the press can reproduce.

This approach works fine for many images, but it can cause difficulties with images that have important detail in the highlights or shadows.

Highlight problems. One source of trouble in setting the highlight is the *transition zone*—the point at which the press can no longer handle a dot and simply drops out to white paper. It's especially problematic with newsprint (or desktop laser printers), where the minimum dot is often quite large—in the region of 10 percent or so.

We see a lot of newspaper images where highlights on faces appear as large, leprous white patches, or where skies have huge white holes in them. The jump from white paper to a 10-percent dot is sudden and obvious, so when you're dealing with output that has a large minimum dot size, you often want to be a little more conservative and set the minimum dot even larger. The trade-off is that you lose contrast, because the brightest areas in the image are still being reproduced as a 10-percent gray (see Figure 6-26).

Figure 6-26
Trouble in the transition zone

Because of the sudden jump from no dot to a ten-percent dot, images printed to newsprint can display a severe case of "highlight psoriasis."
To emphasize the newsprint effect, we've printed this image with an 85-lpi screen.

Shadow problems. If you set the black point in your image to the maximum shadow dot, and the image has significant detail in the shadows stretching up through level 20 or so, the image will appear flat when it prints, because there will be very little true, solid black in the shadows.

You can deal with this using Levels by setting the black Output slider to a lower value than the maximum dot the press can produce. For example, if the press plugs up at anything over 85 percent, instead of setting the black Output slider to 38, you may want to set it to 35 instead.

Specular highlights. The compress-the-output-levels approach outlined above works well in many images, but it doesn't work well at all when the image contains small specular highlights—the very bright highlights that appear on shiny surfaces such as glass, metal, or a well-polished apple. If you compress this type of image with the normal output controls, you'll get a flat, low-contrast look. Your images will have much more snap on the page if you let those highlights blow out to white paper, rather than printing with the minimum dot. You want to reserve the minimum dot for those parts of the image that are very bright, but still contain some detail.

You can do this with the Output sliders in Levels, but not with any great degree of precision. If you set the white Output slider to a value a little higher than the minimum highlight dot, the very brightest pixels in the image will blow out to white paper. But you won't really know just how much highlight detail is going to blow out, or which parts of the image will actually print with the minimum highlight dot.

You can also run into problems with the transition zone in newsprint. The specular highlights *may* drop out to white. It's equally likely, though, that some will and some won't. Fortunately, Photoshop offers some more precise ways of setting endpoints; we'll look at those next.

Setting Endpoints with the Eyedropper Tools

When you're dealing with specular highlights, you want to set the minimum highlight dot to a level a little darker than the absolute whites in your image. You want the minimum highlight dot to reproduce the lightest parts of the image that still hold detail, and let the small specular highlights blow out to white paper.

The same holds true for deep shadows, though to a much lesser extent. In theory, the maximum shadow dot is the point at which the press plugs up the dots and prints solid ink. In practice, this isn't a hard-and-fast rule. If the press can only print a 95-percent dot and you have a few theoretically unprintable 97-percent dots sprinkled in your shadows, they'll probably provide a little more texture than if you simply set a 95-percent limit.

Photoshop's black and white eyedropper tools (in both the Levels and

Curves dialog boxes) let you set your minimum highlight and maximum shadow dots very accurately. These tools are shrouded in mystery, and provoke more than their fair share of confusion, in part because they can do so many things. For a detailed description of what the eyedroppers do, see the sidebar "The Math Behind the Eyedroppers," later in this chapter.

Eyedropper confusion. Many people find the eyedropper tools in the Levels and Curves dialog boxes so confusing that they give up on them after trying them once or twice. Others believe that they're as useless as Brightness and Contrast (until recently, we were in that camp). There are four sources for the confusion.

▶ The tools give misleading feedback. When you use them, they move the Levels sliders or change the endpoints of the curve in Curves. But those changes *don't reflect what the eyedroppers are really doing!* If you try to duplicate their effect by moving the sliders or changing the curve, you get a different result. This is incredibly frustrating, because you have to ignore the signals the dialog box is giving you.

▶ Using either eyedropper sets the tonal curve to a straight line, so if you make a Levels or Curves tweak and then use the eyedroppers, your tweak is immediately undone. If you use the eyedroppers first, and then do a Levels or Curves tweak, you're likely to change what you did with the eyedroppers!

▶ People keep trying to use these tools for tonal correction rather than targeting. Since they're really designed to make small tonal moves, the larger moves involved in tonal correction tend to push their limits.

▶ The tools live in the Levels and Curves dialog boxes, which apply non-linear transformations, but they apply a linear transformation. Nonetheless, this linear transformation is not necessarily bad.

This may make the eyedroppers sound almost useless, but if you understand how and when you should use them, they let you set your minimum and maximum dots very precisely.

What the eyedroppers do. The black, white, and gray eyedroppers do similar things, but each is specialized to operate on a different part of the tonal range. For now, we'll discuss the black and white eyedroppers. The gray eyedropper is a color-correction tool—it isn't available for grayscale images—so we'll deal with it in the next chapter, *Color Correction*.

Each eyedropper lets you choose a target color and a source color. All pixels in the image with the value of the source color are turned to the value of the target color, and all the other pixels in the image are changed proportionally. The black eyedropper operates on the shadows without affecting the highlights, while the white eyedropper operates on the highlights without affecting the shadows.

The advantage they offer over the other methods of tonal compression is that they let us set a specific pixel value *other than black or white* to the minimum and maximum dot values we know the press can hold. This allows us to hold detail in highlight areas while still letting our specular highlights blow out, and maintain texture in deep shadows without making them go flat.

Using the eyedroppers. You can use the eyedroppers from either the Levels or the Curves dialog box, but we prefer using Levels, because of the cool black-point/white-point clipping display in the Levels dialog box. This tool makes it much easier to identify good candidate values for black and white source colors, and to find pixels in the image that have those values.

1. Set the target value by double-clicking the black or white eyedropper, and entering the value in the color picker that appears. You can specify the color in any color space, but for grayscale images, just enter identical values for red, green, and blue.

   Set the target black and white colors to the maximum shadow and minimum highlight values that the output process can handle. For example, a target black value of 13 and a target white value of 243 correspond to a 95-percent maximum shadow dot and a minimum 5-percent highlight dot.

2. Option-drag the black or white Input Levels slider, and note the value at which detail starts to appear. Make sure you return the Input Levels sliders to their original places (at 0 and 255).

3. Now comes the tricky part: find a pixel in the image with that exact value, and click on it with the eyedropper. Photoshop changes that pixel to the output value, and compresses or expands the tonal range to compensate for that change.

The Math Behind the Eyedroppers

For the terminally curious, or for those who want to know exactly what will happen to each value in the image, this is what the two eyedroppers do.

White eyedropper. The white eyedropper simply multiplies all the pixels in the image by *target value ÷ source value*. For example, if we choose a target value of 243 (a five-percent dot), and click the tool on a pixel with a value of 248, all pixels at level 248 are turned to level 243. All the other values in the image are multiplied by 243/248, or approximately 0.98. So pixels with an input value of 255 produce an output value of 250, because 255 * 0.98 = 249.85. Pixels with an input value of 128 produce an output value of 125, and so on down the tonal range until we get to

level 25, which remains unchanged, because 25 * 0.98 = 24.5, which gets rounded back up to 25.

If we make a much smaller move by choosing a source value of 246 and a target of 243, the multiplier is 0.99, so an input value of 255 produces an output value of 253, 128 produces an output value of 127, and values below 50 remain unchanged.

Note that you can use the white eyedropper to stretch the highlights (rather than compressing them) by choosing a source color that's darker than the target color. This produces a multiplier with a value greater than 1, so the pixel values are increased rather than decreased.

Black eyedropper. The black eyedropper essentially does the

reverse of the white eyedropper, but the arithmetic is a little more complicated. To limit the effect to the shadows, the algorithm uses the inverse brightnesses of the input value and of the difference between source and target color— the inverse brightness of any value x is 255-x. If we call the difference between source and target values y, then for each pixel value x, the output value equals $((255-x) ÷ (255-y) * y) + x$.

If this makes your head hurt, don't worry—the net result is very similar to that produced by the white eyedropper, only in reverse. The source value is changed to the target value, and all other values in the image change proportionally, with the change becoming progressively smaller as you go toward the highlights.

This takes a little practice. Use the clipping display in Levels to get a general idea of where to look, check values in the Info palette as you go, and if necessary zoom in and out using Command-spacebar and Command-Option-spacebar or Command-plus and Command-minus.

Tip: Use a Gray Wedge to Select Your Source Color. It's easy to identify the value where your highlight detail really lies using the clipping display in Levels. It's much harder to find a pixel with that value to set as the source, using the eyedropper tool. Fortunately, you can pick up the source color for the eyedropper from any open image—it doesn't have to be in the active image.

To make it easy to find source values, keep a file containing a gray wedge open while you're targeting images.

1. Create a 300-pixel-wide, 72-ppi image, and use the Gradient tool to fill it with a ramp from black to white; turn off dithering first in the Gradient Tool Options palette.

2. Use the clipping display to identify the value you want to select for the source pixel. For this example, let's assume your highlight detail goes up to level 252.

3. Select an eyedropper and, while holding down the mouse button, drag the white eyedropper through the gray wedge until the Info palette reads 252. Release the mouse button, and you've picked up your source value. Just make sure you don't make the gray wedge the active image, or you'll change it instead of the image you were working on.

Tip: Keep the Mouse Button Down. If you're picking up the source value from the active image, it's still handy to hold down the mouse button while searching for the perfect pixel. When you find the one you want, you can just release the mouse button to select it. When the cursor hits the edge of the window, the image autoscrolls, which is sometimes useful.

Depending on where you click the eyedropper, the Input or Output sliders may move (or if you're in Curves, the endpoints of the curve may change). *Ignore this feedback*—it doesn't provide an accurate picture of what's going on. Trust the values in the Info palette instead.

If you don't like the result, or if you click on the wrong pixel by accident, you can click on another pixel to undo the bad tweak and apply another one. To undo both a black and a white eyedropper tweak, hold down the Option key to change the Cancel button in the dialog box to Reset. The changes aren't made permanent until you click OK to close the Levels (or Curves) dialog box.

Setting Endpoints with Curves

The beauty of using the white eyedropper tool to set the minimum highlight dot is that it lets values brighter than the one you select as the source

Figure 6-30 The lighthouse after correction with Levels

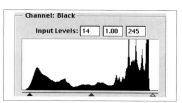

This Levels adjustment results in the image at left and the histogram below.

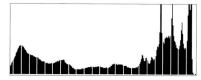

Figure 6-31 The lighthouse after targeting

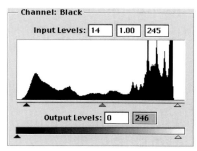

Our measured dot gain curve maps the highlights and shadows accurately to the dot limits, so we need to do relatively little in the way of targeting. We'll combine the targeting move with the tonal-correction move to minimize data loss.

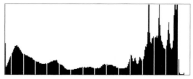

The final histogram after correction and targeting

Using the Info palette as our guide, we pull the white Output slider back to make sure that we hold a dot in the highlights. Setting the white Output slider to 246 gives us a 4% dot.

In this case we target the image with the fast-and-dirty approach: set the output sliders to compress the tonal range, and make a quick curve move to compensate for projected dot gain. But by being conservative in our compression, we can avoid graying out our whites and blacks and flattening the image excessively.

Correcting an Archival Image with Levels

The old photograph in Figure 6-32 presents more of a challenge. The picture of Bruce's grandmother is scanned using an Agfa Arcus Plus from a very old print (c. 1928) that has been stored for years under less-than-ideal conditions. The ink in the inscription is much darker than anything in the photograph itself, and insects have eaten through the emulsion in other areas to produce tiny white spots that are brighter than any real image detail. Together, they fooled the scanner's autoexposure algorithm into using a much wider tonal range than the image really contains, so the scan appears washed out even though the histogram shows some data

Figure 6-32 The uncorrected Ella scan

The black and white points for this scan were wide of the mark, resulting in an excessively flat image.

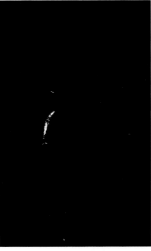

Shadow clipping at level 28   Highlight clipping at level 225

Figure 6-33 Ella corrected and targeted

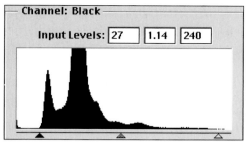

This Levels adjustment results in the image at left and the histogram below.

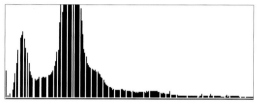

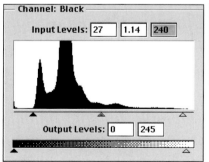

As with the lighthouse image, we combine the tonal correction with Output Level compression to hold a highlight dot, checking our highlight values with the Info palette. You can see the result in the image and histogram at right.

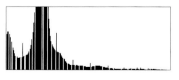

at almost every level. As with the lighthouse image, we apply a 1.8 gamma adjustment to the high-bit data at scan time.

The clipping display for this image tells a very different story. Setting the white Input slider to 240 creates small specular highlights on the bracelet, without clipping anything else in the image. At the shadow end, approximately the first 25 levels are taken up by the ink on the inscription. The darkest pixels in the image itself are in the shadows on the dress, but they also display the noise that's characteristic of flatbed scanners, so we set the black Input slider to level 27. A gamma tweak of 1.14 retrieves a little shadow detail.

If we were in a hurry, this is pretty much all we'd do to the images before sharpening and using the eyedroppers to fine-tune the endpoints. Given more time, we'd cancel out of the Levels dialog box and use Curves instead, remembering what we'd learned about the shadow and highlight values from the clipping display.

Deep Fixes with Curves

Levels lets you produce decent-quality images, but with Curves you can do much more. Curves lets you isolate specific parts of the tonal range and adjust them. Usually there's a trade-off involved—you emphasize some parts of the image at the expense of others. Learning how to manipulate images is easy; learning what needs to be done for each image is hard, and takes practice. The examples we give here are based on our subjective opinions; you may have different ideas on what we should have done.

Lighthouse. Our first three curve points establish the overall contrast. Remembering what we've learned from the clipping display in Levels, we clip the extreme shadows to add density to the blacks. The midtones are still too bright, so we darken them with a second point. This makes the whole image too dark, so a third point brings the midtones and highlights back to a reasonable range.

Our remaining points bring out specific features in the image. We Command-click on the whitecaps to place point 4, and on the water to place point 5, then move them apart to increase the contrast between the whitecaps and the water. This drastically blows out the highlights, so we add point 6 by Command-clicking the bright area on the lighthouse. We pull it back to 240 to bring some detail back into the highlights.

Figure 6-34 Correcting the lighthouse with Curves

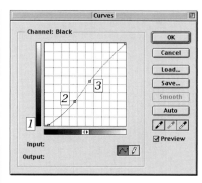

Point 1. 11 in, 0 out. Gives us solid black in the shadows.

Point 2. 94 in, 74 out. Brightens the midtones on the rocks.

Point 3. 141 in, 137 out. Brings the highlights back under control.

Point 4. 161 in, 192 out. Brightens the whitecaps.

Our first three curve points establish the overall contrast. We clip the shadows slightly (1) to get solid blacks and disguise noisy pixels, then darken the midtones (2), concentrating on the rocks. This makes the sky too dark, so we use point (3) to bring the highlights back into a reasonable range. Curve points 4 and 5 increase the separation between the whitecaps and the water.

Brightening the whitecaps blows out all our highlights, so we add point 6 to bring the highlights on the lighthouse down to a manageable level. Point 7 darkens the sky a little further, and adds some solidity to the shadow on the lighthouse.

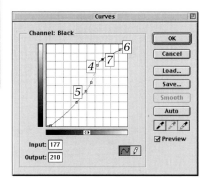

Point 7. 177 in, 210 out. Darkens the sky and strengthens the shadow on the lighthouse.

Point 6. 233 in, 240 out. Corrects for point 4, bringing the highlights back under control.

Point 5. 124 in, 110 out. Darkens the water.

We're left with a tight kink in the curve, so we add point 7 by Command-clicking the shadow on the lighthouse, and pull it back to level 210 to add some solidity to the shadow, and to darken the sky.

Clicking on the title bar of the Curves window to get a quick before-and-after, we can see that we've improved the contrast in almost all areas. The rocks have solidity, and the whitecaps on the waves snap. The image is now ready for sharpening and targeting with the eyedroppers.

Your's Ella. Remembering what we saw in the Levels clipping display, we set the endpoints of the curve first. In this case we clip both the shadows and the highlights considerably because they contain no real image information (dealing, we hope, with any scanner-induced noise that may have been lurking in the shadows). We make sure that our highlight detail is still well below level 250, so we can target it later. A third curve point deepens the shadows, improving the overall contrast.

Three further moves go after specific areas in the image. The first increases contrast in the face, but it makes the highlights on the shoulder a little hot. If this were a modern image, we might let it go, but part of the charm of this photograph is its obvious age. We don't want to make the contrast too harsh, so our fifth curve point pulls back the highlights on the shoulder. A quick before-and-after obtained by clicking on the title bar shows us that we've lost some contrast around the left eye, so our final move lightens that side of the face slightly, and improves its contrast with the background.

Save the Curves

We're done with the curves for now—this is as close as we can get without pulling a proof. But before we press OK to apply them to the image, we save the final curve by pressing the Save button. Because we're working on a copy of the image, if something goes wrong or we decide that some of the changes aren't quite to our liking, we can go back to the original file and load this curve as a new starting point.

After we see proofs, we may want to make some changes, and these are better made by going back to the original data and modifying the curve. A look at the histograms reveals why. We already have some gaps of more than one level; so if we want to do more manipulation, we're better off going back to the original eight bits, rather than stretching and squeezing the remaining ones even further (see figure 6-36).

Figure 6-35 Ella corrected with Curves

Point 3. 52 in, 23 out.
Darkens the background.

We clip the highlights (1) to 250 (the lightest point on the shoulder, reserving the higher levels for the small specular highlights on the bracelet), and the shadows (2), spreading the real image information across the tonal range, and increasing contrast. Point 3 deepens the shadows, so that the darkest areas are almost the same shade as the ink of the inscription.

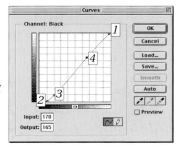

Point 4 lightens the face and also increases its contrast—too much, in fact. It also makes the highlights on the shoulder uncomfortably hot. Point 5 pulls back the highlights on the shoulder, and softens the contrast on the face, producing a result we feel is more in keeping with the photograph's obvious age. Point 6 produces just a hair more contrast on the shadowed side of the face, bringing out the sparkle in the eyes.

Point 1. 250 in, 255 out. Clips and brightens the highlights.

Point 2. 28 in, 0 out. Clips unwanted noise and creates true blacks.

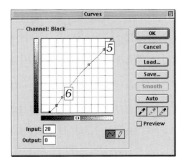

Point 6. 73 in, 51 out. Emphasizes the catchlight in the right eye.

Point 4. 170 in, 165 out. Brightens the lighter tones of the face and increases its contrast.

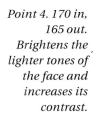

Point 5. 225 in, 219 out. This pulls back the highlights on the shoulder.

Figure 6-36

Histograms of
corrected lighthouse
and Ella images

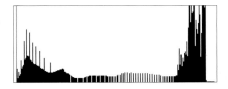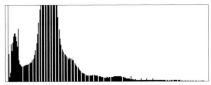

Sharpen Before Final Tonal Compression

Every scanned image needs some unsharp masking, and it's a rich and complex enough subject that we've devoted an entire chapter to it later in the book. For now, trust us on the sharpening we apply to the two images before we do final tonal compression.

Figure 6-37

Sharpening settings
for lighthouse and
Ella images

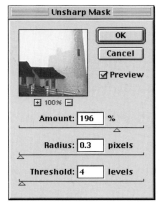

The lighthouse image both needs and benefits from considerably more sharpening than the studio portrait, which we deliberately leave soft since it preserves more of the feel of the original. Note that we also use a much smaller sharpening radius for the lighthouse image, because it contains more small details than the portrait.

Final Compression with the Eyedroppers

You can use the eyedroppers from either the Levels or Curves dialog box, but we always use Levels, because we find the clipping displays indispensable. We use them to check where our highlight and shadow details really are after sharpening.

We set the highlight target for a four-percent dot (our printer told us that they could probably hold a three-percent dot, but we decided to err on the side of caution), and set the shadow target for a 96-percent dot.

Figure 6-38

Setting eyedropper targets

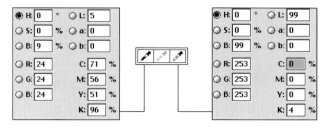

If you have Grayscale setup set to Black Ink, the fast, easy way to set the eyedropper targets for grayscale print work is to use the K field in the CMYK color picker. .

The moves we make with the eyedroppers are small and have a barely perceptible effect on the images overall, but they let us nail the extremes of the tonal range precisely.

Figure 6-39 Lighthouse, sharpened and targeted

We need to set 4 percent as the source value for the white eyedropper, because that's what our press can hold. The edge of the middle attic window has several pixels in the 0-3 percent range, so we zoom into that area, find a 3-percent pixel along the edge of the window, and click on it. We may end up with a very few pure white highlights, but we've ensured that anything that contains detail will print with a dot. Repeating the process for the black eyedropper, we click on a 98-percent pixel in the extreme shadow along the left side of the image.

Tonal Magic

Levels and Curves are real powerhouses, and becoming fluent with them is key to mastering Photoshop's production capabilities. We've introduced these tools by looking at grayscale manipulation, but they play an even more important role in color correction.

Figure 6-40

Ella, sharpened
and targeted

We want to make sure that we hold a dot in the skin tones, but we also want the specular highlight on the bracelet to blow out to white paper, so we choose a 3-percent pixel in the necklace as the source color, forcing it to 4 percent. This ensures that the only area in the image that won't hold a dot on press is the small specular highlight on the bracelet.

When you correct color, you're still stretching and squeezing 8-bit grayscale channels; but you're working with several channels simultaneously, so it's a lot more complex. If you master the operation of the tools thoroughly in grayscale, the color-correction techniques we present in the next chapter will come much more easily.

Color Correction

Thinking in RGB and CMYK

If you opened this book and went straight to this page looking for easy answers, stop. Go directly to jail. Do not pass Go. Do not collect $200. While you're in jail, you should take some time and read through a few other chapters.

First off, take a look at Chapter 4, *Color Essentials*. Then, if you're looking to convert your image from RGB to CMYK, or if you're trying to make decisions based on what you see on the monitor, or if you're confused about the brave new world of color management systems and device profiles, you're going to need to know about RGB Setup, CMYK Setup, Grayscale Setup, and Profile Setup (so go read Chapter 5, *Color Settings*). And when you make color corrections in Photoshop, you're really manipulating the tone of the individual color channels, so you need to understand how to tweak grayscale images before you touch color ones—they're at least nine times more complicated! (So you'd better read the last chapter, *Tonal Correction*, too.)

That said, if you want to plunge in, go ahead. Just bear in mind that when things get sticky, you may want to refer back to those chapters to get a better handle on what you've actually been doing.

Changing Modes and Losing Information

We've stressed throughout this book that almost everything you do to an image in Photoshop throws away some information. But a great many people, including some of the so-called experts, don't realize that switching to a different color mode throws away information faster than just about anything else.

The subject of mode conversion is surrounded by confusion and by more than its share of mythology. We'll discuss the arguments in detail throughout this chapter, but let us say up front that mode changes (color-space conversions) lose considerable amounts of information, no matter which color space you're going to or from (with one exception—the conversion from grayscale to RGB). Mode changes between RGB and Lab, Lab and CMYK, and RGB and CMYK all discard image information to a greater extent than most people realize.

RGB to Lab

There's a general impression in the Photoshop community that you can switch between RGB and Lab color without losing significant amounts of image information. Until we did some real tests, we shared this assumption, but we were surprised to find that the conversion between RGB and Lab is far from lossless. You lose a significant number of differences between levels—remember, difference is detail.

For instance, try converting an RGB step wedge to Lab—one quick, simple selection from the Mode menu—and examine the results: *about 35 of the possible 256 levels simply disappear* (see Figure 7-1). This loss may not be visually significant—you can't see it on the screen, and you're unlikely to see it in print—but if you try to stretch the now-degraded tonal range after the conversion, it will start to show up as posterization.

Figure 7-1
RGB-to-Lab-to-
RGB data loss

Histogram of a gray wedge in RGB mode (not terribly interesting)

Histogram of gray wedge after RGB-to-Lab-to-RGB conversion

The gaps in the histogram show unused levels after RGB-to-Lab mode conversion, but they don't tell the whole story about the loss of image information. The spikes in the histogram indicate where values have been rounded (made the same). These also represent loss of image detail. It may not have been visible detail, but it was there waiting to be exploited, and perhaps made visible. Now it's gone, never to return.

CMYK and Lab

The conversion from CMYK to Lab (and vice versa) loses a little more information than from RGB to Lab, and the pattern is a little different (see Figure 7-2). You're likely to get subtle color shifts, in addition to losing tonal distinctions. Basically, you get more rounding errors switching between a three-channel and a four-channel color space than you do switching between two three-channel color spaces.

Figure 7-2

Data loss when going from CMYK -to-Lab-to-CMYK

A gray wedge histogram looks like this after CMYK-to-Lab-to-CMYK conversion.

RGB to CMYK

Converting an image from RGB to CMYK in Photoshop—the most common and necessary of conversions—loses a lot of image information (see Figure 7-3). It has to. The RGB color space contains 16.7 million colors, of which (at most) a few thousand are printable using four-color process printing. When the conversion is done right, the printed CMYK piece will bear a reasonably close resemblance to the RGB image on the screen, even though it contains far fewer colors, a smaller dynamic range, and a much narrower color gamut (see the sidebar, "CMYK Myths," later in this chapter).

Figure 7-3

Data loss in RGB-to-CMYK conversion

The best you can hope for in the RGB-to-CMYK conversion is a perfect translation of the RGB original squeezed into the smaller gamut of press-ready CMYK. You may not get even that, because Photoshop's Classic Separation engine tends to clip out-of-gamut colors during the conversion rather than compressing the whole gamut proportionally. (This is a crucial concept which we discuss in more detail in "Gamut compression and gamut clipping," later in this chapter.) You lose differences between colors, and as we've said several times, difference is detail.

RGB to RGB

The only real drawback to Photoshop 5's implementation of an RGB working space is that we're now faced with the necessity of converting both our legacy images and our new scans into our chosen working space. Like other color space conversions, this one too involves some data loss, and unfortunately, you're forced to do the conversion right at the start of the editing process, when you open the file.

How much data loss are we talking about? It depends on the specific RGB spaces you're converting from and to. Figure 7-4 shows the histograms of some typical conversions.

Figure 7-4
Data loss in
RGB-to-RGB
conversions

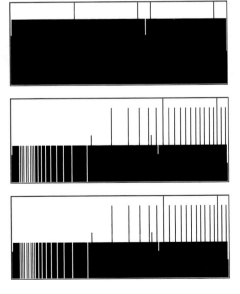

A gray wedge histogram after conversion from AppleRGB to ColorMatch RGB.

A gray wedge histogram after conversion from AppleRGB to BruceRGB.

A gray wedge histogram after conversion from AppleRGB to Adobe RGB (1998), (formerly incorrectly known as SMPTE-240M).

Figure 7-4

Data loss in RGB-to-RGB conversions, cont'd

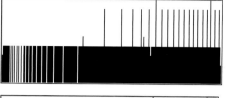

A gray wedge histogram after conversion from ColorMatch RGB to BruceRGB.

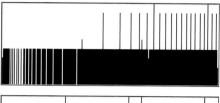

A gray wedge histogram after conversion from ColorMatch RGB to Adobe RGB (1998).

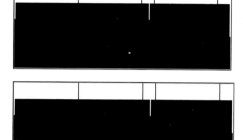

A gray wedge histogram after conversion from sRGB to Adobe RGB (1998).

A gray wedge histogram after conversion from sRGB to BruceRGB.

Some of the histograms in Figure 7-4 look scarier than others, and some don't look scary at all. The loss occurs when there's a mismatch between the gammas of the two RGB spaces involved: going between two gamma 1.8 spaces, such as Apple RGB and Colormatch RGB, or between two gamma 2.2 spaces, such as Adobe RGB (1998) and BruceRGB, is practically, if not theoretically, lossless. We discuss several ways to avoid losing data when bringing new scans into the working space in Chapter 13, *Capturing Images.* The main concern is with gamma 1.8 legacy files, and it applies only to Mac users and to those rare Windows users who calibrate their monitors to a gamma of 1.8.

We're pretty strong advocates of gamma 2.2 for editing spaces, because it's more perceptually uniform than gamma 1.8, and it devotes more bits to the shadows, which is usually where we need them. But there's no getting around the fact that converting a gamma 1.8 image into a gamma 2.2 working space loses some data, though not nearly as much as an actual Mode change. Most Windows users' legacy images are already in a gamma 2.2 space, so they don't have a problem.

Bruce's legacy images were all in ColorMatch RGB, and he's routinely been converting them into either BruceRGB or Adobe RGB (1998). He's run into a few images that were too far gone to withstand the transformation—they'd already been heavily edited, or were marginal to begin with—and for those, he's switched back to ColorMatch RGB. But for the vast majority, he feels the benefits of the gamma 2.2 spaces outweigh the one-time hit. Make your own call, but unless your images are on the verge of posterization already, we think the loss is a worthwhile trade-off.

RGB versus CMYK

The debate over whether to work in RGB or CMYK has been the subject of countless magazine articles, several online flame wars, and even a few books. Of course, if your work is destined for a film recorder, the computer screen, or videotape, then CMYK is quite irrelevant; but if you're working in the print medium, it's very important indeed.

Some experts go so far as to say that if your work is destined for print, you should work exclusively in CMYK. When confronted, they usually give four reasons for this.

▶ It's the only color space that matters.

▶ RGB is meaningless.

▶ Monitor calibration is inherently impossible.

▶ All that matters are the CMYK dot percentages.

While all these points have some validity, we beg to differ with the philosophy as a whole. As we've noted before, when all you have is a hammer, everything starts to look like a nail. People who tell you to do everything in CMYK undoubtedly have excellent traditional prepress skills and a deep understanding of process-color printing, but they just don't realize how much image information Photoshop loses during the conversion, and they probably are not comfortable working in RGB.

As a result, they convert raw scans (or even worse, badly acquired Photo CD images) to CMYK immediately, damaging the scan irretrievably. Then they make huge corrections in CMYK, trying to salvage a printable image from what's left. Once they're done, they congratulate themselves on

CMYK Myths

One of the reasons we wrote this book was to dispel a number of myths that have cropped up during the short life of desktop prepress (and some others that have been around even longer)—especially those regarding CMYK and RGB issues. Here are our answers to two common areas of confusion.

CMYK has more colors (false).

We've heard experts deride the notion that CMYK contains fewer colors than RGB. "Do the math, stupid," they say. "CMYK has 256^4, or more than 4 *billion* colors." We wish that were the case. CMYK has more than 4 billion color *specifications*, but a large number of them are simply alternate ways of specifying the *same* color using a different balance of black to CMY inks. And many of them (for example, 90C 90M 90Y 100K) are "illegal" specifications that would turn the paper into a soggy mess scattered all over the pressroom floor. When you also take into account the constraints imposed by the black-generation curve and the total ink limit, you end up with far fewer colors than RGB.

CMYK is more accurate (true, sort of).

Other experts say, "CMYK may have a narrower gamut, but the data points in CMYK are packed much closer together than they are in RGB, so CMYK specifies colors *more accurately* than RGB."

Here they have a point. You *can* specify smaller differences between colors in CMYK than you can in RGB, because the same number of bits are being used to describe a smaller color gamut. (Whether these smaller color differences are detectable by the human eye is a question we'll leave to someone willing to carry out the empirical research.)

But this is only relevant if your RGB original is being converted to CMYK by a scanner (probably a drum scanner) that captures 12 bits of data per color, and uses them *all* in the RGB-to-CMYK conversion. If you use Photoshop to do the conversion, you won't gain any accuracy, because all Photoshop has to start with is 8-bit-per-channel RGB data. It can't get any better in the conversion—only worse.

---

their exquisite skills while pointing out the limited quality you can attain with desktop color.

These limits are self-imposed and largely illusory. If you follow these people's recommendations, you too will throw away about a third of your image right off the bat; then you'll be able to labor mightily, use all sorts of nifty tricks, and be rewarded with mediocre results for your efforts.

We have a very simple rule: *Don't change color spaces unless or until you have to, and do as much of your correction as possible in the image's original color space. The ideal number of color-space conversions is one or none.*

All images ultimately come from an RGB source, so even if the desired end result is a set of CMYK separations, you should do as much of your image correction as possible in the RGB file. This is not a universally accepted view, but we believe that the arguments in its favor are compelling. When you prematurely convert to CMYK, you restrict yourself in at least five ways.

▶ You lose a great deal of image information, making quality tonal and color correction much more difficult.

▶ You target the image for a particular set of press conditions (paper, press, inks, etc.). If press conditions change, or if you want to print the image under various press conditions, you're in a hole that's difficult to climb out of.

▶ Because the CMYK image is targeted to specific output conditions, it's much more difficult to proof on color printers than it is with a repurposable RGB image.

▶ You increase your file size by a third, slowing most operations by that same amount.

▶ You lose several convenient Photoshop features that only work in RGB, such as the Levels clipping display (see "Levels," later in this chapter).

More important, correcting images in RGB prior to CMYK conversion just plain works.

For the vast majority of Photoshop users, that means working in RGB for as long as possible, and only converting your image to CMYK after you're finished with your other corrections. There's no doubt that it's important to keep an eye on the CMYK dot percentages while you work, but you don't need to work in CMYK to do that—they're always available in the Info palette, even when you're working in RGB.

We're not saying that you should never make corrections in CMYK—far from it. Your CMYK separations will often benefit from fine-tuning. Editing the black plate is a particularly powerful technique, but it's most effective as a fine-tuner, making small moves. Similarly, Hue/Saturation changes in CMYK are generally more delicate than in RGB. If you work in print, you must learn to edit in CMYK. But it isn't the only game in town.

When to Use CMYK

If your images come from a traditional drum scanner in CMYK form, it makes no sense to convert them to RGB for correction. You should stay in CMYK. If you find that you have to make major corrections, though, you'll almost certainly get better results by rescanning the image instead of editing it in Photoshop. In high-end prepress shops, it's not unusual to scan an image three times before the client signs off on it.

Tip: Ask for RGB. Color houses are so used to providing CMYK scans that they sometimes forget that their high-end drum scanners are actually reading RGB values, which an internal color computer is converting to CMYK on the fly. These color computers are usually set to make a better CMYK conversion than Photoshop's defaults will, but productivity, not quality, is the main reason color houses use them.

But if you're going to be manipulating the image yourself in Photoshop, or need an image that can be targeted to multiple devices or press conditions, you can ask the shop to save the image in RGB format. They may tell you they can't do it, but a growing number of color houses are now RGB-capable. Of course, you're then responsible for correcting the color balance and making the conversion to CMYK.

When you start with RGB images, certain kinds of fine-tuning, such as black-plate editing, can *only* be done on the separated CMYK file. But if you find yourself needing to make large moves in CMYK after a Photoshop mode change, it's time to look at your Color Settings: RGB Setup, CMYK Setup, and Profile Setup, because the problem probably lies there (see Chapter 5, *Color Settings*). In that case, it makes more sense to go back to the RGB original and reseparate it using new settings that get you closer to the desired result.

If all you have is a CMYK file, work in CMYK if at all possible. In dire emergencies, such as when you have a CMYK file targeted for newsprint and you want to reproduce it on glossy stock, you *may* want to take the desperate step of converting it back to RGB, applying corrections, and reseparating to CMYK; but in general, you should view RGB to CMYK as strictly a one-way trip.

Tip: CMYK to RGB. We can think of two reasons to convert a CMYK image to RGB: You need to prepare an image for the web or multimedia, and a CMYK scan is all you have, or you need to repurpose the CMYK image for a larger-gamut output process. In either case, you need to expand the tonal range and color gamut—if you just do a mode change from CMYK to RGB, you'll get a flat, lifeless image with washed-out color, because the tonal range and color gamut of the original were compressed in the initial RGB-to-CMYK conversion, and a Photoshop Mode change always tries to reproduce the compressed gamut and squashed tonal range faithfully in RGB.

We used to resort to some insane workarounds that involved telling Photoshop major untruths. Fortunately, that's no longer necessary, because we can now use the Profile-to-Profile command to do the transformation using a perceptual rendering, with Black Point Compensation turned on. But there's a trick involved: if you simply choose From: CMYK Color and To: RGB Color, the rendering intent and Black Point Compensation options aren't available. You need to create an ICC profile of your CMYK Setup (if it isn't one already), and choose it by name in the From: field. (If you really want to know why this is the case, see "Profile-to-Profile" in Chapter 5, *Color Settings*.) You'll find it works surprisingly well.

That said, this is a last-resort technique. Work on a copy of the file, and watch for color shifts and posterization.

When to Use RGB

If your image comes from an RGB source, such as a desktop scanner or a digital camera, you should do as much of your work as possible in RGB. The files are smaller, so your work goes faster, and you have the entire tonal range and color gamut of the original at your disposal, allowing you to exploit the small differences between pixels that you want to emphasize in the image. It's also much easier to repurpose RGB images for different kinds of output than it is to do so with CMYK.

RGB has some less obvious advantages, as well. Some features (such as the clipping display in Levels) are only available in RGB, not in CMYK. And when you work in RGB, you have a built-in safeguard: it's impossible to violate the Black and Total Ink Limit values you specify in CMYK Setup (because they'll always be imposed when you convert to CMYK).

When you edit CMYK files directly, you have no such constraint—you can build up so much density in the shadows using Levels or Curves that you're calling for 400-percent ink coverage. On a sheetfed press, this will create a mess. On a web press, it will create a potentially life-threatening situation! In any case, it's something to avoid unless you're printing to the rare desktop color printer that can handle 400-percent total ink.

Even if you prefer using a different program to create separations, you'll find that Photoshop is just about the best image editor around, but frankly, Photoshop now offers so many different separation options that we find little reason to use anything else.

Image Correction and Targeting

In Chapter 6, *Tonal Correction,* we drew the distinction between correction and targeting. Correction is the process of compensating for flaws in the original and for distortions introduced in the image-capture process. Targeting compensates for the shortcomings of the output process.

The distinction is less important than it used to be. Photoshop now handles targeting of grayscale images for press output the same way it handles targeting of color images, automatically. If you're using dot gain curves or a good ICC profile, Photoshop will do a pretty good job of setting the endpoints to the print process's minimum and maximum dot. This can be both a blessing and a curse, as we'll see.

Correcting Color Images

Correcting color images is very much like correcting grayscale images, but with a catch. You're still stretching and squeezing the bits, but you're doing so on three (RGB) or four (CMYK) channels instead of only one, so it's nine or sixteen times more complicated!

The classic order for preparing color images for print is as follows.

1. Spotting, retouching, dust and scratch removal.

2. Global tonal correction.

3. Global color correction.

4. Selective tonal and/or color correction.

5. Targeting (sharpening, handling out-of-gamut colors, compressing tonal range, converting to CMYK).

We generally adhere to this, but it depends on the image and on the quality of the image capture. For instance, you often have to lighten an image before you can even consider retouching it.

And sometimes it's impossible to separate tonal correction and color correction. Changes to the color balance affect tonal values too, because you're manipulating the tone of the individual color channels. For example, if you add red to neutralize a cyan cast, you'll also brighten the image because you're adding light. If you reduce the green to neutralize a green cast, you'll darken the image because you're subtracting light. In any case, we try wherever possible to make a single set of curve adjustments that take care of all the global problems.

Fix the biggest problem first. The rule of thumb we've developed over the years is simple: *fix the biggest problem first*. This is partly plain common sense. You often have to fix the biggest problem before you can even see what the other problems are. But it's usually also the most effective approach, the one which requires the least work, and the one that degrades the image the least.

With many desktop flatbed scanners—especially 8-bit scanners—the biggest problem is usually that the midtones and shadows are too dark, so we start with global tonal correction. If, on the other hand, we're faced with a badly acquired Photo CD image, the overall tone may be fine, but the image will have a global color cast which we go after first. With a purely synthetic image bound for a printing press, such as one created by a 3D rendering program, we might first desaturate the whole image a little.

Tip: Look at the Image Before You Start. This may seem obvious, but stop for a moment. Look at the image carefully. Zoom to 100% and look at every pixel. Have you missed dust or scratches? Are there particularly noisy areas that might cause problems? Look at each channel individually. Are there details (or defects) lurking in one channel that are absent from others? Is noise concentrated in one channel? (It's usually most prevalent in the blue.) Look at the histogram. Is the image using the full tonal range? If not, should it? A few minutes spent critically evaluating the image can save hours later on. Develop a plan, and stick to it unless it obviously isn't working (in which case, see below).

Tip: Leave Yourself an Escape Route. The great Scots poet Robert Burns pointed out that the best-laid plans o' mice and men gang aft agley. He didn't have the benefit of the History palette, or the Undo and Revert commands, but you do. History is a great feature, but it's a RAM-hog, and eventually it starts dropping states, so foster good habits. If a particular move doesn't work, just undo (Command-Z)—you can reload Levels, Curves, Brightness/Contrast, Color Balance, and Hue/Saturation with the last-used settings by holding down the Option key while selecting them either from the menu or with a keyboard shortcut. If a whole train of moves has led you down a blind alley, revert to the original version.

If you're working on a complex or critical problem, work on a copy of the image. When you apply a move using Levels, Curves, or Hue/Saturation, save it before you apply it. That way, you can always retrace your steps up to the point where things started to go wrong.

Photoshop's Adjustment Layers feature lets you avoid many of the pitfalls we've just discussed. You don't need to get your edits right the first time because you can go back and change them at will. You automatically leave yourself an escape route because your edits float above the original image rather than being burned into them, and it really doesn't matter what order you choose to make the edits in, because they'll all be applied simultaneously when you flatten the image.

But sometimes it's impractical to use Adjustment Layers because of RAM constraints, and to use Adjustment Layers effectively, you need to know how the various controls operate on a flat file. So even if you plan to use Adjustment Layers for as much of your editing as possible—and we encourage you to do so—you still need to master the techniques we discuss in this chapter, and the pitfalls they entail. For a much more thorough discussion of Adjustment Layers, see Chapter 8, *The Digital Darkroom.*

Targeting Color Images

As with grayscale images, you can choose to separate the process of correcting color images from that of targeting them, or you can do both at once. The trade-off is speed versus flexibility. If you target an image, it's often difficult to reproduce satisfactorily using a different output process.

You may be able to convert a magazine separation for newsprint, but going the other way is likely to be a nightmare, because you've compressed the image into the small gamut of newsprint. And repurposing a newsprint separation for output to a continuous-tone film recorder is well-nigh impossible. If you try to stretch the tonal range back to the gamut of film, it will probably fall apart; and if you don't try, it'll be flat and lifeless (see Figure 7-6 on page 270, and "Tip: CMYK to RGB," earlier in this chapter).

So if you think you may want to use the image for more than one kind of output, you should treat correction and targeting as two separate processes: you can save the corrected image while still in RGB, and then use it to create versions targeted for the specific output conditions. If you just want to get it on the page and out the door, you can make all your corrections with the final output in mind, targeting as you correct, and save yourself some time.

Automatic versus manual targeting. When you convert an RGB image to CMYK using Photoshop's separation engine, it automatically compensates for both dot gain and for the reduced color gamut of CMYK. The results that you get depend—critically—on the settings you make in the RGB Setup and CMYK Setup settings, so it's important to get these right (see Chapter 5, *Color Settings*). But even with the best-possible global settings, you may still want to adjust some things manually before doing the conversion. The dot gain compensation works better than ever, but Photoshop's handling of out-of-gamut colors is another story.

Gamut compression and gamut clipping. As we discussed back in Chapter 4, *Color Essentials*, RGB colors that can't be reproduced in CMYK are called out-of-gamut colors. There are two ways to handle these colors, and now, fortunately, Photoshop offers both.

▶ Reduce the color gamut of the entire image proportionally, so that differences in color saturation are preserved (*gamut compression*). You can get this kind of rendering from Photoshop 5 by choosing ICC in CMYK Setup, and setting the rendering intent to Perceptual.

▶ Clip the out-of-gamut colors to their nearest printable equivalents, while leaving the in-gamut colors unchanged (*gamut clipping*). The Photoshop Classic engine has always worked this way, as do ICC profiles when you set the rendering intent to Relative or Absolute Colorimetric.

Each approach has its strengths and weaknesses. The disadvantage of the former approach is that, if your image contains no out-of-gamut colors, you'll lose saturation unneccesarily. The disadvantage of the latter approach is that differences in saturation between out-of-gamut colors are lost, and so detail in highly saturated areas goes away. For example, if you have a pixel that's really hot pink and another one that's even hotter, they'll both get clipped to the same dull pink color; the difference between them is gone.

The Photoshop Classic separation engine has improved with each release of Photoshop, including Photoshop 5, but it still does a colorimetric rather than a perceptual rendering, clipping out-of-gamut colors rather than compressing the source gamut into that of the target.

Unless you take care of the out-of-gamut colors yourself, Photoshop will take care of them for you during separation, and it may not give you the results you want (see Figure 7-5 on page 269). In fact, Photoshop Classic's gamut-clipping behavior is one of the main reasons that we often use ICC profiles with one of the available CMMs instead.

That said, the Photoshop Classic separation engine has been much maligned by its detractors. It can create great color seps. It just takes some extra work, and you have to do the work *before* you convert the image to CMYK. Once Photoshop has clipped those out-of-gamut colors, you can never bring back the subtle details they may contain.

Tip: Targeting Color Images for RGB Output. Some output processes—notably film recorders, computer screens, and many inexpensive inkjet printers—use RGB data. This presents a special problem, because Photoshop 5, like earlier versions, still allows only one RGB space at a time. You can fool Photoshop into providing a soft-proof of the RGB output device (See "Custom RGB-to-RGB Tables" in Chapter 5, *Color Settings*), allowing you to use CMYK Preview to soft-proof your RGB output, but this doesn't provide a reliable method of creating the print file.

The best solution is to obtain a good ICC profile for the RGB device. Then, if the printer driver offers ICC color management, you can simply do the transform on the fly at print time. If the driver doesn't support color management, you can use Profile-to-Profile to create the print file—we usually duplicate the image, do the Profile-to-Profile transform, print the result, then close the duplicate without saving.

In the absence of an ICC profile, you *can* create a custom RGB Setup space with the primaries, white point and gamma of the output device. We don't really recommend this approach—it's definitely out on the bleeding edge—but in some cases it may be your only option. See "Custom RGB Spaces" in Chapter 5, *Color Settings*.

Fine-tuning CMYK files. No matter how well you tweak the various preferences that control the RGB-to-CMYK conversion, it's likely that your separated CMYK files can benefit from some judicious fine-tuning to optimize them for your press conditions. We strongly advise pulling a proof before you do any corrections on the CMYK image unless you know appropriate CMYK dot percentages cold, or you know from experience that you can really trust your monitor's simulation of CMYK. With a proof, you can see what needs to be changed. Without one, you're either guessing or flying on instruments.

Color-Correction Tools

For color correction, we rely heavily on the same four tools that we use for grayscale correction—the Histogram, the Info palette, and the Levels and Curves dialog boxes (and the eyedropper tools they contain). They operate in the same way as they do in grayscale, but their effects are sometimes significantly different because we're dealing with three or four channels instead of one.

With Levels, Curves, and Histogram, you can operate on the color channels individually or on a composite of all of them. The Info palette shows what's happening in each of the channels, and warns you when RGB colors are outside the CMYK gamut. We also use the CMYK Preview command for a visual check of our predicted CMYK values while we're still working in RGB.

In addition to those four tools, we also use the Hue/Saturation command for both global and selective corrections, and its close relative, the Replace Colors command, for selective corrections. The Selective Color command, despite its name, is as useful for global corrections to the entire image as it is for selective corrections to parts of the image, but we generally reserve it for fine-tuning CMYK files.

Let's look at each of these tools in more detail.

Histogram

As we noted in the last chapter, the Histogram command is a simple bar chart that plots the levels from 0 to 255 along the horizontal axis, and the number of pixels at each level along the vertical axis. But it works a little differently with color images than it does with grayscale ones. In a grayscale image you have only one histogram, but in color images, you have a histogram for each channel (three for RGB and Lab, four for CMYK), plus a composite histogram for the combined channels.

Figure 7-5 Out-of-gamut color handling

In addition to overall color variation, note the detail differences in the saturated gloves and water bottle.

Separated with Photoshop Classic

Separated with Photoshop ICC

Separated with Color Access

Hand-tuned, then separated with Photoshop

When you choose Histogram from the Image menu and only one channel is visible, the Histogram dialog box displays the histogram for that channel. When you display the composite image and choose Histogram,

Figure 7-6 Retargeting an image that's been prepared for reproduction on newsprint

The image above left was separated for newsprint. The separation settings resulted in a flat image that would reproduce well in that medium, but that had lost a great deal of its tonal and color range.

For the image above, we started with the newsprint-targeted CMYK file, pulled it back into RGB (see "Tip: CMYK to RGB," earlier in this chapter), then reseparated for this book's wider gamut. The results aren't great, but they're much better than with previous versions of Photoshop.

The image at left was created from the original RGB file, and separated using the proper settings for these printing conditions.

the Histogram dialog box sports a Channel menu that lets you choose the histograms of the individual channels, or a composite histogram labeled Luminosity (see Figure 7-7).

The histograms of the individual channels are identical to those displayed in Levels. The composite Luminosity histogram, however, is different. Moreover, it's different in a useful way. The composite Luminosity histogram shows the overall tonal range of the image—it's analogous to the histogram for a grayscale image or for a single channel. Hence, it's useful for determining how bright your highlights and how dark your shadows are. For reasons we'll see in "Levels," later in this chapter, the composite histogram in Levels doesn't do this.

Info Palette

The Info palette is a vital tool for working in color, particularly when we work in RGB. It lets us read the RGB values under the cursor, and equally important, it can show us the approximate CMYK values that we'll get when we do a mode change to CMYK.

We say "approximate" because if you examine the CMYK values for an RGB file, then convert to CMYK and examine the values again, they differ very slightly. With rare exceptions (we've only seen one), the CMYK values match to within a percentage point, which is a closer match than any imagesetter operator will promise you.

So, we can work on RGB images in their native color space, and still keep an eye on the CMYK values Photoshop will produce when we make color separations. We get the best of both worlds (see Figure 7-7).

When you're working on an RGB file, the CMYK values displayed by the Info palette are governed by the settings in the Printing Inks Setup

Figure 7-7 Histograms, Levels, saturation, and brightness

The Histogram command with the Luminosity option selected depicts the overall brightness distribution of the image—how the histogram would look if you converted the image to grayscale.

The RGB histogram in Levels shows how many pixels are at a given value in any of the channels. Note the spike at the right (255), even though there are no pure whites in the image.

The Levels highlight clipping display (here set to level 220) shows more about saturation levels. The green areas are fully saturated (255G) at this clipping level. The cyan areas are at 255G 255B. And so on. The white areas are truly white—255R 255G 255B.

The Info palette's gamut alarm shows that the fully saturated blue-green sleeve colors can't be printed, along with the CMYK values that will result.

The Gamut Warning display—here set to display in red—shows the saturated areas of the image that can't be reproduced with the current separation settings.

and Separation Setup dialog boxes. If these preferences are set correctly, you should have to do little or no work on the CMYK file after you've made the conversion from RGB to CMYK. See Chapter 5, *Color Settings,* for detailed strategies for setting up these key preferences.

We prefer working visually—relying on a well-calibrated monitor—rather than going strictly by the numbers, but even the best monitor and the best calibration have inherent limitations. Some things are almost impossible to detect visually. For example, without looking at some kind of printed reference under controlled lighting, it's difficult to tell from the monitor whether or not a gray is really neutral. But the numbers in the Info palette provide an infallible guide. Without a well-calibrated monitor, they're your only real guide to what's going on.

Likewise, it's very hard to see differences of one or two levels between adjacent pixels, but the Info palette lets us find these differences, and as we've pointed out, difference is detail. It's even possible to do color correction using a black and white monitor. This is a ridiculously macho practice—we don't recommend or enjoy it—but in a pinch, it works. You need to have a good sense of the target values you're aiming for, and that only comes with experience, but a big part of gaining that experience comes from examining the values on the Info palette for key areas of your images.

Info palette setup. For color work, we use the same Info palette setup more than 90 percent of the time. We set the first color readout to RGB, the second color readout to CMYK, and the mouse coordinates to pixels. You can set all these options with the Palette Options menu on the Info palette, or you can set individual readouts using the individual popup menus.

Setting eyedropper options. You can set the Info palette to show the values of the individual pixels under the cursor, a 3-by-3-pixel average, or a 5-by-5-pixel average, by setting the options for the Eyedropper tool to Point Sample, 3-by-3 Average, or 5-by-5 Average in the Tool Options palette (double-click on the Eyedropper tool). David generally chooses 3-by-3 Average unless he's working with a very high-resolution image (destined for high-screen-frequency or continuous-tone output), in which case he might go to 5-by-5. Bruce sticks with point sample, but double-checks the values by zooming in at 100 percent view. Checking at 100 percent view is absolutely necessary because the zoomed-out displays are now antialiased, so sampled values at less than 100 percent view may be misleading.

Color samplers. A new eyedropper tool, the color sampler, allows you to place up to four locked eyedropper probes, or color samplers, each of which has its own Info palette readout. (See Figure 7-8.) The color samplers are saved with the image, so they'll still be there even if you close and reopen the image. With the Color Sampler tool selected, you can move a sampler by holding down the Shift key and dragging, and you can delete a sampler by Option-clicking it.

When you're using one of the editing or painting tools, you can always get the eyedropper by holding down Option. If you add the Shift key, you get the color sampler tool instead. However, to delete color samplers, you must choose the Color Sampler tool from the tool palette either using the mouse or the keyboard shortcut (I, or Shift-I, depending on whether the tool was set to the eyedropper or the color sampler).

Each color sampler has its own readout on the Info palette. These behave just like the other Info palette readouts. You can change the color space each sampler displays by clicking its individual pop-out menu, and you can hide or show all the color samplers by choosing Show/Hide Color Samplers from the Info palette's pop-out menu.

Figure 7-8 Color Samplers and the Info palette

You can place up to four color samplers in an image, each of which has its own Info palette readout.

When you work with any of the adjustment tools, the samplers show before-and-after values.

We use the color samplers to track what's happening to critical areas in the image when we edit. Typically, we'll place one color sampler for the highlight, a second for a neutral midtone, a third for a neutral three-quarter-tone, and the fourth on any critical color we're trying to adjust, or, just as often, to maintain.

Using the Info palette with other controls. While you're editing an image using any of the controls on the Adjust submenu under the Image menu (Levels, Curves, Hue/Saturation, Replace Colors, and so on), the Info palette provides a before-and-after reading (see Figure 7-8, and 7-9). This allows you to see what is happening while you're making the adjustments.

Tip: Add Swatches for Critical Colors. The new Color Sampler tool lets you lock down up to four samplers, which you can then read from the Info palette, but if you need to track more than four colors, you can use the following workaround.

1. Before opening the Levels or Curves dialog box (or whatever adjustment you're making), increase the size of the image canvas by 50 or 100 pixels.

2. For each pixel that you want to track, pick up its color with the Eyedropper tool.

3. Fill a part of the new white space with the picked-up color—drag out a selection and press Option-Delete to fill it with the foreground color (see Figure 7-9).

Now, while you make color corrections, you can always place the cursor over that color swatch to see how it's changing. When you're finished, crop out the swatches and you're back to normal.

CMYK Preview

If you've gone through the process described in Chapter 5, *Color Settings*, for calibrating your monitor's display of CMYK files to the printed output, you can get a good visual idea of what will happen to your image once it's been converted to CMYK by choosing CMYK Preview from the Mode menu. This doesn't change the file itself—it just changes the way it

Figure 7-9 Adding color swatches

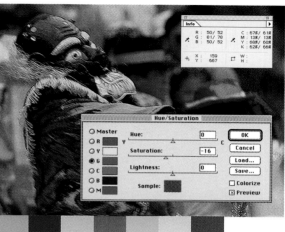

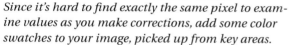

Since it's hard to find exactly the same pixel to examine values as you make corrections, add some color swatches to your image, picked up from key areas.

This allows you to see, measure, and evaluate the changes you're making in key color ranges.

displays on the screen. (This simulation is based—yet again—on the settings in RGB Setup, CMYK Setup, and your monitor profile.)

We often work with CMYK Preview turned on, especially when we're fine-tuning out-of-gamut colors prior to CMYK conversion.

Tip: Use CMYK Preview for Before-and-Afters. Photoshop lets you open more than one window for an image. This is particularly useful in conjunction with CMYK Preview. When you choose CMYK Preview, it only applies to the currently active window, so you can open two windows for the image—use one to view it in RGB, and the other in simulated CMYK.

Gamut Alarm

When you're working in RGB mode, Photoshop displays an exclamation point next to color specifications (in the Info palette and the Color Picker) to warn you when an RGB color is outside the printable CMYK gamut (see Figure 7-7 on page 271).

This gamut alarm is telling you that when you convert the image from RGB to CMYK, Photoshop will clip the RGB color to the closest available CMYK equivalent.

Gamut Warning

Photoshop's Gamut Warning shows you which colors in the image are out of gamut by displaying them with the color you choose in the Gamut Warning Preferences. We don't find this particularly useful—we'd rather just *see* what's going to happen to our colors using CMYK Preview and the Info palette, but we thought we'd mention it for the sake of completeness.

Occasionally we'll turn on Gamut Warning just to see if we've overlooked a trouble spot (such as a highly saturated color in an important area of the image), but nine times out of ten, it just tells us that most of our deep shadows are out of gamut.

Unless we see a glaring problem with the shadows in the CMYK Preview, we just leave them alone and accept the CMYK values that Photoshop produces when we do the conversion. Doing a lot of work to bring very dark colors into gamut manually is just a waste of time. Instead, let Photoshop do it when it converts to CMYK; it's unlikely that you'll be able to see the difference in print.

Tip: Don't Sponge Saturated Colors. The fact that you can load the out-of-gamut colors as a selection using Color Range may tempt you to use the Sponge tool to desaturate them and hence bring them into gamut. Don't, because if you do, you're simply doing manually what Photoshop does automatically during RGB-to-CMYK conversion—clipping out-of-gamut colors. Besides requiring a lot of handwork, it can distort the relationship between the in-gamut and out-of-gamut colors, changing the appearance of the image in odd ways.

Levels

The Levels command operates on color images exactly as it does on grayscale images. The only difference is that, unless you tell it otherwise, it operates simultaneously on all the color channels in the image. We usually find Levels too coarse a tool to use for correcting problems with color balance (though we know people who've developed incredible skills doing so), but we still use it in three ways on color images.

▶   As an image-evaluation tool, using the histograms and clipping display.

▶   When we have a color image that has no problems with color balance, but needs some lightening (or much more rarely, darkening) in the midtones. Often, a move with the gamma slider is all that's needed.

▶ As an image-targeting tool. If the image doesn't contain specular high-lights that we want to blow out to white, we use the black and white Output sliders to limit the minimum highlight and maximum shadow dots. If there are specular highlights, we use the eyedropper techniques (outlined later in the chapter) instead.

The Levels composite histogram. Like the Histogram dialog box, Levels displays the histogram for an individual channel if that's what you have displayed, and offers a Channels menu when you're viewing the composite image. But the composite histogram it displays (labeled RGB or CMYK depending on the image's color space) is different from the Luminosity histogram shown in the Histogram dialog box (see Figure 7-7 on page 271).

In the Luminosity histogram, a level of 255 represents a white pixel. In the RGB or CMYK histograms in Levels, however, a level of 255 *may* represent a white pixel, but it could equally well represent a saturated color pixel—the histogram simply shows the maximum of the individual channels. This means that you have to be extremely careful with the black and white Input Levels sliders, because you can easily drive colors to saturation in a misguided attempt to clip highlights.

Figure 7-7 on page 271 shows the Luminosity histogram and the RGB Levels histogram for the same image. As you can see, they're very different. The image has no pure whites, and the Luminosity histogram shows this. The RGB histogram, in contrast, shows a distinct spike at level 255. In this particular image, rather than indicating clipped highlights, the spike shows the presence of saturated colors—a saturated color always has at least one of the primaries at level 255.

A look at the Levels clipping display shows this quite clearly. If we press Option and hold down the mouse button on the white Input Levels slider, we don't see any white areas, but we do see areas of saturated red, green, and blue.

How Levels works on color images. As the composite histogram implies, any moves you make to the Levels sliders when you're working in the composite channels apply equally to each individual color channel. In other words, you get identical results applying the same move individually to each color channel as you would applying the move once to the composite channel.

However, since the contents of the individual channels are quite different, applying the same moves to each can sometimes have unexpected results. The gamma slider and the black and white Output sliders operate straightforwardly, but the black and white Input sliders can be dangerous.

The white Input slider clips the highlights *in each channel* to level 255. This brightens the image overall, and neutral colors stay neutral. But it usually has an undesirable effect on non-neutral colors, ranging from oversaturation to pronounced color shifts. The same applies to the black Input slider, although the effects are usually less obvious. The black Input slider clips the values in each channel to level zero, so when you apply it to a non-neutral color, you can end up removing all trace of one primary from the color, which also increases its saturation.

Because of this behavior, we use the black and white Input sliders primarily as image-evaluation tools in conjunction with the Option-key clipping display. They let us see exactly where our saturated colors are in relation to our neutral highlights and shadows. If the image is free of dangerously saturated colors, we may make small moves with the black and white Input sliders, but we always try to avoid clipping, staying well outside of the significant areas of the histogram. And we keep a very close eye on what's happening to the saturation—it's particularly easy to create out-of-gamut saturated colors in the shadows.

The image shown in Figure 7-10 is a good candidate for correction using Levels. It has no real color problems, and no dangerously saturated colors, but it's a little flat. Three quick moves with the black and white Input Levels sliders and the gamma slider improve the contrast immensely.

Curves

The Curves command is probably the single most useful tool Photoshop offers for making corrections to tone and color, both globally and locally, and mastering it is an essential Photoshop skill. Almost every color image we work with gets some treatment with Curves; in many cases, a single round of curve adjustments is the only correction we make.

In Chapter 6, *Tonal Correction,* we likened Levels to an automatic transmission and Curves to a stick shift. When you work in color, the difference is more like that between a chain saw and a scalpel.

Figure 7-10 Image correction using Levels

Note that we've targeted and sharpened these images to give a better impression of what we see on screen.

The raw scan, and the tone-distribution histogram

Black clipping at level 25   *White clipping at level 220*

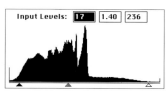

Input Levels: 17 1.40 236

The Levels move above yields the image at left and histogram below.

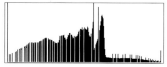

The Curves command works the same way with color images as it does with grayscale ones, save that you can operate on all channels simultaneously (useful for tonal corrections) or on individual channels (useful for changing the color balance).

Curves tips for color images. All the options that exist for Curves in grayscale apply to working in color, too (see "Tip: Customizing the Curves Dialog Box" in Chapter 6, *Tonal Correction*). We always use the fine grid (Option-click on the grid area), and we generally use the Levels values with RGB files and the Percentage values with CMYK files—we're used to thinking of RGB in terms of levels and CMYK in terms of dot percentages.

To adjust the shape of the curve, we almost always use the point tool instead of the freehand (pencil) tool. The freehand tool is useful in some special situations that we discuss in Chapter 6, *Tonal Correction*, but the point tool keeps the curve as smooth as possible, and hence avoids sudden unnatural shifts in tone and color.

We use two distinct methods of placing curve points: one when we're going strictly by the numbers, and the other when we're relying more on what we see on the monitor.

▶ **By the numbers.** If we're going by the numbers, we use the fields at the bottom of the dialog box to type in the input and output coordinates we want. This places the point and automatically bends the curve so that it passes through that point.

▶ **By eye.** If we're operating visually, we Command-click in the image to place the point on the curve, then drag it to where we want it to be.

Tip: Channel Menu Shortcut. When you're working in either Curves or Levels, the "display channel" shortcuts (pressing Command-1 through Command-4 for individual channels, and Command-~(tilde) for the composite channel) operate the Channel menu in the dialog box. However, this only changes the popup menu; if you want to view an individual channel, you must cancel out of Levels or Curves, make the desired channel visible, then reopen Levels or Curves.

We've seen how we can use Levels to make a straightforward tonal adjustment. Figure 7-11 shows the same image adjusted a little more precisely with a master RGB curve instead.

Maintaining tone when correcting. Whether you're working in RGB or in CMYK, the individual channel curves often offer the easiest way to take care of color-balance problems. Remember that cyan is the inverse of red, magenta is the inverse of green, and blue is the inverse of yellow. To remove a red cast, for example, you'd pull down on the red curve in an RGB file, or pull up on the cyan curve in a CMYK file.

However, in cases where the image has a severe color cast, working on a single channel may have too drastic an effect on the overall tone of the image, because each curve adds or subtracts light (in the case of RGB) or ink (in the case of CMYK). In the case of a severe red cast, for example, rather than eliminating it using the red or cyan curve exclusively, you

Figure 7-11 Image correction using Curves

The adjustment with Curves provides more control for fine-tuning particular tonal ranges. The highlights are slightly brighter, and the shadows contain more contrast, than in the image corrected with Levels.

may need to adjust the other curves as well. That way, the overall tone of the image is preserved.

Editing the black plate. We prefer to do all our work with Curves in RGB, with one important exception: editing the black plate in CMYK files. It's very rare for us to make curve-based adjustments to the C, M, and Y plates, but the black plate is a different matter. Small changes to the black plate can have a profound effect on both the contrast and the apparent purity of the colors in the image.

We've come to trust our monitors more than in any previous version of Photoshop, but we almost always have a proof made before we use Curves on the CMYK file, because it's quite difficult to judge the effect of a black plate tweak on the monitor. If the colors in the proof appear muddy, it's usually a sign that the black plate is too heavy. In extreme cases, we'll go back and reseparate the RGB image using a lighter black, but often a small tweak that brightens the quartertones in the black plate can do wonders.

Likewise, small adjustments to the black plate can fix contrast problems, without having to go back to the original and reseparate. But if you're running into color-balance problems, it's a sign that your RGB Setup or CMYK Setup settings, or your monitor profile, need further refinement. You can fix the image at hand by working the CMY curves, but you'll have to fix every other image you produce using these settings, too. It's much more efficient to go back and fix the fundamental problem (see Chapter 5, *Color Settings*, for a detailed discussion of these all-important settings).

Tip: Fix the Neutrals and the Rest Will Follow. When you're wrestling with a global color cast, the easiest way to fix it is to find spots in the image that should be neutral, and make them so. If you do that, the rest of the color will generally fall into place. If you're working in RGB, equal amounts of red, green, and blue produce a neutral tone. If you're working in CMYK, it's a little more challenging. You'll have to determine by experience what combination of C, M, Y, and K produce a neutral tone.

Changing the ink limits and black generation will give you different numbers, but if your Separation settings are based on SWOP inks, you'll always get more cyan than magenta and yellow in your neutrals. When you work in RGB, Photoshop's separation engine adjusts for the impurities in the cyan ink and boosts cyan accordingly. When you work in CMYK, you have to determine the neutral combinations yourself.

Finding neutrals isn't always easy: a great many images simply don't contain any. Sometimes you can find neutrals hiding in the shadows or lurking in the highlights—the Info palette is invaluable for hunting them down (see "Info Palette," earlier in this chapter).

If you're having trouble with scanner-induced color casts, consider scanning a gray wedge with your scanner; you know for a fact that it includes neutral highlights, midtones, and shadows.

Figure 7-12 shows an example of correcting a color cast using Curves. In this case it's a pretty simple correction, mainly adjusting for a yellow cast by tweaking the blue curve. It may be of interest to note that the curve we applied to the blue channel is almost exactly analogous to performing traditional dot etching on the yellow plate of the separation. If we had to make the same correction to a CMYK file, we'd have applied the inverse curve to the yellow channel. Then we'd increase the cyan slightly in the midtones.

Black, White, and Gray Eyedroppers

The eyedropper tools in Levels and Curves function identically in both places, and they operate quite differently from the main controls in those dialog boxes, so it's worth looking at them separately.

We don't always use these tools. Besides an understanding of how they work, it takes experience to decide whether or not an image would benefit from using them. We encourage you to experiment with them, while

Figure 7-12 Correcting a color cast with Curves

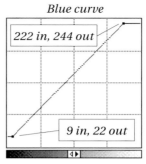

Blue curve

222 in, 244 out

9 in, 22 out

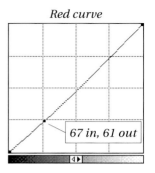

Red curve

67 in, 61 out

To remove the yellow cast in this image, we start with the shadow inside the lower-left window, adjusting the dark end of the blue curve to make it neutral. Then we neutralize the highlight at the bottom of the upper-left window by adjusting the highlight end of the blue curve.

These two moves kill the color cast, but leave the midtones slightly red. We check the values in the lighter shadows, and adjust the red curve to make them neutral.

thinking about what they do. That way, you'll gain a much better understanding of both their possibilities and their pitfalls.

The black and white eyedroppers operate on color images in the same way they do on grayscale images, except that you set a target and source value for each channel in the color image. (See "White Points and Black Points and Grays, Oh My!" in Chapter 6, *Tonal Correction,* for a full discussion of how these tools work, including tips, tricks, and various inherent limitations.)

The biggest difference between using the black and white eyedroppers in color and in grayscale is that in color images, the relationship between the source and target colors becomes much more critical, because it affects color balance as well as tone. If you set a neutral target color and click on a non-neutral source pixel, the color balance of the whole image changes. To get a feel for this, it's worth experimenting by clicking the eyedroppers on a few different pixels in the image.

The gray eyedropper. Back in Chapter 6, *Tonal Correction*, we described how the black and white eyedroppers work. We put off our discussion of the gray eyedropper until now, however, as it is only available with color images. The gray eyedropper does something similar to the other two eyedroppers, but it's different in one major way.

Where the other two eyedroppers always set the color you click on in the image to the target color you specify, the gray eyedropper does not. Instead, it adjusts the gamma values for each channel in an attempt to map the source color you click on in the image to a color with the same *hue and saturation* as the target color, but with the *luminance* of the source color. It's trying to adjust the color without affecting the tone.

Using the Eyedroppers

Now that you understand a little more about what the eyedroppers do, let's look at how you can use them. You can use the eyedropper tools in (at least) three ways.

▶ As highlight/shadow limit tools for targeting.

▶ As color-balancing tools.

▶ As arbitrary color-matching tools.

Whichever way you use them, you have to be careful with the relationship between your target color and your source color. Dramatic (read: "incredibly ugly") shifts in the color balance can ensue when you set a neutral target color and click on a non-neutral source color. Basically, the tools work better for making small moves than for making large ones.

Setting the highlight dot. We use the white eyedropper primarily as a targeting tool, for setting the minimum highlight dot *after* sharpening and immediately prior to converting the image to CMYK. But we only do so when we have an image that has clearly defined neutral highlights *and* contains specular highlights that we want to blow out to white.

Unless both of these apply, it's easier to limit the highlight and shadow dots using Curves, or using the black and white Output sliders in Levels. Here's the procedure to set the minimum highlight dot.

1. Determine the highlight point. We work with the Levels command because it offers the clipping display. We Option-drag the white Input slider to identify the pixel we want to set as the minimum highlight dot (the lightest area where there is actual detail), then return it to a setting of 255.

2. Set the target color. We set the target color according to our printing conditions, but since we're usually working in RGB we specify it using RGB values. The Printing Inks Setup and Separation Setup preferences, when correctly set, give us the desired CMYK values. For example, using our preferred Separation Setup for sheetfed printing, a 243R 243G 243B highlight translates to 6C 3M 4Y 0K. If we're working on a CMYK file, we just specify the CMYK values directly.

3. Select the source pixel/color. Use the white eyedropper to click on a pixel that has the values we want to set to the minimum highlight dot. Typically, it'll have a value somewhere in the 247–251 range. Pixels brighter than that are allowed to blow out softly to white paper, so we preserve the highlight detail with a printable dot, but still get the sparkle from the true specular highlights.

Setting the shadow dot. We use the black eyedropper to set the maximum shadow dot in a different situation. Photoshop's separation engine seems to produce the best results when the Total Black Ink Limit is set to 100 percent, but most presses plug up the black long before it reaches 100 percent. Rather than changing the Separation Setup, we use the black eyedropper to back off the maximum black in the image to the maximum value the press can hold, without changing the percentages of CMY.

The procedure for setting the maximum shadow dot is essentially the same as it is for setting the minimum highlight dot. We identify the darkest pixels in the image that still contain useful detail, and use them as the source pixels for the black eyedropper. We set the target color to the maximum dot the press can hold without plugging up; the difference is that we specify the target color as CMYK, as follows.

The Color Balance Command

We'd be remiss if we didn't at least mention Photoshop's Color Balance command (see Figure 7-13), which lets you make separate color adjustments to the shadows, midtones, and highlights. While we'll mention it, we don't use it—for two reasons.

▶ It doesn't do anything we can't do with Curves.

▶ The things it does are more difficult to control than they are with Curves, because there are some hidden moves happening that are hard to understand.

The command works by warping three preset gamma curves that cover the highlight, midtone, and shadow ranges. Problems can crop up in the areas where the curves overlap—it's easy to get unnatural color shifts, particularly when you shift one range in one direction and another in the opposite direction. You can get the same effect with Curves, but you aren't limited to the preset ranges of the Color Balance tool, and you know exactly what's going on.

Figure 7-13 (Not) using Color Balance

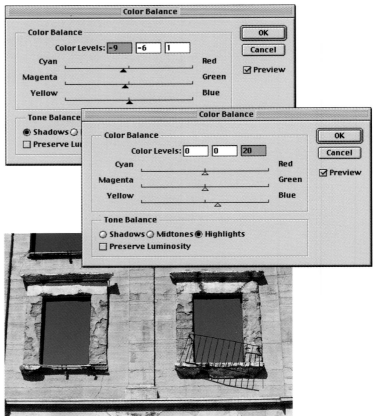

While it's possible to use Color Balance to neutralize color casts (as its name implies), it's more difficult than using Curves, because you can't target particular tonal ranges—only the generalized "Shadows," "Midtones," and "Highlights."

1. Double-click the black eyedropper to set the target color.

2. Click on the pixel you've identified as the source pixel to load its color as the target color. With a typical setup for a sheetfed press, it might read something like 73C 62M 65Y 100K.

3. Reduce *only* the K component of the target color to your desired maximum black value. This can range from 97 percent for very high-quality sheetfed presses with coated stock to 75 percent for newsprint.

4. Click OK to set the new target color.

5. Click the black eyedropper on the source pixel in the image to map it to the new target color.

When you convert the image to CMYK, your maximum shadow dot will have the values you set for the target color, and your black plate won't have plugged-up shadows.

Color balancing. We generally use curves to fix color-balance problems, but if we're in a hurry and the problem isn't too severe, the eyedroppers can be used for a quick fix. Again, this technique works best in images with clearly defined neutrals.

We set the target colors for the black, white, and gray eyedroppers to neutral RGB values (letting Photoshop's separation engine translate them to neutral CMYK values at separation time). The exact values depend on the image and press conditions, but generally the white eyedropper works best in the range from 200 to 255, the gray eyedropper works best in the range from 100 to 156, and the black eyedropper works best in the range from 0 to 64. All these numbers are approximate, but they're good general guidelines.

The trick here is to match the source pixel and the target color so that you're making a transformation that changes the source pixel to a neutral color without greatly affecting its brightness (remember, adding or removing color changes tone). The gray eyedropper does this as a matter of course, but you have to do some figuring with the black and white eyedroppers. For example, if your source pixel is 242R 234G 241B, try a target color that's a loose average of the three, perhaps 239R 239G 239B.

In the example shown in Figure 7-20 on page 302, we were able to eliminate most of the red cast by applying the white eyedropper to the water inside the glass, the gray eyedropper to the light shadow under the teapot, and the black eyedropper to the deep shadows.

Arbitrary color matching. In some cases, you can use the eyedroppers to match colors between images. For example, a classic problem comes up when you shoot an event like a daytime football match, where the light changes over the course of the game. If you're going to run several shots of the game, you want the uniforms to be a consistent color in all the images. The eyedroppers can (sometimes) help you do this.

Are All Color Casts Bad?

Some images simply don't (and shouldn't) contain neutrals. An image shot half an hour before sunset will almost certainly have a reddish yellow cast, and removing it probably isn't a good idea, particularly if the photographer spent several hours waiting for that magical golden light.

Determine the origin. Think about where the color cast originated. Scanners often introduce color casts—sometimes they even introduce color crossovers, where the highlights have a cast in one direction and the shadows have a cast in the opposite direction. (Scanning a gray wedge on your scanner is an easy way to determine what color casts are being introduced by the scanner.) Some film stocks have crossovers too (photographers call them "crosscurves"). Early 1980s Kodachrome is noted for a red-green crosscurve, for example, while some Ektachrome tends to turn blue in deep shadows.

Scanner-induced color casts can and should be corrected. Some color casts are more ambiguous. Whether or not you should correct them depends on the nature of the image. Distant shadows in landscapes actually appear blue to our eyes, and if you make them neutral, you'll end up with an unnatural-looking image. But on a tabletop product shot, you almost certainly want neutral shadows.

Look at the original. The best recourse is (obviously) to look at the original. The usual request is to match the original image. Strictly speaking, this is impossible—film has a much wider tonal range and color gamut than you can hope to achieve with four-color printing. What you can do is to provide the illusion of matching the original within the limits of the output process.

Preserve relationships. The trick here is to preserve the relationships between the important colors in the image. Our eyes are very good at detecting color relationships, but they're easily fooled when it comes to detecting absolute color values—to judge color, they rely heavily on context.

If the original is not available, you just have to guess. We almost hesitate to call this "color correction," because it's unlikely that you'll produce anything that resembles the intentions of the photographer—you're essentially making things up. But you can at least make educated guesses.

Look for memory colors. If the image doesn't contain neutrals, it may contain some *memory colors*. Memory colors are so called because we have an automatic expectation of how they should look. Blue skies, green grass, red fire engines, and foods like apples, oranges, green peppers, and carrots are good examples. If these colors look wrong, the whole image will look wrong.

Note that this technique is not what the designers of these tools had in mind. When we mentioned it to a senior engineer on the Photoshop team, he commented that the technique "will work in many cases; but as the algorithms get stressed with larger moves, it will fail, sometimes dramatically, so don't come crying to me if it doesn't work."

Use the white eyedropper to match highlights, the gray eyedropper to match midtones, and the black eyedropper to match shadows. You need to have both images that you're trying to match open on the screen.

1. Double-click the appropriate eyedropper tool to bring up the Color Picker to choose the target color.

2. Pick up the target color from the "correct" image (the one you aren't changing) by clicking the cursor on the color you want to match. Then click OK to confirm the new target color, and close the Color Picker.

3. In the image you want to change, find the color you want to change, and click the eyedropper on it to convert it to the target color.

If it works, great! If it doesn't work, you may want to give it one more try, being a little more careful when choosing target and source colors. The technique works well with small moves, but if it isn't working it will quickly become obvious. In that case, use curves instead. It's more work, but you'll get more predictable and controllable results.

Hue/Saturation

The Hue/Saturation command (see Figure 7-14) allows us to address saturation problems much more easily than we can using curves, and also lets us make changes to the hue of specific colors. We use it both for correction and for targeting our images. In previous versions of Photoshop, Hue/Saturation was a fairly limited tool, but the all-new Hue/Saturation controls in Photoshop 5 turn it into a powerhouse. Where previous versions of Photoshop let you adjust hue and saturation either globally or in one of six preset ranges (red, green, blue, cyan, magenta and yellow), now new you can tailor the range you're adjusting to fit the image.

Hue/Saturation lets you make tweaks to the hue, the saturation, and the lightness of the entire image using the Master setting. This is mainly useful for controlling saturation—desaturating oversaturated scans or (more rarely) beefing up washed-out scans. The Hue control may seem like a useful tool for dealing with global color casts, but in practice we've found we get much better results using Curves, or the eyedroppers in either Levels or Curves.

Besides the Master setting, Hue/Saturation lets you adjust the hue, saturation, and lightness of the individual primary and secondary colors (R, G, B, C, M, and Y). You can accept the preset ranges, but you can also fine-tune the range of color you're adjusting using the slider at the bottom of the dialog box. The center bar in the slider lets you adjust the color range, while the lighter bars on each end let you control the "fall-off." This is basically like feathering a selection. (See Figure 7-14).

Hue/Saturation is useful, but also dangerous. The effects you'll get depend very much on the original image, but when you're working in

Figure 7-14

Hue/Saturation
dialog box

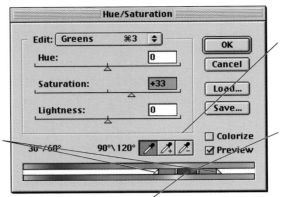

*The eyedroppers let you
select a color range by
clicking in the image.*

*The slider lets you
control the range of
colors you're affecting.
Drag the center bar to
change the hue, widen
or narrow it to change
the range.*

*Drag the ends of the
slider to change the
fall-off. This is like
feathering a color
range selection.*

*We clicked this point in
the image to customize
the range of greens the
adjustment will affect.
Doing so sets the
position of the color
range slider in the
dialog box.*

RGB, it's easy to oversaturate colors. If you're trying to increase the saturation of a color, keep a watchful eye on the gamut warnings in the Info
palette—you can create colors that look wonderful on the screen, but simply aren't reproducible in print. Remember that those out-of-gamut colors get clipped when you go to CMYK, so detail in those areas will vanish.
You can always turn on CMYK Preview for a more realistic view. For delicate saturation adjustments, we usually work on the CMYK file: in CMYK
mode, Hue/Saturation is changing the amounts of ink, and the adjustments tend to be much more subtle than in RGB.

Hue/Saturation versus Levels and Curves. Unlike Levels and Curves, Hue/
Saturation doesn't use Video LUT Animation to provide real-time feedback. If you want to see what you're doing, you must check the Preview

Interpreting RGB and CMYK Values

As we noted back in Chapter 4, *Color Essentials*, RGB and CMYK are both device-dependent—the color that you get from a given set of values varies quite dramatically depending on the device to which those values are sent. But RGB is somewhat more predictable than CMYK. If a sampled color has equal amounts of R, G, and B, you can be sure it's a neutral gray, although if your monitor isn't properly calibrated, it may not look that way. (And of course you're relying on your separation preferences to render

a neutral CMYK gray on press from those neutral RGB values.)

Likewise, you can tell if a color is overly saturated for the CMYK gamut if it contains a large amount of one or two RGB primaries and almost none of another.

CMYK numbers need considerably more interpretation—they only make sense in the context of a specific printing process. Every expert has their own set of magic numbers. They're all correct, but only for the situation in which they're being used.

Recommendations such as 5C 2M 2Y 0K for a neutral highlight, 60C 46M 45Y 11K for a neutral 50-percent gray, or 15C 24M 25Y 0K for Caucasian flesh tones (for instance) are good starting points, but they aren't sacrosanct. After proofing, you may find that you get better results with slightly different values. The same caveat applies to process-color swatch books. The CMYK values they contain were the ones used to print the swatch book. You'll get different results printing on a different press with different paper.

button. This makes it somewhat less interactive than Levels or Curves, because there's always a wait for the image to redraw to show the effect of your changes (the bigger the image or selection, the longer the wait).

Even without real-time feedback, it's a great deal easier to manipulate saturation or to make slight hue changes with this tool than with Levels or Curves. To change a color's saturation with those tools, you have to manipulate each channel separately. In the simplest case—desaturating a saturated primary color such as red (255R 0G 0B)—you have to reduce the amount of red and add equal amounts of blue and green, which is quite hard to do with Levels or Curves.

With a saturated orange (255R 160G 0B), you have to reduce the amounts of red and green proportionally, and add an amount of blue proportional to the amount by which you reduced the red and green. This would be insanely difficult with Curves, and just about impossible with Levels! Hue/ Saturation lets you do it with one move.

Creative uses. Hue/Saturation is often particularly effective when it's used in nonobvious ways. The image in Figure 7-15 has screaming reds that almost overwhelm the rest of the image. The obvious solution would be to desaturate the reds, but they give the image much of its impact.

Instead, we go after the colors that aren't readily apparent in the image. We pump up the greens, increasing the green saturation to 43, and increasing the cyan saturation slightly to 11. Finally, since the reds in the RGB original tend to go slightly yellow when we convert to CMYK, we shift the Hue of the reds by -3, making them a hair more magenta. For each move, we selected the range of color we wanted to affect by clicking in the image, then fine-tuning with the slider in the Hue/Sat dialog box. The effect is subtle, but we think it improves the image considerably.

Tip: Colorizing Grayscale Images. You can also use Hue/Saturation to colorize grayscale images, or to make a color image look like a hand-toned black-and-white print. Convert the grayscale to RGB, choose Hue/Saturation, and turn on the Colorize checkbox. For a warm sepia-tone look, try setting Hue to around 50, Saturation to between 25 and 30, and Lightness to 0. For normal color work, you *must* leave the Colorize button unchecked. (For more information on colorizing grayscale images, see "The Color of Grayscale" in Chapter 15, *Essential Image Techniques*.)

Hue/Saturation in CMYK. Hue/Saturation is also a powerful tool when working in CMYK, but unless you have an unusually clear idea of exactly what you're doing, it's best used as a fine-tuning tool after you've seen a proof. When we got the proof of the drummers image in Figure 7-15, we felt it was still a little flat. Increasing the saturation of the yellow, and shifting and saturating the reds, produced the result shown in the last image in Figure 7-15.

Unlike Curves, Hue/Saturation won't let you violate the ink limits specified in Separation Setup when you work on a file that's already been converted to CMYK. You may think that you could fool it into doing so by increasing the Total Ink Limit in Separation Setup, and to a *very* limited extent, you can—but we've yet to find a practical use for this. If you want to override the ink limits in a CMYK file, use Curves instead. Just remember that you're playing with fire when you do so.

Replace Color

The Replace Color command (see Figure 7-16) takes the features of Hue/Saturation even closer to those of the Color Range selection command (see "Color Range" in Chapter 14, *Selections*). It offers a quick, easy way

Figure 7-15 Hue/Saturation enhancements in RGB and CMYK

The image at left was captured from negative film on a LeafScan 35, with quite a bit of curve correction on the high-bit data using the LeafScan software. The reds overwhelm the rest of the image, but desaturating them would weaken the overall image, so instead we go after the other colors.

Working on the RGB image, we used Hue/Saturation to increase the green saturation—pumping up the background—and bring up the cyan saturation to provide a little more contrast in the red shirts.

Switching to CMYK preview, we see that the reds are more orange than we want, so we shift the hue of the reds slightly toward magenta to produce the result below.

Brings out the greens in the trees, the sweater, and the awning.

Provides contrast in the red shirts (because cyan, the inverse of red, is carrying most of the detail).

Makes the hue of the shirts slightly less orange and more red.

A proof of the above image shows that the reds are still too dominant and too orange, so we make some changes to the CMYK file.

Brings out the few splashes of yellow in the background.

Stops the increased yellow from turning the shirts orange, and sends them toward magenta instead.

Truth in Imaging

We often have to make decisions as to whether we try to reproduce an image as accurately as possible and perhaps settle for some flaws, or adjust it to make it less accurate but also more pleasing. This is a subjective decision, and it leads us to a tricky area.

Photographers commonly lament that prepress people screw up their color. Prepress people commonly lament that photographers shoot images that can never hope to be reproduced in print. Both viewpoints have some justi-

fication. We don't believe that prepress people should simply override the intentions of the image creator—if you want to make stuff up, just paint a picture and leave the poor photographer's work alone—but we also realize that image creators sometimes have unrealistic expectations of the printing process.

We don't have a magic answer here, but we'd like to suggest that this is a situation where communication can prevent engendering a good deal of ill-will. In a

commercial situation, the person who signs the check has the final say, but unless the job is done as work for hire, the photographer has an interest in how the image is reproduced.

In the case of the image in Figure 7-16, we're working on our own photograph, so we can do whatever we like with it and no controversy arises. But we ask you to at least give some thought to the intentions of the image creator when you're faced with a situation like this.

Tip: Use a New Window to See Selective Color in Action. When we use Selective Color, we like to see what it's actually doing to the individual color plates, but unless you're viewing the composite color image, the command is dimmed. The easy workaround is to open new windows for the image, and set each one to view a different channel. Then you can make the composite color window active, choose Selective Color, and turn on the Preview checkbox. You can see the effect on each plate as you make adjustments, though it's a little slow even on a fast Macintosh.

Channel Mixer

We debated whether to mention the Channel Mixer as a color-correction tool. We find it useful for getting grayscale images out of color ones (see "The Color of Grayscale" in Chapter 15, *Essential Image Techniques*), but its usefulness as a color-correction tool is less obvious.

We've been known to use Channel mixer on an RGB image, (see "Extracting Invisible Detail" in Chapter 8, *The Digital Darkroom*), but we're more likely to use it on CMYK files for which no RGB version is available. We show one such scenario in Figure 7-17. The original separation setup put black into the skin tones, making them muddy. We'd rather fix this by going back to the RGB original, changing the separation parameters, and reseparating the image, but that's not always possible. Lightening the black plate with levels or curves would destroy the image contrast—we only want to change the skin tones—and the Channel Mixer provides a very easy, if somewhat rough-and-ready, means of doing so. In the Channel Mixer dialog box, we set Black as the output channel, then, while sampling values from the image and checking them on the Info palette, we subtract some of the magenta and yellow channels from the black. We also boost the black so that the black values in the shadows remain unchanged.

Figure 7-17 Removing black from skin tones

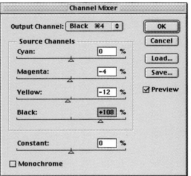

The image shown at left has black in the skin tones. We subtract some yellow and rather less magenta (the pink background relies on magenta), and boost the black slightly to produce the result shown at right.

Color Correction in Practice

Let's look at some practical examples of how we put all these tools to work on images, from start to finish. Here is a representative sampling of originals, each with its own set of problems, and our proposed solutions.

Fixing a Bad Scan

In Figure 7-18 we have a flawed original further compromised by a scan from an ancient 8-bit flatbed scanner. The Levels clipping display and histogram show no detail at all above level 225, and there's heavy posterization in the shadows. In short, we're faced with quite a challenge!

Figure 7-18 Fixing a really bad scan

We obey our own admonition to fix the biggest problem first. The scan is far too dark.

Original scan

Shadow clipping (level 3). The shadows are heavily posterized, with huge tonal jumps between levels 0, 1, 2, and 3.

Highlight clipping (level 210). The deck is the brightest part of the image, and the red channel is brighter than the others.

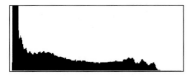

The histogram shows that the highlights are completely empty, and the shadows are clipped.

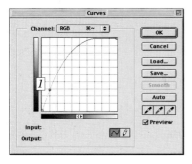

Working with Curves, we drag the cursor over the image and find that the values in the face lie around level 26, so we place point 1 to make the face visible. This blows out the highlights, so we place point 2 to bring them back into a reasonable range.

Point 3 clips the empty values in the extreme highlights. Point 4 brings down the brighter areas of the deck, and point 5 flattens the curve slightly to bring back detail in the sweater. We prefer to make all of our curve adjustments at once, but in this case we need to fix the color before we can go much further.

Point 1. 26 in, 73 out. Makes the face visible, but it blows out the highlights.

Figure 7-18 Fixing a really bad scan, continued

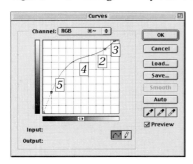

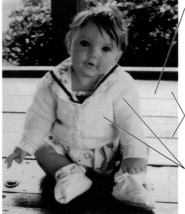

Point 2. 209 in, 228 out. Brings the highlights under control.

Point 3. 240 in, 255 out. Clips the unused highlight values.

Point 4. 152 in, 203 out. Controls posterization on the deck.

Point 5. 68 in, 143 out. Puts detail back into the sweater.

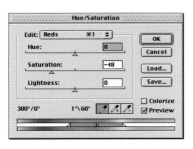

The red is heavily oversaturated, so we need to desaturate it before we can apply a final curve. Using the Hue/Saturation command to desaturate the red by 48 points produces the image seen at right.

  The color looks more natural, but the contrast on the face is still too harsh and the spotless white outfit doesn't snap. We fix this with a second set of curve moves.

  Normally we would have done any necessary spotting—fixing blemishes, dust, and scratches—before starting our tone and color moves, but in this case we couldn't because we couldn't see them! So we spotted the image before applying the final curve.

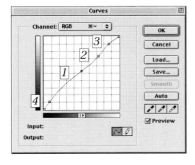

The image is still a little dark, and there simply is no detail in the shadows to be pulled out, so we limit our moves to avoid obvious posterization in the shadows.

  Point 1 lightens the image overall, and points 2 and 3 bring back some detail to the bright areas of the sweater. Point 4 simulates a little fill-flash on the shadowed side of the face without posterizing it too much.

After sharpening, we get the image at right. It isn't wonderful—there's some unavoidable posterization in the face, and there's no shadow detail at all—but it's much better than the original scan.

Given the option, we'd reject this scan as unsuitable for reproduction, but you've probably noticed that clients typically don't go for that argument. And if you're working with a typical 8-bit desktop scanner, you may have to work with this kind of scan every day.

Fixing Contrast and Color

The preceding example was an extreme case. The next example (Figure 7-19) may seem similar at first glance, but a more detailed examination tells a different story. The image looks dark, but it contains good image data throughout the tonal range—it just needs to be redistributed. We can work more precisely with this image than with the previous one because we have much more information to work with. We use the same tools as before—Curves and Hue/Saturation.

Figure 7-19 Fixing a dark image

The clipping display and histogram show that there's detail in both the highlights and the shadows. There are a few white pixels at level 255, but the true whites lie around a more comfortable level 236.

In the shadows, most of the darker pixels represent the saturated flowers in the foreground.

Shadow clipping (15)   *Highlight clipping (238)*

We need to make the midtones and three-quarter tones brighter, which will compress the highlights and reduce the harsh contrast on the sunlit side of the building.

Correcting Color Balance with Eyedroppers

The eyedropper tools in Levels and Curves can be difficult to control, but they can make short work of fixing color balance, particularly in images with well-defined neutrals (see Figures 7-20 and 7-21). The key to successful use of the eyedroppers is careful matching of the target color to the source color that you click on in the image. The eyedroppers don't work well for large moves, but they're very effective with small ones.

Figure 7-21 Partial cast removal with eyedroppers

You don't have to limit yourself to neutral target values with the eyedroppers. You can set any target color, and click on any source color, although large differences between source and target colors can produce unpredictable results. Curves let you control color casts very precisely, but they can be a lot of work, and you can only manipulate one channel at a time. The gray eyedropper can be both faster and more flexible.

The image has a yellow cast, but no obvious neutrals to use as a reference for correction by the numbers. When we make the background neutral using the curves shown below, the result is the rather ugly and austere rendition shown here.

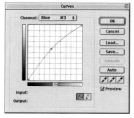 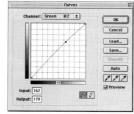

The gray eyedropper provides a more flexible solution. We decide to try removing half of the yellow cast instead of neutralizing it completely.

   We sample the background and see that it has about 25 points less blue than red or green. Halving the difference, we set the gray eyedropper target color to 127R 132G 122B, then try clicking various source pixels in the background.

   Clicking a source pixel of 111R 107G 80B produces the result at right, which looks much more natural than the strictly neutral one above.

Figure 7-22 Correcting a Photo CD image of unknown origin

The Universal Negative 3.0 profile worked better than others in acquiring this image, but the resulting image, top, is flat, and the fleshtones have a cyan cast. Not a bad starting point, though.

We apply the curves at right to get the result above, which represents our best guess.

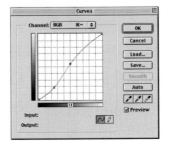

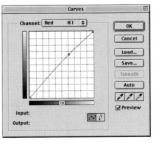

Correcting an Old Photo CD Image

Photo CD got a bad rap when it first appeared, and you still hear people saying that scans from Photo CD are usually flat, with a color cast. This isn't true; a properly made and properly acquired Photo CD scan usually looks great right off the bat. But we understand how Photo CD got its reputation, and this exercise illustrates it.

Color management has always been at the heart of Photo CD—when you open a Photo CD image, you're always asked to choose a source and destination profile. But when Photo CD first appeared, parts of the system were still under construction. With modern Photo CDs, you can use the Image Info button in the Photo CD Open dialog box to find out which profile to use as the source profile for the image.

But most early Photo CDs don't have this information embedded, and they were often scanned using early film profiles (or film "terms," in Kodak jargon) that provided less accurate results than today's. You have to guess which source profile to use (or try them all), and the images often need tweaking for color balance and contrast. This is the case with the image in Figure 7-22, from Kodak's first Photo CD Sampler.

A little experimentation suggested that the best profile for this image was the Universal Negative 3.0 profile—it gave us a better starting point than either the Kodachrome or Ektachrome profiles. So we took a first pass at the image using that profile and a few curve corrections.

But we were guessing, so we cheated and asked a friend at Kodak for a print made from the original negative. As it turns out, our guess wasn't too far off—it was a little on the conservative side. The image did indeed come from a negative. It has the characteristic orangey fleshtones and strong saturation of the Ektar25 stock on which it was shot.

With the print as a reference, we created the curves shown at left, then sharpened it using the techniques described in Chapter 9, *Sharpening*.

The result is the final image at upper right on the facing page, which is about as close a match to the color and appearance of the original print as our output process will allow.

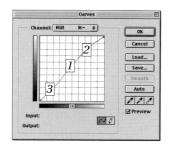

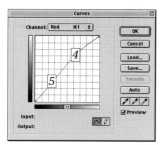

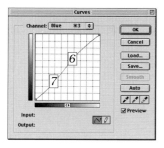

We created the tone curve at left and the color curves below to match the print we used as a reference. We used them to create the upper-right image on the facing page. We also desaturated the reds (see Chapter 8, The Digital Darkroom), and emphasized the eyes with some sharpening tricks (see Chapter 9, Sharpening).

The RGB curve improves the overall contrast, concentrating on the midtones and quartertones. Point 1 lightens the hair slightly, point 2 brightens the highlights on the face, and point 3 pulls back the curve to prevent the shadows from washing out.

The red curve kills the cyan cast. Point 4 puts red back into the fleshtones, and point 5 pulls back the red curve to avoid making the whole image too red.

The blue curve is the fine-tuner. Point 6 takes a little yellow out of the fleshtones, and point 7 pulls back on the blue curve to avoid a blue cast.

Working with a High-Bit Scan

Until Photoshop 5, we used high-bit files only for difficult images — support for them was limited, and since Photoshop treats any high-bit file as a 48-bit image, the memory footprint is twice as big as that of a 24-bit image. But Photoshop 5 offers much better support for high-bit files than previous versions—Hue/Saturation, Channel Mixer, Color Balance, the Rubber Stamp tool, the Lasso, the Pen tool, and Transform Selection, Rotate Canvas and Image Size all work on high-bit files in addition to the selection Marquee, Levels, and Curves offered by previous versions.

We find that this is a pretty complete toolset: the only major omission is Unsharp Mask, but fortunately our good friends at ImageXPress have produced the Alius Deep-Bit Filters package, which along with several other handy filters that operate on high-bit files, includes a very capable Unsharp Mask filter. The majority of today's scanners allow you to bring high-bit data (16 bits per channel) into Photoshop instead of downsampling it to 24-bit color (8 bits per channel) with the scanner software, and we're finding more and more reasons to do so. See "The high-bit advantage" in Chapter 13, *Capturing Images,* for a fuller discussion of the case for using high-bit scans.

The major advantage is that you're working on all the data the scanner can capture. Instead of stretching and squeezing 24 bits, you're stretching and squeezing 48 bits, only 24 of which are visible. This lets you make multiple edits without degrading the image, and hence lets you work much more precisely. And instead of making corrections during the scan (using the scanner's software on a small preview), you can work on the full-size image.

With a 48-bit image, most of the caveats about multiple rounds of Levels or Curves disappear. In fact, you can get better results making a series of small moves than you do making one large one, because each move can be gentler, so you aren't putting tight kinks in the curve. In the bad old days, we had to take this approach to ridiculous lengths, because Leaf Systems, who pioneered 16-bit-per-channel image capture, used their own method of scaling high-bit data which worked at cross purposes to Photoshop, with the result that the images came in very dark from Leaf scanners, and very light from the Leaf DCB digital camera. We're pleased to report that this issue has finally been resolved in Photoshop 5.0.2. As far as we know, no other high-bit capture device has had this problem.

With high-bit images, we don't have to worry about getting everything right with a single set of Curves, Levels or Hue/Saturation adjustments. Instead, we can make many small edits, each one of which addresses a specific problem, as shown in Figure 7-23.

Figure 7-23 Fixing a high-bit scan

The raw 48-bit scan contains good data, holding the highlights in the clouds, and pulling out what little detail in the shadows the film could record, but the contrast is a little harsh, the midtones and three-quarter-tones are too dark, and the color needs a saturation boost.

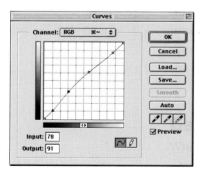

Our first curve opens up the midtones and three-quarter-tones. We placed anchor points near the highlight and the shadow to prevent the curve from affecting them.

Figure 7-23 Fixing a high-bit scan, continued

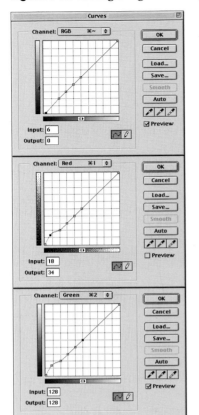

When we inspect the shadows, we find that they're distinctly blue, as often happens at high altitudes, and they're also quite noisy. This round of curves neutralizes the shadows by bringing the red and green channels up to the same levels as the blue, and also clips out some of the noise by moving the endpoint of the RGB curve.

Three quick saturation tweaks use custom color ranges to pump up the dark jungle greens, the yellowish green of the grass, and the blue of the sky, respectively.

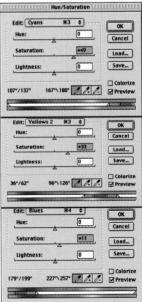

Figure 7-23 Fixing a high-bit scan, continued

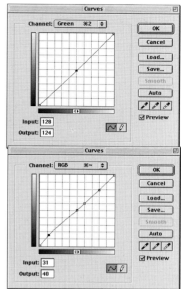

*The image has a slight green cast which became more pronounced
from the saturation moves, so we bring down the midpoint of the green curve. The shoulder of the mountain
at the right is too dark, so we open it up a little with the RGB curve.*

*The shadows are a little washed out. A quick look at the levels clipping display reveals that the first 14 levels
are largely noise, so we clip them. Finally, we sharpen the image using the Alius Deep-Bit-Filter Unsharp
Mask, then we archive the corrected, sharpened RGB image before converting a copy to CMYK and
downsampling to 8 bits per channel.*

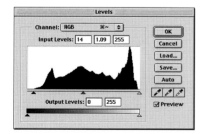

Color is Personal

It has been argued that no two people see the same color, and we know from bitter experience that an individual can see the same color differently on different occasions, or in different contexts. We don't pretend to have all the answers, and you may disagree with some of the decisions we've made with some of the images. That's fine. Our aim isn't to wow you with our color expertise. Instead, we've tried to show you how to evaluate images, how to see problems, and how to use a wide range of Photoshop's tools to address them.

8

The Digital Darkroom

Photographic Techniques in Photoshop

What would you say if we told you that you could perform color correction, use dodging and burning, build up density in overexposed areas, open up underexposed areas, and more—all with a minimum of image degradation and with an unlimited number of undos? You'd probably just laugh at us. But in this chapter we'll show you how.

When we first saw Layers in Photoshop 3, we realized that they opened up new ways of editing images, ways that bore a much greater resemblance to printing in the darkroom than they did to operating prepress equipment. Adjustment Layers, introduced in Photoshop 4, made the whole business of editing with layers much easier. The controls in Adjustment Layers behave exactly as they do when you're working on a flat file, only with far more freedom and flexibility. You can change your mind at any time about a global edit, going back and changing it, you can vary its strength globally by varying the Adjustment Layer's opacity, or even vary it locally by painting on the Adjustment Layer's Layer Mask. In effect, you have not just unlimited Undo, but selective, partial Undo.

The techniques in this chapter can help you get a better image with less degradation and more control of your changes. But much more important, they're designed to give you maximum flexibility so that you can experiment and play with your images more. While we'll give you some places to jump off from, it's really in this playing around that you'll see the myriad of options that these techniques make possible.

Why Use Adjustment Layers?

Whenever you apply a Curves or Levels tweak (or even a Hue/Saturation adjustment) to an image, you're degrading it a little by throwing away some image data. Once that data is gone, you can't get it back. In the digital darkroom, this degradation is no longer an issue because you make edits to layers *above* the image rather than to the image itself.

If you're a photographer, think of it this way: your raw image is like a negative that you can print through many different filter pack combinations on many different contrast grades of paper: you can make huge changes from print to print, but the negative itself doesn't change. If the raw image is analogous to a negative, adjustment layers are like enlarger filter packs on steroids. You can change the color balance as you would with a filter pack, but you can also change the contrast, and do local, selective editing akin to dodging and burning. However, unlike their analog counterparts, you can always undo digital dodging and burning.

There are several other reasons why we love working in the digital darkroom.

▶ **Changing your mind.** Adjustment layers give you the freedom to change your mind. If you make successive edits with Curves or Levels on a flat file, your image will quickly degrade. With adjustment layers, you can go back and change your edits at any time without further degrading the image. This gives you endless freedom to experiment, and because you can fine-tune your edits with no penalty, you're more likely to get the results you want.

▶ **Instant before-and-afters.** You can always tell exactly what you're doing when you use adjustment layers. Because all your edits are on layers, you can easily see "before and after" views by turning off the visibility for the layer you're working on, and then turning it back on again (by clicking on the eyeball in the left column of the Layers palette).

▶ **Variable-strength edits.** The Opacity slider in the Layers palette acts as a volume control for your edits (this is similar to using the Fade Filter feature; see Chapter 2, *Essential Photoshop Tips and Tricks)*.

▶ **Apply the same edits to multiple images.** You can use the same adjustment layer on a number of different images, and even script the layer with Actions to batch-apply to a folder full of images.

▶ **Brushable edits.** You can make selective, local edits to a particular area of an adjustment layer. This means you not only have essentially unlimited undo, but also *partial* undo.

▶ **Doing the impossible.** You can use adjustment layers in conjunction with Apply modes to do things that are usually extremely difficult, if not impossible–such as building density in highlights or opening up shadows without posterizing the image.

You can use adjustment layers as effectively on CMYK or Lab images as on RGB (though we still typically work with RGB images when we can). If you prefer to work by the numbers, the Info palette shows before-and-after values while you're working an adjustment layer's controls, and you can place Color Samplers to track key values just as you can on a flat file. If you'd rather work visually, you can use CMYK Preview to see how your edits will work on the printed result. In fact, in Photoshop 5 you can even preview the individual CMYK plates while working in RGB.

Why Not Use Adjustment Layers?

With all these advantages, why not use adjustment layers for all your edits? We think the only good reasons not to use this powerful feature for making tonal or color adjustments are when you are in a severely RAM-impaired environment, or when you're working on a high-bit image.

Adjustment Layers and RAM. The primary downside to using adjustment layers is that they can use a lot of RAM (or hard drive scratch space, if you don't have enough RAM). The major penalty comes when you add the first adjustment layer—Photoshop requires about two times the size (in RAM) of your base image. Subsequent adjustment layers add very little to the RAM requirements because adjustment layers themselves contain almost no data (unless you do a significant amount of local editing by painting on the Layer mask).

This isn't actually as bad as it sounds; Photoshop needs at least twice the size of your base image in RAM to make any edit, because Photoshop puts a copy of the unedited file into the Undo buffer. So the scratch requirements for an adjustment layer are really only a little more than for a flat file.

In fact, even if using an adjustment layer exceeds the RAM you have, it probably won't be that big of a deal because of the way Photoshop handles its image cache. This means that making an edit with an adjustment layer is often faster than making the same edit on a flat file, even if the adjustment layer needs more RAM than you have available (see Chapter 2, *Essential Photoshop Tips and Tricks,* for a much more detailed discussion of the image cache).

Adjustment Layers and Video LUT Animation. There's one other potential problem with adjustment layers: Video LUT Animation doesn't work with them. So you lose the real-time (though slightly inaccurate) feedback and you can't use the Levels clipping display (see Chapter 6, *Tonal Correction*). This isn't a big deal, either—at worst, it means you just have to leave the Preview checkbox turned on in the various Adjustment Layer dialog boxes (Curves, Levels, and so on).

Tip: The Two-Step Clipping Display. We really like the clipping display feature in the Levels dialog box (hold down the Option key when dragging the white- and black-point sliders). Because they rely on Video LUT Animation, however, they don't work in adjustment layers. Here's one workaround.

1. Target the Background layer by clicking on it in the Layers palette.

2. Use the clipping feature to find good white and black points, as we discussed back in Chapter 6, *Tonal Correction.* Either write down the values on a piece of paper, or save them using the Save button in the Levels dialog box.

3. Cancel out of the Levels dialog box.

4. Create a Levels adjustment layer (we'll discuss how to do this in the next section) using the values you copied in step 2. If you saved the values to disk, load them by pressing the Load button.

All things considered, the disadvantages to using adjustment layers are minimal. We believe that most people will get better, faster results using them.

Adjustment Layer Basics

Before adjustment layers, our digital darkroom techniques involved duplicating the Background layer to use as an editing layer. Because all the edits were made to the duplicate, the original image was never damaged. Every additional change required an additional copy of the image on its own layer. Adjustment layers do exactly the same thing, but they do it "behind the scenes" automatically, and with a much smaller RAM footprint. We mention this because it's much easier to get your head around what happens with an adjustment layer if you think of it as a copy of the base image, particularly when you start using adjustment layers in conjunction with Apply modes.

The controls in adjustment layers work exactly as they do in flat files. You can make adjustment layers using Levels, Curves, Brightness/ Contrast, Color Balance, Hue/Saturation, Selective Color, Channel Mixer, Invert, Threshold, and Posterize. Of these, we tend to use Curves and Hue/Saturation far more often than the others, but we encourage you to experiment. You can't do any harm, because your original image stays intact on the Background layer until you flatten it.

Creating Adjustment Layers

The first step in working with adjustment layers is (obviously) to create one. Photoshop offers three different methods for creating an adjustment layer.

▶ **The Layer menu.** You can create an adjustment layer by choosing Adjustment Layer from the New submenu (under the Layer menu; see Figure 8-1). This is the method to use when you're working by the hour.

Figure 8-1

Creating an adjustment layer

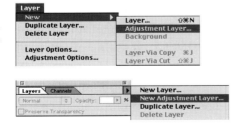

Photoshop offers three different methods for creating an Adjustment Layer.

▶ **The Layers palette menu.** You can choose New Adjustment Layer from the Layers palette popout menu. We find this method a little quicker than the last, because you don't have to navigate through a submenu.

▶ **The New Layer button.** Our favorite method of creating an adjustment layer is to Command-click on the New Layer button at the bottom of the Layers palette.

No matter how you create the adjustment layer, Photoshop asks you what kind of adjustment layer and options you want—the name of the layer, its Apply mode, and its opacity (see Figure 8-2).

Figure 8-2

Creating an adjustment layer

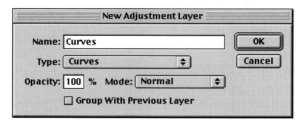

Tip: Adjustment Layer Actions. If you're going to be making a number of adjustment layers, you'll do yourself a favor by creating a "Make Adjustment Layer" action in the Actions palette (see "Actions and Automating Photoshop" in Chapter 2, *Essential Photoshop Tips and Tricks)*. While Bruce has a single action (assigned to an F-key for one-stroke replay) that opens the New Adjustment Layer dialog box and lets you choose which kind of adjustment layer you want, David takes a different approach. He has three different actions—one to automatically add a Curves adjustment layer, another to add a Hue/Saturation adjustment layer, and a third for Levels. After creating the type he wants, David double-clicks on the adjustment layer in the Layers palette to adjust the layer's settings.

Controlling Adjustment Layers

The big difference between using adjustment layers and editing a flat file is that adjustment layers give you much more freedom to control and refine your edits. You have four ways to control your editing when using an adjustment layer that you don't have with a flat file.

Variable strength. You can control the opacity of the adjustment layer by changing the Opacity slider in the Layers palette. This lets you change the intensity of the adjustment globally. We often make edits that are slightly more extreme than we really want, then back off the opacity of the editing layer to reduce the effect to just where we want it. We find this faster than trying to fine-tune the adjustment in the Adjustment Layer dialog box.

Fine-tuning. Whenever you want to make a change to the adjustment layer, you can edit it (changing the curve or choosing other options) by double-clicking on the Adjustment Layer tile in the Layers palette. When you do this, Photoshop displays the settings you last used in the Adjustment Layer dialog box. Not to beat a dead papaya, but you can do this as often as you want without degrading the image because the edits aren't actually applied until you flatten the file.

Multiple edits. You don't have to limit yourself to a single adjustment layer. You can have as many as you want, each stacked on top of the next to make successive edits without degrading the image. This technique is particularly useful when you want one curve to correct the image globally while another curve edits the image in selective places.

Note that adjustment layers apply to all visible layers beneath them. When you stack two or more adjustment layers of the same type—all Curves, or all Hue/Saturation, for example—you'll get the same results no matter what order they're stacked in. But when you mix adjustment layers of different types, you'll get different results depending on the stacking order. Usually the differences are fairly subtle—you may need to check the numbers in the Info palette to see them—but occasionally the difference can be significant, especially when working with Hue/Saturation and Color Balance.

Oddly enough, you can't merge adjustment layers; if you want to reduce the number of layers, your only option is to flatten the whole image. We don't recommend doing this, since you'd lose all the advantages of adjustment layers. Instead, keep all your adjustment layers live until you're finished with the project, then use Save a Copy to save a flattened version of the image.

Selective editing. While the Opacity slider applies to the entire adjustment layer, you can vary the opacity of the layer in distinct, local areas by painting on the adjustment layer's layer mask. To paint on the layer mask, simply click on the adjustment layer tile in the Layers palette and paint; the paint automatically goes on the layer mask. Black paint removes the effect of the adjustment layer; white paint brings it back; gray paint applies the effect partially (25-percent black ink would apply 75 percent of the adjustment layer's effect). By varying the opacity of the brush in the Options palette, you can achieve very precise control over the opacity of the adjustment layer in specific areas of the image.

Note that a new channel is automatically added to the Channels palette whenever you select an adjustment layer in the Layers palette. This is the channel that you're actually drawing on. You can use all the usual layer mask tricks, such as Shift-clicking on the layer mask (in the Layers palette) to turn the mask on or off, and Option-clicking to view (or hide) the layer mask (see "Selections and Layers" in Chapter 14, *Selections)*.

Tip: Use Painting Shortcuts. There are some little shortcuts that we use so often, we need to mention them again here. When painting on the layer mask, don't forget that you can press D to reset the foreground and background colors (to white and black). Press X to switch the foreground and background colors. Press the number keys (0–9) to set the opacity of the paintbrush—for instance, 0 sets the opacity to 100 percent, 9 sets it to 90 percent, 45 to 45 percent, and so on.

Saving adjustment layers. You can save an adjustment layer separately from an image. We find this most useful when we want to apply the same color- and tonal-correction edits to multiple images.

Here's how to save an adjustment layer into a new or different document.

1. Select the adjustment layer you want to save.

2. Choose Duplicate Layer from either the Layer menu or the Layers palette popout menu.

3. Pick a file in the Duplicate Layers dialog box to save the adjustment layer into. If you choose New for the destination, Photoshop creates

a new document for you; if you choose an existing document, Photoshop copies the adjustment layer into that image.

4. Press OK.

The ability to copy adjustment layers also opens up some new workflow possibilities. Before we had the Adjustment Layer feature, we always took care of retouching our image (dust and scratches, and so on) before we did any editing for tone or color. However, with adjustment layers, the order of these tasks doesn't matter. Two people can even work on the same image at the same time—one doing the retouching while the other edits tone and color—then later, you can apply the adjustment layer(s) to the retouched image.

Another workflow option is to make your color- and tonal-correction edits on a low-resolution version of a large image. The edits may go faster on the low-resolution version, and when you're done you can apply the adjustment layers to the monster 300 MB high-resolution version of the image. Of course, if you've done any painting on the layer mask, that won't translate properly when placed into the high-resolution file (see "Tip: Making Masks Meet," below).

Tip: Copying Adjustment Layers Quickly. The Duplicate Layer feature is useful, but we find it faster to copy an adjustment layer simply by dragging it from the Layers palette in one image on top of another image. Again, if the two images have different pixel dimensions, any layer mask will probably transfer incorrectly (see the next tip).

Even better, you can use Actions to script the creation of adjustment layers, then apply exactly the same edits to a whole folder of images using the Batch Processing features (see "Actions" in Chapter 15, *Image Techniques)*. The only limitation is that you can't script edits that you've made by brushing on the layer mask.

Tip: Making Masks Meet. Trying to match an adjustment layer's layer mask in one image to its layer mask in another image is easy, as long as the pixel dimensions of the two images are the same. When you use the Duplicate Layer technique to move an adjustment layer to a different document, Photoshop centers the layer mask in the new document. If the two documents have the same pixel dimensions, this works great; if they don't, you'll have problems.

When you drag an adjustment layer from one document into another, any pixels on the layer mask are placed exactly where you drop the layer (where you let go of the mouse button). This is almost never where you want them to be. Instead, as long as the two images have the same pixel dimensions, you can hold down the Shift key while dragging the layer; this way, Photoshop pin-registers the layer to the target image.

Remember, to match the pixel dimensions of an image, open the Image Size dialog box in the target image (the one you want to change), then select the source image (the one you're copying) from the Window menu.

Tip: Adjustment Layers and Disk Space. At first glance, adding one or more adjustment layers to your image seems to double its size when you save it to disk in the Photoshop format (the only format that lets you save layers; see Chapter 16, *Storing Images)*. That's odd, because the adjustment layer is essentially an empty layer. The key is to turn off Include Composited Image with Layered Files in the Saving Files Preferences dialog box (under the File menu). As we noted back in Chapter 2, *Essential Photoshop Tips and Tricks,* almost no one needs this feature turned on. Turn it off, and your Photoshop file sizes get much, much smaller.

Note that if you paint on the adjustment layer's layer mask (to do local editing), the file size increases a little, but the increase is relatively small.

When you're ready to save a nonlayered version of the image, you can use Flatten Image (from the Layer menu), or use Save a Copy to save a flattened file without damaging your original layered document.

Using Adjustment Layers

In many ways, these tools are more difficult to explain than they are to use, so let's look at some examples. We'll start off with relatively simple examples, and work up to more complex ones.

Simple Adjustment Layers

The image in Figure 8-3 is a well-exposed original, but it's a little flat. We'll fix it with a curve, but instead of burning the curve permanently into the image, we'll use a Curves adjustment layer.

Figure 8-3

The raw image

This image is well exposed, holding detail in both shadows and highlights, but it's a little flat.

Figure 8-4

Applying a Curves adjustment layer

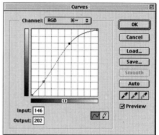

We deliberately exaggerated the curve because we plan to fine-tune it by reducing the adjustment layer's opacity, which in turn lessens the curve's intensity.

A single adjustment layer. We create a new adjustment layer, and choose Curves in the New Adjustment Layer dialog box. We leave Opacity at 100 percent and the Apply mode set to Normal.

Working with a curve on an adjustment layer is very much like working with a curve on a flat file. But this time we'll deliberately make the curve a little more extreme than we would for a flat file.

This curve makes the subject pop, but it's a little too much—the blues of the boat are starting to look washed out, and the white trim is perilously close to blowing out. We reduce the opacity of the adjustment layer to 65 percent, using the Opacity slider in the Layers palette to produce the final result in Figure 8-5. In this case, we deliberately exaggerate the curve and the opacity change to make the difference obvious. Normally, we'd push the curve just slightly past the result we wanted and make far smaller moves with the Opacity slider.

Figure 8-5
The final result

Reducing the adjustment layer's opacity to 65 percent produces this result.

Multiple adjustment layers. Figure 8-6 shows a second, slightly more complex example. Again, the image is well exposed, but it has a greenish color cast and it's dark. In the past, we would have tried to construct a single set of curves that took care of both the color and the tone, but with

Figure 8-6
Killing the color cast

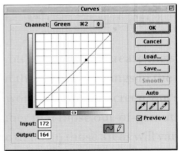

We create a Curves adjustment layer, then bring the green curve down to get rid of the green color cast. Note that a relatively small change to the green curve has a big effect on the water and on the grays of the hull.

adjustment layers we can use multiple sets of curves, each aimed at a single problem. The curves are easier to construct, and the results are better. We usually try to fix the biggest problem first (though again, when you use adjustment layers, the order in which you correct an image is less important). In this case, the worst offender is the color cast, which we'll correct using a Curves adjustment layer. We could probably achieve similar results using a Levels or Color Balance adjustment layer, but for reasons we've explained elsewhere, we generally use Curves for problems like this.

At this point in the process we don't worry about getting the color exactly right, because we can go back and fine-tune the curve later. We just want to tame the color cast sufficiently to let us make good judgments about the contrast without being distracted by the color balance problems. Then by breaking the contrast adjustments out into a different adjustment layer, we can control the color balance globally, and adjust contrast locally (in specific areas of the image). Here, our second Curves adjustment layer brightens and improves the contrast of the image.

Figure 8-7
Fixing the contrast

We create another Curves adjustment layer, and apply an S-shaped curve that brightens the image and increases the contrast, making the subject pop.

Now we can return to the first adjustment layer to fine-tune the color balance. We take the water as our starting point. A sample of the pixel values in the water shows us that it's a little orange—the red channel is high and the blue channel is low. We like the water to be fairly neutral, so we adjust the color balance by double-clicking on the adjustment layer's tile in the Layers palette. Once we've made the water neutral, we check for any other color balance problems, and fix them. At this stage, small changes to the curves have a relatively large impact on the color balance.

Figure 8-8

Fine-tuning the color

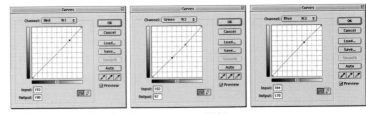

We make the water appear neutral by making very small alterations to the red and blue channels. This in turn makes some of the grays on the hull of the boat look a little magenta. A second point on the green curve neutralizes them.

The image looks much better now, but we've lost almost all the detail in the sky. To bring it back, we target our second Curves layer, the one we used to brighten the image. Using a fairly large soft-edged brush with an opacity of around 40 percent, we paint on the adjustment layer's layer mask with black paint; this "erases" the effect, returning the detail to the image. If we darken the sky too much, we can simply press X to switch foreground and background colors, then paint with white to build back the opacity of the layer. If you find that you need to see exactly where you're painting, remember that you can turn on visibility for the layer mask by Shift-clicking on the layer mask, or by clicking on the layer mask's eyeball in the left column of the Channels palette—however, we rarely find this necessary.

Figure 8-9

Brushing the layer mask

We brush detail back into the sky by targeting our second Curves layer and using a soft brush at a medium opacity to apply black paint to the layer mask.

This image is destined for print, so we turn on CMYK Preview to get an idea of how it will look in CMYK mode. Here, we find the image looks a little unsaturated, so we create one more adjustment layer, this time choosing Hue/Saturation as the adjustment type. Increasing the global saturation by 18 points produces the final result shown below.

Figure 8-10
Adding a Hue/Saturation layer

We add a Hue/ Saturation layer to increase the saturation by about 18 points.

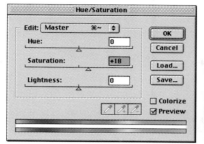

At this point, we save the file with the adjustment layers. Finally, we use the Save a Copy command to save a flattened version of the edited image. We sharpen the copy, set our highlight and shadow points, convert it to CMYK, and send it off for proofing.

Advanced Adjustment Layers

The previous examples were relatively simple, using straightforward adjustment layers for global editing, with some painting on the layer mask for local corrections. However, when you combine adjustment layers with the power of Apply modes, you open up a whole new world of possibilities. We tend to use Multiply and Screen much more than the other Apply modes, but we encourage you to experiment—there are plenty of new techniques waiting to be discovered.

Building density with Multiply. The best analogy we've found for Multiply mode is that it's like sandwiching two negatives in an enlarger. Mathematically, Multiply takes two values, multiplies them by each other, and divides by 255. Practically speaking, this means the result is always darker than either of the sources.

If a pixel is black in the base image, the result after applying an adjustment layer with Multiply is also black. If a pixel is white in the base image, the adjustment layer has no effect (white is the neutral color for Multiply). We use Multiply with Curves adjustment layers to build density, particularly in the highlights and midtones of overexposed images like the one in Figure 8-11.

Figure 8-11

A washed-out image

This scene contains a huge range of contrast from the rising sun to the backlit boat. The image holds detail at both extremes, but the contrast is flat.

This image represents a scene with a huge dynamic range—a backlit boat against the sun rising over the Ganges—and thanks to the wonders of modern color negative film, we were able to capture it. Our scan has detail in both the brightest part of the sun and in the darkest part of the boat, but the distribution of the midtones is quite wrong—they're much too light, rendering what is a quite dramatic image merely pleasant. We can fix it very quickly with a single Curves adjustment layer, using the Multiply mode.

We create a new Curves adjustment layer, but this time we set the mode to Multiply. If we make no changes to the curve, and instead just press OK, the difference is dramatic. This is equivalent to duplicating the Background layer on top of itself and changing the new layer's Apply mode to Multiply.

Figure 8-12

Applying a Curves adjustment layer with Multiply

Applying a Curves layer set to Multiply results in a dramatic increase in contrast.

In fact, the difference is a little too dramatic, so we go back and adjust this adjustment layer's curve by adding two points which open up the midtones slightly while keeping the quartertone and highlight adjustments unchanged. Now the edited image does a much better job of conveying the oppressive heat, the omnipresent smoke and dust, and the languor of the millenia-old ritual that takes place at dawn on the Ganges.

If we want to, we can open up the detail on the boat by brushing black on the layer mask, but after trying it, we decide that the image works better when we leave the boat as a near-silhouette.

Figure 8-13
Adjusting the curve

 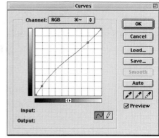

This simple two-point curve opens up the midtones and shadows a little, to produce this final result.

Opening shadows with Screen. Screen is literally the inverse of Multiply. The best real-world analogy we've heard comes from Adobe's Russell Brown: Screen is like projecting two slides on the same screen. The result is always lighter than either of the two sources.

If a pixel is white in the base image, the result is white, and if it's black in the base image, the result is also black (black is the neutral color for Screen). Intermediate tones get lighter. We use Screen mostly to open up dark shadows, like in underexposed film.

If you're a techno-dweeb like we are, you probably want to know what Screen does behind the scenes. Photoshop inverts the two numbers (subtracts them from 255) before performing a Multiply calculation (multiplies them by each other and divides by 255); then the program subtracts the result from 255. That's it. Now, don't you feel better knowing that?

Figure 8-14
A dark, muddy image

This image holds detail in both the highlights and the shadows, but the midtones are much too dark and the color is muddy.

The image in Figure 8-14 was shot using a midrange digital camera, a Polaroid PDC-2000. The image holds detail in both highlight and shadow, but it's dark and muddy. A quick three-layer fix can make huge improvements to the contrast, color balance and saturation.

Our first step is to open up the shadows using a Curves adjustment layer with the Apply mode set to Screen. Our bizarre-looking curve limits the effects of the Screen mode to the shadows and three-quarter tones, and avoids washing out all the detail in the sky.

Figure 8-15

Applying a Curves adjustment layer with Screen

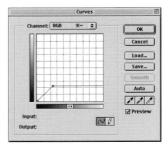

We arrive at this strange-looking curve by determining the lightest point in the image we want to affect, then chopping off the top of the straight-line curve at that point. This limits its effect to the shadows and three-quarter-tones.

Our next step is to pump up the color with a Hue/Saturation adjustment layer. We boost the overall saturation by 35 points, and the yellow and green by an additional 12 points each. This works well for everything except the clouds, which begin to look a little too cyan (sometimes after a long day at the office, the real world starts to look a little too cyan, too).

Figure 8-16

Applying a Hue/Saturation adjustment layer

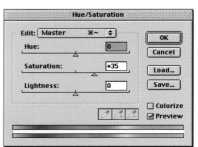

A Hue/Saturation adjustment layer pumps up the color, but makes the clouds too cyan.

We could brush out this color cast from the clouds, but it's probably quicker and easier to use a Color Range selection. First we select the top half of the image with the Marquee tool, including all of the skyline, to narrow down the area on which Color Range will operate. Then we choose Color Range from the Select menu. Even though we have the empty Hue/Saturation adjustment layer targeted, Color Range still works because it operates on visible pixels in all layers. We select the clouds using a low Fuzziness setting, Shift-clicking to build up the selection. Once we have a selection that includes the clouds and excludes the blue sky and the bridge, we click OK to accept the selection. Then we fill it with black (remember that the Hue/Saturation adjustment layer is still selected, so this paints on its layer mask), reducing the opacity of this part of the Hue/Saturation layer to zero—the color cast disappears.

Figure 8-17

Local editing using Color Range

 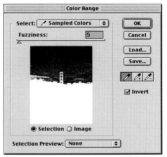

We select the clouds with Color Range, then fill the selection with black paint on the Hue/ Saturation adjustment layer's mask.

For our final step, we create another Curves adjustment layer, and use it to darken the sky and to lighten the foreground, producing the final image. If we had attempted to do these same edits on a flat file without adjustment layers, our image would be hopelessly posterized by now.

Figure 8-18

Making final contrast edits with a Curves adjustment layer

 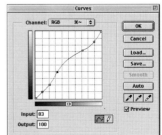

To produce the final image, we create a Curves adjustment layer and apply this fairly gentle curve. It darkens the sky and brightens the foreground, bring more depth to the image.

Reversing lens flare. While Photoshop's Lens Flare filter does a great job of simulating lens flare, more often than not we find that lens flare is something we're trying to remove from images (not introduce). We think the following example does a passable job. In case you're wondering, Bruce is fifth from the left.

Figure 8-19

A problem image with lens flare

Although the sky was overcast, the sun shining through the clouds created enough lens flare to wash out the contrast in the center of the image.

Our first step is to increase the contrast in the lens flare area. We create a Curves adjustment layer, apply an S-shaped curve to increase contrast, then confine the edit to the center of the image by making a radial gradient on the layer mask. We also brush some contrast into the tree at the left by applying white paint to the layer mask.

Figure 8-20

Increasing contrast in the center

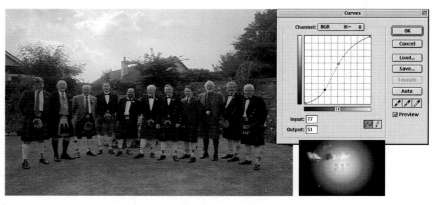

We create a Curves adjustment layer with an S-shaped curve to boost contrast, then mask it using a radial gradient and some local brushing in the layer mask.

Our next step is to build some contrast in the sky. We do this by creating a Curves adjustment layer set to Multiply, then masking it with a linear gradient to limit its effect to the top quarter of the image. We adjust the curve to increase the contrast in the highlights, and to correct the color balance of the sky (it's turning a little magenta). We also brush some contrast into the faces on the left, again using white paint on the layer mask.

Figure 8-21

Fixing the sky with Multiply

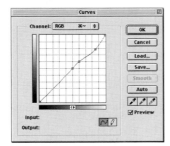 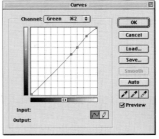

We add a Curves layer set to Multiply, and mask it using a linear gradient and some local brushing to limit its effect to the top of the image. The curves add a little more contrast and fix the color balance.

We have one remaining problem: the complexions of some of the braw lads in the center of the image are excessively florid. We take care of

Figure 8-22

Desaturating the faces

We add a Hue/Saturation layer with the master saturation reduced by about 25 points, and mask it using the same radial gradient we used in the first Curves layer. Then we brush some saturation back into the kilts using white paint on the layer mask.

this by adding a Hue/Saturation layer with the master saturation reduced by 25 points, then we copy the radial mask from our first Curves adjustment layer into this Hue/Saturation adjustment layer; this limits the desaturation to the center of the image (note that you can copy a layer mask by selecting the adjustment layer, pressing Command-A to select all, and then pressing Command-C). Finally, we brush some saturation back into the kilts using white paint on the layer mask.

We don't even want to think about how hard this sort of correction would be without adjustment layers. To make all these edits on a flat file, carefully building selections and then applying the curves and saturation moves to them, would be extremely difficult if not impossible.

Extracting invisible detail. The Channel Mixer isn't a terribly intuitive color-correction tool, but Figure 8-23 shows a situation where it comes in handy. The shadows appear completely blocked, but there's a lot more detail in the blue channel than in the other two. We can pull out that detail by feeding the blue channel into the other two channels, working on an Adjustment Layer through a Layer Mask to confine the effect to the shadows.

Figure 8-23
Blocked-up shadows

The shadows in this image appear completely blocked, but when we look at the individual channels, we see that there's much more detail in the blue than in the red or green.

We create a Channel Mixer Adjustment Layer, and create a Layer Mask to constrain its effect to the shadow areas. In this case, we simply brushed the Layer Mask, but you could also use Color Range to create it. We replaced 90 percent of the red and green channels with blue, producing the image in Figure 8-24.

Figure 8-24

Mixing the channels

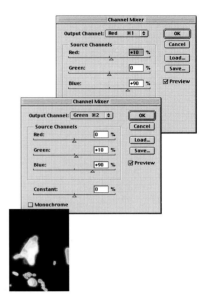

Applying the Channel Mixer through a layer mask, we replace 90 percent of the red and green channels with blue, bringing out the hidden detail.

Figure 8-25

Returning color to the shadows

Using the same layer mask as for the Channel Mixer layer, we create a Hue/Saturation Layer and bump up the saturation to bring back a little color into the shadows, which would otherwise be very neutral indeed.

To produce the final image in Figure 8-25, we create a Hue/Saturation layer and copy the Layer Mask from the Channel Mixer layer, then we bump up the saturation. Since the three color channels are now almost identical, there's very little color left, so we can make a fairly extreme saturation boost of 68 percent to bring back a little color and prevent the shadows from looking flat.

Darkroom Experiments

Don't get the idea that you have to work exclusively using adjustment layers, layer masks, and Apply modes. We just present them as interesting and often useful approaches. You can mix and match the techniques in this chapter with more conventional curve-based editing.

Nonetheless, working with these tools offers a huge amount of freedom to experiment. Because you aren't touching the original image, you can take chances, drive your image to extremes, and generally do things you'd never do if you were working on a flat image. Of course, once you've got the image the way you want it, you still have to deal with all the issues around targeting it for a particular output process, which we discuss in just about every other chapter in this book.

9

Sharpening

Getting an Edge on Your Image

The human visual system depends to a great degree on edges. Simply put, our eyes pass information to our brain, where every detail is quickly broken down into "edge" or "not edge." An image may have great contrast and color balance, but without good edge definition, we simply see it as less lifelike.

As it turns out, no matter how good your scanner and how crisp your original may be, you always lose some sharpness when the image is digitized. Images from low-end flatbed scanners and digital cameras always need a considerable amount of sharpening. High-end scanners sharpen as part of the scanning process. Even a high-resolution digital camera back on a finely focused view camera produces images that will benefit from sharpening. Remember, you *cannot* solve the problem of blurry scans by scanning at a higher resolution. It just doesn't work that way.

Your images also lose sharpness in the output process. Halftoned images (almost anything on a printing press) and dithered ones (such as those printed on thermal-wax and ink-jet printers) are the worst offenders. But even continuous-tone devices such as film recorders and dye-sublimation printers lose a little sharpness.

To counteract the blurries in both the input and output stages, you need to sharpen your images. Photoshop offers several sharpening filters, but Unsharp Mask is the only one that really works as a production tool. Sharpen, Sharpen More, Sharpen Edges, and the Sharpening tool may be useful for creative effects, but they'll wreck your images very quickly if you try to use them to compensate for softness introduced during either acquisition or output.

Unsharp Masking

Unsharp masking (often abbreviated as USM) may sound like the last thing you'd want to do if you're trying to make an image appear sharper, but the term actually makes some sense; it has its origins in a traditional photographic technique for enhancing sharpness.

The things we see as edges are areas of high contrast between adjacent pixels. The higher the contrast, the sharper the edges appear. So to increase sharpness, you need to increase the contrast along the edges.

In the traditional process, the photographic negative is sandwiched in the enlarger along with a slightly out-of-focus duplicate negative—an unsharp mask—and the exposure time for printing is approximately doubled. Because the unsharp mask is slightly out of focus and the exposure time has been increased, the light side of the edges prints lighter and the dark side of the edges prints darker, creating a "halo" around objects in the image (see Figure 9-1).

As we'll see throughout this chapter, this halo effect is both the secret of good sharpening, and its Achilles' heel—depending on the size and intensity of the halo, and where it appears in the image. Photoshop lets you control the halo very precisely, but there's no single magic setting that works for all images, so you need to know not only how the controls work, but also what you're trying to achieve in the image.

How the Unsharp Mask Filter Works

The Unsharp Mask filter works pixel by pixel, which explains why it takes so long, even on a very fast machine. It compares each pixel to its neighbors, looking for a certain amount of contrast between adjacent pixels—which it assumes is an edge. It then increases the contrast between those pixels according to the parameters you set. This creates a halo that, when viewed from normal distances, increases apparent sharpness.

Figure 9-1 Edge transitions and sharpening

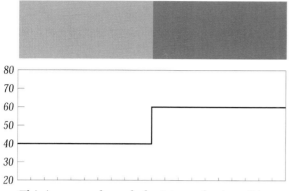

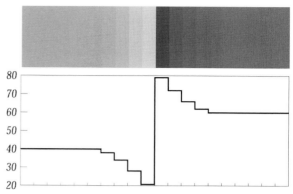

This image and graph depict an edge transition— from 40 to 60 percent. Each tick mark across the graph represents a column of pixels.

After sharpening, the transition is accentuated— it's darker on the dark side, and lighter on the light side, creating a halo around the edge.

Unsharpened   Sharpened

The effect on images ranges from subtle to impressive to destructive. This image is somewhat oversharpened to make the effect clear.

These samples are darker after sharpening.

These samples are lighter.

The net result is a sharper-looking image.

But Photoshop can't actually detect edges—it just looks at contrast differences (zeros and ones again). So unsharp masking can also have the undesired effect of exaggerating texture in flat areas, and emphasizing any noise introduced by the scanner in the shadow areas.

You need to walk a fine line, sharpening only where your image needs it. Fortunately, the controls offered by the filter let you do this very precisely (see Figure 9-2). Here's a rundown of the settings you can control in Photoshop's Unsharp Mask filter, what they do, and how they interact.

Figure 9-2

The Unsharp
Mask filter

Unsharp Mask

OK

Cancel

☑ Preview

⊞ 100% ⊟

Amount: 136 %

Radius: 0.6 pixels

Threshold: 0 levels

Amount

We think of Amount as the volume control of unsharp masking. It adjusts the intensity of the sharpening halo (see Figure 9-3). High Amount settings—you can enter up to 500 percent—produce very intense halos (with lots of pixels driven to pure white or solid black); low Amount settings produce less intense ones. Amount has no effect on the width of the halos—just on the amount of contrast they contain.

Figure 9-3

Varying the USM
Amount setting

Image resolution: 225 ppi
Radius: 1.2
Threshold: 4

Amount: 50   *Amount: 200*   *Amount: 350*

As you increase the Amount setting, the blips around big tonal shifts (edges) can be pushed all the way to white and black. At that point, increasing Amount has no effect whatsoever—you can't get more white than white! Worse, the all-white halos often stand out as artifacts and can look really dumb.

We almost always start out by setting Amount to between 200 and 400. Then we adjust downward from there, depending on the image (see "Working the Controls," later in this chapter).

Radius

Radius is the first thing to consider when you're setting up sharpening; it sets the width of the halo that the filter creates around edges (see Figure 9-4). The wider the halo, the more obvious the sharpening effect. Choosing the right Radius value is probably the most important choice in avoiding an unnaturally oversharpened look, and there are several factors to take into account when you choose, starting with the content of the image itself, the output method, and the intended size of the reproduction (see "Image Detail and Sharpening Radius," later in this chapter).

Figure 9-4
Varying the USM
Radius setting

Image resolution: 225 ppi
Amount: 200
Threshold: 4

Radius: 0.6　　　　*Radius: 1.2*　　　　*Radius: 2.4*

Note that a Radius value of 1.0 does not result in a single-pixel radius. In fact, the halo is often between four and six pixels wide for the whole light and dark cycle—two or three pixels on each side of the tonal shift. However, it varies in width depending on the content of the image.

Threshold

Unsharp Mask only evaluates contrast differences: it doesn't know whether those differences represent real edges you want to sharpen, or areas of texture (or, even worse, scanner noise) that you don't want to sharpen. The Threshold control lets you specify how far apart two pixels' tonal values have to be (on a scale of 0 to 255) before the filter affects them (see Figure 9-5). For instance, if Threshold is set to 3, and two adjacent pixels have values of 122 and 124 (a difference of two), they're unaffected.

You can use Threshold to make the filter ignore the relatively slight differences between pixels in smooth, low-contrast areas while still creating a halo around details that have high-contrast edges. And, to some extent at least, you can use it to avoid exaggerating noisy pixels in shadow areas.

Figure 9-5
Varying the USM
Threshold setting

Image resolution: 225 ppi
Amount: 300
Radius: 2

Threshold: 12   *Threshold: 6*   *Threshold: 0*

Low Threshold values (1 to 4) result in a sharper-looking image over-all (because fewer areas are excluded). High values (above 10) result in less sharpening. We typically begin with a low Threshold value—somewhere between 0 and 4—and then increase it as necessary.

Tip: The Preview Checkbox. The Preview checkbox applies the Unsharp Mask filter to the entire image or selection on the fly, but we keep this turned off most of the time. Even on Bruce's dual-Pentium Intergraph, the preview can take a long time, particularly on large files. And every time you change the filter settings, Photoshop has to recalculate and re-draw the entire screen. Of course, the larger the image, the longer it takes.

We turn on Preview when we're fairly sure we've arrived at the correct settings, and want to check them on the whole of the visible image.

Tip: Select a Critical Area to Preview. When you're working interactively with the Unsharp Mask settings, you may want to strike a happy medium between relying on the tiny proxy and previewing the whole image. You can do this with an additional step or two.

1. Select a critical area in the image, then select Unsharp Mask and turn on the Preview checkbox.

2. When you've arrived at the correct settings, press OK.

3. Press Command-Z (to undo the change you just made), Command-D (to deselect the area), and Command-F (to reapply the filter with the last-used settings).

This is one of those tips that takes longer to explain than it does to do!

Tip: Look at Every Pixel Before You Proceed. Like any other Photoshop effect, you can undo Unsharp Mask as long as you don't do any further editing. After we've applied Unsharp Mask, and before we do anything else, we make a point of looking at the entire image at a 100% view to make sure that we haven't created any problems. If we find a stray noisy pixel, we may just spot it out with the Rubber Stamp tool, or we may decide to redo the sharpening to avoid the problem.

It's a temptation, especially with Unsharp Mask, to zoom in to see the effects more closely. Resist! Especially when you're just getting used to unsharp masking, you should only pay attention to the 1:1 zoom factor.

Tip: Recalling the Filter. If you don't like the results of the filter after seeing them, you can press Command-Z to undo, then Command-Option-F to reopen the filter's dialog box with the last-used settings. (This works with all filters that have user-settable parameters, but we use it more with Unsharp Mask than with any other filter.)

Tip: Fade Filter. If your sharpening is a little too strong, you can reduce the effect of the Unsharp Mask (or any other) filter using the Fade command from the Filter menu (see "Filters and Effects" in Chapter 15, *Essential Image Techniques*). This is one of the best uses of Fade we've come across.

Everything's Relative

One of the most important concepts to understand about sharpening is that the three values you can set in the Unsharp Mask dialog box are all interrelated. For instance, as you increase the Radius setting, you generally need to decrease Amount to keep the apparent sharpness constant. Similarly, at higher Radius settings, you can use much higher Threshold values; this smooths out unwanted sharpening of fine texture, while still applying a good deal of sharpness to well-defined edges.

Correction versus Targeting

Figuring out how the Unsharp Mask filter works is only half the problem, though. The other half is figuring out what you need to do to the image at hand. There are two things you can do with unsharp masking.

▶ **Restore sharpness that was lost in the image-acquisition process.** You can't bring an out-of-focus or blurry original back into focus, but even a blurred original such as a fast-moving motion-blurred subject needs sharpening (it'll still be blurred, but it won't be blurred *and* soft).

▶ **Introduce extra sharpness to compensate for the output process.** In this case, you're targeting the image for your output size and method.

When you correct for softness introduced on input, you need to take into account the image content and the resolution. When you compensate for softness introduced on output, you have to take into account the output process, and the size at which the image will be reproduced.

One-pass sharpening. You can make both sets of corrections in a single move, if you know how and where the image will be output. This approach is certainly faster, and you run less risk of blowing out highlights. However, you end up with an image that's been targeted to a particular output process, and probably won't reproduce as well using another process. For instance, an image sharpened for newspaper output won't look good when it's printed at a much higher halftone frequency, and will look hideous when sent to a continuous-tone device such as a dye-sublimation printer or film recorder (see Chapter 17, *Output Methods*).

But if you're in a hurry, and you're preparing an image for one-off reproduction (particularly if you're printing with a low screen frequency that can only show a limited amount of detail anyway), one-pass sharpening makes sense.

Two-pass sharpening. Because our mothers taught us to keep our options open as long as possible, we often perform two rounds of sharpening: one for correction early in the image-manipulation process, and a second (usually much later) for targeting. The first brings back the sharpness of the original, while the second compensates for shortcomings in the output process. When using the two-pass approach, we take great care in the first pass to avoid creating spurious specular highlights and accentuating image flaws and noise, because these will be further accentuated during the second pass. We apply only enough sharpening to restore the sharpness of the original.

The results of two-pass sharpening often justify the extra pains, especially with images we plan to reuse for several different types of output.

When to sharpen. The first sharpening pass should be done after your global tonal corrections and retouching work, but before any targeting. For instance, when we're preparing a repurposable RGB image, we make our first sharpening pass just before saving the document. Then we target the image to our output method (see "Correction versus Targeting" in Chapter 6, *Tonal Correction*).

When you're sharpening as part of the targeting process—irrespective of whether it's the first or the second round—sharpening should be your third-to-last task. Do all your tonal and color correction first, including any adjustments you make to out-of-gamut colors. Then sharpen for output. Next, set your minimum highlight and maximum shadow dots (see Chapter 6, *Tonal Correction*), and—finally—convert from RGB to CMYK.

There are two exceptions to this order. First, there are times it's helpful to sharpen the individual CMYK channels selectively (see "Sharpening Channels," later in this chapter). Second, you can't sharpen before converting to CMYK if your image is already in CMYK mode. In both these cases, sharpening should be your penultimate step, just prior to setting your highlight and shadow dots.

Note that you need to sharpen *before* you set your highlight and shadow dots, because the sharpening halos can easily end up being driven beyond those limits: if you set the endpoints first, you can wind up creating unwanted specular highlights and plugged-up shadows.

Correcting for Input

With the sole exception of synthetically rendered images, any time you turn an image into pixels, some sharpness is lost. There are many factors that cause loss of sharpness when you digitize an image, and experts differ as to the relative importance of each; whatever the reasons, the bottom line is that almost every image you deal with in Photoshop needs some sharpening.

When you restore the sharpness of the original, or even make the digital file appear sharper than the original, the image doesn't actually contain any more detail—it won't really *be* sharper—but you can fool the eye into seeing it that way.

Consider the source. You should always consider where the image came from first, because each image source has different characteristics.

▶ CCD scanners almost always introduce some noise in the shadows. If you accentuate the noise in your first sharpening pass, it'll probably overwhelm the image in the second pass.

▶ Digital-camera images can present a different set of challenges: some cameras produce artifacts that need to be removed before you can sharpen the images. With a little ingenuity, you can sharpen and re-move artifacts as part of the same process (see "Sharpening Channels," later in this chapter).

▶ Drum scans shouldn't need further sharpening unless they've been downsampled. Drum scanners don't introduce noise into the image, but they can sometimes exaggerate film grain, which has the same visual effect.

We cover techniques for dealing with all these problems in "Unsharp Masking Tricks," later in this chapter.

Consider the image. You also need to consider the content of the image. A head shot needs a different kind of sharpening than a landscape, for example, because one may be more "busy" or detailed than the other. The key to making two-pass sharpening work is to get the correct Radius setting on the first pass, and that depends almost entirely on the content of the image (see sidebar, "Image Detail and Sharpening Radius," later in this chapter).

Sharpening for Output

Different output processes also introduce varying degrees of softness, and you need to sharpen the image prior to printing to compensate for this. With contone output, the situation is fairly simple. Halftone output is a different matter entirely.

Contone output. When you're working with continuous-tone output, your monitor provides a reasonably reliable guide to the sharpness you'll get on output: simply look at the image at a 1:1 zoom factor (slide your chair back, if necessary), and sharpen it so that it looks good on the moni-tor. It should look very much the same on output, at least as far as the apparent sharpness is concerned. In fact, when we're printing on contone output devices, we find that if we take care of the softness that was introduced during image acquisition, we often don't need to apply any further sharpening to compensate for the output device. When we do, we use low Radius and Amount settings with a Threshold value of around 3 or 4.

Halftone output. With halftone output, on the other hand, we definitely need to compensate for the output device, because halftoning breaks up the image detail into halftone dots. The Radius setting we use depends mostly on the image's resolution and halftone screen frequency, while the Amount setting depends on both the image content and the physical size at which it's being reproduced.

If we're trying to do all our sharpening at once, a host of image-specific problems can occur. The problem areas usually lie with detail that is just barely reproducible at the selected output size and halftone screen frequency, and the most common artifact is *aliasing*—jagged edges on fine diagonal lines. You'll run into aliasing problems whenever you try to reproduce detail that's too fine for the halftone screen to handle. Sharpening just exaggerates the jaggies; it doesn't create them.

If we've already performed a light sharpen to restore sharpness lost on input, it takes care of most image-specific problems; so we usually perform two rounds of sharpening on images destined for halftone output, particularly if the images are being reproduced at a relatively small size with a screen frequency of 133 lpi or less.

At low screen frequencies and small sizes, the demands of the image and the demands of the output process are often in conflict. To bring out details in the image, you usually need a fairly small Radius setting. But low screen frequencies need a higher Radius that produces a more exaggerated halo, because the coarse halftone screen simply can't show enough detail to reproduce a very narrow one (if your halo is much smaller than your halftone dot, it will simply disappear, and so will your sharpening). With higher screen frequencies and/or very-large-size output, you can use a much smaller, less-intense halo, as the smaller details in the image are more easily mapped onto the halftone grid.

The other big problem you have to face is that there's really no way to get an accurate on-screen representation of how the sharpened halftone output will look—the continuous-tone monitor display is simply too different from the bilevel halftone. You have to learn by experience. In general, an image well-sharpened for halftone output will appear decidedly oversharpened on the monitor.

Resolution dependency. The Radius setting for halftone sharpening is related directly to the output resolution of the image (in pixels per inch), and indirectly to the sampling ratio of the image—the ratio between output resolution and screen frequency. Assuming your sampling ratio is between 1.5:1 and 2:1, a good starting point for the Radius setting is *image resolution ÷ 200*. (Remember: we're talking about final image resolution, after it's been placed on a page and scaled to fit.)

Thus, for a 300-ppi image, you'd use a Radius of 1.5 (300 ÷ 200). For a 200-ppi image, you'd use a Radius setting of 1. This creates a halo about ⅟₅₀th of an inch in width (⅟₁₀₀th of an inch on each side of the contrast transition), which at normal viewing distances is big enough to give the impression of sharpness, but not so big that it will overwhelm the image.

This is a suggested starting point, not a golden rule, but it's a good one. As you gain experience, you'll find situations where the rule has to be bent, but if you use image resolution ÷ 200, you'll get acceptable sharpening that will keep you out of trouble (as long as you keep your Amount setting within reasonable limits).

Size dependency. The other factor you need to take into account when you're sharpening for halftone output is the physical size of the printed image. Small images need a bit more sharpening than large ones. We find that it's better to handle this by varying the Amount and Threshold settings rather than increasing the Radius; and as always, you have to keep an eye on the highlight values. Bear in mind, though, that if you're using a 2:1 sampling ratio, a single blown-out pixel won't create a white space, since each halftone dot is calculated from four image pixels.

Tip: Radius Settings for Very Large Images. The one situation where you may want to use very high Radius settings is for large images that people will never look at up close, such as billboards and (some) posters. In this case, you may need a higher Radius value to make the sharpness really pop at the intended viewing distance (a hundredth of an inch ain't much at 100 feet). Try the following formula to determine an appropriate Radius setting.

viewing distance (inches) * resolution (ppi) * .0004

This formula is based on some theories about the eye's sensitivity to cycles of amplitude modulation over a given viewing arc (we love throwing around big words like that). We haven't had the chance to test this on a billboard, so we suggest you use it as a starting point, and take it with a pinch (if not a bag) of salt.

Working the Controls

When we're trying to determine the right sharpening settings for an image, we start by setting the Radius. We usually start out with exaggerated Amount and Threshold settings (400 percent and 0 are typical), and then we start experimenting with the Radius value. The exaggerated Amount and Threshold make it easy to see what's happening as we adjust the Radius (see Figure 9-6).

As you increase the Radius, the apparent sharpness also increases—often to an undesirable extent. This is where the aesthetic considerations come in. Some people like more sharpening than others. We find over-sharpened images more disturbing than slightly soft ones, but that's a matter of taste. It's up to you to decide how much sharpening you want.

However much sharpening you decide to apply, you'll find that as you increase the Radius setting, you need to decrease the Amount to keep the apparent sharpness constant. You can work these controls in opposition to achieve a wide range of sharpening effects.

Figure 9-6 Radius versus Amount versus Threshold

Very different USM settings can combine to provide equivalent apparent sharpness.

Image resolution: 225 ppi

   230/0.6/12   *390/0.6/33*   *79/4/19*   *300/5/113*

Threshold is the third part of the equation. You can think of it as a selective smoothing function. At small (less than 1 pixel) Radius settings, a Threshold value as low as 15 or so will probably wipe out most of the sharpening effect. At higher Radius settings, you can use much higher

Image Detail and Sharpening Radius

You can achieve the same apparent sharpness using many different combinations of Amount, Radius, and Threshold settings, but the difference between good and bad sharpening lies largely in matching the Radius setting to the image content.

Look closely at the image at hand. How big, in pixels, are the details that you want to sharpen? You need to match the size and intensity of the sharpening halo to the size of the details in the image.

High-frequency images contain a lot of detail, with sharp transitions between tonal values, while *low-frequency* images have smoother transitions and fewer small details. Whether a given image is high frequency or low frequency depends on the content of the image and on its pixel density. High-frequency images, where the edges of objects are reproduced using only one or two pixels, need a smaller Radius setting than low-frequency images, where the edges may be a dozen or so pixels wide.

An image containing fine detail, such as a picture of trees, is likely to have many more high-frequency transitions than a head shot, for example. But if you scan the trees at a high enough resolution, even the edges on the tiniest leaves will be reproduced several pixels wide in the scan. So it isn't *just* the content that dictates the sharpening, it's the relationship between content and resolution.

Unpleasant settings. Too large a Radius is the prime cause of unpleasantly oversharpened images. Moreover, an overly large Radius can actually wipe out the detail it's supposed to be accentuating. Too small a Radius can result in too little apparent sharpening. This might in turn seduce you into cranking up the Amount setting so far that you create spurious specular highlights, and exaggerate textures such as skin in undesirable ways. With extreme settings, you can change the overall contrast of the image—which in most cases isn't what you want.

Figure 9-7 shows two images that need quite different sharpening settings. The trees image contains a lot of fine detail that needs a low Radius setting and a fairly high Amount setting to bring it out. If we apply the same sharpening to the pumpkin, it fails to bring out the necessary detail (while threatening to create unpleasant mottling).

Conversely, sharpening settings that work well on the pumpkin don't work at all well on the trees. The larger Radius sharpens the larger elements well, but the more

Threshold values to smooth out unwanted sharpening of fine texture, while still applying a good deal of sharpness to well-defined edges.

There are dangers lurking here, though. As you use higher Amount and Threshold settings, you run an increased risk of driving pixels to solid black or solid white. The solid black ones aren't usually too much of a problem, but the blown-out white ones can appear as noticeable artifacts, especially when they're large due to higher Radius settings.

With very high Threshold settings, you get dramatic unnatural sharpening of high-contrast edges, while leaving smaller details soft. This makes the image look quite disturbing—it's hard for the eye to reconcile the sharp edges and the soft detail, so the image looks like there's something wrong with the focus.

Figure 9-7 Unsharp Mask settings for high- and low-frequency images

Settings that work for one image can be ineffective or destructive on another type. Resolution: 266 ppi

Unsharpened

High-frequency settings:
Amount 275, Radius .6,
Threshold 3

Low-frequency settings:
Amount 200, Radius 2,
Threshold 9

delicate elements are lost. It creates a very confused appearance, where the same element in the image appears sharp in some places and soft in others.

If you get the Radius correct first, it's easy to set the Amount to achieve the degree of sharpness you want. Then you can adjust the Threshold to suppress noise, and to avoid oversharpening patterns, film grain, and the like.

In short, the three parameters provided by Unsharp Mask give you a very fine degree of control over the sharpening effect, but it takes a while to get your head around the way they interact.

Unsharp Masking Tricks

There are a host of tricks you can use with unsharp masking—some obvious, others less so. Most are designed to avoid the problems that result when sharpening accentuates dust and scratches in images, scanner noise (especially in the shadows, and especially in color images), and film grain.

Mia

Sometimes a simple Threshold adjustment solves the problem, but when it doesn't, we use two different techniques.

▶ Selectively sharpen individual color channels.

▶ Apply the sharpening through a mask.

Sharpening Channels

Applying separate sharpening to each channel in a color image is a handy technique that can go a long way toward suppressing noise, while bringing out important image detail. We use this technique on RGB images; we'll talk about selective sharpening of CMYK channels a little later.

RGB. If you examine the individual channels of most RGB scans, you'll find that the blue channel is, almost invariably, by far the noisiest of the three. It's also usually the one with the least important detail—our eyes are less sensitive to blue than they are to red or green.

We despeckle the noisy blue channel (or use the Dust and Scratches filter for more control), and sharpen the red and green channels with an Amount of 200, Radius of 1.2, and Threshold of 4 (see Figure 9-8).

There are a couple of important caveats here. First, this technique works best with fairly small Radius settings—1.4 or less. Second, we always use similar Radius settings for both the red and green channels, although we'll usually use a higher Amount on green than on red.

Figure 9-8 Sharpening RGB channels (image resolution: 266 ppi)

Unsharpened   *Noisy blue channel*   *All three channels sharpened*   *Blue despeckled, red and green sharpened*

If you use a very different Radius on the different channels, watch out for color fringing. If you need to use a large Radius, sharpen the blue channel using the same Radius, but keep the Amount setting low.

Lab. Another technique that works well in many situations is to despeckle the blue channel, then convert the image to Lab mode and sharpen the Lightness channel. This eliminates the risk of color fringing, but the mode change does degrade the image (see "RGB to Lab" in Chapter 7, *Color Correction*). We use this trick mostly with images that need a large Radius, but have a lot of noise in the blue channel, but as shown in Figure 9-9, it can also work wonders on images with artifacts from digital cameras.

Figure 9-9 Using Lab to sharpen while removing color artifacts

This 266-ppi image, captured with Kodak's DCS 420 digital camera, displays the orange and blue artifacts that one-shot digital cameras are subject to.

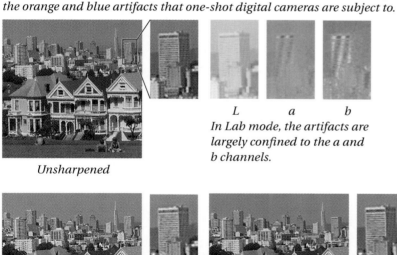

L   a   b
In Lab mode, the artifacts are largely confined to the a and b channels.

L   a   b
A Gaussian blur on the a and b channels—typically around two pixels on b and one pixel on a—removes many of the artifacts. Then we sharpen the Lightness channel (which contains most of the detail) using a Radius of 0.4–0.7 (depending on the image content), an Amount of 300–400, and a Threshold of 2–4.
    Try out the Dust and Scratches filter—the Unsharp Mask of blurring—for more control over the blurring step.

Unsharpened

Globally sharpened

Sharpened in Lab

This same technique can often work to suppress obvious film grain, which creates the appearance of noise, even on drum scans. It can appear at relatively low resolutions: the problem isn't that you're scanning down to the film grain, but more that the grain creates an interference pattern with the pixel grid. You generally need to be more aggressive with the Gaussian Blur and less aggressive with sharpening than on digital-camera images, but the basic technique is the same.

Figure 9-10 Sharpening through a mask

With the noisy blue areas protected by a mask, we're able to sharpen the rest of the image much more aggressively without accentuating artifacts.

  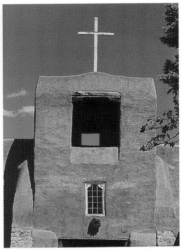

Sharpening the whole image brings out noise in the sky. *We use a mask created from the red channel, with some touchup.* *This protects the sky, allowing for the level of sharpening required.*

Figure 9-11 Sharpening the eyes

This image can benefit from extra sharpening of the eyes.

 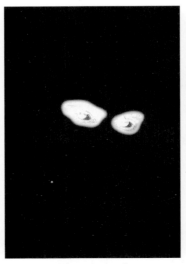 

Sharpened globally (200/0.4/1) *The eye mask* *Selectively sharpened*

CMYK. We generally prefer to do our sharpening before we convert to CMYK, unless we're dealing with CMYK drum scans—in which case little sharpening should be required (because drum scans are sharpened and separated at scan time). But if the scan has been downsampled, you'll need to resharpen—the downsampling lessens or removes the halo that provides the appearance of sharpness. We also run into situations that can best be handled by sharpening individual channels in the CMYK file.

The classic example of this is a head shot, where we want to sharpen the eyes, the eyelashes, and (usually) the hair, but we don't want to sharpen the skin texture. Glossy lipstick can also look very strange when it's sharpened. In this situation, sharpening the black plate only, or the black and the cyan plates, sharpens the hair and eyelashes but leaves the skin tones and the lipstick (which are primarily composed of magenta and yellow) unsharpened.

Suppressing Noise with Masks

For more intractable problems with noise, we apply sharpening through a mask. Most of the noise in CCD scans lies in the shadows—and there's often very little significant detail in the shadows anyway—so we create a simple mask that protects the noisy shadow areas from sharpening, yet allows us to apply full-strength sharpening to the more important areas of the image.

Another situation where we often use a sharpening mask is when the image contains large areas of blue sky (see Figure 9-10). Most such scans contain a lot of noise in the sky—even in drum scans, where it's caused by the interaction of the pixels and the film grain. In this case, we want to mask out the sky and focus our sharpening on the rest of the image.

1. Select the image channel that has the greatest contrast between the areas you want to sharpen and those you don't.

2. Duplicate the channel, and apply a steep contrast curve. In Figure 9-10, we duplicate the red channel, apply a curve, and do a little local touch-up with the Paintbrush to create a sharpening mask that protect both the shadows and the sky (see Chapter 14, *Selections*).

3. To avoid abrupt transitions, apply a two-pixel Gaussian blur to the mask. This softens the edges of the selection, so there isn't an abrupt edge to what gets sharpened and what doesn't.

4. Finally, load this mask as a selection, and apply Unsharp Mask to the composite color channel.

Selective Sharpening

We also use selective sharpening through a mask to emphasize details in images. Probably the single most common situation where we use this technique is in our handling of eyes. Eyes can almost always benefit from a little extra selective sharpening, and it's usually easy to make a mask by copying the red channel (because it usually has the best contrast between eyes and skin), inverting it, and blacking out everything except the eyes. Figure 9-11 shows the effect of selective sharpening through such a mask.

Avoiding the Crunchies

The Unsharp Mask filter is a powerful tool. Used well, it can give your images the extra snap that makes them jump off the page. Used badly, it gives images the unpleasant "crunchy" look we see in all too many Sunday newspaper color supplements. In overdoses, it can make images look artificial, or even blurry. With that in mind, we leave you with two final pieces of advice.

First, it's better to err on the side of caution. An image that's too soft will generally be less disturbing than one that's been oversharpened.

Second, always leave yourself an escape route. Make sure that you archive an unsharpened copy of the image before you proceed.

Use of the Unsharp Mask filter is definitely one of those things that improves with experience, and a considerable part of that experience can be gained from revisiting your earlier efforts and figuring out what went wrong. If you save an unsharpened copy, you can always go back and refine your sharpening to get closer to the result you want.

10

Spot Colors and Duotones

Special Inks for Special Projects

The fundamental problem with printing presses is that they can only print one color at a time. It's like pixels on a black-and-white screen: the color is either on or off. We may have a gloriously rich full-color image on screen, but we've got to be mighty clever to get that image out the back side of a printing press, and no matter what we do, there will be trade-offs involved.

There are two methods for printing color on a press: spot color and process color. Both can give you a wide variety of colors. But they are hardly interchangeable.

Process color. Process color, as we've noted throughout the book, is the method of printing a wide range of colors by overlapping halftones (tints) of only four colors: cyan, magenta, yellow, and black. The colors themselves do not mix on paper. Rather, the eye blends these colors together so that ultimately you see the color you're supposed to.

Spot color. If you are printing only a small number of colors (three or fewer), you probably want to use spot colors. The idea behind spot color is that the printing ink is just the right color you want. With spot color, for example, if you want some type colored teal blue, you print it on a plate (often called an overlay) which is separate from the black plate.

Your commercial printer prints that type using a teal-blue ink—probably a PMS ink—and black for the rest of the job.

Because process colors simply cannot simulate some colors—like deep blues, and metallics like gold—spot colors are also used as "bump" plates and varnishes that print alongside or on top of process-color images. For instance, a picture of a fancy car might be printed with the four process colors, plus a spot blue to highlight ("bump up") some areas of the car, plus a varnish over the image to make it glossy.

This is relatively easy to print on a six-color press. The hard part has always been building the spot color and varnish plates.

Spot Colors from Photoshop

"How can I print spot colors from Photoshop?" has long been one of the most common questions we hear. Until version 5, Photoshop had only a very limited ability to create, preview, and print spot-color overlays. The program was really designed to do process-color work (or continous tone RGB output), not spot color. Fortunately, Photoshop 5 has made the process somewhat simpler (though still not simple). There are three ways to do spot-color work in Photoshop.

▶ Use spot-color channels for all the spot-color image information, and save the file in DCS 2.0 format. This new feature in Photoshop 5 lets you place spot colors in specific areas (like in text or a logo).

▶ Use the Duotone mode. Duotones (or tritones or quadtones) are used to print neutral grayscale images with two or more colors (we'll discuss why you'd want to do this later in this chapter).

▶ Simulate spot colors in CMYK mode. You can use this technique for either duotones or specific-area spot colors.

Tip: Don't Pick Spot Colors. Note that choosing a Pantone (PMS) color from Photoshop's Color Picker and then painting with that color does *not* provide you with a spot-color ink. Rather, as you apply the "spot" color, it's actually being broken up into RGB or CMYK components. We've always felt that it was a particularly cruel joke by the programmers to offer people the chance to see and pick spot colors without the opportunity to print these colors out on spot-color plates.

Tip: Bézier versus Raster Spot Color. Remember that Photoshop is an image-editing tool, so any spot color you create here is going to be bitmapped. If you need crisp high-resolution edges (like for text or a logo), you'll probably get a better result creating the spot-color art in a program like QuarkXPress, FreeHand, or Illustrator. (See Chapter 3, *Image Essentials*, for more on the difference between bitmapped and vector artwork. Also, see "Tip: Spot-Color Plug-Ins," later in this chapter.)

Spot-Color Channels

Until the release of version 5, Photoshop users who wanted to use spot colors generally had to content themselves with painting on an alpha channel and then using a commercial plug-in to save the file out to disk in the DCS 2.0 format (which supports spot colors; see "DCS" in Chapter 16, *Storing Images*).

For years we did this, patiently hoping that Adobe would come up with some magical feature that would make it easier. No such luck. Instead, Adobe simply co-opted this workflow by adding spot-color channels and the ability to save DCS 2.0 files without the aid of a plug-in.

Spot-color channels are, in most respects, identical to normal channels on the Channels palette. To create a new spot-color channel, select New Spot Channel from the popout menu on the Channels palette (or, faster, Command-click the New Channel button at the bottom of the palette).

The New Spot Channel dialog box offers you three controls for your new spot color: Name, Color, and Solidity (see Figure 10-1).

Figure 10-1

Making a new
spot color channel

Name. You should generally leave the naming of the spot color up to Photoshop (it assigns one when you choose a color). The important thing is this: to ensure that your spot color appears on the correct plate when printing from a page-layout program, you must make sure the name of the spot channel matches the name of the same ink in the page-layout program.

Color. You can choose a spot color by clicking on the color swatch and then clicking on a color (if the Color Picker appears, click the Custom button to display the Custom Colors dialog box). The default color model here is Pantone (Coated), but you can choose a different swatch-book type from the Book popup menu (see Figure 10-2). Curiously, the Book popup menu displays several process-color swatch books (like Trumatch and Focoltone) along with the spot-color swatch books (like Pantone and Toyo), even though the process-color books are meaningless here.

Figure 10-2
Picking a spot color

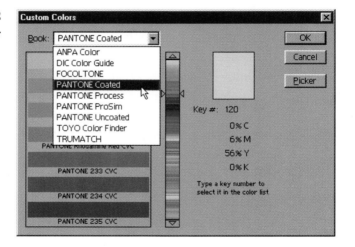

Actually, to be honest, all the colors here are meaningless, because they're only used for screen display. You can pick any color you want (even a regular RGB color), and as long as the name is right, it'll print fine. This is handy if you need to create an image even before you know what PMS color you'll be using on press. Just pick a color and name it "My Spot Color" (or whatever). Later, you can either change the name or just tell your printer that this piece of film should be printed with such-and-such a color.

Solidity. The Solidity feature lets you control how opaque the color is on screen (this is similar to the Opacity setting for regular alpha channels). Again, like Color, this only determines your on-screen preview; it has no effect on the final printed image.

Picking the correct Solidity value for a spot color is almost impossible because every spot-color ink has a slightly different opacity, depending on how it was mixed, what colors it's printed over, and so on. In general, metallic inks are almost totally opaque, letterpress inks are usually more opaque than offset inks, and inks that include a good dose of Opaque White in their ingredients are less transparent than those without.

Ultimately, however, you just have to make up a number and move on, knowing that your screen display of the spot color will almost certainly be somewhat inaccurate. We almost always use a value of about 85 percent for spot colors. If we used 100 percent, we might forget that other colors might show through the spot color, causing mottling (see "Building Traps," later in this section). Of course, if the spot color is a varnish, we'd set the Solidity value to zero, because varnishes are almost transparent (here's one place that Solidity is not the same as Opacity: zero-percent Solidity can still be slightly seen).

Applying Spot Colors

Spot-color channels appear on the Channels palette, though some people erroneously look for them on the Layers palette because spot colors always appear on top of the underlying original image. When you first create a spot-color channel, Photoshop automatically selects it for you; so if you start painting, the "ink" appears on this channel and not the RGB or CMYK channels. When you're finished working on the spot-color channel, you must manually switch to the RGB or CMYK channels (the fastest way to do this is to press Command-~).

Annoyingly, because spot colors appear on their own special channel, you cannot use the Layers feature with spot colors. In fact, even if you use the Type tool to place text on your spot-color channel, the text is automatically rendered and dropped into the channel, not on a layer. (You can still move it and adjust its mode and opacity by choosing Fade from the Filter menu while it's selected, but once you deselect it, it's rendered onto the layer.)

Remember that when you're painting on a spot-color channel, you're always painting in black, white, or gray, even when it looks like you're painting in color. Black is solid spot color; white is no ink at all; gray is a tint of the spot color.

By the way, you can always change the spot-color channel's settings by double-clicking on its tile in the Channels palette.

Tip: Converting a Layer to a Spot-Color Channel. David finds the inability to use spot colors on layers to be frustrating at best (it's like going back to the Photoshop 2.x days). So he'll often lay out his spot colors on one or more layers first, using black rather than a color. Then this trick converts the layers into spot colors.

1. Fill a new layer with white and place it underneath all the spot-color layers on the Layers palette.

2. Merge the "spot color" layer(s) down into this white layer so you end up with just one layer.

3. Select the whole layer (Command-A), and copy it (Command-C).

4. Hide the layer (by turning off the Layer's visibility eyeball) or delete it.

5. In the Channels palette, create a new spot-color channel, or select one you've already made.

6. Paste (Command-V). If you're pasting onto a spot-color channel that already has something on it, you'll probably have to select Fade from the Filter menu and set the Mode to Multiply in order to merge the pasted information with the underlying information.

That's it! The information that was on the layer is now on your spot-color channel.

Tip: Converting Alpha Channels to Spots. If you find yourself wanting to convert a regular alpha channel into a spot-color channel, don't panic; just open the Channel Options dialog box by double-clicking on the channel's tile. There you can select the Spot Color radio button. When you click OK, the channel is changed.

Tip: Building Bump Plates. Putting text or basic shapes on a spot-color channel is relatively easy. Creating quality bump plates for scanned images is much harder. One method is to use the Color Range feature (under the Select menu) to select the kinds of colors you're trying to enhance. For instance, if you're trying to bump up the color in a shiny red bicycle, you might use Color Range to select the Reds in an image. When you create a spot-color channel after making a selection, Photoshop automatically converts the selection into spot color (the fully selected parts become solid spot color, and so on).

If you need to create a lot of bump plates or you need better precision, you might consider using Visu Technology's CoCo. Besides having one of the stranger names in the software industry, CoCo is an excellent tool for building high-quality spot-color bump plates. CoCo's color-range selection is optimized for building bump plates, and it tends to give rather better results than the one built into Photoshop.

Merge Spot Channel. Photoshop also lets you convert your spot-color channel into its RGB or CMYK color equivalents (choose Merge Spot Channel from the popout menu on the Channels palette). Generally, you only need to do this when sending an on-screen comp to a client or putting the image on the Web. (Make sure you save your file first!) Note that the Photoshop documentation implies that you have to merge spot colors before printing to a color printer, but this isn't necessarily true. Just make sure you choose RGB from the Space popup menu in the Print dialog box; that way, Photoshop simulates the spot colors in the RGB it sends to the printer.

Knocking Out versus Overprinting

As we said earlier, spot-color inks are rarely fully opaque, so if you try to print a solid PMS ink on top of your CMYK image, it'll probably look mottled. What's more, it may result in too much ink on the page, causing troubles at print time. (Of course, if you're using a spot color as a bump plate or a varnish then you *don't* want to knock out the image behind it.)

To avoid these overprinting problems, you'll need to manually knock out the parts of your image that lie underneath the spot colors. (This knocking-out process is taken care of for you in other programs, such as when you place spot-color type over an image in QuarkXPress or PageMaker.) Here's one way to do this.

1. Load the spot-color channel as a selection. (You can use Load Selection if you want, but we find it faster simply to Command-click on the spot-color channel's tile in the Channels palette.)

2. Create a new layer in the Layers palette.

3. Use the Fill command on the Edit menu to fill the selection on this new layer with White. (It may not look like much has changed, because the spot color is probably still overlapping the area you just filled with white. Try turning off the visibility of the spot-color channel to see the "knocked out" area below.)

Creating a new layer is optional—you could just fill the background image with white—but we find it more flexible to "knock out" the portions of the image with a layer, just in case you have to make a change later. Of course, you'll still have to flatten the file before saving it in the DCS 2.0 format.

On the other hand, if you have two spot colors that overlap, and you want one to knock out the other, you won't be able to use this layer trick (because spot colors always sit on top of layers). In this case, you have to fill the selection with white on the lower spot-color channel.

Building Traps

There's only one problem with the step-by-step outlined above: it doesn't take trapping into account. Trapping compensates for the slight paper misregistration that is inevitable on a printing press. For instance, if a cyan box abuts a magenta box, but the paper is slightly misregistered when the magenta plate is printed, there'll be a white sliver between the cyan and magenta (see Figure 10-3).

Scanned images generally don't need trapping because there are gradual transitions between colors. For example, if you scanned a picture of a cyan and a magenta box, the edge between the two would actually be made up of both cyan and magenta, creating a natural trap. If one plate misregisters, there's still enough overlap to avoid a white gap.

As soon as you knock out the background behind a spot color, however, you'll almost certainly need to think about trapping. There are three

Figure 10-3
Trapping colors

*The image looks
great on screen . . .*

*. . . but if the press
misregisters, an ugly
gap appears.*

*A trap ensures that
misregistration won't
cause problems.*

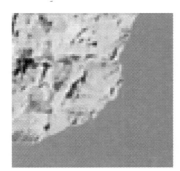 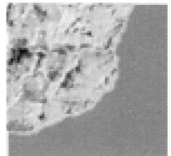

*Scanned images rarely need trapping because shared
colors usually mask press misregistration.*

methods of trapping spot colors in Photoshop: choking the background, spreading the spot color, and the Trap feature.

Choking the background. The general rule of trapping is to spread the lighter color so that it slightly overlaps the darker color. If the spot color is dark, you can effectively spread the background colors "into" the spot color by making the area that you knock out (set to white) smaller. After loading the spot-color channel as a selection in the last step-by-step instruction, choose Contract from the Modify submenu (under the Select menu). A value of one pixel chokes the selection (shrinks it) by a single pixel, which is enough for most trapping problems. (A single pixel is about .25 point—.0033 inch—in a 300-ppi image.)

As it turns out, we often find ourselves using this method even when the spot color is lighter, especially when the spot-color channel contains type or other fine detail.

Spreading the spot color. If the spot color is lighter, you can spread it (make it bigger) so that it slightly overlaps the background. One way to do this is to select the channel in the Channels palette and choose the Minimum filter from the Other submenu on the Filters menu. Minimum spreads the image on a channel (makes it bigger), so that it slightly overlaps whatever is behind it. Again, a one-pixel value here should work well for most images. (Some printing processes—such as printing newspapers—require larger traps.) Watch out for muddying up the fine detail on the spot-color channel with this process, however.

Trap. While the previous technique works pretty well when you're trapping a spot color that is completely surrounded by other colors (because it spreads everything on the spot-color plate), it's not as effective when the spot color only partially overlaps another color. The Trap feature (under the Image menu; see Figure 10-4) lets you build some basic trapping

Figure 10-4

Trap

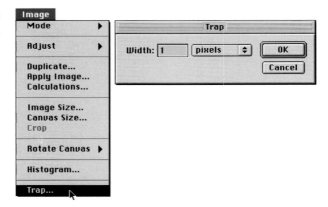

between channels in your image, and only traps where two or more colors intersect.

To trap one spot-color channel, make sure both the background image and the spot-color channel are visible, but select the spot-color channel in the palette. To trap two channels, select them both (you can select multiple channels with the Shift key).

The Trap feature lets you specify a trap in millimeters, points, or pixels. Unfortunately, Photoshop currently seems to have some troubles interpreting these values, so you'll probably need to specify a trap significantly larger than your printer prescribes. For instance, a .25-point trap doesn't have any effect at all on most images; you need to use a value of one point to get even a negligible trap. Note that if you enter a value too small, Photoshop won't perform any trapping at all (it's as though you didn't even use the feature), so you should always check to make sure some trapping really occurred.

(To be honest, while we find the Trap feature occasionally useful, we generally find ourselves using the "choking the background" method the most.)

Saving Images with Spot Colors

While we're going to hold off providing details about the various graphic file formats until Chapter 16, *Storing Images*, it's important to note that you'll generally want to save images that contain spot-color channels in the native Photoshop format (which you can only open in Photoshop) and the DCS 2.0 format (which you can import into QuarkXPress or PageMaker).

Tip: Don't Save Alpha Channels. As we go to press, Photoshop contains a bug: it doesn't distinguish between regular alpha channels and spot-color channels when saving DCS 2.0 files (version 5.02 fixed this partly, but not completely). This can cause havoc when your page-layout program tries to print the image. There's a second bug, too. You can't use the Exclude Alpha Channels checkbox in the Save a Copy dialog box when you save the file, as this excludes both alpha channels and spot colors.

Therefore, it's important that you manually delete all extra channels (not the spot-color channels, of course) before saving the file. We're hoping that a newer version of Photoshop 5 will fix these problems by the time you read this.

Screen angles. When you print two colors on top of each other, and the colors are tinted, each halftone screen has to have a different angle or else you'll end up with distracting moiré patterns (see Chapter 17, *Output Methods*, for more on halftone screens and how to set them). If your spot colors are solid (100 percent), then you don't have to worry about screen angles. If your spot colors are tinted but they don't overlap any other colors, you don't have to worry about it. But you'd better pay attention if you place 50 percent of some Pantone color on top of 20-percent black, or if you're building a spot-color bump plate to enhance a color in your image.

You can set the halftone screen angles in Photoshop (in the Page Setup dialog box) or in your page-layout program. Generally, halftone angles should sit either 45 or 30 degrees apart. (For more information, see the discussion on screen angles in "Saving and Outputting," later in this chapter.)

In the case of bump plates, all the available angles are typically taken up by the cyan, yellow, magenta, and black inks. You can either print the image with stochastic screens, or match the bump plate to one of the process-color inks. It's generally safe to match it to the closest color. For example, if you're printing a bright-red bump plate over a dull-red process-color image, you can probably get away with matching the bump plate's angle to the magenta screen (often 75 degrees). The two colors are similar enough, and the percentage of tint is high enough (almost solid) that you probably won't have any patterning.

Tip: Spot-Color Plug-Ins. As we said earlier, until Adobe built the DCS 2.0 file format into Photoshop 5, people used commercial plug-ins that could save in this format. Plug-ins—such as PlateMaker, from a lowly apprentice productions, and PhotoSpotCT from Second Glance Software—are far from obsolete, however; they offer many DCS-related features that Photoshop 5 lacks. For example, you could fill a whole spot-color channel with black (so it appears as a solid color), then assign a clipping path to it using PlateMaker. If that clipping path is in the shape of text, then the final result is spot-color text that prints at the resolution of your printer, not the resolution of your image. (No more fuzzy edges!)

PhotoSpotCT offers some additional controls (but is also more expensive), including separating an RGB image into a continuous-tone spot-color image and creating bump plates. Again, if you have specialized needs, check out one of the many specialized plug-ins.

Multitone Images

In the old tale of the four blind men and the elephant, each man describes the animal according to the piece he's experienced. "It's a snake-like creature with wrinkled skin," says one, holding the trunk.

"No, it's a hairy animal with giant wings," says another, feeling the ear.

Printing a grayscale image is similar to this experience. Printing presses are powerful and delicate instruments, but depending on the press, the operator, the ink, and the paper, they're often limited to printing far fewer than the 256 shades of gray we can theoretically achieve with an 8-bit image. So after you've gone through a lot of trouble adjusting tone, those tones are pummeled when the image is slapped onto paper. In other words, the final printed result is only a fraction of the whole image, and the viewer is blind to the richness of the original.

There are ways, however, to coax more gray levels, more detail, and more depth out of a printed image. Printers have traditionally tackled this problem by printing the grayscale image more than once, each time with a different-colored ink. These are called duotones, tritones, and quadtones (depending on the number of inks you use). When talking about the genre as a whole, we call these *multitones*, because we're too lazy to keep typing "duotones, tritones, and quadtones." Remember, multitones differ from color images in that they almost always represent an underlying neutral, grayscale image.

Expanding the Tonal Range

While they're often used to colorize grayscale images, the original purpose of multitones was to expand the tonal range of the image. For instance, a 50-percent tint in gray ink may be lighter than a 10-percent spot of black ink; so a 10-percent spot of the gray ink is far lighter than the tonal range of black ink can achieve. If you print black ink in the shadows and gray ink in the highlights, you can achieve more levels of highlight grays.

On the other end of the spectrum, we usually think of 100-percent black ink as solid—you can't get darker than that. But in reality, printing 100-percent black on top of 100-percent gray results in a darker, richer, denser black. Therefore, by adding the gray in the shadows, you expand the tonal range of the image even further toward real black.

Adding an ink is like listening to two of the blind men instead of just one; you get that much more information, and can see the whole of the image that much more clearly.

Colorizing Images

When most designers think about duotones, they don't think about expanding tonal range; they think about colorizing grayscale images. For
instance, many newsletters are printed with two inks—black and some
Pantone color. When given the opportunity to print with a second ink,
many designers immediately think, "Oh, I can give color to my grayscale
images by making them duotones."

There's nothing wrong with colorizing a grayscale image. But colorizing images without thinking about the expanded tonal range usually
looks pretty bad. In this chapter we talk about both, and how they relate
to one another.

Tip: Dumb, Fast Duotones. If we didn't know how hectic life can get in a
production setting, we would hardly believe how many people (printers,
especially) still use the flat-tint duotone trick. The idea is that you can
fake a duotone by laying a flat tint behind the grayscale image. For example, let's say you want to add some blue to a grayscale image. To fake
the duotone look, you could lay down a 10-percent tint of magenta or
PMS 485 behind the entire image (see Figure 10-5), and set the image to
overprint in your page-layout program.

Note that this really is an old printer's trick, and it doesn't look very
good. Because you're making no allowance for the tonal shift, fake duotones are often too dark and muddy. Photoshop makes creating real duotones so easy that faking it is hardly worth the effort. It's faster, but it's not
that much faster.

Photoshop's Duotones

There are two ways to create multitone images in Photoshop: switch
from Grayscale to Duotone under the Mode sub-menu, or create them
in CMYK mode. We're focusing our discussion on the Duotone mode, and
will cover CMYK mode later in this chapter.

In every other color mode in Photoshop, the color is made of multiple
channels—CMYK color is made of four channels, RGB is made of three.
Multitones are different. In a multitone image, Photoshop saves a single
grayscale image along with two curves—one for each color plate. These
curves are just like those in the Curves or Transfer Function dialog boxes
(see Figure 10-6). Note that you can only create a duotone from a grayscale

Figure 10-5 Fake versus real duotones

Just dropping a flat magenta tint behind this grayscale image does little to enhance it. Adjusting the curves for the two inks adds tonal range and depth.

The original grayscale   *Fake duotone*   *Real duotone*

image. (If you've got a color image, see "The Color of Grayscale" in Chapter 15, *Essential Image Techniques*.)

Because you're typically replacing a single gray level with two or more tints of ink, you almost always need to adjust the amounts of ink used by each channel. Otherwise, the image appears too dark and muddy (see Figure 10-7). For instance, if you replace a 50-percent black pixel with 50-percent black and 50-percent purple, it appears much darker. Instead, replacing that 50-percent black with something like 30-percent black and 25-percent purple maintains the tone of that pixel. On the other hand, if the second color were much lighter, like yellow, you'd need much more ink to maintain the tone. You might, for example, use 35-percent black and 55-percent yellow.

The duotone curves give you the ability to make these sorts of tonal adjustments quickly and with a minimum of image degradation because applying a duotone curve *never* affects the underlying grayscale image data. You can make forty changes to the duotone colors or the curves and never lose the underlying image quality.

Note that we say the "underlying image quality" won't suffer. We're not saying that you can go hog-wild with the curves, and your final image will always look good. Far from it. In fact, duotones, tritones, and quadtones

Figure 10-6

Duotone curves

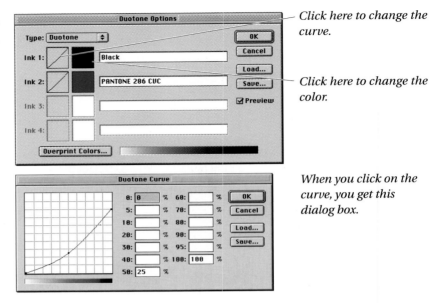

Click here to change the curve.

Click here to change the color.

When you click on the curve, you get this dialog box.

are often very sensitive and can quickly succumb to "lookus badus maximus." But the image data saved on disk is unchanged by adjusting these curves; they're like filters that are applied to the image data, but only when you view it on screen or print it out.

Tip: Use Stephen's Curves. Unless you really know what you're doing, just use the duotone curve sets built by photographer Stephen Johnson

Figure 10-7 Adjusting multitone curves

The three inks are way too heavy, darkening the image considerably, and obscuring shadow detail (far left).

These curves complement each other, maintaining and enhancing the tone of the grayscale image (left).

that ship with Photoshop. We almost never create a multitone image from scratch. Instead, we load in one of Steve's curves (using the Load button in the Duotone dialog box) and then start making small tweaks to the curves, depending on the image.

Most of the curves come in sets of four.

▶ The first and second colorize the image (the first does so more than the second).

▶ The third curve of the set affects the midtones and three-quarter tones primarily, and does very little to the highlights. The effect is to warm or cool the image significantly without colorizing it much.

▶ The final duotone curve makes the image slightly warmer or cooler (still mostly neutral), primarily affecting the three-quarter tones.

If we're using a Pantone color that's not included in the canned presets, we usually pick a canned set for a color that has similar brightness to the one we're using, and replace the color with ours. Then, depending on the two colors' tones, we adjust the curves accordingly.

Tip: Checking Each Duotone Channel. The biggest hassle with images in Duotone mode is that you can't see each channel by itself. If you make a tonal adjustment to an RGB or CMYK image, you can always go and see what that did to each channel. With a duotone, however, you're in the dark. Here's one way out: convert the image to Multichannel mode.

While you're in Multichannel mode, you can view each channel of the multitone image. The first channel corresponds to the first ink, the second to the second ink, and so on. When you're done playing voyeur, select Undo (Command-Z), and you're back where you started.

Adjusting Screen Colors

No one is more aware than Adobe that colors on screen may not match colors on paper. Tech support gets calls all the time from people screaming that they followed the manual's directions, but their images are always different from what they see on the screen.

Calibrating your system and adjusting your monitor is one way to get results that more closely match your display. But the color settings (RGB

Spot versus Process Color

When dealing with printed color, you need to understand the differences between process and spot color. Both can give you a wide variety of colors. But they are hardly interchangeable.

Process color. Process color, as we've noted throughout the book, is the method of printing a wide range of colors by overlapping halftones of only four colors: cyan, magenta, yellow, and black. The eye blends these colors together so that ultimately you see the color you're supposed to.

Spot color. If you are printing only a small number of colors (three or fewer), you probably want to use spot colors. The idea behind spot colors is that the printing ink is just the right color you want. With spot color, for example, if you want some type colored teal blue, you print it on a plate (often called an overlay) which is separate from the black plate. Your commercial printer prints that type using a teal-blue

ink—probably a PMS ink—and black for the rest of the job.

Spot colors from Photoshop. "How can I print spot colors from Photoshop?" is one of the most common questions we hear these days. The answer is that Photoshop has only a very limited ability to create, preview, and print spot-color overlays. It's really designed to do process-color work (or contone RGB output), not spot color. However, there are three ways to do spot-color work in Photoshop.

► Use the Duotone mode. We talk about this throughout the first two-thirds of this chapter.

► Use alpha channels for all the spot-color image information, and save the file in DCS 2.0 format with PlateMaker or Channel/24 (see "DCS version 2.0" in Chapter 16, *Storing Images*).

► Simulate spot colors in CMYK mode. We discuss this later in the chapter.

Multitones. In this chapter, we're focusing on multitones—images that are primarily representing a neutral, grayscale image. Multitones can be printed with either spot or process colors. For example, many newsletters are printed with black and one PMS color. Here, you could include a *spot-color duotone*. On the other hand, many printers charge less if your second color is a process color—cyan, magenta, or yellow. In that case, you still may be printing with only two colors, but your image is technically a *process duotone*.

If you're printing a four-color piece, you can create duotones, tritones, and quadtones easily by using the four process colors already available to you. We're seeing quite a trend toward this in advertising these days. People take color images, convert them to grayscale (see "The Color of Grayscale" in Chapter 15, *Essential Image Techniques*), and then make process-color quadtones out of them.

Setup, CMYK Setup, and so on) are really only designed to handle process-color printing and RGB monitors. Duotones, on the other hand, are often printed with spot-color inks such as Pantone or Toyo.

Fortunately, Photoshop not only lets you pick custom spot colors in the Color Picker (press the Custom button); it also lets you adjust how they appear on screen. This is crucial for duotone work, where you want your monitor display to be as accurate as possible.

Note that your monitor simply cannot display many spot colors (including metallic and fluorescent inks) accurately, or even closely. If you want to produce metallic duotones, you have to use a great deal of imagination. A custom proof such as DuPont's Cromalin is a good idea, too.

Adjusting Colors

While Photoshop does a reasonably good job of representing spot colors on screen, we find that we occasionally want to make adjustments so that what we see on screen is closer to what we see in our swatch book. Once you've selected a spot color from the Color Picker's Custom dialog box, press the Picker button (see Figure 10-8). You can now adjust the RGB, HSB, or Lab values for that color to make it appear closer to your printed swatch.

If you use a colorimeter, such as LightSource's Colortron, you can read the Lab values directly from your printed swatch and type those into the Picker's Lab fields. However, if your screen isn't calibrated, then this representation may look even worse than Photoshop's.

Don't adjust the color's CMYK values, however. As soon as you change one value here, Photoshop assumes you want to adhere to the process-color gamut (not necessary for spot colors). For instance, if you're adjusting the color of a rich blue such as PMS 2738, making even a one-percent change to the CMYK values makes Photoshop snap the color to a pale

Figure 10-8 The Color Picker and Custom Color dialog boxes

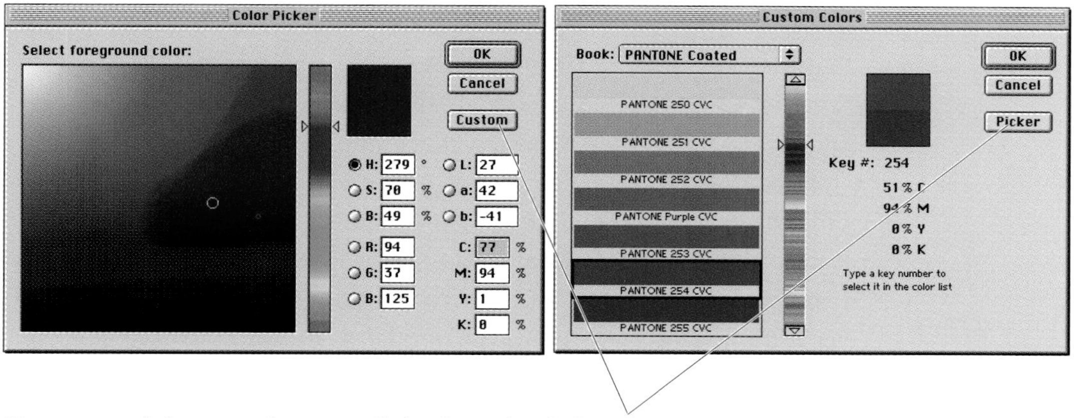

You can toggle between these two dialog boxes by clicking here.

imitation of the blue. (It's in gamut, but who cares? This is for screen representation only; the real color will only appear when ink hits paper.)

Then, if you switch back to the Custom Picker, Photoshop finds the closest match to this new, blah color: PMS 653. Again, it's just for on-screen display, but we're trying to get as close as we can.

Overprint Colors

Once you've told Photoshop how you want each of your colors to display individually in the multitone, you need to tell it how you want the colors to look when printed on top of each other. Duotones are easy, because most duotones are printed with black and another color. Overprinting these two colors results in a darker, richer black, but it's black nonetheless. Unfortunately, Photoshop won't distinguish between the two blacks.

However, when you add more colors to the image (as in a tritone or a quadtone), or don't use black in the mix, telling Photoshop how to display the overprinted colors becomes significantly more important. To set the overprint color, click the Overprint button in the Duotone dialog box (see Figure 10-9).

The basic advice for the Overprint dialog box is to leave it alone unless you have a printed sample of what the overprinted colors *should* look like, or you're really certain that Photoshop has built it wrong.

On the other hand, with some cajoling (and perhaps a pint of Haagen-Dazs sorbet or, for really big favors, Laphroiag), you can often get your printer to "draw down" a sample of the two colors overprinting. Place that under a 5,000-degree Kelvin light, and adjust away. Or, if you're using Pantone inks, you may want to purchase the Pantone Tint Effects Color Suite, which shows various tint builds of Pantone inks, including 100-percent overprints (which is the relevant swatch here).

Changing the Overprint colors has no effect on your printed output. It only affects how the colors appear on screen. It does affect mode changes, however; if you switch from Duotone mode directly to CMYK, RGB, or Lab, the overprint colors are taken into consideration. However, this conversion would be a silly thing to do unless you're printing to a color printer (see "Printing Proofs of Spot Color Images," later in this chapter).

Figure 10-9

Setting the overprint color

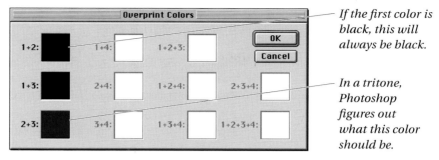

If the first color is black, this will always be black.

In a tritone, Photoshop figures out what this color should be.

Setting Curves

Once you've specified the colors you want in your multitone image and adjusted the tonal range of the grayscale image, it's time to start adjusting your multitone curves. If you followed our advice in "Tip: Use Stephen's Curves," you may have already loaded in a curve set that's somewhat appropriate for your image. However, we'd like to emphasize that every image (and every spot-color ink) is different, so your curves probably need some kind of tweaking. Whether or not you go through the trouble is up to you, but here are some things to think about if you want to give it a go.

Expanding Highlights and Shadows

There are two ways in which you can expand your tonal range with multitones: focusing inks and using ink tones.

Focusing inks. You can focus an ink plate on a particular area of the tonal scale by increasing the contrast in that area. Let's say you want to increase the detail in the shadows. From Chapter 6, *Tonal Correction*, you know that you need to increase the slope of the tonal curve in the shadow areas. However, that means you have to decrease the slope (and therefore the contrast) in the highlights, so you lose detail there.

With one ink, that could be an unacceptable trade-off. But with two or more inks, you can use one to focus on the shadows—increasing the contrast there and bringing out detail—and use another to focus on the highlight detail (see Figure 10-10). When the page comes off press, you have greater detail in both areas. This is one methodology behind double-black duotones (where you print with black ink twice).

Curves Is Curves

If you're wondering about the difference between Duotone curves and regular curves (and transfer curves), the answer is: there's hardly any difference at all. It's mostly a matter of when the corrections are applied to the image.

When you use the Curves dialog box, the image data is affected immediately; you're actually changing the image. Curves also lets you use arbitrary maps (a fancy way of saying that you can draw a line with the Pencil tool).

Curves that you create in Duotone mode, on the other hand, don't get applied until you print the image. In fact, Photoshop just saves the grayscale image plus the curves. When you print, each curve is sent down along with the image data in the form of a transfer function. So you can always go back and change the curves without degrading the image.

Duotone curves have their pros and cons, though. You can't preview how a single channel changes as you move the curve; you can't even see how the mix of curves and inks looks on your image until you press OK in the Duotone dialog box. On the other hand, the Duotone Curves dialog box has an excellent feature: you can type in values instead of simply clicking on the curve. This is especially handy when it comes to targeting by compressing the tonal range.

Because a curve is a curve is a curve, you can save a curve from one dialog box and load it into another (see "Save the Curves" in Chapter 6, *Tonal Correction*). The exception: you can't load curves with arbitrary maps into the Duotone or Transfer dialog boxes.

Tip: Save and Load Curves. As we said earlier, it's a hassle not being able to see how each "channel" of the image changes as you adjust its curve. This is especially frustrating to new users who have a difficult time picturing what the curves are doing without the visual feedback. Whether you're a beginner or a seasoned pro, you may find this technique useful.

1. Duplicate the image. (Remember that if you hold down the Option key while selecting Duplicate from the Image menu, Photoshop won't bother you with a superfluous dialog box.)

2. If the duplicate image isn't already in Grayscale mode, select Grayscale from the Mode menu. This simply throws away the duotone curves. It doesn't affect the image data.

3. Use Curves (Command-M) to create the curve you're trying to achieve for the duotone ink. You can use Preview or any of the other curve tricks we talk about in Chapter 6, *Tonal Correction*. You cannot, however, use Arbitrary Maps (curves made with the pencil tool). Duotones don't understand those at all.

4. Save the curve to disk, then press OK or Cancel in the Curves dialog box. (It doesn't matter at this point; we usually cancel to save time.)

Figure 10-10 Focusing inks on different tonal ranges

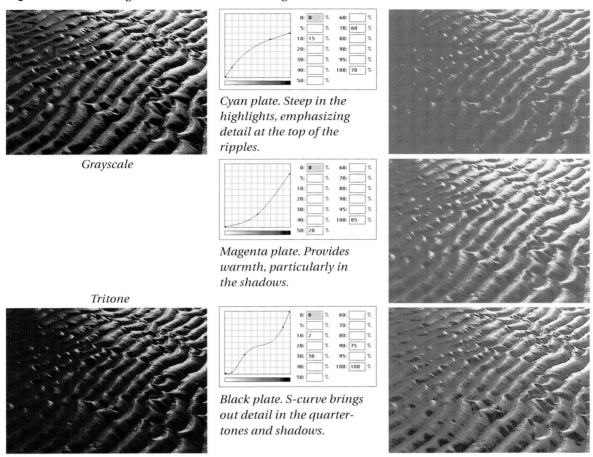

Grayscale

Tritone

Cyan plate. Steep in the highlights, emphasizing detail at the top of the ripples.

Magenta plate. Provides warmth, particularly in the shadows.

Black plate. S-curve brings out detail in the quarter-tones and shadows.

5. Switch back to the Duotone image, open the Duotone dialog box (by selecting Duotone from the Mode menu again), and load the curve you've made into the ink's Curves dialog box.

   If the curve you've made isn't quite right, you can always adjust it in the duotone image, or if you want to get visual about it, go back and load the curve into the grayscale image's Curves dialog box again.

Ink tones. The second method of expanding your image's tonal range, ink tones, is almost always performed in conjunction with the first method, focusing inks. As we said earlier in the chapter, by printing with a gray ink along with black you immediately expand the tonal range, because a tint of gray is lighter than a tint of black; plus, gray printed over black is darker than black alone. Therefore, you can affect the tone of your image by picking appropriate second, third, and fourth colors.

For instance, printing with two dark colors may make less sense than printing with a dark and a light color. If you're printing with three colors, you may want to use black plus a lighter gray (to extend the highlights) plus a darker color (to enrich the shadows).

Creating the Curves

To ensure tonal consistency throughout the image, you need to think carefully about adjusting curves for each ink, depending on their relative tones. For example, let's say you're printing with black plus a PMS ink, Warm Gray 6 (which we can't show you, since we only have process inks to work with).

▶ The black is going to make up the skeleton of the image, with a lot of contrast in the shadows. To do this, we pull the black entirely out of the extreme highlights by setting the 5-percent field to zero. Then we compress the tonal range of the image slightly by setting the 100-percent black to 94 (that way, no pixels become totally black). Finally, to add even more contrast, we pull the 70-percent value down to 45.

▶ The warm gray will be the flesh of the image, holding the contrast in the midtones, and especially focusing on the highlights. To do this, we're going to boost the contrast in the highlights by raising the curve from 5 percent up to 9 percent. Next, we'll lower the 100-percent mark to 90 percent, so that the shadows don't get too dark when both inks print on top of each other. Finally, the curve in the highlights and midtones is steep, but we want it even steeper, so we'll raise the 50-percent mark to 75 percent.

While these adjustments flatten out the contrast in the shadows, we don't care, because the details there are handled by the black ink.

Note that this example is only that: an example. Change the ink and you had better change the curve. Change one curve and you had better change the other. Most of all, the curves you make and use must be dependent on the image you have, the data that makes up the image, and

Figure 10-11

The Info palette
for duotones

*The Info palette shows
how much ink is in
each channel.*

what you want to do with that data. Again, every image is different; so
you should tailor the curves to bring out the detail where you want it
most. (One of our favorite new features in Photoshop 5 is a subtle one:
you can preview your duotone image as you adjust its colors and curves,
making it easier to get it right the first time.)

The Info Palette

When we work on multitone images, we like to set up the Info palette so
that the First Color Readout is Actual Color. This way, we can always see
how much ink is being laid down in an area (see Figure 10-11). Then we
set the Second Color Readout to Grayscale, which tells us what the original underlying grayscale data is. Finally, we set the Mouse Coordinates
in the Info palette to Pixels (so that we can easily refer back to the same
pixel coordinate if we need to).

Tip: Make Gray Wedges Match. One of the most complicated challenges
of creating multitone curves is maintaining the overall tone of the image
while attempting to expand its tonal range. One method we use while
adjusting multitone curves is to work with a gray wedge.

1. Create a new grayscale document as wide as your duotone image and
    perhaps an inch or so tall.

2. Turn off the Dither checkbox in the Gradient Options palette, then fill
    this document with a gradient from black to white.

3. Select Posterize from the Adjust submenu under the Image menu,
    and type "21" in the Posterize dialog box. Press Return.

4. You've now created a 21-step gray wedge, ranging from 0 to 100 per-
    cent in 5-percent increments.

5. In the original image (the one that's going to be turned into a duo-
    tone), increase the height dimension of the image by a little more than
    the height of the gray wedge (select Canvas Size from the Image menu,

Figure 10-12

Using a gray wedge
when adjusting tone

*By comparing the two
gray wedges, you can get a
feel for how the shades in
your multitone are being
affected by the curves.*

click in the bottom-middle square, then increase the number of pixels in the Height field).

6. Back in the gray-wedge document, Select All (Command-A) and copy
   the gray wedge into the duotone-to-be. You can use Copy and Paste,
   but we prefer to simply drag the selection from one document to the
   other and then place it properly in the blank white area above the image (see Figure 10-12).

Now, as you make adjustments to the duotone curves, you can watch
for two important things. (Ordinarily we'd say, "Watch the Info palette."
However, we haven't been able to extract information that's relevant to
comparing images. Let us know if you know something we don't!)

▶ Watch the gray wedge in the duotone image to see if some gray levels
  are blending into their neighbors. This way you can quickly see when
  the highlights, midtones, or shadows are losing definition.

▶ If you align the two document windows (the duotone/image gray
  wedge and the grayscale gray wedge), you can compare their tones.
  For instance, if the duotone gray wedge is significantly lighter than

the grayscale gray wedge, you know that you probably need to bump one or more of the duotone curves.

Again, the goal of making a duotone is most often to maintain the overall tonality, so the two gray wedges should be approximately the same in tone (even if one is colorized and the other is not). However, sometimes your goal is to alter the tone—perhaps to make the highlights lighter or darker. In those cases, the grayscale wedge is still useful as a benchmark.

Unthinkable Curves

In the example above, we created two curves that we would *never* ordinarily apply to an image, because they can result in severe posterization in some areas and lack of contrast in others. We can get away with these unthinkable curves, however, because the posterization and lack of detail are masked, in part, by the overprinting of the two inks. However, these curves are still timid compared to some you might want to create.

For instance, you may want to lay down a heavy solid swath of a light-gray ink under almost the entire image, in order to boost the feeling of depth, or to colorize the image slightly (see Figure 10-13).

Or you may want to hit only a certain highlight area with an ink. In this case, it may be tempting to make the curve return to zero so that this ink won't fall into the shadows. Instead, we suggest you level off the

Figure 10-13 Boosting depth by adding gray

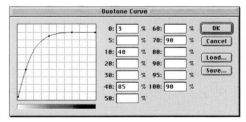

This curve can add depth to, or colorize, the entire image.

Original image   *After the curve is applied*

Figure 10-14 Adding ink in the highlights

It's usually better to extend an ink through the tonal range (top and left), rather than restricting it (bottom and right).

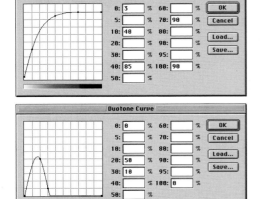

curve so that the ink enriches the midtones and shadows as well (see Figure 10-14). That way you get extra benefit from the ink, and avoid the hue shift caused when one ink is totally absent from part of the tonal range.

Compressing Tones for Targeting

There's no doubt that printing presses have difficulty printing extreme highlights or shadows—the tiny halftone spots disappear to white, and the white areas in the shadows fill in, resulting in solid ink. This is the reason we're so adamant about compressing the tonal range of your images so that all the gray values and details appear in a range that can successfully print on press (see "White Points and Black Points and Grays, Oh My!" in Chapter 6, *Tonal Correction*).

Nonetheless, one of the goals of multitone images is to expand the tonal range and recapture some of that highlight and shadow detail lost in the horrors of the printing process. If you compress the image data significantly before you start adjusting duotone curves, you've simply lost your chance to bring out those details.

We suggest avoiding the targeting step during tonal correction, and instead using the duotone curves to compress the data (see Figure 10-15).

Figure 10-15

Examples of curves for compressing data

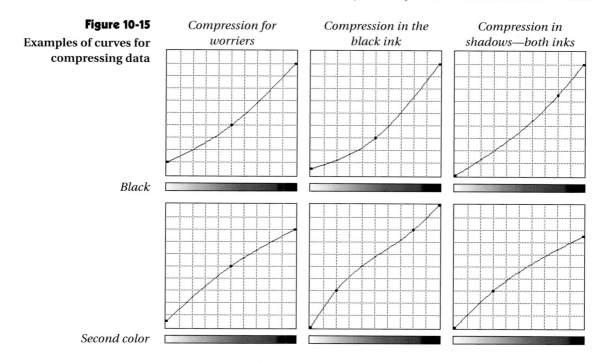

Compression for worriers

Compression in the black ink

Compression in shadows—both inks

Black

Second color

Turning Grayscale to Color

Until now, we've been exploring how to create multitones using the Duotone mode. However, just because you want a multitone doesn't mean that you need to use the Duotone mode to get it. In fact, you can often get just as good results by manipulating the grayscale image in CMYK mode. There are, however, pros and cons to either technique.

▶ **File size.** An image in Duotone mode, whatever the number of inks, is saved as an 8-bit grayscale image along with curves. CMYK images, then, are four times the size, because each pixel is described with 32 bits of information, even if you're only using two channels.

▶ **Single-color areas.** In Duotone mode, there's almost no way to create a single area in which only one color is present. For example, it's a pain to make a 20-percent blue square in the middle of an image, without black also printing in it. However, this is easy to do in any other mode.

▶ **Blends.** There's also no way to create a gradient blend between two spot colors while in Duotone mode. In CMYK mode, it's easy.

▶ **Outputting images.** When you output a multitone image, the mode it's in may have an impact on your output process. For instance, you cannot transfer an image in Duotone mode to a high-end imaging system (like Scitex). Also, because duotone images must be saved in an EPS format (see "Saving and Outputting," later in this chapter), you cannot take advantage of any tricks your page-layout software may be able to do with TIFF images (see Chapter 16, *Storing Images*).

▶ **Adjusting tone.** In Duotone mode, you can always change the duotone curves without affecting the underlying grayscale image data. That means you can quickly repurpose the image to a number of different output devices. Or if your art director decides to print with green instead of yellow ink, you can quickly change the tonal curve to adjust for the difference in ink density.

On the other hand, if you're creating multitones in CMYK mode, you're changing the image data in each channel, so you want to minimize the number of adjustments you make to avoid image degradation. Working in CMYK mode, however, gives you the chance to actually see (interactively) how your curves are affecting the image data. And you can use features like the white-and-black-point clipping display in Levels to make decisions about your curves. This can be very helpful, especially when making small tweaks to the curves.

▶ **Screen representation.** Photoshop knows how to represent most spot colors reasonably well on screen when you're in Duotone mode. However, if you're creating spot-color multitones rather than process-color multitones in CMYK mode (see the sidebar "Spot versus Process Color," earlier in this chapter), you'll either have to ignore the colors you see on the screen (which are RGB representations of CMYK colors) or look ahead in the chapter to "Simulating Spot Colors in CMYK."

Converting Grayscale Images to Color

Because a multitone image typically represents a grayscale image using color, you generally begin with a grayscale image. (If you've got a color image, see "The Color of Grayscale" in Chapter 15, *Essential Image Techniques*.) In this section we're discussing using CMYK to create duotones, so you'll want to switch your image from Grayscale mode to CMYK mode. You can use two methods—simple conversion, or copying into a new file.

Figure 10-16 Grayscale reproduction with the four process inks

The grayscale image

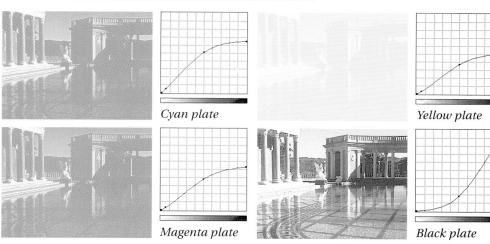

Cyan plate

Yellow plate

Magenta plate

Black plate

Printed using the four process inks

Figure 10-17 Creating curves for duotone and tritone images

By focusing inks on different tonal ranges, you can colorize a grayscale image, and emphasize otherwise-hidden details. The tables show the values entered in the Duotone Curves dialog boxes.

Cool neutral, details held with black

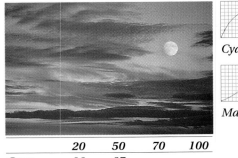

Cyan

Black

	20	50	70	100
Cyan	–	15	60	–
Black	10	–	60	–

Cyan holds highlights, magenta holds shadows.

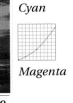

Cyan

Magenta

	20	50	70	100
Cyan	36	67	–	–
Magenta	–	33	–	90

Cyan and yellow in the midtones, black elsewhere

Cyan

Yellow

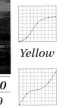

Black

	20	50	70	100
Cyan	6	–	75	89
Yellow	10	52	65	70
Black	30	42	52	92

Magenta and yellow emphasize the shadows.

Magenta

Yellow

Black

	20	50	70	100
Magenta	5	15	–	85
Yellow	4	15	35	85
Black	15	40	–	95

Magenta and yellow carry the highlights.

Magenta

Yellow

Black

	20	50	70	100
Magenta	30	57	–	82
Yellow	30	50	–	68
Black	4	30	–	95

Cyan for the highlights, black for the shadows

Cyan

Black

	20	50	70	100
Cyan	34	48	–	80
Black	5	–	55	–

Simple conversion. You can simply switch your image from Grayscale mode to CMYK mode using the Mode menu. However, many people seem to think that this simply adds three new channels (cyan, magenta, and yellow), and leaves all the grayscale information in the black channel. Not so. Photoshop uses the color settings preferences (see Chapter 5, *Color Settings*) to convert the neutral grays into colors. The amount of black generation (based on the UCR or GCR settings in Separation Setup) determines what appears in the Black channel.

In effect, the curves in the CMYK Setup dialog box are equivalent to creating a quadtone using the Duotone dialog box. We rarely use this method; it's clunky and nigh-on impossible to make adjustments to each plate after the conversion. Plus, Photoshop's separation curves are not designed to expand the tonal range of a grayscale image, so you're losing the opportunity to enhance your image.

Nonetheless, if you *do* use this method, we strongly suggest you set Black Generation to Heavy in the Separation Setup dialog box first. That way, the black channel contains more information, and small press anomalies won't result in large color shifts.

Copy into New. A second, more reasonable, way to convert your grayscale image into CMYK form is to create a new document with the same pixel dimensions as the grayscale image.

1. Select the whole grayscale image (Command-A).

2. Copy it (Command-C).

3. Create a new document (Command-N) and set the mode to CMYK. Photoshop should have automatically set the dimensions of the new document to the size of the image on the clipboard, so there's no need to change them.

4. Switch to the cyan channel (Command-1) and paste the grayscale image into it. Repeat this with each of the four channels that you want to use. (For a tritone, fill three channels; for a duotone, fill two.)

Now it's time to start adjusting curves for each of the channels. This is a tricky proposition because, as we said back in Chapter 6, *Tonal Correction*, you typically don't want to make tonal adjustments to a channel more than once or twice. You can work around this by using a Curves

Adjustment Layer to tune the curves, then flatten the image when the curves are the way you want them.

Tip: Keep the Copy on Hand. If you're using the Copy into New method, and you mess up the curves in one of the channels, don't forget that you may have the original grayscale image still copied in the clipboard. To revert the channel back to where it was when you started, you can simply paste the image back into that channel.

Simulating Spot Colors in CMYK

If you've decided to create or adjust your multitone in CMYK mode, you'll likely want to see a reasonable representation of the image on your screen. If the image is a process-color multitone, this isn't a problem at all. But if you're using one or more spot colors, Photoshop balks at the proposal—it only thinks in cyan, magenta, yellow, and black.

Figure 10-18

CMYK Setup and Ink Colors dialog boxes

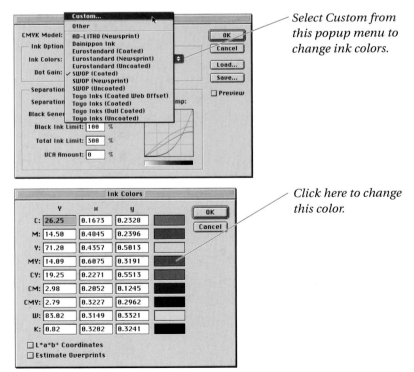

Select Custom from this popup menu to change ink colors.

Click here to change this color.

Converting from Duotone to CMYK Mode

While we wouldn't do this with most images, we have occasionally found it helpful to do much of our multitone work in Duotone mode, then convert to CMYK mode to take advantage of capabilities like solid color tints, blends, interactive tonal adjustments, and output benefits (see "Turning Grayscale to Color," earlier in this chapter). This gives us the best of both worlds, and it gives us one additional advantage: we can print to a color printer for proofing (see "Saving and Outputting," later in this chapter).

As in the conversion from Grayscale to CMYK mode, there are two methods for converting from Duotone mode to CMYK. The easiest method is simply to select CMYK from the Mode menu. This is easy and effective when preparing to output to a color printer, but useless if you need to make further changes to the duotone curves. It's useless because while the result is an image that looks almost exactly the same, it's built with four process colors (like converting RGB to CMYK)—all your painstaking work on the duotone curves goes down the toilet.

If you're planning on converting the image in order to make further adjustments to it while in CMYK mode, it's much better to convert the image to Multichannel mode first. When you convert to Multichannel mode, Photoshop gives you two, three, or four channels (depending on the number of inks you're using), each with the proper curve automatically applied to the original grayscale image. From Multichannel mode, you can convert the image to CMYK mode with two changes.

▶ If there are only two or three channels (if the image is a duotone or a tritone), add channels until you have four. We suggest naming them (double-click on the channel tile in the Channels palette) so you know which is which.

▶ Make sure the channels are in the correct order in the Channels palette. When you convert to CMYK mode, the first channel tile in the palette is always read as the cyan plate, the second is magenta, and so on. However, when you convert a quadtone into Multichannel mode, Photoshop makes black the first tile in the list. You have to drag it into its correct place, or the image will turn out incorrectly.

This, by the way, is how you can convert a duotone image into a CMYK format that Scitex (and other CMYK-only systems) can read and use.

The answer is found by choosing Custom from the Ink Colors popup menu in the CMYK Setup dialog box. As we discussed back in Chapter 5, *Color Settings*, Photoshop knows what color inks you're using by what ink set you've chosen in this dialog box (see Figure 10-18). If you change the color cyan to hot pink here, Photoshop adjusts and displays hot pink wherever you ask for cyan.

Here's how you can change these values to simulate spot colors and get a reasonably good on-screen representation of your image.

1. Find the Lab values for the inks you'll be printing with. (If you've already picked a Pantone or other spot color in the Duotone dialog box, click on the color swatch there. If you haven't picked one yet, you can

find one by opening the Color Picker, clicking Custom, then clicking the Picker button to go back to the Color Picker.)

2. Note the Lab values for the color. (Yes, you have to write them down.)

3. Go to the CMYK Setup dialog box and select Custom from the Printing Inks popup menu.

4. Click on the cyan color swatch and type in the Lab values for the spot color you chose. (If you have precise Lab or xyY values from a spectrophotometer, you can skip clicking on the color swatch and simply turn on the Lab Coordinates checkbox.)

Click OK to save these settings; Photoshop now thinks of cyan as the spot color. If your image is a tritone or quadtone, you have to repeat these steps for the other color(s).

If you're printing with more than one nonblack ink (in the case of a tritone or quadtone), you also need to specify what the *combined* spot-color values are. Otherwise your screen representation will be way off. It's easy enough to find the values for the solid inks, but how can you find out the Lab values for two overprinting spot-color inks? The hard (but most accurate) way is to use a colorimeter, such as the Colortron, to read a drawdown from your printer. We found an easier way (one which is usually reasonably accurate) in Rob Day's *Designer Photoshop*.

1. Create a new small grayscale document, and convert it to Duotone mode. This is just a dummy document that you'll throw away later.

2. While in the Duotone dialog box, select the two or three colors in your tritone or quadtone. Don't bother with the curves; they don't concern us here.

3. Click on Overprint Colors to see how Photoshop believes these colors should overprint.

4. Click on the 2+3 color swatch, and write down the Lab value of the color. Repeat this with any other nonblack color swatch.

5. Leave these dialog boxes, and open the Custom Ink dialog box inside CMYK Setup.

6. Click on the overprinting color swatches for the corresponding spot colors (for instance, the one labeled CM is the overprinting color for cyan and magenta). The hardest part here, we find, is remembering what spot colors correspond to what process-color labels.

When you save this printing ink setup, your multitone images should appear correctly—more or less—on the screen. Note that making changes in this dialog box has no effect on CMYK image data. *It has a radical effect,* however, on any image that you convert *to* CMYK mode, and on the way Photoshop displays CMYK images. Therefore, we strongly suggest you save the custom ink settings in the CMYK Setup dialog box (use the Save button). Then switch back to a standard SWOP ink set (or whatever you usually use) whenever you're not working on your spot-color image.

Saving and Outputting

While we explore printing and saving from Photoshop in depth in Chapter 16, *Storing Images,* and Chapter 17, *Output Methods,* multitones have some specific requirements that we can better discuss in the privacy of this chapter. The two most relevant issues in getting a duotone out of Photoshop and onto paper or film are saving and screen angles.

The file format that you use when saving a multitone document depends entirely on the mode the image is in: Duotone or CMYK.

Duotone mode. You can save Duotone-mode images in three formats—Photoshop, EPS, and Raw. But the only file format that's useful in page-layout programs is EPS, because Photoshop has to save the duotone curves in the form of transfer curves—something only EPS files can handle.

In order for the EPS duotone to separate properly from the page-layout program, however, you have to make sure that the color names in the duotone exactly match the names in your page-layout program's color list. For instance, if you used "Pantone 286 CVC" in your duotone, you should also have a color named "Pantone 286 CVC" in QuarkXPress or PageMaker. Fortunately, if you haven't defined the color name when you import the multitone, the latest versions of these programs add the name to the color list automatically on import.

Tip: Don't Exclude Image Data. It quacks like a bug: If you turn on the Exclude Non-image Data option in the Save a Copy dialog box when saving a duotone image in Photoshop 5.0, the duotone information is stripped out. Oops! (This should be fixed in a future version.)

Tip: Use Short Pantone Names. If you've already created and applied a Pantone color in your page-layout program before you import your duotone, you need to be twice as careful about ensuring the names are the same. Let's say you've added "Pantone 240 CV" to your PageMaker color list. Then you use the same color in your Photoshop duotone and import it into PageMaker. What you may or may not notice is that Photoshop, by default, named its PMS color "Pantone 240 CVC". Because of the one-letter difference, PageMaker thinks it's a different color, and will separate it onto a different plate.

There are tricks in PageMaker and QuarkXPress to combine spot colors onto a single plate, but you can avoid some of these troubles by turning on the Use Short Pantone Names checkbox in Photoshop's General Preferences dialog box. That way, it leaves off the final character, just the way PageMaker does. If you're using XPress, don't worry about it; it's smart enough to merge the colors onto a single plate automatically.

CMYK mode. If you've created your multitone image in CMYK mode, you have a choice, just as with any other CMYK image, to save in either EPS or TIFF (of course, you have more choices than this, but these are the only *good* choices). However, if you need to specify particular halftone screen angles in your duotone—and you often do—you have to use EPS (TIFFs don't let you save that sort of information). Plus, if you've built custom ink colors, you may have to save as EPS in order to see the proper preview in your page-layout program. (If the program is smart enough to read and interpret an embedded color profile, TIFF files may work properly.)

The most important thing to remember when creating duotones, tritones, or quadtones in CMYK mode is this: if you're not intending to use process-color inks, be very careful at separation time. If you import a CMYK image into a page-layout program and print color separations, the cyan channel ends up on the cyan plate, the yellow channel ends up on the yellow plate, and so on. This is what you'd expect and want if you were using process-color inks in your image; but if you're using spot-color inks (as in the earlier section, "Simulating Spot Colors in CMYK"), this could be a disaster.

Screen Angles

Every topic in digital imaging must have at least one controversy. One of the controversies surrounding duotones is what screen angles you should use when printing them. People fall into two camps : those who favor 30 degrees between inks, and those who favor 45. We are in the latter camp: 45 degrees between the halftone screens results in the least obvious patterns. (You always get *some* patterning when you overlap screens; the trick is to minimize it.) The angles you pick, however, may vary.

We typically print black ink at 45 degrees because people tend to "blur out" this angle the most (important for a dark color). But that only leaves zero degrees for the second ink. If that ink is very light, like yellow or a light gray, you can print it at zero degrees. With a darker color like burnt sienna, cyan, or dark gray, however, a zero-degree screen may appear too obvious. Our second choice is printing the inks at 30 and 75 degrees.

With these screen combinations, be aware that the RIP might think it knows better, and substitute "optimized" process-color angles. Ask your service bureau to turn off Balanced Screens, or HQS, or whatever.

The more traditional among us usually print with 30-degree offsets. We suspect there may be an element of superstition in this, but many people who've built more duotones than we've had hot dinners use angles 30 degrees apart. However, when pressed, most confess that they do so because that's what they were taught to do.

Conventional wisdom puts the strong color at 45 degrees and the weak one at 75 degrees. But this can have the effect of making one screen more obvious than the other, so in many cases angles of 15 and 75 degrees are used instead.

In a tritone image, of course, we always revert to the second opinion: 30-degree offsets, usually using 15, 45, and 75 degrees (with 45 used for the ink/curve combination that is dominant—that has the greatest density). Finally, for quadtones, we use the four standard process-color angles: 0, 15, 45, and 75. (Note that many people state these angles as 45, 90, 105, and 165; they're the same thing, but three of them are rotated 90 degrees.) The lightest ink is always printed at zero degrees.

Printing Order

In order for the inks to match their proper halftone screen angles automatically, arrange them from darkest to lightest in the Duotone dialog box (bearing in mind the curves you've set up for each ink; a dark ink with a very light curve may not be terribly dominant on press).

If you want to specify angles manually, however, you can use the Screens button in the Page Setup dialog box (see Figure 10-19 and "Imaging from Photoshop" in Chapter 17, *Output Methods*).

Figure 10-19

Setting screens for duotones

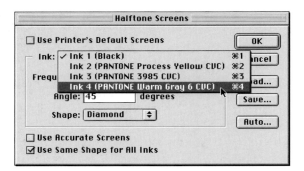

There's often little you can do about the order in which the inks are printed on press, however, even though this order may have a significant effect on the image. We suggest discussing the topic with your printer and relying heavily on their experience with inks.

Printing Proofs of Spot Color Images

Seeing spot colors (or representations of them) on screen is one thing. Proofing them on paper is quite another. You really only have two choices when trying to proof your multitone images: custom inks and converting to process colors.

Custom inks. Some service bureaus provide proofing systems that attempt to match Pantone and other spot colors. For instance, the Cromalin system lets you build proofs using Pantone's spot colors (Match Prints cannot do this, by the way). Have no doubt, this is an expensive proposition, but it's the closest approximation you can get this side of a press check.

For this type of proofing, it doesn't matter whether you've used Duotone or CMYK mode to create your multitones, or what type of inks you'll finally be printing with. You're dumping a piece of black film for each ink color; the color (spot or process) only appears when the proofs are made.

Process colors. An alternative is to print proofs on a color printer with CMYK colorants. Most spot inks just can't be reproduced faithfully with CMYK, but with skill, luck, and a good dose of experience, you can get something meaningful out of these devices.

There are three ways to print a multitone image on a color printer.

▶ **Just print it.** If your image is in Duotone mode and you simply select Print from the File menu, Photoshop sends the grayscale image to the printer along with four transfer curves (one for each process color). If the printer can only print grayscale, it throws away the transfer curves and just prints the grayscale image. If it's a color printer, it renders the image as faithfully as it can.

The primary problem with this approach is that Photoshop makes the assumption that your multitone colors are spot colors—even if they're specced as process colors—so it pushes them through its color engine (via the color preferences dialog boxes; see Chapter 5, *Color Settings*). This is more or less the same as simply converting to CMYK mode yourself and then printing. If you have really good values set up in the appropriate dialog boxes (especially CMYK Setup) and your system is well calibrated, there's a reasonable chance you'll get a nice-looking image. Otherwise, your images may look bizarre.

If the multitone image is in CMYK mode when you print, Photoshop simply sends the raw CMYK data to the printer. This usually looks like dreck because the CMYK data is probably targeted to a device other than your color proofer.

▶ **Convert to RGB.** A second method of printing multitone images is to convert them to RGB mode first (whether they're in Duotone or CMYK mode), and then tell Photoshop to send the RGB data to the printer (select RGB in the Print dialog box). While this sometimes works, it often gives you even stranger colors than printing the CMYK data. The reason: the printer doesn't know what that RGB data is supposed to look like; it doesn't know what you're seeing on your screen (see Chapter 4, *Color Essentials*).

▶ **Use Profile to Profile.** Our favorite choice is to use the Profile to Profile feature (in the Mode submenu, under the Image menu) to convert the image to the appropriate RGB or CMYK values for the output device. If the image is in Duotone mode, you'll have to switch to RGB mode before using Profile to Profile, however.

Note that no matter which method you use, the color you see from a color printer is almost certainly going to be different from your final image, and no printer worth his or her salt would take something like this as a contract proof. But it may be helpful in the process of creating good curves.

Tip: Be There During the Print Run. Stephen Johnson has made more duotones than anyone else we know, and he maintains that even after printing hundreds of multitone images, he still doesn't know exactly what he's going to get until he shows up for the press run. Take his advice. If you're doing critical duotones, you *must* be present during the press run— the way the press operator controls the inks can make or break the final printed piece.

Billions of Shades of Gray

If the real world would simply perform as all the theories tell us, grayscale images would fly off the printing press with deep, rich tones and an incredible dynamic range and CMYK images would simulate every color in the rainbow. Unfortunately, the real world doesn't pay much attention to theories, so we need to help the process along. Spot colors— whether in the form of bump plates, solid spot areas, or duotones—are great ways to do this. After all, if you're trying to faithfully reproduce an elephant, you want to listen to (or see) as many perspectives as you can.

Line Art

Dreaming in Black and White

With all the frenzy on the Photoshop scene that surrounds cool effects like fractalization, motion blurs, and drop shadows, it's easy to lose sight of the basics. And there are few scanned images more basic than line art.

Line art—those black-and-white images (or "bitmap images," in Photoshop terminology) with no halftoning, dithering, or anything else—are as simple as can be. Each pixel is either on or off, black or white, and you're not concerned with gray levels or halftones. Scanning, manipulating, and printing these things should be easy. And it is, at least compared to the vagaries that surround grayscale and color images.

Nonetheless, we've found that most people's line art images don't begin to approach the quality of (even mediocre) photographic reproduction. Edges are jaggy, fine lines break up, and dense patterns clog up. Many of you are going to be surprised when we tell you that it doesn't have to be that way.

With line art, you can actually produce an image that matches the original to an extent that just doesn't happen with grayscale and color images. With just a few techniques under your belt, you can achieve that ethereal, Platonic state of perfect line art reproduction, and with very little effort. The tricks lie in scanning mode, resolution, sharpening, and thresholding.

Scanning in Grayscale

It's *essential* that you scan in grayscale mode to take advantage of the techniques covered in this chapter. If you scan in line art (1-bit) mode, you can't do much of anything to improve your image. In Grayscale mode, however, you can sharpen, adjust the black/white threshold to control line widths, and increase your effective line art resolution; each of these techniques helps create a beautiful reproduction.

So avoid the temptation to scan line art *as* line art, and scan it as grayscale instead. Sure, your files are eight times as large, but it's only temporary. You can convert them to Bitmap mode when you're done with your manipulations. And the quality difference with these techniques is like the difference between . . . well . . . black and white.

Resolution

When you're printing to an imagesetter, you need very high image resolution to match the quality of photographically reproduced line art. That means 800 ppi minimum image resolution. You *can* see the difference between 800- and 1,200-ppi line art (see Figure 11-1), so you may want to opt for the higher resolution if your printing method can hold it.

Of course, you never need image resolution higher than output resolution. If you're printing your final artwork on a 600-dpi laser printer, for instance, you don't need more than 600-ppi image resolution. The additional data just gets thrown away.

Tip: Fast Line Art Imagesetting. It may seem like 800- and 1,200-ppi images are going to make for big files and slow print times, and that's often the case. But there's a little-known back-door trick that might speed things up for you. Most imagesetters that are based on Adobe PostScript RIPs (and perhaps some others) can process same-resolution bilevel images very quickly.

For example, if you send a 1,200-ppi line art (bitmap) image to a 1,200-dpi imagesetter, it can say, "Hey! That's a 1,200-dpi bitmap, and I'm printing 1,200-dpi bitmaps, so I'll just blast it down onto the page, dot for dot." The end result? A 1,200-ppi line art image may print much, much faster than an 800-ppi image. Try it on your system and see if it works.

(By the way, this doesn't work with desktop laser printers, at least according to the testing we've done.)

Figure 11-1 Line art resolution

Grayscale scan

144 ppi

300 ppi

600 ppi

800 ppi

1,200 ppi

Tip: Scan Big for High Resolution. "Great," you're saying. "They say we need 800-ppi images, but all we've got is a 300-ppi scanner. And they said back in the Image Essentials chapter that upsampling is useless. What are we supposed to do with this business card the client gave us?"

You've got two options to get a higher resolution out of a low-resolution scanner. First, you can scan a large original at your scanner's highest optical resolution and scale it down, increasing resolution. If you reduce the image to 50 percent, for instance, you double the resolution.

You can either scale the image in a page-layout program, or adjust the size in Photoshop's Image Size dialog box while the File Size checkbox is turned on (see Chapter 3, *Image Essentials*).

If you don't have a larger version of the artwork, you can enlarge your small version on a stat camera or quality photocopier, and scan that. You still get a higher-quality image because the photographic enlargement doesn't cause pixelization (there may be some cleanup work involved after the scan, of course).

The second solution (which you can use in combination with this enlargement/reduction technique) is covered in the next tip.

Tip: Doubling Your Scanner's Line Art Resolution. The second method for going beyond your scanner's resolution essentially "steals" information from an 8-bit grayscale scan, converting that information into higher line art resolution.

1. Scan your artwork as a grayscale image at your scanner's maximum optical resolution (let's use 300 ppi for this example).

2. Double the image resolution (quadrupling the file size) using the Image Size dialog box (make sure the Resample Image checkbox is turned on with Bicubic as the resampling method). In our example, you'd upsample to 600 ppi. Note that if your scanning software can interpolate up to this same resolution, you can use that as you scan, and save yourself a step.

    If you're yelling, "Hey! You said interpolation was useless," you're right—we did. This is the exception (we can't think of any others).

3. Sharpen and threshold the image as outlined later in this chapter.

4. Switch to Bitmap mode at the same resolution (600 ppi in our example), with the 50% Threshold option selected (see Figure 11-2).

Figure 11-2

Converting to
Bitmap mode

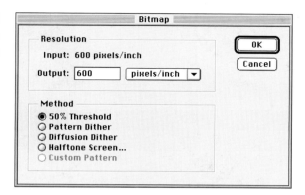

Voilà! A 600-ppi line art image from a 300-ppi scanner. While it isn't a true 600-ppi scan, it's so close that we dare you to find a difference. You may be able to raise the image's resolution above two times optical resolution, but that's pretty much the point of diminishing returns.

Note that you can use this tip alongside the previous one to res up to 800 ppi or higher.

If the arithmetic of scaling and resolution is giving you trouble, you might want to take a look at the tip "Figuring Scaling and Resolution" in Chapter 13, *Capturing Images*.

Sharpening

Nothing will do more for the quality of your line art images than sharpening the grayscale scan (see Figure 11-3). 'Nuf said. We recommend running the Unsharp Mask filter twice with the settings 500/1/5. If your scanning software can sharpen, you may be able to save yourself a step (Hewlett-Packard's DeskScan software does it, for instance, though not as well as Photoshop's Unsharp Mask filter).

Thresholding

When you scan line art in Grayscale mode, lines aren't captured as hard lines, but as a collection of pixels with different values (see Figure 11-4). But although you scanned in grayscale, you ultimately want a straight black-and-white image. The way you get there is via the Threshold command (from the Adjust submenu under the Image menu). Threshold turns gray pixels above a certain value to black, and pushes all other pixels to white.

Figure 11-3
Line art with and
without sharpening

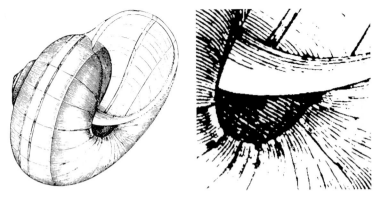

Without sharpening

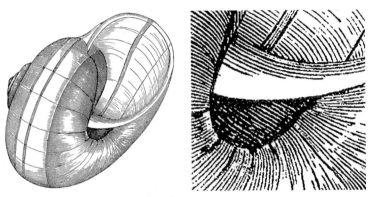

With sharpening

By adjusting the break point in the Threshold dialog box where pixels go to black or white, you can control the widths of lines in your scanned-as-grayscale line art image (see Figure 11-5).

For simple line art images that don't include very detailed and dense shadow areas, just set Threshold to 2 and press Return. With images that do include densely detailed shadows, try values up to about 55. As you move the slider to the left, you can see the fine lines start to break up. As you move right, the shadow areas start to clog. It's a lot like working the trade-off between shadow and highlight detail with the Levels dialog box on a grayscale image.

Figure 11-4
Line art scanned
as grayscale

Scanned as line art   *400%*

Scanned as grayscale   *400%*

Scanned as grayscale with sharpening   *400%*
and thresholding applied

Scanning Prescreened Art

Rescreening—scanning images that have already been halftoned—is one of the toughest quandaries you'll encounter in Photoshop. We cover it in some detail in Chapter 15, *Essential Image Techniques,* but it's worth a note here, as well.

Figure 11-5

Threshold settings for line art

Threshold: 2

Threshold: 80

Threshold: 185

One way to avoid the screen conflicts (moiré patterns) that you can get by scanning black-and-white halftoned images is to use the line art techniques described in this chapter. In other words, don't try to make Photoshop convert the halftone spots into gray levels; just leave them as halftone spots. This works best with images screened at 85 lpi or less, because you can pick up the detail you need to hold the screen.

If you work for a newspaper and are forever getting veloxed camera-ready art, this may be the trick for you. However, if you scan a *lot* of previously halftoned images, you should definitely check out the ScanPrep Pro Plug-in from ImageXPress (see the *Resources* appendix). Its Copy Dot mode does a better job of scanning veloxes than anything we've seen.

Perfect Forms

There are few absolutes in the imaging business, and it's nice to find something that gets close. Get these line art techniques down pat (or better yet, automate them using Photoshop's Actions), and you can get great line art every time, without hardly trying.

12

Scanners

The Right Tool for the Right Job

The vast majority of images that end up in Photoshop come via some kind of scanner. But digital cameras and Kodak's Photo CD are becoming increasingly important as image sources. Photoshop doesn't care where your images come from, but you should.

All digital images share similarities, but the devices they come from are often radically different and impose their own idiosyncracies on the image. Knowing a little about the unique aspects of each kind of capture device is helpful, whether you're shopping for one, looking to have images digitized by a service provider, or simply having to work with the images in Photoshop.

In this chapter we take a look at three types of image capture devices—scanners, digital cameras, and Photo CD—along with their strengths, weaknesses, and quirks.

Scanners

Scanners come in all shapes, sizes, and prices, but they all do the same thing—they take an original print or transparency and convert it to pixels. But scanners differ considerably in resolution (the number of pixels they can "see" per inch), in their ability to see into the shadow areas of an original, and in the kinds of original they're best equipped to scan.

405

Many factors go into building a good scanner, and manufacturers' specifications often confuse more than they illuminate. It's impossible to judge a scanner by its specs—more often than not, the spec sheet is incomplete—but it's worth taking a quick look at the various specs anyway. There are several items that we always look for.

▶ CCD versus PMT

▶ Optical resolution versus interpolated resolution

▶ Bit depth

▶ Dynamic range and dMax

▶ One-pass versus three-pass

▶ Scanner type: flatbed, drum, or transparency

CCDs vs PMTs

One of the most important differences among scanners is whether they sense light with *CCDs* (charge-coupled devices) or *PMTs* (photomultiplier tubes). Almost every drum scanner on the market uses PMTs; they typically offer superior performance in reading shadow detail while minimizing noise. But they're expensive.

A drum scanner has three or four PMTs, and the entire image spins past them. Most other scanners use CCD arrays—rows of hundreds or thousands of tiny CCDs that capture many pixels of data simultaneously. CCDs are much less expensive than PMTs, but in most cases they aren't as sensitive to low levels of light.

Debate continues to rage over the relative merits of CCDs versus PMTs, but the gap in quality is narrowing dramatically (particularly with the introduction of high-end CCD scanners such as the Scitex SmartScanners and the Linotype-Hell Topaz). It's clear that PMTs have reached the end of their evolution—they're one of the very few instances of vacuum tube technology still in production—whereas CCDs are continuing to improve and evolve. If you're trying to decide whether to buy or use a PMT or a CCD scanner, we suggest you focus on all the other factors that apply instead.

Resolution

Scanner resolution is probably the most misunderstood of all scanner specifications, and the lion's share of the blame for this goes to flatbed scanner vendors. Drum scanner resolutions are usually stated in an unambiguous way—most are around 2,700 ppi (over res 100; see "Terms of Resolution" in Chapter 3, *Image Essentials*). The same holds true for transparency scanners, though the resolutions are sometimes higher—the Imacon Flextight Precision II, and the older Nikon LS3510AF and Leafscan 35 and 45 all boast resolutions over 5,000 ppi (res 200).

Flatbed resolution. Flatbed scanners are a different story. Two factors determine the *optical* resolution of a flatbed. The resolution *across* the bed is determined by the number of elements in the CCD array—typically 300, 400, or 600 per inch, although some mid-range flatbeds have increased this to 1,000 or even 1,400 per inch. The resolution *along* the bed is determined by the increments in which the stepper motor moves the scanning head.

Stepper motors are cheap and CCD arrays are relatively expensive, so it's easy to produce a scanner that steps in $1/1,200$-inch increments, but if the CCD array is only 400 ppi, it's really a 400-ppi scanner. (Once you get into the 1,000-by-2,000-ppi realm, the distinction may be less clear-cut.)

Interpolated resolution. Most flatbeds also offer *interpolated* resolution. Interpolated resolution is useful for smoothing curves in line art, but it's essentially useless for continuous-tone image scanning. If a flatbed scanner's specs mention more than one number for resolution, the real resolution is invariably the lowest one. Interpolation only adds data—not information. You could interpolate image resolution up to a million ppi (with your scanning software, with Photoshop, or whatever), and not improve image quality a whit.

Dual resolution. A few flatbed scanners, such as the Agfa DuoScan and the Umax PowerLook 3000, use two sets of lenses to provide two different optical resolutions. The lower resolution covers the entire image area, but you can switch to a higher resolution with a reduced image area to scan transparencies or small reflective originals.

Bit Depth

One of the big advances in desktop scanners has been the emergence of scanners that capture more than eight bits of data ("high-bit" scanners)—often 9, 10, 12, or even 16 bits per color channel. While you still end up outputting eight bits per color, these scanners offer you a great deal of flexibility in choosing the right eight bits to output.

When you perform tonal correction on 8-bit data, you throw away information—you end up with substantially less than 256 shades of gray in each channel (see "Stretching and Squeezing the Bits" in Chapter 6, *Tonal Correction*). But when you make those same corrections on a high-bit scanner, they operate on all the bits the scanner can capture, before downsampling to eight bits. The result is that you get a full eight bits of output, using all 256 possible levels. We discuss this more fully in "Getting a Good Scan" in Chapter 13, *Capturing Images*.

Dynamic Range and dMax

A scanner's *dynamic range* is the range of densities it can see, and the maximum density—or *dMax*—is the deepest shadow into which it can see. For example, if a scanner has a dynamic range of 3.0 and a dMax of 3.2, then the deepest shadow it can see has an optical density (sometimes called *O.D.*) of 3.2. But if you set the black point to capture shadow detail going down to the dMax of 3.2, you'll blow out any highlights lighter than 0.2 to white, because the scanner's total density range is only 3.0.

If you're scanning transparencies, dynamic range is very important because of the large range of tones possible in transparencies. It's somewhat less important with reflective-art scanning (like on most flatbeds), but we still see plenty of scanners out there that can't handle even the limited dynamic range of a good print.

While dMax is important, the value printed in the manuals should be read with a grain of salt, at least with CCD scanners. Scanners work by shining a bright light on or through artwork, and reading how much light gets bounced back (for reflective art) or comes through the film (for transparencies). In the shadow areas, very little light does either, and the CCD has a difficult time seeing the differences between one very dark area and another. The dMax that vendors quote is typically the point at which the noise inherent in the CCD overwhelms the weak signal produced in the dark areas of the image. Usually you'll see significant amounts of noise in the shadows that are quite a bit lighter than the dMax.

Unfortunately, neither the dynamic range nor the dMax spec tells you anything at all about how finely the scanner can discriminate between the shades of gray that it *can* see. A spec that quotes only the dMax without stating the dynamic range is basically meaningless. One that states both dMax and dynamic range is slightly more useful—it will at least give you a ballpark idea of the kinds of original for which it's suitable.

Very high-contrast prints may have a dynamic range approaching 2.0, although 1.4–1.8 is more typical. Negative film generally has a dynamic range of 2.4 or so, while that of slide film may approach 3.4 or even 3.6. (Note that if film has a dynamic range of 3.6, it's implicit that the dMax is 3.6, too; *dMin*, on the other hand, is film plus fog.) But no one has yet developed a spec that measures how accurately a scanner records all the intermediate shades between black and white.

One-Pass versus Three-Pass

Some scanners capture RGB colors in one pass; others do it in three passes (one each for red, green, and blue). This is ultimately a non-issue. We've seen three-pass scanners that were faster and had better registration than some one-pass scanners. All that's important is that the design is well implemented.

Flatbed Scanners

Flatbed scanners are by far the most common type of scanner. They operate very much the same way photocopiers do—you place the artwork on the scan bed, where it's read by a moving CCD array which is stepped along the image by a stepper motor. Each movement of the scanning head produces one row of pixels. Flatbed scanners are very easy to use, particularly for scanning reflective artwork.

Some flatbeds offer transparency adapters, but the results from these are mixed. Mid-range ($3,000–$5,000) flatbeds can do a good job on 120-format or larger transparencies, but they may have insufficient resolution to get much out of a 35 mm slide. Older flatbeds tend to be optimized for the much narrower dynamic range of reflective artwork, so they produce a limited amount of shadow detail from transparencies.

However, the latest generation of midrange flatbeds such as the Agfa DuoScan, Umax PowerLook 2000 and Linotype-Hell Saphir Ultra II have a dynamic range of around 3.4 and enough resolution to handle everything except 35 mm film. We've obtained surprisingly good results from these scanners using 2,000-dpi scanning, which involves interpolation in one dimension, despite what we said earlier about *avoiding* interpolated resolution. For medium- and large-format transparencies, flatbed scanners provide scans that approach drum scanner quality.

Drum Scanners

Drum scanners are the workhorses of the prepress industry. The original artwork is attached to a transparent cylinder (the drum), which then spins rapidly and moves the image under the sensor. Drum scanner sensors are almost always photomultiplier tubes (PMTs).

High-end drum scanners have color computers that convert the RGB scans to CMYK on the fly, and perform unsharp masking as well (see Chapter 9, *Sharpening*). High-end drum scanners excel at producing high volumes of tightly purposed CMYK scans, but they aren't well suited to producing RGB output for film recorders, and they're gross overkill for multimedia work.

It usually takes three people to keep a high-end drum scanner busy. One loads images on a drum, a fairly finicky process that involves using tape, oil, gel, or powder to attach the original to the drum. The second takes a drum loaded with images to an offline station where the scanning parameters are set for each image. The third runs the scanner itself, scanning the drum loaded by the second person, and returning the drum that's just been scanned to the first person.

Desktop or "baby" drum scanners are much less expensive than their full-size siblings, though they're still far from cheap ($20,000 and up). They usually leave RGB-to-CMYK conversion to the host computer, and most have fixed (rather than removable) drums, so they don't have the productivity advantage of the full-size models.

If you need absolutely noiseless shadows, and you're prepared for the general inconvenience of mounting images on the drum (plus slow scanning once the images are mounted), a baby drum might be worth your consideration.

Drum scanners are generally designed with transparencies in mind. It's possible to scan reflective art, but the results are frequently disappointing, and you can't scan books, paintings, or any other original that can't tolerate being wrapped around the drum.

Transparency Scanners

Transparency scanners are usually CCD-based scanners, but unlike flat-beds, they're optimized for scanning transparencies, both positive and negative. Cheaper transparency scanners are usually dedicated to 35 mm format, while more expensive ones can usually handle 2¼-inch and 4-by-5-inch formats as well.

Good transparency scanners can provide results that approach or equal those of drum scanners, and they subject the originals to a good deal less wear and tear. If you work in 35 mm format, a relatively inexpensive slide scanner will give you much better results than you'll ever get from scanning prints.

Digital Cameras

Digital cameras, like scanners, come in all shapes and sizes. It's unlikely that digital cameras will replace film anytime soon, but in some niche markets they can offer compelling advantages—in some cases more than economic. Our friend Stephen Johnson has shown us comparisons of images from the BetterLight digital camera back (an image-capture device that attaches to the back of the camera) with 4-by-5 film that show the digital camera clearly outresolves the film in both spatial detail and dynamic range (but only at the cost of exposure times measured in minutes).

Digital cameras that offer film-like exposure times typically have a *much* lower resolution than film. High-volume catalog work and time-critical news photography are two major growth areas for the use of (different types) of digital cameras. In both cases, they're attractive because they eliminate the time and cost of film processing and scanning.

The term "digital camera" is really an umbrella that covers several approaches to capturing images. But they all share two common features: they use some kind of lens-and-shutter setup that's recognizable as a camera, and they replace the film plane with some kind of CCD array.

Area array cameras. Digital cameras that use an *area array* work more or less like conventional cameras—the image is captured all at once by a flat array that sits behind the lens where the film usually is. They can even use flash lighting. However, because high-resolution area arrays are very expensive, these cameras tend to have limited resolution. Area array cameras based on conventional film-camera bodies also have a couple of other interesting wrinkles.

The array usually takes up a far smaller area than film would, so the effective focal length of each lens is increased. A normal lens becomes a telephoto, and a wide-angle lens becomes a normal lens—the Kodak DCS 420, for example, ships with a 28 mm wide-angle, which gives approximately the same field of view as a 50 mm lens on a 35 mm camera. To get true wide-angle coverage, you'd need a lens in the 16 mm range—a very expensive lens indeed!

The smaller image area can also play havoc with the camera's built-in metering system, which is designed to deliver a good exposure on a full frame of film. The smaller area and the narrower dynamic range of the CCD behave very differently than film does.

When it comes to capturing color, area array cameras use one of two approaches: one-shot or three-shot. In the three-shot approach, you make three separate exposures through red, green, and blue filters. You get the full resolution of the CCD, but you're pretty much limited to static subjects. The one-shot approach might seem more tempting, but again it involves some significant compromises.

We call one-shot color cameras *decal* cameras, because the color filters are applied directly onto the CCD elements as decals, and each sensor element is dedicated to capturing a single color. Kodak's and Nikon's cameras use two green, one red, and one blue element to create each full-color image pixel (in varying arrangements), while Leaf's Catchlight has extended the filter set to include a fourth color.

One trade-off with either approach is that you need four sensors to make a single color pixel, so your final image has only one-quarter the resolution of the CCD itself. A second trade-off is that all the decal cameras we've seen are plagued by image artifacts. Each vendor's offerings have their own signature artifacts, ranging from color fringing to aliasing to strange combinations of blurring and edge sharpening as the raw image is converted into RGB pixels.

These artifacts can be mitigated by postprocessing the image—Kodak uses a special Photoshop filter, and Leaf uses a stand-alone application—but they can't be eliminated completely. (See Figure 9-9 in Chapter 9, *Sharpening* for more information about dealing with artifacts.)

Linear array cameras. To avoid the problems inherent in decal cameras, higher-resolution digital cameras generally use *linear arrays* and a stepper motor that moves the array across the image area. These getups are often called *scanning backs* because they're just like flatbed scanners stuck on the back of a camera.

Scanning backs offer much higher resolutions than area array cameras, so you can produce much bigger images. They're also free of the artifacts that come with the decal approach. The disadvantage is that they require exposure times measured in minutes, which limits their use to static subjects, and prohibits the use of flash or strobe lighting.

Tip: Scaling Up from Digital Cameras. Any photographer knows all too well what happens when you enlarge an image too much: you see the grain of the film. One interesting property of digital camera images is that, because there's no film grain, you can upsample them without running into an unsightly conflict between film grain and the pixel grid. You do, however, have to keep a watchful eye out for lingering artifacts from decal color cameras.

Acquiring digital camera images. Note that almost everything we say in Chapter 6, *Tonal Correction*, about capturing images from scanners applies also to images from scanning back cameras. Most capture 12 bits internally, and provide the same kinds of tone- and color-correction features found in high-bit scanners. Use them.

None of the decal cameras as yet offers any real degree of control over the way images are acquired into Photoshop, but it's worth saving the raw files these cameras produce because the postprocessing software will undoubtedly improve in the future, and you may be able to tame artifacts that today appear almost impossible.

Photo CD

When Photo CD first appeared, it seemed like one of those occasional Kodak aberrations (like the disc camera)—we thought it very unlikely that people would want to view their family snapshots on TV. We were right about the consumer market's indifference to Photo CD, but we've come to recognize it as a simple and cost-effective method of acquiring and storing images.

If you have your images scanned to Photo CD when the film is being processed, the cost can be as low as 90 cents per image (at a "quickie" photo lab). But if you want mounted slides scanned, or you want to be sure your scans are free of dust and scratches, you should probably spring for a professional photo lab—even an expensive Photo CD scan is only three dollars or so (Pro Photo CD can run between $12 and $30).

Through an incredibly ingenious compression scheme, Photo CD manages to squeeze about 120 color images, each available at five different resolutions (see Table 12-1), onto a CD-ROM. The exact number of images depends on the content; some images compress more than others.

Table 12-1
Photo CD resolutions

Photo CD resolution	Size in pixels	Size at 225 ppi	File size
Base/16	192 × 128	.85″ × .57″	72 K
Base/4	384 × 256	1.7″ × 1.1″	288 K
Base	768 × 512	3.4″ × 2.3″	1.13 MB
4Base	1,536 × 1,024	6.8″ × 4.5″	4.5 MB
16Base	3,072 × 2,048	13.6″ × 9.1″	18 MB
64Base*	6,144 × 4,096	27.3″ × 18.2″	72 MB

*Pro Photo CD only

Don't confuse a Photo CD scan made by a pro lab with Pro Photo CD. While Photo CD is limited to 35 mm format, Pro Photo CD can handle up to 4-by-5-inch transparencies. But the addition of the 64Base resolution reduces the number of images that can fit on the CD (and increases the price per scan).

Working with Photo CD isn't quite as simple as one might expect (see Chapter 13, *Capturing Images*), but the format offers reasonably high-quality scanning at a hitherto unheard-of price, and it comes with its own archival-quality storage medium.

From Photons to Pixels

If you're doing your own scanning, you need to be aware of both the limitations of the scanner and the ways in which you can take advantage of the scanner's strengths. In the next chapter, we'll explore the scanning process, from preparing the original to controlling the scan with the scanner software.

13 Capturing Images

Good Data In, Good Data Out

Ansel Adams often said that the key to getting a great print was to start with a great negative. Of course, even with great negatives he still did massive amounts of manipulation in the darkroom. It's the same in Photoshop. You may do lots of postscan tweaking in Photoshop, but if you didn't start with a good image capture in the first place, you're unlikely to get great results from Photoshop.

When we say "capture an image," we mean using a scanner; but with only a few minor exceptions, everything we say about scanning applies equally well to capturing images with digital cameras or video boards, rendering images in a 3D rendering application, or bringing in images from Photo CD (see Chapter 12, *Scanners*).

What Makes a Good Scan (and Why You Should Care)

If there's a single generalization we're comfortable making about working with Photoshop, it's the golden rule of computing: GIGO, or Garbage In, Garbage Out. Photoshop's tools may let you make all sorts of corrections to an image after you've opened it, and if push comes to shove, you can sometimes rescue a shot that would otherwise be unusable. But if you start with a good scan, you'll have less work to do, and your final results will be better than if you had to fight the image all the way.

The Original

At the risk of pointing out the obvious, the first thing that makes for a good scan is a good original. We've seen scanners blamed for introducing shadow noise when the problem was actually in the print.

Starting with a good original is particularly important when you're using a low-end scanner, because low-end scanners offer less flexibility in the corrections you can make during the capture process. Flawed originals can sometimes be saved—for instance, if the image has an obvious color cast or is plagued with dust marks and scratches—but only by dint of applying considerable skill and effort.

Tip: Dealing with Scratched Film. Each piece of film has two sides, with different characteristics. The emulsion side, which is usually the less shiny of the two, is delicate and should never be handled. The base side is more robust. If you have scratches on the emulsion side, about all you can do is to have the image oil-mounted and scanned on a drum scanner—the oil will help fill the scratches. Fingerprints on the emulsion are hopeless.

Scratches on the base side can be filled in using either a special compound available from any good photo store, or—a much cheaper alternative—a judicious application with a Q-Tip of some grease from the side of your nose! Fingerprints on the base side can be carefully removed using a Q-Tip and film cleaner. *Don't* use Windex, 409, or alcohol.

Shadow and highlight detail. Look closely at the dark areas: are they really black, or do they have random speckles of color? Are the highlights blown out? Are the shadows plugged up? None of these problems is easily correctable, and some aren't correctable at all. If you usually get your prints done by Joe's One-Hour Photo and Bait, and you find yourself fighting with the images in Photoshop, you may want to consider using a professional photo lab that monitors its chemistry more carefully.

Lower-contrast originals. In general, most steps in the printing process increase contrast, so it's better to start with an image that's slightly flat than one with too much contrast. You can boost the contrast of a flat image, but it's harder to decrease contrast without compromising quality.

Why Good Scans Are Important

If you're really good at Photoshop, you can make a bad scan look almost as good as a good scan—at least on easy images with a narrow tonal range and no heavily saturated colors. However, doing so involves a continuous battle to avoid posterization, artifacts, and unnatural color shifts. With difficult images that are heavily saturated and have a wide tonal range, a good scan is indispensable.

As we explain in Chapter 6, *Tonal Correction*, when you adjust the tone or color balance in Photoshop, you're throwing away image information. If you're scanning images for print or for screen display, the photographic original will contain far more image data than you can reproduce in your output, so information will be lost somewhere—either in your manipulations, in the separation process, or on press. The trick, of course, is to be selective in what you throw away, and to keep what you need to make the image look its best for your intended purpose.

The closer your original scan is to the desired result, the less manipulation you'll have to do in Photoshop, and the less of the image you'll have to chuck. If you need to make radical changes to the tone or the color balance in Photoshop, you run the risk of posterizing the image. If you make your tone and color balance moves at scan time, you'll have a much easier time than if you have to make huge moves in Photoshop. We'll discuss these issues more in the next section.

Getting a Good Scan

You have three primary concerns when you're scanning: tone, color balance, and resolution. A good scan captures detail (with little noise) in both the highlights and shadows, captures both pastels and saturated colors, and contains clean neutrals that are free of obvious color casts. It also contains the right number of pixels for reproduction at the desired size.

Without proper resolution, you either lose details in your image or slow down your workflow with files bloated with data you don't need. Bad contrast or color balance, however, can have even more dire consequences for your images.

Resolution

Whether you're using a digital camera, a drum scanner, or a flatbed scanner, you first need to make sure that you're capturing the right number of pixels. If you're unsure of what this is, see "How Much Is Enough?" in Chapter 3, *Image Essentials*. Note that even if you only need a 200- or 266-ppi image, you may want to scan higher than that. Then, later, you can downsample the image to the resolution you need using Photoshop's Image Size dialog box.

Scanning and downsampling. David always scans at the maximum optical resolution (*not* interpolated resolution!) of the scanner, then downsamples in Photoshop as necessary. Bruce believes that scanning at an integral multiple of the optical resolution is okay; in other words, on a 400-ppi scanner he'll scan at 200 or 100 ppi (the optical resolution divided by two or four), but not at 250. Then he downsamples as necessary, too.

We have to admit that there are elements of superstition and simplification in this two-step process. We haven't tested how every scanner on the market downsamples from its maximum resolution, but from what we've seen, Photoshop does a better job than most of them. If you're in a real hurry, and you want to save yourself the extra step of downsampling in Photoshop, try scanning at the resolution you need.

We recommend you test this first, though. Compare the results you get by scanning the same image at full optical resolution, then downsampling in Photoshop, to those you get by scanning at a lower resolution to begin with. If you find that your scanner does as good a job of downsampling as Photoshop does, or if the difference is minor, by all means save yourself some time and use its capabilities.

Tip: Figuring Scaling and Resolution. The arithmetic of resolution and scaling is always hard to wrap your brain around. Here's a fast way to use Photoshop as a calculator to figure out the numbers, given that you know the final size of the image on the page. (You can get it from PageMaker's Control palette or XPress's Measurements palette: draw a box where the image goes, and read out the height and width numbers.)

1. Choose New from the File menu, and enter the dimensions and resolution of the image you want. If it's a grayscale or line art image, choose Grayscale from the Mode popup menu. Otherwise, choose RGB.

2. Note the pixel dimensions and file size, then press Cancel to leave the dialog box.

3. Back in your scanning software, select the area you want to scan, then adjust the resolution setting until the resulting pixel dimensions are close to the numbers you got in step two. When they match you know you've got the right scan size. If your scanner software doesn't report pixel dimensions, you can try to match the file size instead (it's just a little less accurate).

4. Scan the image, manipulate it as necessary in Photoshop, place it on the page, and scale it to fit.

Tip: Lose the Noise. You can often reduce the noise from a scanner considerably by scanning at the scanner's maximum optical resolution, then downsampling to the resolution you need.

This works particularly well if you scan at 200 percent or more of the required resolution, because the noise tends to show up as single pixels. When you downsample, each pixel in the downsampled image is created from four pixels in the original scan, and those four pixels are averaged into one, so the noise is reduced significantly.

Tip: Don't Bother Upsampling. We never scan at a low resolution and sample up in Photoshop (except when creating line art; see "Tip: Doubling Your Scanner's Line Art Resolution" in Chapter 11, *Line Art*). Photoshop can interpolate pixels, but it can't add detail through interpolation that wasn't there before you resized it. The result? The resized image usually ends up looking soft or blurry.

Tone and Color—Defining Your Goals

In the process of reproducing an image, you need to make two sets of tonal and color corrections.

▶ **Tonal correction.** This fixes defects in the original and distortions in the image-capture process.

▶ **Targeting.** This compensates for the output process.

How and when you make these corrections depend on the capabilities of your image-capture hardware and software, and on your workflow. We discuss this distinction throughout Chapters 6 and 7, *Tonal Correction* and *Color Correction*.

With some capture devices, it's possible to correct and target the image at the same time—in fact, this is standard operating procedure in prepress houses that use drum scanners. The advantage is productivity: you need to do less to the image in Photoshop once it's been captured. The disadvantage is loss of flexibility: you end up with an image targeted for a particular set of output conditions—it contains only the image information needed for that output process.

Obviously, if you don't know what the output process will be when you're capturing the image, you can't target the image for it during the capture. If you do know the output process, you may be able to realize some significant productivity and quality gains by targeting at capture time, but desktop scanners generally don't let you do so very easily, and most digital cameras don't let you do so at all.

Targeting is almost invariably a matter of going from a wider range of tone and color to a narrower one. It's easy to do this in Photoshop without introducing posterization or color shifts (see Chapter 6, *Tonal Correction*). So as a rule, we recommend that you simply try to capture as much good image information as you can, and take care of targeting the image in Photoshop.

Correcting the image is another story: you can often get better images with less work if you handle some or all of the tonal correction as you scan. However, the introduction of RGB working spaces in Photoshop 5 creates a new problem that the majority of scanner vendors have not yet addressed. The vast majority of scanner drivers, including those that work as Photoshop plug-ins, simply send the scanner RGB values straight to the monitor. The result is that the image you see in the prescan window of the scanner software will often look different from the final image the scanner delivers into Photoshop.

We hope this is a temporary problem. It should be relatively easy for scanner plug-in vendors to revise the software to use Photoshop's display mechanism. Thus far, the only one we know of that's doing so is Second Glance's Scantastic, but we hope that others will follow suit.

Other scanners allow you to scan into a profiled color space, including all the Heidelberg CPS scanners that use LinoColor, the Nikon LS-

2000, and the Imacon Flextight Precision scanners. With these scanners, you can simply designate your Photoshop RGB working space as the target profile. (See Chapter 5, *Color Settings*, for instructions on how to save your RGB Setup space as an ICC profile.)

The majority of scanners, though, don't allow scanning to a profiled space, and don't use Photoshop's display mechanism to display the prescan image. We've developed several strategies for dealing with this. Your choice will depend largely on the capabilities of your scanner and its accompanying software, and on your workflow requirements.

Scanning Strategies

If you're using an 8-bit-per-channel capture device, your options are fairly limited, which at least makes the choice easy. But almost every scanner sold today—even the very inexpensive entry-level flatbeds—capture at least 10 bits per channel, and if you don't optimize the image using all the bits the scanner can capture, you're wasting the high-bit capabilities of the scanner.

Eight-bit capture devices. If you have an 8-bit-per-channel capture device such as an older entry-level flatbed scanner, your best choice is to use a scanner profile. There are several relatively inexpensive packages for creating scanner profiles, including Candela's ColorSynergy, Monaco Systems' MonacoSCAN, and Heidelberg CPS's ScanOpen. The main limitation of most profile-driven scanning is that you're limited to using the same scanner settings you used to create the profile whenever you scan an image.

With 8-bit capture devices, this isn't really a problem, because it's almost certain that the software controls—such as brightness, contrast, and gamma curves—are affecting the eight bits of data *after* the capture—exactly what Photoshop does when you correct an 8-bit image. Since the controls are likely to be less flexible versions of Photoshop's own features, there's little point in using them—you can achieve the same or better results more easily using the tools and techniques described in Chapter 6, *Tonal Correction*. In this case, your concern is simply to make sure that you're capturing all the data the device can grab, without damaging it on the way.

To do so, you need to find the "sweet spot" in the controls, where the data is simply being passed on unfiltered. Sometimes, this is just a matter of leaving the software at its default settings, but often it's not. The only way to be sure is through trial and error. With scanners, you can simply tweak the controls. If you're working with an 8-bit digital camera, you also have lighting and exposure to take into consideration, but the same principles apply.

1. Try capturing a range of representative images that have real blacks, real whites, and a good range of tones in between. (If you have access to a gray-step wedge, or to a color target such as the IT8 or Kodak's Q60, use it instead.)

2. Start with the scanner's defaults, and look at the histogram of the resulting scan. Check to see if the scanner is clipping the highlights or shadows (see Figure 13-2 on page 428). If it's doing one or the other, reduce or increase the brightness and try again. If it's clipping both, try reducing the contrast.

3. If the image has real blacks and whites, but the scan isn't covering the full tonal range, you might try increasing the contrast. Once you've found settings that work, save them, and use them for all your scans.

Note that these settings may not produce very good-looking images. That doesn't matter—you're just trying to get as much good image information as possible to tweak in Photoshop.

Although you want to capture the entire tonal range of the image without clipping the shadows or blowing out the highlights, sometimes you may find that your scanner or camera can't do this. In that case, you'll have to decide whether you want to sacrifice highlight detail or shadow detail. The image content is the final arbiter, but when in doubt, remember that blown-out highlights usually look worse than plugged-up shadows.

Once you've found the scanner's sweet spot, you can use these settings to scan the target that comes with the profiling systems mentioned earlier in this chapter. Then, scanning simply becomes a matter of setting your crop and resolution—you leave the tone and color controls alone. When the final scan is delivered into Photoshop, the Missing Profile dialog appears: set the scanner profile as the source, and RGB Color as the target. Note that the initial release of Photoshop 5 had a bug that allowed images opened through Acquire plug-ins to bypass the profile mismatch handling mechanism. It's fixed in Photoshop 5.0.2, but if you haven't upgraded, you can do a Profile-to-Profile transform instead.

The high-bit advantage. If your scanner captures more than eight bits
per color internally, you want to get the image as close as possible to its
desired state while it's still in high-bit form. If you don't, you're just wasting those extra bits for which you almost certainly paid a premium (see
Figure 13-1).

Figure 13-1

Using the
extra bits

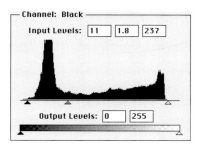

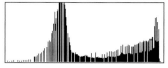

*If you apply this kind of big tonal move to
an 8-bit scan, you lose a lot of data, resulting in this depopulated histogram below,
and an image that's harder to work with.*

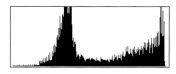

*With tonal correction of a high-bit image, you
can make big moves and still end up with a
full 256 gray levels in the 8-bit file—making
further corrections much easier.*

A 12-bit scanner, for instance, uses 4,096 levels internally for each color.
When you use the scanner's controls, you're performing tonal correction
on this high-bit data. Rather than stretching and squeezing eight bits of
data, you're choosing which 256 out of the possible 4,096 gray levels will
appear in the final output. You can set the tone of the image the way you
want it and still have a full 256 gray levels. If you make those same adjustments after scanning instead, operating with eight bits of data, you
lose tonal information and end up with substantially fewer than 256
shades of gray.

Of course, you can only exploit the high-bit capabilities of your capture device if the software has the necessary features (see "Software
Tools," later in this chapter), *and* the scanner software displays the image accurately in the prescan. If you're lucky enough to have a scanner
that fills both these criteria, you can use the scanner controls to optimize
the image. Then, when the Missing Profile dialog appears, you can tell
Photoshop to simply open the image with no conversion.

If your scanner supports scanning to a profiled RGB space, you can
simply designate your RGB Setup space as the target profile. We expect
this capability to become increasingly common, but it's not yet widespread.

An alternate strategy, which works very well indeed, is to bring the high-bit data into Photoshop and make all your tone and color corrections there. Photoshop 5 offers much more support for high-bit files than did previous versions, and it also offers a more complete toolset than most scanner drivers. The only downside to this approach is that high-bit files are twice as large as 8-bit-per-channel ones, with a concomitant increase in RAM and storage requirements.

If the larger footprint makes bringing the high-bit data into Photoshop impractical, or if your scanner doesn't allow you to export the high-bit data to Photoshop, you can take one of the following approaches:

▶ Use the prescan controls in the scanner software to get the image the way you want it, then when you go through the Missing Profile dialog, set your monitor profile as the source and RGB Color as the destination profile. (You've been correcting the image in monitor RGB in the scanner plug-in, since it's sending RGB directly to the screen.) The downside to this approach is that you're limiting your scans to the gamut of the monitor, which may be smaller than the scanner is capable of producing.

▶ If you use ColorMatch RGB as your RGB Setup space, you're probably doing so to make your editing space essentially the same as your monitor space, so there shouldn't be a mismatch, assuming that your monitor is actually calibrated to the ColorMatch standard. Use the scanner controls to optimize the image, then when the Missing Profile dialog appears, tell Photoshop to open the image with no conversion. As with the previous strategy, the downside is that the ColorMatch RGB gamut is on the small side.

▶ Ignore any color issues while you're scanning, and simply concentrate on capturing the full tonal range of the image and optimizing the contrast. Open the final scan in Photoshop with no conversion, and fix saturation and color balance problems there. You lose some of the benefit of the high-bit data, but you'll capture a full gamut and tonal range.

None of these strategies is ideal, but until the scanner vendors update their software to take full advantage of Photoshop's new color capabilities, they're about the best you can do.

Targeting

If you're working with a typical desktop scanning setup, which delivers RGB or grayscale scans to Photoshop, your options for targeting the image to a particular output process during the scan are pretty limited.

Grayscale. When capturing grayscale images with some scanners, you can set the highlight and shadow limits to values you know your output process can handle. This is reasonable *if* your scanner also lets you set the tone the way you want it. While this can work well for images that don't have specular highlights or solid blacks, with most images you're better off just using Photoshop's tools for targeting the image, as described in Chapter 6, *Tonal Correction*.

Color. With color, your options are even more limited. Unless your output is destined for an RGB output process such as the computer screen or a continuous-tone film recorder, you need to convert the RGB scan to a targeted set of CMYK values.

Most desktop scanner/software combinations can't deliver CMYK scans. They rely on the host computer and software like Photoshop to convert RGB into CMYK, so you should simply concern yourself with getting a good RGB capture that represents the whole tonal range of the image. If you've got a high-bit scanner, you can also try to get good color balance with clean neutrals. Then you can use Photoshop to target the image after the capture (see "Image Correction and Targeting" in Chapter 7, *Color Correction*).

The notable exception to this rule is the growing number of scanners that allow you to scan to a profiled color space. We generally prefer to scan to RGB, converting to CMYK only when we have to. But if you know at scan time what your printing process will be, and you aren't worried about being able to repurpose the scan, you can scan to a CMYK profile just as easily as to an RGB one.

Correcting and targeting at once. High-end scanners let you do both sets of corrections—adjusting for scanned imperfections and targeting for the output process—at once. In fact, the biggest difference between a $2,000 scanner and a $200,000 scanner isn't quality—it's productivity. The $200,000 scanner lets you create targeted CMYK scans, ready for printing, where the tone and color are tightly matched to a particular set of output conditions—paper, ink, and press. This offers a huge productivity advantage over most desktop scanners.

If your scanning software has all the tools you need to target your scans—tonal and color correction, color separation, and sharpening—then you can pick up some real workflow advantages by using those capabilities. Scans can land on disk ready for print, and you need never go near Photoshop. This is a book on Photoshop, however, so we'll limit our discussion to targeting images after they've arrived in Photoshop.

For now, here's how to get good scans into Photoshop, so you can work your will on them with its tools.

Software Tools

We can't hope to cover every piece of image-acquisition software on the market, but fortunately most of them offer features very similar to Photoshop's tone- and color-correction tools. We recommend you look at the discussion of those tools in Chapters 6 and 7, *Tonal Correction* and *Color Correction*; the techniques discussed there also apply when scanning.

Whatever image-capture method you use, there's a definite order for making adjustments. First, determine the cropping and resolution; then set the tonal range; and finally, fix any problems with the color balance. If you have to do major surgery to fix the color balance, you may have to go back and adjust the overall tone again. For example, a strong magenta cast can be neutralized by adding a lot more green, but doing so will brighten the image, because you're adding light.

Five key tools help you get the tonal range and color balance right when you capture images.

▶ Histograms

▶ On-screen densitometers

▶ Black/white-point settings

▶ Gamma settings

▶ Curve controls

The first two help you evaluate the image, the last three help you fix it. If you're lucky, your image-acquisition software will offer all five, but it's more typical to get two or three out of the five in any given scanning software package.

Tip: Make Sure Your Scanner Controls Really Work. It's important to determine that the scanner's gamma and/or curves controls are really affecting the high-bit or analog data that the scanner produces, rather than just being applied to 8-bit data as a postscan filter. If they're being applied post-scan, you're better off making the same adjustments in Photoshop after the scan. (If the tools are acceptable, however, use them! There's a real workflow advantage to correcting at scan time.)

How can you tell if your scanner is working on high-bit data? One easy way is to apply a fairly extreme curve or gamma adjustment to a scan—say, a gamma of 2.2 or thereabouts. First, pull an uncorrected scan into Photoshop and make the move using Photoshop's Levels command, then go back and rescan the image applying the same gamma tweak in the scanner software. Compare the histograms of the two images. If the one with the gamma tweak applied during the scan isn't substantially cleaner, with fewer spikes and missing levels, the scanner software is almost certainly applying the tweak as a filter on the 8-bit data. In that case, simply treat the scanner as an 8-bit capture device. (Console yourself with the fact that it's probably at least capturing eight good bits of data, unlike many 8-bit-only scanners.)

Experimenting in Photoshop is an excellent way to get a feel for how these controls operate. Work in Photoshop with an image scanned using the scanner's default settings. When you've figured out exactly what needs to be done to the scan in Photoshop, try going back to the scanner software and rescanning the image using settings that duplicate your Photoshop tweaks as closely as possible. After a while, you'll find that your initial scans are getting much closer to the desired results as you exploit the power of the scanner's controls. But you'll be retaining much more image detail than you would if you did the same tonal moves on the 8-bit data in Photoshop.

Image-Evaluation Tools

Almost all scanners and most digital studio cameras let you do a quick prescan, a low-resolution capture that you can use to set the cropping rectangle. You can also use it as a basis for tone- and color-balance adjustments. But even with a perfectly-calibrated monitor, there's only so much you can tell from looking at the typical postage-stamp-sized prescan.

Instead, you can use two other tools (when available) to evaluate your image before your final scan: the histogram and the densitometer.

Histogram. The histogram is simply a bar chart that shows the number of pixels in the image at each gray level from 0 to 255 (see Figure 13-2). This gives you a quick look at how the information is distributed in the scan. Good scanning software lets you see the histogram before and after correction. Photoshop displays a histogram in the Levels dialog box, or when you choose Histogram from the Image menu. In most scanning software, the histogram is simply a static display, though with a few scanning packages, you can make adjustments using something like Photoshop's Levels dialog box.

The histogram is a key tool for evaluating tonal range; it can tell you a lot about your scan at a single glance. A histogram that ends in a "cliff" at the left (shadow) end of the scale indicates a scan where shadow detail is lost. If it ends in a cliff at the right (highlight) end of the scale, you've blown out the highlight detail. A correctly exposed scan produces a histogram with a slope (rather than a cliff) at each end, indicating relatively few pixels at either the darkest value (0) or the lightest value (255).

Figure 13-2 **Evaluating scans with the histogram**

Note that these images have not been through final correction. They represent what comes in from the scanner.

An overly dark scan	*A too-light scan*	*A well-exposed scan*

All this assumes a "normal" image—if you have a picture of a black cat in a coal cellar, or a polar bear in the snow, your histogram will look different; but in each case, you want to try to hold as much detail in shadows and highlights as possible.

Densitometer. An on-screen densitometer lets you read the value of the pixel under the cursor. Like Photoshop's Info palette, this lets you get a little deeper into analyzing the image, particularly if the tool offers before-and-after readouts. Some scanner software use a palette for the densitometer information, while others put it in the prescan window itself.

Tip: Use the Densitometer to Find Detail. You can use the densitometer to check for detail in the highlight and shadow regions, which can be hard to see on your monitor. Pass the cursor over very bright or very dark areas in the image. If the pixel values *change* as you move around, there's detail in there, even if you can't see it. As you make gamma moves to brighten the midtones, you emphasize detail in the shadows and suppress it in the highlights. By evaluating the detail with the densitometer, you can play the trade-off between the two.

Image-Adjustment Tools

To capture the tonal range of an image correctly, you have to set the black point and white point properly to avoid plugging up the shadows or blowing out the highlights, and you have to set the gamma to distribute the midtones properly. For a detailed discussion of tonal correction, see Chapter 6, *Tonal Correction*.

Scanning software that comes with 8-bit scanners often limits your adjustments to changing brightness or contrast. But using brightness or contrast is like bungee jumping without a cord—you may live through it, but you'll probably lose something in the process (see the sidebar "The Non-Linear Advantage" in Chapter 6, *Tonal Correction*).

Unfortunately, a few high-bit scanners (such as the Kodak RFS 2035 Plus) also limit the controls to brightness and contrast. They're better than nothing, but keep an eye on the histograms for shadow or highlight clipping. Most high-bit scanners offer more sophisticated methods for adjusting the tone and color: black- and white-point settings, gamma settings, and arbitrary curves.

Setting black and white points. Most high-bit image-capture software offer one or more of the following methods of setting the black point and white point.

▶ **Autoexposure.** Though they can be a little brain-dead, these features are often a good place to start. They look for the darkest and lightest pixels in the image to set the white and black points.

One problem with these features, particularly with film scanners, is that they're easily fooled by dust or scratches. If the software lets you designate an area of the image to consider when determining the endpoints, you can simply change the area under consideration to avoid the offending spot. If not, you'll have to resort to manual methods.

▶ **Black and white input levels.** These work identically to, and usually resemble, the black and white input sliders in Photoshop's Levels dialog box. They're almost invariably accompanied by a histogram that lets you see the amount of shadow or highlight clipping taking place.

▶ **Black and white eyedroppers.** Eyedropper tools let you set the black and white points by clicking on specific areas in the image preview. These tools work roughly the same way as the eyedroppers in Photoshop's Levels and Curves dialog boxes, but they don't always let you choose a target color—they just set the area you clicked to black or white.

In some cases, if you click a non-neutral pixel in a color image, they'll maintain the color of the pixel while setting its brightness to the maximum or minimum value possible. In other cases, they'll also eliminate the color cast. To use these features effectively, you need an on-screen densitometer. This will also let you determine exactly what the eyedropper is doing.

Tip: Determining Black and White Points. To determine the white point and black point for an image, follow these steps.

1. Scan the image with your "optimum" gamma (see "Tip: Determining Optimum Gamma," below), and white and black point set to 0 and 255.

2. Bring the image into Photoshop, choose the Levels command, then Option-drag the black-point and white-point triangles to display where the shadow and highlight detail lie (see "Black-point/white-

point clipping display" in Chapter 6, *Tonal Correction*). Use this clipping display to determine appropriate white- and black-point settings.

3. Use those settings in the scanning software, perhaps allowing yourself two or three extra levels to make sure that you really aren't clipping any detail.

Gamma controls. Unlike Brightness and Contrast controls, gamma adjustment lets you make large changes to the midtones with (usually) only minimal effects on the shadows and highlights. In Photoshop, you make gamma adjustments using the Levels command (Command-L). The middle (gray) slider in the top bar changes the gamma as you drag it, or you can type a number into the middle field. Many scanner drivers only offer numeric control over gamma—you just type in the gamma value you want. For a full discussion of gamma adjustments and how to use them, see Chapter 6, *Tonal Correction.*

Almost all scans need a gamma adjustment. Typically, scans come in looking dark. Most scanners have a native gamma of 1.0—the output values are exactly the same as the input values. But neither our eyes nor our monitors have a linear response to changes in brightness. Usually you'll need to scan with a gamma setting somewhere between 1.4 and 2.2. In theory, if you want your on-screen image to match the original, your scanner gamma setting should match that of your RGB Setup space. But as the EPA says, your mileage may vary. If you're scanning for print, a gamma setting of around 1.8 is a good starting point.

Also note that changing the gamma setting for many high-bit scanners tends to change the appropriate white- and black-point settings. This shouldn't happen, but it does, so adjusting these three settings can be an iterative process—at least until you get to know the settings.

Tip: Determining Optimum Gamma. To figure out what gamma setting on your high-bit scanner will provide an accurate midtone reading, scan a gray target with a known gray value, such as the ubiquitous Kodak 18-percent gray card, which reflects 18 percent of the light striking it. Scan at a variety of gamma settings, and use the one that renders the gray card somewhere around level 100 to 120.

Curves. Curves are by far the most flexible way of controlling both the overall tonal characteristics of the scan and the color balance of the individual channels. Curves appear in various places within scanning software, and often have the same appearance and functionality as the Curves dialog box in Photoshop.

We believe that all high-bit scanners should offer some kind of curves controls. They are essential for correcting color balance while tapping the full capabilities of these scanners. Fortunately, most vendors seem to be coming around to that view. For a full discussion of curve-based adjustments, see Chapters 6 and 7, *Tonal Correction* and *Color Correction*.

Sharpening

Note that even though some scanners allow you to sharpen images on the fly, we almost never do, for two reasons.

▶ Photoshop's Unsharp Mask filter offers far more control than the sharpening in most scanner software.

▶ It's always best to do sharpening after you've made all your tone and color adjustments. This is because sharpening relies on minute adjustments in the contrast of neighboring pixels. If you make tonal adjustments after sharpening, you can wipe out the effect of sharpening, or possibly even worse, exaggerate it.

Unless you have a great deal of faith in your scanner's sharpening algorithms and don't plan on doing anything more with the image in Photoshop, we recommend that you simply leave sharpening to Photoshop.

Photo CD Revisited

Photo CD got off to a rocky start. Most pros found the early results from Photo CD pretty disappointing, because there were two things that Kodak failed to make clear in Photo CD's early days. (Of course, back then they still thought people would look at their pictures on TV.) To get good results from Photo CD, you have to know two things: what to ask for when you have scans made, and how to bring the scans into Photoshop.

Unfortunately, this makes it necessary to learn some Photo CD jargon.

Photo CD Lingo

Photo CD was originally conceived as a mass-market consumer product. So, Kodak put a great deal of effort into building a scanning software and hardware system that would reproduce the color of the *original scene*, not the color on the film. They thought Photo CD users would be the kind of people who had their film developed by the corner drugstore—they'd want happy Kodak color rather than what was actually on the film.

To do this, Kodak developed film-specific lookup tables—called *film terms*—that would neutralize each film stock's particular biases, and an autoexposure feature called the Scene Balancing Algorithm (SBA) that would bring underexposed or overexposed images back into a normal tonal range.

These features have caused professional photographers no end of grief, for two reasons. First, professionals choose specific film stocks precisely because they want to exploit the films' unique biases. Second, they want the tonal range they put on the film rendered faithfully, not normalized to lowest-common-denominator average-one-hour-print values.

Knowing What to Ask For

Fortunately, Photo CD is capable of reproducing quite faithfully what's on the film. The key is in knowing what to ask for when you buy the scans. You need to treat reversal (slide) film and negative film differently.

Slide film. To get faithful Photo CD scans of slides, you must ask the Photo CD lab to do three things.

▶ Use Universal Film Terms (Universal Kodachrome for Kodachrome, Universal E-6 for everything else).

▶ Use Locked Beam Scanning (which means the operator makes no corrections to the image).

▶ Turn the Scene Balancing Algorithm off.

This should give you scans that faithfully capture the contents of the slide—with one limitation. The dynamic range of the original PIW scanner was only about 2.8, so you won't get great shadow detail on very contrasty slides. Kodak has made an upgrade available for the PIW scanner that increases the dynamic range to 3.3. If you're dealing with contrasty slides, it's worth seeking out a lab that has sprung for the upgrade.

Negative film. The smaller density range of negative film has a much better fit to the dynamic range of the Photo CD scanner, but it also presents a problem. You don't want what's literally on the film, because the film is a negative—it's inverted and has an orange mask. Instead, you want a positive image—a scan that's as close as possible to the tone and color you'd get from a good print. This takes human intervention.

If possible, you should have negatives scanned using the film term for that film stock. If the negatives are perfectly exposed and processed, you can ask the lab to create a custom film term for your negatives. This is worthwhile if you're doing measured photography under controlled studio lighting, but it's unlikely to work in most real-world situations where people shoot negs.

Most negs aren't perfectly exposed—a big reason people use negative film is precisely because it allows more latitude in the exposure. For negatives shot under available light, or under a variety of different lighting conditions, you'll get better results if you ask the scanner operator to intervene, and to apply the Scene Balancing Algorithm where necessary. You won't get this kind of service at the 69¢-a-scan Photo CD labs, but many professional labs that charge two or three dollars per scan will do this for you, and the results are usually worth the extra cost.

Bringing Photo CD Images into Photoshop

Getting the scans done right is half the battle when you use Photo CD. The other half is bringing them into Photoshop correctly. You can't simply open Photo CD images in Photoshop. There's always a conversion process involved.

Photo CD images are stored in a proprietary color space, called Photo YCC, developed by Kodak. This color space contains only 24 bits of data per pixel, but the data is in a highly compressed form—Kodak claims to encode 12 bits of luminance data plus two 8-bit color channels into the YCC format. To work with Photo CD images in Photoshop, you have to convert them into one of the color spaces that Photoshop can use—RGB, CMYK, or Lab—so the way you acquire Photo CD images makes a big difference to the final result.

When you open a Photo CD image, you're always asked to choose a source and destination profile (see Figure 13-3). For the source profile, you should choose Kodak Photo CD Color Negative V 3.2 for negative scans, Kodak Photo CD Universal K-14 V 3.2 for scans from Kodachrome,

Figure 13-3 Opening a Photo CD image

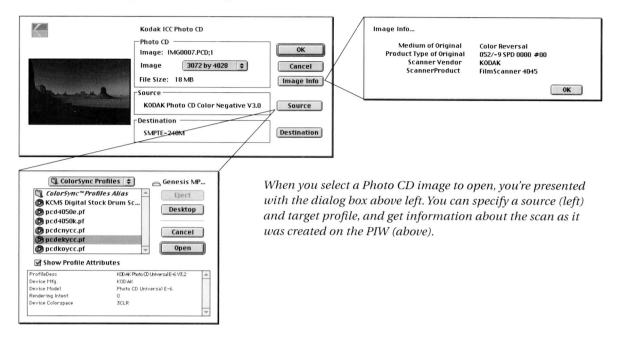

When you select a Photo CD image to open, you're presented with the dialog box above left. You can specify a source (left) and target profile, and get information about the scan as it was created on the PIW (above).

and Kodak Photo CD Universal E-6 V 3.2 for all other scans from slide film. Note that the actual file names for the Photo CD profiles are pretty cryptic, there are some subtle mnemonic hints that "pcdnycc" is color neg, "pcdekycc" is E-6, and "pcdkoycc" is Kodachrome. For the destination profile, choose the profile for your RGB or CMYK Setup space (depending on whether you want to acquire the image as RGB or CMYK), or Adobe Photoshop CIELAB if you want to acquire the image as Lab. If you don't know the original film type, you can click the Image Info button to find out. A few early Photo CDs lacked this info, but just about any Photo CD made in the last four years should have it. The first line tells you whether the film was negative or reversal (slide) film. If it's a scan from neg film, that's all you need to know to choose the right profile. If it's from slide film, you need to know whether it's E-6 or Kodachrome: If the first three numbers on the second line are 052, it's from E-6 film; if they're 014, it's from Kodachrome.

There's one more wrinkle to this. The bug fix that stopped images opened through an Acquire module from bypassing the profile mismatch handling mechanism causes the Missing Profile dialog to appear when you open a Photo CD image. Since you've already specified the conversion into the appropriate working space, you should tell Photoshop to open the image with no conversion.

Is That All There Is?

No matter how good a job you do of capturing the image, you'll almost certainly need to massage it some more using Photoshop's own tools. But if you've captured the image to be as close as possible to the way you want it, the tweaks you make in Photoshop will be small and subtle, so you'll run far less risk of losing valuable image data, and introducing posterization and artifacts. Plus, you'll preserve the shadow and highlight detail that make the difference between a so-so image and one that leaps off the page and grabs you.

Go back and revisit Chapter 6, *Tonal Correction*, and Chapter 7, *Color Correction*. Given a little ingenuity, almost all the techniques we discuss in those chapters can be applied during the scan itself. You'll get better results, and you'll have less work to do in Photoshop after the scan.

Selections

Paths, Masks, and Channels

You love the painting and retouching tools that Photoshop offers; you love layers; you even love all the options it gives you for saving files. But as soon as someone says "alpha channel" or "mask," your eyes glaze over. And when someone strings together a sentence like, "Edit your selection in Quick Mask mode and then intersect it with the eighth alpha channel," you drop your mouse and head for the door.

It doesn't have to be this way. Masks, channels, and selections are actually really easy (if you get past their bad reputation). And they are the essential tools for silhouetting and compositing images—two of the most common production tasks.

The first part of this chapter covers all the tools in Photoshop for working with selections, channels, and masks, along with a lot of tips for using the tools the smart way. At the end of the chapter, we run through some step-by-step selection techniques to show how you can use all these tools together to handle both simple and complex situations.

Masking-Tape Selections

The key to understanding selections, masks, and channels is to realize that they're all basically the same thing down deep. No matter what kind of selection you make—whether you draw out a rectangular marquee, or draw a path with the Lasso, or use the Magic Wand to select a colored area—Photoshop internally sees the selection as a grayscale channel (see Figure 14-1).

Figure 14-1

Selections are channels, too

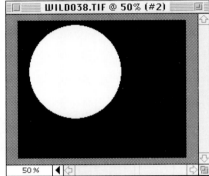

This selection is the same . . .   *. . . as this mask/channel.*

If you've ever carefully painted around a window (the kind in the wall of your house), you've probably used masking tape to mask out the areas you didn't want to paint. If you apply the masking tape to the window, you can paint right over it, knowing that the window remains untouched. Selections, masks, and channels are electronic forms of masking tape.

In Photoshop, the masking tape is typically colored black. Let's say you use the elliptical marquee to select a circle. Behind the scenes, Photoshop sees this circle as a grayscale channel. In this selection channel, the areas that you selected (the parts with no masking tape over them) are white, and the unselected areas (the parts with masking tape over them) are black.

Why Digital Tape Is Better

However, like everything else in life, there's also a spectrum of gray area between the two extremes. In real life, you can't have partially opaque masking tape. The wood or window or whatever is either covered and no paint touches it, or it's not (all the paint touches it). Fortunately, we're not dealing with real life; we're dealing with computers, and they're much more flexible than normal ol' tape.

If you look carefully around the edges of that circle we selected, you'll notice that there are gray areas between the black and the white.

The gray parts of a selection channel are areas that are partially se-lected. If an area in a selection channel is 25-percent gray, then that area is 75-percent selected. Remember, the lighter the gray, the more selected the area is.

Benefits of Partial Selection

There were gray areas in that circle we selected because the elliptical marquee was anti-aliased (see Figure 14-2). If you turn the Anti-aliased checkbox off in the Marquee Options palette, the selection you'd get would have no gray, partially selected pixels.

Figure 14-2
Anti-aliased
edges

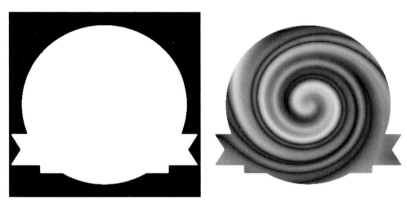

Aliased edges make for poor masks because they're too jaggy.

Smooth, anti-aliased masks create nicer, smoother edges.

Smooth transitions between selected (white) and unselected (black) areas are incredibly important for compositing images, painting, cor-recting areas within an image—in fact, just about everything you'd want to do in Photoshop.

When you paint over an area that is fully selected (no black masking tape), 100 percent of the paint is applied to each pixel. When you paint over an area that isn't selected (fully covered with black masking tape), no paint is applied. And when you paint over an area that is partially selected, only a percentage of the paint is applied to the underlying image.

The same thing goes for deleting, smudging, applying a filter, or any other action you can take on a pixel in Photoshop. The more selected the pixel is, the more the effect is applied (see Figure 14-3).

Figure 14-3
Partially selected pixels

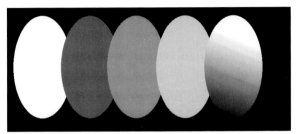

This is the selection mask; the ovals are selected by varying amounts (the one on the left is fully selected; the one on the right has a gradient selection).

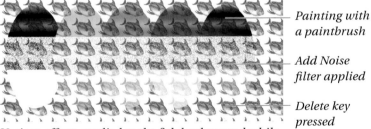

Painting with a paintbrush

Add Noise filter applied

Delete key pressed

Various effects applied to the fish background while the above selection is active

Tip: You Can Always Move Your Selection. One of the most frequent changes you'll make to a selection (which is why this tip is way up here at the beginning of the chapter) is moving it without moving its contents. For instance, you might make a rectangular selection, then realize it's not positioned correctly. Don't redraw it! In Photoshop 3, you had to hold down the Command and Option keys to drag the selection. In Photoshop 4 and 5, you don't have to worry about modifier keys; just click and drag the selection with the selection tool. The selection moves, but not the pixels underneath it.

Or, press the arrow keys to move the selection by one pixel. Add the Shift key, and the selection moves ten pixels for each press of an arrow key.

Tip: Moving a Selection While Dragging. One of the coolest (and least known) selection features is the ability to move a marquee selection (either rectangular or oval) while you're still dragging out the selection. The trick: hold down the Spacebar key while the mouse button is still held down.

Selection Tools

Although there are a mess o' ways to make a selection in Photoshop (we'll look at them all in this chapter), there are three basic selection tools in the Tool palette: the Marquee tool, the Lasso tool, and the Magic Wand (see Figure 14-4). While some people eschew these tools for the more highfalutin' selection techniques, we find them invaluable for much of our day-to-day work.

Figure 14-4
Selection
tools

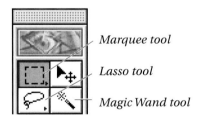

Marquee tool

Lasso tool

Magic Wand tool

The important thing to remember about these selection tools (and, in fact, every selection technique in Photoshop) is that they can all work in tandem. Don't get too hung up on getting one tool to work just the way you want it to; you can always modify the selection using a different technique (this idea of modifying selections is very important, and we'll touch on it throughout the chapter).

Tip: Adding to and Subtracting from Selections. No matter which selection tool you're using, you can always add to the current selection by holding down the Shift key while selecting. Conversely, you can subtract from the current selection by holding down the Option key. Or, if you want the intersection of two selections, hold down the Command and the Shift keys while selecting (see Figure 14-5).

Figure 14-5

Adding, subtracting, and intersecting selections

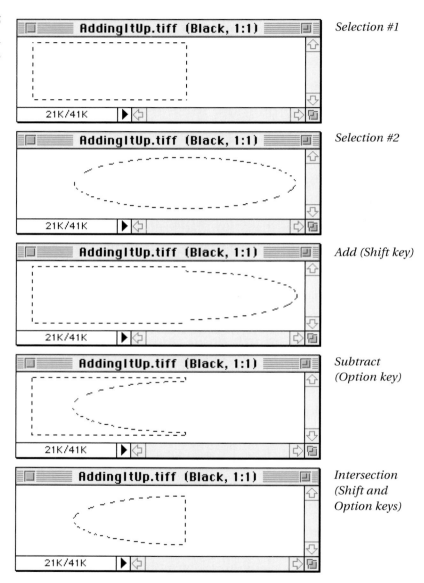

Selection #1

Selection #2

Add (Shift key)

Subtract (Option key)

Intersection (Shift and Option keys)

Note that this is different than in Photoshop 3, where the Command key subtracted from a selection, and Command-Shift gave you the intersection. (Now the Command key always switches to the Move tool.)

Tip: Select It Again. While Bruce is the steady-and-sure type, David tends to rush through Photoshop like a madman. One result is that David often deselects a selection without having thought through the implications (like "will I need this again?"). Fortunately, when he finds he does need that old selection again, he can recall it (in Photoshop 5) by pressing Command-Shift-D (or choosing Reselect from the Select menu).

Tip: Transforming Selections. Getting a selection right the first time you make it is a rarity (we keep a bottle of '96 Côtes du Rhône ready for those few occurrences). For instance, an object might look rectangular, but once you try to select it with the Marquee tool you find that the selection needs to be rotated, stretched, and skewed slightly. In the past, we found ourselves succumbing to all sorts of horrible workarounds to tweak our selections. Now we just use the Transform Selection feature in the Selection menu (sorry, we don't know of any keyboard shortcut here).

When you choose Transform Selection, Photoshop places the Free Transform handles around your selection and lets you rotate, resize, skew, move, or distort the selection however you please. When you're done, press Enter.

Less obvious is that after you choose Transform Selection, you can pick options from the Transform submenu (under the Edit menu). For example, if you want to mirror your selection, turn on Transform Selection, drag the center point of the transformation rectangle to the place around which you want the selection to flip, then choose Flip Vertical or Flip Horizontal from the Transform submenu (see Figure 14-6).

Marquee

The Marquee tool is the most basic of all the selection tools. It lets you draw a rectangle or oval selection by clicking and dragging. If you hold down the Shift key, the marquee is constrained to a square or a circle, depending on whether you have chosen Rectangle or Ellipse in the Marquee Options palette. (Note that if you've already made a selection, the Shift key adds to the selection instead.) If you hold down the Option key, the selection is centered on where you clicked.

Tip: Toggle Between Tools. You can switch between the rectangular and elliptical selection tools on the Shape popup menu in the Marquee

Figure 14-6
Transforming a selection

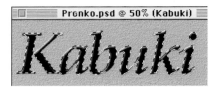

The type is selected by Command-clicking on the type layer.

By dragging the center point to here, the transformation is centered at this location.

You can skew a selection by Command-dragging one of the side handles.

Here the selection is skewed and scaled.

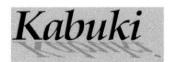

Here, Levels was used to adjust the background color.

Options palette, but it's faster to press M once to select the tool, and then Shift-M to toggle between the tools (Option-clicking on the Marquee tool in the Tool palette also toggles between them).

Tip: Pull Out a Single Line. If you've ever tried to select a single row of pixels in an image by dragging the marquee, you know that it can drive you batty faster than Mrs. Gulch's chalk scraping. The Single Row and Single Column selection tools (click and hold the mouse button down on the Marquee tool to get them) are designed for just this purpose. These are godsends when a low-end scanner glitches and slightly (or severely) throws off a row or column of pixels. We often use them to clean up screen captures, or to delete thin borders around an image. They're also useful with video captures, because each pixel row often equals a video scan line.

Tip: Selecting Thicker Columns and Rows. If you want a column or row that's more than one pixel wide/tall, you need to use a different method. Set the selection style to Fixed Size in the Marquee Options palette, and type the thickness of the selection into the Height or Width field. In the other field, type some number that's obviously larger than the image, like 10,000. When you click on the image, the row or column is selected at the thickness you want.

Tip: Selecting that Two-by-Three. You've laid out a page with a hole for a photo that's 2 by 3 inches. Now you want to make a 2-by-3 selection in Photoshop. Ordinarily, trying to select that with the Marquee tool would be nigh-on impossible without patience and a scratch pad full of math. However, when you choose Constrained Aspect Ratio from the Style popup menu, Photoshop lets you type in that 2-by-3 ratio in the Marquee Options palette (see Figure 14-7).

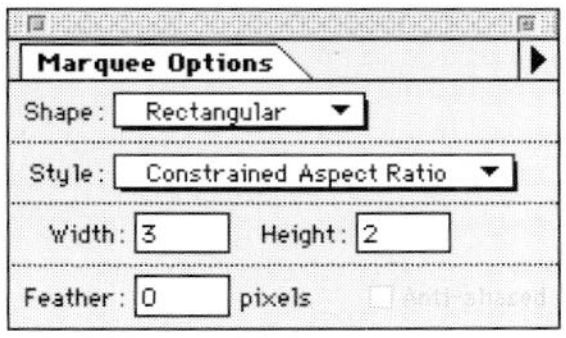

Figure 14-7
Constrained
Aspect Ratio

If you're looking to select a particular-sized area, you can select Fixed Size from the Style popup menu. The problem is that you have to type the measurement in pixels. If you don't usually think in pixels, try this.

1. Option-click on the document size area in the lower-left corner of the document window to find the resolution of the image.

2. Multiply the resolution by the number of inches you want the selection to be, horizontally and vertically.

3. Type these numbers into the horizontal and vertical fields of the Marquee Options palette.

4. Click where you want to specify the upper-left corner of the selection (or Option-click to specify the center of the selection).

For instance, let's say your image is at 300 ppi and you want a 2-by-3 selection. When you multiply the resolution by the dimensions, you know to type 600 and 900 into the Options palette fields.

Lasso

The Lasso tool lets you create a freeform outline of a selection. Wherever you drag the mouse, the selection follows until you finally let go of the mouse button and the selection is automatically closed for you (there's no such thing as an open-ended selection in Photoshop; see Figure 14-8).

Figure 14-8 Lasso selections

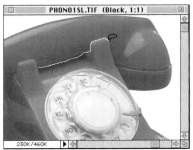  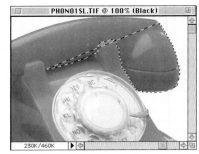

Beginning the selection   *End of selection*   *Closed on mouse release*

Tip: Let Go of the Lasso. Two of the most annoying attributes of selecting with the Lasso are that you can't lift the mouse button while drawing, and you can't draw straight lines easily (unless you've got hands as steady as a brain surgeon's). The Option key overcomes both these problems.

When you hold down the Option key, you can release the mouse button and the Lasso tool won't automatically close the selection. Instead, as long as the Option key is held down, Photoshop lets you draw a straight line to wherever you want to go. This solves both problems in a single stroke (as it were).

The folks at Adobe saw that people were using this trick all the time and decided to make it easier on them. Photoshop includes a Straight-line Lasso tool that works just the opposite from the normal Lasso tool: when you hold down the Option key, you can draw non-straight lines. If you press the L key once, Photoshop gives you the Lasso tool; then press shift-L, and you get the Straight-line Lasso tool.

In order to close a selection when you're using the Straight-line Lasso tool, you have to either click at the beginning of the selection or double-click anywhere (this automatically closes the selection for you).

Tip: Select Outside the Canvas. You may or may not remember at this point in the book that Photoshop saves image data on a layer even when it extends past the edge of the canvas (out into that gray area that surrounds your picture). Just because it's hidden doesn't mean you can't select it. If you zoom back far enough, and enlarge your window enough (or switch to full-screen mode) so that you can see the gray area around the image canvas, you can hold down the Option key while using the Lasso tool to select into the gray area. (Ordinarily, without the modifier key, the selections stop at the edge of the image.)

Magnetic Lasso. New to Photoshop 5 is the Magnetic Lasso tool, which lets you draw out selections faster than the regular Lasso tool. This tool can seem like magic or it can seem like a complete waste of time—it all depends on three things: the image, your technique, and your attitude.

To use the Magnetic Lasso tool, click once along the edge of the object you're trying to select, then drag the mouse along the edge of the selection (you don't have to—and shouldn't—hold down the mouse button while moving the mouse). As you move the mouse, Photoshop "snaps" the selection to the object's edge. When you're done, click on the first point in the selection again (or triple-click to close the path with a final straight line).

So the first rule is: Only use this tool when you're selecting something in your image that has a distinct edge. In fact, the more distinct the better because the program is really following the contrast between pixels. The lower the contrast, the more the tool gets confused and loses the path.

Here's a few more rules that will help your technique.

▶ Be picky with your paths. If you don't like how the selection path looks, you can always move the mouse backward over the path to erase part of it. If Photoshop has already dropped an anchor point along the path (it does this every now and again), you can remove the last point by pressing the Delete key. Then just start moving the mouse again to start the new selection path.

▶ Click to drop your own anchor points. For instance, the Magnetic Lasso tool has trouble following sharp corners; they usually get rounded off. If you click at the vertex of the corner, that forces the path to pass through that point.

▶ Vary the Lasso Width as you go. The Lasso Width (on the Options palette) determines how close to an edge the Magnetic Lasso tool must be to select it. In some respects it determines how sloppy you can be while dragging the tool, but it becomes very important when selecting within tight spots, like the middle of a "V". In general, you should use a large width for smooth areas, and a small width for more detailed areas.

Fortunately, you can increase or decrease this setting while you move the mouse by pressing the square bracket keys on your keyboard. (For extra credit, set Other Cursors to Precise in the General Preferences dialog box; that way you can see the size of the Lasso Width.) Also, Shift-[and Shift-] set the Lasso Width to the lowest or highest value (one or 40). If you use a pressure-sensitive tablet, turn on the Pressure checkbox on the Options palette; the pressure then relates directly to Lasso Width.

▶ Sometimes you want a straight line. You can get a straight line with the Magnetic Lasso tool by Option-clicking once (at the beginning of the segment) and then clicking again (at the end of the segment).

▶ Occasionally, customize your Frequency and Edge Contrast settings. These settings (on the Options palette) control how often Photoshop drops an anchor point and how much contrast between pixels it's looking for along the edge. In theory, a more detailed edge requires more anchor points (a higher frequency setting), and selecting an object in a low-contrast image requires a lower contrast threshold. To be honest, we're much more likely to switch to a different selection tool or technique before messing with these settings.

The last rule is patience. Nobody ever gets a perfect selection with the Magnetic Lasso tool. It's not designed to make perfect selections; it's designed to make a reasonably good approximation that you can edit. We cover editing selections in "Quick Masks," later in this chapter.

Tip: Scrolling While Selecting. It's natural to zoom in close when dragging the Magnetic Lasso tool around. Nothing wrong with that. But unless you have an obscenely large monitor, you won't be able to see the whole of the object you're selecting. No problem: the Grabber Hand works just fine while you're selecting—just hold down the Spacebar and drag the image around.

Magic Wand

The last selection tool in the Tool palette is the Magic Wand, so-called more for its icon than for its prestidigitation. When you click on an image with the Magic Wand (you can't drag after clicking), Photoshop selects every neighboring pixel with the same or similar gray level or color. "Neighboring" means that the pixels must be touching on at least one side (see Figure 14-9).

Figure 14-9
Magic Wand
selections

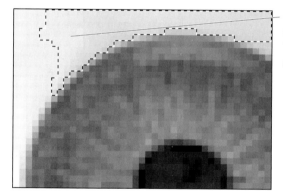

We clicked here with the Magic Wand tolerance set to 18.

How similar can the neighbors be before Photoshop pulls them into the selection? It's up to you. You can set the Tolerance setting in the Magic Wand Options dialog box from 0 to 255.

In a grayscale image, this tolerance value refers to the number of gray levels from the sample point's gray level. If you click on a pixel with a gray level of 120 and your Tolerance is set to 10, Photoshop selects any and all neighboring pixels that have values between 110 and 130.

Tip: Sample Small, Sample Often. The Magic Wand tool can be frustrating when it doesn't select everything you want it to. When this happens, novice users often set the tolerance value higher and try again. Instead, try keeping the tolerance low (between 12 and 32) and Shift-click to add more parts (or Command-click to take parts away).

Tip: Sample Points in the Magic Wand. Note that when you select a pixel with the Magic Wand, you may not get the pixel value you expect. It all depends on the Sample Size popup menu in the Eyedropper tool's Options palette. If you select 3 by 3 Average or 5 by 5 Average in that popup menu, Photoshop averages the pixels around the one you click on with the Magic Wand. On the other hand, if you select Point Sample, Photoshop uses exactly the one you click on.

Bruce prefers Point Sample because he always knows what he's going to end up with. David, on the other hand, only uses Point Sample when using the eyedropper tools in Levels or Curves (see Chapter 6, *Tonal Correction*); when he's just trying to pick up a color, he uses 3 by 3 Average.

In RGB and CMYK images, however, the Magic Wand's tolerance value is slightly more complex. The tolerance refers to each and every channel value, instead of just the gray level.

For instance, let's say your tolerance is set to 10 and you click on a pixel with a value of 60R 100G 200B. Photoshop selects all neighbors that have red values from 50 to 70, and green values from 90 to 110, and blue values from 190 to 210. All three conditions must be met, or the pixel isn't included in the selection.

Bruce almost never uses the Magic Wand; he finds it too limiting, so he uses Color Range instead (which we talk about later in this chapter; see Figure 14-29 on page 475). David finds himself using the Magic Wand frequently. However, he almost never gets the selection he wants out of it, so he uses other tools to fine-tune the selection.

Tip: Select on a Channel, Not Composite. Because it's often hard to predict how the Magic Wand tool is going to work in a color image, we typically like to make selections on a single channel of the image. The Magic Wand is more intuitive on this grayscale image, and when you switch back to the composite channel (by pressing Command-zero or clicking on the RGB or CMYK tile in the Channels palette), the selection's flashing border is still there.

Tip: Reverse Selecting. One simple but nonobvious method that we often use to select an area is to select a larger area with the Lasso or Marquee tool and then Option-click with the Magic Wand tool on the area we don't want selected (see Figure 14-10).

Figure 14-10
Reverse selecting

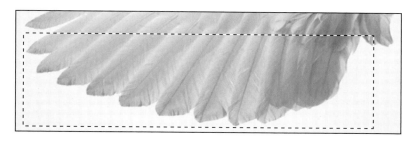

The entire area is selected

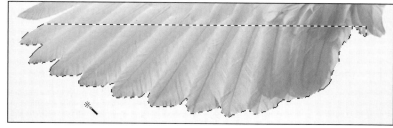

Option-click with the Magic Wand tool to deselect the background

Floating Selections

We need to take a quick diversion off the road of making selections and into the world of what happens when you move a selection. Photoshop has traditionally had a feature called floating selections. A floating selection is a temporary layer just above the currently selected layer; as soon as you deselect the floating selection, it "drops down" into the layer, replacing whatever pixels were below it.

In Photoshop 3, whenever you pasted pixels in to an image, you got a floating selection; whenever you moved pixels you got a floating selection; whenever you placed type, you got a floating selection. Floating selections were everywhere. But since version 4, Photoshop hardly ever uses floating selections because when you add type or paste pixels in, the program automatically creates a new layer.

Selections from Channels

Why would you go through all the trouble of creating a selection if the selection was already made for you? More often than not, the selection you're looking to make is already hidden within the image; to unlock it you only have to look at the color channels that make up the image (see "Channels," later in this chapter).

Here's one way to tease a selection mask out of an image (see Figure 14-11). We demonstrate these techniques in more detail in the step-by-step examples at the end of this chapter.

1. Switch though the color channels until you find which channel gives the best contrast between the element you're trying to select and its background.

2. Duplicate that channel by dragging the channel tile onto the New Channel icon in the Channels palette.

3. Use Levels or Curves to adjust the contrast between the elements you want to select and the rest of the image.

4. Clean up the mask manually. We typically use the Lasso tool to select and delete areas, or the Brush tool with one finger on the X key (so you can paint with black, then press X to "erase" with white, and so on).

Using Levels and Curves. The real key to this tip is step number 3: using Levels or Curves. With Levels, concentrate on the three Input sliders to isolate the areas you're after.

In the Curves dialog box, use the Eyedropper tool to see where the pixels sit on the curve (click and drag around the image while the Curves dialog box is open, and watch the white circle bounce around on the curve). Then use the Pencil tool in the dialog box to push those pixels to white or black. The higher the contrast, the easier it is to extract a selection from it.

Some people use the Smooth button after making these sorts of "hard" curve maps. However, in this case, we typically run a small-value Gaussian Blur after applying the curve, so we don't bother with smoothing the curve.

Using RGB. It's usually easier to grab selection masks from RGB images than from CMYK images. However, if you're going to switch from CMYK to RGB, make sure you do it on a duplicate of the image, because all that mode switching damages the image too much.

Figure 14-11 Starting with a channel

Red channel

Green channel

Blue channel (best contrast)

Quick and dirty Levels adjustment to blue channel

Fine-tuned version of blue channel

The one time that Photoshop 4 does still use floating selections is when you move a selection of pixels within an image. As soon as you move the selected pixels, Photoshop creates a new temporary floating selection layer. In version 4 you could even see this temporary layer in the Layers palette; in version 5, even this last vestige of visibility is gone.

Tip: Forcing a Float. In version 3, you could make Photoshop float a selection of pixels by pressing Command-J. Now, that keystroke copies the pixels into a whole new layer (and deselects them). As we said earlier, the only time Photoshop floats a selection is when you move pixels.

▶ If you want to cut out the pixels and float them (so that a blank spot remains where the pixels were), you can drag the selection with the Move tool. Remember that you can get the Move tool temporarily by holding down the Command key.

▶ If you'd rather copy the pixels into a floating selection, you can hold down the Option key while dragging.

▶ David's favorite way to force pixels to float is to make a selection then press Command-Left Arrow (or any other arrow key; they all do the trick). This cuts the selection out, floats it, and moves it over one pixel. Again, if you add the Option key, you copy the pixels instead of leaving a blank spot.

Tip: Floating Selections Are Layers, Too. As we've said about a bazillion times, a floating selection is simply a temporary layer in your Photoshop document. The layer appears whenever pixels are floating, and disappears when you deselect. And that means you can play with it just as you can with a layer. For instance, you can change its mode to Multiply, Screen, Overlay, or any of the others. You can change its opacity. But if this layer no longer appears in the Layers palette, where do you make these changes? After floating pixels, select Fade from the Filter menu. (Non-intuitive, but true.)

However, as soon as you try to paint on it, or run a filter, or do almost anything else interesting to the floating selection, Photoshop deselects it and drops it back down to the layer below it.

Tip: The Lasso Placeth and Taketh Away. The Lasso tool isn't only good at selecting stuff. It's good at removing pieces of floating selections, too. It was Greg Vander Houwen who first showed us how useful this can be for compositing images when you don't want to add new layers.

1. Make a quick 'n' dirty selection with the Lasso tool around the area you want.

2. Drag the selection to approximately where you want it (this creates a floating selection). Don't deselect or defloat it yet.

3. In the Options palette, give the Lasso tool a Feather value, such as 5 or 6 pixels (the feather radius depends entirely on the image content; see "Anti-aliasing and Feathering," later in this chapter).

4. Finally, hold down the Option key and use the Lasso tool to "eat away" at the edges of the floating selection (see Figure 14-12). You might want to change the opacity of the floating selection while you do this so you can see what's beneath it (press a number on your keyboard;

Figure 14-12

Eating away at a floating selection

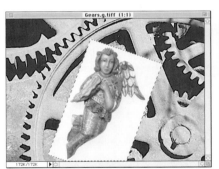

The angel is on a floating layer.

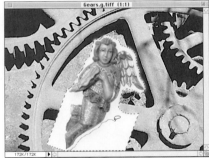

Option-dragging with the Lasso tool eats away at the floating selection.

The final image

then press zero to go back to 100 percent when you're done). The portions of the selection that are eaten away simply disappear as though they were never copied.

This gives you a great deal of control over shaping and sizing the selection when you most need it: while the selection is floating in position.

Quick Masks

When you select a portion of your image, you see the flashing dotted lines—they're fondly known as marching ants to most Photoshop folks. But what are these ants really showing you? In a typical selection, the marching ants outline the boundary of pixels that are selected 50 percent or more. There are often loads of other pixels that are selected 49 percent or less that you can't see at all from the marching ants display.

Photoshop 3 had an exception to this: when there were no pixels more than 49-percent selected then the marching ants showed you every selected pixel, no matter how selected it is. For some reason, Adobe took this feature out in version 4; it's incredibly annoying now, so if we're lucky they'll decide to put it back in to the program later.

Tip: Hide the Marching Ants. The human eye is a marvelous thing. Scientists have shown us that one of the things the eye (and the optical cortex in the brain) is great at is detecting motion (probably developed through years of hunting and gathering in the forests). However, evolution sometimes works against us. In Photoshop, the motion of a selection's marching ants is so annoying and distracting that it can bring production to a halt.

Fortunately, you can hide those little ants by selecting Hide Edges from the Select menu (or pressing Command-H). We do this constantly. In fact, we almost never actually apply a filter or do much of anything in Photoshop while the ants are marching.

The only problem is that you actually have to use your short-term memory to remember where the selection is on screen. With complex operations, you also have to remember that you have a selection—we've lost count of the number of times we've wondered why our filter or curve was having no visible effect on the image, only to remember belatedly that we had a 6-pixel area selected, usually one that currently wasn't visible.

But seeing cut-and-dried marching ant boundaries is often not helpful. So Photoshop includes a Quick Mask mode to show you exactly what's selected and how much each pixel is selected. When you enter Quick Mask mode (select the Quick Mask icon in the Tool palette or type Q), you see the underlying selection channel in all its glory. However, because the quick mask is overlaying the image, the black areas of the mask are 50-percent-opaque red and the white (selected) areas are even more transparent than that (see Figure 14-13). The red is supposed to remind you of rubylith, for those of you who remember rubylith.

Figure 14-13
Quick Mask mode

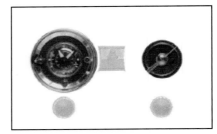

The marching ants show some of the selected areas of the image.

The quick mask shows all the selected pixels (fully and partially selected). Here the quick mask is set to white instead of the usual red.

You can change both the color and the transparency of the quick mask in the Quick Mask Options dialog box (see Figure 14-14)—the fast way to get there is to double-click on the Quick Mask icon. If the image you're working on has a lot of red in it, you'll probably want to change the quick mask color to green or some other contrasting color. Either way, we

Figure 14-14
Quick Mask
Options dialog box

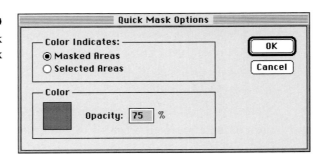

almost always increase the opacity of the color to about 75 percent, so it displays more prominently against the background image.

Note that these changes aren't document-specific. That is, they stick around in Photoshop until you change them.

Tip: How Selected Is Selected? Even when you're in Quick Mask mode it's difficult to see partially selected pixels (especially those that are less than 50-percent selected). Note that the Info palette shows grayscale values when you're in this mode; those gray values represent the "percentage selected" for each pixel. It's just another reason always to keep one eye on that palette.

Tip: Moving Selections of Under 50 Percent. As we said earlier, it's very annoying that Photoshop does not display the marching ants when there are no pixels in a selection more than 49-percent selected. Even worse, because there are no marching ants, there's no way to "grab" the selection to move or copy it! These are the only three remedies we know of.

▶ Float the selection first (see "Tip: Forcing a Float," earlier in this chapter).

▶ Copy or cut the selection into a new layer.

▶ E-mail Adobe and tell them you want this ability put back in the program.

Editing Quick Masks

The powerful thing about quick masks isn't just that you can see a selection you've made, but rather that you can edit that selection with precision. When you're in Quick Mask mode, you can paint using any of Photoshop's painting or editing tools, though you're limited to painting in grayscale. Painting with white (which appears transparent in this mode) adds to your selection; black subtracts from it.

If the element in your image is any more complicated than a rectangle, you can use Quick Mask to select it quickly and precisely. (We do this for almost every selection we make.)

1. Select the area as carefully as you can, using any of the selection tools (but don't spend too much time on it).

2. Switch to Quick Mask mode.

3. Paint or edit using the Brush tool (or any other painting or editing tool) to refine the selection you've made. Remember that partially transparent pixels will be partially selected (we often run a Gaussian Blur filter on the quick mask to smooth out sharp edges in the selection).

4. Switch out of Quick Mask mode. The marching ants update to reflect the changes you've made (see Figure 14-15).

Figure 14-15 Editing quick masks

Original, quick-and-dirty selection with the Lasso tool

In Quick Mask mode, you can clean up the selection using any tool, including the brushes.

When you leave Quick Mask mode, the selection is updated.

Note that if you switch to Quick Mask mode with nothing selected, the quick mask will be empty (fully transparent). This would imply that the whole document is selected, but it doesn't work that way.

Tip: Filtering Quick Masks. The Quick Mask mode is also a great place to apply filters or special effects. Any filter you run affects only the selection, not the entire image (see Figure 14-16). For instance, you could make a rectangular selection, switch to Quick Mask mode, and run the

Figure 14-16
Filtering
quick masks

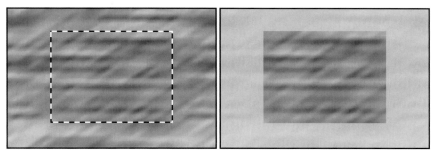

 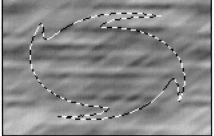

Original selection   *Quick mask of original selection*

Quick mask after Twirl filter applied   *Post-Twirl selection*

Twirl filter. When you leave Quick Mask mode, you can fill, paint, or adjust the altered selection.

Tip: Reversal of Color. Some people are just contrary. Give it to them one way and they want it the other. If you're the kind of person who likes the selected areas to be black (or red, or whatever other color you choose in Quick Mask Options) and the unselected areas to be fully transparent, you can change this in Quick Mask Options. Even faster, you can Option-click on the Quick Mask icon in the Tool palette. Note that when you do this, the icon actually changes to reflect your choice.

If you do change the way that Quick Mask works, you'll probably want to reverse the way that channels and layer masks work, too (double-click on the channel in the Channels palette). Otherwise, you'll have a hard time remembering whether black means selected or unselected. Bruce doesn't worry about keeping these things straight—he just uses Inverse (from the Select menu, or press Command-Shift-I) when the selection winds up being the opposite of what he wants.

Anti-Aliasing and Feathering

If you've ever been in a minor car accident and later talked to an insurance adjuster, you've probably been confronted with their idea that you may not be fully blameless or at fault in the accident. And, just as you can be 25-percent or 50-percent at fault, you can partially select pixels in Photoshop. One of the most common partial selections is around the edges of a selection. And the two most common ways of partially selecting the edges are anti-aliasing and feathering.

Anti-Aliasing

If you use the Marquee tool to select a rectangle, the edges of the selection are nice and crisp, which is probably how you wanted them. Crisp edges around an oval or nonregular shape, however, are rarely a desired effect. That's because of the stair-stepping required to make a diagonal or curve out of square pixels. What you really want (usually) is partially selected pixels in the notches between the fully selected pixels. This technique is called "anti-aliasing."

Every selection in Photoshop is automatically anti-aliased for you, unless you turn it off in the selection tool's Options palette. Unfortunately, you can't see the anti-aliased nature of the selection unless you're in Quick Mask mode because anti-aliased (partially selected) pixels are often less than 50-percent selected (see "Quick Masks" earlier in this chapter).

Note that once you've made a selection with Anti-aliased turned off in the Options palette, you cannot then anti-alias it—though there are ways to fake it.

Feathering

Anti-aliasing simply smooths out the edges of a selection, adjusting the amounts that the edge pixels are selected in order to appear smooth. But it's often (too often) the case that you need a larger transition area between what is and isn't selected. That's where feathering comes in. Feathering is a way to expand the border area around the edges of a selection. The border isn't just extended out; it's also extended in (see Figure 14-17).

To understand what feathering does, it's important to understand the concept of the selection channel that we talked about earlier in the

Figure 14-17
Feathering

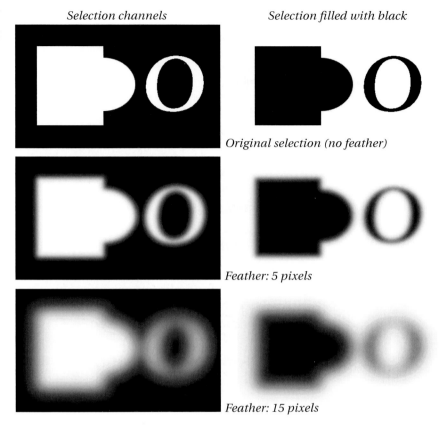

Selection channels   *Selection filled with black*

Original selection (no feather)

Feather: 5 pixels

Feather: 15 pixels

chapter. That is, when you make a selection, Photoshop is really "seeing" the selection as a grayscale channel behind the scenes. The black areas are totally unselected, the white areas are fully selected, and the gray areas are partially selected.

When you feather a selection, Photoshop is essentially applying a Gaussian Blur to the grayscale selection channel. (We say "essentially" because in some circumstances—like when you set a feather radius of over 120 pixels—you get a slightly different effect; however, there's usually so little difference that it's not worth bothering with. For those technoids out there who really care, Adobe tells us that a Gaussian Blur of the quick mask channel is a tiny bit more accurate and "true" than a feather.)

There are three ways to feather a selection.

▶   Before selecting, specify a feather amount in the Options palette for the selection tool.

▶ After selecting, choose Feather from the Select menu (or press Command-Option-D).

▶ Apply a Gaussian Blur to the selection's quick mask.

Tip: Tiny Feathers. It's not in the manuals, but Photoshop has the ability to feather using something other than a whole number. It has always bothered us that there was no way to feather with a radius of .5 or 1.75 (only 1, 2, 3, and so on). In earlier versions we would have to switch to Quick Mask mode (press Q), run a Gaussian Blur at the amount you want, then switch out of Quick Mask (press Q again). No longer.

Tip: Faking Anti-aliasing. Let's say that after you've spent five minutes making a complicated selection, you realize that Anti-aliased was turned off in the Options palette. You can fake the anti-aliasing by feathering the selection by a small amount, like .5. This blurs the selection slightly (the edges contain partially selected pixels), giving an anti-aliased look.

Tip: Feathering a Portion of a Selection. When you choose Feather from the Select menu, your entire selection is feathered. Sometimes, however, you only want to feather a portion of the selection. Maybe you want a hard edge on one half of the selection and a soft edge on the other. You can do this by switching to Quick Mask mode, selecting what you want feathered with any of the selection tools, and applying a Gaussian Blur to it. When you flip out of Quick Mask mode, the "feathering" is included in the selection.

Note that if you want a nice, soft feather between what is feathered and what isn't, you first have to feather the selection you make while you're in Quick Mask mode (see Figure 14-18).

Channels

Back in "Masking-Tape Selections," we told you that selections, masks, and channels are all the same thing down deep: grayscale images. This is not intuitive, nor is it easy to grasp at first. But once you really understand this point, you've taken the first step toward really surfing the Photoshop tsunami.

Figure 14-18 Feathering part of a selection

Original image	*Anti-aliased selection*	*After Gaussian blur*	*Mustache and neck "feathered"*

A channel is a solitary 8-bit, grayscale image. You can have up to 24 channels in a single image in Photoshop 4. (Actually, there are two exceptions: first, images in Bitmap mode can only contain a single 1-bit channel; second, Photoshop allows one additional channel per layer to accommodate layer masks, which we'll talk about later in this chapter.)

But in the eyes of the program, not all channels are created equal. There are three types of channels: alpha, color, and spot color channels (see Figure 14-19). We'll discuss the first two here, and the third in Chapter 10, *Spot Colors and Duotones*.

Figure 14-19
The Channels
palette

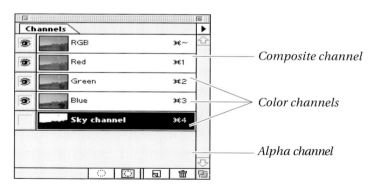

A channel is a solitary 8-bit, grayscale image.

Alpha Channels

People get very nervous when they hear the term "alpha channel," because they figure that with such an exotic name, it has to be a complex feature. Not so. An alpha channel is simply an 8-bit grayscale image. Alpha channels let you save selections, but you can use them in a number of other ways, too (see "Tip: Tissue Overlay Channels," in Chapter 15, *Essential Image Techniques*).

Saving selections. Selections and channels are really the same thing down deep (even though they have different outward appearances), so you can turn one into the other very quickly. Earlier in this chapter we discussed how you can see and edit a selection by switching to Quick Mask mode. But quick masks are ephemeral things, and aren't much use if you want to hold on to that selection and use it later.

When you turn a selection into an alpha channel, you're saving that selection in the document. Then you can go back later and edit the channel, or turn it back into a selection.

The slow way to save a selection is to choose Save Selection from the Select menu. It's a nice place for beginners because Photoshop provides you with a dialog box (see Figure 14-20). But pros don't bother with menu selections when they can avoid them. Instead, click the Save Selection icon in the Channels palette. Or, if you want to see the Channel Options dialog box first (for instance, if you want to name the channel), hold down the Option key while clicking the icon (see Figure 14-21).

Figure 14-20
Save Selection
dialog box

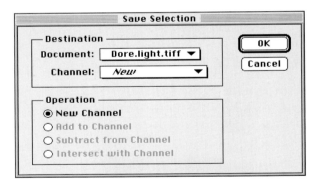

Figure 14-21
Saving a selection

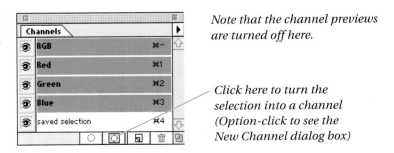

Note that the channel previews are turned off here.

Click here to turn the selection into a channel (Option-click to see the New Channel dialog box)

Tip: Loading Selections. Saving a selection as an alpha channel doesn't do you much good unless you can retrieve it again. Again, the slowest method is to use the Load Selection item from the Select menu (though there are benefits to this method; see "Tip: Saving Channels in Other Documents," later in this chapter.

One step better is to Command-click on the channel that you want to turn into a selection. Even better, press Command-Option-#, where the number is the channel you want. For instance, if you want to load channel six as a selection, press Command-Option-6.

Note that if you press Command-Option-~(tilde), you load the luminosity mask. This is not the "lightness" of the image; rather, it's approximately the same as selecting Grayscale from the Mode menu. It's rare that you'd need it, but isn't it great to know that it's there?

Tip: Be a Packrat! Every time it takes you more than 30 seconds to make a selection in your image, you should be thinking: Save This Selection. We try to save every complex selection as a channel or a path until the end of the project (and sometimes we even archive them, just in case). The reason? You never know when you'll need them again. Photoshop doesn't let you go back and change what you've done too often, and we've just been burned too many times by having to re-create selections from scratch (of course, the new selection never matches the old one exactly).

Saving selections as channels takes up lots of memory, though. If you don't think you'll need a selection for a while, offload that channel into another file (see "Duplicating Channels," below). This still swallows disk space, but hey—it's cheap compared to RAM.

Tip: Don't Save Channels as TIFFs. If you're saving a mess of channels along with the image you're working on, don't save the file as a TIFF. Even though you can save all those channels in a TIFF image, you're not taking advantage of Photoshop's compression techniques, so your files end up being much larger than necessary. Instead, save in Photoshop format. Of course, if you need those extra channels saved in a TIFF, then go ahead and save as in that format (see Chapter 16, *Storing Images*, for reasons why you might want this ability).

Tip: Adding, Subtracting, and Intersecting Selections. Let's say you have an image with three distinct elements in it. You've spent an hour carefully selecting each of the elements, and you've saved each one in its own channel (see Figure 14-22). Now you want to select all three objects at the same time.

Figure 14-22 Adding, subtracting, and intersecting selections

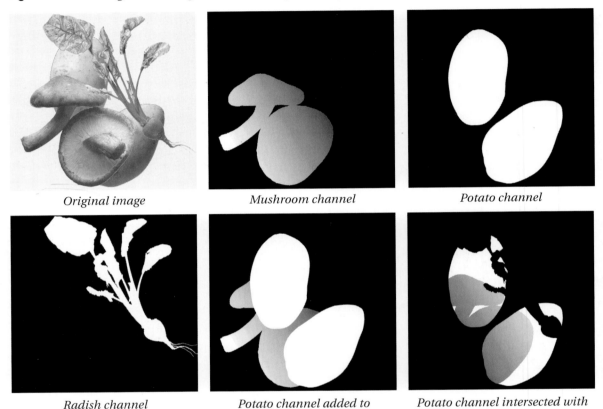

Original image

Mushroom channel

Potato channel

Radish channel

Potato channel added to
mushroom channels

Potato channel intersected with
mushroom and radish channels

In the good old days you would have sat around trying to figure out the appropriate channel operations (using Calculations) to get exactly what you wanted. But it's a kinder, gentler Photoshop now. After you load one channel as a selection, you can use Load Selection from the Select menu to add another channel to the current selection, subtract another channel, or find the intersection between the two selections.

Even easier, use the key-click combinations in Table 14-1. Confused? Don't forget to watch Photoshop's cursor icons; as you hold down the various key combinations, Photoshop indicates what will happen when you click.

Table 14-1	Do this to the channel tile . . .	. . . to get this result
Working with selections	Command-Shift-click	Add channel to current selection
	Command-Option-click	Subtract channel from selection
	Command-Shift-Option-click	Intersect the current selection and the channel

Multidocument Channels

As we said earlier, your alpha channels don't all have to be in the same document. In fact, if you've got more than 24 channels, you have to have them in multiple documents. But even if you have fewer than 24, you may want to save off channels in order to reduce the current file's size. Here are a bunch of tips we've found helpful in moving channels back and forth between documents.

Tip: Saving Channels in Other Documents. From what we've said earlier in this chapter, you might infer that we think only a dolt trying to waste time would use the Load or Save Selection items on the Select menu. Not true! Taking the extra time to use the menu items can pay off in certain circumstances. Here's one: you can save selections to or load selections from other documents.

As long as another file is currently open, you can save a selection into it using Save Selection, or load a selection (from a channel) from it using the menu items. You can even save selections into a new document by selecting New from the Document popup menu in the Save Selection dialog box.

If you have two similar documents open and you've carefully made and saved a selection in one image, you might want to use it in the other image. Instead of copying and pasting the selection channel, take a shortcut route and use the Load Selection dialog box (see Figure 14-23). You can load the selection channel directly by choosing it from the Document and Channel popup menus.

The catch here is that both documents have to have exactly the same pixel dimensions (otherwise, Photoshop wouldn't know how to place the selection properly).

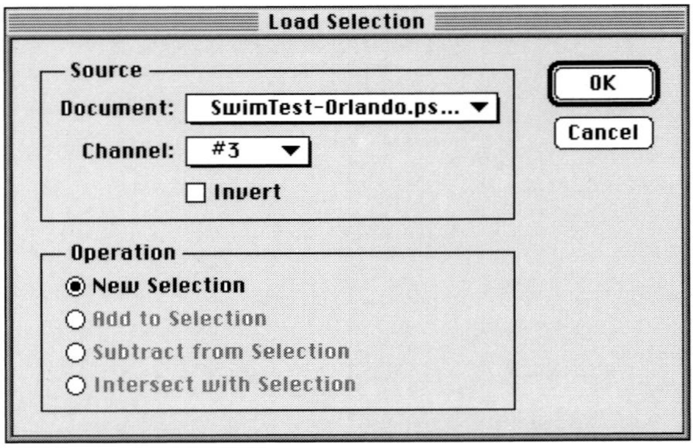

Figure 14-23

Load Selection
dialog box

Figure 14-23

Load Selection
dialog box

Load Selection

Source
Document: SwimTest-Orlando.ps... ▼

Channel: #3 ▼

☐ Invert

OK

Cancel

Operation
◉ New Selection
○ Add to Selection
○ Subtract from Selection
○ Intersect with Selection

Tip: More Saving Off Channels. If you've already saved your selection into a channel in document A, how can you get that channel into document B? One method is to select the channel and choose Duplicate Channel from the Channel palette's popout menu (see Figure 14-24). Here you can choose to duplicate the channel into a new document or any other open document (as long as it has the same pixel dimensions as the one you currently have open).

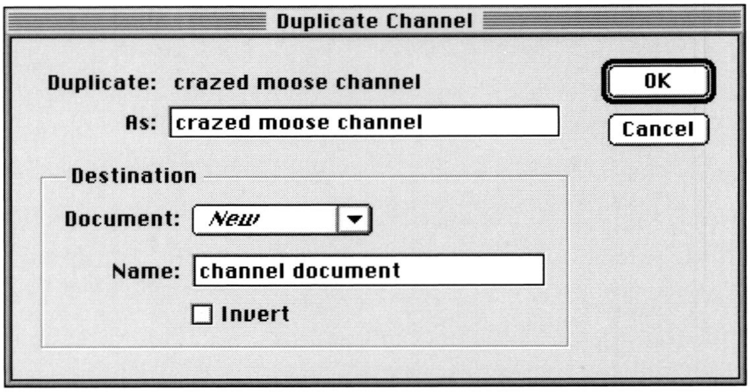

Figure 14-24

Duplicating a channel to
another document

Duplicate Channel

Duplicate: crazed moose channel

As: crazed moose channel

OK

Cancel

Destination
Document: New ▼

Name: channel document

☐ Invert

Tip: Saving Off Channels Using Copy and Paste. We hear you asking, "Why not just copy and paste the channel from one document into another?" The answer is that Copy and Paste can really bog down in larger files ("large" meaning any file so big that Photoshop has to start writing it to disk; see Chapter 1, *Building a Photoshop System*). In smaller files, however, Copy and Paste works just as well.

Tip: Copying Channels the Fast Way. However, when it comes right down to it, the fastest way to copy a channel from document A to document B is simply by dragging the channel's tile (in the Channels palette) from document A onto document B. It's nice, quick, simple, and elegant. The problem is that the two documents have to be the same size or else Photoshop won't align the channels properly.

Tip: Dragging Selections. Photoshop is full of little, subtle features that make life so much nicer. For instance, you can now drag any selection from one document into another document using one of the selection tools. (The Move tool actually moves the pixels inside the selection; the selection tools move the selection itself.)

Normally, the selection "drops" wherever you let go of the mouse button. However, if the two documents have the same pixel dimensions, you can hold down the Shift key to pin-register the selection (it lands in the same location as it was in the first document). If the images aren't the same pixel dimension, the Shift key centers the selection.

Color Channels

When a color image is in RGB mode (under the Mode menu), the image is made up of three channels: red, green, and blue. Each of these channels is exactly the same as an alpha channel, except that they're designated as color channels. You can edit a color channel separately from the others. You can independently make a single color channel visible or invisible. But you cannot delete or add a color channel without changing the image mode.

The first tile in the Channels palette (above the color channels) is the Composite channel. Actually, this isn't really a channel at all. Rather, the composite channel is the full-color representation of all the individual color channels mixed together. It gives you a convenient way to select or deselect all the color channels at once, and also lets you view the composite color image while you're editing a single channel.

Tip: Selecting and Seeing Channels. The tricky thing about working with channels is figuring out which channel(s) you're editing and which channel(s) you're seeing on the screen. They're not always the same thing!

The Channels palette has two columns. The left column contains little eyeball checkboxes that you can turn on and off to show or hide individual channels. Clicking on one of the tiles in the right column not only displays that channel, but lets you edit it, too. The channels that are selected for editing are highlighted (see Figure 14-25). The two columns are independent of each other because editing and seeing the channels are not the same thing.

Figure 14-25

Selecting multiple channels

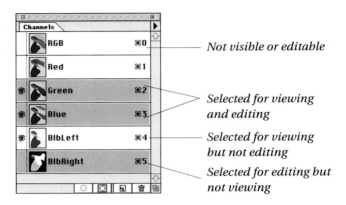

Not visible or editable

Selected for viewing and editing

Selected for viewing but not editing

Selected for editing but not viewing

When you're jumping from one channel to another, skip the clicking altogether and use a keystroke instead. Command-# displays the channel number you press; for instance, Command-1 shows the red channel (or whatever the first channel is), and Command-4 shows the fourth channel (the first alpha channel in an RGB image).

In earlier versions of Photoshop, Command-0 would select the color composite channel (deselecting all other channels in the process). Now, the keystroke is Command-~ (tilde). Sorry, there's no way (that we know of) to select channels above number nine with keystrokes.

You can see as many channels at once as you want by clicking in the channel's eyeball checkboxes. To edit more than one channel at a time, Shift-click on the channel tiles.

Note that when you display more than one channel at a time, the alpha channels automatically switch from their standard black and white to their channel color (you can specify what color each channel uses in Channel Options—double-click on the channel tile).

The Select Menu

If making selections using lassos and marquees and then saving or loading them were all there was to selection in Photoshop, life would be simpler but duller. Fortunately for us, there are many more things you can do with selections, and they all—well, almost all—help immeasurably in the production process.

You can find each additional selection feature under the Select menu: Grow, Similar, Color Range, and Modify. Let's explore each of these and how they can speed up your work.

Grow

Earlier in the chapter, when we were talking about the Magic Wand tool, we discussed the concept of tolerance. This value tells Photoshop how much brighter or darker a pixel (or each color channel that defines a pixel) can be and still be included in the selection.

Let's say you're trying to select an apple using the Magic Wand tool with a tolerance of 24. After clicking once, perhaps only half of the apple is selected; the other half is slightly shaded and falls outside the tolerance range. You could deselect, change the tolerance, and click again. However, it's much faster to select Grow from the Select menu. (In Photoshop 3 you could press Command-G, but that keystroke does something else now.)

When you choose Grow, Photoshop selects additional pixels according to the following criteria. (By the way, the manuals are wrong about how Grow works . . . it's weird but we figured it out.)

1. First, it finds the highest and lowest gray values of every channel of every pixel selected—the highest red, green, and blue, and the lowest red, green, and blue of the bunch of already selected pixels (or the highest cyan, magenta, yellow, and black, and so on).

2. Next, it adds the tolerance value to the highest values and subtracts it from the lowest values in each channel. Therefore, the highest values get a little higher and the lowest values get a little lower (of course, it never goes above 255 or below 0).

3. Finally, Photoshop selects every adjacent pixel that falls between all those values (see Figure 14-26).

Figure 14-26
The Grow
command

After Magic Wand click   *After Grow*

In other words, Photoshop tries its hardest to spread your selection in every direction, but only in similar colors. However, it doesn't always work the way you'd want. In fact, sometimes it works very oddly indeed.

For instance, if you select a pure red area (made of 255 red, and no blue or green), and a pure green area (made of 255 green, and no red or blue), then select Grow, Photoshop selects every adjacent pixel that has any red or green in it, as long as the blue channel is not out of tolerance's range. That means that it'll pick out dark browns, lime greens, oranges, and so on—even if you set a really small tolerance level (see Figure 14-27).

Tip: Controlled Growing. If you switch to a color channel (like red or cyan) before selecting Grow, Photoshop grows the selection based on

Figure 14-27
Anomalies with the
Grow command

When the two center squares are selected, Grow selects all the bottom squares and none of the top squares. Why? Because of slight blue "contamination" in the top squares.

Many of these colors are selected unexpectedly with Grow.

that channel only. This can be helpful because it's much easier to predict how the Magic Wand and Grow features will work in grayscale mode than in color.

Tip: Instead of the Magic Wand. While the Magic Wand tool is pretty cool and provides a friendly point-and-click interface, it's often not very useful because colors in a natural image (like a scan) are typically pretty varied. Even if you click in what looks like a representative spot, you might not get the full range you expect.

Instead, try selecting a larger representative area with the Lasso or Marquee tool. Then, select Grow or Similar from the Select menu (see below for a discussion of Similar). Bruce maintains that the best method is just to use Color Range instead (see "Color Range," later in this chapter).

Similar

Grow and the Magic Wand have a common downfall: they only select contiguous areas of your image. If you're trying to select the same color throughout an image, you may click and drag and grow yourself into a frenzy before you're done. Choosing Similar from the Select menu does the same thing as choosing Grow, but it chooses pixels from throughout the entire image (see Figure 14-28).

Figure 14-28
The Similar command

Selection made with Magic Wand. A Tolerance setting of 24 manages to avoid the shadows and green areas.

After Similar is selected. Some brighter areas of the apples are still not selected.

Note that Similar and Grow are both attached to the Magic Wand's options; Photoshop applies both the Wand's tolerance and its anti-alias values to these commands. We can't think of any reason to turn anti-aliasing off, but it's nice to know you have the option.

Color Range

One of the problems with Similar and Grow is that you rarely know what you're going to end up with. On the other hand, Color Range lets you make color-based selections interactively, and shows you exactly which pixels will be selected. But there's one other advantage of Color Range over the Magic Wand features (we think of Similar and Grow as extensions of the Magic Wand).

The Magic Wand–based features either select a pixel or they don't (the exception is anti-aliasing around the edges of selections, which only partially selects pixels there). Color Range, however, only fully selects a few pixels and partially selects a lot of pixels (see Figure 14-29). This can be incredibly helpful when you're trying to tease a good selection mask out of the contents of an image.

We rarely use Color Range to create a final selection mask. Rather, we find it great as a first or second step in building the mask, and then we follow it up with other tools (including Levels or Curves), adding and removing pixels. There are four areas you should be aware of in the Color Range dialog box: selection eyedroppers, the Fuzziness slider, canned sets of colors, and Selection Preview.

Adding and deleting colors. When you first open Color Range, Photoshop creates a selection based on your foreground color. Then you can use the eyedropper tools to add or delete colors in the image (or, better yet, hold down the Shift key to get the Add Color to Mask eyedropper, or the Option key to get the Remove Color from Mask eyedropper). Note that you can always scroll or magnify an area in the image. You can even select colors from any other open image.

Tip: Avoid Sample Merged. Color Range is always in Sample Merged mode. It sees your image as though all the visible layers were merged together. If you've got an object on a layer that you don't want included in the selection mask, hide that layer before opening Color Range.

The Fuzziness factor. Every Photoshop book we've seen (including Photoshop's manuals) says that the Fuzziness slider in the Color Range dialog box is more or less the same as the Tolerance field in the Magic Wand Options palette. That's sort of like saying that Republicans are more or less the same as Democrats. Yes, they're both in the business of running the country, but . . . .

As we said earlier, pixels that fall within the tolerance value are either fully selected or not; pixels that fall on the border between the selected and unselected areas may be partially selected, but those are only border pixels. Color Range uses the fuzziness value to determine not only whether a pixel should be included, but also how selected it should be.

Figure 14-29 Magic Wand versus Color Range

While you can make similar selections with the Magic Wand and Color Range, each is more efficient in particular situations. Magic Wand is faster for big, consistent areas, while Color Range excels for finer details.

The original image. It is photographed on a good, uniform white background, and includes an area of relatively solid color (the reds) that is an obvious target for change.

Three quick Shift-clicks with the Magic Wand yield a very serviceable silhouette mask. A bit of feathering or a Gaussian Blur of the mask (combined with a Levels tweak to adjust the blur) deals with the hard edges.

Because the object is hard-edged to begin with, the Magic Wand's inability to partially select pixels doesn't pose much of a problem in compositing.

A mask created with Color Range (here with few sample points and a high Fuzziness setting) is more appropriate for subtle selections.

A detail of the mask shows that there are partially selected pixels (the gray areas).

This more subtle mask is just the ticket for a Hue/Saturation tweak, changing the red areas to blue without an artificial look.

We're not going to get into the hard-core math (you don't need to know it and we're not entirely sure of it ourselves), but Figure 14-31 should give you a pretty good idea of how Fuzziness works.

Tip: Sampling versus Fuzziness. Should you use lots of sample points or a high Fuzziness setting? It depends on the type of image. To select large areas of similar color, tend toward a lower fuzziness (10–15) to avoid selecting stray pixels. For fine detail, you need to use higher Fuzziness settings, because the fine areas are generally more polluted with colors spilling from adjacent pixels.

Either way, try adding sample points to increase the selection range before you increase fuzziness.

Tip: Return to Settings. If you want to return to the Color Range dialog box with exactly the same settings as you last used, hold down the Option key when selecting Color Range from the Select menu.

Canned colors

Instead of creating a selection mask with the eyedroppers, you can let Photoshop select all the reds, or all the blues, or yellows, or any other primary color, by choosing the color in the Select popup menu (see Figure 14-30). If you choose one of these, Photoshop only selects a pixel if it contains more of that color than any other. For instance, if you choose Reds, Photoshop selects a pixel with an RGB value of 128R 115G 60B;

Figure 14-30

Color Range
dialog box

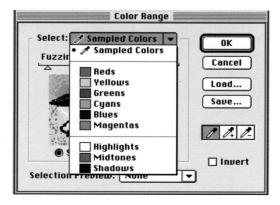

Figure 14-31 Fuzziness versus sample points for Color Range

Four selections created with Color Range. At right is the result of a Hue/Saturation move on the selection.

Few sample points, low fuzziness.

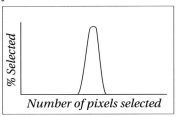

Few sample points, high fuzziness.

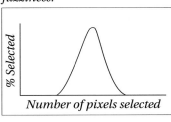

Many sample points, low fuzziness.

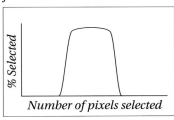

Many sample points, high fuzziness.

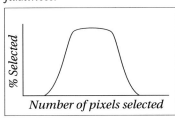

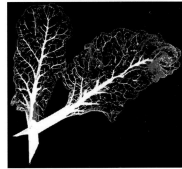

but it won't even partially select a pixel that has an RGB value of 128R 130G 60B.

The greater the difference between the color you choose (in this example, red) and the other primaries (e.g., blue and green), the more the pixel is selected. (To get really tweaky for a moment: the percentage the pixel is selected is the percentage difference between the color you choose and the primary color with the next highest value.)

Do you really need to know any of this? No. Probably the best way to use these features is just not to use them at all (we almost never do).

On the other hand, you can also choose Highlights, Midtones, or Shadows, which we find a bit more useful. When you choose one of these, Photoshop decides whether to select a pixel (or how much to select it) based on its Lab luminance value (see Table 14-2 and Chapter 5, *Color Settings*, for more information on Lab mode).

Table 14-2

Ranges for Color Range (L value in Lab mode)

Select name	Fully selected pixels	Partially selected pixels
Shadows	1–40	40–55
Midtones	55–75	40–55 and 75–85
Highlights	80–100	75–85

We find selecting Highlights, Midtones, and Shadows most useful when selecting a subset of a color we've already selected (see "Tip: Color Range Subsets," next).

Tip: Color Range Subsets. If you're trying to select all the green buttons on a blouse using Color Range, you're going to pick up every other green object throughout the image, too. However, you can tell the Color Range feature to only select green items within a particular area—the blouse, for instance—by making a selection first. Draw a quick outline of the area of interest with the Lasso tool, then choose Color Range. Photoshop ignores the rest of the image.

Similarly, you could select all the green items in the image, then go back to Color Range again and select only those greens that are in Highlight areas.

Tip: Invert the Color Range Selection. Do you often find yourself following up a Color Range selection with an Invert from the Select menu?

If you are trying to select the opposite of what's selected in the Color Range dialog box, you can remove that extra step by turning on the Invert checkbox in the Color Range dialog box; Photoshop automatically inverts the selection for you.

If you already have a selection made when you Invert the Color Range selection, Photoshop deselects the Color Range pixels from your selection.

Selection Preview. The last area to pay attention to in the Color Range dialog box is the Selection Preview popup menu. When you select anything other than None (the default) from this menu, Photoshop previews the Color Range selection mask.

The first choice, Grayscale, shows you what the selection mask would look like if you saved it as a separate channel. The second and third choices, Black Matte and White Matte, are the equivalent of copying the selected pixels out and pasting them on a black or white background. This is great for seeing how well you're capturing edge pixels. The last choice, Quick Mask, is the same as pressing OK and immediately switching into Quick Mask mode.

Because the Selection Preview can slow you down, we recommend turning it on only when you need to, then turning around and switching back to None. It can be really helpful in making sure you're selecting everything you want, but it can also be a drag to productivity.

Tip: Changing Quick Mask Options. If you're a hard-core Color Range user, you may one day have the strange desire to change your Quick Mask options settings while the Color Range dialog box is open. You can do it (believe it or not). Hold down the Option key while selecting Quick Mask from the Selection Preview popup menu. Don't say we don't strive to give you every last tip!

Tip: Forget the Color Range Radio Buttons. Here's another little tip that can speed up production by a moment or two: if you frequently use the Image and Selection radio buttons in the Color Range dialog box, stop! Instead, press the Command or Control key—either one works on the Mac—on your keyboard. This toggles between the Selection and Image previews much faster than you can click buttons. This is sometimes helpful if you need a quick reality check as to what's selected and what is not.

Modify

When you think of the most important part of your selection, what do you think of? If you answer "what's selected," you're wrong. No matter what you have selected in your image, the most important part of the selection is the boundary or edge. This is where the tire hits the road, where the money slaps the table, where the gavel slams the podium, where the invoice smacks the client. No matter what you do with the selection—whether you copy and paste it, paint within it, or whatever—the quality of your edge determines how effective your effect will be.

When making a precise selection, you often need to make subtle adjustments to the boundaries of the selection. The four menu items on the Modify submenu under the Select menu—Border, Smooth, Expand, and Contract—focus entirely on this task.

Border. Police officers of the world take note: there's a faster way to get a doughnut than driving down to the local Circle K. Draw a circle using the Marquee tool, then select Border from the Modify submenu under the Select menu. You can even specify how thick you want your doughnut (in

Figure 14-32
Border

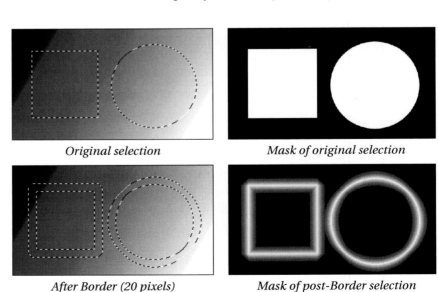

Original selection

Mask of original selection

After Border (20 pixels)

Mask of post-Border selection

pixels, of course). Border transforms the single line (the circle) into two lines (see Figure 14-32).

The problem with Border is that it only creates soft-edged borders. If you draw a square and give it a border, you get a soft-edged shape that looks more like an octagon than a square. In many cases, this is exactly what you want and need. But other times it can ruin the mood faster than jackhammers outside the bedroom window.

Tip: Level Borders. If selecting Border gives you a super-soft edge when what you want is a harder, fatter edge, try this quick-mask trick. Switch to Quick Mask mode (press Q), then use the Levels or Curves dialog box to adjust the edge of the selection (see "Tip: Finer Spreads and Chokes," later in this chapter). If you find that the edge of the selection becomes too jaggy, you can always apply a 0.5 Gaussian Blur to smooth it out. Remember that when you're in Quick Mask mode, you can select the area to which you want to apply the levels or blur.

Tip: More Border Options. Here's one other way to make a border with a sharper, more distinct edge.

1. Save your selection as an alpha channel.

2. While the area is still selected, choose Expand from the Modify submenu under the Select menu (we discuss this command later in the chapter).

3. Save this new selection as an alpha channel.

4. Load the original selection from the alpha channel you saved it in.

5. Choose Contract from the Modify submenu.

6. Mix the two selections (the expanded and the contracted) together by Command-Option-clicking on the channel that contains the expanded version.

You can now save this selection and delete either one or both of the other alpha channels you saved. Note that you don't have to expand and contract the selection; this method lets you choose to only contract or expand, too.

Tip: Using Borders When Compositing. One of the positive aspects of Photoshop giving you a soft-edged border when you select Border from the Modify submenu is that you can use it to touch up the edges of objects you're placing over a background. For instance, if an object on a layer is not feathered or anti-aliased enough, you can use Border to blur its edges into the background. Or, if the edge of a composited object has some edge spill from the previous background, you can touch it up with Border.

1. Paste the object and place it exactly where you want it. In Photoshop 4 and 5, this automatically creates a new layer.

2. Make sure the edges around the object are selected. One fast way to do this is to select the layer's transparency mask by Command-clicking on the layer in the Layers palette (see "Selections and Layers," later in this chapter).

3. Select Border from the Modify submenu.

4. Feather the border selection slightly (with a radius like .5).

5. Hide the marching ants (Command-H).

6. If you want to get rid of aliasing, apply a Gaussian Blur to the area. If you're trying to rid yourself of some background color spill, you can use the Rubber Stamp tool to clone some of the object's color into the border selection (we'll discuss this in more depth in "Step-by-Step Silhouettes," later in this chapter). Or you can just press Delete to remove the edge pixels, blending the foreground and the background images together.

Finally, you may want to apply some unsharp masking to sharpen the edge a little. Therein lies the art: blurring enough and sharpening enough to get a smooth but clean edge.

Smooth. The problem with making selections with the Lasso tool is that you often get very jaggy selection lines; the corners are too sharp, the curves are too bumpy. You can smooth these out by selecting Smooth from the Modify submenu under the Select menu. Like most selection operations in Photoshop, this actually runs a convolution filter over the

Figure 14-33
Smooth

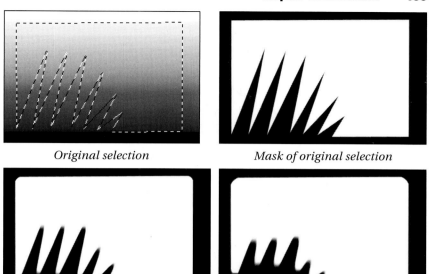

Original selection

Mask of original selection

After Smooth with 10-pixel radius

After Smooth with 16-pixel radius

selection mask—in this case the Median filter. That is, selecting Smooth is exactly the same thing as switching to Quick Mask mode and choosing the Median filter.

Smooth has little or no effect on straight lines or smooth curves. But it has a drastic effect on corners and jaggy lines (see Figure 14-33). Smooth (or the Median filter, depending on which way you look at it) looks at each pixel in your selection, then looks at the pixels surrounding it (the number of pixels it looks at depends on the radius value you choose in the Smooth dialog box). If more than half the pixels around it are selected, then the pixel remains selected. If fewer than half are selected, the pixel becomes deselected.

If you enter a small Radius value, only corner tips and other sharp edges are rounded out. Larger values make sweeping changes. It's rare that we use a radius over 5 or 6, but it depends entirely on what you're doing (and how smooth your hand is!).

Expand/Contract. The Expand and Contract features are two of the most useful selection modifiers. They let you enlarge or reduce the size of the selection. This is just like spreading or choking colors in trapping (if you don't know about trapping, don't worry; it's not relevant here).

Figure 14-34
Expand and Contract

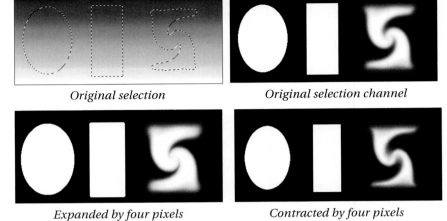

Original selection

Original selection channel

Expanded by four pixels

Contracted by four pixels

Once again, these modifiers are simply applying filters to the black-and-white mask equivalent of your selection. Choosing Expand is the same as applying the Maximum filter to the mask; choosing Contract is the same as applying the Minimum filter (see Figure 14-34).

Note that if you enter 5 as the Radius value in the Maximum or Minimum dialog box (or in the Expand or Contract dialog box), it's exactly the same as running the filter or selection modifier five times. The radius value here is more of an "iteration" value; how many times do you want the filter applied at a one-pixel radius?

While we frequently find these selection modifiers useful, they aren't very precise. You can only specify the radius in one-pixel increments (see "Tip: Finer Spreads and Chokes," next).

Tip: Finer Spreads and Chokes. You can make much finer adjustments to the size of a selection by using Levels rather than Expand or Contract from the Select menu. Here's how.

1. Once you have your selection, switch to Quick Mask mode.

2. Apply a Gaussian Blur to the area you want to expand or contract (if it's the whole selection, then blur the whole quick mask). We usually use a low Radius value, such as .5 or 1.

3. In Levels (Command-L), adjust the middle (gamma) slider control to make the area darker or lighter. Making it darker contracts the selection; lighter expands the selection (see Figure 14-35).

Figure 14-35

Precision control
over expanding and
contracting

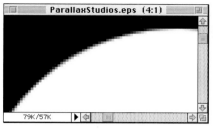

Original selection channel

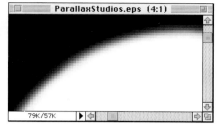

*Selection channel after Gaussian Blur
and Levels*

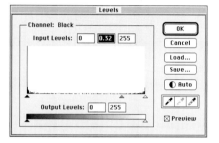

*The gamma slider controls the
expansion or contraction of
the mask channel's gray levels—
hence the abruptness of the blur.*

What's nice about this tip is that it's a very gentle method of expanding or contracting the selection. Instead of "Wham! Move one pixel over," you can say, "Make this selection slightly bigger or smaller."

Selections and Layers

Photoshop 3 gave us the ability to have multiple layers in a single document, and Photoshop 4 made it nigh on impossible not to use multiple layers. There's very little difference between painting or editing on a background or on a layer. There is, however, a big difference in making a selection on a layer. Plus, Layers opens up three new features that are related to selections: transparency masks, layer masks, and using layers as a mask.

When reading about these new features, don't forget that masks are just channels, which are 8-bit grayscale "images," just like we talked about earlier in this chapter.

Transparency Masks

Most of the time when you create a new layer, the background is transparent. When you paint on it or paste in a selection, you're making pixels opaque. Photoshop is always keeping track of how transparent each pixel

Figure 14-36

Transparency masks

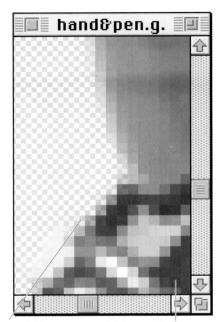

This area is transparent.

This area is partially opaque.   *This area is opaque.*

is—fully transparent, partially transparent, or totally opaque. This information about pixel transparency is called the transparency mask (see Figure 14-36).

Remember the analogy we made to masking tape earlier in the chapter? The selection/channel/mask (they're all the same) acts like tape over or around your image. In this case, however, the mask doesn't represent how selected a pixel is; it's how transparent (or, conversely, how visible) it is. You can have a pixel that's fully selected, but only 10-percent opaque (90-percent transparent).

Tip: Load the Transparency Mask. You can load the transparency mask for a layer as a selection in the Load Selection dialog box, but it's much faster to Command-click on the layer's tile in the Layers palette. (In Photoshop 3, you had to press Command-Option-T.) For instance, if you have some text on a type layer and you want to make a selection that looks exactly like the type, Command-click on the type layer's tile. This loads the selection and you're ready to roll.

Tip: Loading the Transparency Mask and Moving. In Photoshop 3, it was important not to load the transparency mask as a selection and then try to move the image. The reason: loading the transparency mask didn't select everything completely. Some pixels (those that were partially transparent) are only partially selected. So if you moved the selection in Photoshop 3, you left some behind. Fortunately, the folks at Adobe have changed this "feature" so that all the pixels get moved in this instance.

While it's great that they changed this behavior, the real lesson is "don't load the transparency mask if you're only trying to move the pixels on a layer." There's really no need; you can just use the Move tool, target the layer, and drag it.

Layer Masks

The task: to composite several images on a background. You've placed each object on a separate layer, then used the techniques in this chapter to carefully select and delete the portion of each object that must be hidden. But, after hours of sweat and mouse-burn, when you show the result to your art director, she says, "Can't you move this over a little and crop out that, and we need a little more of this showing here . . . ."

Fortunately, you can use layer masks to avoid this sort of nightmare in your work. Layer masks are just like transparency masks—they determine how transparent the layer's pixels are—but you can see layer masks and, more important, edit them (see Figure 14-37).

If you had used layer masks in the example above, you would have smiled at your art director and made the changes quickly and painlessly. Here's how you do it.

Creating and editing layer masks. You can apply a layer mask to a layer by selecting Add Layer Mask from the Layer menu. When a layer has a mask—it can only have one—the Layers palette displays a thumbnail of the mask (see Figure 14-38).

The first tricky thing about using layer masks is that it's often difficult to tell whether you're editing the layer or the layer mask. The only two differences are that the layer mask thumbnail has a dark border around it (on a high-resolution screen, the two borders look about the same; and if you have Previews turned off in the Layers palette, there's no difference here at all), and the document title bar says "Layer x Mask." We typically

Figure 14-37 Layer masks

The earth is on a separate layer above the background image of the car.

The layer mask

After the layer mask is applied to the Earth layer

Figure 14-38

Adding a
layer mask

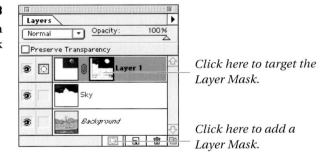

*Click here to target the
Layer Mask.*

*Click here to add a
Layer Mask.*

glance at the title bar about as often as we look in our car's rear-view mirror; it's a good way to keep a constant eye on what's going on around us.

Once you have a layer mask, you can edit it by clicking on its icon in the Layers palette (see "Tip: Layer Mask Keystroke," below).

We may be breaking a record for redundancy here, but it's important to remember that a mask is the same as a selection, which is the same as a channel. Underneath, they're all grayscale images. Editing a mask is as simple as painting with grays. Painting with black is like adding masking tape; it covers up part of the adjoining layer (making those pixels transparent). Painting with white takes away the tape and uncovers the layer's image. Gray, of course, partially covers the image.

Tip: Faster Layer Masks. While there's no built-in keyboard shortcut to add a layer mask, it is a little faster to click on the Add Layer Mask icon in the Layers palette. If you Option-click on the Add Layer Mask icon, Photoshop inverts the layer mask (so that it automatically hides everything on the layer).

Note that you can make a selection before clicking on the icon. In this case, the program "paints in" the non-selected areas with black for you (on the layer mask). This is usually much easier than adding a layer mask, then using the paint tools to paint away areas. (Of course, Option-clicking on the icon with a selection paints the selected areas with black, so that whatever was selected "disappears.")

Tip: Layer Mask Keystroke. When you're working on a layer, you can jump to the layer mask (make it "active" so all your edits are to the mask rather than the image) by pressing Command-\ (backslash). When you're ready to leave the layer mask, press Command-~ (tilde) to switch back to the layer itself.

Tip: Getting Rid of the Mask. As soon as you start editing layer masks, you're going to find that you want to turn the mask on and off, so you can get before-and-after views of your work. You can make the mask disappear temporarily by selecting Disable Layer Mask from the Layer menu. Or, if you need to get your work done quickly, do it the fast way: Shift-click on the Layer Mask icon.

If you want to hide the mask with extreme prejudice—that is, if you want to delete it forever—select Remove Layer Mask from the Layer menu (or, even faster, drag the Layer Mask icon to the Trash icon). Photoshop gives you a last chance to apply the mask to the layer. Note that if you do apply the mask, the masked (hidden) portions of the layer are actually deleted.

One last way to get rid of a mask: all layer masks go away when you merge or flatten layers.

Displaying layer masks. The second tricky thing about layer masks is that when you create one, you can't see it, so editing the mask can seem difficult. The trick is to Option-Shift-click on the Layer Mask icon in the Layers palette (just so that you Photoshop 3 users don't think you're losing your mind: yes, this used to be Shift-click). This displays the mask on top of the layer, like any other channel would display.

If you don't like the color or opacity of the layer mask, you can Option-Shift-double-click on the icon to change the mask's color and opacity. Then, when you're ready to see the effects of your mask editing, Option-Shift-click on the icon again to "hide" it.

If you want to only see the layer mask (as its own grayscale channel), Option-click on its icon. This is most helpful when touching up areas of the layer mask (it's sometimes hard to see the details in the mask when there's a background visible).

Tip: When Masks Move. As we explained back in Chapter 2, *Essential Photoshop Tips and Tricks*, the best way to move an image that's floating on a layer is to use the Move tool. However, note that the layer mask is tied to its layer, so when you move the layer with the Move tool, the layer mask moves, too.

While this is usually what you'd want, you can stop this from happening by clicking on the Link icon that sits between the layer and layer mask previews in the Layers palette. When the Link icon is on, the layer and layer mask move together; when off, the layer and layer mask can be moved independently.

Layers as Masks

Layers not only have masks, but they can act as masks for other layers. The trick is to use "clipping groups." For instance, if you place a circle on a layer with a transparent background, then make a new layer and fill it entirely with some bizarre fractal design, the strange texture totally obliterates the circle. However, if you group the two layers together, the lower

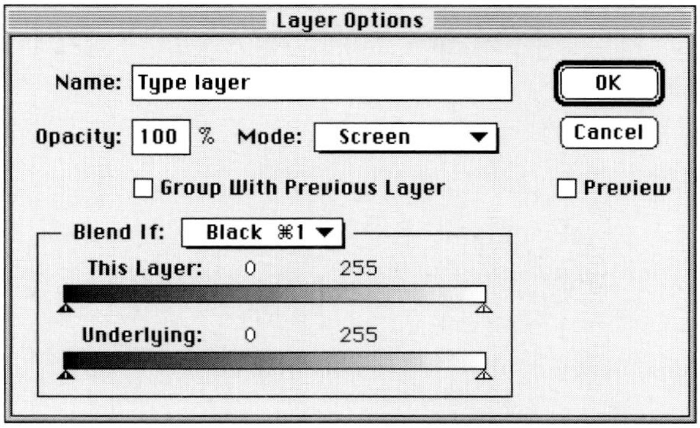

Figure 14-39

Layer Options
dialog box

Figure 14-39

Layer Options
dialog box

one acts as a mask for the higher one (so the fractal design only appears within the circle).

You can group layers together in one of three ways.

▶ You can turn on the Group with Previous Layer checkbox in the Layer Options dialog box (double-click on the layer tile in the Layers palette; see Figure 14-39).

▶ You can select Group with Previous Layer from the Layer menu (or, even faster, press Command-G).

▶ You can Option-click between their tiles in the Layers palette (yes, the layers have to be next to one another, in any of these cases).

You don't have to stop with grouping two layers. You can group together as many as you want, though the bottommost layer always acts as the mask for the entire group (see Figure 14-40).

By the way, the Photoshop manuals say that you can't use different layer modes for each layer in a clipping group. Not true. You can adjust the opacity or mode for each layer, and they act just as they normally would.

Paths

After we explored the differences between bitmapped graphics (made of pixels) and object-oriented graphics (made of lines, curves, and other objects) back in Chapter 3, *Image Essentials*, we pretty much ignored the latter—until now. Photoshop does offer limited support for object-

Figure 14-40
Layers as masks

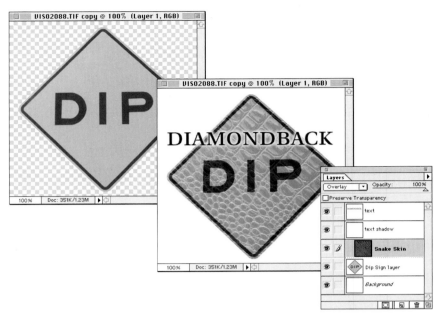

Layer 2 (the dip sign layer) is acting as a mask for Layer 3 (the snake skin texture). The text layers are not part of the mask group, so they appear unchanged.

oriented drawing, via the Pen tools and the Paths palette. Photoshop lets you do several things with paths.

▶ Draw, edit, delete, and save paths

▶ Copy and paste paths between Photoshop and Adobe Illustrator or Macromedia FreeHand

▶ Convert paths into selections

▶ Convert selections into paths

▶ Rasterize paths into pixels (stroking and filling)

▶ Save EPS images with a path applied as a clipping path

Curiously, the primary strength and weakness of Paths as a selection tool stem from the same attribute: paths have no connection to the pixels below them; they live on a separate mathematical plane in Photoshop, forever floating above those lowly bitmapped images.

The strength of this is that you can create, edit, and save paths without regard for the resolution of the image, or even for the image itself. You can create a path in the shape of a logo (or better yet, import the path from Illustrator or FreeHand) and drop it into any image. Then you can save it as a path in Photoshop, ask the program to rasterize the path (turn it into a bitmapped image) and drop it down into the pixel layers, or convert the path to a selection.

The weakness of paths' separateness is that paths used as selections can't capture the subtlety and nuance found in most bitmapped images. A path can't, for instance, have any partially selected pixels; you can only achieve hard-edged selections (see Figure 14-41).

While we occasionally use paths for selections, we more typically use them for clipping images that will be placed in other programs (read: PageMaker or QuarkXPress) for output. We discuss the use of clipping paths in some detail in Chapter 16, *Storing Images*.

Tip: The Space-Saving Paths Myth. There's a lot of folklore floating around in electronic imaging circles. One little piece of gossip is that you can save a lot of disk space if you convert your channels into paths before saving your document. Sorry, not true.

The myth's argument is that paths take up almost no space at all in a document (they're just tiny mathematical descriptions of lines and curves). However, what people miss is that Photoshop compresses simple alpha channels—ones that are mostly black and white—down to almost nothing, anyway. And any channel that you can successfully

Figure 14-41 Paths versus channels

The original image

Selection masks can partially select pixels.

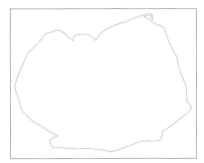

Paths are good at clean outlines, but they can't select image detail.

convert into a path (that is, without ruining essential elements of the channel) will most certainly have to be one of these simple types.

A simple channel may take up between 40 and 100 K in a 6 MB document, while a path may only take 1 or 2 K. But if you're worried about saving 100 K, you might reconsider working with Photoshop in the first place.

Creating and Editing Paths

In Photoshop, Paths (as its name suggests) lets you draw paths. If you've ever used Adobe Illustrator or Macromedia FreeHand, you're already familiar with drawing and editing paths. Photoshop's Paths interface is most similar to Adobe Illustrator's (no surprise there; see Figure 14-42).

As we noted earlier, paths are xenophobic creatures, and they don't like mixing with those weird, bitmappy pixels. Photoshop keeps them separate by floating paths above the pixels on their own layer. This layer doesn't appear in the Layers palette, though. Rather, it's only visible when the path is selected in the Paths palette (in Photoshop 3, the Paths palette had to be visible, too, but no longer).

Figure 14-42
Paths

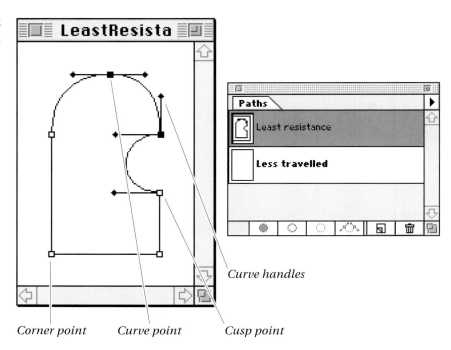

Curve handles

Corner point   *Curve point*   *Cusp point*

The Paths palette displays all the paths in your document, and gives you some control over what to do with them. To draw a path, however, you must select one of the Pen tools in the Tools palette. There are seven Pen tools (click on the Pen tool in the Tool palette to see the other six), but we only use two or three of them, using modifier keys to get to the rest.

Pen tool. The Pen tool (press P) is the only tool we ever select to draw paths. Without modifier keys, you can draw straight-line paths by clicking, or curved paths by clicking and dragging. You can also easily access any of the other tools. For instance, if you move this tool over a point on a line, it automatically changes to the "delete point" tool. If you move the Pen tool over a segment, it lets you add a point (click or click-and-drag).

Selection tool. The Selection tool (press A for "arrow," or hold down the Command key when any other Pen tool is active) lets you select a point or points on the path. As in Illustrator, if you hold down the Option key when you click on the path with this tool, all the points are selected (so, Command-Option works with the Pen tool).

Once a point or a path is selected (note that you can select points with the Selection tool by clicking on them or by dragging a marquee around them), the Selection tool lets you move them. As in most other programs, if you hold down the Shift key, Photoshop only lets you move the points in 90- or 45-degree angles. If you hold down the Option key when you click and drag, Photoshop moves a copy of the entire path.

Convert Point tool. When you're working with the Pen tool, you can create a sharp corner by clicking, or a rounded corner by dragging. When you have two round corners on either side of a corner point, that corner point is called a cusp point. But what if you change your mind and want to make a corner into a curve, or a curve into a cusp?

The Convert Point tool lets you add or remove curve handles (those levers that stick out from the sides of curve or cusp points). If you click once on a point that has curve handles, the curve handles disappear (they get sucked all the way into the point), and the point becomes a corner. If you click and drag with the Convert Point tool, you can pull those handles out of the point, making the corner a curve.

Similarly, you can make a cusp by clicking and dragging on one of the control handles on either side of the point. Note that if you have the Pen tool selected, you can get the Convert Point tool by holding down the Option key.

Tip: Use Cusp Points. Eric Reinfeld, live from New York, tells us that he makes all his points cusp points while he's drawing his paths. Here's how.

1. To create the first two points of the path, just click and drag them to set the angle of the first curve.

2. All subsequent points on the path are created by clicking, dragging to set the angle of the previous curve, and then Option-dragging from the point to set the "launch" angle of the next curve.

3. Finally, to close the path (if you want it closed), Option-click or Option-drag—depending on if you want the final segment to be a curve or a straight line—on the first point of the path.

While it takes some getting used to and takes a bit more work, this technique gives you much more control over the angle and curve of each segment in the path because each point is independent of the ones on either side.

Freeform Pen tool. David got into this business because he can't draw worth beans, but if you've got a a steady hand and a sure heart—and a graphics tablet wouldn't hurt either—you might find yourself wanting to draw paths with the Freeform Pen tool. When you let up on the mouse button, Photoshop converts your loose path to a smooth path full of corner, curve, and cusp points. (Exactly how closely Photoshop follows your lead is up to the Curve Fit setting in the Options palette.)

Note that, like the Lasso tool, you can draw a straight line with the Freeform Pen tool by holding down the Option key and lifting the mouse button. Then you can either click to "connect the dots" or release the Option key to return to freeform drawing.

Magnetic Pen tool. Once the engineers at Adobe figured out how to make the Magnetic Lasso tool, it was a snap for them to add the functionality to the Pen tool, too. Thus, the Magnetic Pen tool was born. The two tools work so similarly that it's hardly worth discussing twice; instead go read that section earlier in this chapter (if you haven't already). Also similar is a result that you will almost certainly have to finesse; these are not precision tools.

Tip: Multiple Path Segments in the Path. You don't have to limit yourself to one path per path tile (in the Paths palette). You can have two or more path "segments" in a single path tile. To some, this is obvious, but some people just never think of it.

Tip: Paths as Guides. Photoshop makes it easy to get guides on your image (see "Guides and Grids" in Chapter 15, *Essential Image Techniques*). But Photoshop only offers horizontal and vertical guides. If you want a diagonal or curved guideline, you can fake them using paths. Make a path using the Pen tools. When you're done making paths, save the path by giving it a name (double-click on the Working Path tile in the Paths palette, or Option-drag the Working Path tile onto the New Path icon).

When you want to hide the guide lines, click off the path's tile in the Paths palette or Shift-click on the tile.

Tip: Arrow Keys and Paths. If you have pixels and a path selected at the same time, using the arrow keys moves the path, not the selection. The arrow keys move the path one pixel at a time (one screen pixel). Or, if you hold down the Shift key, the arrow keys move the path ten image pixels (not screen pixels). At 100-percent view, image pixels and screen pixels are the same thing, of course.

Tip: Drag Segments, Too. When editing your paths, don't get too caught up with having to move the paths' points and the curve handles around. As in FreeHand and Illustrator) you can also drag the path segment itself. If it's a curved segment, Photoshop adjusts the curve handles on either side of it automatically. If there are no curve handles to adjust (if it's a straight-line segment), Photoshop actually moves the corner or cusp points on either side of the segment.

Tip: Connecting Paths. You've got two paths you want to connect? It's not as hard as you think.

1. Use the Path Selection tool to select one of the path's endpoints.

2. Switch to the Pen tool.

3. If you want that point to be a cusp, Option-drag out a handle.

4. Click and drag on the other path's endpoint. (Or alternatively, Option-drag to make it a cusp point.)

Tip: The Scissors Tool. Illustrator and FreeHand both have Scissors tools that let you cut a path in two. Photoshop does not. But there's always a workaround! Use the Add Point tool (or the Pen tool with the Control key held down) to add three points really close to each other where you want the break to be. Then select the middle point and delete it.

Tip: Flipping, Rotating, and Modifying Paths. For years, we've been frustrated that Adobe Systems, creators of PostScript and Illustrator, hadn't gotten around to putting basic path transformation tools into Photoshop. The only way to rotate or scale a path was to drag it into Illustrator, transform it, and then drag it back. Fortunately, Photoshop 5 now lets you transform paths without leaving the program: just select the path you want to edit in the Paths palette and choose Free Transform from the Edit menu (or press Command-T). Similarly, you can select from the many options in the Transform submenu (under the Edit menu).

You don't have to transform the entire path, either. If the path has several subpaths, you can select one of them (by Option-clicking on the subpath) before transforming. You an even select one or more points on the path; in this case, Photoshop only changes those points and the segments around them.

Tip: Paths Outside Image Boundaries. Paths are like floating selections in that they live on their own layer above the mundane world of pixels. They're also like floating selections in that you can drag them off the side of the image boundary and they don't get clipped.

Paths to Selections

Paths for paths' sake are pretty useless (except for clipping paths, and that tip earlier on using paths as guides). Rather, once you've got a path, you typically need to convert it into a selection or rasterize it into pixels. Let's look at converting to selections first. Photoshop makes this process easy for you: you can convert a path to a selection in one of four ways.

▶ Select Make Selection from the Paths palette's popout menu.

▶ Click on the Make Selection icon (see Figure 14-43).

Figure 14-43

Converting a path
to a selection

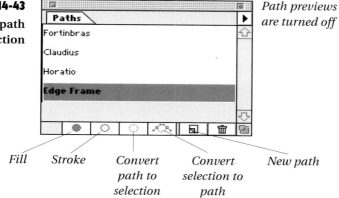

*Path previews
are turned off*

Fill   *Stroke*   *Convert
path to
selection*   *Convert
selection to
path*   *New path*

▶ Command-click on the path's tile in the Paths palette.

▶ Drag the path tile onto the Make Selection icon.

▶ Press Enter. (Enter does something different when you have a painting tool selected; see "Tip: Stroking on Enter," later in this chapter).

If you hold down the Option key while dragging a path on top of, or clicking on, the Make Selection icon, Photoshop displays the Make Selection dialog box (Figure 14-44).

Figure 14-44

Make Selection
dialog box

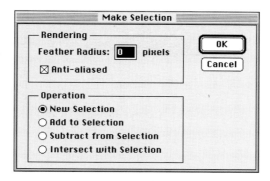

This dialog box lets you add, subtract, or intersect selections with selections you've already made (if there is no selection, these options are grayed out). It also lets you feather and anti-alias the selections. The default for selections (if you don't go in and change this dialog box) is to include anti-aliasing, but not feathering.

Tip: Avoiding the Make Selection Dialog Box. You know we avoid dialog boxes and menu items whenever we can get away with it. So it should be no surprise at all that we tend to avoid the Make Selection dialog box.

If you're using the Make Selection dialog box to add, subtract, or intersect paths, you can use these keystrokes instead.

▶ Shift-Enter adds the path's selection to the current selection.

▶ Option-Enter subtracts the selection.

▶ Shift-Option-Enter intersects the two selections.

Each of these works when clicking on the Make Selection icon or dragging the tile over the icon, too. It's just that the Enter key is so much easier. We still haven't found keystrokes for adding or removing feathering or anti-aliasing, though. (Caveat to this tip: as we explain below in "Rasterizing Paths," Enter does something different when you have a painting tool selected; in this case, you'd want to use the icons instead.)

Selections to Paths

To turn a selection into a path, choose Make Work Path from the popout menu in the Paths palette. When you ask Photoshop to do this, you're basically asking it to turn a soft-edged selection into a hard-edged one. Therefore, the program has to make some decisions about where the edges of the selection are.

Fortunately, the program gives you a choice about how hard it should work at this: the Tolerance field in the Make Work Path dialog box. The higher the value you enter, the shabbier the path's representation of the original selection. Values above 2 or 3 typically make nice abstract designs, but aren't very useful.

Tip: Making Paths with Icons. There's one more way to convert a selection into a new path: click on the Make Path icon in the Paths palette. Note that this uses whatever tolerance value you last specified in the Make Work Path dialog box unless you hold down the Option key while clicking on the icon, in which case it brings up the dialog box.

Rasterizing Paths

The second thing you can do with a path is rasterize it into pixels. As we said back in Chapter 3, *Image Essentials*, rasterizing is the process of turning an outline into pixels. Photoshop lets you rasterize paths in two ways: you can fill the path area and you can stroke the path.

Filling. To fill the path area with the foreground color, drag the path's tile to the Fill Path icon, or click on the Fill Path icon in the Paths palette. Or, better yet, Option-click the icon, and the Fill Path dialog box appears (this is the same dialog box you get if you choose Fill Path from the Paths palette's popout menu). The dialog box gives you options for fill color, opacity, mode and so on.

Stroking. Stroking the path works just the same as filling: you can drag the path tile to the Stroke Path icon, or simply click on the icon in the Paths palette (while a path is visible). When you do this, Photoshop strokes the path with the Pencil tool. That's pretty lame, so instead, change the tool it uses by Option-clicking on the Stroke Path icon (or select Stroke Path from the popout menu in the Paths palette).

Tip: Stroking on Enter. If you were paying attention, you noticed that we've said a few times that the Enter key sometimes does something other than converting paths to selections. When you have a painting tool selected in the Tool palette, pressing Enter strokes the path with that tool. We like using this because we almost always want a different painting tool than the one we wanted last time.

Tip: Working with Multiple Paths. As we said earlier, you can have more than one path within a path "layer." For instance, you can have three circular paths together, and save them all under one path name. If you want to stroke or fill just one of those three, select it with the Path Selection tool (Option-click on the path to select the entire path) before stroking or filling.

Tip: Rasterizing Paths Inside Selections. If you make a selection before filling or stroking your path, Photoshop only fills or strokes within that selection. This has tripped up more than one advanced user, but if you're aware of the feature, it can really come in handy.

Step-by-Step Silhouettes

Now that we've gone through all of Photoshop's tools for working with selections, channels, and masks, it's time to bring all those tools to bear. And the best place to demonstrate these tools in practice is in the process of creating silhouettes—that oh-so-common and (sometimes) oh-so-difficult of production techniques.

We'll start by showing how to create a simple silhouette, and work our way up to some of those images that seem like they're totally impossible.

The Spill's the Thing

If there's one thing that makes silhouettes difficult, it's the edge detail. In most cases (especially when you're trying to select fine details), some of the color from the image background spills over into the image you want. So when you drop the silhouetted image onto a different background (even white), the spill trips you up, making the image look artificial and out of place.

A Simple, Hard-Edged Silhouette

When the image you're trying to select has been photographed on a white background with good studio lighting so the background's free of colors that contaminate the edges, your selection is relatively easy. We typically jump in with several clicks of the Magic Wand along with Grow or Similar. We almost never get a perfect fit, however, so we usually clean up the edges in Quick Mask mode. In Figure 14-45 we use Gaussian Blur and Levels to choke the edges of the selection mask. That way, we can be sure no background color spills over in our final composited image.

Figure 14-45 Silhouetting a hard-edged element

The original image. Our goal: to select the object from its background.

The Magic Wand, Grow, and Similar get us most of the way there.

We switch to Quick Mask mode and lasso the areas that should not be included in the selection.

After fixing the edge detail (see below), we incorporate a new background into the image.

The original selection left some edge pixels unselected, causing edge spill.

We apply a small-radius Gaussian Blur to the quick mask, which appears to worsen the edge spill.

A radical Levels gamma shift on the mask darkens the edge pixels.

When the mask is partially transparent, the dark areas around the edge tell us that there will be no edge spill.

Pulling Selections from Channels

Trying to build a selection mask for the tree in Figure 14-46 with the basic selection tools would drive you to distraction faster than having to watch Barney reruns with your four-year-old. Instead, we found the essence of a great selection hiding in the color channels of the image. While you can often pull a selection mask from a single channel of the image, in this case we made duplicates of both the blue and green channels. Then, using Levels, we pushed the tree to black and the background to white. After combining the two channels, it only took a little touch-up to complete the mask.

Figure 14-46 Creating subtle masks from multiple channels

The original. Our goal: to select the tree and make it more green.

The blue channel has the best contrast between sky and tree.

The green channel has the best contrast between sky and grass.

We copy the blue channel and force the sky to white and the tree to black with the Levels dialog box.

A similar move on the green channel creates a mask for the lower part of the tree.

We delete the "garbage" areas from each mask with the Brush and Lasso. To edit the channels better, we make them and the color channels visible at the same time.

We use Calculate (Add) to merge the two channels into one, providing the final mask.

After loading the selection mask, we use curves to brighten and saturate the greens in the tree, and pull back the reds and blues slightly.

Removing Spill from Fine-Edged Selections

The finer the pixel selection, the harder it is to remove edge spill. It doesn't get much tougher than the detail in Figure 14-47, so we used a variation of a trick Greg Vander Houwen taught us: replacing the border pixels with pixels from the background. In this case, once we realized how bad the edge spill was in the composited image, we built a border mask for the dandelion with the Border command and cleaned it up in Quick Mask mode.

Finally, we chose the new background image's layer, and—using our border selection—copied pixels to a new layer using Command-J. Then, to get rid of dark green pixels at the edges, we placed the new layer above our foreground object and set the layer mode to Lighten. This doesn't touch the lighter pixels in the dandelion. In other images we might have used Normal, Darken, Hue, or Color; it depends on the relationship between the foreground and the background colors.

Figure 14-47 Removing edge spill in detailed areas by filling from a background

The original image. The goal: to composite the dandelion onto another background.

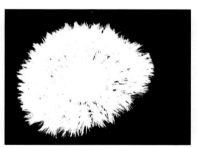

A selection mask created using Color Range with many sample points and a low Fuzziness level.

The edge spill is obvious. We select the transparency mask by Command-clicking on the foreground layer.

We use Border with a large radius, then feather the resulting selection.

We copy pixels from the background to a new layer and set it to Lighten.

The green fringe disappears, without sacrificing edge detail.

Removing Spill with Preserve Transparency

Edge spill is insidious, and—as we saw in the last example—can be a disaster when compositing images. Here's one more method of removing spill that we like a lot. If you place the pixels on a transparent layer, you can make use of the Preserve Transparency feature in the Layers palette to "paint away" the edge spill.

In the example in Figure 14-48, the color from the blue sky is much too noticeable around the composited trees. So we place the trees on a layer and build a selection that encompasses just their edges. This step is really just a convenience—it makes our job of painting out the edge spill easier. With Preserve Transparency turned on, we select the Rubber Stamp tool and clone interior colors over the blue edge pixels. In some areas, we also use Curves to pull the blue out (because our border selection is feathered, these moves affect only the pixels we're after).

This is a trick you can use with all sorts of variations. If the edge color is relatively flat, you might be able to use the Brush tool (we usually add a little noise after painting in order to match the background texture); this is also an area where it behooves you to test out different Apply modes (Lighten, Multiply, and so on).

Enhancing Edges with Filters

We're naturally wary when it comes to using Photoshop filters; while very powerful, they're almost always used to create funky effects. However, every now and again we see how we can use the same filters to increase our productivity and enhance our work life. Deke McClelland taught us about one such application: using filters to get better selections.

The two filters that we use most often for this sort of thing are the High Pass and the Find Edges filters (usually one or the other; not both at the same time). We typically duplicate the image we're working on, then use one or more filters on the copy to extract the selection we want.

Find Edges is a very blunt instrument when it comes to making selections, but it can often draw out edges that are very hard to see on screen.

The trick to using High Pass is to use very small values in the High Pass dialog box, usually under 1 or 2 pixels. Then, we use the Levels or Curves dialog box to enhance the edges in the mostly-gray image.

Figure 14-48 Painting out edge spill using layers, a border mask, and Preserve Transparency

The original image

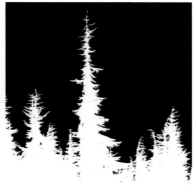

A mask created using Color Range

The trees are copied onto a layer above the sunset image. The blue spill ruins the compositing effect.

A closeup of the composited image shows the blue edge spill from the original sky.

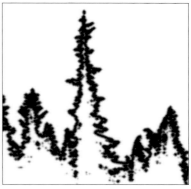

We create a border mask by using Border on the transparency mask, then running a Gaussian Blur.

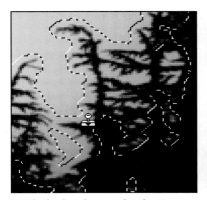

With the border mask selection loaded and Preserve Transparency turned on, we rubber stamp dark interior pixels over the blue pixels.

The final image after the blue edge spill has been removed

A closeup of the final image

Tip: Complex Masks with Plug-Ins. After working with Photoshop's selection tools for a while, you begin to know instinctively when you're up against a difficult task. For instance, trying to create a selection mask for a woman in a gauzy dress, with her long, wispy hair blowing in the wind, could be a nightmare. And if you have to perform twenty of these in a day . . . well . . . 'nuf said. It's time to plunk down some cash for one of the several masking programs on the market. For instance, MaskPro from Extensis, KnockOut from Ultimatte, or MagicMask from Chroma.

We're not saying that these plug-ins are perfect. In fact, far from it. But they can often get you 90 percent of the way to a great selection in 10 percent of the time it would take you with Photoshop's own tools. From there, you'll still have to tweak using the various methods throughout this chapter.

Enhancing Edges with Adjustment Layers

Adjustment Layers are almost always used for tonal or color adjustments (we talk about Adjustment Layers in quite some detail in Chapter 8, *The Digital Darkroom*). But here's a method that Greg Vander Houwen showed us that uses Adjustment Layers to help make selections. This is particularly useful when you're trying to select a foreground image out of a background, and the two are too similar in color (see Figure 14-49).

First, add an Adjustment Layer above the image (Command-click on the New Layer icon in the Layers palette). The type of Adjustment Layer depends on what you're trying to achieve. You can make a radical adjustment in this layer, knowing that you're not actually hurting your original image data. Use the Adjustment Layer to boost the contrast between the foreground and background, so that you can make a better selection.

Masks, Channels, and Life

While you can get by with performing global manipulations on images, the vast majority of images you'll work with require making a selection. We hope that after seventy pages we've done more to allay your fears than to cause you panic when selecting pixels in your image. Remember the two golden rules of selections:

Figure 14-49 Using adjustment layers to emphasize elements and build masks

The original image

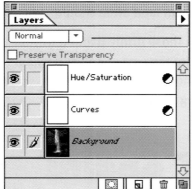

We added two adjustment layers: a Curves layer that drastically increased the image contrast, and a Hue/Saturation layer that desaturated the image slightly.

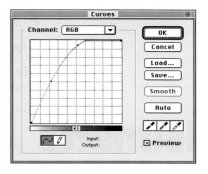

The Curves dialog box of the Curves adjustment layer. Note that the shadows have been completely blown out to black. The curve has also been tweaked on the red, blue, and green channels.

After these extreme adjustment layers are applied, the image looks almost unrecognizable.

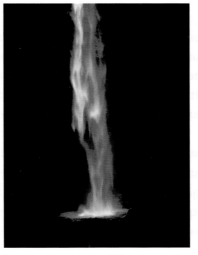

We duplicate one of the channels of this "extreme" image and clean it up for our water mask. Now we can throw away the adjustment layers (they've done their job).

Finally, we load our new mask into the layer mask of a new, more subtle Hue/Saturation adjustment layer. This way, the effect only affects the water.

in your image. People often zoom in closer than this, thinking "the closer the better." Not so. Sure, you can see the pixels, but you're not really seeing the image (Zen koan or sage advice? You be the judge).

If you can't fit the image on your screen, start at the upper-left corner (press the Home key) and use the Page Down key to move down until you reach the bottom. Scroll once to the right (press Command-Page Down), and start over. We can't overstress the importance of this procedure.

If you like working zoomed in or out and can't be bothered with getting back to 100-percent view, check out "Tip: Use New Window" in Chapter 2, *Essential Photoshop Tips and Tricks*.

Build a base camp. Our friend and colleague Greg Vander Houwen (you've probably read about him elsewhere in this tome) turned us on to the mountaineering phrase "base camp." The concept is simple: while you're working on an image, don't just save every now and again; instead, create an environment that you can return to at any time. That means taking snapshots in the History palette or—better yet—using Save As and Save a Copy at strategic moments in your image manipulation. It also means saving your curves before applying them, and sometimes even writing down the various settings you use in dialog boxes (like Unsharp Mask).

When you've built a solid base camp, you can always return to it, get your bearings, and start up the hill again. As Greg noted, "I might build a few base camps along the way, depending on how high the mountain is."

The Color of Grayscale

Even though many more people are printing in color these days, most people are not. Therefore, one of the most common procedures in Photoshop is converting color images into grayscale. If you convert images by selecting Grayscale from the Mode menu, there's a good chance you're not getting the best-quality image you can. Most color images contain a usable grayscale version, but you often have to wrestle to find it. Getting a good grayscale out of a CMYK image is particularly challenging, but even with RGB images it isn't always easy.

Let's first take a look at three relatively obvious ways to get grayscale information out of a color file.

Tip: Scan in Color. Almost every scanner on the market these days is built to scan color images. If your original image is a color picture, you'll often get a better final result by scanning it in color and then converting it to grayscale in Photoshop using one of the techniques below—it's like using color filters when you shoot black-and-white film . If you're scanning a grayscale picture, you may also get a better result scanning in color; it depends on how neutral gray the image really is. For instance, we're more likely than not to scan an ancient yellowed black-and-white photograph as an RGB color image.

Convert to Grayscale. The most obvious way to convert an image to grayscale is simply to choose Grayscale from the Mode submenu (under the Image menu). When you do so, Photoshop mixes the red, green, and blue channels together, weighting the red, green, and blue channels differently (according to a standard formula that purports to account for the varying sensitivity of the eye to different colors). It works (more or less) at least on some images, but the results are often far from ideal.

For instance, there are many images in which this weighting loses more information than it keeps. Remember, detail is in the differences between pixels, and if the gray pixels are too similar, you can lose important information.

Take a channel, any channel. Look at the individual color channels in the image. Occasionally you'll find the perfect grayscale image sitting in one of them. Then you can copy and paste it out, or use Calculations to pull it into a new document (see "Tip: Saving Off Channels Using Calculate" in Chapter 14, *Selections*). Or just delete the other two channels by displaying the channel you want, then selecting Grayscale from the Mode menu.

Desaturate. You can select Desaturate from the Adjust submenu (under the Image menu, or press Command-Shift-U). This is the same as reducing the Saturation setting in the Hue/Saturation dialog box to zero—it literally pulls the color out of each pixel in the document. The image is still in RGB, but if you then convert it to grayscale you'll get a very different result than if you'd simply converted it to grayscale without desaturating first.

Convert to Lab. For a more literal rendering of the luminance values in an image, you can convert the image to Lab, then discard the color channels (A and B). This gives you yet another different rendering.

Devious methods. Sometimes none of the above methods provide the grayscale image you want. Photoshop offers some more devious alternatives. In the past you had to use the dreaded Calculations dialog box to custom mix channels; we still use Calculations sometimes, because it lets you do things you can't do any other way, but Photoshop 5's Channel Mixer feature offers an easier method of doing simple blending of channels, so we often turn to it first.

The Channel Mixer dialog box is more utilitarian than you'd hope from a program like Photoshop (see Figure 15-1), but it lets you do one thing extremely well: mix together the color channels of your image. You mix channels by percentage, and the result is a single channel (you can choose which channel the result will end up on in the Output Channel popup menu).

Figure 15-1

Channel Mixer dialog box

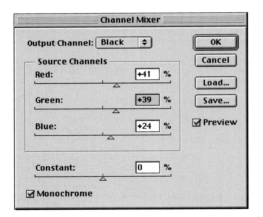

When converting an RGB image to grayscale remember two things. First, the percentages in the dialog box should always add up to 100 percent to maintain the same overall tone of the image (though there may be situations where you don't *want* to maintain the overall tone of the image). We wish there were a way to constrain the percentages in this way, but unfortunately, you have to just do the math in your head (or on a calculator, if it has come to that). Second, turn on the Monochrome checkbox; this ensures that the result will be neutral gray (in an RGB image, the result ends up on all three channels; in a CMYK image, the result is placed solely on the black channel).

(Note that the Channel Mixer works fine with CMYK images, but it's much harder to maintain the image's tone; we prefer working from an RGB image when building grayscale images with the Channel Mixer, even if it means converting from CMYK to RGB first.)

Calculating images. Like the Channel Mixer, selecting Calculations from the Image menu lets you mix and match new grayscale images from the existing channels, but with much more power and flexibility (see Figure 15-2). The options on the Blending submenu are the same as the ones in the Layers palette, and the Opacity field serves the same function as the Layers palette's Opacity slider. Calculations lets you combine channels in much more complex ways than the simple addition and subtraction offered by the Channel Mixer.

Figure 15-2

The Calculations dialog box

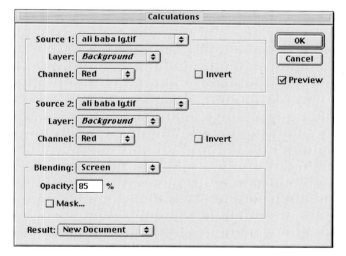

Tip: Use Preview in Calculations. At first glance, the Calculations dialog box seems a lot less interactive than the Layers palette. But it doesn't have to be that way. When you turn on the Preview checkbox, you can actually watch how the various combinations work in real time (or at least as fast as your machine can compute).

For instance, changing Opacity can be a real bear, but when you turn on Preview, you get to see the effect before pressing OK. Then you can

Figure 15-3 Finding the hidden grayscale

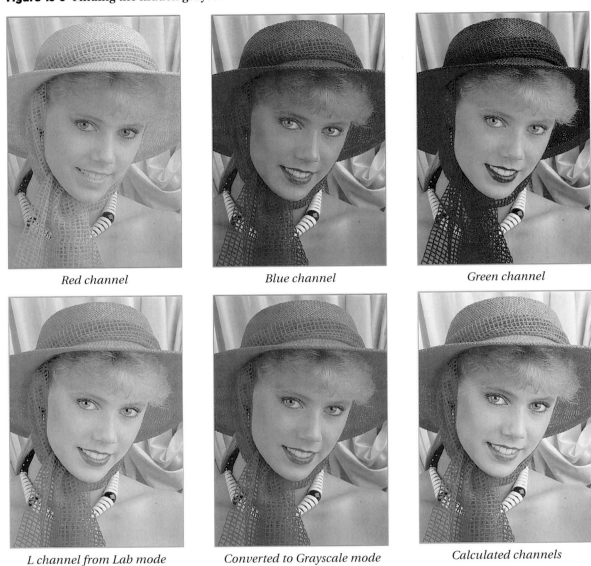

Red channel   *Blue channel*   *Green channel*

L channel from Lab mode   *Converted to Grayscale mode*   *Calculated channels*

type a new Opacity setting almost as quickly as you can move the slider in the Layers palette.

Figure 15-3 shows an image's individual color channels and the results obtained using conventional methods of producing grayscales. None of them really work.

We could proceed in any number of ways, but here's one that works well. We present it as an example rather than as the "correct" solution—you could achieve similar results using several different methods. Again, we encourage you to experiment.

1. We start out by screening the blue channel into itself at 70-percent opacity, creating a new channel 4. We choose the blue channel as our starting point because it has closest-to-normal contrast, other than being very dark. The lipstick and hat in the green channel are almost black, and the red channel just looks strange.

2. In a second calculation, we apply the red channel to channel 4, using Hard Light at 40-percent opacity, to create channel 5. This lightens up the midtones, and fixes the unsettling effect created by the eyes being much lighter than the skin.

3. At this point we have a decent image, but the contrast is still too harsh, and the hat and lipstick are still a little dark. We take the red channel (the one with the least contrast) and screen it into channel 5 at 30-percent opacity. Rather than creating a new channel, we select a new document as the destination.

We settle on 30-percent opacity as providing pleasing contrast, but anything in the 10-to-50-percent range gives a decent image. At settings higher than 50 percent the image is too flat, and at less than 10 percent it's too contrasty, but even fairly large changes in the opacity on this calculation have relatively subtle effects on the overall contrast.

The result is a creditable monochrome rendering of the color original. If the hidden grayscale is hard to find in your color image, experiment with Calculations. You may be surprised at what you can find.

Retouching

Every time we get into an argument (sorry, we mean "discussion") about the ethics of digital imaging, we find that everyone has their own tolerance level of what can or should be changed in an image. We've heard photographers argue convincingly that each time you manipulate an image, especially when you add or remove real objects, it erodes the credibility of photography as a representation of the real. But we also recognize that people have to make a living, and sometimes (for better or worse) that involves improving the purported reality the photograph represents. We don't have an answer to this debate, but we urge you to at least consider the question.

In this section, we want to relay a few key pointers that we've learned over the years about retouching images, in the hope that they'll make you more efficient in retouching to whatever degree is right for you.

Tip: Use Feathering. Often, the smallest thing can make the biggest difference. Feathering, for example (see Figure 15-4). When you're retouching a local, selected area—whether you're adjusting tone, painting, using a filter, or editing pixels—it's often important to feather the selection (see "Feathering and Anti-aliasing" in Chapter 14, *Selections*).

Figure 15-4 Feathering as a retouching tool

This trick only works when covering an element with an area of uniform color and texture.

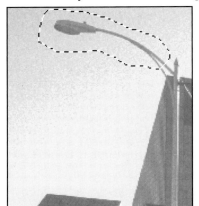 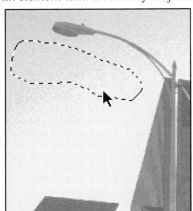 

Make a loose selection with the Lasso tool and feather 4 pixels.

Drag the selection to another location.

Command-Option-drag back to cover the original. The feathering ensures a seamless edge.

Feathering is like applying a Gaussian Blur to the edges of a selection: it blends the selected area smoothly into the rest of the image. How much to feather depends entirely upon the image and its resolution, but even a little feathering (two or three pixels) is much better than nothing.

Tip: A Myriad of Small Spots. Mildew, dust, corrosives, abrasive surfaces, or even a mediocre scanner can cause hundreds or thousands of tiny white or black spots in an image. And when it comes to sharpening, these spots can pop out at you like stars on the new moon. If you're like us, you're already cringing at the thought of rubber-stamping all those dots out.

However, photographer Stephen Johnson showed us a technique that can stamp out thousands of spots in a single move. It works best in flat areas without much texture or detail.

1. Select the area with the spots, and feather the selection.

2. Copy the selection to a new Layer (Command-J).

3. In the Layers palette, set the mode of the new layer to Darken (for white or light-gray spots) or Lighten (for black or dark-gray spots).

4. Use the Command key (to get the Move tool) along with the arrow keys to move the new layer left, right, up, or down by one or two pixels. The number of pixels you need to move the floating selection depends on how large the spots are. However, if you move too far, the duplication effect becomes more obvious than the spots, defeating the purpose.

5. If you want, you can press Command-E to merge the new layer back into the original. (We usually leave these as separate layers as long as we can, so we don't damage the original until it's necessary.)

You're effectively getting rid of thousands of spots at the same time. You still may have to use the Rubber Stamp to get rid of a few artifacts and some of the larger spots, but most of your work is already done. This technique works well on flat areas, but it often wipes out texture such as film grain, making the edit appear unnatural. For textured areas such as skies, we use a variant of the above technique (see Figure 15-5).

1. Select the area with the spots, and feather the selection.

2. Copy the selection to a new Layer (Command-J).

3. Use the Command and arrow keys to move the new layer left, right, up, or down by a few pixels—just enough that you see the dust spots move (if the spots are tiny, a one- or two-pixel move does the trick).

4. Open the Layer Options dialog box by double-clicking the new layer's tile in the Layers palette. Make sure the Preview checkbox is turned on.

Figure 15-5
Getting rid
of spots

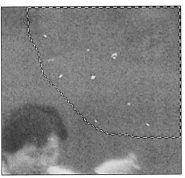

*Screen capture of a feathered
selection around some of
the white spots*

*Selection copied to new layer,
moved, and set to Darken: the
background texture is damaged*

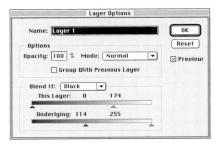

*The new layer is set to Normal, and
the blending controls are activated.*

The final despotted image

5. If you're trying to remove white spots, drag the right "This Layer" slider to the left to encompass the darker half of the spectrum. You should drag it just far enough so that the majority of the white spots disappear (if you drag it too far over, some spots will reappear).

6. Drag the left "Underlying" slider as far to the right as you can without the white spots reappearing. In most cases, this won't be very far, and the "Underlying" sliders will encompass a much wider range than the "This Layer" sliders.

7. Press OK. You can see a "before and after" by turning on and off the visibility of the new layer.

8. If you want, you can press Command-E to merge the new layer back into the original. (We often leave these as separate layers, so we don't damage the original image before we have to.)

At first, this variant seems like it takes much more work, but with experience, you'll find that you can make the right blending settings very quickly, and the dust spots just disappear.

Tip: Blurry Layer Blending. When you set the right "This Layer" slider (in the Layer Options dialog box) to 20-percent gray, you're telling Photoshop *not* to include any pixels in the layer that are lighter than 20-percent. The problem is that this is a very hard edge, so you get a jaggy composite. The solution: you can Option-click on each of the sliders to break it into two half-triangles. This provides a smooth blend between what is included and what is not. We almost never use Layer Options without blurring the transitions, even if only a little.

Tip: Tissue Overlay Channels. Greg Vander Houwen showed us one of the more innovative ways to use alpha channels: as a place to store his client's retouching notes (see Figure 15-6). If you scan your client's tissue overlay and add it to your image as an alpha channel, you can see the notes as you work.

When you want to see the client's notes, you can make that channel visible. When you want them hidden (you know what's best for your client, right?), just hide the channel by clicking on its eyeball in the Channels palette. Of course, you could also use layers for this, too.

Tip: Alignment via Opacity and Mode. If you've been using Photoshop for years, you've probably wondered what happened to floating selections,

Figure 15-6

Channels as
tissue overlays

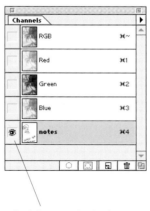

*Click here to hide the
tissue overlay.*

those hybrids between layers and selections. They're still there, but you don't run into them very often. One instance is when you make a selection, then hold down Command- or Command-Option while dragging it. The resulting pixels are moved or copied and—until you deselect—sit on a floating selection. The problem is that Photoshop 5 hides the Opacity and Mode controls for these floating selections: To change these, select Fade from the Filter menu before deselecting.

In general, however, we tend to prefer placing selected pixels on a separate layer for accurate positioning. You can do this by pressing Command-J (or choosing New Layer via Copy from the Layer menu). For example, a photographer on an online service recently wrote, "I was working on a group portrait of a family in which everyone's expressions were great except the teenage son's, whose eyes were closed. There was another shot in the same basic pose where he looked good, so of course I decided to replace the head in image A with the one from image B."

When doing this kind of massive image editing, it's often difficult to align the new image with the old.

One way to ensure their alignment is to change Opacity in the Layers palette to 50 percent or less, so you can see the image underneath. In this example, the photographer positioned the top head's eyes with the original image's eyes (using the arrow keys to nudge one pixel at a time; see Figure 15-7). Finally, he set Opacity back to 100 percent, and retouched the edges of the overlying layer.

Note that instead of changing the opacity, you can change the overlying layer's Apply mode. When trying to align two objects in an image, we often set the mode to Darken or Lighten. Then we watch the pixels lighten and darken, to give us clues.

Rubber Stamp

The Rubber Stamp tool (please don't ask us why it's called that; last time we used a rubber stamp was in KidPix) is the Swiss army knife of retouching tools. You can use the Rubber Stamp tool to copy pixels from any place in your image (or even another image) and then paint them someplace else: Option-click to pick up a source point, and then paint away elsewhere to copy those pixels. Remember that you can control the Opacity and the blend mode of the tool using the Option popup menu in

Figure 15-7 Aligning floating selections

The original image

When the new selection is dropped over the original image, it's hard to see where it should be placed.

Opacity set to 60 percent so that positioning is easier

The final image

the Rubber Stamp Options palette or with keystrokes (see Chapter 2, *Essential Photoshop Tips and Tricks*).

Tip: Retouch on a Layer. However you retouch your image—with the Rubber Stamp tool, painting, copying pixels from other portions of the image, and so on—try to do the work on a separate layer. When your edits are on a separate layer, it's easy to erase a change, and it's easy to see "before and after" views by turning the layer's visibility off and on. Remember that if you're using the Rubber Stamp tool when painting on a separate layer, you need to turn on the Use All Layers checkbox in the Options palette.

Tip: Unlimited Cloning Supply. Don't let the boundaries of your image's window restrict you. If you want to clone from another open document, go right ahead and do it. You don't even have to switch documents, as long as you have a large enough monitor.

Tip: Keep Jumping Around. The single biggest mistake people make when using the Rubber Stamp tool to clone from one area to another is dragging the mouse in a painting fashion. You should almost never paint when cloning. Instead, dab here and there with a number of clicks. Note that the behavior of the Rubber Stamp tool has changed: in previous versions of Photoshop, once a brush-stroke passed over an area you'd already cloned in the same stroke, the brush would pick up the cloned material rather than the original image, which resulted in an ugly "striping" effect. In Photoshop 5, the Rubber Stamp always clones from the original image, but it's still a good idea to use dabs rather than strokes.

A second mistake is continuing to clone from the same area. Keep changing the source point that you're cloning (the point on which you Option-click). For example, if you're erasing some specks of dust on someone's face, don't just clone from one side of the specks. Erase one speck from pixel information to the left; erase the second speck from the right, and so on. That way, you avoid creating repeating patterns, and make the retouch less obvious (see Figure 15-8).

There are times, of course, when both these pieces of advice should be chucked out the window. For example, if you're rebuilding a straight line by cloning another parallel line in the image, you'd be hard-pressed to clone it by any other method than painting in the whole line. The following tip provides a way to do so relatively painlessly.

Tip: Stroking Paths. If you're trying to get rid of long scratches in an image, or to clone out those power lines that are always much more noticeable in a photograph than they were in reality, you can use the Pen tool to define a path, then use the Rubber Stamp tool to stroke the path, obliterating the offending pixels in one swell foop.

1. Draw the path, keeping it as close to the center of the scratch (or powerline, or whatever) as possible, and save it (double-click on the Work Path in the Paths palette).

2. Select the Rubber Stamp tool, and set the Option to Clone (aligned); if you're removing a light-colored scratch, set the mode to Darken, and if you're removing a dark powerline, set the mode to Lighten.

3. Choose a soft-edged brush that's somewhat wider than the widest point of the scratch.

Figure 15-8

Cloning with
the Rubber Stamp

The original image

*Close-up of the original image.
Note the dark stain on the door.*

*Using the Rubber Stamp tool like
a paintbrush (making long
dragging movements) can cause
obvious repeated patterns.*

The final image after retouching

*Instead, use the Rubber Stamp
tool with lots of little clicks, often
picking up a new "origin" spot by
Option-clicking.*

4. Option-click beside the start of the path to set the source point for the cloning operation, just as you would if you were going to rubber-stamp the scratch by hand.

5. Turn off the path in the Paths palette pop-out menu (Shift-click on the path) to hide it, and then drag the path over the Stroke button at the bottom of the palette (see Figure 15-9).

Figure 15-9

Path retouching

The original image

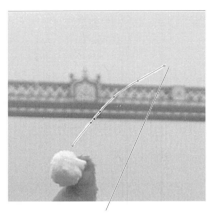

Draw the path, choose the Rubber Stamp tool, and click here to set the source point for the rubber stamp.

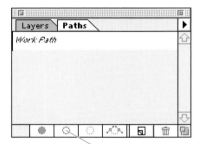

Drag the path tile over the stroke button to stroke it and produce the result at right.

Presto, the scratch is gone. The keys to making this technique work are careful selection of the brush size and source point. If the brush is too big (or small), or your source point isn't aligned correctly, you may wind up duplicating the scratch instead of removing it. However, with a little practice you can make this work very quickly and easily.

Dust and Scratches

The Dust and Scratches filter isn't all that useful for removing dust and scratches. It removes them, but it destroys so much detail and texture in the process that the cure is generally worse than the disease. We're still experimenting with it—we think of it as being a reverse Unsharp Mask filter, which should surely be useful for *something*. The best use we've found so far is removing halftone patterns when rescreening (see "Rescreens," later in this chapter).

One situation where it may prove useful is in blurring the A and B channels in Lab images to get rid of digital-camera artifacts or film grain (see "Sharpening Channels" in Chapter 9, *Sharpening*, for a discussion of this technique). The Dust and Scratches filter is slower than the Gaussian Blur filter, but the Threshold slider makes it more controllable.

Tip: Maintain the Texture. The danger with these retouching techniques is that they tend to destroy texture, and hence appear unnatural. You can sometimes simulate texture that's been lost by running the Add Noise filter on the affected area at a low setting. However, it's generally better to keep a close eye on what's happening to your texture as you retouch. (Also, see "Tip: Snapshot Patterns," below.)

Tip: Snapshot Patterns. Sometimes it's nice to be able to paint in a texture or a pattern with one of the brush tools. For instance, instead of adding noise to a selection, you might want to paint in noise selectively. It was Luanne Cohen who first showed us this step-by-step procedure for applying textures or patterns to an area.

1. Draw a selection surrounding the general area to which you want to apply the texture.

2. Fill the area with that pattern or texture by filling it, or applying a filter to the selection. (For instance, if you want to paint with noise, use the Add Noise filter here.)

3. Set the source state in the History palette to the most recent action (in this case, the filter or fill) by clicking to the left of it.

4. Move back to the previous state (either click on the previous state's tile in the History palette or press Command-Option-Z). This grays out the source state, but that's okay.

5. Now you can paint with the History Brush tool, adjusting brush size, opacity, and mode as you see fit. For instance, when painting textures, it's often helpful to paint in Multiply or Screen mode, adjusting Opacity as you wish (see Figure 15-10).

Figure 15-10 Painting with textures

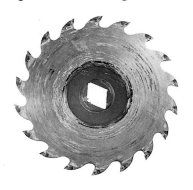

The original image

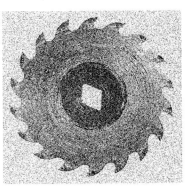

We set the source state in the History palette after running a filter.

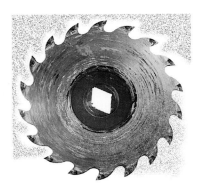

We move the current state back one state and paint with the History brush.

By the way, if you paste a pattern or texture into your file in Step 2, you need to merge the new pasted layer with the background layer before setting the source state. Then, you should step back two states in Step 4 (to a state before you pasted in the new pixels).

Also, note that as we go to press Photoshop 5 has a bug that might catch you unawares: After you set the source state and step back to a earlier state, Photoshop grays out the source state, right? At this point, Photoshop starts ignoring the Maximum History States setting in the History Options dialog box (see Chapter 2, *Essential Photoshop Tips and Tricks* for more on this option), and the states start really piling up. The answer: after you're done with painting from that source state, reset the source state to any other active state or snapshot.

Objects versus Pixels

Wasn't it Robert Frost who said, "Bitmaps are bitmaps, and objects are objects, and never the twain shall meet"? As we've seen with Photoshop's Paths features, they may not meet, but they certainly interact. In this section, we want to look at how you can convert images between pixels and objects (such as paths or Illustrator documents), and why you'd want to.

Open versus Place

We all know that clients are notorious for asking the impossible. They want Pantone colors in the middle of a process-color image (without paying for another ink). They want a tiny photograph blown up to poster size (retaining the sharpness, of course). Or they want their crisp, clean logos added to a product shot. Wait—that last one isn't so hard, after all.

In early versions of Photoshop, you could only open Adobe Illustrator EPS files in Photoshop. Now you can open *any* EPS file, no matter the program or the platform. This is a major step forward, and we're shocked that Adobe hasn't widely advertised this feature.

There are two ways to import EPS files: Open and Place.

Open. When you select an EPS file in the Open dialog box, Photoshop recognizes it as such and gives you additional options (see Figure 15-11). The additional options you get with an EPS file let you specify the resolution and size of the final bitmap image. When you press OK, Photoshop creates a new document and *rasterizes* the EPS (turns it into a bitmap). Any areas of the EPS that don't have a fill specified come in transparent.

Figure 15-11

Opening a
Generic EPS file

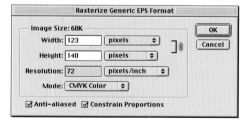

Tip: Forcing the EPS Point. If you can't see the EPS file in Photoshop's Open dialog box, it probably means that the file type, creator, or suffix is missing (depending on whether you're on a Macintosh or a PC). Your best bet is to try changing the file's name so that it ends in ".eps". If this still doesn't work, the file may have become corrupted, and Photoshop only lets you open the PICT or TIFF preview of the EPS file (usually only a 72-dpi representation of the image).

Tip: Opening Previews. You can, if you want, open the PICT or TIFF preview of an EPS file instead of rasterizing the EPS itself. This might come in handy, for instance, if you need a placeholder for the EPS, but the whole EPS file would be enormous and take too long to rasterize.

1. On the Macintosh, turn on the Show All Files checkbox in the Open dialog box. In Windows, select Open As from the File menu.

2. Select EPS PICT Preview (or EPS TIFF Preview) from the Format menu (on the PC, this is the Open As dialog box).

Now when you open the file, you only get the low-resolution preview.

Place. When you select Place rather than Open, Photoshop drops the EPS file into your current document and then lets you scale and rotate it to fit your needs (you can scale it by dragging a handle, rotate it by dragging outside the rectangle, and move it by dragging inside the rectangle). When you're finished scaling the image, press Return or Enter. Photoshop doesn't rasterize the image into pixels until you do this, so scaling won't degrade the final image. (Note that you can always press Command-period—Escape on Windows—to cancel the Place command.) Like Paste, Place almost always creates a new layer for your incoming image (it won't if you place an EPS on a spot color channel for instance).

Tip: Proportional Scaling. When you dragged one of the corner handles in a placed EPS image in version 3, Photoshop scaled it proportionally unless you held down the Command key. Now the default behavior is to scale it disproportionally unless you hold down the Shift key.

Tip: Colorizing Black and White Images. For some reason, David keeps finding himself in the position of opening a black-and-white EPS file (like a logo) in Photoshop and needing to colorize it. However, the Colorize feature in Hue/Saturation—the tool he'd usually use for this sort of thing—doesn't work because it doesn't colorize any pixels that are fully black, or white. Turns out there are many different ways to get around this, but our favorite is to remove the image from every color channel but one (for instance, in an RGB image, press Command-1 to get to the red channel, then select all and delete it; do the same thing to the green channel). Now you can switch back to the color composite (Command-~) and use Hue/Saturation to change the color and tone to whatever you want.

Tip: Maintaining Objects. What we'd really like is for Photoshop to let us open or place an EPS file, and give us paths instead of bitmaps. Unfortunately, we can't figure out how to do that. You can, however, *paste* or drag a path from Adobe Illustrator or Macromedia FreeHand into Photoshop (see "Paths" in Chapter 14, *Selections*). If you paste the path in, Photoshop asks if you want to rasterize the path into pixels or leave it as a path. If you drag objects across from FreeHand or Illustrator, Photoshop automatically rasterizes . . . unless you hold down the Command key, in which case you get paths instead.

If you're creating images for multimedia or the Web, check out "Tip: Maintaining Colors" in Chapter 18, *Multimedia and the Web*, for more information on moving objects from Illustrator to Photoshop.

Tip: Opening Non-Illustrator EPSes. Although Photoshop lets you import and rasterize any EPS file, sometimes it's helpful to use some other program to rasterize the images for you. For instance, you may want more control over how the image is opened than Photoshop allows you, or perhaps Photoshop won't rasterize an EPS file from some program properly (no one's perfect). In these cases, it's good to know about a few other programs on the market.

▶ **Epilogue**, from Total Integration, is a high-end Photoshop plug-in solution to your rasterizing needs (see Figure 15-12). It's expensive, but it's a true Adobe CPSI RIP, which means that it's really solid, as long as you have enough RAM and scratch drive space. Many professional color houses and service bureaus use Epilogue because it lets you import EPS images that have embedded OPI or DCS tags. It also lets you preview and crop EPS images before importing them, and gives you control over how much the image should be anti-aliased.

▶ **Transverter Pro**, from TechPool, is a utility that rasterizes PostScript images. It's relatively inexpensive, and it almost always works. Transverter Pro also has the added benefit of converting between a number of other formats. For instance, you can convert CorelDraw EPS files to Illustrator files, and so on.

▶ **GhostScript** is a freeware PostScript interpreter (you can find it on the Internet at www.ghostscript.com) that will rasterize just about any PostScript file. GhostScript is available for Macintosh, Windows, and

Figure 15-12
Epilogue

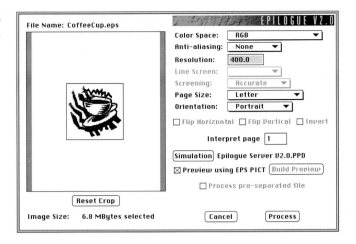

Unix, and it's very flexible. It's not the most intuitive program to use (you save a TIFF out by printing to a device called TIFF, for instance), but it's worth looking at.

Tip: Add Your Page Layout to Images. We suppose many advertising agencies are doing this now, but it was Kurt Karlenzig at an agency in Tokyo who showed us how effective it can be to use Photoshop to build photorealistic comps of ads. The client can see their ad in place—on a billboard or a bus, or wherever—before the ad is even created (see Figure 15-13).

You can create the ad in PageMaker or XPress, as usual, then save it as an EPS. Once you rasterize it and import it into Photoshop, you can rotate it, scale it, and so on, so that it fits the ad space (don't forget to add a little noise so that it looks more realistic in the photograph).

Drop Shadows

Is there any single image technique more ubiquitous than the drop shadow? Every catalog and ad seems to require at least one (and often many) of the little beasts. Because earlier versions of Photoshop offered no simple, built-in method for building drop shadows, everyone developed their own special techniques, some of which used dozens of steps to achieve the effect. Fortunately, Photoshop 5 has simplified the process

Figure 15-13 Adding your page layout to images

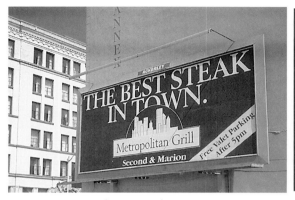

The original image

The ad created in QuarkXPress and saved as an EPS

The ad incorporated into the street scene, ready to show the client

significantly with the new Effects feature. (While David rejoiced upon seeing this new feature, Bruce, a latter-day John Henry, still does drop shadows the hard way, mostly because he refuses to admit that an automatic routine could do as good a job.)

Tip: Use a Plug-in for Drop Shadows. Even David agrees that Photoshop's Effects feature is not the end-all and be-all of drop shadow creation. For anything but the most basic drop shadow, you need to either create the effect yourself, spend time tweaking what Photoshop provides, or use a commercial plug-in. For instance, PhotoTools from Extensis lets you add noise automatically to shadows (see "Tip: Add Noise to Your Drop Shadows," later in this section) and even build multiple light sources. Andromeda Software's Shadow Filter lets you create incredibly complex shadows, even projecting them onto a different 3-D plane. EyeCandy from Alien Skin, too, offers some fascinating drop shadow effects.

Photoshop Effects

While we tend to shy away from anything resembling a special effect in Photoshop, the Drop Shadow effect in Photoshop 5 is so great from a productivity standpoint that we need to cover it, if only briefly. While Photoshop's other automatic effects are kind of fun (halo, inner shadow, and so on), we'll let those of you with spare time play with those yourselves.

There are several key reasons why you should use Photoshop's drop shadow effect rather than trying to build your own.

▶ You can apply a drop shadow to any layer by simply selecting Drop Shadow from the Effects submenu (under the Item menu) and changing the settings in the Drop Shadow dialog box (see Figure 15-14). Or, if you don't like menus, Control-click on the layer's tile in the Layers palette to bring up the context-sensitive menu (right-click on Windows) and choose Effects.

▶ Drop shadows transform along with their layer, so you can move or rotate a layer's pixels and the shadow follows along.

▶ You can edit an effect (change its color, blend mode, position, intensity, and so on) by double-clicking the little "f" symbol that appears in the Layers palette (see Figure 15-15).

▶ You can turn off the effect by Option-double-clicking on the "f" symbol. To turn it back on again, press Command-Z, or reselect Drop Shadow from the Effects submenu. You can also temporarily turn off all the effects in your image by choosing Hide All Effects from the Effects submenu (or from the context-sensitive menu you get when Control-clicking or right-clicking on the "f" symbol in the Layers palette).

But perhaps the best thing about automatic drop shadows is that once you get them looking just the way you want 'em, you can convert them into a regular layer by selecting Create Layers from the Effects submenu.

Figure 15-14
Automatic drop shadows

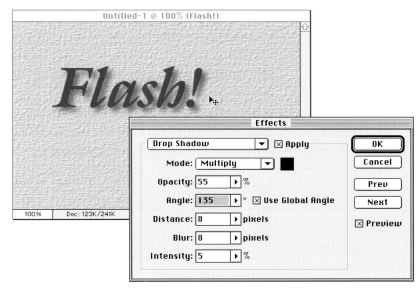

You can click and drag on the image to position the shadow.

Figure 15-15
Layer effects

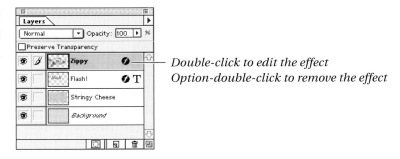

— *Double-click to edit the effect*
Option-double-click to remove the effect

Once they're a regular layer, you can tweak them to your heart's content using any of the pixel editing, transformation, and filter features in Photoshop. In the next section we'll explore why you might want to save these drop shadow layers out as their own files, too.

Tip: Consistent Drop Shadows. After years of hunting and gathering, the human eye and brain (for it's actually difficult to tell where one ends and the next begins) has developed into an astonishingly good pattern recognition device. In the midst of chaos, we can slowly see patterns emerging. More importantly, in the midst of pattern, we very quickly see anything that breaks the pattern, even by a hair. This, then, brings us to drop shadows.

Tip: Use Light Drop Shadows. Another common mistake people make when building drop shadows is making them too dark. It's easy to control this in the Drop Shadow dialog box; just change the Opacity setting. (A 30- or 40-percent shadow is usually sufficient.) When building drop shadows manually, or when tweaking shadows on their own layer, we typically use Levels to constrain the gray values in a drop shadow to under 30 percent. You can do this by setting the black Output Level to 180 (either drag the lower-left triangle, or type this value into the first Output field). Often, you can get by with even less; even an eight- or ten-percent drop shadow can appear quite dark enough.

Tip: Add Noise to Your Drop Shadows. A friend of ours kept claiming that Scitex drop shadows always printed better than Photoshop's, but he didn't know why. Finally, after comparing the two carefully, he realized the difference: Scitex drop shadows are slightly noisier, and therefore more lifelike. The solution: use the Add Noise filter with a low setting (between 2 and 10) on the shadow. Because you don't want to add noise to the rest of your image, make sure your shadow is on a transparent layer when you do this. (If you've already merged the shadow in with background, you can try selecting just the shadow area before adding noise.)

Troubles in Page-Layout Land

The trouble, then, isn't in creating a drop shadow so much as getting that drop shadow into (and back out of) a page-layout program such as PageMaker or QuarkXPress. If the drop shadow blends into the background of the image, there's no problem (the drop shadow is simply part of the image itself). But when the drop shadow must sit on top of a colored background or another graphic in PageMaker or XPress, or even on top of text, life gets . . . well . . . interesting.

The essential problem is giving the appearance of transparency, so that the background looks like it's showing through the drop shadow. Since color and grayscale images are opaque in PageMaker and XPress, you need to use some workarounds. Here are several methods we use, depending on the image, the background, the program, and the time of day.

Separate the shadow. If you're trying to print a black drop shadow over solid black text, and not over a background color or another image, you can add a grayscale drop shadow to your page separately from the original image (see Figure 15-17). Although the drop shadow appears to be over the text, it's really printing beneath it.

Figure 15-17
Separate shadows

The drop shadow is on the bottom level, then the text above it, then the image of the scissors on top (with a clipping path). This example is from XPress.

The final image

The image is brought in as an EPS with a clipping path. Of course, this tip is pretty limited, but the idea of separating the drop shadow from the image is the starting point for several techniques.

Tip: Lower Shadow Resolution. Remember how we said that the resolution of your images should always be at least 1.2 times your halftone screen frequency? Here's an exception: if you're creating a separate drop-shadow image, you can lower its resolution considerably (there's no detail in a drop shadow, so there's no detail to lose). We rarely use more than a 1:1 ratio (where resolution equals screen frequency), and sometimes we'll even go lower. For instance, a colleague of ours printed a catalog at 150 lpi, and every one of his drop shadows (there were a *lot*) was set to 120 ppi.

Overprinting grayscales. If your drop shadow is a separate file (as above), you can import the TIFF as a grayscale, and make sure it overprints whatever is beneath it. For instance, you can bring a grayscale drop shadow into QuarkXPress and set it to Overprint (in the Trap Information palette). Or in PageMaker, apply an overprinting black color to the shadow (define a new black, and turn on the Overprint checkbox in the Edit Color dialog box).

There are two problems with this method, however. First, it only works when there's no black in the color beneath it. If the background color is 30C 20M, the grayscale image will overprint fine. However, if the shadow is overprinting a colored background of 50C 30M 10K, the drop shadow image (the whole square) overprints the magenta and cyan, but *knocks out* the black. This happens because in PostScript, whatever tint is printed last wins (if a lighter shade is printed over a darker shade, the lighter one is printed). Of course, this means that if the drop shadow were set to print in cyan, then the background could have black . . . but no cyan.

The second problem is that these overprinting grayscale images don't look right on screen or in most color printer output. Nonetheless, this is a handy technique when printing over colors that don't contain any black.

(Note the corollary to this tip: You can put the grayscale image over the image in PageMaker or XPress and then set the "background color" to overprint. This works, but has the same two drawbacks as overprinting the grayscale image.)

By the way, let's say you import a TIFF into a picture box in QuarkXPress and set the background color of the box to some solid color. In XPress 3.x, this wouldn't work because XPress 3.x always knocks out the image from the background color of the picture box. In QuarkXPress 4, however, it works great; by default, XPress 4 overprints grayscale images over the box's background color. This makes life much simpler!

Bitmap shadows. One of the more clever methods of overprinting drop shadows on top of a colored background in a page-layout program is to make the drop shadow a separate, 1-bit, black-and-white bitmap file. This technique works no matter what color background you have, though some people find the effect less aesthetically pleasing than a regular halftone (see Color Plate 4 on page 679.)

1. Place or make your grayscale drop shadow in a separate document.

2. Select Bitmap from the Mode menu. You have several choices for converting the gray values into black and white (see Figure 15-18). We typically use Halftone Screen. However, if we know we're placing the drop shadow on top of another black screen, or on another screen which might conflict with this one, we use Diffusion Dither instead (so that the two overlapping screens don't create a moiré pattern).

Figure 15-18

Converting to bitmap

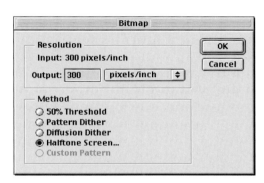

The value you enter for Output resolution is crucial. You need enough image resolution to get a decent range of grays for the drop shadow, given your screen frequency (see "The Rule of Sixteen" in Chapter 3, *Image Essentials*). And try to ensure that your image resolution is an integral divisor of output resolution (for 2,400-dpi output, for instance, use 300, 600, 800, or 1,200 ppi), to avoid ugly patterns.

If you're using the Diffusion Dither option, then you should set Output resolution to around 150 ppi (if your final output device is a desktop laser printer) or 300–800 ppi (for imagesetter output). The resolution choice here is dependent on how fine a dither the press can hold, but again, shoot for an integral divisor of output resolution.

3. Save the bitmap drop shadow as a TIFF. You can also save it as an EPS, with the Transparent Whites checkbox turned on in the EPS Options dialog box (see Figure 15-19)—but only if the background you're dropping it on is black and white. If you put one of these EPSes over color, the whites knock out, which ruins the whole trick. Also note that PageMaker has trouble with these transparent EPSes. We stick to TIFFs.

Figure 15-19

EPS Options
dialog box

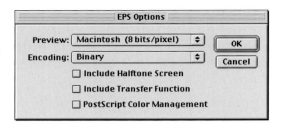

4. Bring the drop shadow into XPress or PageMaker and drop the real image (typically with a clipping path) on top of it. The preview image of the drop shadow you see on screen is often just a horrible black blob; but the image prints properly.

If you're in PageMaker and you're printing the drop shadow over a colored background, you must apply an overprinting color to the TIFF drop shadow. Otherwise, all those little black dots will knock out of the color beneath, with disastrous trapping problems. (XPress overprints these 1-bit TIFFs automatically.)

Note that you can generally get a smoother effect by using Isis Imaging's IceFields to convert the shadow to a 1-bit Bitmap image, rather than Photoshop's diffusion dither.

Incorporating background. The very best way to make a drop shadow integrate with a color, texture, or an image is to integrate it in Photoshop first. That way, you have full control over how the drop shadow blends into the background (we usually like using Multiply mode). Plus, you can easily color the drop shadow, so it's not just black (which often looks a little lifeless).

There are two potential problems with this technique.

▶ If your drop shadow hangs partially off a colored box, you face the problem of aligning the box edges in Photoshop and in the page-layout program. We can only suggest careful measurement and proofing.

▶ You have to be working in CMYK mode when you define the background color in Photoshop, so you're *sure* that the CMYK background values match those in the page-layout program. The colors probably won't *look* like they match on screen when you bring this incorporated image into PageMaker or XPress, because every program has its own way of displaying CMYK colors on your RGB screen. For instance, 30-percent cyan in Photoshop looks different from 30-percent cyan in XPress. But they'll print the same.

Drop Shadows of Text and Objects

The above techniques are all well and good if your drop shadow is of a Photoshop image. But what if you're trying to create a drop shadow of some text, or a shape in QuarkXPress or PageMaker? The key to bringing elements from XPress or PageMaker into Photoshop is first saving the page as EPS. Then you've got two choices for bringing the EPS into Photoshop.

▶ **RIP the EPS.** Remember, Photoshop can open any EPS file. If you want a drop shadow behind some text, place that text in a separate document and save this new document as an EPS file. Now, open that image in Photoshop. For a drop shadow, we recommend using Grayscale mode at 120 ppi. Make sure you don't change the size of the image in inches or picas, though!

▶ **Use the PICT resource.** The truth of the matter is that rasterizing an entire EPS in order to build a drop shadow is often major overkill. If it's going to take too long to rasterize, you can open the low-resolution PICT (Macintosh) or .tif (Windows) preview that PageMaker or XPress creates instead (see "Tip: Opening Previews" earlier in this chapter). Then you can build the drop shadow from that. Note that in Windows, only XPress can save an EPS with a preview suitable for opening.

The reason you can use the low-resolution preview for this is that you're blurring it so much that you'd never know the difference. Note that this only works reliably for grayscale drop shadows. You can do it with color, but you have to be mighty careful to avoid color shifts.

Once you've opened the text or object in Photoshop, you can quickly turn it into a drop shadow (see Figure 15-20).

1. Crop out everything but the text or object you want to create a drop shadow for.

Figure 15-20
Creating drop shadows
from PageMaker or
QuarkXPress

Shadowed Text & Objects ✳ ● ⧗

The EPS artwork from the page-layout application.

EPS artwork rasterized in Photoshop, blurred with Gaussian Blur and lightened with Levels

Shadowed Text & Objects ✳ ● ⧗

Final artwork back in the page-layout program

2. In the Image Size dialog box (under the Image menu), increase the resolution of the image to 120 (or whatever resolution you feel comfortable with; see "Tip: Lower Shadow Resolution," earlier in this chapter). Make sure the physical size of the image doesn't change (that means keeping the Dimensions popup menus set to Inches or Picas or anything but Pixels).

3. Use Levels, Brightness/Contrast, or Curves to make the entire image lighter (we often set the black point to about 30-percent gray).

4. Blur the entire image with the Gaussian Blur filter, and add noise (see "Tip: Add Noise to Your Drop Shadows," earlier in this chapter).

5. Save the file as a TIFF, and import it back into your page-layout application, offset slightly from the type.

Tip: Use an XTension. One more tip for XPress users. If you find yourself building your own shadows from QuarkXPress elements (like type, or boxes, or lines, or whatever) more than once a week, go buy an XTensions. There are several XTensions that are very good at making drop shadows, including ShadowCaster from a lowly apprentice production, and QX-Effects from Extensis. You can just select a text box (or anything else) and tell it to make a drop shadow. If the text partially (or fully) overlays a TIFF image, the XTensions are even able to "burn" the drop shadow into the underlying image. (This tip has nothing to do with Photoshop, but it might make your life much, much easier.)

Filters and Effects

Sure, you can paint and retouch and composite within Photoshop, but you know as well as we do that the most fun comes from playing with filters. But if you're like most people, you could make filter-fooling a lot more fun. Here are some methods we've found useful.

Tip: Float Before Filtering. Standard protocol leads people to make a selection, then choose a filter from one of the Filter submenus. We suggest adding one step to the process: copy the selection to a new layer first (Command-J). Doing so gives you much more flexibility in how the filter is applied. For instance, once the filter is applied on the new layer, you can move it, change its Apply mode, run an additional filter, soften the effect by lowering the layer's Opacity, and so on. Best of all, you don't actually damage your original pixels until you're sure you've got the effect just right. If you don't like what you've done, you can undo, or delete the entire layer.

Tip: Filter Keystrokes. Like many other features of Photoshop, working with filters can be sped up with a couple of little keyboard shortcuts. You can tell Photoshop to run a filter again by pressing Command-F. However, this doesn't let you change the dialog box settings. As Bill Niffenegger (the king of filters) says, "Never leave a filter alone . . . always change it!"

If you'd like to follow this advice, you'll need to press Command-Option-F; this reopens the dialog box of the last-run filter, so you can change the settings before applying it.

Tip: Fading Filter Effects. Photoshop 4 introduced a nifty new feature to the Filter menu, Fade, which allows you to reduce the opacity of a filter, or even change the Apply mode, immediately after running it (as soon as you do anything else—even make a selection—the Fade feature is no longer available). You can get to the Fade dialog box quickly by pressing Command-Shift-F (see Figure 15-21).

The Fade feature not only works with filters but also with any of the features in the Adjust submenu (under the Image menu). For example, you can run Hue/Saturation on an image, then reduce the intensity of the effect. We almost never use this, because we prefer to use Adjustment Layers, which are even more powerful (see Chapter 8, *The Digital Darkroom*).

Note that you can also run Fade on brush strokes you've made with the Brush tool (or any other painting tool). As with filters, if you perform any other action, the Fade feature stops working.

Tip: Filters on Neutral Layers. Instead of burning filter effects directly into an image, you can filter a neutral-colored layer. Using filters in conjunction with neutral layers gives you much more freedom to change your mind later.

When you select New Layer from the Layer menu or the Layers palette, Photoshop gives you the choice of filling that layer with the neutral color for the mode you choose for the layer. For instance, if you set the layer to Screen mode, Photoshop can fill the layer with black—screening with black has no effect on the image below, so it's "neutral."

Now, when you apply a filter to that layer, the parts that get changed are no longer "neutral." They change the appearance of the pixels below. Then you can run filters on this layer and they begin to affect the image below (see Figure 15-22).

There are some great benefits of working this way. First, you can always go back and change the filter—move it, re-create it with different settings, or even change the effect entirely with a different filter. Second, you don't have to actually apply the filter to the pixels below until you

Tip: Get Permissions First. This should be obvious, but all too often it is not: if the printed image isn't yours, you should always get permission to use it *before* you scan it in. Ethics aside, there are certainly copyright issues involved here. Most copyright violations in digital imaging occur when people scan in pictures from magazines or books without thinking.

Frequency Considerations

One of the first things to consider when working with rescreens is the screen frequency of the printed images. Our techniques vary, depending on whether we're working with low-, mid-, or high-frequency halftones.

Low-frequency halftones. Low-frequency images are both hard and easy. They can be easy because you can reproduce them as line art, as mentioned above. But they're frustrating because there's so little detail; scanning as grayscale is almost always futile. If the line-art techniques aren't working for you, however, you can try using the methods for medium-frequency images described in the next section.

Medium-frequency halftones. Capturing medium-frequency halftones—80 lpi to 120 lpi—is perhaps the hardest of all. These halftone spots are too small to re-create in line art, but they're too large and coarse to blend together as a grayscale without blurring the image unacceptably (see "High-frequency halftones," later in this chapter). You know a halftone falls into this category if you can see the halftone dots when the paper is six inches away from your face, but you can't see them (at least, not clearly) when the paper is two feet away.

There are five techniques that we commonly use when scanning midfrequency halftones (there are other techniques, but we usually find these ones effective). All five attempt to capture grayscale information and remove the moiré patterns that typically occur (see Figure 15-24).

▶ **Median, Despeckle, and Dust and Scratches.** The Median filter is probably the most effective method of removing dot patterning, but it comes at a cost. Median averages several pixels together to get a median value for the group. That means your image gets blurry

Figure 15-24 Rescreening mid-frequency halftones often causes moirés

A 400-ppi scan of the screened image, printed with a 75-lpi screen

After using the Despeckle, Median, and Unsharp Mask filters (75 lpi)

After downsampling (133 lpi)

quickly. Often you can retrieve some of the edges with Unsharp Mask, but sometimes you have to apply Median so much that the image is damaged. Nonetheless, even a one-pixel Median filter can smooth out many of the problem areas in an image.

If the resolution of the printed image is above 100 lpi, the Despeckle filter might work better than Median. We often try Despeckle first, and if it doesn't work well enough (or it damages the image in ways we don't like), we undo it and revert to Median.

Earlier in this chapter, we said that the Dust and Scratches filter must be good for something. Removing halftone moiré patterning is one area in which we've had some success. You get an effect similar to using Median, but you get a little more control over it.

▶ **Downsampling.** Downsampling using bicubic interpolation (see Chapter 3, *Image Essentials*) is one of the best ways we know to get rid of patterning, because Photoshop groups together a number of pixels and takes their average gray value. The problem, of course, is that you can also lose detail. Your goal is to downsample just enough to average out the halftone dot pattern, but not so much that you lose details in the image.

▶ **Upsampling.** After you downsample, you might need to upsample again to regain image resolution. You never get lost details back, of course, but sometimes sharpening the higher-resolution image can make it appear as though you did.

▶ **Rotating.** When you rotate an image in Photoshop, the program has to do some heavy-duty calculation work (see "Rotating," later in this chapter), and those calculations typically soften the image somewhat, breaking up the halftone pattern. If you have a very slight patterning effect after scanning a prehalftoned image, you might try rotating the entire image 10 or 20 degrees, and then rotate the same amount back again. This double rotation can average out some patterning.

Once you've managed to break up the halftone pattern, you'll need to go after the image with the Unsharp Mask filter to give the impression of sharpness for the detail that remains. Since the image will probably be fairly blurry, you'll have to make the more extreme sharpening moves that we suggest in Chapter 9, *Sharpening*, while being careful to avoid bringing the halftone pattern back out.

High-frequency halftones. Scanning pre-halftoned images with high screen frequencies—over 133 lpi—is often easier, because the dot patterns blur into gray levels while maintaining detail. You often need to use the techniques listed above, but you don't have to work as hard at salvaging the image. In fact, we often find that just scanning at the full optical resolution of the scanner and downsampling to the resolution you need (see Chapter 13, *Capturing Images*) is enough to get rid of patterning.

Tip: Pay Attention to 1:1. Remember that the most important magnification view in Photoshop is 1:1. If you scan an image and you see horrible moiré patterns at 1:3 view, don't panic. Zoom in to 1:1 view and see what's going on. The damage is often much less than you first thought. Even if you see no patterning at 1:1 view, you still may opt to do a little smoothing work (especially if you see patterning when zoomed in to 2:1 or 4:1), but it's not essential.

Rotating

We find ourselves rotating images all the time. Perhaps we didn't scan the image right; perhaps a piece of the image needs to be straightened out. Whatever the case, here are a few little tips that should make your rotating go a little more easily.

Tip: When to Rotate Images. If you don't know if or how much you'll rotate an image in PageMaker or XPress, go ahead and rotate it on pages first (see "Imaging from a Page-Layout Program" in Chapter 17, *Output Methods*). When you know the degree of rotation you're using and you want to save time printing, go back to Photoshop, rotate the image the same amount, save it as a new file (so your original unrotated version isn't marred), and import the new pre-rotated file onto your pages in place of the original image. It will print much faster.

Tip: Use Transform, not Arbitrary. Let's say you make a selection, then rotate it 15 degrees by selecting Numeric Transform from the Transform submenu (under the Layer menu). It's not rotated quite enough, so you use Numeric Transform again to rotate an additional five degrees. What you may not know is that each time you rotate this selection, Photoshop is interpolating and throwing away data, so your image slowly degrades. The more times you rotate, the worse the image gets.

Instead, if you're not absolutely sure how much you want to rotate the selection, choose Free Transform or Rotate instead. These let you rotate the selection as many times as you want—Photoshop gives you a preview each time—until you get it right. When it's perfect, you can press Enter or Return to finalize the rotation. Photoshop only performs the rotation math once, so the selection is degraded the minimum amount necessary.

If you have a clear frame of reference in the original—a horizon that needs to be straightened, or the edge of a building that should be vertical—you can measure the angle of rotation you need with the Measure tool.

Tip: Rotation Increments. If you're using Free Transform (Command-T) and you're having difficulty getting just the right angle (the angle appears in the Info palette), try pulling the cursor out away from the selection while you rotate. Now you have more leverage, so you can rotate in finer increments.

Also note that when you hold down the Shift key while rotating, Photoshop constrains the rotation to 15-degree increments.

Text and Bitmapped Images

Sure, a picture is worth a thousand words. But that doesn't mean we're going back to hieroglyphics. People often want to overlay text on top of pictures, then ask us, "Should we use the Type tool in Photoshop, or the features in our page-layout program?" The answer, almost always, is to use PageMaker or QuarkXPress. We say this for three reasons.

▶ Text that you create in Photoshop is always bitmapped. If you're working with a 225-ppi image, that means any text you add to that image in Photoshop is similarly 225 ppi. That's high enough for most images, but it looks crummy for hard-edged type. Sure, you can anti-alias the text in Photoshop; that looks great on screen, but it just looks fuzzy in final output (see Figure 15-25).

Figure 15-25

Text from Photoshop
versus PageMaker or
Quark XPress

Now is the winter of our discontent
Made glorious summer by this sun of York,
And all the clouds that loured upon our house
In the deep bosom of the ocean buried.

Text from Photoshop (250 ppi)

Now is the winter of our discontent
Made glorious summer by this sun of York,
And all the clouds that loured upon our house
In the deep bosom of the ocean buried.

Text from PageMaker

▶ The Type tool in Photoshop is pretty short on typographic flexibility. Even though you can now kern letter pairs and set character-level formatting, PageMaker and QuarkXPress are still superior typographic tools.

▶ Unless your text is on a separate type layer in Photoshop, there's no way to change a word once it's placed (absolutely inevitable if you've got a client looking over your shoulder).

On the other hand (we always try to be evenhanded), there are three reasons why you might want to create text directly in Photoshop.

▶ If your final output is to a color printer such as an ink-jet or dye-sub printer, anti-aliased type within the bitmapped image often looks better. The hard-edged type from a program such as XPress looks too jaggy off these low-resolution devices.

▶ If the text is integrated into your image, instead of being a separate element overlaying the image, there's a good chance that you'll have to create it in Photoshop.

▶ Finally, you'll probably have to create the text in Photoshop if the text is filtered, textured, or has an image within the letterforms (though see the next tip for a workaround).

Tip: Textured Text with Smooth Edges. As we said above, one of the main reasons you'd want to add type over your image in a separate program (like QuarkXPress or PageMaker) is that otherwise the type will look blurry or jaggy. But what if you want the text to be textured, or filled with some kind of cool bitmapped-image effect (like putting a weird blend into the letterforms)? The trick is to either crop or clip your Photoshop image into the proper shape.

For instance, you could save your bitmapped image from Photoshop as a TIFF or EPS and place it into Illustrator, FreeHand, or QuarkXPress 4 (make sure the image is slightly larger than the type will be). Now, create the type, convert it to outlines, and place the image so that it's clipped by these outlines. (In Illustrator, use the Mask feature; if you've got more than one character, don't forget to make them all a single compound path first. In FreeHand, use the Paste Inside feature. In QuarkXPress 4, just select Get Picture to import the image into the picture box you get after choosing Text to Box; see Figure 15-26.)

Note that if there's a lot of text, using the compound path as a clipping path may result in a PostScript error. The simpler, the better (and don't forget to increase flatness if you can).

Figure 15-26
Placing images
inside text

Here, the text is placed over the image in QuarkXPress 4.

The text is converted to outlines, and the background picture is duplicated using Step and Repeat with zero offsets.

The duplicate picture and the text outlines are selected. Choose Intersection from the Merge submenu (under the Item menu). Now you can edit the image within the text.

Tip: Smooth Textured Type in Photoshop. You can perform a workaround similar to the last tip, but export all your EPSes from Photoshop. Here's how we do it.

1. Create your text in Adobe Illustrator or Macromedia FreeHand, convert it to an outline, and copy it to the clipboard.

2. Paste the text into Photoshop; when the program asks you, tell it to paste it in as paths. (As an alternative, you can drag the paths from the illustration program to Photoshop while holding down the Command key.)

3. Position the path where you want it, and save it by giving it a name (double-click on the Working Path tile in the Paths palette).

4. Use Save a Copy from the File menu to save the file as a TIFF or EPS image (see "Clipping Paths" in Chapter 16, *Storing Images*, for more on file formats and clipping paths). From the Clipping Path popup menu, choose the text's path you saved in step 3.

You can now import this text into QuarkXPress or PageMaker and place it on top of the image (see Figure 15-27). Note that you don't *have* to create the text path in Illustrator. You could also create the text on your new layer in Photoshop, then immediately convert the text outline into a path in the Paths palette. However, the path is almost always rougher and of lesser quality than a true outline from Illustrator or FreeHand.

Figure 15-27

Textured type in Photoshop

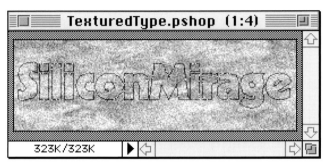

The text is created in Illustrator and pasted into Photoshop over the texture, then the whole image is saved as an EPS with a clipping path.

Actions

The trick to being really productive and efficient with computer technology is being lazy. Yes, it's a paradox, but it's true—the lazier you are, the more likely you are to find the really efficient ways of doing things so you can get out of work faster and go to the beach (or the mall, depending on your particular geographic options and avocational preferences). If you've got an overzealous work ethic, you probably don't mind repeating the same mind-numbing tasks four hundred times, but you won't be exploiting the power of the computer in front of you.

So, instead of performing the same task over and over again, why not automate the process? Photoshop's Actions palette lets you automate a number of tasks and can make your life a happier place to be. For example, Bruce works with a lot of digital cameras, and each digital camera's images need a particular kind of tweaking. Rotate the image 90 degrees, run this filter, use that Curves setting, resize the image to such-and-such . . . Instead of performing each task one at a time, he can run through them all with a keystroke. Even better, actions can batch process all the images in a folder so you don't even have to open them in Photoshop.

Note that there are also ways to automate Photoshop with Apple-Script, if you're on a Macintosh. We'll cover that at the end of this section.

Action limitations. But before you get too heady with your newfound actions power, you should know that Photoshop doesn't let you record everything you might want. While Photoshop 5 offers many new recording possibilities—like the ability to record blend modes, opacity, and even selections—you still cannot record paint strokes (like those made with the Brush, Airbrush, or Rubber Stamp tools), zooms, switching windows, and scrolls. And there are many features which aren't necessarily recordable, but you can force them into an action (see "Editing Actions," later in this chapter).

Also, note that actions that while you can use your old Photoshop 4 actions in version 5, those you create in Photoshop 5 cannot be used in the older version.

Keep in Mind

Besides the limits of what you can and cannot record in the Actions palette, there are a few more things to thing to keep in mind.

Difficulty. While recording and playing simple actions (those with only two or three steps) may be easy, trying to build complicated actions can be damaging to your head (and the wall you're banging it against).

Think it through. You should always think the action through completely *before* you start recording it. You might even write down each step on paper and then record it after you're pretty sure everything will work out the way you think.

Generic actions. Try to make your actions as generic as possible. That means they should be able to run on any image at any time. Or, barring that, provide the user with a message at the beginning of the action noting what kind of image is required (as well as other requirements, such as "needs text on a layer" or "must have something selected"). This is a good idea even if you're the only one using your actions, because (believe

we don't like the effect, we can revert back to this snapshot. Another option is to simply save your document first, and then use the Revert command (in the File menu) to undo the action.

Tip: Making Buttons. You can change the Actions palette into a palette full of buttons by choosing Button Mode in the palette's popout menu. When it's in button mode, you only have to click once on a button to run it. Switch out of button mode to create new actions or edit existing ones.

Sets. Photoshop 5 lets you create sets of actions, which will be a godsend to anyone who works with dozens of actions. Sets are pretty self-explanatory.

▶ You can create a new one by choosing New Set from the Action palette's popout menu (or by clicking the New Set button in the palette). You can delete a set by selecting it and choosing Delete from the same popout menu.

▶ You can move actions between sets by dragging them.

▶ You can rename a set by double-clicking on its tile in the Actions palette.

▶ You can show or hide the actions within a set by clicking on the triangle to the left of the set's name.

▶ You can also save sets (see "Saving Actions," below).

▶ You can play all the actions in a set (in order) by selecting the set and clicking the Play button.

Editing actions. Once you've built an action, you can edit it (in fact, you'll almost certainly want to edit it unless it worked perfectly the first time). If you want to record additional steps somewhere in the middle of the action (or at the end of the action), select a step in the action and press the Record button. When you're done recording actions, press the Stop button. All the new actions fall after the step you first selected.

If you want to add a step that cannot be recorded for some reason (perhaps it's an item in the View menu), you can select Insert Menu Item from the Action palette's popout menu. This lets you choose any one feature from the menus, and then inserts it into the action (after whatever step it currently selected). If the menu item is currently grayed out, you can select it by typing the first few characters of the name into the text field, and then clicking Find (see Figure 15-29).

Figure 15-29

Insert Menu Item

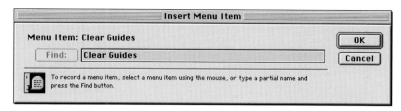

To change the parameters of a step, double-click on it in the Actions palette. For example, if a step applies a curve to the image (using the Curves dialog box), but you want to change the curve, double-click on the step and choose a different curve. Note that when you do this, you may actually change the current image; just press Command-Z to undo the change (this undoes the change to the image, not the change to the action).

Annoyingly, some steps cannot be re-recorded. For instance, a step that sets the foreground color to red should be able to change so that it changes it to blue . . . but you can't. Instead, you have to record a new step, then delete the original.

If you want to change the action's name, tile or button color, or keyboard shortcut, just double-click on the action's name.

Tip: Duplicating Actions. Option-dragging a step within an action duplicates it. For instance, if you want to use the same Numeric Transform step in two scripts you can Option-drag that step from one action into the proper place in the second action.

Tip: Stop Where You Are. Normally, Photoshop won't display any of the usual dialog boxes when you run an action. For instance, if you include a Numeric Transform step in an action, Photoshop will just perform the transform without displaying the dialog box. However, you can force Photoshop to display the dialog box, stop, and wait for the user to input different settings before continuing. To do this, click once in the second column of the Actions palette, next to the step. A black icon indicating a dialog box appears next to the step, and a red icon appears next to the action's name.

Don't click on a red dialog box icon! If you do, it turns black *and* Photoshop adds a black "stop here" icon next to every step in the action that can have one. There's no Undo here, so the only way to reset the little black icons is to turn them on or off one at a time.

Note that if you insert a step using the Insert Menu Item command, Photoshop always opens the appropriate dialog box and doesn't even offer you the chance to turn this icon on or off. (This is because steps inserted in this way are meant to simulate the user actually selecting the item.)

Tip: Talk to Your Users. You can insert a command at any point in your action that stops the action and displays a dialog box with a message in it. This message might be a warning like "Make sure you have saved your image first," or instructions such as "You should have a selection made on a layer above the Background." To add a message, select Insert Stop from the Actions palette's popout menu. Photoshop asks you what message you want to appear and whether or the message dialog box should allow people to continue with the action (see Figure 15-30).

Figure 15-30
Adding a message

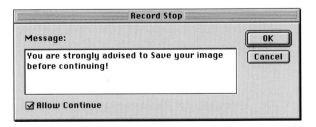

If the message is a warning, you should turn on the Allow Continue option, but if the message consists of instructions, you may want to leave this checkbox off. When Allow Continue is turned off, Photoshop stops the action entirely. After the user presses the OK button in the message dialog box, Photoshop automatically selects the next step in the Actions palette, so the user can continue running the action by pressing the Run button again (this works even if the Actions palette is in Button mode).

Saving actions. After you've created the world's most amazing action, you may want to share it with someone else. You can get actions out of your Actions palette and on to your hard drive by selecting Save Actions from the Actions palette's popout menu. Unfortunately, you cannot save a single action; the Save Actions feature only saves sets of actions. Fortunately, the workaround isn't too painful.

1. Create a new set (click on the New Set button at the bottom of the Actions palette), and name it something logical.

2. Either move or duplicate the action you want to save by dragging it or Option-dragging it into the new set.

3. Select the new set and choose Save Actions from the palette's popout menu.

4. If you want, delete the set you just created.

Of course, you can load sets of actions in just as easily with the Load Actions or Replace Actions features in the palette's popout menu. Watch out for Replace Actions and its cousin Clear Actions; these replace or clear *all* the actions in the palette; not just the selected one.

Tip: Curves and Adjustments. We love the fact that Photoshop can record the exact settings of the Curves, Levels, and Hue/Saturation dialog boxes. Nonetheless, you should note that if you record loading a Curves file from disk (or a Levels or Hue/Saturation file or any other adjustment), Photoshop records the name of the file rather than the curve itself.

The workaround: record loading the setting in the Curves dialog box (or whatever), then change the settings just a tiny bit before pressing OK. As long as there is a difference, Photoshop records the settings in the dialog box rather than the file's name. Remember that you can always go back and change the settings back to the way you want them.

Troubleshooting Actions

Sometime, somewhere, something will go wrong when you're building actions. That's where troubleshooting comes in. When troubleshooting (or debugging, as it's often called), the most important thing to keep in mind is that there *must* be a logical solution to the problem. (Of course, this isn't always true, but it's good to keep a positive attitude.)

Dummy files. The first thing you should do after building an action is *not* test it on some mission-critical image. Rather, try it on a dummy image. Even better, try it on several dummy images, each in a different mode (RGB, CMYK, Grayscale, Indexed Color), some with layers, some without, some with selections made, others without, and so on. If it doesn't perform correctly on any of these, you can decide whether to work at making it work or to add a message at the beginning of the action that says "don't try it on such-and-such-type of images" (see "Tip: Talk to Your Users," earlier in this section).

Step-by-step. You can force Photoshop to pause between each step and redraw the screen by selecting Step-By-Step in the Playback Options dialog box (you can choose this from the popout menu in the Actions dialog box). This is often useful, but the best troubleshooting technique in the Actions palette (in fact, probably the only troubleshooting technique) is to select the first item in the action and press the Run button while holding down the Command key. This plays just this first step. Now go check out all the relevant palettes. Is the channels palette the way you expect it? What about the Layers palette? What are the foreground and background colors?

When you're convinced that all is well, press Command-Run again to check the second step in the action. And so on, and so on . . .

If at any time you find the palettes or colors set up improperly, now is the time to replace the last step or double-click on it to change its settings. If something is really messed up, then don't forget the Revert feature.

Tip: Batching Files. If you've gone through the trouble to make an action, you probably want to apply it to a bunch of different files. You can automate an action by selecting Batch from the Automate submenu under the File menu (note that this used to be in the Actions palette in Photoshop 4). The Batch dialog box is pretty utilitarian; you need to step through it carefully or a whole lot of images could be messed up (see Figure 15-31).

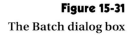

Figure 15-31

The Batch dialog box

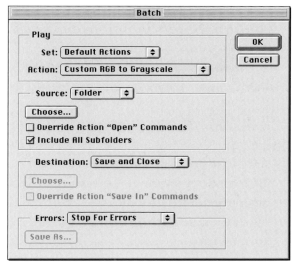

- ▶ **Play.** Choose which action in which set you want to run.

- ▶ **Source.** If your files are on disk, set this to Folder (and then choose a folder). If, for some reason, your action includes an Action command, you need to decide whether or not to override it (in general, you would want to). If the files are coming from a device such as a digital camera (via an Import filter,) then choose Import.

- ▶ **Destination.** There are three settings in the Destination popup menu: None, Save and Close, and Folder. None simply leaves the files open after processing them (not very helpful, and takes up too much RAM). Save and Close saves over the original files (we never use this). Folder lets you choose where the final images will be saved (this is just right).

It's really important to test this on a small number of images before attempting a larger batch process. For instance, if the action has added layers or channels, Photoshop may have to save the file in a different format, forcing the Save As dialog box to appear and stopping the batch process short. It'd be good to know this sooner rather than later.

Tip: Batching Multiple Folders. If you've got several folders worth of images that you need to process, you can speed up your work by creating aliases (on the Mac) or shortcuts (on Windows) for each image folder, and then placing them into one folder. Finally, in the Batch dialog box,

turn on the Include All Subfolders checkbox. Photoshop sees the   ʲaʳ
as subfolders, and acts on all the images.

Tip: AppleScript and Photoshop. If Actions has gotten you all
about automating Photoshop and you use a Macintosh, you shou
nitely check out what you can do with Photoshop and Apple   ⸬
AppleScript is a way for one application (or your system) to talk
other application behind the scenes. For instance, in System 8.5, ᵧ   ᵼca
attach a script to a folder so that as soon as you drop an image i
folder, your system launches Photoshop, performs several actions on it,
saves the file, and then closes it again; it's all handled automatically. (You
can run AppleScripts in operating systems earlier than 8.5, too; it's just
the folder actions that are new in that version.)

The problem is that Photoshop is not fully scriptable by itself. In fact,
the only AppleScript command that Photoshop really knows about is
DoScript, which runs a pre-built action. Nonetheless, this can still be
very powerful. For instance, David has long been frustrated that he can
only use function keys to trigger actions, so now he assigns his own keystrokes using CE Software's QuicKeys: The QuicKey runs an AppleScript,
which runs an action.

If you need more automation than Actions allows, check out Main
Event Software's PhotoScript, which actually adds the ability to write
scripts that directly control and query Photoshop. For example, if you use
QuarkXPress (which is also scriptable), you could write a script that
would automatically "see" how you've rotated, sized, and cropped images within your XPress picture boxes. It could then open the images in
Photoshop, perform those manipulations on the original images, resave
them, and then re-import them into XPress. Powerful stuff!

New Techniques

Even though Photoshop is an amazing tool, it still won't do everything for
you. Creating drop shadows, silhouettes, special edges, or text in
Photoshop can be a chore. But we hope that with these new methods,
your work will fly faster and you'll be able to focus on more fun stuff.

16

Storing Images

Managing Files for Fast Production

We've been barking at you for a few hundred pages that what we're really talking about is not images, but rather zeros and ones. But the zeros and ones that one program writes to disk may not be readable by another program. Why? Because the same data can be written to disk in a variety of ways, called *file formats*. Different file formats may be as different as two different languages (like Spanish versus Chinese), or as similar as two dialects of the same language (like American versus British English).

The world would be a simpler place if everyone (and all software) spoke the same language, but that's not going to happen. Fortunately, programs such as Photoshop, QuarkXPress, and PageMaker can read and sometimes even write in multiple file formats. The important thing, then, is not for us to understand exactly what makes one different from the others, but rather what each file format's strengths and weaknesses are, so that we can use them intelligently. (Wouldn't it be great if we could speak in French to our lovers, German to our bosses, and oh-so-polite Japanese to our acquaintances?)

In this chapter, we're taking an in-depth look at each of the many file formats that Photoshop understands. (Note that we won't cover Photo CD here, because Photoshop can't write Photo CD files—it can only read them; they're discussed in Chapter 13, *Capturing Images.*) More to the point, we'll explore why you'd want to use some of them and avoid others. One of the key issues in storing images is saving disk space, so we also discuss how various file formats handle compression internally. At the end of the chapter we explore the nitty-gritty of compression in file formats: how it works, what it does to your files, and how it's different from archival compression methods.

Tip: Hide Formats You Don't Use. Photoshop itself actually only knows how to read and write about half of the file formats we're discussing in this chapter. But it can read and write the other types because of plug-ins that came with the program. For instance, when the CompuServe GIF and FilmStrip plug-ins are in Photoshop's Plug-ins folder, Photoshop can read and write in these "languages."

However, if you don't use these formats, you don't have to leave them cluttering up your Save As popup menu. Instead, you can move any formats that you don't want out of the File Formats folder (inside the Plug-ins folder in the Photoshop folder) into another folder (outside the Plug-ins folder). Don't just hide them inside another nested folder; Photoshop can still find them there.

In this section, we'll focus on each file format that appears in the Save As dialog box's popup menu. Before we get to that, however, we'll cover one feature that applies to every file format in Photoshop: previews.

Preview Options

When you use Save As or Save a Copy with Photoshop's default preferences, Photoshop also creates two miniature preview images within your file: Icon and Thumbnail (in Windows, you just get the Thumbnail). You can control this behavior, and—on the Macintosh—add a third type of preview, by turning on the Ask When Saving checkbox in the Saving Files Preferences dialog box (select Saving Files from the Preferences submenu under the File menu. From then on, you get a choice in the Save As dialog box—in Windows, you get a Save Thumbnail checkbox; on the Mac, you get three checkboxes, one each for saving an Icon, a Thumbnail, and a Full Size preview (see Figure 16-1). Here's a rundown of what the different previews are.

Figure 16-1
Preview options

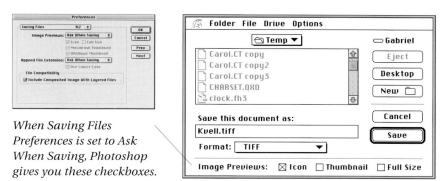

When Saving Files
Preferences is set to Ask
When Saving, Photoshop
gives you these checkboxes.

Icon. The first preview, Icon, acts as a desktop picture, so you can see (with a little imagination) what the image is when you're staring at the file on your Macintosh desktop (see Figure 16-2). For the technoids in the audience: it adds an 8-bit, 32-by-32-pixel icl8 resource (that's geekspeak for a color icon) to the file.

The only way to get an icon in Windows is to save the file in Photoshop format with the Save Thumbnails checkbox turned on. The icon that you see on the desktop is really cruddy, but a better preview is hidden in the Properties dialog box (click on the file with the right mouse button and then select Properties).

Figure 16-2
Icons on
the desktop

This document
has an
Icon preview.

This document
does not.

Thumbnail. The second preview is a slightly larger image that Quick-Time-savvy applications can display in their Open dialog boxes. This way, you can see what's in the image before you open it. Again, for those who like to know: this image is a 128-by-128-pixel, JPEG-compressed, 24-bit PICT in the file's resource fork (though on Windows, it's actually saved in the image's header itself).

Note that you must have Apple's QuickTime extension loaded in order to read thumbnail previews on the Mac (you can still write them, but they won't show up in Open dialog boxes).

Saving and Opening Images

Throughout this chapter we discuss "reading" and "writing" various file formats, but we should, just for a moment, explore the mechanisms in Photoshop for performing these acts. The four relevant menu items—Open, Save, Save As, and Save a Copy—are all found under the File menu. (Some third-party color management systems use the Export command to save images that have been color-corrected for a specific device; we'll deal with those later.)

Open. You can open, or "read," an image by selecting Open, choosing the file, and pressing OK. Simple enough. The one exception to this (and this is why we mention it at all) is when the Show All Files checkbox is turned on. (Note that the Open As feature in Photoshop for Windows is equivalent to turning on Show All Files in the Open dialog box.) In that case, you can specify what file format ("language") you'd like Photoshop to read in.

This is particularly helpful when trying to open images that were created on a PC or some other sort of machine. When you bring the file across to the Mac, Photoshop may not recognize it as a TIFF file or EPS file or whatever it may be. In this case, you must turn on Show All Files, and explicitly tell it what file format the image is saved in.

Save. Selecting Save in Photoshop works the same as in every other Macintosh program: it replaces the previously saved image data with the current image data. Photoshop saves in whatever format the original image was saved in. If you haven't saved your document when you select Save (or press Command-S), Save performs a Save As instead.

Save As. If you want to save the image you're working on but change its name, its file format, and/or the place it's saved, use Save As instead of Save. This doesn't change the original image (the one already on disk). We use Save As all the time as we go through the process of adjusting an image. That way, we can always go back two or three (or more) steps.

Note that if your document has layers or alpha channels, you may not be able to save in a different file format with Save As.

Full Size. When Ask When Saving is turned on in Saving Files Preferences, Photoshop on the Mac gives you one additional choice: Full Size preview. This one adds a considerably larger JPEG-compressed 24-bit PICT resource to the file; its dimensions are the actual physical output size of the image, downsampled to the resolution of your monitor.

The primary benefit to Full Size preview is that it can be used by many third-party image browsers. Unfortunately, it's ignored by both PageMaker and QuarkXPress.

Note that there's no reason to select Full Size Preview with an EPS file; it's equivalent to saving the EPS file with a Macintosh (JPEG) preview (see "Encapsulated PostScript (EPS)," later in this chapter).

Save a Copy. The Save a Copy feature first arrived in version 3.0, and like all new features, it took some getting used to. However, now we find ourselves using it daily. Save a Copy is the same as Save As, except for two things.

▶ If you have multiple layers, Save a Copy lets you save a flattened version of the image (in which all the layers are merged together).

▶ If you have multiple channels, it gives you the option of including them or not.

Selecting Save a Copy is like saying, "Save the current image to disk, but let me keep working on the one I have open now." Or, it's like making a photocopy of your artwork, and then continuing to work on the original.

Tip: Save QuicKey. David has been working on Macintoshes

Figure 16-3 QuicKeys saves the day

for more than ten years, but he still gets into hot water with Photoshop's Save command. Because of long-standing habits, he occasionally presses Command-S, even when he wants to use Save As or Save a Copy.

This usually means disaster for Photoshop images. (For instance, he might be working on original image data from a scanner, which he may want to return to later.)

His solution: he made a little QuicKey that stops him from saving so easily. Now when he presses Command-S, a little dialog box

appears, asking him if he really wants to save (see Figure 16-3).

If he clicks OK (or presses Return), it saves just as usual. But he has a chance to cancel out of this dangerous maneuver and avoid risking his original image data.

For those of you who'd like to try this, the QuicKey is a Sequence with two steps: there's a Message Extension shortcut (which makes the dialog box appear with a Cancel button option) followed by a Menu Item shortcut (which selects Save from the File menu).

Tip: Save Time Saving Previews. Saving an Icon or Thumbnail preview considerably lengthens the time it takes to save your image. However, if you save one type of preview, saving the other type as well takes hardly any additional time—one or two seconds at most. Saving a Full Size preview takes still longer, so you should only do so if the image is going to an application that will benefit from it.

File Formats

You've probably noticed by now that a lot of this book focuses on prepress; nonetheless, we've done our best to include vital information for those whose output is continuous-tone film or the computer screen. Most people use Photoshop to prepare images that they're going to take elsewhere, be it PageMaker, QuarkXPress, a Scitex system, the World Wide Web, or whatever. So, while Photoshop can read and write a number of different file formats, we're going to focus on just a few at first.

While you're working on an image in Photoshop, you should save the file in Photoshop's native file format. It's the best possible format, in that it supports all of Photoshop's nifty features such as layers and channels, and it uses a robust lossless compression scheme. The only problem is that Photoshop is just about the only application that can read it, so if your images are destined for another application, you usually need to save them in some other format to make them readable.

If your image is destined for a presentation program, a multimedia program, or another screen-based application, PICT and JPEG are the best formats to use. But if the image is going to a page-layout program, you should always use TIFF or EPS.

Some page-layout programs will tell you that they can accept and print images in PICT, or .BMP, or .WMF, or various other weird formats. This may even be true on the third Tuesday of the month, when it coincides with the full moon, and the wind is coming briskly out of the southwest; but in general, using anything other than TIFF or EPS in a print-based application is courting disaster, no matter what the software publisher says. So TIFF and EPS are the formats that we'll cover in detail first and foremost, along with a more brief discussion of PICT and JPEG. Then we'll cover the other options at a brisk pace.

Photoshop

The Photoshop file format—otherwise known as Photoshop's "native" format—is the most flexible format around. In fact, it's the only way to save everything that Photoshop is capable of producing: multiple layers, paths, multiple channels, clipping paths, screening and transfer settings, and so on. (Note that histories and snapshots are not saved in any file format.) This is typically the best format in which to save your documents until you know how you're going to use them.

One of the coolest things about the Photoshop format is that it automatically compresses the image using *run length encoding*, or RLE. (We explain the various compression methods in "Compression," later in this chapter.) There's no way to turn this compression off, but it's fast and transparent, so we don't worry about it, and neither should you.

Compression in the Photoshop format is especially helpful when you're saving files with multiple alpha channels, because basic selection channels often compress down to a tiny fraction of their original size with RLE (see Figure 16-4). The same thing goes for saving files that have multiple layers, because transparent space on layers is compressed to almost nothing (not that you have a choice on this one; as we said earlier, the Photoshop format is the only one that supports multiple layers).

Figure 16-4
Compressing
channels

Photoshop automatically compresses
this simple channel to 11 K.

This more complicated image only
gets compressed to 130 K with RLE.

At the time of this writing, very few other programs can read native Photoshop files, layers and all, though some programs can read the flattened version that Photoshop saves along with your document when the Include Composited Image with Layered Files preference is turned on.

Photoshop 2.0

No one we associate with still uses Photoshop 2.0. However, we *do* know some folks who still use version 2.5.1 (people on computers with only 8 MB of RAM). If you need to open your Photoshop documents in Photoshop 2.5.1, you may be tempted to save your files in the Photoshop 2.0 format. Don't bother. We have not yet found any advantage of saving documents in this format. (Note that this format is not even available in Photoshop for Windows.)

Most images saved in the Photoshop format open just fine in older versions of the program. Similarly, Photoshop 2.5.1 can read TIFF or EPS images saved with multiple channel or path information. The catch here is that the file can't have layers and must have fewer than 16 channels (this is a limitation of versions earlier than 3.0). Also note that versions earlier than 3.0 don't understand compression, so Photoshop won't compress them in the Photoshop 2.0 format; thus, your file sizes may increase dramatically.

Tip: Don't Include Flattened Layers. By default, Photoshop saves a flattened version of your layered files along with the regular version. This is great if you *are* using layers and want to open the file in Photoshop 2.5.1 or some other program that claims to open "native Photoshop documents," like Illustrator or FreeHand (they don't really read the layers, only the flattened version). For most of us, however, this behavior is useless and just makes our files bigger on disk.

Unless your workflow depends on opening Photoshop files in another program, we strongly suggest that you turn off the Include Composited Image with Layered Files option in the Preferences dialog box (Command-K).

File Formats for Print

If your image is destined for multimedia or the internet, you may want to use the GIF formats. But if the image is going to a page-layout program, you should always use TIFF, EPS, or DCS.

Some page-layout programs will tell you that they can accept and print images in PICT, or .BMP, or .WMF, or various other weird formats. This may even be true on the third Tuesday of the month, when it coincides with the full moon, and the wind is coming briskly out of the southwest; but in general, using anything other than TIFF, EPS, or DCS in a print-based application is courting disaster, no matter what the software publisher says. So these are the formats that we'll cover in detail first and foremost; then we'll look at formats appropriate for non-prepress applications.

Encapsulated PostScript (EPS)

As we said back in Chapter 3, *Image Essentials*, Encapsulated PostScript (EPS) is really an object-oriented file format, but Photoshop can save images as *bitmap-only* EPSes. That's the only kind of EPS file we're going to talk about here. Note that the only time you should use an EPS file is when you're saving an image that you're about to import into a page-layout program. That's what EPS is made for.

While many people prefer working with EPS files over everything else (see sidebar, "TIFF versus EPS," later in this chapter), they have some serious limitations. Sure, you can save grayscale, RGB, or CMYK data in EPS format. Sure, you can save an any-sized file with or without compression. Sure, you can save clipping paths and transfer functions. But once you've saved the file, it's set in mud. Once you bring the image into a page-layout program, you're stuck with it.

Plus, you can only print EPS files on a PostScript printer (or with software that acts as a software PostScript interpreter). That means those low-cost ink-jets are usually ruled out. But we often *do* want to make some changes to images while on pages—colorizing the image, or setting a special halftone screen—and in those cases we switch to a different file format, such as TIFF.

When you save an image as an EPS, Photoshop lets you set the file's preview style and encoding, and it gives you a choice as to whether or not you want to include halftone screening, transfer curve, and PostScript Color Management information (see Figure 16-5). Let's look at each of these. (Note that earlier versions of Photoshop let you choose a clipping path here, too; see "Clipping Paths," later in this chapter, for more on how Photoshop 5 handles clipping paths.)

Figure 16-5

Save as EPS

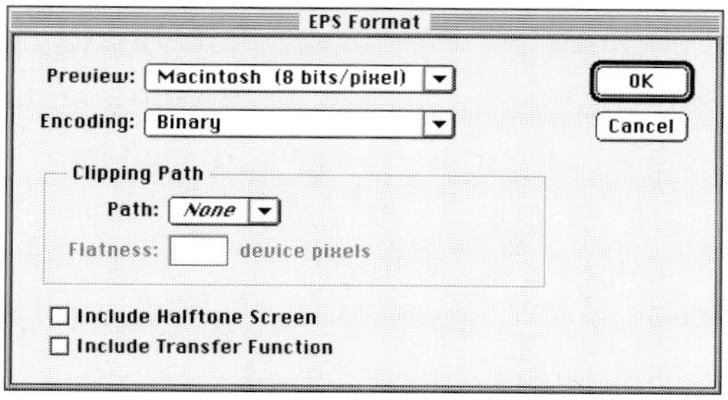

TIFF versus EPS

As we travel around the world doing seminars and conferences, we are forever hearing people say things like "My service bureau told me to only use EPS files," or "I was told I'd get better images if I used TIFFs," or "Don't EPS files print better?" While we try to appear calm and collected, inside we're just waiting to scream, "Who told you this nonsense? Were they raised by wolves?"

While the confusion is understandable, we want to make a few points about TIFFs and EPSes that will, we hope, clear the air a little.

TIFFs and EPSes contain *exactly the same image data*. The way in which it's written (encoded) may be somewhat different, but that doesn't change the image one iota.

The key difference between TIFFs and EPSes is not what they are or how they're written, but what other programs can do to them.

Encapsulated data. The entire philosophy behind EPS (Encapsulated PostScript) files is that they're little capsules of information. No other program should have to—or even be able to—go in and change anything about the data that's there.

EPS files were designed to be imported into other programs so that those programs wouldn't have to worry about what's in them at all. When it came time to print, that program would simply send the EPS down to the printer, trusting that the PostScript inside would image correctly.

Open TIFF format. TIFFs, on the other hand, were designed not only to be imported into other programs, but also to be exchanged among image editors.

That is, the program that imports the TIFF can actually access the information inside it and, potentially, change it.

Programs such as QuarkXPress and PageMaker have exploited this property of TIFFs by incorporating features that let you make changes to the TIFF image. On pages, for instance, you can apply a color to a grayscale TIFF image. When you print the page, the program literally changes the image data on its way to the printer. It almost never changes the data on your disk, but it changes it in the print stream. There's no way for these programs to change EPS image data at all.

Downsampling and cropping. More important, both PageMaker and XPress have the ability to downsample TIFF data at print time. If you import a 300-ppi TIFF into XPress and print it to a desktop laser printer at 60 lpi (see

Previews. EPS files typically have two parts: the high-resolution PostScript data and a low-resolution screen preview. When you import an EPS into a page-layout program (or a word processor or whatever), the computer displays the low-res image on the screen, and when you print the page, the computer uses the high-res PostScript code. (If you don't have a PostScript printer, the low-res preview prints out instead—not terribly useful except for simple proofing.)

On the Macintosh, Photoshop lets you save EPS files with five different types of previews, or no preview at all, via the Preview popup menu in the EPS Format dialog box. In Windows, you have only two preview choices. As we said in "Preview Options," with EPSes there's no reason to

Chapter 17, *Output Methods*, for more on halftone screen frequency), XPress automatically downsamples the image to 120 ppi (two times the halftone frequency).

XPress does this because it knows that sending the additional data is wasted time. The result is that your page prints faster. In PageMaker, you can achieve the same thing by choosing Optimized in the Print: Options dialog box. There's no way to downsample an EPS at print time.

Similarly, have you ever tried importing a full-page, 20 MB EPS file into one of these page-layout programs and cropping it down to a 1-by-1-inch square? The program is forced to send the entire 20 megabytes to the printer, even though all you want is a little bit of the image.

With a TIFF image, however, only the data that is necessary to print the page at that screen frequency is sent to the printer, again saving printing time and costs.

Previews and separations. One of the biggest hassles of TIFF images, however, is that they can take a long time to import, because the page-layout program has to read the entire file in order to create a screen preview for the image. EPS files can import quickly because Photoshop has already created a preview image.

On the other hand, CMYK TIFF files usually print separations much faster than EPS files because the data can be separated into discrete 8-bit chunks (only sending yellow data for the yellow plate, and so on). With EPS files, however, PageMaker and XPress have to send all 32 bits (cyan, yellow, magenta, and black) for each plate. This slows down printing considerably. (There are exceptions to this; see "DCS," later in this chapter, and "Tip: Send Eight Bits, Not 32" in Chapter 17, *Output Methods*.)

Workflow considerations. There are plenty of other differences between EPS and TIFF files—like the fact that you can save transfer funtions and halftone-screening information in EPS files—but we're going to leave them for later in the chapter. Our purpose is simply to show that TIFF and EPS files are equals in stature if not in aim.

As for us, when we have a choice, we almost always use TIFF files; we prefer their flexibility, and we do a *lot* of page proofing with large grayscale images, so the downsampling at print time helps a lot. However, if we need fast importing of large files, or a duotone image, we switch to EPS. But don't listen to us. The most important reason why you should use one over the other is not "my consultant/service bureau/guru told me so," but your own workflow. The sorts of images you work with, the kind of network and printers you have, and your proofing needs all play a part in your decision.

turn on the Full Size preview option in the Save As dialog box. The specific EPS options do the same thing, and give you more control.

▶ **TIFF.** In Windows, Photoshop only offers 1-bit or 8-bit TIFF from the Preview popup menu. The default is 1-bit, which seems strange to us; we always change this to 8-bit. On the Macintosh, the only time you should select one of these is when your image needs to be imported into a page-layout program on a PC. If you choose one of the PICT formats, the preview is lost when the file is moved to the PC (an EPS without a preview just looks like a gray box on pages, though it prints correctly). Some programs on the Macintosh, such as PageMaker and

QuarkXPress, can import PC EPS files with the preview image intact; but no programs that we know of on the PC can read Mac previews.

▶ **PICT.** Files that will stay on the Mac should be saved with a PICT preview. Photoshop gives you three choices: 1-bit, 8-bit, and JPEG. Until recently, David always used the 8-bit Macintosh preview when creating EPS files that were destined to stay on the Mac. Somehow it just seemed safer than using JPEG. Then Bruce showed him the light, and David hasn't gone back to 8-bit since.

When you save an EPS file with a Macintosh JPEG preview, Photoshop has to take the time to build a JPEG preview. However, we gladly take the minor performance hit to get the benefits. JPEG previews are better looking and take up less space on disk than their 8-bit brethren. (A JPEG preview for a 300-dpi tabloid-sized image is about 90 K.) Plus, they occasionally even redraw faster in a page-layout program.

Bear in mind that you can't read JPEG previews unless you have the QuickTime system extension loaded, and then only with QuickTime-aware applications (yes for QuarkXPress and PageMaker 6, no for PageMaker 5).

If you're concerned about disk space, you may choose to have no preview (None) or a black-and-white preview (1-bit, either TIFF or PICT). Personally, we'd rather suffer thumbscrews than use either of these when hard drive prices are so low.

ASCII versus binary. When you save an image in Photoshop, you have the choice of how to encode the data (see Figure 16-6). *Encoding* is simply a fancy-schmancy way of saying "the way the data is written to disk." The first two choices in the Encoding popup menu, ASCII or binary, are like choosing between words with one or two syllables. If you always said "feline" instead of "cat," it would take twice as long to communicate, right? If you choose ASCII, the image takes up twice as much space on your hard drive and takes twice as long to send to the printer.

You only need to use ASCII when you're printing PostScript over a PC or UNIX serial port, or passing files through some esoteric networks or gateways. Binary images can confuse these pipelines (and PostScript devices that are connected to them), because some of the binary data is interpreted as control characters that say things like "End of File!" (For the propeller-

Figure 16-6
Encoding in EPS

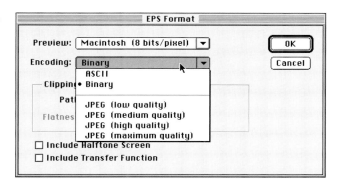

heads in the audience, this doubling effect occurs because ASCII data is saved in hexadecimal, which uses two 8-bit characters—0 to 9 and A to F—to describe the same information as eight bits of binary data.)

JPEG compression. Instead of saving the EPS file with binary or ASCII encoding, you can choose some level of JPEG compression, which we describe in more detail in "Compressing Images," later in this chapter. (Nope, sorry, there's no way to save an EPS file with lossless compression from Photoshop, even though PostScript Level 2 and 3 interpreters can decompress several lossless compression methods.)

Photoshop offers four choices for JPEG quality—Maximum, High, Medium, and Low. The better the quality, the less compression you can achieve. The great benefit of JPEG compression in EPS files is that you not only keep the image small on your hard drive, but you also can send a (much) smaller file down the network lines to your printer, reducing transmission time.

There are two downsides to creating JPEG EPS files, though. The first is that you can *only* print them on a printer that has Level 2 or 3 PostScript, because only they know how to decompress JPEG. Older desktop laser printers and imagesetters may not be able to handle JPEG images.

The second problem with JPEG EPS files is that they won't separate properly when printed. They *should*, but for some reason the entire image comes out on the black plate. However, if you save the file as a DCS file (see "DCS," later in this chapter), the separation works like a charm! So, while DCS files can be a hassle in their own right, if your workflow can handle them, the JPEG DCS option can really save a lot of time.

Tip: Removing the JPEG Compression. If you need to print a JPEG-compressed EPS on a non-Level 2 printer, open the file in Photoshop and save it in an uncompressed format. Or you might try the DeBabelizer utility if you have a lot of files to decompress.

Halftone screens and transfer functions. If you want to save halftone-screening or transfer-curve information in the image, you must save it as an EPS file. You can set the halftone screens and transfer functions in the Page Setup dialog box (see Chapter 17, *Output Methods,* for details). Our basic opinion is that it's rare that you need to save an EPS with a transfer curve; best just to leave that checkbox turned off.

Saving halftone screens in an EPS file, however, is sometimes useful. For instance, when saving duotone, tritone, or quadtone images, you almost always want to set specific screen frequencies and angles for each ink. If you want to import that image into a page-layout program, you have to save it as an EPS (that's the only non-native format you can save duotones in), and to maintain your angles, you have to turn on the Include Halftone Screen checkbox. (Note that PageMaker and QuarkXPress let you specify angles, too; though they cannot override the settings you make in an EPS.)

PostScript Color Management. Some years ago, the folks at Adobe had the clever idea that color management could be made simpler if output devices themselves could do the conversions from one color space into their own color space. They built a basic color management engine into PostScript Level 2 (and made it a bit more robust in Level 3), and waited for the world to get excited. They're still waiting.

It appears that they added the PostScript Color Management checkbox in the Save as EPS dialog box in order to drum up some interest in their technology. When this is turned on, Photoshop includes an ICC profile in the EPS file. If you've got a PostScript output device that knows about profiles, it can manage the data "appropriately." Otherwise, the printer should ignore it.

There are so many problems with this workflow (and with the technology itself) that we don't know where to begin. Instead, we recommend you leave this checkbox turned off and handle your color management on the software side of life.

Tip: Send Eight Bits, Not 32. Earlier, we stated that when you print a single-file CMYK EPS from a page-layout program, that program has to send down all 32 bits of information for each plate; it can't "pull apart" the data, transmitting only the eight bits of cyan for the cyan plate, and so on. It turns out that in some cases, that's not true anymore.

The folks at Quark figured out how to break down the data in Photoshop CMYK EPS files in order to print faster. They implemented this feature in version 3.31, but it broke in some later 3.x versions. Fortunately, it now works again in QuarkXPress 4. You can test this easily: save an image as both a CMYK TIFF and a CMYK EPS. Import the TIFF version and write a PostScript file to disk. Now replace the image with the EPS version and write the file to disk. If the second PostScript file is four times larger than the first, then you know that XPress has simply included the entire EPS four times; if they're approximately the same size, you know that the program has "pulled apart" the EPS the way you'd want.

As we go to press, PageMaker 6.5 still does not have this feature.

DCS

The DCS (Desktop Color Separation) format is a newcomer to Photoshop's Save As popup menus, but it's not a new format. That's because it used to be an option inside the Save as EPS dialog box. It made sense: DCS is really just a special case of the EPS file format. However, it's weird (and important) enough that Adobe added it as two separate file formats: Photoshop DCS 1.0 and Photoshop DCS 2.0.

Originally, DCS was designed to separate the high-resolution image data from the low-resolution preview image. In version 1.0, the DCS format always resulted in five files. The first four held the high-resolution data for each color place (cyan, magenta, yellow, and black). The fifth file, also called the *master file*, was the one that you actually imported into a page-layout program, and it contained three things: a low-resolution screen preview, a low-resolution composite CMYK version of the image, and pointers to the other four files.

There were two problems with DCS 1.0. First, some people didn't like to keep track of five files for each image (though to be fair, many other people thought this was great because they could leave the high-resolution data on a server and just use the master file on their own systems). Second, there was no way to include spot colors.

Figure 16-7

Saving Desktop Color
Separation (DCS) files

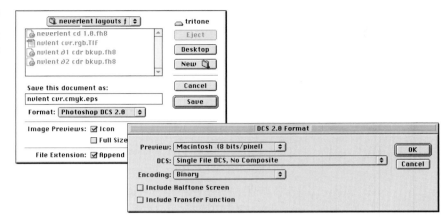

DCS 2.0 solves both problems. If you've already preseparated your image (converted to CMYK mode) you have the choice of saving the image in either a DCS 1.0 or a DCS 2.0 format (see Figure 16-7). However, we know of no good reason to use DCS 1.0, so we'll focus on version 2.0, which does everything that 1.0 does and more.

Of the various options in the Save as DCS 2.0 dialog box, most of them are equivalent to the ones in the Save as EPS dialog box (which we discussed in the last section). For instance, Preview lets you determine the quality and kind of RGB screen preview; Encoding determines the format of the data within the file; and so on. The only new feature here is the DCS popup menu, in which you can choose whether you want one single file or multiple files on disk, and what sort of composite image you want.

DCS composites. Many people confuse the EPS's composite image with the preview image. This is understandable; they're almost exactly the same thing. Both are low-resolution (72-ppi) representations of the original image; both can be used instead of the high-res image for proofing.

The real difference is in their uses. The preview image is always in RGB mode and is designed for screen use only. The composite image is saved in CMYK mode (literally, it's the same as downsampling the high-res CMYK image to 72 ppi using Nearest Neighbor interpolation), and is meant to be printed to a low-resolution color printer for proofing purposes.

For color-proofing devices that require color separations, you can force XPress to send the high-resolution data with an XTension, such as Total Integration's SmartXT. We don't know of any way to do this in

PageMaker other than trying to get the color printer to recombine the separations.

Multi-file or single file. Whether you tell Photoshop to write a single file or multiple files is up to you and your workflow. Probably the best reason to use multiple files is if you need or want to keep your high-resolution data in a separate place (like on a server or at your service bureau). This is especially helpful with very large files (we leave the definition of "very large" up to you).

On the other hand, keeping track of a number of files can be a pain in the left buttock, and the links to the high-res images can be "broken" if you rename or move those files (see "Tip: Recovering Lost Links in DCS," below).

Note that either way, DCS files typically print faster from a page-layout program than either TIFF or EPS files. For instance, with a single-file EPS, PageMaker or QuarkXPress typically has to send the entire EPS to the printer for each and every plate. However, with DCS files, they can send only the cyan to the cyan plate, and so on. (Actually, XPress can sometimes "break down" single-file EPS files, too; see "Tip: Send Eight Bits, Not 32" earlier in this chapter.)

Tip: Naming Spot Colors. As we explain in Chapter 17, *Output Methods*, if your DCS file includes spot colors, your page-layout software must also have colors named exactly the same way (yes, PageMaker and XPress import these names automatically when you import a DCS 2.0 file).

Tip: Recovering Lost Links in DCS. Occasionally, when working with multi-file DCS files, the master file gets lost or the link between the master file and the high-res color files is broken (this can happen if you move or rename the high-res files). Don't fear; you can always reassemble the DCS files in Photoshop.

1. Open each of the high-res images in Photoshop. They're all EPS files, and they're all in Grayscale mode.

2. When all four of the files are open, select Merge Channels from the Channels palette's popout menu.

3. Make sure the mode is set to CMYK and the Channels field is set to 4 (see Figure 16-8); press OK.

Figure 16-8
Merge Channels
dialog box

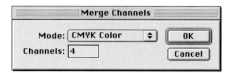

4. Photoshop is pretty good at guessing which file should be set to which color channel in the Merge CMYK Channels dialog box (see Figure 16-9), but if it guesses wrong, set the popup menus to the proper files.

Figure 16-9
Merge CMYK
Channels dialog box

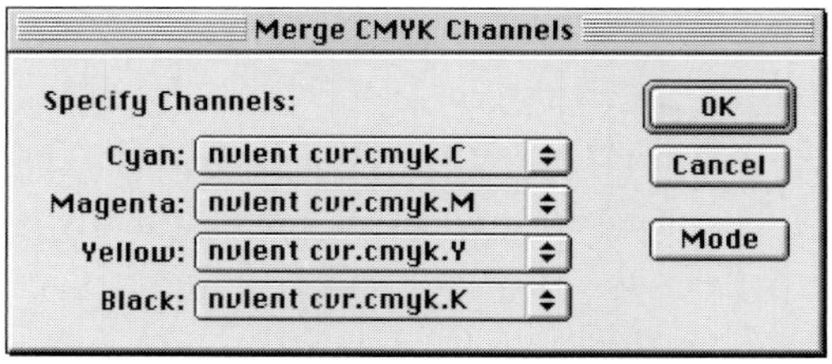

When you press OK, Photoshop merges the four grayscale files into a single, high-resolution CMYK file. You can now create the five DCS files again, if you want. (Note that if you have spot colors in your DCS file, you'll have to add the additional channels manually, after you merge the CMYK channels.)

TIFF

The Tagged Image File Format (TIFF, pronounced just as it reads) is *the* industry-standard bitmapped file format. Almost every program that works with bitmaps can handle TIFF files—either placing, printing, correcting, or editing the bitmap. TIFF is a very straightforward format—in general, the only information it contains beyond the actual pixels themselves is the output size and resolution.

A Photoshop TIFF can be any dimension and any resolution (at least we haven't heard of any limits). You can save it in Grayscale, RGB (indexed or 24-bit), CMYK, or Lab color mode. You can even include as many additional channels as you want (up to the maximum 24 Photoshop allows;

bear in mind, however, that few programs other than Photoshop can *understand* a multichannel TIFF).

TIFF images must be bitmap-only, though you can include clipping paths (if your page-layout program uses them; see "Clipping Paths," later in this chapter). You can't save layers in a TIFF file. And you cannot include screening or transfer-curve information in a TIFF. These are both controlled by the application that's printing the TIFF image.

Previews. When you save an EPS, you almost always ask Photoshop to save a preview image with it. To get a preview for a TIFF file, however, you have to select Full Size Preview in the Save As dialog box. The problem is that no software packages (other than some image browsers) currently read those previews, so they're useless. (Earlier versions of QuarkXPress *did* read them, but the image was often messed up at print time; see "Preview Options," earlier in this chapter.)

When you import a TIFF image into a page-layout application, the program reads the entire file and creates a low-resolution preview for you. This is hardly any trouble in a 1 MB image. But you could wait for many minutes while PageMaker or QuarkXPress reads and downsamples a 40 MB image. We prefer TIFFs for most of our work, but when we work with larger images, we often switch to EPS files for this reason alone.

Color models. You can save a preseparated CMYK image as a TIFF. When you place that file in a page-layout program or the like, no further separation is required. The program can simply pull the cyan channel when it's printing the cyan plate, the magenta channel when it's printing the magenta plate, and so on.

There is a facility in TIFF files to use indexed color, but using indexed color is a prime cause of compatibility problems, in our experience (see "Indexed Color" in Chapter 3, *Image Essentials*). If someone gives us an indexed-color TIFF to work with, we immediately convert it to straight RGB or CMYK and damn the file size. (Of course, if we're resaving it as a PICT or GIF file, we'll leave it in Indexed Color mode.)

IBM versus Mac. For some reason, the IBM and the Mac have different versions of TIFF. It has something to do with the file's byte order and the processing methods of Motorola versus Intel chips. For whatever reason, you sometimes need to convert TIFFs when you move them between platforms. Happily, programs like Photoshop, HiJaak, and DeBabelizer can read *and* write both Mac and IBM TIFFs.

One addition to make you breathe easier: PageMaker and QuarkXPress on both Windows and Mac can import either Intel- or Motorola-type TIFFs, so saving in one format or the other is less crucial in the prepress world.

Compression. Photoshop lets you save TIFF files with LZW (lossless) compression. Unlike the Photoshop or PICT formats, if you want compression in a TIFF file, you have to ask for it when you save the image (see Figure 16-10).

Figure 16-10
Saving TIFF files

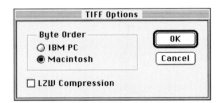

We've met people who claim that they always save their files in PICT format because it gives them the best compression. Not so. LZW-compressed TIFFs are almost always more compact (see "Compressing Images," later in this chapter, for an explanation of why). They're also more reliable than PICT images for most page-layout work. On the other hand, they often take longer to save and open than non-compressed TIFFs, sometimes much longer (isn't that always the trade-off, though?).

Compatibility. TIFF may sound like the ideal bitmapped file format, but in fact the picture is not totally rosy. As it turns out, there are several different "flavors" of TIFF. It's such a flexible format that TIFFs written by some programs are incomprehensible to some others.

This isn't as much a problem today as it was in past years when TIFFs varied widely, but we still occasionally hear about people who can't open their TIFFs—usually saved by scanning software—in Photoshop. Their only recourse is to open them in an intermediary program first, save them, and then try opening them in Photoshop. Compressed TIFFs are generally more prone to this kind of behavior than uncompressed ones.

Tip: Use File Info for Captions. Let's say you're doing production work in Photoshop on the eighth floor, and the pages are being laid out in QuarkXPress on the fourteenth floor (those designer types always get a better view). You're all on an Ethernet system, so it's easy to transfer the files up there. But what about all those captions and credits that they need? In the old days, you might have written on the back of the photograph, or perhaps slapped a Post-it note down somewhere. Now, there's nothing to write *on*.

Fortunately, Photoshop lets you save caption information inside TIFF or EPS files. You can select File Info from the File menu and type all sorts of information about the image and where it came from, and so on. The problem is that unless they're opening those files again in Photoshop, it's hard for them to get at that information.

XPertTools Volume 1 and XTSee are two XTensions for QuarkXPress for the Macintosh that let you see the caption information saved in a TIFF or (with XPertTools) EPS file (see Figure 16-11). If the layout folks are using one of these XTensions, they can quickly see the image's caption. Even better, they can copy and paste the caption into a text box in XPress. Talk about workgroup efficiency!

Figure 16-11
Reading caption
information

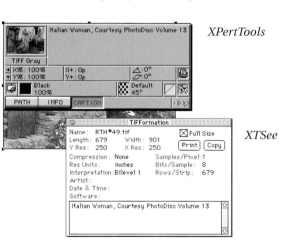

Note that this only works with the Caption field of File Info. There are still many more fields that you can't get at unless you use proprietary software from AP or some other company.

Tip: Color Management Systems. If you're relying on a color management system to control your color, it's generally a great deal easier to do so using TIFF than it is using EPS files, because as yet there's no standard way of attaching device profiles to EPS files, whereas there is for TIFFs. It's possible to build a color-managed workflow around EPS using commercial XTensions and utilities (such as Color Solution's Parachute, which intercepts all the color elements in a PostScript stream and applies color transformations based on rules that you set in advance, or PraxiSoft's ColorSyncXT for QuarkXPress, which allows you to apply profiles to imported EPS files), but both XPress 4 and Pagemaker 6.5 include support for color-managing TIFF files with no additional software.

Clipping Paths

The old art of cutting silhouettes out of paper is mostly gone now, though it lives on at street fairs and tourist spots. If you've ever seen someone cutting one of these, you know how painstaking a process it can be. We wonder why, then, people expect creating a silhouette in Photoshop to be as easy as snapping their fingers. Far from it: masking out the background of an image—leaving only the foreground object—is a difficult proposition. Unfortunately, it's something that many of us in production work have to do every day (see Figure 16-12).

Figure 16-12
The effect of
a clipping path

The biggest problem is often not that of making a selection to silhouette (we cover a lot of selection and silhouetting techniques in Chapter 14, *Selections*). Rather, it's bringing that selection into a page-layout program without unnaturally harsh edges resulting. In this section we'll discuss getting silhouettes to print properly from PageMaker or XPress.

The secret to clean silhouettes is Photoshop's paths feature. Remember that Bézier paths are generally smoother than raster (bitmap) data because they're always imaged at the resolution of your output device, whereas bitmapped images print at whatever resolution they're set to, or at the coarseness of your halftone screen. Once you use the Pen tools to create a path in Photoshop (and then save that path in the Paths palette by double-clicking on the Working Path tile), you can specify that your path be used as a clipping path upon output.

1. Select Clipping Path from the popout menu in the Paths palette.

2. Choose the path that you want as a clipping path.

3. Give it a flatness value (see "Tip: Bump Up Your Flatness," later in this chapter) and press OK. The name of the path (in the Paths palette) should now be in outline style, indicating it's a clipping path.

4. Save the image as a TIFF or EPS and import it into PageMaker or XPress.

(Note that in earlier versions of Photoshop, you could choose a clipping path from within the Save as EPS dialog box, but no longer.)

TIFF or EPS. Photoshop can save—and the newest versions of Quark-XPress and PageMaker can read—clipping paths in either TIFF or EPS files. Because we tend to use TIFF files, this is great news. Remember that clipping paths don't really delete the data itself; the entire image gets sent to the printer along with the instructions on how to clip it down.

Why use paths. People use paths most often when they want to place a silhouette of an object over a colored background in a page-layout program. For instance, many catalogs have a colored tint over the entire page, with irregularly-shaped objects—shoes, toaster ovens, cars—floating as if in mid-air. If you try to achieve this effect by simply making the background transparent (white) rather than using a clipping path, you'll get an object surrounded by a white box. (Even if it looks like there are transparent areas on screen, it still prints as white; see Figure 16-13.)

Because paths are mathematical lines and curves, they're always as sharp as the printer you print on. That's almost always sharper than the resolution of your image, so be prepared for your edges to look overly

Figure 16-13

When what you see isn't what you get

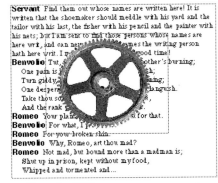

How the EPS appears on screen in QuarkXPress

How the EPS prints from XPress

How an EPS with a clipping path prints

crisp. No, you can't make a soft, fuzzy edge with a clipping path—so, no drop shadows or clouds! (See Chapter 15, *Essential Image Techniques*, for more information on these sorts of effects.)

Soft edges. The main problem with clipping paths is that you cannot clip a soft or semitransparent edge. So, drop shadows are out. Clipping around a gauzy dress is out. If your subject is having a bad hair day, clipping around the head is going to make it look even worse.

There are several ways of making soft edges interact with your background on pages (see "Drop Shadows," in Chapter 15, *Essential Image Techniques*). The best one, however, is simply to design your page so that the image doesn't overlap any other colors in your page-layout application.

Alternatively, you can forget about clipping paths, and composite the image with the background in Photoshop, using the techniques described in Chapter 14, *Selections*.

Tip: Bump Up Your Flatness. You can often speed up print times dramatically and/or avoid PostScript "limitcheck" errors by raising the PostScript flatness value in the Save as EPS dialog box.

If you've worked with flatness in FreeHand or Illustrator (before version 5), you know that the flatness value determines how hard the PostScript interpreter works to give you smooth curves. The higher the flatness value, the faster the graphic prints, but the more choppy the curve gets. If you raise your flatness too high, the curve turns into a set of straight lines. However, you can almost always raise your flatness to between 3 and 5 and never see the difference, regardless of output resolution.

Of course, flatness only applies to PostScript curves, so if you're not using clipping paths, there's no need for a flatness value.

Tip: Inset Paths Slightly. When you're drawing paths around objects to silhouette them in Photoshop, make sure you draw the path very slightly inside the object's border—we typically place the path one or two pixels inside the edge. This usually avoids most of the spillover from the background color. If spillover is a significant problem with an image, you should be thinking about building a Photoshop composite instead of using a clipping path.

Tip: Clipping Paths and QuarkXPress 4. Not only can QuarkXPress 4 see (and use) a clipping path in your Photoshop TIFF image, but it can see (and use) any other path saved with the file, too. In fact, XPress is a little overzealous about its clipping path functionality: If it sees even a single path saved in a TIFF file, it will use it as a clipping path. If you don't want it to be a clipping path, you must manually turn it off on the Clipping tab of the Modify dialog box.

On the other hand, there are two positive effects of XPress's feature.

► You don't have to specify that a path be a clipping path within Photoshop. Just save the TIFF file with a regular path and XPress can use it.

► If you have more than one path saved with your TIFF file, you can choose which path you want to use from within XPress. This is great if you won't decide which portions of a picture you want to use until you see it alongside the rest of your page layout.

Tip: Clipping Paths and QuarkXPress 3.x. If you import a TIFF image with a white background into an XPress 3.x picture box and set the background of that picture box to None (transparent), XPress attempts to figure out what white areas in the picture are *supposed* to be transparent. However, it's pretty clumsy at doing this, and the result is often very jaggy edges (see Figure 16-14). There are two reasons for this.

Figure 16-14

Transparent TIFFs
versus clipping paths

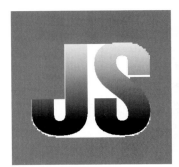

A grayscale TIFF in a XPress 3 picture box, Background color: "None." A 72-dpi outline, opaque interior pixels.

Saved as an EPS with a clipping path. Works in XPress or PageMaker.

▶ XPress 3.x only uses the low-resolution preview image when figuring out where the edge of the image is. That could be either 36 or 72 ppi.

▶ XPress 3.x can't see around corners. It figures the silhouetted edge by finding the first nonwhite pixel on the left and right of each row of pixels. As soon as it sees a nonwhite pixel, it stops and says, "Here's the edge of the image." The program can't tell if that single pixel accidentally floating an inch from the edge of the image is an accident or not, so it assumes that it's part of the image—causing lots of problems.

If you want to bring a silhouetted TIFF (or, in fact, any TIFF with a partially white background) into XPress 3.x, make sure that the background of the picture box is set to an opaque color (like white). Otherwise, use a clipping path saved in an EPS file.

File Formats for Multimedia and the Web

Where TIFF and EPS (and the DCS variant) file formats are designed for print, there are plenty of other formats that you can use for multimedia and Internet publishing, including PICT, JPEG, and GIF. Again, the file format is like the envelope that holds the image data; there is usually no inherent difference in the image itself, just how it's presented to whatever program you're trying to view the image with.

PICT

The PICT format (pronounced just as it looks) is the Mac-standard object-oriented file format. A PICT graphic can contain a bitmap as one of the objects in the file, or as its only object ("bitmap-only PICT"). Bitmap-only PICTs can be any size, resolution, and bit depth. While Photoshop for Windows can open a PICT (".pct") image, few other programs on the PC can. If the PC is your final destination, it'd be better to use some other file format.

PICT is a respectable format for saving bitmaps that are in the editing process, but still not as flexible as the Photoshop format—PICT files can't handle multiple layers, CMYK data, or more than four channels (that's RGB plus one channel total).

You should certainly plan on converting to TIFF or EPS before placing the image in a page-layout package; PageMaker and QuarkXPress, at least, are limited in their ability to manage PICTs effectively.

Nonetheless, PICT is the primary format when you're printing to non-PostScript devices—like most film recorders—or for multimedia work (like working with QuarkImmedia, mTropolis, or Macromedia Director); in these cases, you rarely need to move out of RGB mode. PICT file formats are not generally appropriate for Web publishing.

As in the Photoshop format, you can't turn compression off in the PICT file format, although Photoshop makes it look like you can. When you save a file in the PICT format, Photoshop asks whether you want to use JPEG (and if so, how lossy do you want it) or no compression at all (see Figure 16-15). However, if you pick None, Photoshop still uses RLE compression. (By the way, you can only save or open PICT images in JPEG format when you've got QuickTime loaded on your Mac.)

Figure 16-15

Saving PICTs

If you select None, Photoshop still uses RLE compression.

If you select one of the other options, the image is compressed with JPEG instead of RLE.

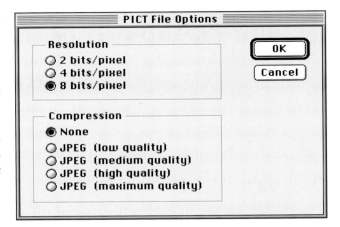

Tip: Photoshop's Compression is Better. If you're on a quest to save hard disk space, you might try saving your images in PICT format to take advantage of its lossless RLE compression. Don't bother. Saving images in the Photoshop format is not only faster, but compresses them more (on average) than PICT. The reason? PICT's RLE compression is done by QuickTime; Photoshop's is done by Photoshop.

The difference is in how they save the data (for the technoids out there: PICT saves image data in a "chunky" format—like RGB RGB RGB—while Photoshop saves image data in a "planar" format—like RRR GGG BBB).

CompuServe GIF

The Graphics Interchange Format (commonly known as GIF, pronounced "jiff" or "giff," depending on your upbringing), is the "house-brand" image file format of the CompuServe online information service. However, GIF images have long since broken free of CompuServe's corporate walls and are now the industry standard on almost every online service, including the Internet (notably for Web pages).

GIF files are designed for on-screen viewing, especially for images where file size is more important than quality, and for screens that only display 8-bit color (256 colors). Photoshop GIFs are always 8-bit indexed color images, making them reasonable for on-screen viewing, but certainly not for printing.

Macintosh File Types and PC Extensions

One important thing to know about file formats is that Macintoshes and PCs "see" files differently. On the Macintosh, every file has several attributes attached to it, including two codes specifying the file type and creator. These are mysterious four-letter labels that tell the Macintosh what sort of file it is and what program generated it. For example, when you double-click on a file, the Mac looks at the file's creator to see what application to launch; Photoshop's creator code is 8BIM (we're sorry to say that they didn't change it when they went from 2.x to 3.0). The file type is determined by the file format. The important ones are easy: TIFF is TIFF, and EPS is EPSF.

If you move an image from some other platform to the Macintosh, you may not be able to open or place it, because it has a file type of TEXT or DATA or some such, while the opening application is looking for EPSF or TIFF. You can view and change a file's type using Laurence Harris's shareware classic, File Buddy (see Figure 16-16), Apple's free ResEdit, and various other commercial and shareware programs.

In the PC world, everything is different. There are no file types, no file creators . . . there are only file names. PC files (at least those in Windows 95, 98, or NT) must end with a three-letter extension such as .TIF, .EPS, or .BMP. This

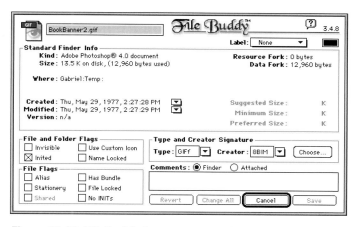

Figure 16-16 FileBuddy lets you see and change file types

extension provides all the information (and it ain't much) about the file's type and creator. Even Windows 95 doesn't stretch the file information beyond that.

Tip: File Name as File Type. As we said earlier, when you bring a file from a PC (or any other kind of computer system) over to the Mac, the Macintosh typically can't tell what kind of file it is, so it assigns it a file type of DATA or TEXT or something like that. Photoshop, in turn, can't figure out what

file type it's supposed to be, so it may not appear in the Open dialog box. However, Photoshop doesn't just look at the file's type; it also looks at the name.

Photoshop thinks any file with the suffix ".eps" is an EPS file, whether or not it really is one (see Table 16-1). Therefore, when you transfer the file to the Macintosh, make sure you give it the proper suffix. That way, Photoshop can read it properly even if Show All Files isn't turned on in the Open dialog box.

Table 16-1 File type suffixes that Photoshop recognizes

Amiga IFF	.iff	Pixar	.pxr
Encapsulated PostScript	.eps	Raw	.raw
Filmstrip	.flm	Scitex CT	.sct
JPEG	.jpg	Targa	.tga
PCX	.pcx	TIFF	.tif
Photo CD	.pcd	Windows bitmap	.bmp
PICT	.pct		

GIFs are automatically compressed using lossless LZW compression (see "Compressing Images," later in this chapter). We discuss GIF images, and how to make them in Chapter 18, *Multimedia and the Web*.

JPEG

Most people talk about JPEG as a compression method within another file format—like JPEG EPS—but it turns out that JPEG is also a file format all by itself. Obviously, you can't get around compressing the image when you save a file in JPEG format, and you wouldn't want to.

While there are plenty of people who use JPEG images for prepress work, the vast majority of JPEG images are found on the World Wide Web. The only problem with using the JPEG format for printing (besides the fact that it's lossy; see "Compressing Images," later in this chapter) is that few programs other than Photoshop can read this format. QuarkXPress can, if you have the JPEG filter XTension loaded (it comes with all new versions of XPress). PageMaker 6.x can, but PageMaker 5.x can't.

And even if the program can read it, neither XPress nor PageMaker sends the JPEG information down to the printer for decompression (as they do with JPEG-encoded EPSes). Instead, they decompress it and send it down just as they would a TIFF file. So you get the hard disk savings, but it actually takes longer every time you print the file because the printing program has to decompress the JPEG image each time.

JPEGs on the Web is a different matter. JPEGs are ubiquitous on the Internet because they're the only good way to display full color (24-bit) images in a Web page (see "PNG" later in this chapter for one other possibility). We discuss JPEG images and how to make them in Chapter 18, *Multimedia and the Web*.

Niche File Formats

As we noted back in the Preface, this book only covers a fraction of the potential uses of Photoshop—those centered around production. People use this program for so many different things that we couldn't hope to cover them all here. In the last section, we discussed each of the file formats that are relevant for most professionals who are putting images on paper or film. You, however, might be doing something interesting, different, or just plain odd. Don't worry; Photoshop can probably still accommodate you.

Reasonable Niche File Formats

In this section, we'll explore six file formats that Photoshop can read and write, and why you might have cause to use them. In all but one, FilmStrip, there's no need to save in these file formats until you absolutely need to. And even then, you should save the original image in Photoshop format as well.

Scitex CT. Whether to use the Scitex CT file format is a no-brainer: if you own a Scitex system or are trying to output via a Scitex system, you *may* want to save your document in this format as the last stage before printing. If you don't have any contact with a Scitex system, ignore this one.

It may be important to note that the Scitex CT format is not actually the CT ("continuous tone") format that Scitex folks usually talk about. It's actually the Handshake format, which is less proprietary and more common (QuarkXPress can even import these files).

Scitex CT files are always CMYK or grayscale; however, Photoshop lets you save RGB images in this format, too. We can't figure out why. If you can figure out a good use for them, let us know. By the way, if you're trying to get Photoshop duotones through a Scitex system, you should sprint directly to "Converting Duotones to CMYK" in Chapter 10, *Spot Colors and Duotones.*

PNG (Portable Network Graphic). For a while there it looked like the GIF file format would take over the Internet, and therefore the world. Then, in early 1995, CompuServe and Unisys shocked the world by demanding that developers whose software wrote or read GIF files pay a royalty fee for the right to use the format. Legally, they were entitled; but no one had to pay before, and it jarred the electronic publishing community enough that a group of dedicated individuals decided to come up with a new file format for web graphics.

The result of their work is the PNG format (which is pronounced "ping," and officially stands for "Portable Network Graphic," though it unofficially stands for "PNG's Not GIF"). Not only is it a free format that any developer can use, but it does so much more than GIF, that it's likely that it will slowly become the next major graphic file format standard.

For instance, PNG can support both 8-bit indexed color and full 24-bit color. Where GIF can include 1-bit transparency (where each pixel is either transparent or not), PNG has full 8-bit transparency with alpha channels, so a graphic could be partially opaque in some areas. PNG also includes some limited ability to handle color management on the Internet, by recording monitor gamma and chromaticity. There are many other features, too (among which is the significant bonus of, unlike GIF, having a relatively unambiguous pronunciation).

With the speed that the Internet is changing these days, it would be foolish for us to predict when PNG will become commonplace. However, ultimately, PNG is not likely to replace GIF or JPEG anytime soon. Few people's Web browsers currently support PNG, and even when they do, it will take years for people to switch images over to the PNG format.

Fortunately, Photoshop is ready and waiting, and can save and open PNG format files. There are some reports that it is not fully PNG-compliant, however, and that several features—such as gamma support—don't work quite yet. Look for updates to Photoshop as PNG becomes more widely used.

PICT Resource. Are you authoring multimedia or developing software on the Macintosh? If so, you may find yourself needing to save an image into the resource fork of a file. Here's where the PICT Resource file format comes in. To be honest, it's not really a different file format; the Macintosh lets you place PICT information in the data or resource fork of a file. Photoshop, however, is a convenient way to move the image from one to the other. (Windows programs don't have a resource fork, so PC users can ignore this file format.)

Note that Photoshop lets you open PICT resources in two different ways. First, if the file has a PICT resource numbered 256, Photoshop lets you open that particular resource directly from the Open dialog box. If there are multiple PICT resources, you can access them only by selecting PICT Resource from the Acquire submenu (under the File menu; see Figure 16-17).

PDF (Portable Document Format). Adobe's Acrobat Portable Document Format (PDF) is very slowly becoming more accepted in both the prepress and Internet industries, though not nearly as quickly or widely as Adobe had hoped. Photoshop 4 could save an image in PDF format

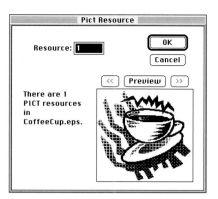

and it could open its own image-only PDF files. Version 5 now lets you open any PDF file, rasterizing it into a bitmapped image.

Note that Photoshop uses a little JPEG compression when saving the PDF, so the file size is reduced. However, the image quality does suffer very slightly.

Ultimately, the best use of PDFs from Photoshop may be the ability to make easy to transport "portfolios" of images by saving a number of images in PDF format, then using Acrobat Exchange to fit them together into a multi-page document.

FilmStrip. Video, film, and animation all have a similar popular appeal, and the tools that let mere mortals create this sort of stuff (like Adobe Premiere) have finally begun to find a market. But that doesn't mean that programs that create or edit still images will go away. For what is video but a bunch of still images strung together over time?

Programs like Premiere let you save movies in a file format that Photoshop can open, called Filmstrip (see Figure 16-18). You can then edit each frame individually in Photoshop, save the file out again, and import the clip in the video/animation program. This technique not only lets you make small retouching changes, but even perform rotoscoping (a form of animation), colorizing, or any number of other special effects.

When you open a Filmstrip file in Photoshop, it looks like a tall and narrow noodle. But when you double-click on the Zoom tool to scroll in to 1:1 view, you can see each image frame clearly, along with its time and frame code. Note that changing the file's size, resolution, or pixel dimensions may be disastrous, or at least unpredictable. Instead, constrain your edits to the pixels that are already there.

Figure 16-18
Filmstrip format

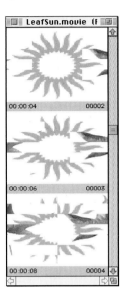

Raw. The last file format that we can even remotely recommend using is the file format of last resort: the Raw format. If you've ever traveled in a foreign country, you've probably found yourself in situations where you and the person in front of you share no common language. The answer? Reduce communication to gestures and sounds.

The Raw format is a way to read or write image data in a "language" that Photoshop doesn't know. It relies on the basics of bitmapped images (see Figure 16-19).

▶ All bitmapped images are rectangular grids of pixels.

▶ Some bitmapped images have header information at the beginning of the data.

▶ Color data is usually either interleaved (such as alternating red, green, blue, red, green, blue, and so on) or noninterleaved (such as all the red information, then all the green, and finally all the blue).

If you're trying to import from or export to some strange computer system, you may have to rely on the Raw format because that system might not know from TIFF, EPS, or any other normal, everyday file format. This is becoming less of a problem as mainframe systems (especially imaging systems that are used for scientific or medical imaging) learn the newer, better file formats we've been discussing up until now.

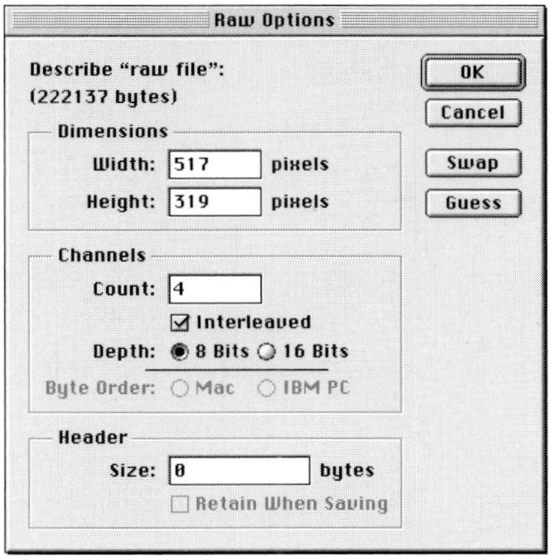

Figure 16-19

Opening Raw data

Note that Photoshop can only read data using the Raw data format if it's saved as binary data; hex is out.

Tip: Make Photoshop Guess for Raw Data. Okay, someone gives you a file and you find you can't open it using any of Photoshop's standard file format options. You decide to take a leap and attempt the Raw format. But when you ask your so-called friend about the file's vital signs—"What are the pixel dimensions? Interleaved or noninterleaved color? Is there a header?"—he just stares at you blankly.

Fortunately, Photoshop can do a little guessing for you. If you press the Guess button in the Open as Raw dialog box when the Width and Height fields are blank, Photoshop figures out a likely height/width combination for the image. If it's a color image, you need to know if it's RGB (three channels) or CMYK (four channels).

If there's a header and your friend doesn't know how big it is (in bytes), then it's probably a lost cause. On the other hand, if your friend knows the pixel dimensions but not the header, you can press the Guess button while the Header field is blank.

Unreasonable Niche File Formats

We don't mean to be harsh, but there are some file formats that are like putting matches in the hands of small children. For instance, some people still save images from FreeHand or MacDraw as PICT and expect them to print properly. It can happen, but it ain't likely. The object-oriented PICT format is very unreliable and should be avoided in professional work. Here are a few file formats that we just ignore most of the time when it comes to bitmapped images. Unless you have a clear, specific, and compelling reason to use them, we strongly recommend that you do likewise.

Amiga IFF. The Amiga computer story reads like that of the Tucker car or the PublishIt! desktop publishing software. Most people have never heard of these products, much less realized how great they were. Each one of the select group of people who used the Amiga had their own theories about why most of the world shunned the love of their computing life, but when it came right down to it, the computer simply shuffled away in obscurity until it died an ignominious death.

However, perhaps out of a sense of obligation to the would-be contender, or perhaps from a real need in the market (though we don't see it), Photoshop still lets you open and save in the Amiga IFF format. However, unless you really need it, or you want to see a format that features rectangular rather than square pixels, ignore it.

MacPaint. The MacPaint format is ultimately the most basic of all graphic formats on the Macintosh, but it's so outdated that there's almost no reason to use it anymore. Paint files (more rarely called PNTG, or "pee-en-tee-gee," files) are black and white (one bit per pixel), 72 pixels per inch, 8-by-10 inches (576-by-720 pixels). That's it. No more and no less. The MacPaint format is useful for capturing and placing black-and-white Mac screen shots (especially since it's so compatible with every Mac program), but TIFFs are more flexible, so we use those instead.

PCX. Whereas many formats (such as TIFF) are industry standards, the PCX format was developed by ZSoft Corporation, the developers of Publisher's Paintbrush. It's a granddaddy of bitmapped formats, predating Windows 1.0 when it hit the streets as part of PC Paintbrush. The current version of PCX supports adjustable dimensions and resolutions, and 24-bit color, but only a 256-color palette (indexed to 24-bit color), up from earlier 4- and 16-color versions.

Since a variety of palette-color techniques have been applied to PCX files over the ages, files from earlier programs can have serious color-mismatch problems. But if you're satisfied with the results of working with the PCX images you have, then go for it. We typically recommend using TIFF files instead of PCX whenever possible.

Pixar. To understand why Photoshop still saves and opens Pixar files, you have to understand that Photoshop was born from the minds of Tom and John Knoll as a way to do some of the low-level grunt work that goes into the cool special effects produced at George Lucas's Industrial Light and Magic (ILM), which is a close cousin of Pixar. As far as we're concerned, someone should put this file format out of our misery.

Targa. The Photoshop manuals maintain that the Targa file format is designed for TrueVision video boards, though other programs (especially DOS programs) also use it. Like PixelPaint, this format is almost entirely obsolete, as far as we can tell (though it lingers on in some mainframe and minicomputer databases).

Windows Bitmap (BMP). Windows Bitmap (typically called "BMP", pronounced by saying the letters) is the bitmap format native to Windows Paint. It is rarely encountered outside of Windows and OS/2 Presentation Manager, and is hardly considered a professional's choice of file format. While you can store a 1-, 4-, 8-, or 24-bit image of various dimensions and resolutions, we still prefer TIFF, given its strong support by desktop-publishing applications and compatibility across different computer systems.

If you're creating wallpaper for your Windows desktop, this is the format for you!

Compressing Images

One thing that can be said of all bitmapped images is that "they're pigs when it comes to hard disk space." We've often wondered why Adobe doesn't bundle a gigabyte hard disk with every copy of Photoshop they sell. It would make sense. Except that maybe a gigabyte isn't big enough.

Our aim, then, is to stretch out the scarce resources we have on hand, especially hard drive resources. And we've got three methods to accomplish this goal: work with smaller images (no, seriously!), archive our images when we're not using them, and work with compressed file formats.

Lossy versus Lossless

As we keep saying, bitmapped images are made simply of zeros and ones. In an 8-bit grayscale image, each pixel is defined by eight zeros or ones. If images are already reduced to this level of simplicity, how can they be reduced further? By bundling groups of bits together into discrete chunks.

Lossless Compression

Let's take the example of a 1-bit (black-and-white) bitmap, 100 pixels on each side. Without any compression, the computer stores the value (zero or one) for each one of the 10,000 pixels in the image. This is like staring into your sock drawer and saying, "I've got one blue sock and one blue sock and one black sock and one black sock," and so on. We can compress our description in half by saying "I've got one blue pair and one black pair."

Run Length Encoding. Similarly, we can group the zeros and ones together by counting up common values in a row (see Figure 16-20). For instance, we could say, "There are 34 zeros, then 3 ones, then 55 zeros," and so on. This is called Run Length Encoding (RLE), and it's automatically used for Macintosh PICT images (fax machines use it, too). We call it "lossless" because there is no loss of data when you compress or decompress the file—what goes in comes out the same.

Figure 16-20
Run Length Encoding
lossless compression

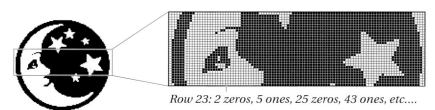

Row 23: 2 zeros, 5 ones, 25 zeros, 43 ones, etc....

LZW and Huffman. There are other forms of lossless compression. For instance, RLE compresses simple images (ones that have large solid-colored areas) down to almost nothing, but it won't compress more complex images (like most grayscale images) very much. LZW (Lempel-Ziv-Welch, though you really don't need to know that) and Huffman encoding work by tokenizing common strings of data.

In plain English, that means that instead of just looking for a string of the same color, these methods look for trends. If RLE sees "010101", it can't do any compression. But LZW and Huffman are smart enough algorithms to spot the trend of alternating characters, and thereby compress that information.

Lossy Compression

The table of contents at the front of most books is a way of compressing information. If you ripped the table of contents out of this book and mailed it to someone else (we're not actually suggesting that you do this!), they would be able to "unpack" it and read what's in this book. But they wouldn't actually be seeing the words you're reading now. Instead, they'd read an "average" of each chapter. The more detailed chapters have more headings, so your friend would see more detail in them than he or she would in a simple-headed chapter like this one.

Bitmapped images can be similarly outlined (compressed), transmitted to someone else, and unpacked. And similarly, when you look at the unpacked version, you don't get all the detail from the original image. For example, if nine pixels in a 3-by-3 square are similar, you could replace them all with a single averaged value. That's a nine-to-one compression. But the original image data, the variances in those nine pixels, is lost forever.

This sort of compression is called *lossy* compression because you lose data when compressing it. By losing some information, you can increase the compression immensely. Where an LZW-compressed TIFF might be 40 percent of original size, a file saved with lossy compression can be two percent or less of the original file size.

Levels of JPEG compression. Lossy compression schemes typically give you a choice of how tight you pack the data. (The primary method—the only method Photoshop offers—is JPEG, for Joint Photographic Experts Group.) With low compression, you get larger files and better quality. High compression yields lower quality and smaller files. How much quality do you lose? It depends on the level of the compression, the resolution of the image, and the content of the image.

Different programs implement JPEG differently, and with varying results. Note that JPEG is both a compression method and a file format in its own right (see "File Formats," earlier in this chapter), but both are based on similar algorithms.

Two other forms of lossy compression—fractal compression and wavelet compression—look promising as future compression technologies, but Photoshop currently supports neither of them without a plug-in.

JPEG warnings. Here are a few things to remember when working with JPEG. First, note that images with hard edges, high contrast, and angular areas are most susceptible to artifacts from JPEG compression. For example, a yellow square on a green background in a lower-resolution image looks pretty miserable after lossy compression. On the other hand, compressing natural, scanned images using JPEG—especially those that are already somewhat grainy or impressionistic—probably won't hurt them much at all.

You should *only* use JPEG on finished images (those on which you've finished all editing and correction). Tone or color correction on a JPEGed image exaggerates the compression artifacts. Sharpening a JPEGed image produces an effect that might one day find its way into Kai's Power Tools, but it's difficult to envisage a use for it in a production setting.

Also, compressing and decompressing images repeatedly can make images worse than just doing it once. But since we just told you that you should only JPEG finished images, the point is moot—you can just open them, look at them, and close them again.

Tip: Great Preview, Small Files. If you're primarily concerned with getting a good preview image in your page-layout or multimedia program, and are not concerned with printing color separations, try saving your image as an EPS file with a JPEG preview. The 24-bit color JPEG preview is the smoothest you'll find. Because you're not going to print this puppy, you can make the file size really small by setting the Encoding popup menu to JPEG (low quality).

Another choice would be to save the file in the JPEG file format (again, if the multimedia or page-layout program you're using can read it). The preview is usually not quite as good (though it's still better than TIFF or regular EPS), but the file size on disk is even smaller. In this case, you'll probably want to use Medium compression or better, so the image quality won't be too poor.

To Compress or Not to Compress

Over the years, we've found only a few universal truths. One of those is: "Fast, Cheap, or Good: you can have any two of the three." Compression is certainly no exception to this rule. Compressing files can be a great way to save hard drive space (read: "save money") and sometimes to cut down on printing times (read: "save more money"). But compressing and decompressing files also takes time (read: "lose the money that you just saved").

Optimally, if you have way too much hard drive space, you may never need or want to compress your images. For those of us less fortunate, you may only want to compress those images you're finished with into a lossless archive.

On the other hand, if you still need access to the files (you can't use images that are stored in archives until you extract them) but you need to make your files smaller and you don't mind the performance hit, you may opt for either a lossless or a lossy compression file format. The benefit of compressing data in this way is that you don't have to decompress the file manually before opening it. Rather, Photoshop does all the decompression for you, on the fly, when you open it. Most compressed file formats can also be opened directly in page-layout programs (in this case, PageMaker or QuarkXPress does the automatic decompression for you).

The downside of compressed file formats is that Photoshop has to compress or decompress the file each and every time you save or open the file. That means time sitting and staring at your computer screen. The smaller the document, or the faster your machine, the less time you have to grab a cup of coffee. In the case of page-layout applications, the program may decompress the image once when it opens it, but it typically has to decompress it *every time you print the page*. (There are exceptions to this, though; see "Encapsulated PostScript (EPS)," earlier in this chapter.)

To be honest, we almost never compress files until we archive them, unless we have to modem them, and in a hurry. It's a hassle to save TIFF files with LZW compression, and too often these compressed TIFFs are mysteriously less reliable. When we absolutely need to save a file in a compressed file format, our choice is JPEG (if we *need* to compress a file, we probably need to compress it more rather than less, and only JPEG will do the trick). However, we never use anything other than Maximum quality in JPEG; we find the increase in compression at Good, Medium, or Low simply isn't worth the degradation in quality.

Ultimately, storage space is getting so inexpensive these days that it's almost silly to worry about compression. The Iomega Zip drive, with 96 MB disks that cost $15, is so inexpensive that you might as well buy one and another for your dog. The Jaz drives offer gigabyte storage for around $100; CD-ROMs are becoming easier and cheaper to produce; and DAT cartridges can store more than eight gigs for under $20. If time equals money, then time spent compressing and decompressing files (whether it's manual or automatic) is money down the big porcelain doughnut.

Archiving

You may have worked with programs such as StuffIt, Compact Pro, or Disk-Doubler (if you don't already work with one of these, you probably should). They all have pretty much the same function: to compress files—any kind of files—and save space on your hard drive. This sort of compression is called *archiving* because people typically use it on files that they're not currently using.

Archiving a file is like folding up a piece of paper and putting it into an envelope. It takes a little time to fold it up (compress it) and a little time to unfold it (decompress it), and while it's in the envelope, you can't read it. The archive file (the "envelope" that contains the compressed file) takes up less room on your hard drive, but in order to work on the enclosed file, you have to decompress it, usually with the same program that compressed it.

All archival compression programs use lossless compression methods, so you never have to worry about degrading the image. However, that also means they may not compress down as much as you'd like. Because it often takes a long time to compress very large files, we just buy additional removable media (such as SyQuests, Bernoullis, CD-ROMs, or magneto-optical drives) and store our files uncompressed.

Tip: Archiving Small Files. By the way, archiving programs can almost always store multiple files in the same "envelope." One of our favorite uses for archiving programs (we prefer Compact Pro but StuffIt is good, too) is to store tens or hundreds of small files together. Because of the way the Macintosh file system works, each file (no matter how small it is) takes up a minimum amount of space on disk, and the larger the hard

Figure 17-1
Halftoning

Figure 17-2
A representation of
digital halftone cells

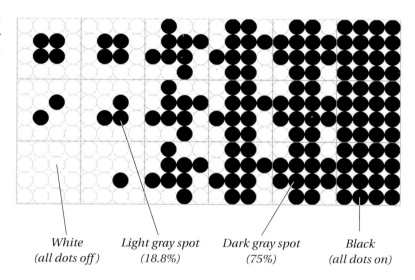

*White
(all dots off)*   *Light gray spot
(18.8%)*   *Dark gray spot
(75%)*   *Black
(all dots on)*

Figure 17-3
Tint percentages

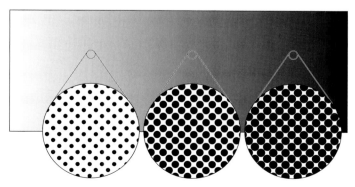

You can print multicolor images by overlaying two or more color halftones (typically cyan, magenta, yellow, and black). Again, our eyes fool us into thinking we're seeing thousands of colors when, in fact, we're only seeing four.

David coauthored a book with Glenn Fleishman and Steve Roth, called *Real World Scanning and Halftones*, that covers halftoning in much more detail than we can get into here. However, we should at least cover the basics. Every halftone has three components, or attributes: screen frequency, screen angle, and spot shape.

Screen frequency. Halftone spots on a grid are like bitmapped images; they have resolution, too. The more spots you cram together within an inch, the tighter the grid, the smaller the spots, and so on. The number of halftone spots per inch is called *halftone screen frequency*. Higher frequencies (small spots, tightly packed, like those in glossy magazines) look smoother because the eye isn't distracted as much by the spots. However, because of limits in digital halftoning, you can achieve fewer levels of gray at a given output resolution. Also, higher screen frequencies have much more dot gain on a printing press, so tints clog up and go muddy more quickly (see "Image Differences," later in this chapter).

Lower screen frequencies (as in newspapers) are rougher looking, but easier to print (less dot gain) and you can achieve many levels of gray at lower output resolutions. Screen frequencies are specified in lines per inch, or *lpi* (even though we're really talking about "rows of spots per inch").

Screen angle. Halftone grids are not like bitmapped images; you can rotate them to any angle you want. (In a bitmapped image, the pixels are always in a horizontal/vertical orientation.) Halftones of grayscale images are typically printed at a 45-degree angle because the spots are least noticeable at this angle. However, color images are more complex.

When you overlap halftone grids, as in color printing, you may get distracting moiré ("mwah-RAY") patterns which ruin the illusion. In order to minimize these patterns, it's important to use specific angles. The greater the angle difference between overlapping screens (you can't get them any farther apart than 45 degrees), the smaller the moiré pattern. With four-color process printing, the screens are typically printed 30 degrees apart at 15, 45, and 75 degrees (yellow, the lightest ink, is generally printed at 0 degrees—15 degrees offset from cyan).

Spot shape. The last attribute of halftones is the shape of each spot. The spot may be circular, or square, or a straight line, or even little pinwheels (see Figure 17-4). The standard PostScript spot shape is a round black spot in the highlights, square at 50 percent, and an inverted circle (white on black) in the shadows. Changing the shape of the spot is rarely necessary. However, if you're producing cosmetic catalogs, or need to solve tonal shift problems printing on newsprint at coarse screen frequencies (to use two examples), controlling the halftone spot can definitely improve the quality of your job.

Figure 17-4
Spot shape

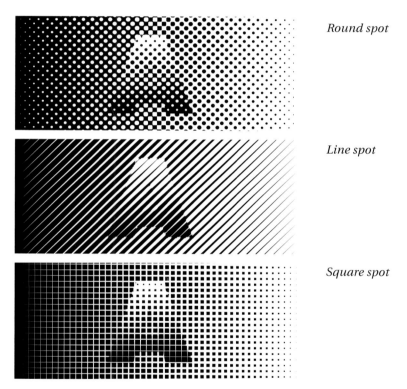

Round spot

Line spot

Square spot

Screen Settings: What Overrides What?

When you send a grayscale or color bitmapped image to a PostScript printer, the computer inside the printer converts the image into a halftone. That means that the printer sets the halftone screen frequency, angle, and spot shape. However, there are plenty of times when you want to override the printer's default settings to use your own halftone screening

The Rule of 16

It's simply a rule of the universe: in digital halftoning, the higher the screen frequency you request at a given output resolution, the fewer levels of gray you can achieve. The problem, in a nutshell, is that higher screen frequencies mean smaller halftone spots; and because these halftone spots are made of groups of printer dots, the smaller the spot, the fewer printer dots it contains. The fewer printer dots in a halftone spot, the fewer gray levels that spot can simulate (see Figure 17-5).

There's a simple equation that lets you figure out approximately how many gray levels you can achieve at a given halftone screen frequency on a given printer:

$$(\text{printer resolution} \div \text{screen frequency})^2 + 1$$

However, we can make it even simpler for you. We know that there is a maximum of 256 levels of gray possible on any PostScript printer. Therefore, you can figure out (with a little behind-the-scenes arithmetic) the highest screen frequency you should use on a given printer by dividing the resolution by 16.

Or conversely, if you know you want to print at a given screen frequency, you can figure out what resolution printer you need by multiplying the frequency by 16.

If you break this rule—going to a higher screen frequency than the output device can support—you start losing gray levels. If you lose enough gray levels, you start seeing posterization. Try it for yourself: print a grayscale image at 106 lpi on a 300-dpi laser printer (see Figure 17-6).

For instance, if you know that you're going to print on a 2,400-dpi imagesetter, the highest frequency you should use is 150

Figure 17-5 Gray levels versus screen frequency

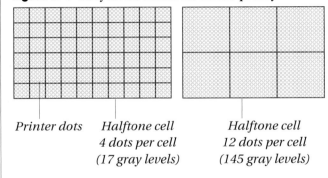

Printer dots   *Halftone cell*
                   4 dots per cell
                   (17 gray levels)

Halftone cell
12 dots per cell
(145 gray levels)

information. Fortunately, most programs give you some help in doing this, and Photoshop gives you a *lot* of help.

Figure 17-7 shows, in brief, the order in which screening controls override each other. Let's look at each of them in order.

Device's default setting. Every PostScript output device has a built-in default screen setting. On most desktop laser printers, it's 53 lpi at 45 degrees. Imagesetters vary widely, but are typically above 100 lpi at 45 degrees.

Driver setting. Printer drivers are the software modules that "drive" printers in the background; PostScript drivers actually write much or all of the PostScript code that gets sent to the printer. Although the Windows PostScript

(2,400 ÷ 16). Or, if you know that you want to print at 133 lpi, you should print on an imagesetter with resolution of at least 2,100 dpi (133 x 16).

On the other hand, we know that most printing presses can't handle anywhere near 256 levels of gray (especially on uncoated stock). So there's a corollary rule: if you think you don't really need a full range of grays, adjust accordingly. Perhaps use the Rule of 13, which would give you 170 levels of gray, but might save you a little money—it's usually cheaper to run film at a lower resolution because it images faster, saving the service bureau time.

When your output device doesn't have enough resolution to support the full range of 256 grays at the line screen you want, you have a choice. You can lower the screen frequency, which loses fine detail, or you can settle for fewer shades of gray, which increases the amount of posterization. Some

Figure 17-6 Posterization due to insufficient output resolution

Printed at 133 lpi on a 2,400-dpi imagesetter

Printed at 106 lpi on a 300-dpi laser printer

images are better served by going with the higher screen frequency and fewer grays; others need the full range of grays and can sacrifice detail. The trade-off is particularly important when you're printing to a desktop laser printer. With a 60-lpi screen, a 600-dpi laser printer can produce about 100 gray levels. With a 100-lpi screen, it only produces 36 gray levels.

Tip: See Posterization in Action. If you use the Rule of 13, you're going to posterize your image. That's life. But is that so

bad? Oftentimes, it's not. You can see approximately what the effect of posterizing your image to 170 levels of gray would be with the Posterize command on the Map submenu under the Image menu. The effect you get by selecting Posterize and typing 170 is more or less what you'd get if you printed your image at 175 lpi on a 2,400-dpi imagesetter, or at 110 lpi on a 1,270-dpi imagesetter.

If your image is not very posterized to begin with, this level of posterization may have very little effect on it.

Figure 17-7
What screen settings override what

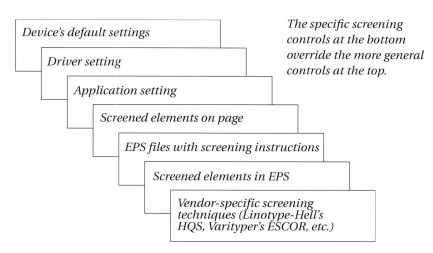

Device's default settings

Driver setting

Application setting

Screened elements on page

EPS files with screening instructions

Screened elements in EPS

Vendor-specific screening techniques (Linotype-Hell's HQS, Varityper's ESCOR, etc.)

The specific screening controls at the bottom override the more general controls at the top.

Making Halftones in Photoshop

When you print an image from Photoshop or a page-layout program, the PostScript printer converts your grayscale or color data into halftones. That doesn't mean, though, that you couldn't do it yourself in Photoshop if you really wanted to. In fact, there are a few times when it's advantageous to convert images into halftones in Photoshop.

▶ You are printing to a non-PostScript printer and want controllable halftones and smaller image files.

▶ You want a diffusion dither—a stippled screen very similar to the stochastic screening available on many imagesetters, but

useful for lower-resolution output as well (see Figure 17-9 for an example).

▶ You want to create some special halftone-like effects.

▶ You want to learn about how halftones work. Creating halftones in Photoshop is a great way to learn what halftoning is all about. (When we do halftoning seminars, it's not until we show people how to do halftoning in Photoshop that they really understand what we've been talking about.)

Here's how to convert a grayscale image into a halftone in Photoshop (yes, this only works

with grayscale images; if you're working on a color image, select Grayscale, or duplicate a color channel into a new grayscale document).

1. Select Bitmap from the Mode submenu in the Image menu (see Figure 17-8).

2. In the Bitmap dialog box, choose an output resolution appropriate for your output. All the same rules for line art images that we talked about back in Chapter 11, *Line Art*, apply here.

   So if your final output is on a 300-dpi laser printer, you don't need more than 300-ppi image resolution. If your final

driver lets you control the halftone screen for the print job, most Macintosh drivers do not.

Application setting. Many applications provide control over halftone screens for your print jobs. In both QuarkXPress 4 and PageMaker 6.x, it's in the Print dialog box. In Photoshop, you get at it via the Screens button in the Page Setup dialog box. Anytime you set screening information at the application level, it overrides both the device default and the driver settings.

Individual screened elements within publications. In some applications—FreeHand is a good example—you can select individual objects (text or graphics) and set a screen for those objects. In others (such as PageMaker and QuarkXPress), you can apply screens to individual bitmapped images (TIFF only). These are called *object-level settings*, and they override the application-level settings, which still apply to the rest of the job.

output is on an imagesetter, you may need to raise this to 800 or 1,000 ppi.

3. Select the Halftone Screen radio button in the Bitmap dialog box, and press OK. (While you're here, you should also check out the Diffusion option; it's a totally different look.)

4. In the Halftone Screen dialog box, set the frequency (bearing in mind the Rule of 16), angle, and spot shape, then press OK.

If you don't like the halftone effect that results, you can undo the mode change and start over with different settings.

Note that once you halftone a grayscale image, you can no longer make many edits to it—no tonal adjustments, filters, or the

like (there's nothing there for the tools to work with). Also, you shouldn't scale the image, even a little, or you can expect to get very strange patterning when you print.

We generally let the imageset-ter's RIP take care of the screening for us. We certainly never do this Photoshop halftoning on color images (unless we're trying to create a special effect). But for drop shadows and the like, this is a great technique.

Figure 17-8 Bitmap dialog box

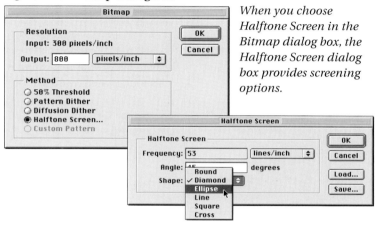

When you choose Halftone Screen in the Bitmap dialog box, the Halftone Screen dialog box provides screening options.

EPS files that include screening instructions. When you save a file as EPS from Photoshop, you can tell the program that you want to include screening information. Then, if you import that EPS file into a program such as PageMaker or QuarkXPress, the screening information in the EPS overrides the program's settings when you print the whole page—but for that object only.

You almost never need to save screening information with your EPS image. Of course, there are always exceptions; for instance, you often want to save particular angles in duotone images (see Chapter 10, *Spot Colors and Duotones*).

Individual screened elements within EPS files. An EPS file that contains screening instructions can also include individual elements within the file that have their own screening instructions. For example, an EPS from FreeHand might have a gray box that has an object-level halftone screen applied to it. That item would be screened as specified, and the rest of the EPS would be screened as *it* was specified (or if there is no screen specified for the whole EPS, using the settings of the printing application—probably PageMaker or QuarkXPress).

Vendor-specific screening instructions. If you're printing to an imagesetter that uses a specialized screening technique such as Linotype-Hell's High-Quality Screening (HQS), Agfa's Balanced Screens Technology (BST), or Prepress Solutions' ESCOR, you may not get the screen settings you expect.

These techniques use screening "filters" which catch *all* screening instructions, and replace the frequency/angle combinations with the closest settings that are available in their optimized sets. So even if you specify angles in Photoshop and save as an EPS, you still may not get your exact request. This is mostly significant if you're after a specialized spot shape. If you are, tell your service bureau to turn off HQS, or BST, or whatever.

Contone Output

With binary devices such as imagesetters and printers, we need to use a halftone to fool the eye into seeing shades of gray because we can't create color or gray pixels. With a contone device, we *can* vary the color or gray shade of each pixel. Continuous-tone imaging, usually called *contone*, is different from halftone imaging in two other ways.

▶ The pixels touch each other so that without very close inspection no paper or clear film shows through between marks.

▶ Each pixel is a specific color, made by building up varying densities of primary colors in the same spot.

The most common contone imaging device is your computer monitor. The color of each pixel you see (or don't see, if the screen's resolution is high enough) is made by mixing together varying amounts of red, green, and blue. For example, to make a pixel more red, the monitor must increase the number of electrons that are bombarding the red element of the pixel.

There's no threat of moiré patterns, because there are no grids involved. But then again, there's no chance of mass-reproducing the image, as no printing press can handle continuous-tone images (see "Hybrid Color Screening," later in this chapter). Aside from the monitor, there are two

pitfalls are specifying too high an ink density and underestimating dot gain. Color laser printers don't have dot gain in the usual sense, and they use dry toner, so one might think that you could go all the way to a 400-percent total ink limit and 100-percent black ink limit. If you do, you'll get very dense shadows and saturated colors that look as though they belong in some other image. As a starting point, try 260-percent total ink with an 85-percent black limit in the CMYK Setup dialog box.

Image Differences

Now that we've explored the various imaging methods, we should recap and highlight some of the different techniques you must use in building images suitable for output on halftone and contone devices. We say "recap" because we've mentioned most (if not all) of these in previous chapters, though never in one place.

Resolution. The first and foremost difference between contone and half-tone imaging is the required image resolution. It's quite a bit more complicated to work out the resolution needed for halftone output than it is for contone, so we'll deal with halftone output first.

▶ **Resolution requirements for halftone output.** The resolution of the output device isn't directly relevant in determining the resolution you need for the image. It's the halftone screen frequency that matters. You never need an image resolution above two times (2×) the halftone screen frequency (and often you can get almost-equivalent results with as little as 1.2× or 1.4×). That means that even if you're printing on a 2,400-dpi imagesetter, your image resolution can (and should) be much lower. For instance, printing at 150 lpi, you never need more than a 300-ppi image, and usually no higher than 225 ppi (we generally use the 1.5 multiplier). (See Figure 3-7 on page 87, and Color Plate 2 on page 678.)

▶ **Resolution requirements for contone output.** The required resolution for a contone output device is easy to figure, but it can sometimes be hard to deliver. Your output resolution should simply match the resolution of the output device. If you're printing to a 300-dpi dye-sub printer, your image resolution should be 300 ppi. When printing to a

4 K film recorder, your image should have a horizontal measure of 4,096 pixels, or about 60 MB for a 4-by-5 print. An 8 K film recorder really wants 240 MB—an 8,192 x 10,240-pixel image.

In truth, many high-resolution film recorders are more forgiving, and you can halve the resolution. For instance, we know of few people who actually send a 960 MB image to a 16 K film recorder, and we know quite a few who get good results sending a 60 MB file to an 8 K film recorder (about half the amount of data it "requires"). Sending less than a full 60 MB to a 4 K film recorder, however, is a much more marginal proposition. Make sure, though, that you send an integral multiple of the device's resolution. If you send 4,095 pixels to a device that wants 4,096, it'll either barf when it gets the file, or you'll get some very strange interpolation artifacts.

The appropriate resolution for stochastic screening is less clear, but in general you rarely need over 300-ppi images.

Tonal and color correction. We talk a great deal about tonal compression for halftone output in Chapter 6, *Tonal Correction*, and Chapter 7, *Color Correction*, so we won't go into it here. Contone output needs less in the way of tonal and gamut compression than halftone output, because contone devices generally have a greater dynamic range and a wider gamut than do halftone devices. However, this can bring its own problems, particularly when you have a scanner with a tendency to over-saturate some colors, as do many inexpensive scanners (and even some expensive ones). Keep a watchful eye on saturated colors. Some dye-sublimation printers feature a magenta that's almost fluorescent!

Sharpening. As we noted back in Chapter 9, *Sharpening*, contone images need much less sharpening than halftone images. But that doesn't mean they don't need any at all. Halftones, again because of their coarse screens and significant dot gain, mask details and edges in an image; sharpening can help compensate for both the blurriness of the scan and the blurri-ness of the halftone. And, halftones being what they are, you have a lot of room to play with sharpening before the picture becomes oversharpened (most people end up undersharpening).

In contone images, however, there's a real risk of oversharpening. Not only should you use a lesser Amount setting for unsharp masking, but also a smaller Radius. Where a Radius less than one is often lost in a halftone image, it's usually appropriate in contone images.

Image mode. This last item, *image mode*, isn't really dependent on what output method you're using. However, because we still see people confused about image mode, we thought we'd throw in a recap here, too.

Again: if you're printing to a color contone device that outputs to film (or if the image is only seen on a color screen), you should leave your image in RGB mode. Contone *and* halftone devices that print on paper (or film that will be used to image paper later) require CMYK images, but in many cases you'll get better results sending RGB and letting the printer handle the conversion. Or, if you have a good profile for the output device, you can try using Profile-to-Profile to convert the image from your RGB editing space to the device's space before printing.

We've tried many times to build Photoshop Classic CMYK setups for dye-sublimation printers, but it simply doesn't work. Photoshop's separation engine is geared toward halftone output, where the ink density remains constant and the dot size varies. It simply can't handle the variable density on dye-sublimation printers.

Hybrid Screening

When printing with hybrid screening, such as to a color laser printer or to film with stochastic screening, keep in mind that your image requires the sharpening and resolution of a contone image, but also the tonal and color corrections of a halftone image. In fact, these images often result in so much dot gain that you need to compress the image's tonal range significantly more than you'd think.

Imaging from Photoshop

We haven't taken a poll, but it appears that most people who use Photoshop don't print directly from it; instead, they save their images in some other format and then import them into some other program to print later. Nonetheless, perhaps out of admiration for the underdogs out there, or perhaps just because, we're going to tackle the topic of imaging directly from Photoshop before we move out of Photoshop and into QuarkXPress, PageMaker, or other programs.

As in almost every other Macintosh or Windows program, there are two menu items (and accompanying dialog boxes) tied to imaging: Page Setup and Print, both found under the File menu.

Page Setup

Most of the items in the Page Setup dialog box tell Photoshop how to print the document. Almost any other software developer in the world would have put this stuff in the Print dialog box, but the engineers at Adobe code to a different drummer. In fact, it makes sense for a couple of these items to be here, because they also apply when saving files in various formats (see Chapter 16, *Storing Images*).

The features in the top half of the dialog box (see Figure 17-10) are determined by what printer driver you've got selected in the Chooser

Figure 17-10

The Page Setup
dialog box

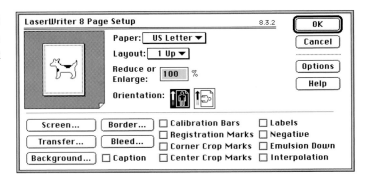

Figure 17-11
Halftone Screens
dialog box

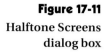

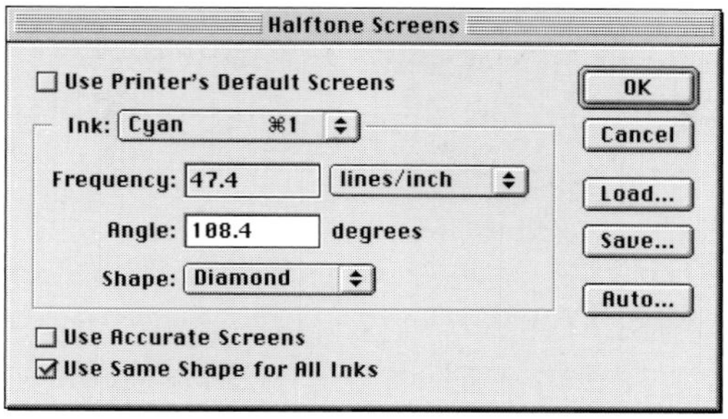

(Macintosh) or Page Setup dialog box (Windows). Because these are standard system-level features, we're going to skip them and get right to the good stuff: the Photoshop items in the lower half.

Screen. When you click the Screen button, Photoshop brings up the Halftone Screens dialog box, where you can specify the halftone screen angle, frequency, and spot shape for your image (see Figure 17-11). When the Use Printer's Default Screens checkbox is turned on (it is unless you go and change it), Photoshop won't tell the printer anything about how the image should be screened.

Unless you want to take explicit responsibility for setting your own halftone screens, you should leave Use Printer's Default Screens checked. When you do so, you make sure that the resulting file has no halftone screens built in, so unless someone intervenes downstream, the RIP will handle the screening. In the vast majority of cases, the RIP will do a better job than you can. Tell your service bureau what screen you want, and then it's their responsibility.

On the other hand, if you want or need to specify your own screens, turn this checkbox off. Photoshop gives you a wide array of possibilities for setting the halftone screen. And when you have a color image, you have even more choices.

▶ **Frequency and Angle.** The frequency and angle are self-explanatory.

▶ **Shape.** When the Use Same Shape for All Inks checkbox is on, the Shape popup menu applies to each process color. We can't think of any reason you'd change this, except for special low-frequency effects.

▶ **Use Accurate Screens.** When you turn on the Use Accurate Screens checkbox, Photoshop includes the PostScript code to activate

Accurate Screens in your imagesetter. However, if your imagesetter doesn't have Accurate Screens technology, or if it uses some other screening technology—such as Balanced Screens or HQS—you should just leave this off. (We almost always leave it off, unless our service bureau tells us to turn it on.)

▶ **Auto.** If you don't know what frequency/angle combinations to type in, check with your service bureau. If your service bureau doesn't know, you're probably in trouble. However, as a last resort, you could try pressing the Auto button and telling Photoshop approximately what screen frequency you want and what resolution imagesetter you're using. The program has canned settings that sometimes work. Again, if you're using an imagesetter with HQS or Balanced Screens technology, you can ignore this feature; those technologies override the screen values. (See "Screen Settings: What Overrides What," earlier in this chapter.)

Note that you can include these screen settings in EPS files (see "Encapsulated PostScript (EPS)" in Chapter 16, *Storing Images*).

Tip: Use Diamond Spot. Peter Fink's PostScript prowess perfected the diamond spot (say that ten times fast). The diamond spot is better in almost every instance than the standard round spot because it greatly reduces the optical tonal jump that is sometimes visible in the mid-to-three-quarter tones—the 50-to-75-percent gray areas. We've also been told that the diamond spot is much better for silkscreening.

Whatever the case, on those rare occasions when we print from Photoshop, or save halftone screens in an EPS using our own screening parameters, we use the diamond spot. Again, there's a good chance that this will be overridden or replaced by the imagesetter's specialized screens, unless you tell your service bureau to turn them off.

Transfer. Back in Chapter 6, *Tonal Correction*, and in Chapter 10, *Spot Colors and Duotones*, we discussed the idea of input/output contrast curves. Well, here they are once again, in Page Setup (see Figure 17-12). A transfer curve is like taking a curve that you made in the Curves dialog box and downloading it to your printer. It won't change the image data on your hard drive, but when you print with the transfer curve, it modifies the printed gray levels.

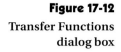

Figure 17-12

Transfer Functions
dialog box

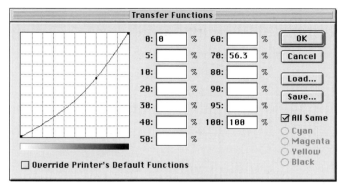

It's a rare occasion that you'd need to use a transfer curve these days. Here are a few examples of why you might, however.

▶   If you're printing from Photoshop to an uncalibrated imagesetter, you can use transfer curves (plus a lot of proof pages and a densitometer) to calibrate the device. We'd rather get calibration software that's made for this sort of thing. (Even better, we'd prefer our service bureau to own this software and calibrate their devices regularly.)

▶   You may have a single grayscale or CMYK image that you want to print on several different presses or paper stocks. Because each type of press or paper requires slightly different targeting (see "White Points and Black Points and Grays, Oh My" in Chapter 6, *Tonal Correction*), in a perfect world you'd want to retarget an "ideally" corrected image for each output method. However, this is often not possible. Transfer curves let you make these sorts of minor adjustments at print time.

Note that you can only save a transfer curve in a Photoshop or EPS-format file. But there's a danger in doing this, particularly with EPS images, because there's no obvious signal that tells anyone working with the image that it contains a transfer curve, except that the values in the file aren't the same as those that print. The only way to tell is to open the image in Photoshop and check to see if there's a transfer curve specified. If you do use a transfer curve, make sure that whoever is responsible for printing the file knows it's there!

Tip: Interchangeable Curves. While Bruce can think about transfer curves in terms of numbers, David needs a more touchy-feely approach. So he tries out his transfer curves in the Curves dialog box first. When he gets a curve just the way he wants it, he saves the curve to disk (using the Save button in the Curves dialog box), then goes to the Transfer Functions dialog box and loads it in.

You can go the other way, too, setting points by just typing numbers into the Transfer Functions dialog box, saving them to disk and loading them into the Curves dialog box. But this is less relevant, now that you can key in values numerically in the Curves dialog box. (Also, you can only transfer a "master" curve like this; not the individual color channels.)

Tip: Setting and Retrieving Defaults. There's a hidden feature in the Transfer Functions dialog box. When you hold down the Option key, the Load and Save buttons change into "<-Default" and "->Default" buttons. For some reason it took us a moment before we realized those hyphens and angle brackets were supposed to be arrows. The first, "<-Default", means replace the current transfer curve with the default curve. The second means just the opposite: replace the default curve with the current curve (the one in the dialog box).

The default curve is the curve that all new Photoshop documents are created with. The default curve is also applied when you convert to a new color mode. Note that there are actually two default curves—color and grayscale—so if you set the default for a grayscale image, it won't be applied to color images, and vice versa.

All in all, we never change the default curves from their straight, 45-degree settings. However, if you're using transfer curves as your primary imagesetter-calibration, tonal-correction, or targeting method, this may save you some time.

Note that at the bottom of the Transfer Functions dialog box, Photoshop provides you with a checkbox: Override Printer's Default Curves. Don't turn this on unless you really know what you're doing with transfer functions. If your service bureau is using calibration software, turning this checkbox on will override their carefully adjusted settings, and could give you nasty results. While it's nice that Adobe gives us this control, this is one we tend to ignore.

Background. Background and the next eleven features are only relevant when you're printing from Photoshop; you cannot save them in an EPS format (or any other, for that matter) and expect them to carry over to other programs, like you can with Screen and Transfer.

When you print your image from Photoshop to a color printer, the area surrounding the image is typically left white (or clear if you're printing on film). The Background feature lets you change the color that surrounds the image, using the standard Photoshop color picker. The background color that you pick acts like a matte frame around the image to the edges of the paper (or whatever size you picked in Page Setup's Paper popup menu).

Border. If you specify a border around an image (the border can be up to .15 inches, 10 points, or 3.5 millimeters), Photoshop centers the frame on the edge of the image when you print; that is, half the frame overlaps the image, and half the frame overlaps the background. You cannot, unfortunately, change the color of the frame; it's always black.

We can't think of any reason to use this feature, except perhaps to print an image with a pretrapped frame directly from Photoshop, then strip it in with the rest of the film manually. Yuck. We'd rather import the file into QuarkXPress or PageMaker and keyline it there.

Bleed. Setting a bleed value adjusts where Photoshop places the corner crop marks. You can choose a bleed up to 9.01 points, 3.18 millimeters, or .125 inches (who knows who came up with these values). Again, this is most useful if you're planning on doing manual stripping later.

Caption. David loves Photoshop's ability to save a caption with a file because of its tie-in to QuarkXPress (see "Tip: Use File Info for Captions" in Chapter 16, *Storing Images*), but it's also helpful when printing a whole mess of images that you need to peruse, file, or send to someone. When you turn on the Caption checkbox in Page Setup, the program prints whatever caption you have saved in File Info (under the File menu) beneath the image. If you haven't saved a caption, this feature doesn't do anything.

We often include our names or copyright information in the Caption field of the File Info dialog box. It won't stop people from stealing, but at least your name travels with your images.

Newspapers and stock photo agencies can make much more elaborate use of the File Info feature, including credit lines, handling instructions, and keywords for database searches.

Calibration Bars. When you turn on the Calibration Bars checkbox in Page Setup, Photoshop prints one (for grayscale images) or several (for color images) series of rectangles around the image (see Figure 17-13). Beneath the image is a ten-step gray wedge; to the left is the same gray wedge, but on each color plate; to the right is a series of colors, listed below. Each color is 100 percent (solid).

▶ Yellow

▶ Yellow and Magenta

▶ Magenta

▶ Magenta and Cyan

▶ Cyan

▶ Cyan and Yellow

▶ Cyan, Magenta, and Yellow

▶ Black

Figure 17-13
Page Setup options

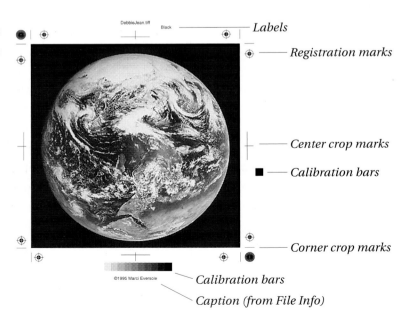

Labels

Registration marks

Center crop marks

Calibration bars

Corner crop marks

Calibration bars

Caption (from File Info)

Registration Marks. If you're outputting separations, you need to add registration marks so that the printer can align the four colors properly. Turning on the Registration Marks checkbox adds ten registration marks (eight bull's-eyes and two pinpoint types).

Corner Crop Marks. Even if your printer is going to strip your image into another layout, it's helpful to print with corner crop marks, which specify clearly where the edges of the image are. This can help the stripper align the image with a straight edge. In fact, it's essential if the image has a clear white background (like a silhouette); without crop marks, it's impossible to tell where the image boundaries are.

Center Crop Marks. If you need to specify the center point of your image, turn on the Center Crop Marks checkbox. We always turn this on along with Corner Crop Marks as an added bonus, although we aren't always sure *why* we do so. Note that when you turn this feature on, Photoshop also adds two pinpoint registration marks, even on grayscale images.

Labels. When you're printing color separations, turning on the Labels checkbox is a must. This feature adds the file name above the image on each separation, and also adds the color plate name (cyan, magenta, yellow, or black, or whatever other channel you're printing).

Negative and Emulsion Down. When it comes to the Negative and Emulsion Down options in the Page Setup dialog box, our best advice is to ignore them. Both of these effects are better performed at the imagesetter rather than in Photoshop. On the other hand, if your service bureau specifically tells you to set these a certain way, or if you're an imagesetter operator and you think it's right to do so on your system, go right ahead.

Interpolation. The last item in the Page Setup dialog box, Interpolation, does absolutely nothing. In a perfect world, this feature would tell your printer to smooth out low-resolution images at print time. Unfortunately, we don't know of any devices that can actually do this. But thanks, Adobe, for giving us the choice!

Print

At long last, we arrive at the Print dialog box (see Figure 17-14). The features and "look" of the Print dialog box depend on which output driver you have selected in the Chooser. However, there are four items that Photoshop puts there which are almost always present: Encoding, Print Selected Areas, Printer Color Management, and Space. (Note that recent Macintosh PostScript printer drivers hide these options; you have to select "Adobe Photoshop 5" from the dialog box's popup menu to get to them.)

Figure 17-14

The Print
dialog box

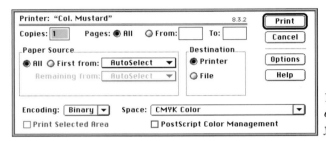

*You may have
other options with
your driver.*

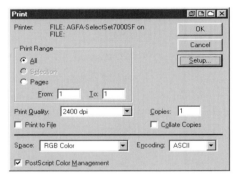

Encoding. We mentioned the concept of encoding in Chapter 16, *Storing Images*. The idea is that image data can be stored and sent to a printer as ASCII or binary data. ASCII takes twice as much space to describe the data as binary, but it's universally understandable by PostScript devices, no matter how they're connected to the world; so it's often preferable on networks that are administered using DOS or UNIX machines. We recommend saving time and using Binary; if it doesn't work, try ASCII.

The Print dialog box gives you one more option: JPEG. While JPEG is much more compact than either Binary or ASCII, and therefore is sent down the wires to the printer faster, the compression is lossy, so image quality degrades slightly. However, when printing with JPEG encoding,

Photoshop only compresses the image slightly, so degradation is kept to a minimum. (We'd be surprised if you could see the difference on a natural scanned image of decent resolution.) Note that JPEG encoding only works when printing to PostScript level 2 or 3 printers, because they know how to decompress JPEG.

Print selected areas. You'd be surprised how many people wonder how to print just a small portion of their enormous image. They go through all sorts of duplicating and cropping convolutions instead of simply drawing a marquee around the area they want printed, then turning on the Print Selected Areas checkbox in the Print dialog box (on Windows, you choose Print Selection). If no pixels are selected, or if the selected area isn't a rectangle, this checkbox is grayed out.

Printer Color Management. Some printers, primarily those with PostScript Level 3 interpreters, include some basic color management functionality. When you turn on the Printer Color Management checkbox in the Print dialog box, Photoshop can convert the appropriate ICC profiles to Color Space Arrays (CSAs) and send them along with your image data (this checkbox is labeled PostScript Color Management when you have a PostScript printer selected). We think this is one of those technologies that sounds better than it plays out. First of all, few printers can actually perform the task properly. Secondly, you won't know if the image looks right until it's printed. Ultimately, we leave this checkbox off, and handle our color management needs in Photoshop.

Space. Earlier versions of Photoshop let you convert your image to another color space on-the-fly at print time, but it really only gave you a handful of choices. Now, Photoshop 5's robust internal color management system gives you many more controls. Of course, with control comes confusion, so let's try to clarify what's going on here.

By default, Photoshop picks the same color space as your current image, so when you print an RGB image, the Space popup menu is set to RGB, and when you print a CMYK image, the popup menu reads CMYK. If you choose a different space, Photoshop performs a Profile-to-Profile transformation to convert your image's colors to the new color space before sending it to the printer (see Chapter 5, *Color Settings*, for more on color space conversions).

Where David likes the simplicity of the Space popup menu, Bruce almost never uses this feature because it tends to behave differently on different printers, and sometimes, differently on the same printer on different platforms. Instead, he duplicates his image, uses Profile-to-Profile with an appropriate ICC profile for the printer, and then sends this new data to the printer. This way, he has more control over the rendering intent, black-point compensation, and so on. When he's done printing, he just closes the duplicate image, usually without saving it.

Generally, when you're printing to a film recorder, you should leave the Space popup menu set to RGB. When printing to a color printer, however, you might assume that you would choose CMYK (because printers use CMYK ribbons or ink). Real life isn't that simple, though.

If you're printing to a color printer, it's unlikely that Photoshop's built-in color separation will give you the results you want unless you've created custom printing inks and CMYK Setups. Also, note that the printer drivers for some CMYK inkjet printers such as the Epson Color Stylus only understand RGB input. You can print a CMYK file to them, but the first thing the driver does is to convert them to RGB. As a result, you'll almost always get better results printing in the RGB color space and letting the printer do its own conversion to CMYK. Even better, if you can make or obtain a reasonably good profile for your color printer, you can choose it from the Space popup menu.

Tip: Printing Separations. Have you been trying to get Photoshop to print color separations of your CMYK and Duotone images? The folks at Adobe hid the controls! To print each color on its own plate (rather than a composite color image), you must select Separations from the Space popup menu in the Print dialog box.

Tip: Printing Single Colors in Separations. Photoshop doesn't give you an obvious way to print fewer than all four process colors when printing color separations; the Print Separations checkbox is either on or off, never "on, but only the cyan and magenta, please." Nonetheless, you can do just this in one of two ways.

▶ Photoshop only prints the color plates that are displayed in the document window. For instance, if you only want to print magenta and black, click on the yellow and cyan eyeballs in the Channels palette to hide them. Now when you print, Photoshop automatically prints separations of the remaining two colors. (The Space popup menu only displays one option, Grayscale, when you do this.)

▶ You can also use the Page Range feature at the top of the Print dialog box to print fewer than four color separations. For example, when Print Separations is turned on, you can tell Photoshop to print from page two to page two; page two in a CMYK image is the magenta plate. If all the colors are not visible (because you've hidden them, as in the last bullet item), then page two is whatever the second *visible* color is. Note that this doesn't work when Print Selection is turned on in Windows.

Be aware that printing different plates for a separation at different times or from different devices can cause problems with registration and tint (hence color) consistency. If you have to rerun a single plate, it's typically better to rerun all four.

Imaging from a Page-Layout Program

As we said earlier, most people don't print directly from Photoshop—at least for their final output. Instead, they print from separation programs, presentation programs, or page-layout programs. In this section, we're going to focus on the latter item: page-layout programs such as PageMaker and QuarkXPress.

Our assumption here is that if you're printing from a page-layout program, you're probably printing to a PostScript printer, resulting in paper or film with black-and-white halftoned images on it.

QuarkXPress and PageMaker

Over the past few years, QuarkXPress has become the imaging tool of choice for graphic designers, service bureaus, ad agencies, and other heavy color users. Whether or not it deserves this title should be (and is) argued anywhere but here (otherwise Bruce and David would debate themselves into a tizzy).

The important thing to note is that if you place CMYK files in TIFF or EPS format, both PageMaker and QuarkXPress will simply pass the CMYK data along to the output device. Needless to say, Photoshop is a much better program for getting your images right than either of our page-layout choices.

No matter which page-layout application you prefer to use with Photoshop, there are some basic rules you should follow.

File formats. In Chapter 16, *Storing Images*, we cover file formats in some detail, including which ones to use for page layout. To recap quickly: when it comes to printing from page-layout programs, PICT is evil; always use TIFF, DCS, or EPS. We tend toward the TIFF format for almost all our files, though we'll occasionally use EPS or DCS for specialized effects—such as spot colors or custom screening—or for very large files.

CMYK versus RGB. The choice between importing RGB and CMYK images involves two decisions—when do you want to do your separation, and what program do you want to do it? You can preseparate all your images with Photoshop (or another program), or you can place RGB images in QuarkXPress or PageMaker, and rely on their color management systems (generally ColorSync or KCMS) to do the separations for you.

Preseparating has a lot going for it. Images land on pages ready to print; the page-layout program just sends the channels down, with no processing at print time. Placing unseparated files has advantages as well, though. You can use the color management systems to produce better proofs off color printers, and you don't have to target the images until the last minute, when you know all your press conditions and are ready to pull final seps. When it comes right down to it, we separate almost all our images in Photoshop first.

Picture linking. Bitmapped images are often big, lumbering creatures that can't be corralled into a single page. That's why both PageMaker and QuarkXPress have picture linking. When you import or place an EPS or a TIFF image on your page, the program only places a low-resolution representation image, sort of like a "For Position Only" (FPO) image. When you print, the program ignores this low-res picture and uses the high-resolution image data on disk instead. That means that QuarkXPress or PageMaker has to be able to find the high-res data on disk. If you've thrown it away, or moved it to a different folder, the program can't find it and prints with the ugly preview version.

PageMaker gives you a little more control over linking than XPress does. In PageMaker you can specify, by file size, whether a file links or is embedded right into the document. This makes some sense; if you've got ten 100 K images, it might be more efficient to embed them rather than maintain the links. On the other hand, PageMaker's screen previews, especially high-resolution data, are often significantly slower than QuarkXPress's unless you turn off High-Resolution Display, in which case they're pretty rough. On the other other hand . . . .

The final note on picture linking is that if or when you send your Page-Maker or QuarkXPress document to a service bureau, make sure you send all the linked graphics, too. We like to think in terms of sending a *folder* to be output, not just a single file. XPress has the Collect for Output feature to help you with this; in PageMaker, use Save As with the Files for Remote Printing option selected.

Tip: Pasting Images. You can always force PageMaker or QuarkXPress to embed an image by pasting it in rather than using the Place or Get Picture commands. However, many people have reported problems with doing this. PageMaker will let you at least try to print separations if you paste in a CMYK image, but not an RGB one. Occasionally it will even work, though often what prints is a 72-ppi screen rendition of the image. XPress will try to separate anything that you paste in, but the results are unpredictable at best.

Often, the image you paste is scaled radically differently than the one in Photoshop, or takes much longer to view on screen (which makes scrolling unbearable). Also, if you need to go back and edit that image, you may be lost; for some reason, most people who paste images also delete the original.

Our recommendation? Just don't do it, unless the image you're pasting in is very small, and not in color.

Tip: Relinking Images. Many people get themselves into a bother when XPress all of a sudden can't seem to find their linked images. For instance, if you create a document on the PC, then bring it (and the graphics) to the Mac, XPress can't seem to find the EPS and TIFF files, and lists them as "Missing" in the Picture Usage dialog box.

Here's a little trick you can use to make the program see them all: put the XPress document in the same folder as all the graphics. Then open the file and select Picture Usage from the Utilities menu. If one or more of the images is listed as "Missing", update one of them; the rest are updated automatically. PageMaker is usually better at cross-platform transfers, but if images do go missing, choose Links from the File menu, navigate to the folder in question, and click Update All.

Rotating. Rotating bitmapped images is a major pain, even on a fast machine. When you import an image into QuarkXPress or PageMaker and rotate it on the page, it seems to rotate very quickly. But the real math work is done at print time inside your PostScript printer. That means that every time you print (either a proof or your final piece), your printer has to do the same time-consuming calculations that you could have done *once* in Photoshop. If you know you're going to rotate an image 15 degrees, do it in Photoshop first, then import it onto your page.

Cropping and clipping. Let's say you've imported a 24 MB photograph of your class of '74 onto your QuarkXPress or PageMaker page, but out of fourteen hundred people, you only want to print the 31 people who were on the lacrosse team. You use the cropping tool (in PageMaker) or the picture box handles (in XPress) to crop out everyone else, duplicate the image, recrop, and so on, for 31 people. And then you print the page . . . .

If you saved the image from Photoshop as an EPS, prepare to wait a while for the page to print. In fact, you might want to consider a quick jaunt to the Caribbean. The entire image, no matter how much is showing, has to be sent to the printer for every iteration. Don't laugh. We've seen this plenty of times (usually in the same publications that are littered with gratuitous tabs and space characters).

On the other hand, if you saved the image as a TIFF, the file shouldn't take too long because QuarkXPress and PageMaker can pull out just the data they need to image your page. However, it does take the program a little extra time at print time to throw away the data it doesn't need.

In either case, the page-layout program has to import and save a low-resolution preview of the *entire* image. That means unnecessary time and file size. The best solution: crop your images in Photoshop before importing them.

Image editing. Both PageMaker and QuarkXPress let you perform some basic tonal manipulation on TIFF files. In PageMaker (with grayscale images only), select Image Control from the Element menu. In QuarkXPress, select Other Contrast from the Style menu (see Figure 17-15). This is like saying that your kitchen knife lets you perform heart surgery. Sure you can do it, but it's gonna get ugly. Except for special effects (and controlling screen settings on an image-by-image basis), we recommend that people simply not use these features; instead, use Photoshop.

Figure 17-15

Changing contrast in
XPress and PageMaker

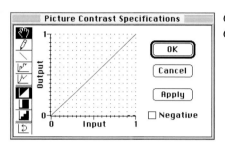

*QuarkXPress's Other
Contrast dialog box*

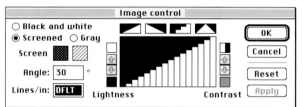

*PageMaker's Image
Control dialog box*

Getting It Out

Photoshop is the best all-around tool we've encountered for working with images, massaging images, and targeting images for specific output devices. However, page-layout programs such as PageMaker and XPress excel at integrating text and graphics into complete pages.

If you keep that distinction clear, you'll use Photoshop to do everything that needs to be done to your images, and give the page-layout program an image file that it can simply pass on to the output device. Your work will proceed more smoothly, and you (or your service bureau) will encounter fewer unpleasant surprises. Sometimes it's nice when life is boring . . . .

18

Multimedia and the Web

Purposing Pixels for the Screen

It's pretty clear that we've spent most of our professional lives focused on preparing images that are destined for a printing press. However, the times they are a-changing, and one of the most common uses for Photoshop today is preparing images for screen display, whether in an interactive multimedia presentation or a World Wide Web site. And just as there are techniques for optimizing an image for paper, there are methods you can use to ensure good quality on screen (as well as tips for preparing your on-screen image efficiently).

In this chapter, we take a look at several important issues you need to consider when preparing images for multimedia or the Web, including deciding on a graphic file format and dealing with indexed-color images. Note that we don't discuss all the cool ways you can make funky buttons, rules, bullets, and other page elements; there are other great books on the market that include those techniques.

By the way, there are several other programs currently on the market that are expressly designed to build Web graphics, such as Adobe's ImageReady (which is almost exactly the same as Photoshop, except that it's optimized for Web images) and Macromedia's Fireworks. However, this is a book on what you can do with Photoshop, so we won't be covering those programs.

Preparing Images

No matter whether an image is destined for print or for screen, we always recommend that you do the tonal correction, color correction, and sharpening in Photoshop. However, the kind of correction and sharpening you need for on-screen images is almost always different than for printed images.

The one rule that almost always applies to images for the screen is that no matter what the image looks like on your screen, it will look different on everyone else's. Preparing images for multimedia and the Internet is an exercise in frustration for anyone who is used to print production; even the whims of a web press seem trivial compared to the variations from one person's screen to another.

Tone

While the display on some computer monitors is darker than on others, monitors connected to a Macintosh tend to display images lighter than those on a PC. This is because the native gamma of Macintosh screens is around 1.8, whereas Windows display systems have a native gamma around 2.3 (see Figure 18-1 on page 659). You can compensate for this to some extent by choosing an appropriate RGB space for your images (see Chapter 5, *Color Settings*), but it's unlikely that the people who view your images will have calibrated monitors, so the above gamma numbers are no more than a general guideline.

There are several strategies for dealing with this mismatch. All involve some compromises. Since the destination monitor is essentially an unknown, you can be fairly certain that until self-calibrating monitors are ubiquitous and all browsers support system-level color management, your images are going to look much better (or worse) on some systems than on others. Ultimately, it's simply impossible to produce images that will look good to every Web user.

Given the current state of the art, the best you can do is to choose an aim point appropriate for the audience you're trying to reach. We suggest you choose one of the following alternatives.

▶ Export your edited images into sRGB, accepting its inherent limitations.

▶ Split the difference, and export your edited images into a gamma 2.0 RGB Setup space. This will result in images that look a little light on Windows and a little dark on the Mac, but they shouldn't be terribly off.

▶ Prepare two sets of images, one at gamma 1.8 and one at gamma 2.2, and set up your site so that Mac users see the gamma 1.8 version while Windows users see the gamma 2.2 version.

▶ Export the images with your RGB working space profile embedded, and rely on browsers to color-manage them correctly.

All four approaches have their strengths and weaknesses. Each of these four strategies optimizes the image for a different set of users. Let's look at each in turn.

Using sRGB. Back in Chapter 5, *Color Settings*, we discussed the sRGB color space, developed by several industry giants to describe the general characteristics of the "typical" Windows monitor. The idea is that if every monitor actually matches sRGB, then people can target their images to this standard, creating sort of a default color management system without resorting to CMMs and profiles.

There are two major problems with sRGB. First, the gamut is on the small side compared to a good, high-quality monitor, and it remains to be seen whether or not it offers a large enough gamut for color-critical e-commerce such as clothing or cosmetics. (Ironically, the logo color of one of sRGB's main proponents, Hewlett-Packard, lies outside the sRGB gamut.)

The second problem is that the sRGB "standard" relies on the assumption that the vast majority of monitors actually display sRGB, which is really quite doubtful. However, given the marketing muscle behind sRGB, it's probably the most sensible choice unless you're trying to sell color-critical merchandise or show fine art on the Web.

Tip: Work in a Big Space. Even if every image you create is for the Web, we still suggest setting your RGB Setup dialog box to a reasonable color space, like Adobe RGB (1998)—formerly known as SMPTE-240M—or

Bruce RGB (if you don't know what we're talking about here, check out Chapter 5, *Color Settings*). If you choose the smaller sRGB space in RGB Setup, you're limiting your color options when editing your images. Then, if you want to compress your images to the sRGB space before saving them, you can use Profile-to-Profile (from the Mode submenu, under the Image menu) to convert from your RGB space to sRGB.

If you're going to save your file in the JPEG format after performing Profile-to-Profile, make sure you either turn off profile-embedding (in the Profile Setup dialog box) or change your RGB editing space to sRGB (in the RGB Setup dialog box). Don't forget to change it back after saving!

Split the difference. Another alternative, which is probably worth considering only if you anticipate a lot of Macintosh users as well as a lot of Windows users visiting your site, is to split the difference between the Mac's gamma 1.8 and Windows' gamma of 2.2, and export your images into a gamma 2.0 space, which should produce reasonable results for most viewers. For details on how to create a custom RGB space, see Chapter 5, *Color Settings*.

However, you'll probably want to use this space only as an output space for your images, and do most of your editing in a larger-gamut editing space. The easiest way to do this is to define your custom space in RGB Setup, save it to disk as an ICC profile, then restore your regular working space. When you've finished editing the image, you can use Profile-to-Profile to convert it to the custom space.

If you're a perfectionist, you could adopt the strategy used by our friend Bill Atkinson on his Web site, www.natureimages.com. His site is set up so that Macintosh users see images prepared with a gamma of 1.8, while Windows users see images prepared with a gamma of 2.2. Of course, this takes more work and a duplicate set of images for each platform, but it's the only way we know to be reasonably sure that viewers will see images with something close to the contrast you intended.

Embedding profiles. Rather than recalibrating your monitor or worrying about what types of screens your audience has, we believe that it is a significantly better approach to embed your working space profile into your scanned images (which Photoshop does by default when you save an RGB file). The profile describes what actual color the RGB values in the image represent, so your Web browser (along with a system-wide color management engine like ColorSync or ICM 2.0) can convert the image's color and tone on the fly to the local machine's monitor color space. (As we said in an earlier chapter, embedding a Photoshop profile only adds about 0.5 K to an image, so file size shouldn't be a consideration.)

There are two problems with this technique. First, the browser must be able to read embedded profiles. As we go to press, only Internet Explorer for the Macintosh, version 4.01 or later, can do this (and even then, only when you turn on the ColorSync checkbox in the Preferences dialog box). Second, your audience has to create a monitor profile for their machine (or else the color management engine won't know what color space to convert the image *to*). On the Macintosh, ColorSync 2.5 lets you do this free (as does Adobe Gamma; remember to use one or the other, but not both). Unfortunately, there is no free way to do this on Windows yet. (There are relatively low-cost methods—like the aforementioned Colorific, or Adobe Gamma, if they have it).

We believe that in the not-too-distant future, all the major browsers will read embedded profiles and there will be a free and easy way to build a basic monitor profile. The reason: electronic commerce demands it; the number one reason for merchandise returns is "it wasn't the color I saw in the catalog." Without passing these two basic hurdles, customers will never be able to tell whether the shirt they're looking at is a dark burgundy or a light red, and e-commerce will flounder.

Note that Photoshop does not embed profiles in GIF files because they're always in Indexed color mode rather than RGB. However, there are ways that you can specify a profile for a GIF file (see the Web site www.colorsync.com for more information on specifying an associated profile within your HTML code).

Color

Not only can you rarely predict tonal shifts in images for screen, you can hardly assume anything about color. Most graphic arts professionals have 24-bit color ("true color") monitors, but just because you have one doesn't mean that your audience will. In fact, many computer users are only able to view 256 colors at a time, due to the constraints of their video hardware. Other computer users (though not nearly as many) only have grayscale screens, so they won't see color at all.

What's even worse, even two people with the same kind of screen and computer system will probably see the same image differently on each of their monitors. Again, monitor calibration can help considerably, but it's too rare to depend upon.

However, there are a few rules you can generally trust.

▶ It's usually more important to retain the contrast between colors than the particular colors themselves. Image details that result from subtle changes in color (like the gentle folds in a red silk scarf) are often lost in translation.

▶ Solid areas of color, including text, should be set to one of the 216 "Web-safe" colors (see "Tip: Web-Safe Colors," below) so that they won't dither on 8-bit screens.

▶ If you built your image on a 24-bit color monitor (which is a good idea, even when making Web graphics), switch your monitor to 8-bit color (256 colors) and 8-bit gray to test how much of the rest of the world will see your image.

▶ While you're testing, also try looking at your image on both Macintosh and Windows systems.

▶ Images for multimedia and the Web should always be in RGB or Indexed Color mode.

Tip: Web-Safe Colors. Every computer system has a built-in palette of 256 colors that it uses, unless some program tells it to use another palette. The problem is that the palettes that Web browsers use on Macintosh and Windows share only 216 of the 256 colors. These 216 colors are called "Web-safe" or "browser-safe" colors because they appear more or less the same on both platforms (given with the earlier caveats about color and tone rarely being quite the same between the two).

If you use a non–Web-safe color in your image, it—by necessity—gets dithered using the system palette's colors when viewed on an 8-bit color monitor (see Figure 18-2 on page 660). The dithering is distracting in many images (especially images with text), but is usually unavoidable in pictures that contain anti-aliasing, gradients, or photographic images.

Web-safe colors are less relevant for screens set to display 16-bit ("thousands of colors") or 24-bit ("millions of colors" or "true color") color because little or no dithering is necessary on these monitors.

There are various ways to choose Web-safe colors for a Photoshop image, including buying the ColorWeb swatch book from Pantone that provides the RGB and hexadecimal equivalents of them all. Here's a method that won't cost you anything.

1. Open the Swatches palette and choose Replace from the palette's popout menu.

2. When Photoshop asks you for a palette, choose the Web Safe Colors file from the Color Palettes folder (this is inside the Goodies folder, inside the Photoshop folder).

The Swatches palette now displays only the 216 Web-safe colors. If you choose among them, you can't go wrong.

If you do the math, you'll find that all the Web-safe colors are in 20-percent steps within the 256-level scale. That is, a typical Web-safe color might be 20-percent red and 60-percent green. You might be tempted with this knowledge to change your color picker in order to specify colors by percentage. Don't do it. Photoshop translates these values based on your RGB Setup dialog box settings, so you won't get the proper values at all. Instead, if you want to type specific numbers into the Color Picker dialog box, use 0, 51, 102, 153, 204, or 255 (these correlate directly with 0, 20, 40, 60, 80, and 100 percent).

Resolution

One of the wonderful advantages to working on images for screen display is that resolution is almost always 72 ppi, making for extremely small images (relative to prepress images, at least). A 4-by-5-inch image at 72 ppi takes up 300 K, where the equivalent prepress image might consume over 4.5 MB of disk space and RAM. With smaller file size comes faster processing time with less of a RAM requirement. You can actually use any resolution you want, but when it comes time to put the image on screen, each image pixel is mapped to a screen pixel. A 300-ppi image will become enormous on screen!

Of course, similar to the vagaries of color and tone on the Internet, you rarely know what resolution screen your images will be viewed on—your 72-ppi illustration quickly becomes much smaller if someone views it on a high-resolution monitor. Because you cannot assume monitor resolution, it's often a good idea to design your 72-ppi images slightly larger in size so they'll look okay on a higher-resolution screen. The "standard" resolution of most Windows monitors is 96 ppi: Bruce runs a 17-inch monitor at 1600-by-1200-pixel resolution, which is close to 150 ppi! (Which makes a Web image on his screen about half-size.)

Note that when scanning images destined for the screen, we still almost always scan them at a higher resolution (often the full optical resolution of the scanner) and then downsample them in Photoshop (see Chapter 13, *Capturing Images*, for more information on this process).

Tip: Hybrid Web-Safe Colors. When it comes right down to it, 216 colors aren't a lot to choose from. If you're feeling cramped, you might want to build your own "hybrid" Web-safe colors. The trick is to build tiny checkerboard patterns of pixels that only include Web-safe colors (see Figure 18-3 on page 661).

1. Create a 2-by-2-pixel image.

2. Make two of the pixels one color and the other two a different color. A checkerboard pattern is best.

3. Select all the pixels (Command-A), and choose Define Pattern from the Edit menu.

4. Now go to some other document and fill a selection with the pattern (choose Fill from the Edit menu, and select Pattern from the Use popup menu).

There are thousands of different colors that you can create just by combining two Web-safe colors (you can see some at www.pixelboyz.com/rwpshop/hybridcolors.htm). If you want to get fancy, you can try building checkerboard patterns of more than two colors to simulate even more colors (though it's tough to get this to work without the pattern being obvious). Lynda Weinman, the author of *Designing Web Graphics,* points out that this technique works best when you choose colors that are close in tone; this way the eye blends the colors together, rather than seeing two separate colors.

By the way, if you have to do this more than a few times, get one of the freeware or low-cost products that produce these patterns for you (such as BoxTop Software's ColorSafe, Auto F/X's WebVise, or RDG's Dither-Box).

Tip: Building Seamless Tiles. Here's one technique for building repeating tiled patterns (rectangular pictures that repeat horizontally and vertically to fill space of any size; see Figure 18-4 on page 661).

1. Create a new document the size you want the pattern to be. It can be square or rectangular.

2. Paint or paste in the image you want to tile.

3. Select Offset from the Other submenu under the Filter menu and choose offset values of about one-quarter the width and height of the image.

4. If your image extended to the sides of the document before you applied the Offset filter, you can now see the sharp edges. You should retouch the image so that the sharp lines are no longer apparent (you might use the Smudge tool or the Rubber Stamp tool to do this). If the image did not touch any side of the document, you may find that there are holes you want to fill in.

5. Select Offset one more time (remember that you can press Command-F to repeat the last filter) to make sure there are no additional holes or sharp edges in the image. (If there are, fix them.) When editing the image, be sure not to paint any edge pixels—if you do, you'll have to repeat steps 3 and 4 again.

The image now tiles without harsh edges. If you want to test the "tileability" of the image without leaving Photoshop, you can select the entire image (Command-A) and choose Define Pattern from the Edit menu. Now use the Fill command (on the Edit menu) to fill some other image with the pattern. Make sure this second file is large enough to see the pattern repeat at least a few times horizontally and vertically.

Tip: Pages to Graphics. People spend so much time trying to figure out how to get their PageMaker or QuarkXPress pages up on the Internet. Converting to HTML is one option, though the page almost never looks the same as it did originally. Saving in the PDF format is another option, but then people need Acrobat Reader to view the page, which is a hassle.

Our favorite method of getting pages from XPress or PageMaker (or any other program) up on the Net is to make a picture out of each one.

1. Save a page from the program as an EPS. PageMaker and QuarkXPress have specific features to do this; if your program doesn't, you can print to disk as an EPS file using the LaserWriter PostScript driver.

2. Open this EPS file in Photoshop. When Photoshop opens the Generic EPS dialog box, choose to open the image as an RGB file at 72 dpi. Small type doesn't convert well to bitmap, but you might get a better result by turning on Anti-alias in the Open EPS dialog box.

3. Select Flatten from the Layer menu.

4. Save the file as either a GIF or a JPEG, depending on the content of the page and how much compression you're likely to achieve (see the next section for more on these file formats).

5. Put this picture on your Web site.

By turning the page into a picture, anyone with a Web browser can see it on the Internet. And surprisingly, even a full-page "page image" can be made very small if it's mostly text. (You can see examples of this at www.pixelboyz.com/rwpshop/pageimage.htm.)

Tip: Remove the Big White Box. The folks at Quark made a tiny change between version 3 and version 4 in how XPress writes its EPS files: XPress used to treat the white background of the page as transparent in the EPS file. Now it draws a big white box in the background so it is opaque. Most people never notice the difference, but it can be a killer depending on what you're doing with those EPS files.

If you dare, here's how you can remove that white box from XPress's PostScript code. Note that this is an industrial-strength tip . . . that means you should always work on a copy of your file, and don't try it at home if you don't feel comfortable with editing PostScript files.

1. Open the EPS file in a text editor or word processor. (If it's a large EPS file, a text editor like BBEdit on the Macintosh is probably your best bet.)

2. Search for the comment `%%EndSetup` in the document. A few lines after that, there should be a line that reads `g np clippath 1 H V G` (or something similar).

3. Delete these three characters: `1 H V`. In the example above, the line would now read `g np clippath G`.

4. Save the file (perhaps under a new name). Make sure the file is saved in "text-only" mode (text editors only work in this mode, so you don't have to worry about it, but word processors like Microsoft Word allow you to format the text, which can cause trouble in PostScript files). Note that saving this file may lose your screen preview; it depends on what text editor or word processor you're using (again, BBEdit on the Macintosh works well).

That's it! Those three characters are the culprits in the opaque background problem. With them gone, the background is transparent again. (Of course, the built-in screen preview won't change; but when you print the document or rasterize it in Photoshop, it will be transparent.)

Tip: Maintaining Colors. If you use Adobe Illustrator or Macromedia FreeHand along with Photoshop, you've probably found that your colors shift when you bring your images from the illustration program to Photoshop. For instance, when you spec a color in FreeHand or Illustrator as 100-percent magenta, it looks really bright on screen; when you bring it to Photoshop (see "Objects versus Pixels" in Chapter 15, *Essential Image Techniques* for more information on how to do this), the image appears muddy and dull. The reason is that the illustration programs and Photoshop display CMYK information on screen in completely different ways. If you're creating images for the Web, this is a disaster. Fortunately, you can get consistent color in one of several ways.

If you're using FreeHand 7.02 or later, there are two simple solutions. First, you can export the document (or just particular objects) using the Photoshop RGB EPS file format (select Export from the File menu). This EPS file specifies colors in RGB mode rather than CMYK, so Photoshop displays them properly. If you are going to do a lot of this, you should change FreeHand's behavior internally (the ReadMe file that comes with FreeHand 7.02 discusses how to alter the Preferences file or run an AppleScript to change this preference).

If you're an Illustrator user, you can make Photoshop display CMYK the same way Illustrator does by making a custom Printing Inks Setup preferences setting in Photoshop (this same technique works for FreeHand and other programs, too). Even better, create your colors in RGB mode in Illustrator 8 (or later), and turn off the CMYK PostScript option when saving your file as an EPS document. This way, when you open the EPS in Photoshop in RGB mode, you get the real RGB values.

Tip: Gang Up Thumbnails. Maybe we're just Type A personalities, but we can't help but gnash our teeth while watching the download of a Web page containing twenty or thirty tiny images. They might be little buttons, or thumbnails of other images, or logos . . . but whatever they are, they will almost always download faster as one big image rather than separate images. Not only are the combined images smaller in file size, but a single image transfers more quickly than multiple images (due to the way that Web servers handle multiple files).

Saving Your Images

We discussed graphic file formats back in Chapter 16, *Storing Images*, but we need to explore two formats—GIF and JPEG—in more depth here because they're key to the way images appear on the Internet. If your images are destined for a multimedia program such as QuarkImmedia, mTropolis, Microsoft PowerPoint, or Macromedia Director, you can probably save them in the PICT, TIFF, or EPS file format (see "Tip: Great Preview, Small Files" in Chapter 16, *Storing Images*). But for Web use, you almost assuredly need to save your images in either GIF or JPEG format.

The most important concern when building images for the Web is file size. It's easy to make flashy graphics that look cool (the books about that subject could fill a wheelbarrow). It's not so easy to make good-looking images that are small enough (in file size) that they transmit quickly. Many people (David included) won't return to any site containing graphics that take more than 15 or 20 seconds to download with a 28.8 Kbps modem, so it's crucial to keep file sizes down.

Figure 18-1

Monitor gamma
and image tone

*Macintosh screen,
gamma 1.8*

*Windows screen,
gamma 2.2*

Tip: Leave Off the Previews. In order to keep your file size to a minimum on the Macintosh, you may want to avoid using Thumbnail or Icon previews (see "Previews" in Chapter 16, *Storing Images*). However, these previews are stripped away if your server isn't a Macintosh or if you upload your images to the server using the Raw Data format, so it may not make much of a difference. In general, though, we avoid the previews altogether for GIF and JPEG images.

Tip: Checking File Size. The file size that Photoshop provides in the lower-left corner of the document window is far from accurate, mostly because it doesn't take into account any form of compression you will achieve with either JPEG or GIF images. The only way to find an image's true (post-compression) file size is to save it to disk and switch out of Photoshop. If you have a Macintosh use Get Info in the Finder (select the file and choose Get Info from the File menu); if you're working on a Windows machine use Properties on the Desktop (click on the file with the

Figure 18-2
Web-safe colors

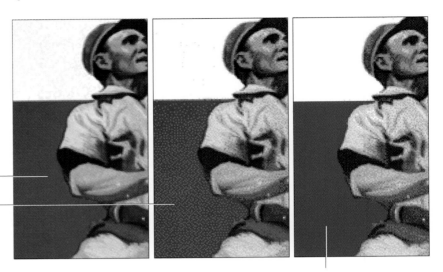

On a 24-bit color monitor, these colors wouldn't dither. On an 8-bit color monitor, however, these colors simply aren't available.

If the color is Web safe, it won't dither on 8-bit color screens

right mouse button and choose Properties from the list of options). See Figure 18-5 on page 662.

If the file size is displayed as "27 K on disk (22,045 bytes used)", only pay attention to the second number. The first value is the amount of space the image takes up on your hard disk: this depends on the minimum block size your hard disk uses. If your disk uses 32 K blocks, a 2 K file will occupy 32 K on disk, and a 33 K file will use 64 K of disk space. The second number shows the actual amount of data someone would have to download to see the image, and it's usually smaller than the disk space number.

JPEG

For best reproduction on the Web, almost all scanned photographic images should be saved in the JPEG file format. This way, people viewing the image on a 24-bit color monitor will see all the colors in the image, and those on 8-bit monitors will see a dithered version. Fortunately, the dithered version is usually pretty good—almost as good as if you had converted the image to 8-bit in Photoshop yourself.

JPEG compresses RGB natural images really well, even if the image does suffer some degradation in the process. On the other hand, JPEG is not suitable for images that have a lot of solid colors, especially

Figure 18-3

Hybrid Web-safe colors

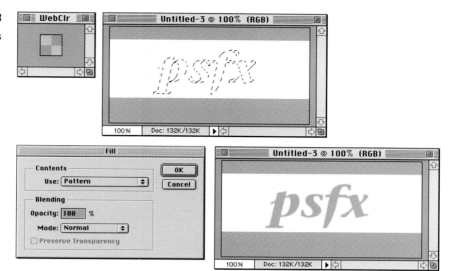

Figure 18-4

Seamless tiles

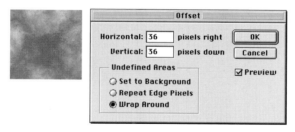

After running the Offset filter, you can see (and fix) hard edges that make a tile obvious.

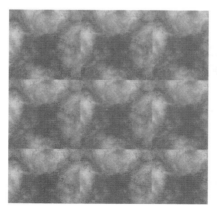

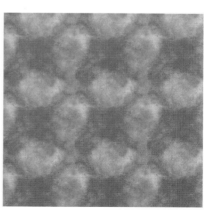

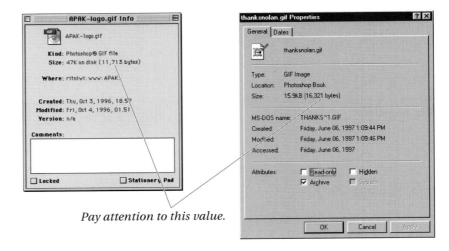

Figure 18-5

Finding file size

Pay attention to this value.

computer-generated images, type, and line art. It's also not appropriate
for images in which you've used Web-safe colors—because colors often
shift in JPEG images—or images that require transparency.

When you save an image in the JPEG file format, Photoshop asks you
how compressed and in what JPEG format you want your image. It also
asks you if you want to save any paths that you've built, but as that's self-
explanatory, we needn't cover it here (Hint: Why in the world would you
need to save paths in an image that's on the Internet?)

Image Quality. The worse the image quality, the more Photoshop can
compress your image. You can ignore the Quality popup menu if you
want; Maximum, High, Medium and Low are just preset options for numeric values you can type in yourself or dial in with the Quality slider.
Because the degradation differs greatly depending on the content of the
image, finding the right compression/quality mix is largely a matter of
trial and error.

While we almost never use a quality setting other than 9 or 10 for
prepress images, we very often find low-quality compression (like 2 or 3)
to be adequate, especially for smaller, thumbnail images where detail is
not essential.

Format Options. Like TIFF and other committee-based standards, there
are various flavors of the JPEG file format, and not all programs can read
or write them all. Photoshop lets you save JPEGs in one of three formats:
Baseline, Baseline Optimized, and Progressive.

▶ Baseline is the lowest common denominator for JPEG images. Almost any program that can open or view JPEGs can open this variety, but you don't necessarily get the best compression. If you're using JPEGs for prepress work, this is the format you should use.

▶ Baseline Optimized provides a slightly smaller file for the same quality setting, and most programs can open or view files in this format.

▶ Progressive JPEGs are even smaller in size, and all the major Web browsers are able to read them (though some lesser-known programs cannot). The benefit to this format is that images saved as Progressive JPEG appear in stages, first very chunky, then successively finer. Photoshop lets you specify the number of steps it takes the browser to complete the image. Some people don't like the step-by-step approach to viewing an image, but this is the format we prefer.

Because the differences in compression among the formats are often extremely minimal—often only one or two K—we rarely make a decision about which to use based on size alone. More important is whether the image will appear the way we want it to our target audience.

Tip: Keep Your Originals. Remember that if you open a JPEG image in Photoshop and then save it out again as a JPEG, the compression damages the image even more. So remember to always keep the original non-JPEG version of your image. That way, you can go back and make edits on the original and save out the JPEG version fresh again.

Tip: Save Blends as JPEG. Blends (or gradients, vignettes, or whatever you want to call them) look much better when saved as JPEG than when saved as GIFs. This way, people who have 24-bit color monitors will see a smooth blend, and people with 8-bit monitors will see the crummy dithered version (but at least some people will be happy).

GIF

While JPEG is the preferred format for natural ("photographic") scanned images, GIF (don't even get us started on the "how should this be pronounced" argument) is currently *the* format for everything else.

▶ Images that contain areas of solid colors (including most blocks of text and computer-generated pictures)

▶ Animations

▶ Transparency in images

▶ Images that rely on Web-safe colors

Theoretically, the GIF specification allows for a full 24-bit color image; however, nobody really supports this, so GIF images are always saved in 8-bit indexed color (for more on this mode, see "Indexed Color" in Chapter 3, *Image Essentials*). That means you cannot have more than 256 colors in your image. Fortunately, you can usually specify which 256 colors you want to use.

Saving a GIF. Most people convert their RGB images to Indexed Color mode (on the Mode submenu) before saving them as a GIF. There's nothing wrong with doing this, but we strongly recommend converting a duplicate of the image to Indexed Color rather than destroy your original RGB image. The RGB mode is much more efficient in the long run because it affords the most flexibility in editing the image.

Note, however, that you don't have to convert the image to Indexed Color mode first. Sometimes it's just faster to choose GIF89a Export from the Export submenu (under the File menu) while the image is still in RGB mode. This lets you convert to Indexed Color mode and save the GIF in one fell swoop, though it doesn't give you as much control over the conversion as the Mode menu method. Whatever layers are visible when you export the image are saved in the GIF file format (see "Tip: Layer Animations," later in this chapter).

The GIF89a Export plug-in gives you several options, including palette type, number of colors, and interlacing (see Figure 18-6). (We discuss how to build transparency into GIFs later in this chapter.) By the way, one of these options, Export Caption, is only available when you've added a caption using the File Info feature (on the File menu). However, we don't know of any software that actually reads this caption.

1. Choose Adaptive from the Palette popup menu. This way, Photoshop determines the 256 colors that will best represent the image. (If you don't like the 256 colors that Photoshop picks, see "Converting to

Indexed Color," later in this chapter.) If you've already built a custom color palette (or you want to use the Web-Safe Color palette that comes with Photoshop), you can choose it by pressing the Load button. (When using the GIF89a Export plug-in with a custom palette, it's important that you turn on the Use Best Match option; otherwise, your GIF may look quite unlike your original RGB image.)

2. Next, in the Colors field, you can choose how many colors Photoshop should include in the palette. There's no reason that you have to use all 256 colors, and it's important to use as few colors as possible in

Figure 18-6

GIF89a Export

order to reduce the image's file size. Most images look just fine with 128 or fewer colors. (If you're using a custom palette, you can typically ignore the value in the Colors field.)

3. Finally, you must decide if you want the GIF to be interlaced or not. Interlaced GIFs appear in several passes, like a venetian blind slowly opening. Some people like this transition effect, but you should be careful not to overuse it. If seeing a partially visible GIF is actually going to be useful to the audience (for example, if the person seeing it might make a decision on whether to click on the picture or not based on a partially visible version), then go ahead and interlace it. If it wouldn't be especially useful, then leave the box unchecked. Note that interlacing a GIF adds slightly to the file's size, so you probably don't want to use it for small images (like buttons, bullets, or lines).

You should always save your images while they're still in RGB mode (usually in Photoshop file format), so you can return to edit them later.

Tip: Preview the Palette. In order to strike a good balance between image quality and file size, set the Colors field in the GIF89a Export dialog box to 255 colors, and press the Preview button. This is the best quality you can expect to get (see Figure 18-7). Now press OK to leave the Preview window, switch to 128 colors, and preview it again. Chances are that in most images you won't see much of a difference. Continue reducing the colors (to 64, 32, and 16) and previewing the result until you find the value below which the quality would be unacceptable. Use that value to save the GIF image.

Figure 18-7
Previewing the GIF

Tip: Layer Animations. Photoshop doesn't let you create GIF animations, but you can use it as a tool to build each frame of an animation and then use some other utility (like GifBuilder) to piece them together. Often, you can build each frame of an animation on a different layer of an RGB image. When you're ready to export the GIFs, you can turn on the first layer (and turn the others off), and export the image with the GIF89a export filter. Then turn off layer 1, turn on layer 2, and export again. Keep going until all the frames are exported.

Converting to Indexed Color. As we said earlier, there are actually a few reasons why you might want to convert your image to Indexed Color mode in Photoshop (see Figure 18-8). Remember, though, that when you

Figure 18-8

Converting to
Indexed Color mode

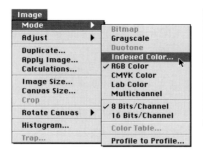

convert an image to Indexed Color, you lose all your layers and a lot of
the subtle details in the image. (Keep your fingers on Command-Z, just
in case you need to undo the conversion.)

> **Prioritizing colors.** When you export an RGB image with the GIF89a
> export filter and ask for an Adaptive palette, Photoshop chooses 256
> colors that best represent the entire image. However, occasionally
> you and Photoshop might disagree as to what colors in the image are
> the most important. For instance, if you convert a photographic por-
> trait of someone against a bright blue background, the color palette
> will include a lot of blues that you might not necessarily care about—
> you probably want Photoshop to include more skin tones instead.
> You can force Photoshop to prioritize colors by selecting the area con-
> taining the colors you want, then converting to Indexed Color mode.
> Note that Photoshop may still change the colors slightly, so it's not a
> particularly good method for ensuring Web-safe colors.

> **Web-safe colors.** If you want to make sure that all the colors in your
> image are Web-safe (see "Tip: Web-Safe Colors," earlier in this chap-
> ter), you can choose Web—rather than Adaptive—from the Palette
> popup menu in the Indexed Color dialog box. This way, Photoshop
> will map every color in your image to a Web-safe color. You might
> want to do this if dithering on 8-bit monitors bothers you more than
> shifting your image colors.

> **Custom palettes.** After converting an image to Indexed Color with an
> Adaptive palette, you can view the palette by selecting Color Table
> from the Mode submenu (under the Image menu). More important,
> you can save this palette to disk in order to use it for other conver-

sions (press the Save button). In this way, you can standardize a number of images on the same palette. For instance, you could convert one image to Indexed Color with a Web-safe color palette, export that palette, and then later use the exported palette with the GIF89a Export plug-in to export subsequent images more easily.

Custom color palettes that you've saved to disk from Photoshop are also used in other programs, such as QuarkImmedia. Note that you need to save the palette with an ".aco" extension if you want it to work on Windows or cross-platform machines.

▶ **Editing colors.** In an indexed-color image, each pixel is assigned a number from 0 to 255. The pixel's color comes only by comparing the number with a color lookup table (*clut*). Fortunately, this is all done behind the scenes, so you don't have to think about it much. One reason to convert an image to Indexed Color is so you can edit the particular colors in an image by editing the clut. If you choose Color Table from the Mode submenu, you can click on any color in the table to edit it. In color tables that have more than eight or 16 colors, this kind of editing is cumbersome, but in some instances, editing an image's color table can be a very powerful tool (see "Tip: Swapping Indexed Colors," later in this chapter).

▶ **Transparency from channels.** We discuss transparency in GIF images later in this chapter, so for now, suffice it to say that one more reason to convert images to Indexed Color before exporting them as GIFs is the ability to use alpha channels as transparency masks on export.

Make sure the Preview option is turned on in the Indexed Color dialog box; it slows things down a bit, but it's much faster than pressing OK, undoing a result you don't like, then returning to the dialog box.

Tip: Converting with Other Utilities. If you have to convert a lot of images to Indexed Color or turn them into GIF or JPEG images, it may behoove you to invest in software that does it better than Photoshop can. For instance, Equilibrium's DeBabelizer can often optimize palettes better than Photoshop does, including creating superpalettes (like making a single color palette that represents colors from fifty different images, perhaps prioritizing five images that you think are most important).

Tip: Eking Out the Bytes. A great many images on the Internet (or "information superhighway" or "Infobahn" or whatever you want to call it) are saved in GIF format, especially those that appear on World Wide Web sites. The reason is simple: they're very compact. However, sometimes they're just not compact enough. For instance, on slower modem lines, there's a significant difference between watching a 30 K image slowly appear on your screen and a 15 K image appear without trouble.

If you're trying to eke out every little bit of compression in a GIF file, keep in mind how LZW compression works: it looks for repeating patterns of colors. For instance, it can tokenize "red, blue, red, blue, red, blue" into one piece of information. Therefore, the images that get compressed the most contain lots of these repeating patterns.

Here are several ways you can make Photoshop use more repeating patterns when you're converting images from RGB to Indexed Color.

▶   Use solid areas rather than gradations or textures.

▶   If you do use gradations (blends), consider unchecking the Dither option in the Gradient tool's Options palette and making the blend vertical (top to bottom) rather than horizontal (side to side). (This ensures that more pixels of the same color will sit next to each other.)

▶   Using specific color schemes is better than using lots of different colors. The fewer colors you use, the better compression you'll achieve.

▶   Use a smaller bit depth (use a 6- or 4-bit palette instead of eight bits). Of course, many images degrade significantly with fewer colors, so you should play around with this.

▶   If you're converting to Indexed Color before exporting the GIF, select Pattern dither instead of Diffusion dither (in the Indexed Color dialog box).

▶   Using System palette (or Uniform, if you're using fewer than eight bits per pixel) instead of Adaptive can save one or two kilobytes, which is important in some cases. If this doesn't matter as much to you, Adaptive is probably better.

With any of these techniques, the image's dither is almost always slightly more obvious, but you can make the image transfer over telephone lines faster.

Tip: Finding Dimensions for HTML Tags. If you're writing your own HTML code, it's always a good idea to include height and width values within the image source tag. For instance: <IMG SRC="mooseattack.gif" WIDTH="200" HEIGHT="200">. If you don't include the image's pixel dimensions, the Web browser has to download the entire image before it can lay out the page properly. One of the fastest ways to find these dimensions is by Option-clicking in the Image Size area at the lower-left corner of the document window in Photoshop (see Figure 18-9).

Figure 18-9

Finding pixel dimensions

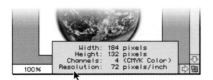

Tip: Swapping Indexed Colors. Let's say you have a logo on your Web page, which you want to be a different color every week. One way to make this color change would be to edit the GIF image's color lookup table (see Figure 18-10).

1. Open the GIF image and select Color Table from the Mode submenu (under the Image menu).

2. Click on the color you want to change, and when Photoshop asks you to, select a new color from the Color Picker (or type in RGB values). You probably want to make sure that the color you select is Web-safe.

    If the image is anti-aliased and all the intermediary colors are clumped together in the palette (they often are), you can change them all at once. For example, if you have five different red swatches—from light pink to bright red—you can drag the mouse from the first swatch to the last. When you let go of the mouse button, Photoshop asks you for the new first color (to replace the light pink) and then for the new last color (to replace the bright red). It will build all the intermediary colors for you based on the two you choose.

3. Press OK and save the image.

Needless to say, this tip works best when the palette has very few colors.

Figure 18-10
Swapping Indexed Color

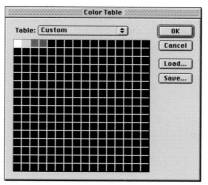

Click on a swatch to change its color. This alters the color throughout the image.

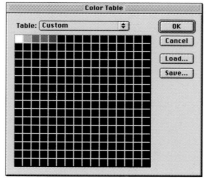

Transparency

Not all images are created rectangular, though bitmapped files always are. If you have an image of an apple on a white background, you can knock out the white, making it transparent, so that the apple sits on whatever background you choose for your Web site.

There are two problems with transparency on the Web, however. First, JPEG images don't support any kind of transparency, so you're stuck with the GIF file format, even for natural scanned images. Second, GIF transparency is 1-bit. That means each pixel in the image is either transparent or it's not; so no matter how semiopaque your image may be in

Photoshop, there's no partial transparency in the GIF image. (The new PNG file format does allow for 8-bit transparency. However, as yet it hasn't become widely accepted by the various Web browsers.)

Transparency from RGB images. When you export an RGB image with the GIF89a Export plug-in, any pixels that are transparent in Photoshop become transparent in the GIF image. An image that has a background layer cannot include transparency. However, you can double-click on the Background layer in the Layers palette to convert it into a regular layer. Then you can erase pixels to achieve transparency (see Figure 18-11).

Even better than erasing the background pixels is to add a layer mask to this layer (select Add Layer Mask from the Layer menu), and to paint black on the mask wherever you want the background to be transparent. This way, you can always go back and quickly edit the transparency and reexport the image.

Figure 18-11
Erasing to transparency

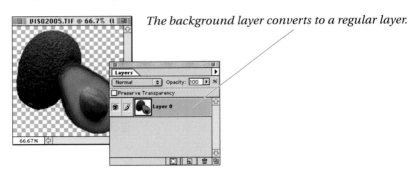

The background layer converts to a regular layer.

Transparency from indexed-color images. Indexed-color images in Photoshop don't inherently support transparency, so if your image is already converted to Indexed Color when you export using GIF89a Export, you must use the plug-in itself to make areas in the GIF transparent. The GIF89a Export dialog box changes when your image is already in Indexed Color mode; it adds tools for specifying which colors should be transparent (see Figure 18-12). There are two ways to specify transparency in this dialog box.

▶ You can use the Eyedropper tool in the GIF89a dialog box to choose colors from the displayed preview image or from the color swatches below the image. Any color you click on becomes transparent (you can click on more than one, and they'll all change). If you change your

Figure 18-12

Transparency in indexed-color images

mind after choosing a color, you can Command-click on it to revert to opacity. Remember that if you click on a white pixel, *every* white pixel in the file becomes transparent, often including white pixels in the image itself.

▶ You can build an additional channel in the image (see Chapter 14, *Selections*), and then choose this channel from the Transparency From popup menu. This is significantly more powerful and flexible– if you don't like the transparency in the first GIF you export, you can quickly edit the channel and export again. Unless there are only a handful of colors in the image, this is a much-preferred method. Remember that while you can make a full grayscale alpha channel, transparency is always on or off; pixels that are more than 50-percent black on the channel translate to transparent and those under 50-percent are ignored.

Anti-aliasing. Anti-aliased images often cause havoc with transparency because you often get edge spill (see "The Spill's the Thing" in Chapter 14, *Selections*). In general, it's a good idea to avoid any kind of anti-aliasing around the edges that will become transparent. However, if your image is already anti-aliased, you can often make the edges transparent without a halo by building a hard-edged channel or layer mask and then using the steps outlined above.

Images that have no anti-aliasing around them often look really jaggy in Photoshop, but when they're placed over a colored or patterned background, you often don't notice the jaggies at all (or if you do, they're still better than a halo around the image; see Figure 18-13).

Figure 18-13
Anti-aliasing images

Anti-aliased to white background

Aliased (jaggy edges)

The anti-aliased version looks terrible on a colored background.

The aliased version looks good.

Tip: Fake Transparency on Solid Colors. Building transparency into your images is an unnecessary step if your Web page has a solid-color background. It's usually faster to build the background color into the Photoshop file, then export it as a GIF image. Plus, you get a better-quality image because you can anti-alias the foreground image with the background color for a smooth blend between the two.

This technique doesn't work when the background of the Web page is patterned, because you'll never (ever) get the background in the image to align with the background of the Web page.

Tip: Anti-aliasing to a Background Color. If you really want anti-aliased edges around your image and you're placing the image over a patterned color background, you can sometimes fake it.

1. Select the predominant color in the background pattern, and make this color the background color of your image. Make sure the foreground image is anti-aliased into this color.

2. If your image is still in RGB mode, build a layer mask to knock out the background color (but not the parts of the foreground image that are anti-aliased), then export the GIF file. If you've already converted to Indexed Color, then build a channel for the transparency and choose it in the GIF89a Export dialog box.

3. Place the image over the patterned background on the Web page.

Now the anti-aliased edges appear to blend into the background at first glance, but on closer inspection they really don't.

The Future of Publishing

Tim Gill of Quark, Inc. drew laughs at the spring 1997 Seybold Conference when he commented that "print publishing has one very important attribute that isn't shared by the Web: you can make money doing it." While much of the wild rush to the Web has been driven by vague fears of being left behind by the competition, people are beginning to invent Web business models that actually make sense and occasionally even make money as well. Whatever your reason for being on the Web, one of the keys to success is to produce images that are small, compress well, and yet still have impact. Photoshop gives you the tools to accomplish this. As for making money at it: if we knew, would we have written this book?

Color Plate 1 When RGB and CMYK combine (page 79)

This figure is somewhat complicated by the need to print the red, green, and blue versions using cyan, magenta, and yellow inks.

REAL WORLD COLOR

Color Plate 2 Resolution and image reproduction (page 86)

How much resolution do you need? All of these images are printed using the same 133-lpi halftone screen, but they contain different numbers of pixels. Look for details, such as readability of type.

2:1 sampling ratio, 266 ppi

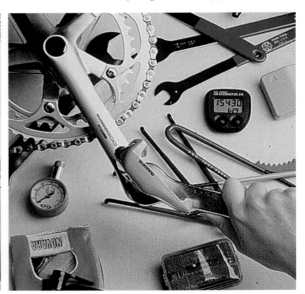

1.5:1 sampling ratio, 200 ppi

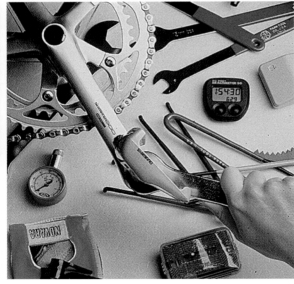

1.2:1 sampling ratio, 160 ppi

1:1 sampling ratio, 133 ppi

Color Plate 3 Indexed Color changes (page 98)

Indexed Color, shown as it's typically used, for 72-ppi display on screen. Since the colors are indexed to a 256-color palette, when the palette changes, the colors in the image change.

The high-resolution, 24-bit image

Macintosh system palette

An optimized or "adaptive" palette

A radical palette switch

Color Plate 4 Drop shadow techniques (page 540)

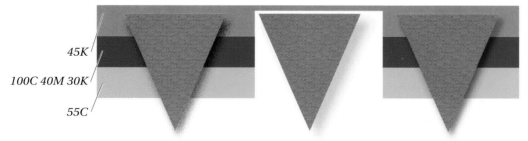

45K

100C 40M 30K

55C

Diffusion dither created with ICEfields and saved as TIFF

Grayscale saved as TIFF and set to overprinting color. It fully knocks out the black plate below it.

Triangle, color drop shadow and background incorporated into one TIFF file

Color Plate 5 Black generation (page 171)

The proportion of black to CMY inks has a considerable effect on image reproduction. Each method of black generation has its strengths and weaknesses. Undercolor removal, or UCR, replaces neutral colors with black ink, but uses CMY inks to reproduce all non-neutral colors. Gray component replacement, or GCR, extends the black plate into non-neutral areas, replacing a neutral amount of CMY with black ink.

A UCR separation uses black ink only in the neutral areas. It produces rich shadows, but can be difficult to control on press because it uses a lot of ink compared to GCR separations.

A Light GCR setting replaces slightly more CMY with K than does a UCR separation. In this image, Light GCR puts slightly more black into the sky and the water than does the UCR separation.

Maximum GCR replaces all neutral components of the CMY inks with black. It's easy to control on press because the black plate carries most of the image, but it can make shadow areas look flat.

Image Credits

And Permissions

Earth image used on chapter opening pages, courtesy National Aeronautics and Space Administration.

Page 7. Space Shuttle and Earth images courtesy National Aeronautics and Space Administration.

Page 15, 17, 20, 22, 24, 39. Taj Mahal image ©1994 by Bruce Fraser. Scanned on Leafscan 35 from Kodak Ektapress 100 negative film.

Page 32. From "Nature, Wildlife and the Environment," courtesy PhotoDisc.

Page 44. From "Nature, Wildlife and the Environment," courtesy PhotoDisc.

Page 49. From "Clouds Gallery," courtesy Mary & Michael.

Page 53. From "Nature, Wildlife and the Environment," courtesy PhotoDisc.

Page 78. From "Retro Americana," courtesy PhotoDisc.

Page 79. From "Faces and Hands," courtesy PhotoDisc.

Page 80. Deep bitmap image courtesy Simon Tuckett.

Page 82. From "Fine Art and Historical Photos," courtesy PhotoDisc.

Page 83. From "Faces and Hands," courtesy PhotoDisc.

Page 86. From "Fine Art and Historical Photos," courtesy PhotoDisc.

Page 87. From "Classic Sampler," courtesy Classic PIO Partners.

Page 91. From "Faces and Hands," courtesy PhotoDisc.

Page 95. From "Object Series 4: Retro Relics," courtesy PhotoDisc.

Page 114. Curraghs at Sunset image ©1995 by Bruce Fraser. Scanned on Leafscan 35 from Kodak Royal Gold 200 negative film.

Page 206 and 231. Special collections division, University Washington Libraries. Photo by Cobb, UW negative #10509.

Page 207. Figure 6-4: "Dia" ©1994 by Susie Hammond. Scanned on Hewlett-Packard Scanjet IIcx from 4x6 print.

Page 207. Figure 6-5: Special collections division, University Washington Libraries. UW negative #80.A.W&S.

Page 208. From "ColorBytes Sampler One," courtesy ColorBytes, Inc.

Page 215. Waterfall photo by Eric Wunrow, from "ColorBytes Sampler One," courtesy ColorBytes, Inc.

Pages 218 through 220. Train photo by Eric Wunrow, from "ColorBytes Sampler One," courtesy ColorBytes, Inc.

Page 222. Boat photo by Eric Wunrow, from "ColorBytes Sampler One," courtesy ColorBytes, Inc.

Page 228. Building photo from "ColorBytes Sampler One," courtesy ColorBytes, Inc.

Pages 242 through 251. Cape Elizabeth Lighthouse, Maine image ©1993 by Bruce Fraser. Scanned on Leafscan 35 from Kodak Lumiere 100 reversal film.

Pages 244 through 252. Your's Ella image by Drummond Shiels Studios,

Edinburgh, Scotland, c. 1926. Photographer unknown. Scanned on Agfa Horizon scanner from 8x10 print.

Page 269 and 678. Bike Parts image ©1991 MacUser Magazine, by Peter Allen Gould. Scanned on Leafscan45 from Kodak Ektachrome 4x5 transparency.

Page 270. Alcatraz image ©1995 by Bruce Fraser. Digital capture from Kodak DCS 420 Digital Camera.

Page 271, 275, and 295. Masked Dancer image ©1994 by Bruce Fraser. Scanned on Leafscan 35 from Kodak PJA-100 negative film.

Page 273. Conservatory, Golden Gate Park image ©1995 by Bruce Fraser. Digital capture from Nikon E2S.

Page 279 and 281. San Francisco Painted Ladies #1 image ©1995 by Bruce Fraser. Digital capture from Kodak DCS 420 Digital Camera.

Page 283 and 286. Rhyolite Windows image ©1988 by Bruce Fraser. Scanned on Leafscan 35 from Kodak Ektar 25 negative film.

Page 290. Machu Picchu #1 image ©1998 by Bruce Fraser. Scanned on Imacon Flextight Precision from Kodak PJA-100 negative film.

Page 292. La Paz Drummers image ©1994 by Bruce Fraser. Scanned on Leafscan 35 from Kodak PJA-100 negative film.

Page 298 and 299. "Dia" ©1994 by Susie Hammond. Scanned on Hewlett-Packard Scanjet IIcx from 4x6 print.

Pages 300 through 302. Conservatory, Golden Gate Park image ©1995 by Bruce Fraser. Digital capture from Kodak DCS 420.

Page 302. Glass image ©Fuji Photo Film, scanned on Agfa Arcus Plus from 4x5 print.

Page 303. La Paz Street Vendor image ©1994 by Bruce Fraser. Scanned on Leafscan 35 from Kodak PJA-100 negative film.

Page 297 and 304. Woman in Red Hat image ©1990 by Eastman Kodak Co., photographer Bob Clemens, from Kodak Photo CD Sampler. Photo CD image scanned on Kodak PIW from Kodak Ektar 25 negative film, acquired into Photoshop using KICC, Universal Negative 3.2 ICC Profile.

Pages 307 through 309. Machu Picchu #2 image ©1998 by Bruce Fraser. Scanned on Imacon Flextight Precision from Kodak PJA-100 negative film.

Page 321 and 322. Blue Curragh image ©1995 by Bruce Fraser. Scanned on Leafscan 35 from Kodak Royal Gold 200 negative film.

Pages 323 through 325. Connemara Fishing Boats ©1995 by Bruce Fraser. Scanned on Leafscan 35 from Kodak Lumiere reversal film.

Page 326 and 327. Dawn at Varanasi image ©1995 by Bruce Fraser. Scanned on Leafscan 35 from Kodak Ektapress 100 negative film.

Pages 327 through 329. Golden Gate Bridge image ©1996 by Bruce Fraser. Digital capture from Polaroid PDC-2000.

Page 330 and 331. Men in Kilts image ©1995 by Pamela Pfiffner. Scanned on Leafscan 35 from Kodak Ektapress 100 negative film.

Page 332 and 333. Machu Picchu #3 image ©1998 by Bruce Fraser. Scanned on Imacon Flextight Precision from Kodak PJA-100 negative film.

Page 337. Photo by Goetzman Photo.

Page 338. Frosted trees image from "Color Digital Photos: Paramount," courtesy Seattle Support Group.

Page 339. Ship masts image from "Color Digital Photos: Paramount," courtesy Seattle Support Group.

Page 340. Bird image from "Color Digital Photos: Paramount," courtesy Seattle Support Group.

Page 347. Eye image courtesy ©1990 by Eastman Kodak Co., photographer Bob Clemens, from Kodak Photo CD Sampler.

Page 349. Trees image from "Signature Series 8: Study of Form and Color," courtesy PhotoDisc.

Page 349. Pumpkin image from "Object Series 1: Fruits and Vegetables," courtesy PhotoDisc.

Page 350. Golden Gate Bridge image ©1995 by Bruce Fraser. Digital capture from Kodak DCS 420 Digital Camera.

Page 351. San Francisco Painted Ladies #2 image ©1995 by Bruce Fraser. Digital capture from Kodak DCS 420 Digital Camera.

Page 352. Mission San Miguel image ©1992 by Bruce Fraser. Scanned on Leafscan 35 from Kodak Gold 100 negative film.

Page 352. Woman in Red Hat image ©1990 by Eastman Kodak Co., photographer Bob Clemens, from Kodak Photo CD Sampler.

Page 369. Barn image from "Signature Series 8: Study of Form and Color," courtesy PhotoDisc.

Page 370. Leaf image from "Signature Series 8: Study of Form and Color," courtesy PhotoDisc.

Page 377. From "Signature Series 8: Study of Form and Color," courtesy PhotoDisc.

Page 380. From "Fine Art and Historical Photos," courtesy PhotoDisc.

Page 381 and 382. From "Signature Series 8: Study of Form and Color," courtesy PhotoDisc.

Page 385. Hearst pool image from "Color Digital Photos: Paramount," courtesy Seattle Support Group.

Page 386. From "Signature Series 8: Study of Form and Color," courtesy PhotoDisc.

Page 399. From "William Morris: Ornamentation & Illustrations from The Kelmscott Chaucer," Dover Publications.

Page 402. From "Animals," Dover Publications.

Page 403. From "Animals," Dover Publications.

Page 404. Special collections division, University Washington Libraries. UW negative #10542.

Page 428. Special collections division, University Washington Libraries. UW negative #80.A.W&S.

Page 438. From "Fine Art and Historical Photos," courtesy PhotoDisc.

Page 446. From "Classic Sampler," courtesy Classic PIO Partners.

Page 454. Floating angel image from "Object Series 4: Retro Relics," courtesy PhotoDisc.

Page 454. Gears image from "Signature Series 8: Study of Form and Color," courtesy PhotoDisc.

Page 452. From "Signature Series 8: Study of Form and Color," courtesy PhotoDisc.

Page 451. From "Object Series 4: Retro Relics," courtesy PhotoDisc.

Page 456. From "Classic Sampler," courtesy Classic PIO Partners.

Page 458. From "Signature Series 8: Study of Form and Color," courtesy PhotoDisc.

Page 463. From "Fine Art and Historical Photos," courtesy PhotoDisc.

Page 466. From "Object Series 1: Fruits and Vegetables," courtesy PhotoDisc.

Page 472. From "Children of the World," courtesy PhotoDisc.

Page 473. Apples image from "The Painted Table," courtesy PhotoDisc.

Page 475. Fishing lure from "Object Series 4: Retro Relics," courtesy PhotoDisc.

Page 477. From "Object Series 1: Fruits and Vegetables," courtesy PhotoDisc.

Page 486. From "Faces and Hands," courtesy PhotoDisc.

Page 488. From "Signature Series 8: Study of Form and Color," courtesy PhotoDisc.

Page 488. Earth image courtesy National Aeronautics and Space Administration

Page 493. From "Object Series 4: Retro Relics," courtesy PhotoDisc.

Page 503. From "Object Series 4: Retro Relics," courtesy PhotoDisc.

Page 504. From "Signature Series 8: Study of Form and Color," courtesy PhotoDisc.

Page 505. From "Signature Series 8: Study of Form and Color," courtesy PhotoDisc.

Page 507. Trees image from "Signature Series 8: Study of Form and Color," courtesy PhotoDisc.

Page 507. Sunset image from "Kais Power Photos," courtesy HSC Software.

Page 509. Waterfall image from "Signature Series 8: Study of Form and Color," courtesy PhotoDisc.

Page 516 and 552. Woman in Red Hat image ©1990 by Eastman Kodak Co., photographer Bob Clemens, from Kodak Photo CD Sampler.

Page 518. "Seattle Lamppost" ©1995 by David Blatner.

Page 520. Shanghai Dancers image (detail) ©1997 by Pamela Pfiffner. Scanned on Leafscan 35 from Kodak Tri-X negative film.

Page 521. "Debbie" ©1995 by David Blatner.

Page 523. From "Fine Art and Historical Photos," courtesy PhotoDisc.

Page 525. From "Fine Art and Historical Photos," courtesy PhotoDisc.

Page 526. "Christmas Hat/London" ©1995 by Pamela Pfiffner. Scanned on Leafscan 35 from Kodak Ektapress 100 negative film.

Page 528. From "Object Series 4: Retro Relics," courtesy PhotoDisc.

Page 533. "Billboard" ©1995 by David Blatner.

Page 536. From "Object Series 4: Retro Relics," courtesy PhotoDisc.

Page 539. From "Object Series 4: Retro Relics," courtesy PhotoDisc.

Page 547. From "Object Series 4: Retro Relics," courtesy PhotoDisc.

Page 550. From "Retro Americana," courtesy PhotoDisc.

Page 575. Cherries image from "Object Series 1: Fruits and Vegetables," courtesy PhotoDisc.

Page 575. Background texture courtesy Artbeats.

Page 590. "Edna Hassinger" courtesy Allee Blatner. Photographer unknown.

Page 615. Taj Mahal image ©1993 by Carol Thuman.

Page 619. Figure 17-6: Special collections division, University Washington Libraries. UW negative #80.A.W&S.

Page 625. From "Object Series 4: Retro Relics," courtesy PhotoDisc.

Page 636. Earth image courtesy National Aeronautics and Space Administration.

Page 660. From "PhotoDisc Fine Art Sampler," courtesy PhotoDisc.

Page 673. "Spleef" ©1996 by Toby Malina.

Page 677. From "PhotoDisc Sampler" courtesy PhotoDisc.

Page 679. From "Fine Art and Historical Photos," courtesy PhotoDisc.

Page 680. Boothbay Harbor, Maine image ©1993 by Bruce Fraser. Scanned on Leafscan 35 from Kodak Lumiere 100 reversal film.

Production Notes

How We Made This Book

In many ways, producing this book was as interesting as writing it. So we thought that something a bit more complete than a normal colophon was in order. What follows is an overview of the systems and procedures that we used to produce this book.

Our Systems

We're often asked about our personal system setups. Here's a quick run-down of what equipment we used while making this book. This isn't everything we use, of course . . . there's always some new toy.

Bruce. **System 1** Daystar Millenium G3/307, 512 MB RAM, Mitsubishi SpectraView monitor, ATI Nexus GA video card, Miles Initio UltraSCSI card, 16 GB total hard drive space, Jaz drive, Gretag Spectrolino spectro-photometer. **System 2** Intergraph ExtremeZ 2D workstation, Matsushita 21-inch monitor, Matrox Millenium II AGP video card, 512 MB RAM, 12.6 GB total hard drive space. **System 3:** PowerMac 8100/100, 136 MB RAM, SuperMatch PressView 21 and Apple 13-inch monitors, Radius Thunder IV and E-Machines Ultura LX video cards, Adaptive Solutions PowerShop DSP accelerator, 8 GB total hard drive space, Zip drive. **System 4:** Daystar Genesis MP 600, 384 MB RAM, Radius Pressview 17SR and Barco PDC 321 monitors, Radius ThunderColor 30/1600 and ATI XClaim/GA video cards, ATTO Express PCI multichannel SCSI card, 9 GB total hard drive space, Wacom Art-Z tablet, Gretag SPM50 spectrophotometer.

David. **System 1:** PowerMac 8100/80, 72 MB RAM, Radius PressView 17SR and Apple 13-inch monitors, 5 GB total hard drive space, Zip drive, Yamaha CD-R, Epson Stylus inkjet printer, Wacom ArtPad tablet, Linotype-Hell Saphir scanner. **System 2:** Dell 200 Mhz Pentium, 32 MB RAM, 3 GB total hard drive space, Windows 95.

Writing, Editing, and Page Layout

We wrote and edited this book in Microsoft Word 5 on the Mac, then poured the Word files into PageMaker 6.5.2.

Design and Type

The body text typeface is Adobe Utopia (various weights)—9.8 on 15 for the main text, 8.8 on 12.5 for sidebars. Heads are set in ITC Kabel Black.

Images

We scanned many of the images on a LeafScan 35, and more recently, on an Imacon Flextight Precision II. When original film wasn't available, we used a variety of flatbed scanners, including an Agfa Arcus Plus, a Linotype-Hell Saphir Ultra, a Heidelberg CPS Opal Ultra, and a UMAX PowerLook 3000. We also used direct digital captures from Kodak DCS 420, Polaroid PDC-2000, and Nikon/Fuji E2S digital cameras. The remaining images came from various CD collections (see "Image Credits"). All the images in this book started out in RGB form; we used no drum scans.

We placed all the color images as preseparated CMYK TIFFs (with the exception of duotones and graphics from Illustrator and FreeHand, all of which required that we use EPS).

Screen to press. One of the central issues that we faced in producing this book was trying to show you what you can expect on press, on continuous-tone output, and on screen. Showing final press output on coated stock is easy; the book is printed on coated stock. But representing what you might see on screen or in an original photographic print (much less a slide or negative) is another story. As a result, some of the figures in this book are constructed to show relationships, rather than actual results.

Most of the images throughout the book, for instance, have been sharpened and targeted so they aren't blurry and dark on pages (they aren't blurry and dark on screen or in the originals). Again, the goal was to depict in print what you can expect to see during the production process.

Separations

With a few exceptions (which we reference specifically), all the color images in this book were separated in Photoshop using the same RGB Setup and CMYK Setup settings.

RGB Setup. Most of the images in this book were edited in Adobe RGB (1998). A few legacy images were edited in ColorMatch RGB or Bruce RGB. For monitor calibration, we used an X-Rite DTP 92 Monitor Optimizer, a Radius ProSense calibrator, and a Minolta BlueEye colorimeter.

CMYK Setup. Since the book was printed using direct-to-plate technology on a web press, we decided that a print test was necessary. In addition to test images, the standard color bars, and gray ramps, we included targets for several ICC profile creation tools. We measured the progressive colors with a Gretag SPM 50 spectrophotometer and entered the CIE xyY values into a Custom Ink Colors file, using the average of three readings each from four different press sheets for a total of twelve sets of measurements.

We also measured the dot gain and entered it into custom Dot Gain Curves. We used Light GCR, 100-percent Black Ink Limit, 300-percent Total Ink Limit, and variable amounts of UCA depending on image content, but never more than 5 percent. For some screen shots of dialog boxes, we used a Heavy GCR separation with the same ink limits.

In addition, we built an ICC profile using Logo ProfileMaker Pro profiling software, again using the average of three readings each from four different press sheets for a total of twelve sets of measurements. For this larger set of measurements, we used a Gretag Spectrolino mounted on a Gretag SpectroScan xy table to automate the data collection. On most images, the difference between the two CMYK Setups was very small. We used whichever one seemed appropriate for the image at hand.

Preproofing

When we compared the test images on the print test with the digital files viewed on our reference monitor, we found that our custom ICC profile in combination with solid monitor characterization gave us a very accurate on-screen view of the CMYK data in Photoshop.

We also used our ICC profile in conjunction with ColorSync to provide accurate viewing of the color within PageMaker. This proved surprisingly useful: in several cases we went back and edited the images after we had seen them in context on the page.

For hard-copy preproofing, we used the press ICC profile as our Separations profile and a custom profile for the NewGen Chromax dye-sublimation printer that we built using ColorSavvy's RTKit Pro profiling software as our Composite profile. PageMaker automatically cross-rendered the CMYK TIFFs to the Chromax's color space when we printed pages to the Chromax for preproofing.

For non-color proofing, we built .pdf files for each chapter and emailed them to our editors. In most cases, the changes were sufficiently minor that they could be conveyed in email messages. We killed as few trees as possible during the production of this book.

Index